The **Rough Guide** to

# The Yucatán

written and researched by

## Zora O'Neill and John Fisher

ROUGH
GUIDES

NEW YORK • LONDON • DELHI

www.roughguides.com

# Contents

◄◄ Diver in Cenote Carwash  ◄ El Paraiso Beach Club, Tulum

## Introduction to

# The Yucatán

**Best known for major tourist attractions like the beaches
of Cancún and the towering pyramid at Chichén Itzá, the
Yucatán Peninsula – the eastern tip of the curving horn of
Mexico, facing the Caribbean Sea to the east and the Gulf
of Mexico to the west and north – is also still very much
the frontier, a swath of untamed greenery that forms a
place apart from the rest of the country. Until the 1960s,
this was literally the case, as roads did not connect the
Yucatán with central Mexico. As a result, residents were
left to develop their own worldview, one that looked to
Europe and Cuba for cultural cues while taking pride in
the indigenous Maya culture. Today, it's not uncommon for
people born in this region to say they're *yucatecos* first,
*mexicanos* second.**

More than anywhere else in Mexico, the Yucatán
and the northeastern part of Chiapas reflect
native American culture at every level of society:
**Maya tradition** is palpable in remote, timeless
villages of thatch-roof palapa homes, but also
in shopping malls, political campaigns and TV
advertisements. Although the Maya as a people
are by no means free of the poverty borne disproportionately by indigenous
cultures throughout the country, many Maya have prospered, and their
culture is incredibly influential, as all *yucatecos* use Maya vocabulary, eat Maya
cuisine and generally take pride in living in "the land of the pheasant and the
deer", as the Maya have called their richly forested terrain for centuries.

Travel in the Yucatán and Mayan Chiapas ranges from blazingly easy, along
smooth toll highways in ultra-cushy buses, to virtually impossible, as rattletrap
minivans packed with machete-carrying farmers get mired in muddy tracks.
In the latter case, you may be the only passenger remotely upset, as there's
a general sense that minor annoyances really are minor, and that there's

▲ Huipiles

always something else to do in the meantime. This **laid-back attitude** can be intensely frustrating – or wonderfully relaxing, if you give in to it. You may also be put off by the extremes of wealth and poverty, though it is not as visible here as in the rest of Mexico; similarly, the smog, slums and crime that mark Mexico City are not nearly as evident in the metropolises of the Yucatán, which are generally kept meticulously clean and have relatively few poor areas. Violent crime is almost nonexistent, and for the most part this is a friendly and enormously enjoyable place to visit. Women travellers in particular will appreciate the overall lack of the *machismo* culture so common in central Mexico; in fact, modesty and almost formal politeness are the norm.

Between the powdery white Caribbean **beaches** and the wild, dense rainforest that covers the inland peninsula and the muggy river valleys of Chiapas and Tabasco, you'll find a huge variety of attractions. Some, such as the Maya **ruins** of Palenque or the mega-clubs of Cancún, are man-made, while others are natural – UNESCO has established five biosphere reserves in this area, the largest being the 1.7-million-acre Calakmul Biosphere Reserve. Travellers who prefer cities will enjoy both the sprawling energy of Villahermosa and the gracious tranquillity of Mérida.

# Where to go

**C**ancún, the largest tourist destination in the Yucatán, has a reputation as a spring-breaker's debauch, but it offers much more: as a built-from-scratch city carved out of the jungle in the 1970s, it's an interesting urban experiment that also happens to have beautiful beaches and world-class hotels and restaurants. Continuing down the Caribbean coast leads to less frenetic towns, such as **Playa del Carmen**, **Tulum** and **San Miguel**, on the reef-ringed island of **Cozumel**, and eventually the utter isolation of the **Costa Maya**, near Mexico's border with Belize.

Away from the Caribbean, you can choose to visit scores of ancient Maya sites (see box, p.9) or a number of modern cities, the largest of which is

5

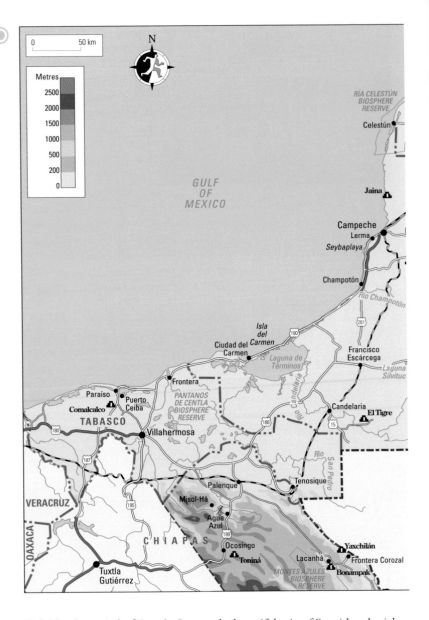

**Mérida**, the capital of Yucatán State and a beautiful mix of Spanish colonial and French- and Italian-inspired architecture. On the Gulf coast of the peninsula, the city of **Campeche** is a tiny gem, with its historic core of pastel-painted buildings. South and west of Campeche lies the state of Tabasco, where the Olmecs – considered the mother of all Mesoamerican

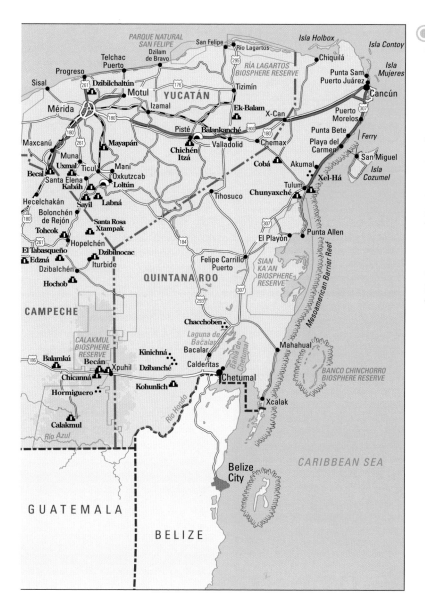

cultures – flourished more than a millennium before the first Maya cities; you can see the enormous stone heads they carved, along with other relics, in the city of **Villahermosa**. Chiapas, directly south of Tabasco, was the centre of the Zapatista uprising in the 1990s, though visitors are little affected these days, and the strength of indigenous traditions here, together

7

## On the beach

The crystalline white sands of the Yucatán's Caribbean coast are so transfixingly beautiful that many visitors never go further than their sun chairs for the whole of their vacation. The coast between Cancún and Tulum, known as the Riviera Maya (see p.115), complies with the best images of the Caribbean – all glassy water and broad sand; as a result, though, development is somewhat dense, and isolated beaches are now quite rare.

Farther south, the Costa Maya (see p.169) around Mahahual and Xcalak offers isolation, but the beaches are narrower and shaded in many places by pine trees, not palms. Another less crowded alternative is the Gulf coast (see pages 263 & 289), along the north and west sides of the peninsula, where the water is not quite so clear but you can enjoy it in perfect solitude. In any case, all of the beaches in Mexico are technically public, and you may lay down your towel anywhere you like. Some hotels will let you use their beach furniture if you order from the bar; elsewhere, beach clubs rent chairs and serve food and drinks, usually for a modest fee.

with the opening-up of a number of lesser-known Maya ruins near the majestic city of **Palenque**, continue to lure travellers.

If it's wildlife you're after, a number of nature reserves are sanctuaries for countless colourful birds and mammals. The **Sian Ka'an Biosphere Reserve**, on the Caribbean coast, comprises a particularly diverse range of ecosystems, while **Ría Celestún** and **Ría Lagartos** (on the west and north Gulf coasts, respectively) enclose bird-filled estuaries. Divers shouldn't miss Cozumel, where lush coral gardens rim the coast; the growths are an outlying part of the **Mesoamerican Barrier Reef**, the longest barrier reef in the western hemisphere, running along the Caribbean coast from just south of Cancún all the way to Honduras.

The typical travel route through the Yucatán Peninsula begins in Cancún and goes counter-clockwise around the main highways, via Chichén Itzá, Mérida and Campeche, with a dip into Tabasco State to see the Olmec ruins, then down to Palenque in Chiapas. A completist will finish the Maya circuit via the **Río Bec** ruins in the southern parts of Campeche and Quintana Roo. Alternatively, many people travel from central Mexico into Chiapas, then traverse the peninsula clockwise, heading up the Gulf coast and across to Chichén Itzá and finishing off their trips with a stint on the Caribbean beaches.

▲ Playa Norte, Isla Mujeres

## Maya present and past

Throughout the Yucatán, Chiapas and neighbouring Belize and Guatemala, the Maya have a total population of approximately four million; nearly one third of the state of Chiapas is Maya. The majority on the peninsula are Yucatec Maya (that is, related to or current speakers of the Yucatec variation of the Maya language), while the Lacandón and Chol Maya live in Chiapas.

The four major Maya sites in Mexico – Palenque in Chiapas, Calakmul in Campeche and Uxmal and Chichén Itzá in Yucatán State – represent separate phases in ancient Maya supremacy. With enough time, you could visit all four ruined cities; alternatively, you can focus on one and explore the surrounding smaller sites as well. Near Palenque sits Bonampak, with its splendid murals, while in the neighbourhood of Calakmul you'll find the odd towers of the Río Bec sites to the west; the elaborately carved city of Edzná and the Chenes sites are to the north and west, near the city of Campeche. Uxmal is the anchor of the Ruta Puuc, a circuit that passes the smaller but equally ornate ruins of Kabah, Sayil and Labná. Not far from Chichén Itzá lie Ek-Balam, noted for its stucco decoration, and Cobá, an excellent place to spot wildlife. And if you're planning no more than a beach vacation, you can visit the ruins at Tulum, a small but exceptionally scenic site overlooking the Caribbean, with its own lovely arc of sand.

▲ Chichén Itzá

## Yucatecan cuisine

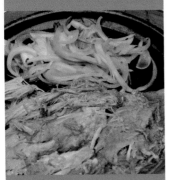

Even if it weren't so tasty, the food of the Yucatán Peninsula would be remarkable for its colour alone: candy-pink pickled onions top dishes spiced with lurid orange annatto, while bright green *chaya*, a spinach-like leafy green, turns up in everything from scrambled eggs to fruit-juice blends. Many of the most typical dishes reflect the earthy traditional foods that the Maya have eaten for millennia: maize, beans, pumpkin seeds, bitter oranges, turkeys and game animals like deer. Dried and fresh chillies find their way into many things, but they're not relied on to the extent they are in central Mexican cuisine. Instead, the tiny, deadly *habañero* pepper provides all the heat; luckily, it's always served on the side in a rough-cut raw salsa. In a pinch, you can kill the heat with a cold shot of *xtabentun*, a honey-flavoured liqueur that was allegedly first made by the ancient Maya.

# When to go

To a great extent, the physical terrain in Mexico determines the climate – certainly far more than the expected indicators of latitude and longitude. You can drive down the coast all day without conditions changing noticeably, but turn inland to the mountains, and the contrast is immediate: in temperature, scenery, vegetation and even the mood and character of the people around you.

**Summer**, from late May to October, is in theory the **rainy season**, but just how wet it is varies from place to place. In the heart of the Yucatán you can expect muggy air and a heavy but short-lived downpour virtually every afternoon; Chiapas is the wettest state, with many minor roads washed out by autumn. On the Caribbean coast, the rains culminate in **hurricane season** from mid-September to mid-October – you'll get wet weather and choppy seas (as well as plenty of mosquitoes), if not an actual storm.

▲ Mangrove tunnel at Celestún

**Winter** is the traditional tourist season, with dry air, mild temperatures and clear skies, and in the beach resorts like Cancún and Playa del Carmen, hotels are packed from late December to April.

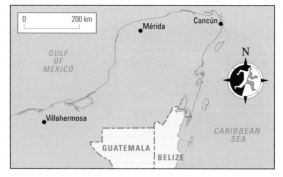

But the inland part of the Yucatán Peninsula and the highlands of Chiapas, which are not quite so affected by the winter tourist influx, can get chilly then: indeed, nights in the mountains can be cold at any time of year.

Visitors now come all year round – sticking on the whole to the highlands in summer and the coasts in winter. **November** is probably the ideal time to visit, with the rains over, the land still fresh and the peak season not yet begun. Overall, though, the climate is so benign that any time of year will do, so long as you're prepared for some rain in the summer, some cold in winter and the sudden changes that go with the altitude at any time.

## Average temperatures and rainfall

| | Jan | March | May | July | Sept | Nov |
|---|---|---|---|---|---|---|
| **Cancún** | | | | | | |
| Max °F | 81 | 84 | 88 | 90 | 89 | 84 |
| Min °F | 67 | 71 | 77 | 78 | 76 | 72 |
| Max °C | 27 | 29 | 31 | 32 | 32 | 29 |
| Min °C | 19 | 22 | 25 | 26 | 24 | 22 |
| Rainfall (inches) | 3.5 | 1.6 | 4.6 | 4.3 | 9 | 3.8 |
| Rainfall (mm) | 88.9 | 40.6 | 116.8 | 109.2 | 228.6 | 96.5 |
| **Mérida** | | | | | | |
| Max °F | 82 | 90 | 93 | 91 | 90 | 84 |
| Min °F | 64 | 68 | 70 | 73 | 73 | 66 |
| Max °C | 28 | 32 | 34 | 33 | 32 | 29 |
| Min °C | 18 | 20 | 21 | 23 | 23 | 19 |
| Rainfall (inches) | 1.2 | 0.6 | 2.9 | 5.0 | 7.7 | 1.4 |
| Rainfall (mm) | 30.5 | 15.2 | 73.7 | 127 | 195.6 | 35.6 |
| **Villahermosa** | | | | | | |
| Max °F | 76 | 83 | 89 | 86 | 85 | 79 |
| Min °F | 66 | 69 | 73 | 74 | 73 | 68 |
| Max °C | 24 | 28 | 31 | 30 | 29 | 26 |
| Min °C | 18 | 20 | 22 | 23 | 22 | 20 |
| Rainfall (inches) | 3.6 | 1.9 | 3.3 | 5.2 | 13.1 | 9.4 |
| Rainfall (mm) | 91.4 | 48.3 | 83.8 | 132.1 | 332.7 | 238.8 |

## things not to miss

*It's not possible to see everything the Yucatán has to offer in one trip – and we don't suggest you try. What follows is a selective and subjective taste of the region's highlights, from stunning ancient ruins and spectacular beaches to folk dancing and traditional crafts. They're arranged in five colour-coded categories, so you can browse through to find the very best things to see, do and experience. All highlights have a page reference to take you straight into the Guide, where you can find out more.*

**01** **Pirámide del Adivino** Page **248** • Rising from a unique oval base, the most striking of all Maya pyramids is found at Uxmal, south of Mérida.

**02** **Mahahual** Page **176** • In this remote town on the Costa Maya, a small crew of beach bums is dedicated to preserving the hammock-lounging lifestyle.

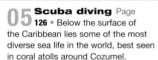

**05** **Scuba diving** Page **126** • Below the surface of the Caribbean lies some of the most diverse sea life in the world, best seen in coral atolls around Cozumel.

**03** **Trovador serenades** Page **228** • The Yucatán's traditional crooners gather nightly in cafés and on city plazas – hire a trio for a romantic ballad.

**04** **Hammocks** Page **232** • Yucatecans have perfected the craft of hammock-weaving; the best place to buy one is from a specialist in Mérida.

**06** **Chichén Itzá** Page **206** • The giant pyramid that towers over the ruined city of Chichén Itzá is an icon of Maya power in the Yucatán Peninsula.

**07** **The Bonampak murals** Page **314** • Still vivid after more than 1200 years, the wall-paintings at this site in eastern Chiapas depict ancient rituals with precise detail.

**08** **Parque La Venta** Page **296** • Discover relics of the Olmec civilization, the oldest in Mesoamerica, at this lush park in Villahermosa, which also contains a museum and zoo.

**09** **Jarana dancing** Page **234** • Catch this folk dance – a hybrid of Spanish and Maya styles – at a village fiesta if you can; it's also performed weekly in Mérida.

**10** **Palenque ruins** Page **306** • The biggest Maya site in Chiapas is remarkable for both its well-preserved architecture and its beautiful natural setting amid stunning waterfalls and pools.

**12** **Río Hondo** Page **185** • Explore the secluded area along the river that forms the unspoiled border between Mexico and Belize.

**14** **Sian Ka'an Biosphere Reserve** Page **162** • The Yucatán's most diverse nature sanctuary contains over one million acres of empty beaches, vibrant reefs, tangled mangroves and lush forest.

**11** **Whale sharks** Page **110** • At the end of every summer, more than two hundred of these enormous gentle fish gather off the north Gulf coast.

**13** **Cenotes** Pages **121**, **152** & **203** • Filled with cool, crystal-clear water, the numerous caverns and sinkholes that riddle the soft limestone bedrock of the peninsula make for a memorable swimming or diving experience.

**15** **Cobá** Page **160** • Climb Nohoch Mul, the tallest pyramid in the Yucatán, to see the jungle stretch to every horizon.

**16 Flamingos** Page **240** • Flocks of these pink birds gather in two biosphere reserves on the peninsula's Gulf coast. The biggest population feeds in the shallow estuary near the village of Celestún.

**17 Ek-Balam** Page **204** • The flawlessly preserved stucco decoration is the main attraction at this small ruined city north of Valladolid.

**18 Caribbean beaches** Page **92** • Whether hanging up your hammock or bedding down in a plush resort, the powdery white sand and impossibly turquoise water are irresistible.

**19 Calakmul** Page **191** • The Yucatán's largest ruined city is also the most remote, near the border with Guatemala and deep in a jungle where howler monkeys and jaguars still roam.

**20 Shrimp tacos** Page **127** • *La Floresta* in Playa del Carmen does them best, but these scrumptious snacks can be found all along the Caribbean coast.

# Basics

# Basics

# Getting there

The quickest and easiest way to get to the Yucatán is to fly, although you can also reach the peninsula by travelling overland from central Mexico, Guatemala or Belize as part of a longer trip. Unless you've got your own boat, getting there by water is only normally possible on a cruiseship.

Barring special offers and airpasses, the best fares will carry certain restrictions, such as advance booking (an **Apex** ticket, for example, which must be booked at least fourteen days before departure) and fixed dates, with a penalty charge if you change your schedule. They may also limit your stay – typically to between 7 and 21 days. Many airlines offer **youth** or **student fares** to those 25 and younger, though requirements vary; a passport or driving licence are sufficient proof of age, though these tickets are subject to availability and can have eccentric booking conditions. If you qualify, you'll save perhaps eight to ten percent, but you'll need to book as far in advance as possible, as seat availability at these prices is limited. Most cheap round-trip fares involve spending at least one Saturday night away, and many will only give a percentage refund if you need to cancel or alter your journey.

You can often cut costs by going through a **specialist flight agent** – either a consolidator, who buys up blocks of tickets from the airlines and sells them at a discount, or an agent, who in addition to dealing with discounted flights may also offer special **student and youth fares** and a range of other travel-related services such as travel insurance, car rentals, tours and the like. Some agents specialize in charter flights, particularly to Cancún, which may be cheaper than anything available on a scheduled flight, but again departure dates are fixed and withdrawal penalties are high. Don't automatically assume that tickets purchased through a travel specialist will be cheapest, however; once you get a quote, check with the airlines and you may turn up an even better deal. (**Courier flights**, once a bargain traveller's standard, have been cut back sig-

nificantly since September 11, 2001, and no such flights run to Mexico.)

To some extent, the fare will depend on the **season**. Though prices to Mérida and non-resort destinations show little fluctuation, fares to Cancún are highest around Easter, from early June to mid-September and at Christmas and New Year. Prices drop a bit during the "shoulder" seasons of mid-September to early November and mid-April to early June. Note also that flying on weekends adds to the round-trip fare; the typical lowest round-trip Apex prices quoted on p.20 assume midweek travel in high season.

If the Yucatán is only one stop on a longer journey, you might want to consider buying a **round-the-world (RTW) ticket**. Some travel agents can sell you an "off-the-shelf" RTW ticket that will have you touching down in about half a dozen cities; others will have to assemble one for you, which can be tailored to your needs but is likely to be more expensive.

## Booking flights online

Most airlines and discount travel websites offer you the opportunity to book your tickets **online**, cutting out the costs of agents and middlemen, though many now charge a small handling fee. Good deals can also be found through discount or auction sites, though you should read the fine print carefully. In the US, the airlines' own websites are becoming increasingly competitive with larger online travel bookers, so you should include them in your search as well.

### Online booking agents

Ⓦ **www.cheapflights.com** (in US); Ⓦ **www. cheapflights.co.uk** (in UK and Ireland); Ⓦ **www.cheapflights.ca** (in Canada); Ⓦ **www.**

**cheapflights.com.au** (in Australia and New Zealand) Flight deals, travel agents, plus links to other travel sites.

Ⓦ **www.cheaptickets.com** Discount flight specialists (US only).

Ⓦ **www.deckchair.com** Quick means of scanning cheap flights to popular escapes from Britain.

Ⓦ **www.etn.nl/discount** Links to consolidator and discount agents, maintained and vetted by the non-profit European Travel Network.

Ⓦ **www.expedia.com** (in US); Ⓦ **www.expedia. ca** (in Canada); Ⓦ **www.expedia.co.uk** (in UK) Discount airfares, all-airline search engine and daily deals.

Ⓦ **www.flyaow.com** Online air travel info, with search engine for bargain flights.

Ⓦ **www.geocities.com/thavery2000** Extensive list of airline toll-free numbers (from the US) and websites.

Ⓦ **www.hotwire.com** Discount ticket site (US only), best for last-minute savings, that sells off tickets from major US airlines. Request your travel dates only, then receive your times and airlines, plus a fixed rate; you then have one hour to purchase your ticket. Tickets are non-refundable and do not earn frequent-flier miles.

Ⓦ **www.lastminute.com** (in UK); Ⓦ **www. us.lastminute.com** (in US); Ⓦ **www.lastminute. com.au** (in Australia) Offers good last-minute holiday package and flight-only deals.

Ⓦ **www.orbitz.com** Travel booking site funded by five major US airlines, generally offering marginally cheaper fares than competitors Travelocity and Expedia (US only).

Ⓦ **www.priceline.com** (in US); Ⓦ **www. priceline.co.uk** (in UK) Put in a bid for a flight on a certain date, and if the search engine finds a ticket at an equivalent value, a non-refundable, non-transferable and non-changeable ticket will be purchased. Savings run as high as forty percent off standard fares, but you cannot specify flight times or airlines, and you can bid only once on any given itinerary. To get an idea of going rates, visit Hotwire first.

Ⓦ **www.skyauction.com** (US only) Auctions tickets and travel packages. The best strategy is to bid late, with the maximum you're willing to pay, since if you win you'll pay just enough to beat the runner-up. Read restrictions on tickets carefully – dates are often limited, and taxes and surcharges can add up.

Ⓦ **www.smartertravel.com** Tips and tricks for negotiating travel bargains and frequent-flier perks, primarily for US travellers.

Ⓦ **MACROBUTTON HtmlResAnchor www. travelocity.com** Along with Expedia, the most full-service online travel agency, with destination guides,

hot web fares and deals on car hire, accommodation and flights. Based on the travel agent system SABRE, the most comprehensive central reservations system in the US.

Ⓦ **www.travelshop.com.au** Australian website offering discounted flights, packages, insurance and online bookings.

## From the US and Canada

From most places in North America, **flying** is obviously the most convenient way to reach the Yucatán. However, it is also accessible **by bus or car** – especially if you intend to take in more of Mexico on your way to the peninsula – and numerous **cruises** stop off along the coast.

### By air

Flights to Cancún go **from almost every major US city**, but the cheapest and most frequent depart from "gateway" cities in the south and west, most commonly Los Angeles, Dallas, Houston and Miami, though New York City can occasionally be comparably priced. Round-trip flights from LAX, Miami and Dallas **to Cancún** start around US$250, rising to US$400 in peak season; figure an additional US$100 or so from other US hubs. You can also find attractive deals that include a few nights' lodging in Cancún, Playa del Carmen or Cozumel (see "Packages and organized tours", p.21). **For Cozumel**, flights go on several airlines from Charlotte, Chicago, Dallas, Detroit, Houston, Minneapolis and Philadelphia. Rates from southern cities like Houston and Dallas are typically US$275–350 year-round; expect a US$100 or so increase from northern cities like Chicago and New York. You can reach these cities on other carriers via Mexico City.

Continental serves **Ciudad del Carmen, Mérida and Villahermosa** from Houston, while Aeroméxico offers a few additional flights. Tickets to all three cities start around US$275 and go up to US$350 in high season. You can also reach these cities (as well as Cancún and Cozumel), on numerous airlines' codeshare flights if you transfer in Mexico City.

**From Toronto, Vancouver, Winnipeg, Halifax, Calgary and Montréal**, Air Canada flies direct to Cancún, though flights are not very frequent. Prices start at around Can$900, and cheaper charter flights are plentiful in the winter. Note that your options expand greatly if you fly via the US.

### Airlines

**Aeroméxico** ☎1-800/237-6639, 🖥www.aeromexico.com; ☎1-800/021-4010 in Mexico. Atlanta, Cincinnati, Houston, LA, Miami, New York and Salt Lake City to Cancún; LA and Miami to Mérida; Houston and San Antonio to Villahermosa and Ciudad del Carmen.

**Air Canada** ☎1-888/247-2262, 🖥www.aircanada.ca; ☎1-800/719-2827 in Mexico. Halifax, Montréal, Toronto, Winnipeg, Calgary and Vancouver to Cancún.

**Alaska Airlines** ☎1-800/252-7522, 🖥www.alaska-air.com; ☎55/5282-2484 in Mexico. Anchorage to Cancún, via LA.

**America West Airlines** ☎1-800/235-9292, 🖥www.americawest.com; ☎1-800/235-9292 in Mexico. Phoenix to Cancún.

**American Airlines** ☎1-800/433-7300, 🖥www.aa.com; ☎1-800/904-6000 in Mexico. Boston, Chicago, Dallas, LA, Miami, New York, Reno and St Louis to Cancún; Dallas to Cozumel.

**Continental Airlines** ☎1-800/523-3273 in the US and Mexico, 🖥www.continental.com. Cleveland, Detroit, Houston, Memphis, Minneapolis and New York to Cancún; Houston, Minneapolis and New York to Cozumel; Houston to Ciudad del Carmen, Mérida and Villahermosa.

**Delta Air Lines** ☎1-800/241-4141, 🖥www.delta.com; ☎1-800/123-4710 in Mexico. Atlanta, Cincinnati and Salt Lake City to Cancún; Miami to Mérida.

**Mexicana** ☎1-800/531-7921 in the US, 866/281-3049 in Canada, 🖥www.mexicana.com; ☎1-800/509-8960 in Mexico. Chicago, Dallas, Los Angeles, Miami, New York and Toronto to Cancún.

**Northwest** ☎1-800/447-4747, 🖥www.nwa .com; ☎55/5279-5390 in Mexico. Detroit, Houston, Indianapolis, Newark, Memphis, Milwaukee and Minneapolis to Cancún; Detroit, Houston, Newark, and Minneapolis to Cozumel; Houston to Ciudad del Carmen, Mérida and Villahermosa.

**United Airlines** ☎1-800/538-2929, 🖥www.ual.com; ☎1-800/003-0777 in Mexico. Denver, San Francisco and Washington to Cancún; Charlotte and Chicago to Cozumel.

**US Airways** ☎1-800/622-1015 in the US and Canada, 🖥www.usairways.com; ☎1-800/843-3000 in Mexico. Boston, Charlotte, Philadelphia and Washington to Cancún; Charlotte, Chicago and Philadelphia to Cozumel.

### Travel agents

**eXito** ☎1-800/655-4053, 🖥www.exitotravel .com. Independent travel specialists for Latin America. Website features a particularly useful airfare finder and other invaluable information.

**Last Minute Club** ☎1-877/970-3500, 🖥www.lastminuteclub.com. Canada-based travel club specializing in standby flights and packages; membership is Can$40 per year.

**Now Voyager** ☎212/459-1616, 🖥www .nowvoyagertravel.com. New York-based courier flight broker and consolidator.

**STA Travel** ☎1-800/781-4040 in the US, 1-888/427-5639 in Canada, 🖥www.statravel.com. Worldwide discount travel firm specializing in student and youth fares, with branches in the New York, Los Angeles, San Francisco and Boston areas; also offers student IDs, travel insurance, car rental and more.

**Travel CUTS** ☎1-800/592-2887 in the US, ☎1-866/246-9762 in Canada, 🖥www.travelcuts.com. Canada's main student travel firm, specializing in student fares, IDs and other travel services.

## Packages and organized tours

Hundreds of independent companies offer good-value **package tours** to Mexican resorts, as do the tour arms of most major North American airlines. Packages are generally available only for the beach resorts, such as Cancún and Cozumel, and travel time is restricted to one or two weeks. If, however, what you want is a week on a Mexican beach, your best bet is to comb the Sunday newspaper travel sections for the latest bargains, then see if your local travel agent or an online agency like Travelocity can turn up anything better. Prices vary tremendously by resort, season and style of accommodation, but one week in a good hotel will generally start at US$700 per person. Prices may be less than that on last-minute deals available a week or two before the departure date. The busiest times for North Americans travelling to Mexican resorts are during Christmas and the college spring break season, when you'll be less likely to get the flight or the fare you want.

In addition, literally hundreds of **specialist companies** offer tours of the Yucatán based around hiking, biking, diving, birdwatching and the like. See p.63 for just a few of the possibilities; a travel agent should be able to point out others. Remember that book-

## Airpasses in Mexico

If you want to visit several destinations in a fairly short time and venture into central Mexico or neighbouring countries, then an **airpass** is worth considering; these can be especially useful if combined with the flexibility of an open-ended ticket.

The **MexiPass** consists of prebooked and prepaid coupons for internal flights on Mexicana and Aeroméxico (including subsidiary Aerocaribe, serving the Yucatán Peninsula) at discount prices for travellers from outside Mexico. Travel to Mexico can be on any airline (but some fares are lower if you use Mexicana or Aeroméxico); the pass is valid for ninety days, and you'll need to purchase a minimum of two coupons and book routes and dates before you leave your home country. Date (but not route) changes can be made without paying a penalty, provided space is available on the flight you want. Prices are for one-way flights, based on zones, increasing the further you fly, and do not include domestic departure taxes (currently US$24 per flight): Cancún to Mérida, for example, costs US$80, as is Mérida to Cozumel; Cancún to Mexico City runs for US$200. You can also incorporate international flights on the Mexican carriers between the USA, Canada and the Caribbean, in which case you need to buy at least three coupons. Because most flights are routed through Mexico City, the pass isn't ideal for hopping just around the Yucatán, but it can offer real savings on the longer flights: for example, New York–Cancún–Mérida–Mexico City–New York will cost US$615 before taxes. The potential permutations are mind-boggling, but the savings can be considerable; you need to think seriously about what you want to see, and in what order, before you go. The best way to find out how (or if) an airpass will benefit you is to call either the airlines concerned or a specialist flight agent.

ings made through a travel agent cost no more than going through the tour operator – indeed, many tour companies sell only through agents. Unless stated, the prices we've quoted do not include the cost of actually getting to Mexico. For operators that run trips exclusively for travellers with disabilities, see p.69.

More countercultural, and arguably better value, are **overland routes** covered by Green Tortoise Adventure Travel. Converted school buses provide reasonably comfortable transport and sleeping space for up to 35 people; the clientele comes from all over the world, and communal cookouts and remote camping spots are the rule. The routes that currently include the Yucatán are the fourteen-day Maya Trail trip from Cancún to San Cristóbal de las Casas and back up along the Caribbean coast (US$700 plus US$121 for food and park entrances); the Pyramids and Playas tour (also fourteen days) to Tulum and into Belize (US$699 plus US$151 for food); and a 28-day San Francisco–Cancún "Winter Migration" (US$1249 plus US$191 for food). For more information,

contact the main office at 494 Broadway, San Francisco, CA 94133 (☎415/956-7500 or 1-800/867-8647, ⊚www.greentortoise. com). Additional speciality tour operators are listed in the UK (see p.26) and Australia sections (see p.27).

### Package tour operators

**Future Vacations** ☎1-888/788-2545, ⊚www.futurevacations.com. Vacation packages in Cancún and Cozumel.
**Globus** ☎1-800/755-8581, ⊚www.globusjourneys.com. Eight-day tour of the northern Yucatán Peninsula from US$1459.
**International Student Tours** ☎1-888/472-3933 in Canada, ⊚www.istours.com. Student group-travel company offering week-long resort packages to Cancún (from Can$1109 including airfare).
**Majestic Mexico Tours** ☎1-877/783-2485, ⊚www.mexico-tours.com. First-class sightseeing tours around the Yucatán archeological sites starting at US$719 without airfare.

### Specialist tour operators

**Adventure Center** ☎1-800/228-8747, ⊚www.adventure-center.com. Specializes in ecologically sound adventure travel. The ten-day

"Yucatán Panorama", for example, starts at US$600 for the trip from Cancún to Palenque and back. The 22-day "Mayan Adventure" (from US$1205) takes in sites in Belize as well. Prices include transport and hotel only, not meals.

**Adventures Abroad** ☎1-800/665-3998, ⓦ www.adventures-abroad.com. Canada-based travel planners providing small-group tours. A seven-day tour of the Yucatán's ancient sites costs Can$1502 or US$1333.

**Backroads** ☎1-800/462-2848, ⓦ www.backroads.com. Hiking, biking and snorkelling tours to the Yucatán and other destinations, starting at US$2698 per person for a six-day trip. Sporty family packages are available as well.

**Bike Mexico** ☎416-848-0265, ⓦ www.bikemexico.com. Backroads cycling tours led by the bike fanatics you would expect. Trips range from a week-long excursion around the Ruta Puuc (US$620) to a full tour of the peninsula from Cancún to San Cristóbal de las Casas, lasting three and a half weeks (US$1370).

**G.A.P. Adventures** ☎1-800/465-5600, ⓦ www .gap.ca. Guided adventure trips with some camping and trekking; US$1455 for three weeks on the Ruta Maya through the Yucatán, Chiapas, Guatemala and Belize, or US$890 for a two-week "Ancient Civilizations" trip from Mexico City to Cancún.

**Global Exchange** ☎1-800/497-1994 or 415/255-7296, ⓦ www.globalexchange.org. Offers "Reality Tours" to increase American travellers' awareness of real life in other countries; trips to Chiapas to learn about indigenous rights cost US$750 on average.

**S&S Tours** ☎1-800/499-5685 or 520/458-6365, ⓦ www.ss-tours.com. Archeology tour by train, on the deluxe Expreso Maya, between Mérida and Palenque. The eight-day journey starts at US$2650.

**Wilderness Travel** ☎1-800/368-2794, ⓦ www.wildernesstravel.com. Nine days on the Ruta Maya in Chiapas and Guatemala from US$2695 (depending on how many people take the tour).

## By bus

North American **bus travel** is grim compared to the relative comfort of Amtrak's train service, but you have a wider range of US border posts to choose from. Count on at least 45 hours' journey time from New York to a Texas frontier post (around US$120), or at least eleven and a half hours from San Francisco to Tijuana (US$88) – and a further day's travel from either point to Mexico City, from which it's another 20 hours to Mérida.

Because of the North American Free Trade Agreement (NAFTA), many Mexican bus companies also cross the border into the US, which means that you can pick up a bus back into Mexico as far north as Houston or LA.

Greyhound (☎1-800/229-9424, ⓦ www .greyhound.com) runs regularly to all the major border crossings, and some of their buses will take you over the frontier and to a Mexican bus station, which saves a lot of hassle. Greyhound agents abroad should also be able to reserve your through tickets with their Mexican counterparts, which is even more convenient but involves a lot of pre-planning.

A cheap and cheerful alternative to the rigours of Greyhound travel is an overland tour in one of Green Tortoise's summer-of-love style buses (see "Packages and organized tours" on p.22).

## By car

Taking your own **car** into Mexico will obviously give you a great deal more freedom, but it's an option fraught with complications. Aside from the border formalities, you'll have to contend with the state of the roads and the style of driving – these considerations are dealt with in more detail on p.45.

US, Canadian, British, Irish, Australian, New Zealand and most European **driving licences** are valid in Mexico, but it's a good idea to arm yourself with an International Driving Permit – available to US citizens for a nominal fee from the American Automobile Association (☎1-800/222-4357, ⓦ www.aaa.com), and to Canadian drivers from the Canadian Automobile Association (☎613/247-0117, ⓦ www.caa.ca). If you are stopped by a Mexican traffic cop for any reason, show that first, and if they abscond with it you at least still have your own (more difficult to replace) licence.

As a rule, you can drive in Baja and the Zona Libre (the border area extending roughly 20km into Mexico) without any special formalities. To drive elsewhere in Mexico, however, you must obtain a temporary **importation permit** (around US$25) from the Departamento de Migración at the border. You'll need to show registration and title (or rental contract) for the car, plus your driver's licence and passport, and you'll probably be asked to supply photocopies of these and of your tourist card. To make sure you don't sell the car in Mexico or a neighbouring country, you'll be required either to post a cash bond of about US$400 for a car less than four years old (plus nonrefundable tax and commission), deposited at a branch of Banjercito, which has branches at all border posts for this purpose, or to give an imprint of a major credit card. You can get a refund of a cash deposit only at the same border post where you paid the bond; using plastic is preferable because you can return via any border crossing you like. Note that your importation permit is subject to a six-month time limit, during which you can drive your car out of Mexico and return, but there are penalties in force if you exceed the limit, including forfeiture of your vehicle.

Similar conditions apply if you want to **sail** to Mexico in your own boat. For further details, see ⓦ www.tijuana.com/boatcrossing.

With few exceptions, US auto **insurance** policies don't cover mishaps in Mexico. Take out a Mexican policy, available from numerous agencies on either side of every border post. Rates depend on the value of the vehicle and what kind of coverage you want, but figure on US$11 or so a day for basic liability. Fourteen days' liability coverage is US$85 with Mexico Insurance Services (☎619/941-2443, ⓦ www.mexinsure.us) and full coverage for a US$10,000 vehicle is US$130.45. Also well respected is Sanborn's Insurance (☎1-800/222-0158, ⓦ www.sanbornsinsurance.com).

The American Automobile Association and Canadian Automobile Association produce **road maps** and route planners for travel to Mexico, and members may qualify for discounted insurance at affiliated border agencies. However, emergency and breakdown services apply only in the US and Canada.

## By cruise

Several **cruise lines** ply the Caribbean out of Miami, taking in Cozumel, Playa del Carmen and Mahahual. Yucatan Express (☎1-866/670-3939, ⓦ www.yucatanexpress.com) runs a ship from Tampa to Progreso

and Puerto Morelos, starting at just US$65 one way for passage only on the 36-hour crossing to Progreso; **packages** that include meals as well as hotels on land are also available. For posher, full-vacation outings, **prices** start at US$600 per person, plus airfare to the starting point, and go (way) up from there. Agencies specializing in cruises include Cruise Adventures (☎1-800/248-7447, ⓦ www.cruiseadventures.com) and Cruise World (☎1-800/228-1153, ⓦ www.cruiseworldtours.com).

### North American cruise lines

**Carnival Cruise Lines** ☎1-888/227-6482, ⓦ www.carnival.com.
**Norwegian Cruise Line** ☎1-800/327-7030, ⓦ www.ncl.com.
**Royal Caribbean Cruises** US & Canada ☎1-800/398-9819, UK ☎0800/018 2020, ⓦ www.royalcaribbean.com.

## From the UK and Ireland

Aside from charter flights in high season, there are no direct flights between **Britain** and the Yucatán Peninsula; British Airways does fly three times weekly from London Heathrow to Mexico City, or you can take one of the daily flights to Cancún with a connection in Miami or Dallas.

Good deals can be found with a number of European carriers, though most fly to Mexico City **via European hubs**, so you will have to change planes again to reach Cancún or Mérida. Another possibility is to fly **via the US** and either continue overland or buy an onward flight once in the country, although the US immigration process can now be a lengthy hassle. New York is normally the cheapest destination in the US, but it's a long way from Mexico; for speediest connections, it's usually best to fly to Miami (on BA, American or Virgin), Houston (Continental), Dallas (American) or Atlanta (Delta). The cheapest high-season fares are usually on Continental or Virgin (connection at Miami with Aeroméxico), but these probably won't beat flights via Europe. If you want a stopover on a budget flight, you'll generally pay upwards of £100 more, though it may be worthwhile if you also want to spend some time in the US. For more on getting to Mexico from North America, see p.20.

Ticket prices to Mexico are usually lower than to other Latin American destinations, and competition is such that there are often bargains available, especially if you can be flexible with dates. Tickets are typically valid for between three and six months, sometimes up to one year, but some tickets work out cheaper if you're away less than thirty days. If you want to fly into one city and out of another, travel to different destinations in Mexico, or even other countries in the region, then it's worth considering an open-return ticket, perhaps in conjunction with an airpass (see box on p.22).

Official fares, quoted by the airlines, are generally more expensive than those booked through a flight or travel agent. To find discount agents, check the travel pages of the broadsheet papers or listings magazines, Teletext or the Internet, though websites in the UK are not so directly geared to finding Mexican destinations as their US counterparts (for online booking agents, see p.19). STA Travel's website (see p.26) has a reasonable fare finder too. Deciding which flight option is best can be a little complex; as always, a good flight specialist – such as North South, Journey Latin America or Trailfinders (see p.26) – is the best first call to weed through the possibilities.

Prices for scheduled return flights from London to Cancún range from £600 low season to £750 or more in high season, including taxes; flights to Mexico City are about £625, so it's rarely cheaper to fly there and take an internal flight to the Yucatán. Charter flights to Mexico are fairly common now, usually flying out of Gatwick or Manchester to Cancún. Charter fares, sometimes under £350 in the low season, can also be very good value any time outside school holidays, though they can go as high as £870 in August, and your stay will probably be limited to two or four weeks. Try My Travel (℡0870/238 7777, ⓦwww.mytravel.co.uk), whose charters offer the largest choice of Mexican destinations.

There are currently no direct flights **from Ireland** to Mexico. Your cheapest way to get there will almost certainly be to take one of the numerous daily flights **to London** from Dublin, Cork, Shannon or Belfast, then connect with one of the transatlantic flights detailed above. You can also fly from Ireland **via the US**, with Delta from Dublin via Atlanta, or with Continental from Dublin or Shannon via New York (Newark). The cheapest place to buy your ticket will almost certainly be a discount travel agent such as USIT (℡01/602 1904, ⓦwww.usit.ie) rather than from the airlines themselves. Expect to pay around €700 low season, €1000 high season, including tax for the cheapest return tickets from Dublin to Mexico, €50–100 more from Cork or Shannon. From Belfast or Derry, expect to pay around £800 low season, £1300 high season.

## Airlines

**Aer Lingus** Republic of Ireland ℡0818/365000, Northern Ireland ℡0845/084 4444, ⓦwww.aerlingus.com.

**Aeroméxico** ℡0207/801 6234, ⓦwww.aeromexico.com; ℡1-800/021-4010 in Mexico.

**Air France** UK ℡08701/424 343, ⓦwww.airfrance.com/uk, Ireland ℡01/605 0383, ⓦwww.airfrance.com/ie; ℡1 800/123-4660 in Mexico.

**American Airlines** UK ℡08457/789 789 or 020/8572 5555, Ireland ℡01/602 0550, ⓦwww.aa.com; ℡1 800/904-6000 in Mexico.

**British Airways** UK ℡0870/850 9850, Ireland ℡1890/626 747, ⓦba.com; ℡55/5387-0300 in Mexico.

**Continental** UK ℡0845/607 6760, ⓦwww.continental.com/uk, Ireland ℡1890/925 252, ⓦwww.continental.com/ie; ℡1-800/523-3273 in Mexico.

**Delta** UK ℡0800/414767, Ireland ℡01/407 3165, ⓦwww.delta.com; ℡1-800/123-4710 in Mexico.

**Iberia** UK ℡0845/850 9000, Ireland ℡01/407 3017, ⓦwww.iberiaairlines.co.uk; ℡998/986-0243 in Mexico.

**KLM** UK ℡08705/074 074, ⓦwww.klmuk.com; ℡55/5279-5390 in Mexico (Northwest Airlines).

**Lufthansa** UK ℡0870/8377 747, Ireland ℡01/844 5544, ⓦwww.lufthansa.co.uk; ℡55/5230-0000 in Mexico.

**Mexicana** ℡020/8492 0000, ⓦwww.mexicana.com.mx; ℡1-800/509-8960 in Mexico.

**Ryanair** Ireland ℡0818/303 030, UK ℡0871/246 0000, ⓦwww.ryanair.com.

**United** UK ℡0845/844 4777, ⓦwww.unitedairlines.co.uk; ℡1-800/003-0777 in Mexico.

**Virgin Atlantic** UK ℡08705/747 747 ⓦwww.virgin-atlantic.com.

## Travel agents

**Bridge the World** UK ☏ 0870/814 4400, ⓦ www .bridgetheworld.com. Round-the-world tickets and good deals aimed at the backpacker market.
**Joe Walsh Tours** Ireland ☏ 01/241 0800, ⓦ www .joewalshtours.ie. General budget fares agent.
**Lee Travel** Ireland ☏ 021/427 7111, ⓦ www.leetravel.ie. Flights and holiday pakages.
**North South Travel** UK ☏ 01245/608 291, ⓦ www.northsouthtravel.co.uk. Travel agency offering discounted fares worldwide; profits are used to support projects in the developing world, especially the promotion of sustainable tourism.
**Premier Travel** Northern Ireland ☏ 028/7126 3333, ⓦ www.premiertravel.uk.com. Discount flight specialists.
**South American Experience** UK ☏ 020/7976 5511, ⓦ www.southamericanexperience.co.uk. Flight and tailor-made-itinerary specialists; very good airfare prices.
**STA Travel** UK ☏ 08701/600 599, ⓦ www.statravel.co.uk. Specialists in low-cost flights, plus tours for students and those 25 and younger – though other customers welcome.
**Trailfinders** UK ☏ 0845/058 5858, ⓦ www.trailfinders.co.uk, Ireland ☏ 01/677 7888, ⓦ www.trailfinders.ie. One of the best-informed and most efficient agents for independent travellers; produce a very useful quarterly magazine worth scrutinizing for round-the-world routes.
**USIT** Republic of Ireland ☏ 01/602 1600, Northern Ireland ☏ 028/9032 7111, ⓦ www.usit.ie. Ireland's main student and youth travel specialists.

## Packages and tours

Many companies offer **package tours** to Mexico, and there's an enormous choice to suit all budgets. Trips range from two weeks in a luxury beach hotel to trekking around the most remote archeological sites. Wild-life trips are popular too – you can look for manatees off the Caribbean coast or seek rare birds in the cloud forests of Chiapas. Group tours save the hassle of making your own arrangements and can be good value. The tours are generally relaxed and friendly, usually led by someone from the UK who knows the area, and in many cases there's also a local guide. Several firms offer tailor-made itineraries as well. Any High Street travel agent can sell you a basic package to Cancún; the list on the right covers the best and most experienced UK specialist opera-tors. Prices quoted do not include the airfare

unless stated, and are of course subject to supplements for things like single room occupancy. Many tours operate in winter only, though several run year-round. Addi-tional specialist tour operators are listed in the North America (see p.22) and Australia sections (see p.27).

### Specialist tour operators

**Cathy Matos Mexican Tours** UK ☏ 020/8492 0000, ⓦ www.cathymatosmexico.com. A specialist in Mexico for over 25 years, Cathy can arrange almost any sort of Yucatán trip from a Cancún beach stay to jungle exploration, but above all the unusual and the upmarket. Prices start from around £1000 for a week in Cancún, including flights.
**Exodus** UK ☏ 0870/240 5550, Ireland ☏ 01/679 5700, ⓦ www.exodus.co.uk. Sixteen-day Ruta Maya tour in Mexico, Guatemala and Belize from £1000 plus US$150.
**Journey Latin America** UK ☏ 020/8747 8315 or 0161/832 1441, ⓦ www.journeylatinamerica. co.uk. Latin America experts with a wide range of organized groups, mix-and-match tours and holidays, including the haciendas and luxury Riviera Maya hotels, as well as language courses in Mérida. Seven-day Maya city tour from around £970 including flights; 15-day Yucatán self-drive from £1500 inclusive.
**Travelbag Adventures** UK ☏ 0870/794 1009, ⓦ www.travelbag-adventures.com. A good outfit that will tailor itineraries to your needs. Small-group hotel-based excursions include an eight-day "Mayans & Mexicans" tour of central Yucatán from £1119, including airfare, and a sixteen-day "Realm of the Maya" tour in the Yucatán, Chiapas, Guatemala and Belize from £1399.
**Trek America** UK ☏ 0870/444 8735, ⓦ www.trekamerica.co.uk. Small-group adventure trips, camping or staying at budget hotels across Mexico, including a ten-day "Mexican Highlights" tour for £618, or an eighteen-day trek around the Yucatán into Belize. Flights and food are extra.
**Trips Worldwide** UK ☏ 0117/311 440, ⓦ www. tripsworldwide.co.uk. Offers an inspired range of tailor-made itineraries to lesser-visited places, such as Isla Holbox, from £1795 for fourteen days. Also agents for many other recommended tour operators.

## From Australia and New Zealand

The high season for flights to Mexico **from Australia and New Zealand** comprises mid-June to mid-July, and mid-December to mid-January. You can count on paying

A$200–400 more at peak season than the fares quoted below.

From Australia the cheapest flights are with LAN to Mexico City via Santiago, Chile (A$2300). Alternatives are with Air New Zealand via Auckland and United Airlines via Los Angeles (A$2700). From New Zealand, your cheapest choices are again LAN via Santiago (from NZ$2300), as well as Air New Zealand via Los Angeles (NZ$2400).

One of the best deals, mile for mile, on RTW fares from Australia is offered by the Star Alliance airline group (including Air New Zealand, United, Lufthansa, Thai, Singapore and Varig). Prices and deals vary, but the best deal is A$2590/NZ$3099 for 26,000 miles and up to five stops; the only catch is that no Mexican airline is a member of the group, so you can't use the fare to hop around the country. A similar deal is offered by OneWorld (including Qantas, British Airways, Cathay Pacific, American and LAN). Additional specialist tour operators are listed in the UK (see p.26) and North America sections (see p.22).

## Airlines

**Aerolineas Argentinas** Australia ✆ 02/9234 9000, New Zealand ✆ 09/379 3675, Ⓦ www.aerolineas.com.ar/au; ✆ 1 800/123-8588 in Mexico.
**Aeroméxico** Australia ✆ 029/959 3922, ✆ 09/623-4294, Ⓦ www.aeromexico.com; ✆ 1-800/021-4010 in Mexico.
**Air New Zealand** New Zealand ✆ 0800/737 000, Ⓦ www.airnz.co.nz, Australia ✆ 013/2476, Ⓦ www.airnz.com.au; ✆ 55/5705-1717 in Mexico.
**Air Tahiti Nui** New Zealand ✆ 09/308 3360, Australia ✆ 02/9244 2799, Ⓦ www.airtahitinui.com.
**Delta** Australia ✆ 01300/302 849, New Zealand ✆ 09/379 3370, Ⓦ www.delta.com; ✆ 1-800/123-4710 in Mexico.
**Japan Airlines (JAL)** Australia ✆ 02/9272 1111, www.au.jal.com, New Zealand ✆ 09/379 9906, Ⓦ www.nz.jal.com; ✆ 555/242-0150 in Mexico.
**LAN** Australia ✆ 01305/670 9999, New Zealand ✆ 09/977 2233, Ⓦ www.lan.com; ✆ 1 800/700-6700 in Mexico.
**Mexicana** Australia ✆ 03/9699 9355, New Zealand ✆ 09/914 2573, Ⓦ www.mexicana.com; ✆ 1-800/509-8960 in Mexico.
**Qantas** Australia ✆ 13/1313, Ⓦ www.qantas.com.au, New Zealand ✆ 0800/808 767, Ⓦ www.qantas.co.nz.

**United** Australia ✆ 13/1777, Ⓦ www.unitedairlines.com.au; ✆ 1-800/003-0777 in Mexico.

## Travel agents

**Flight Centre** Australia ✆ 13/3133, Ⓦ www.flightcentre.com.au, New Zealand ✆ 0800/243 544, Ⓦ www.flightcentre.co.nz.
**Holiday Shoppe** New Zealand ✆ 0800/808 480, Ⓦ www.holidayshoppe.co.nz.
**STA Travel** Australia ✆ 1300/733 035, Ⓦ www.statravel.com.au, New Zealand ✆ 0508/782 872, Ⓦ www.statravel.co.nz.
**Trailfinders** Australia ✆ 1300/780 212, Ⓦ www.trailfinders.com.au.

## Tour operators

**Mexico.com.au** Australia ✆ 1800/020 700, Ⓦ www.mexico.com.au. Booking agency for accommodation throughout Mexico.
**South America Destinations** Australia ✆ 1800/337050 or 03/9725 4655, Ⓦ www.south-america.com.au. Offers a six-day "Yucatán Explorer" tour that includes Oaxaca.
**South America Travel Centre** Australia ✆ 1800/655 051 or 03/9642 5353, Ⓦ www.satc.com.au. Tours include twelve days in the Yucatán from A$1750, or 22 days on the Ruta Maya in Mexico, Guatemala and Belize from A$2275.
**World Expeditions** Australia ✆ 1300/720 000, Ⓦ www.worldexpeditions.com.au, New Zealand ✆ 0800/350 354, Ⓦ www.worldexpeditions.co.nz. Offers a fourteen-day "Mayan World" tour in Chiapas and Guatemala from A$4290, or a 22-day trip including Oaxaca and Mexico City too from A$5520 (not including airfare). They also have offices in the US (✆ 1-888/464-8735, Ⓦ www.weadventures.com) and UK (✆ 020/8870 2600, Ⓦ www.worldexpeditions.co.uk).

# Overland routes

The Yucatán Peninsula is a highly alluring leg of any extended trip through Mexico and Central America and can be accessed by air as well as by driving.

## From elsewhere in Mexico

If you'll be travelling **by bus** to the peninsula from Mexico City or any point south and east, an invaluable resource is Ⓦ www.ticketbus.com.mx, where you can check schedules and buy tickets for most first-class and deluxe routes, as well as some second-class services. As many bus stations are located outside of town, this website will spare you an extra trip to the terminal.

Mérida, the capital of Yucatán state, is also its transport hub, with constant traffic in and out. The main route to the city **by bus from Mexico City** is via Puebla and Villahermosa, then through Campeche – a nineteen-hour ride (3 daily), so it's worth splurging on UNO, the deluxe bus line operated by ADO. Buses from the capital also alight at Cancún (3 daily; 24hr) and Campeche (3 daily; 17hr). From **Oaxaca**, most buses head north and rejoin the Puebla–Villahermosa highway, then continue on to the lacklustre town of Escárcega.

Mérida's airport also receives frequent internal **flights**, including eight daily from Mexico City (1hr 40min). It's also possible to fly from the capital to Cancún (19 daily; 2hr) and Campeche (2 daily; 1hr 10min).

## From Guatemala and Belize

Travellers coming from the Maya sites in northern Guatemala and Belize will find themselves at some very out-of-the-way border crossings. If you want to bypass the potential bureaucratic hassles that come with isolated posts on borders that see a lot of illegal immigration, you can of course fly. Coming **by air from Guatemala**, Taca International (℡2470-8222 in Guatemala, ⓦwww.grupotaca.com) flies four days a week (Tues, Thurs, Sat, Sun) from Guatemala City to Cancún (3hr). Direct flights from Flores also operate to Cancún (1hr 30min). Tickets for both start at about US$180/£100 one-way.

Travellers have several choices when arriving **by car from Guatemala**. The easiest, most frequented checkpoint is at the Talismán Bridge to Tapachula, though this deposits you in southern Chiapas, beyond the scope of this book; an international **bus** runs from Guatemala City through to Tapachula (4 daily; 5–6hr), and you will have to get off the bus at the border, then re-board on the Mexico side after having your pass-port inspected. If you arrive at the check-point on a second-class Guatemalan bus, you can take one of the many *combis* waiting on the Mexico side.

If you plan to limit your route in Mexico to northern Chiapas and the Yucatán, then the best crossing is at Bethél, on the Rio Usumacinta opposite Frontera Corozal. Buses run from Flores to Bethél (3 daily; 5hr), where you take a thirty-minute *lancha* ride across the river (US$35 for up to four people). From Frontera Corozal, you can head directly to Palenque or stop off at Bonampak and Yaxchilán. Less desirable (for expense and complex transport connections), yet possible, is the crossing at El Naranjo, which requires a four-hour boat ride to the village of La Palma in Mexico.

There are no direct flights **from Belize** to the Yucatán, and given the size of the country, it makes more sense simply to travel **by bus** to the border at Chetumal. Buses run frequently from Corozal, twenty minutes from the border (and not to be confused with Frontera Corozal, in Mexico) to Chetumal, stopping at the checkpoint and the duty-free shopping zone, then depositing passengers at either the main Chetumal bus station or main market just northeast of the centre.

Note that in all cases, you will need a Mexico-issued tourist card (see opposite) in addition to your passport. There is no charge for the cards, but of course that doesn't deter Mexican immigration officials from asking, especially at the smaller border crossings. If you have the opportunity, visit a consulate in Guatemala City or Belize City to obtain a tourist card ahead of your arrival at the border, as the posts can sometimes be out of them. Whenever possible, cross the border during the daytime, and allow plenty of time in your schedule; **posts typically close after 8pm**. Also note that Mexico observes daylight saving time, while Guatemala does not. Keep your passport handy once in Mexico, as buses in the border area are often stopped in additional immigration sweeps.

# Red tape and visas

Citizens of the US, Canada, the UK, Ireland, Australia, New Zealand and much of Western Europe do not require a visa to enter Mexico as tourists for less than 180 days; most Western Europeans can stay for 90 days. Non-US citizens travelling via the US, however, may need a US visa. Visitors entering by land are subject to a M$190 entry fee, which will be included in your ticket if arriving by air.

What every visitor does need is a valid **passport** and a **tourist card** (or FMT – *folleto de migración turística*). Tourist cards are free, and if you're flying direct, you should get one on the plane, or from the airline before leaving. Otherwise Mexican consulates issue them, in person or by post. Note that if you are **entering from Belize or Guatemala**, it's not at all uncommon for border posts to run out of tourist cards, or for officials to (illegally) demand a fee for issuing them.

Though most visitors require a passport to pick up their tourist card, US and Canadian citizens only need proof of citizenship (an original birth certificate or notarized copy, for instance, or naturalization papers), along with some form of photo ID (such as a driver's licence). US and Canadian citizens can enter Mexico without a passport if they carry such documents plus their tourist card with them, but it's not advisable, since officials checking your ID may not be aware of this right. Moreover, as of December 31, 2006, US border officials will require American citizens to show their passport when returning from Mexico by air, and this policy will also apply to land border crossings by the end of 2007.

A tourist card is valid for a single entry for **up to 180 days**, though officials will often write in thirty days or less. Be sure to specify you want the full time limit if you know you'll be visiting for a long stretch, as getting an extension can be a frustrating and time-consuming business. You don't always get the time you've asked for in any case: in particular, along the borders with Belize and Guatemala to the south, you will probably get only thirty days (though they may give you more if you specifically ask), and entering via Chiapas State means you're likely to get only fifteen days (extensions unlikely). You may also be asked to show bank statements or other proof of sufficient funds for your stay, about US$300 for every week you'll be in Mexico.

Be sure not to lose the **tourist card stub** that is given back to you after immigration inspection. You are legally required to carry it at all times, and if you have to show your papers, it's as important as your passport. It also has to be handed in on leaving the country – without it, you may experience delays.

Should you lose your tourist card, or need to have it renewed, head for the nearest **Departamento de Migración**, or immigration department office; there are branches in the largest cities. In the case of renewal, if you are near a border, it's far simpler to cross for a day and get a new one upon re-entry than apply for an extension; if you do apply to the immigration department, it's wise to do so a couple of weeks in advance, though you may be told to come back nearer the actual expiry date. Whatever else you may be told, branches of Sectur (the tourist office) cannot renew expired tourist cards or replace lost ones – they will only make sympathetic noises and direct you to the nearest immigration office.

**Visas**, obtainable only through a consulate (in person or by mail), are required by nationals of South Africa and most non-industrialized countries, as well as by anyone entering the country to work, or to study or for more than six months. Business visitors need a Business Authorization Card available from consulates, and usually a visa too. Anyone under 18 needs written consent from their parents if not accompanied by both of them (if accompanied by one, they need written consent from the other).

## Mexican consulates and embassies abroad

The following **embassies and consulates** all issue visas and tourist cards. To find the address of one not listed here, see ⓦwww. sre.gob.mx/delegaciones/dire

### Australia

**Embassy** 14 Perth Ave, Yarralumla, Canberra, ACT 2600 ☎02/6273 3963, ⓦwww.embassyofmexico inaustralia.org.

### Belize

**Embassy** 18 N Park St, Belize City ☎02/230193 or 230194, ⓦwww.embamexbelize.gob.mx.

### Canada

**Embassy** 45 O'Connor St, Suite 1500, Ottawa, ON K1P 1A4 ☎613/233-8988, ⓦwww.embamexcan .com.
**Consulates** at 2055 rue Peel, Suite 1000, Montréal, PQ H3A 1V4 ☎514/288-2502, ⓦwww.consulmex.qc.ca; 199 Bay St, Suite 4440, Commerce Court W, Toronto, ON M5L 1E9 ☎416/368-2875, ⓦwww.consulmex.com; 710–1117 W Hastings St, Vancouver, BC V6E 2K3 ☎604/684-3547, ⓦwww.consulmexvan.com.

### Cuba

**Embassy** C 12 no. 518, Miramar, Playa, Havana 6 ☎7/204 7722, ⓔembamexc@enet.cu.

### Guatemala

**Embassy** Av 2 no. 7–57, Zona 10, Guatemala City ☎02/420-3433, ⓦwww.sre.gob.mx/guatemala.

### Ireland

**Embassy** 43 Ailesbury Rd, Ballsbridge, Dublin 4 ☎01/260 0699, ⓔembasmex@indigo.ie.

### New Zealand

**Embassy** 111–115 Customhouse Quay, 8th floor, Wellington ☎04/472 0555, ⓦwww.mexico.org.nz.

### UK

**Embassy** 8 Halkin St, London SW1X 7DW ☎020/7235 6393, ⓦwww.mexicanconsulate. org.uk.

### US

**Embassy** 1911 Pennsylvania Ave, NW, Washington, DC 20006 ☎202/728-1600, ⓦwww.embassyofmexico.org.
**Consulates** are in nearly fifty other US towns and cities, among them those in the border states listed below:
**Arizona** 1201 F Ave, Douglas, AZ 85607 ☎520/364-3107, ⓦwww.consulmexdouglas.com.
**California** 1549 India St, San Diego, CA 92101 ☎619/231-8414, ⓦwww.sre.gob.mx/sandiego.
**Texas** 301 Mexico Blvd, Suite F-2, Brownsville, TX 78520 ☎956/542-4431, ⓦwww.sre.gob. mx/brownsville; 910 E San Antonio Ave, El Paso, TX 79901 ☎915/533-3644, ⓦwww.sre.gob.mx/elpaso

## Embassies and consulates in Mexico

Contact information for embassies and consulates can be found at ⓦwww.sre.gob. mx/delegaciones/acreditadas. For further details of consulate locations, see the "Listings" sections for the relevant cities in this book.

# Information, websites and maps

The first place to head for information is the Mexican government's ministry of tourism, the Secretaría de Turismo (Sector), which has offices throughout Mexico and abroad. With the advent of the Internet, however, these offices have been scaled back and do not stock the array of leaflets and maps for walk-in visitors that they once did; you're better off visiting the Sector-sponsored website ⓦwww.visitmexico.com as a starting point, then contacting your local office with specific queries if necessary.

Once you're in the Yucatán, you'll find **tourist offices** (sometimes called *turismos*) run by Sector, in addition to some run by state and municipal authorities. It's quite impossible to generalize about the services offered: some are extremely friendly and helpful, with free information and leaflets by the cartload; others are barely capable of answering the simplest question. These offices are listed in the relevant city and regional sections throughout the guide. You can also call Sector toll-free round the clock in Mexico at ⓣ1-800/903-9200, from the US or Canada on ⓣ1-800/446-3942, or from Europe on ⓣ0800/6666 2211.

## Mexican tourist offices overseas

### In the US

225 N Michigan Ave, Suite 1850, Chicago, IL 60601 (ⓣ312/228-0517, ⓕ228-0515); 4507 San Jacinto St, Suite 308, Houston, TX 77004 (ⓣ713/772-2581, ⓔadhemir_olguin@mia.bm.com); 1880 Century Park E, Suite 511, Los Angeles, CA 90067 (ⓣ310/282-9112, ⓕ310/282-9116); 375 Park Ave, Suite 1905, New York, NY 10152 (ⓣ212/308-2110, ⓕ212/308-9060); 5975 Sunset Dr, Suite 305, South Miami, FL 33143 (ⓣ786/621-2909, ⓕ786/621-2907).

### In Canada

1 Place Ville Marie, Suite 1931, Montréal, PQ H3B 2C3 (ⓣ514/871-1103, ⓕ514/871-3825); 2 Bloor St W, Suite 1502, Toronto, ON M4W 3E2 (ⓣ416/925-0704, ⓕ416/925-6061); 999 W Hastings St, Suite 1110, Vancouver, BC V6C 2W2 (ⓣ604/669-2845, ⓕ604/669-3498).

### In the UK

Wakefield House, 41 Trinity Square, London EC3N 4DT ⓣ020/7488 9392, ⓦwww.mexicotravel.co.uk.

## Websites

In addition to the Sector site (ⓦwww .visitmexico.com), you may find the following **websites** useful for travel planning in the Yucatán, Chiapas and Villahermosa.

### Government advisories

Western governments put out the latest information and advice on travel in Mexico. The tone can be extremely overcautious and generalized – alarmist crime warnings, for instance, are hardly applicable to the Yucatán – but overall, their websites are well informed, regularly updated, and always worth reading before making travel plans, and again before departure.

**Canadian Foreign Affairs Department** ⓦwww .dfait-maeci.gc.ca/latinamerica/mexico-en.asp
**Australian Foreign Affairs Department** ⓦ www.dfat.gov.au/geo/mexico/index
**UK Foreign and Commonwealth Office** ⓦwww.fco.gov.uk
**US State Department** ⓦtravel.state.gov

### Other useful websites

**Amnesty International** ⓦweb.amnesty.org/library/eng-mex/index. Amnesty offers the latest information on the human rights situation in Chiapas and nationwide.
**Diario de Yucatán** ⓦwww.yucatan.com.mx. The oldest and largest newspaper on the peninsula, published daily in Mérida. In Spanish only.

### Exploring Colonial Mexico
Ⓦ www.colonial-mexico.com. Run by *Espadaña Press*, this site concentrates on art and architecture from the colonial era, with an excellent archive of photos and information on Franciscan missions and haciendas in the Yucatán.

**INEGI** Ⓦ www.inegi.gob.mx. Website of the Mexican government's National Institute for Statistics, Geography and IT, with tables of statistical and geographical information, and maps of things like climate and vegetation. Some, but not all, is posted in English.

### Latin American Information Centre (LANIC)
Ⓦ www.lanic.utexas.edu/la/mexico. The premier Latin American academic website, it furnishes an excellent source of background information, logically laid out with extensive links covering topics such as history, politics, culture, religion and food.

**Mesoweb** Ⓦ www.mesoweb.com. A huge collection of articles and resources on pre-Columbian Mexico and Central America, including the latest archeological news, maps, timelines and articles about life in the Maya world.

### Mexico Desconocido
Ⓦ www.mexicodesconocido.com. The online version of the popular magazine that explores Mexico's backcountry and historic heritage. A good portion of the articles are available in English.

**Mundo Maya** Ⓦ www.mayadiscovery.com. The online outlet of a now-defunct magazine devoted to Maya culture, with very readable, non-academic articles.

**Ruins of Mexico** Ⓦ www.geocities.com/atlantis01mx/index. An online guide to Mexico's archeological sites, with photos, plans and explanations, which aims eventually to cover all sites, both major and minor. What's on it so far is excellent.

**US National Weather Service** Ⓦ weather.noaa .gov/weather/MX_cc. Highly detailed reports on weather conditions at locations across Mexico.

**Weather Underground** Ⓦ www.wunderground .com/global/mx. User-friendly reports on weather conditions.

## Maps

You should be able to find a reasonable **map** of Mexico in any of the outlets listed below, and in many large bookshops besides. A number of country maps, such as those published by Nelles (1:2,500,000) make some attempt to show relief, but this tends to make other details harder to read. Detailed maps just of the Yucatán Peninsula, however, are a bit harder to come by. Rough Guides, in conjunction with the World Mapping Project, have produced our own rip-proof, waterproof maps of Mexico and of the Yucatán, with roads, contours and physical features all clearly shown. Obviously we recommend it, and if you compare it for price and clarity with the competition, we are confident that you will prefer it too.

If you'll be travelling to the Caribbean beach towns, look for the excellent maps produced by Can-Do Maps, available for sale at Ⓦ www.cancunmap.com. The finely detailed plans of Cancún, Isla Mujeres, Cozumel, Playa del Carmen and the full Riviera Maya clearly label all hotels, restaurants and rental homes, as well as the usual sites.

In Mexico itself, the best maps are those published by Patria, which cover each state individually, and by Guía Roji, which also publishes a Mexican road atlas. The drawback is that they are not updated frequently, and newer or smaller roads in the Yucatán are often missing. Both makes of map are widely available, though – try large Pemex stations.

More detailed, large-scale maps (for hiking or trekking) are rare. International Travel Maps of Vancouver publishes a good one (1:1,000,000) that includes Villahermosa and parts of Chiapas, though it was last updated only in 2000 and can be hard to find. INEGI, the Mexican government mapmakers, do produce very good topographic maps on various scales. The company has an office in every state capital and an outlet at Mexico City's airport. Unfortunately, stocks can run low, so don't count on being able to buy the ones that you want.

# Insurance

As there are no reciprocal health arrangements between Mexico and any other country, travel insurance is essential. Many policies can be adapted to reflect the coverage you want – for example, sickness and accident benefits can often be excluded or included at will. If you do take medical coverage, verify if benefits will be paid during treatment or only after your return home, and whether there is a 24-hour medical emergency phone number. If you need to make a claim, keep receipts for medicines and medical treatment. Also, if you have anything stolen from you, you must make an official statement to the police and obtain a copy of the declaration (*copia de la declaración*) for your insurance company.

A typical **travel insurance policy** also provides safeguards for the loss of baggage, tickets, and a certain amount of cash or travellers' cheques, as well as the cancellation or curtailment of your trip. Most policies exclude so-called dangerous sports unless an extra premium is paid; in Mexico this can mean scuba diving, windsurfing, kiteboarding or trekking, though probably not kayaking or jeep safaris.

Before paying for a new policy, however, **check that you're not already covered**. Credit-card companies, home-insurance policies, and private medical plans some-times cover you and your belongings when you're abroad. Some package tours may include insurance, too, and holders of official student/teacher/youth cards in Canada and the US are entitled to meagre accident coverage and hospital inpatient benefits. Most travel agents, tour operators, banks, and insurance brokers will be able to help you, or consider the travel insurance deal Rough Guides offers (see box below). Remember that when securing baggage insurance, make sure that the per-article limit – typically under $800/£500 – will cover your most valuable possession.

## Rough Guides travel insurance

Rough Guides has teamed up with Columbus Direct to offer you travel insurance that can be tailored to suit your needs.

Readers can choose from many different travel insurance products, including a low-cost backpacker option for long stays; a short-break option for city getaways; a typical holiday package option; and many others. There are also annual multi-trip policies for those who travel regularly, with variable levels of cover available. Different sports and activities (trekking, skiing, etc) can be covered if required on most policies.

**Rough Guides travel insurance** is available to the residents of 36 different countries with different language options to choose from via our website – ⓦ www.roughguidesinsurance.com – where you can also purchase the insurance.

Alternatively, UK residents should call ☎ 0800 083 9507; US citizens should call ☎ 1-800/749-4922; Australians should call ☎ 1 300 669 999. All other nationalities should call ☎ +44 870 890 2843.

# Health

It's always easier to become ill in a foreign country with a different climate, different food and different germs, still more so in a country with lower standards of sanitation than you might be accustomed to. Most travellers, however, get through Mexico without catching anything more serious than a dose of Montezuma's Revenge. You will still want the security of health insurance (see "Insurance" on p.33), but the important thing is to keep your resistance high and to be aware of the health risks linked to poor hygiene, untreated water, mosquito bites, undressed open cuts and unprotected sex.

What you eat and drink is crucial: a poor **diet** lowers your resistance. Be sure to eat enough – and enough of the right things. Eating plenty of fibre, such as the ubiquitous black beans served with Mexican food, helps avoid constipation. Peeled fresh fruit will keep up your vitamin and mineral intake; don't gorge yourself on all the tropical bounty, though, as this change in diet alone may be a shock to your digestive system. It might be worth taking daily multivitamin tablets with you, but they're really no substitute for fresh fruit and vegetables. You can also fortify your intestinal tract by taking acidophilus pills or eating plenty of yoghurt before and during your trip. Drink plenty of fluids, but keep intake of dehydrating alcohol and caffeine to a minimum. Also try to get enough sleep and rest, as it's easy to become run-down if you're on the move a lot, especially in a hot climate.

The lack of **sanitation** in Mexico is often exaggerated, and it's not worth being obsessive about or you'll never enjoy yourself. Even so, a degree of caution is wise – don't try anything too exotic or extremely spicy in the first few days, before your body has had a chance to adjust to local microbes, and avoid food that looks like it has been on display for a while or not freshly cooked. You should also steer clear of salads, and peel fruit before eating it. Avoid raw shellfish, and don't eat anywhere that is obviously dirty (most Yucatecan restaurants, however, are scrupulously clean) – street stalls in particular are suspect. Equally important, monitor your own hygiene by washing your hands at every opportunity; restaurants often have a dedicated tap and sink to one side in the dining room for this purpose. For advice on water, see box p.37.

For comprehensive coverage of the health problems encountered by travellers worldwide, consult *The Rough Guide to Travel Health,* by Dr Nick Jones.

## Vaccinations

No inoculations are required for Mexico, but it's worth visiting your doctor at least four weeks before you leave to check that you are up to date with **tetanus**, **typhoid** and **hepatitis A** shots. Those travelling from the US or Canada will have to pay for inoculations, available at any immunization centre or at most local clinics. Most GPs in the UK have their own travel clinics where you can get advice and certain vaccines on prescription, though they may not administer some of the less common immunizations. Normal travel clinics can be more expensive, but you won't need to make an appointment. In Australia and New Zealand, vaccination centres are less expensive than doctors' clinics. Most will also sell travel-associated accessories, including mosquito nets and first-aid kits.

## Medical resources for travellers

### Websites

ⓦ **health.yahoo.com** Information on specific diseases and conditions, drugs and herbal remedies, plus advice from health experts.
ⓦ **www.fitfortravel.scot.nhs.uk** Scottish NHS

website carrying information about travel-related diseases and how to avoid them.

ⓦ **www.istm.org** International Society for Travel Medicine site, with a full list of clinics specializing in international travel health.

ⓦ **www.tmvc.com.au** Lists Travellers Medical and Vaccination Centres in Australia and New Zealand, plus general travel health information.

ⓦ **www.tripprep.com** Destination information such as necessary vaccinations for most countries, including Mexico; free registration required for access.

## In the US and Canada

**Canadian Society for International Health** 1 Nicholas St, Suite 1105, Ottawa, ON K1N 7B7 ☏613/241-5785, ⓦ www.csih.org. Distributes a free pamphlet, "Health Information for Canadian Travellers", containing an extensive list of travel health centres in Canada.

**Centers for Disease Control** 1600 Clifton Rd NE, Atlanta, GA 30333 ☏1-800/311-3435 or 404/639-3534, ⓦ www.cdc.gov. Provides outbreak warnings, suggested inoculations, precautions and other background information for travellers. Useful website plus International Travelers Hotline on ☏1-877/394-8747.

**International Association for Medical Assistance to Travellers (IAMAT)** 1623 Military Rd no. 279, Niagara Falls, NY 14304 ☏716/754-4883, and 40 Regal Rd, Guelph, ON N1K 1B5 ☏519/836-0102, ⓦ www.iamat.org. A non-profit organization that can provide a list of English-speaking doctors in Mexico, climate charts and leaflets on various diseases and inoculations.

**International SOS Assistance** 3600 Horizon Blvd, Suite 300,Trevose, PA 19053 ☏1-800/523-8930, ⓦ www.intsos.com. Members receive pre-trip medical referral info, as well as overseas emergency services designed to complement travel insurance coverage.

**MEDJET Assistance** ☏1-800/963-3538, ⓦ www.medjetassistance.com. Annual membership programme for travellers (US$205 for individuals, US$325 for families) that, in the event of illness or injury, will fly members home or to the hospital of their choice in a medically equipped and staffed jet.

**Travel Medicine** ☏1-800/872-8633, ⓦ www.travmed.com. Sells first-aid kits, mosquito netting, water filters, reference books and other health-related travel products.

**Travelers Medical Center** 31 Washington Sq W, New York, NY 10011 ☏212/982-1600. Consultation service on immunizations and treatment of diseases for people travelling to developing countries.

## In the UK and Ireland

**British Airways Travel Clinics** 213 Piccadilly, London W1J 9HQ ☏0845/600 2236 (Mon–Fri 9.30am–5.30pm, Sat 10am–4pm, no appointment necessary) and 101 Cheapside, London EC2V 6DT (Mon–Fri 9am–4.30pm, appointment required), ⓦ www.britishairways.com/travel/healthclinintro. Vaccinations, tailored advice from an online database and a complete range of travel healthcare products.

**Communicable Diseases Unit** Brownlee Centre, Glasgow G12 0YN ☏0141/211 1062. Vaccination centre.

**Dun Laoghaire Medical Centre** 5 Northumberland Ave, Dun Laoghaire, Co Dublin ☏01/280 4996. Advice on medical matters abroad.

**Hospital for Tropical Diseases Travel Clinic** 2nd floor, Mortimer Market Centre, Capper St, off Tottenham Court Rd, London WC1E 6AU ☏020/7387 9600 (Mon–Fri 9am–5pm by appointment only). A consultation costs £15, which is waived if you have injections or buy malaria pills. A recorded Health Line (☏0906/133 7733; 50p per min) gives hints on hygiene and illness prevention as well as listing appropriate immunizations.

**MASTA (Medical Advisory Service for Travellers Abroad)** 40 regional clinics; call ☏0870/606 2782 or visit ⓦ www.masta.org for the nearest one. You can get a personalized health brief, giving written information tailored to your journey by post, for £3.49 online or by calling UK ☏0906/822 4100 (£1 per min).

**Nomad Travel & Outdoor** surgeries at 40 Bernard St, London WC1N 1LE ☏020/7833 4114 and 3–4 Wellington Terrace, Turnpike Lane, London N8 0PX ☏020/8889 7014 (Mon–Fri 9.30am–6pm, call to book vaccination appointment). Advice is free if you show up in person, or you can call their telephone helpline on ☏0906/863 3414 (60p per min).

**Trailfinders** immunization clinics at 194 Kensington High St, London W8 7RG ☏020/7938 3999, ⓦ www.trailfinders.com/clinic. (Mon–Fri 9am–5pm except Thurs to 6pm, Sat 10am–5.15pm). Clinics that do no require appointments.

**Travel Health Centre** Dept of International Health and Tropical Medicine, Royal College of Surgeons in Ireland, Mercers Medical Centre, Stephen's St Lower, Dublin 2 ☏01/402 2337, ⓦ www.travelmedicine.ie. Pre-trip advice and inoculations by appointment (Mon–Fri 9.30am–12.30pm & 1.30–4.30pm).

**Travel Medicine Services** PO Box 254, 16 College St, Belfast BT1 6BT ☏028/9031 5220. Offers medical advice before a trip and help afterwards, in the event of a tropical disease.

Tropical Medical Bureau Grafton Buildings, 34 Grafton St, Dublin 2 ☎01/671 9200, 🌐tmb.exodus .ie. Medical articles, trip advice and inoculations, with ten other clinic locations around the country; by appointment only, but you can book online.

## In Australia and New Zealand

**Travellers' Medical and Vaccination Centres**
This is a partial list of clinics; for a full list, see 🌐www.tmvc.com.au.

27–29 Gilbert Place, Adelaide, SA 5000 ☎08/8212 7522, ✉adelaide@traveldoctor.com.au.

Level 1 Canterbury Arcade, 170 Queen St, Auckland ☎09/373 3531, ✉auckland@traveldoctor.co.nz.

5/247 Adelaide St, Brisbane, Qld 4000 ☎07/3221 9066, ✉brisbane@traveldoctor.com.au.

5/8–10 Hobart Place, Canberra, ACT 2600 ☎02/6257 7156, ✉canberra@traveldoctor.com.au.

270 Sandy Bay Rd, Sandy Bay, Hobart, Tas 7005 ☎03/6223 7577, ✉hobart@traveldoctor.com.au.

2/393 Little Bourke St, Melbourne, Vic 3000 ☎03/9602 5788, ✉melbourne@traveldoctor .com.au.

Level 7, Dymocks Bldg, 428 George St, Sydney, NSW 2000 ☎02/9221 7133, ✉sydney@traveldoctor.com.au.

Shop 15, Grand Arcade, 14–16 Willis St, Wellington ☎04/473 0991, ✉wellington@traveldoctor.co.nz.

## Intestinal troubles

Despite all the dire warnings below, a bout of **diarrhoea** ("Montezuma's Revenge", or simply *turista*, as it's also known in Mexico) is the only medical problem you're likely to encounter. No one, however cautious they are, seems to avoid it altogether, largely because there are no reliable preventive measures. It's caused by the bacteria in Mexican food, which are different from (as well as more numerous than) those found in other Western diets, and is compounded by the change in food intake and routine.

If you go down with a mild dose of the runs unaccompanied by other symptoms, this will probably be the cause. If your diarrhoea is accompanied by cramps and vomiting, it could be **food poisoning** of some sort. Either way, it will probably pass of its own accord in 24 to 48 hours without treatment. In the meantime, it's essential to replace the fluid and salts you're losing, so drink lots of water, preferably with oral **rehydration salts** – *suero oral* (brand names: Dioralyte, Electrosol, Rehidrat) – which are a must for chil-

dren. If you can't get these, dissolve half a teaspoon of salt and three of sugar in a litre of water. Avoid greasy food, heavy spices, caffeine and most fruit and dairy products; some say bananas, papayas, guavas and prickly pears (*tunas*) are a help, while plain yoghurt or a broth made from yeast extract (such as Marmite or Vegemite, if you happen to have some with you) can be easily absorbed by your body when you have diarrhoea. Drugs like Lomotil or Imodium plug you up – and thus undermine the body's efforts to rid itself of infection – but they can be a temporary stop-gap if you have to travel. If symptoms persist for more than three days, or if you have a fever or blood in your stool, seek medical advice (see "Getting medical help" on p.39).

## Malaria and dengue fever

Caused by a parasite that lives in the saliva of Anopheles mosquitoes, **malaria** is endemic in some parts of Mexico, though beach resorts like Cancún, Cozumel and Isla Mujeres are malaria-free. Daytime visits to archeological sites are risk-free, too, but low-lying inland areas can be risky, especially at night. The best strategy is to wear repellent and clothing that covers your skin; if you'll be spending long periods in at-risk areas, you may want to take chloroquine (brand names: Nivaquin, Resochin, Avloclor, Aralen), starting one week before you arrive and continuing for a month afterwards. Chloroquine is unsuitable for sufferers of various conditions, such as epilepsy and psoriasis, but daily proguanil (brand name Paludrine) can be used in its place. (Weekly mefloquine, sold as Lariam, is very controversial, given its potential for severe mental-health side effects.)

If you come down with malaria, you'll probably know. The fever, shivering and headaches are like severe flu and come in waves, usually beginning in the early evening. Malaria is not infectious, but can be dangerous and sometimes even fatal if not treated quickly. If no doctor is available, take 600mg of quinine sulphate three times daily for at least three days, followed by three Fansidar (available from a local pharmacy) taken together.

## What about the water?

In a hot climate, it's essential to increase **water** intake to prevent dehydration. Most travellers – indeed most Mexicans if they can – stay off the tap water, although a lot of the time it is in fact drinkable, particularly in Cancún.

Most restaurants and *licuaderías* use **purified water** (*agua purificada*) in drinks and for ice, but always check; most hotels have a supply and will often provide bottles of water in your room. Bottled water (generally purified with ozone or ultraviolet) is widely available, but stick with known brands, and always check that the seal on the bottle is intact, since refilling empties with tap water for resale is common (carbonated water is generally a safer bet in that respect).

There are various methods of **treating water** while you are travelling, whether your source is from a tap or a river or stream. Boiling it for a minimum of five minutes is the time-honoured method but is not always practical and will not remove unpleasant tastes.

**Chemical sterilization**, using either chlorine or iodine tablets or a tincture of iodine liquid, is more convenient but leaves a nasty aftertaste (which can to some extent be masked with lemon or lime juice). Chlorine kills bacteria but, unlike iodine, is not effective against amoebic dysentery and *giardiasis*. Pregnant women or people with thyroid problems should consult their doctor before using iodine tablets or iodine-based purifiers. Too many iodine tablets can cause gastrointestinal discomfort themselves. Inexpensive iodine removal filters are available and are recommended if treated water is being used continuously for more than a month or is being given to babies.

**Purification**, involving both filtration and sterilization, gives the most complete treatment. Portable water purifiers range in size from units weighing as little as 60g, which can be slipped into a pocket, up to 800g for carrying in a backpack. For those planning to spend an extended period in remote areas where clean water is not available, look into some of the best water purifiers on the market, which are made in Britain by Pre-Mac. For suppliers worldwide contact Pre-Mac International Ltd, Unit 5, Morewood Close, Sevenoaks, Kent TN13 2HU ☎01732/460333, ⊛www.pre-mac.com.

The most important thing, obviously, is to avoid **mosquito bites**. Though active from dusk till dawn, female Anopheles mosquitoes prefer to bite in the evening. Wear long sleeves, skirts or trousers, avoid dark colours, which attract mosquitoes, and put repellent on all exposed skin, especially feet and ankles, which are their favourite targets. Plenty of good brands are sold locally, though health departments recommend carrying high-DEET brands available from travel clinics at home. An alternative is to burn coils of pyrethrum incense such as Raidolitos; these are readily available and burn all night if whole, but break easily. Sleep under a net if you can – one that hangs from a single point is best (you can usually find a way to tie a string across your room to hang it from). Special mosquito nets for hammocks are available in Mexico.

Another illness spread by mosquito bites is **dengue fever**, the symptoms of which are similar to those of malaria, plus aching bones. Dengue-carrying mosquitoes are particularly prevalent during the rainy season and fly during the day, so wear insect repellent in the daytime if mosquitoes are around. The only treatment is complete rest, with drugs to assuage the fever – unfortunately, a second infection can be fatal.

### Other bites and stings

Other biting **insects** can be a nuisance. These include bed bugs, sometimes found in cheap hotels – look for squashed ones around the bed. Sandflies, often present on beaches, are quite small, but their bites, usually on feet and ankles, itch like hell and last for days. Head or body lice can be picked up from people or bedding, and are best treated with medicated soap or shampoo.

Scorpions are mostly nocturnal and hide during the heat of the day under rocks and in crevices, so poking around in such places when in the countryside is generally ill-advised. If sleeping in a place where they might enter (such as a beach cabaña), shake your shoes out before putting them on in the morning, and try not to wander round barefoot. The sting of most scorpions in the Yucatán is not particularly dangerous, only very painful; cold-pack the sting to reduce swelling, and seek medical treatment if pain does not lessen within six hours. Very few of the **snakes** in this area of Mexico are poisonous, and are unlikely to bite unless accidentally disturbed. To see one at all, you need to search stealthily – walk heavily and they will usually slither away. If you do get bitten or stung, remember what the snake or scorpion looked like (kill it if you can do so without receiving more bites), try not to move the affected part (tourniquets are not recommended – if you do use one, it is *vital* to relieve it for at least ninety seconds every fifteen minutes), and seek medical help: antivenins are available in most hospitals.

## Heat

The most common cause of health problems is of course **the sun**. Tolerance takes a while to build up: use a strong **sunscreen** and, if you're walking during the day, wear a hat or keep to the shade. Be sure to avoid dehydration by drinking enough (water or fruit juice rather than beer or coffee, and you should aim to drink at least two litres a day), and don't exert yourself for long periods in the hot sun. Be aware that overheating can cause **heatstroke**, which is potentially fatal. Signs are a very high body temperature without a feeling of fever, accompanied by headaches, disorientation and even irrational behaviour. Lowering body temperature (a tepid shower, for example) is the first step in treatment.

Less serious is **prickly heat**, an itchy rash that is an infection of the sweat ducts caused by excessive perspiration that doesn't dry off. A cool shower, zinc oxide powder and loose cotton clothes should help.

## HIV and AIDS

It is estimated that some 160,000 people are **HIV**-positive in Mexico. While the problem is no worse than in many other countries, **AIDS (SIDA)** is still a concern, and you should take all the usual precautions to avoid contracting it. In particular, to contemplate casual sex without a condom, whether with a Mexican or a fellow traveller, would be madness – carry some with you (preferably from home; if buying them in Mexico, check the date and remember that heat affects their durability). They will also protect you from numerous other sexually transmitted diseases.

Should you need an injection or any invasive procedure, make sure that the equipment is sterile (you may want to bring a sterile kit from home); any blood you receive should be screened, and from voluntary rather than commercial donor banks. If you have a shave from a barber, make sure a clean blade is used, and don't submit to processes such as ear-piercing, acupuncture or tattooing unless you can be sure that the equipment is sterile.

## Hepatitis and other diseases

**Hepatitis A** is transmitted through contaminated food and water or through saliva and thrives in conditions of poor hygiene. It can lay a victim low for several months with exhaustion, fever and diarrhoea, and can even cause liver damage. The Havrix vaccines have been shown to be extremely effective; though expensive (around US$150/£95 for a course of two shots), protection lasts for ten years. Gamma globulin vaccines are no longer used as they are blood products, and there are concerns with regard to the transmission of new variant Creutzfeldt-Jakob disease.

Hepatitis symptoms include a yellowing of the whites of the eyes, general malaise, orange urine (though dehydration can also cause this) and light-coloured stools. If you think you have it and are unable immediately to see a doctor, it is important to get lots of rest, avoid alcohol and do your best not to spread the disease. If medical insurance coverage is an issue, you can go to

## Travellers' first-aid kit

The items you might want to carry with you (in addition to sunscreen, which is a must), especially if you're planning to go trekking or spend time in the more remote areas of Mexico, are:

❏ **Antiseptic cream**

❏ **Bismuth sulfate (Pepto-Bismol)** for nausea and digestive problems

❏ **Hydrocortisone/calamine lotion** or any of the creams designed to take the itch out of insect bites

❏ **Ibuprofen** (to reduce fever, swelling or pain from sunburn)

❏ **Imodium/Lomotil** for emergency diarrhoea treatment

❏ **Insect repellent** (ideally DEET)

❏ **Lint/gauze and sealed bandages**

❏ **Multivitamin and mineral tablets**

❏ **Plasters/Band-aids**

❏ **Rehydration sachets**

❏ **Water sterilization tablets** or **water purifier**

a pathology lab (most towns have them) to get blood tests before paying a greater amount to see a doctor. More serious is **hepatitis B**, which is extremely contagious and passed through blood or sexual contact. Vaccinations are recommended if you will be in contact with those with weaker immunity systems, for example, working around medical patients or with children. Ideally three doses are given over six months but if time is short, other options take one to two months, with a booster given after a year.

Typhoid and cholera are spread in the same way as hepatitis A. **Typhoid** produces a persistent high fever with malaise, headaches and abdominal pains, followed by diarrhoea. Vaccination can be by injection or orally, but the oral alternative is less effective, more expensive and only lasts a year, as opposed to three for a shot in the arm. **Cholera** (*cólera*) appears in epidemics rather than isolated cases – if it's around, you will hear about it and see public health notices. Cholera is characterized by sudden attacks of watery diarrhoea with severe cramps and debilitation. The vaccination is no longer given, as it is ineffective.

Immunizations against **mumps, measles, TB** and **rubella** are a good idea for anyone who wasn't vaccinated as a child and hasn't had the diseases, and you should make sure you are covered for **tetanus**. You don't need a shot for yellow fever unless you're coming from a country where it's endemic (in which case you need to carry your vaccination certificate), and the polio vaccine is no longer necessary as the disease has been eradicated from the Americas.

**Rabies** exists in Mexico, and the rabies vaccine is advised for anyone who will be more than 24 hours away from medical help. The best advice is simply to give dogs a wide berth, and not to play with animals at all, no matter how cuddly they may look. A bite, a scratch or even a lick from an infected animal could spread the disease; rabies is potentially fatal so if you are bitten, assume the worst and get medical help as quickly as possible. While waiting, wash any such wound immediately but gently with soap or detergent and apply alcohol or iodine if possible. If you decide to get the vaccination, you'll need three shots spread over a four-week period prior to travel.

## Getting medical help

For minor medical problems, head for a pharmacy – look for a green cross and the "**Farmacia**" sign. Pharmacists are knowledgeable and helpful, and many speak some English. They can also sell drugs over the counter (if necessary) available only by prescription at home. One word of warning, however: in many Mexican pharmacies you can still buy drugs such as Entero-Vioform and Mexaform, which can cause optic nerve damage and have been banned elsewhere; it is not a good idea, therefore, to use local brands unless you know what they are.

For more serious complaints you can get a list of English-speaking **doctors** from your government's nearest consulate (see p.30) or from MedToGo health and safety travel service, which publishes two handy directories of English-speaking medical facilities, *MedToGo Mexico* and *MedToGo Yucatan*; the latter

includes thorough advice on dive safety. The company's website (🖥 www.medtogo.com) contains honest assessments of the quality of medical care in various Mexican cities, and useful links about travel health as well. Big hotels and tourist offices may also be able to recommend medical services. Every Mexican border town has hundreds of doctors (and **dentists**) experienced in treating gringos, since they charge less than their colleagues across the border. Also, every reasonably sized town should have a state- or Red Cross-run **health centre** (*centro de salud* or *centro médico*), where treatment is free.

# Costs, money and banks

**Mexico is not as cheap as it once was, and, compared to the rest of the country, Cancún and the Caribbean coast have a reputation for being expensive. Although in general costs are lower than you'll find at home, compared with the rest of Central or South America, prices on the peninsula can come as something of a shock.**

In the long term, the North American Free Trade Agreement with the US and Canada (NAFTA) can probably be expected to keep costs (and, one hopes, wages) rising, though inflation has moved in to some extent. Prices in the text of the guide section are quoted in **Mexican pesos** (M$), but in the tourism-centric coastal areas, these prices change almost daily, according to the exchange rate with the US dollar. When appropriate in the Basics section of this book, prices are quoted in both US dollars and British pounds. Check the **Universal Currency Converter** (🖥 www.xe.com) for up-to-date conversions.

## Costs

The developed tourist resorts and big cities are invariably more expensive than remote towns, and certain other areas also have noticeably higher prices – among them the newly wealthy oil region around Ciudad del

Carmen. Prices can also be affected by **season**, and many hotels raise their prices during busy times of the year. Mexicans travel in July and August, the week between Christmas and New Year and the week before Easter (Semana Santa), and these periods overlap with the popular seasons for visitors. Nonetheless, wherever you go you can probably get by on US$380/£200 a week (you could reduce that if you hardly travel around, stay only in campsites or hostels, live on basic food and don't buy any souvenirs, but that requires a lot of discipline), while on US$760/£400 you'd be living very comfortably.

**Accommodation** prices range from around US$10/£5.20 for a beach cabaña to upwards of US$250/£136 for five-star luxury. A double-occupancy room in a cheap hotel costs US$20–25/£10.40–15.60 per person, and a room in the mid-range is about US$40–60/£20.80–31.20. **Food** prices can also vary wildly, but you should always be able to get a substantial meal in a basic Mexican restaurant for around US$4/£2. Most restaurant bills come with fifteen percent IVA (*impuesto de valor añadido*, or valued-added sales tax) added; this may not always be included in prices quoted on the menu. If you intend to travel around a lot, **transport** could be another major expense because distances are so huge. On a per-kilometre basis, however, prices are still quite reasonable: the four-hour run between Cancún and Mérida starts at just US$19/£10.

As always, if you're **travelling alone** you'll end up spending more – sharing rooms and food saves a substantial amount. In the larger resorts, you can get apartments for up to six people for even greater savings. If you have an **International Student or Youth Card**, such as those issued by STA Travel, you might find the occasional reduction on a museum admission price, but don't go out of your way to obtain one, since most concessions are, at least in theory, only for Mexican students.

**Service** is rarely added to bills, except in more expensive restaurants in the resort towns, and the amount you tip is entirely up to you. In cheap places, it's just the loose change, typically about ten percent, while expensive venues tend to expect a full fifteen percent. It's not standard practice to tip taxi drivers, unless they help with your bags, in which case ten percent is appropriate. Attendants at gas stations who wash your windows or perform other routine services on your car should receive an extra M$5 or so.

## Currency

The "new Mexican peso", or **nuevo peso**, usually written $, was introduced in 1993 and is made up of 100 centavos (¢) – it's the equivalent of 1000 old pesos. Bills come in . denominations of M$20, M$50, M$100, M$200 and M$500, with coins of 10¢, 20¢, 50¢, M$1, M$2, M$5, M$10 and M$20. The use of the dollar symbol for the peso is occasionally confusing; the initials MN (*moneda nacional*, or national coin) are occasionally used to indicate that it's Mexican, not American, money that is

being referred to. Make a practice of hoarding small change (though try not to take it out of the country with you), as it comes in handy for numerous small tips and payments in out-of-the-way places where large bills (anything above M$200) are rare.

## Currency exchange

The easiest kind of foreign currency to change in Mexico is **cash US dollars**. US dollar travellers' cheques come second; Canadian dollars and other major international currencies such as pounds sterling, yen and euros are a poor third, and you'll find it difficult to change travellers' cheques in those currencies. Guatemalan quetzales and Belize dollars are best got rid of before entering Mexico (otherwise, your most likely bet for changing them is with tourists heading the other way).

Correspondingly, you'll get the best rates for cash dollars, slightly lower rates for dollar travellers' cheques, and rates lower still for other currencies; indeed, it is a good idea to change other currencies into US dollars at home before coming to Mexico, since the difference in the exchange rate more than outweighs the amount you lose in changing your money twice, and only larger banks in big cities are equipped to make the swap in any case.

You will receive the best rates by far, however, simply by withdrawing pesos from a local **automatic teller machine** (ATM, or *cajero automático*), which can be found in all but the smallest towns; just verify with your home bank that your card will work in Mexico, and that you will not be charged punishing fees for using your card in a foreign country. The local ATM charge, currently levied by only a couple of banks, is about M$3 per transaction, which beats what you'd pay at a *casa de cambio* (exchange office*)*, or exchange kiosk. Likewise, using a **credit card** will secure the better commercial exchange rate as well, and plastic is accepted at many better hotels and restaurants.

**Banks** are generally open Monday to Friday from 9.30am until 5pm, though the international HSBC bank stays open until 7pm on weeknights. The commission charged varies from bank to bank, while the exchange rate, in theory, is the same

– fixed daily by the government. *Casas de cambio* are open longer hours and at weekends, and have varying exchange rates and commission charges; they also tend to have shorter queues and less bureaucratic procedures. They usually give better rates than banks, but it's always worth checking, especially if you're changing travellers' cheques. Occasionally, *casas de cambio* give rates for Canadian dollars, sterling and other currencies that are as good as those they give for US dollars, so again it's worth shopping around, especially if you intend to change a large sum.

In Cancún and to a lesser extent Cozumel and Playa del Carmen, many **hotels**, **shops** and **restaurants** that are used to tourists are prepared to change dollars or accept them as payment, but rates will be very low. There isn't much of a **black market** in Mexico since exchange regulations are relatively loose, and it's not really worth bothering with unless it comes about through trustworthy personal contacts or you want to do someone a favour.

## Travellers' cheques

**Travellers' cheques** have the obvious advantage over cash that if they are lost or stolen, the issuing company will refund them on production of the purchase receipt. For that reason, keep the receipt safe and separate from the cheques themselves, along with a record of the serial numbers and a note of those ones you have already cashed. If your cheques do get lost or stolen, the issuing company will expect you to report the loss to their local office immediately. You pay one to two percent commission to buy the cheques, and usually get a lower rate of exchange for them, but it's worth it for the peace of mind.

When buying travellers' cheques, get a sensible mix of denominations, and stick to the established names – Thomas Cook, American Express or Visa – not only because these will be more recognized, but also because there will be better customer service should they be lost or stolen.

## Credit and ATM cards

Major **credit cards** are widely accepted and handy for emergencies. Visa and MasterCard are the best; American Express and other charge cards are usually accepted only by expensive places, but an Amex card is worth it for the other services it offers, such as mail pick-up points and dollar travellers' cheque purchase. Credit cards are not accepted in the cheapest hotels or restaurants, or for bus tickets on second-class service, but you can use them to get cash advances from banks. Usually there's a minimum withdrawal of around US$75–100.

In addition, you can get cash 24 hours a day from **ATMs** in most towns, using credit cards or bank cards to withdraw cash directly from your account back home. All but a very few ATMs are now connected to all the necessary international networks such as Plus and Cirrus, so you should have no problem with your card; nonetheless, you'll want to carry a small amount of backup cash just in case you encounter problems.

Make sure before you leave home that your **personal identification number** (PIN) will work abroad – it should be a four-digit number. Remember that cash withdrawals on credit cards are treated as loans, with interest accruing daily from the date of withdrawal, plus there may be a transaction fee on top of this. Finally, take the usual care when you're withdrawing money from ATMs, especially at night.

---

### Phone numbers for lost cards or cheques

**American Express** ☏1-866/247-6878 (travellers' cheques); ☏1-715/343-7977 (collect in the US for credit cards)

**Diners Club** ☏+44 1-252/513 500 (for cards issued in UK); ☏1-303/799-1504 (in the US); ☏+61 3/9805 3310 (in Australia); ☏+64 9/359 7797 (in New Zealand)

**MasterCard** ☏1-800/307-7309

**Thomas Cook/MasterCard** (for travellers' cheques) ☏1-800/223-7373

**Visa** ☏1-410/581-9994 (collect in the US)

## Wiring money

**Wiring money** is a fast but expensive way to send funds abroad and should be considered only as a last resort. Money can be sent via MoneyGram or Western Union (see right) and should be available for collection, from the company's local agent, within a few minutes of being sent. Fees depend on the amount being transferred, and MoneyGram charges on a sliding scale, so sending larger amounts of cash is better value. For example, wiring US$100/£52 to Mexico will cost US$5–15/£3–8 whilst US$1000/£520 will cost around US$50–80/£26–42.

It's also possible to have money wired directly from a bank in your home country to a bank in Mexico, although this is somewhat less reliable because it involves two separate institutions. If you take this route, the person wiring the funds to you will need to know the telex number of the receiving bank.

### Money-wiring companies

**MoneyGram** US ☎ 1-800/955-7777, Canada ☎ 1-800/933-3278, UK ☎ 0800/018 0104, Ireland ☎ 1850/205 800, Australia ☎ 1800/230 100, New Zealand ☎ 0800/262 263, ⓦ www.moneygram.com.

**Western Union** US & Canada ☎ 1-800/325-6000, UK ☎ 0800/833 833, Ireland ☎ 1800/395 395, Australia ☎ 1800/173 833, New Zealand ☎ 0800/270 000, ⓦ www.westernunion.com.

# Getting around

**Although distances in Mexico can be huge, if you're just travelling within the Yucatán Peninsula and Chiapas, the longest slog you'll probably face is an overnight bus between Mérida and Palenque, which can take up to ten hours. Public transport at ground level is frequent and reasonably efficient everywhere, though you might want to take an internal flight if you'll be travelling on to central Mexico.**

## Flights

All of the Yucatán's major cities – Mérida, Cancún, Campeche, Ciudad del Carmen, Villahermosa and Chetumal – have **airports** served by Aeroméxico, Mexicana and, in some cases, Aerocaribe, Aeromar and Aviacsa. Generally, only Villahermosa and Mérida, as well as Mérida and Cancún, connect; otherwise, you'll probably have to fly back to Mexico City to transfer (Magnicharters often has good prices to Mexico City from Mérida and Cancún). Overall, tickets are not terribly cheap, but the time saved over bus travel can make them worthwhile.

The price of a ticket on a particular flight doesn't normally vary from agent to agent, so there's no point in shopping around; it's usually twice as much for a round-trip as a one-way ticket.

Mexicana and Aeroméxico offer multi-flight airpasses, available only outside Mexico (see the box on p.22 for details).

### Domestic airlines

**Aerocaribe** Mexico ☎ 1-800/623-4518, ⓦ www.aerocaribe.com. Cancún, Chetumal, Mérida and Cozumel to Mexico City; Cancún to Villahermosa; Mérida to Cancún, Ciudad del Carmen and Villahermosa.

**Aeromar** US ☎ 1-800/950 0747, Mexico ☎ 1-800/237-6627 or 5133-1111, ⓦ www.aeromar.com.mx. Campeche to Villahermosa, and to other points in central Mexico.

**Aeroméxico** US ☎ 1-800/237-6639, Mexico ☎ 1-800/021-4010, ⓦ www.aeromexico.com.

**Aviacsa** US ☎ 1-888/528-4227,

Mexico ☎1-800/006-2200, ⓦwww.aviacsa.com.mx. Cancún, Chetumal, Mérida and Villahermosa to Mexico City; Mérida to Villahermosa.
**Magnicharters** Mexico ☎1-800/703-8300, ⓦwww.magnicharters.com. Mexico City to Cancún and Mérida.
**Mexicana** US ☎1-800/531-7921, Mexico ☎1-800/509-8960, ⓦwww.mexicana.com.mx.

## Buses

Within Mexico, **buses** (long-distance buses are called *camiones*, rather than *autobuses*, in Mexican Spanish) are by far the most common and efficient form of public transport. A multitude of companies run an unbelievable number of them, connecting even the smallest of villages. Long-distance services between major cities use very comfortable and dependable vehicles; remote villages are commonly connected by more rattle-trap conveyances.

There are basically two **classes** of bus: first (*primera*) and second (*segunda*). First-class vehicles have reserved seats, videos and air-conditioning, and an increasing number of second-class lines on the most popular inter-city routes have the same comforts. The main differences will be in the number of stops – second-class buses call at more places, and consequently take longer to get where they're going – and the fare, which is about ten percent higher on first-class services, and sometimes a lot more. Most people choose first-class for any appreciably long distance, and second for short trips or (obviously) for destinations only served by a second-class local bus, but you should certainly not be put off second class if it seems more convenient – and it may even prove less crowded. **Air-conditioning** is not necessarily a boon; there's nothing more uncomfortable than a bus with sealed windows and a broken air-conditioner, or a bus chilled to 16°C/60°F.

**Deluxe buses** also run on important inter-city routes; ADO GL and UNO are the two services in the Yucatán. Fares are around thirty percent higher than for first-class buses, but they have few if any stops, waitress service with free snacks and drinks, air-conditioning that works (be sure to keep a sweater handy, as it can get very cold) and they may also be emptier. The UNO buses have more fully reclining seats with leg rests, comparable to business class seats on airlines. Both ADO GL and UNO have computerized reservations and accept credit cards in payment; you can buy tickets online at ⓦwww.ticketbus.com.mx.

Most towns of any size have a modern bus station, known as the **Central Camionera**. Don't let the word "central" fool you, though, as they can be located a long way from the town centre. Where there is no unified terminus you may find separate first- and second-class terminals, or individual ones for each company, sometimes little more than bus stops at the side of the road. In almost every bus station, there is some form of **baggage storage** office – usually known as a *guardería*, *consigna* or simply *equipaje*, and costing about US$0.30/£0.15 per item per hour. Before leaving anything, make sure that the place will be open when you come to collect. If there's no formal facility, staff at the bus companies' baggage dispatching offices can often be persuaded to look after things for a short while.

Always check your **route** and **arrival time**, and – whenever possible – buy **tickets** from the bus station in advance to get the best (or any) seats. You'll rarely have any problem getting a place on a bus from its point of origin or from really big towns. In smaller, mid-route places, however, you may have to wait for the bus to arrive (or at least to leave its last stop) before discovering if there are any seats. The increased prevalence of computerized ticketing, however, is easing the problem. Alternatively, there's almost always a bus described as *local*, which means it originates from where you are (as opposed to a *de paso* bus, which started somewhere else), and tickets for these can be bought well in advance.

Weekends, holiday season, school holidays and fiestas can overload services to certain destinations; again, the only real answer is to buy tickets in advance. However, you could also try the cheaper second-class lines, where they'll pack you in standing, or take whatever's going to the next town along the way and try for a *local* from there. A word with the driver and a small tip can sometimes work wonders.

## Trains

Mexico's **railways** were privatized in 1995, and since then, though more freight is carried by rail, all passenger services have been withdrawn bar three services run especially for tourists. In the Yucatán, the deluxe *Expreso Maya* runs between Palenque and Chichén Itzá, only on demand by tour groups (☎999/944-9393, ⓦwww.expreso-maya.com). A five-day Palenque–Chichén Itzá trip that includes meals and hotels (the train contains no sleeper cars) starts at US$1330.

## Driving

Getting your car into Mexico **properly documented** (see "Getting there" on p.23) is just the beginning of your problems. Although most people who venture in by car enjoy it and get out again with no more than minor incidents, driving in Mexico does require a good deal of care and concentration, and almost inevitably involves at least one brush with bureaucracy or the law. In general, police have eased up of late in response to pressure from above to stop hassling tourists.

**Renting a car** in Mexico – especially if done with a specific itinerary in mind, just for a day or two – avoids many problems and is often a very good way of seeing quickly a small area that would take days to explore using public transport. In all the tourist resorts and major towns there are any number of competing agencies, with local operations usually charging less than the well-known chains when you compare full insurance (local companies will generally quote rates that include all necessary coverage). Daily **rates** with unlimited mileage start at around US$50/£26; weekly rates usually cost the same as six days. For shorter distances, mopeds and motorbikes are also available in some resorts, but the large, international companies don't deal with them because of the high frequency of accidents.

Drivers from the US, Canada, Britain, Ireland, Australia and New Zealand will find that their **licences** are valid in Mexico, though an international permit can be useful, especially if your domestic one has no photo on it. You are required to have all your documents with

you when driving; insurance is not compulsory, but you'd be foolhardy not to get some sort of policy.

Mexican **roads and traffic**, however, are your chief worry, though if you know the basic road courtesies, the whole driving experience is much less stressful. Traffic circulates on the right, and the normal speed limit is 40kph (25mph) in built-up areas, 70kph (43mph) in open country, and 110kph (68mph) on the freeway. Most important of the **road rules** is that a left-turn signal often means it's clear to overtake. If you wish to make a left turn, pull into the farthest *right* lane, or the hard shoulder if possible, then put on your left-turn signal and turn only when all lanes are clear. A driver who wants to pass will flash his headlights; you're expected to pull to the right and slow a bit to hasten the process. Another convention to be aware of is that the first driver to flash their lights at a junction, or where only one vehicle can pass, has the right of way: they're not inviting you to go first. Any good road map should explain the more common symbols used on Mexican road signs, and Sectur has a pamphlet on driving in Mexico in which they're also featured.

Some of the new highways are excellent, and the toll (*cuota*) **superhighways**, such as the one between Cancún and Mérida, are better still, though extremely expensive to drive on. Away from the major population centres, however, roads are often narrow, winding and potholed, with bicyclists loaded with burdens weaving along the nonexistent hard shoulder. Rural roads (including the free highway to Chichén Itzá) are punctuated by large **speed bumps** (*topes*) in every town or village, however small. If not crossed at an absolute crawl, *topes* can do serious damage to your car's undercarriage. At any sign of population, slow down and be alert, as they're not always well marked. Most people suggest, too, that you should never drive at night – sound advice, even if not always practical. Just proceed with care and look out for wildlife and pedestrians.

Driving in towns can be another hassle – downtown streets are usually designated one-way, but **signage** can be poor (look for small arrows affixed to lampposts). If you're unsure, note the direction in which the parked cars, if not the moving cars, are facing. **Theft** is a small threat, so you might want to pay extra for a hotel with secure parking, or at least for parking in a private lot. If you park on the street, lock everything that might look enticing in your boot. You may well also have to fork out on-the-spot "fines" for traffic offences (real or concocted), though this practice doesn't seem prevalent in the Yucatán.

If you have a breakdown, the free highway mechanic service known as the **Ángeles Verdes** (Green Angels) can help. As well as patrolling all major routes looking for beleaguered motorists, they can be reached by phone on ☎55/5250-8221 and speak English.

Should you have a minor **accident**, try to come to some arrangement with the other party – involving the police will only make matters worse, and Mexican drivers will be just as anxious to avoid doing so. If you witness an accident, you may want to consider the gravity of the situation before getting involved. Witnesses can be locked up along with those directly implicated to prevent them from leaving before the case comes up – so consider if your involvement is necessary to serve justice. In a serious incident, contact your consulate and your Mexican insurance company as soon as possible.

For further sound advice on driving in Mexico, see the ASIRT report, online at ⊛www.asirt.org/roadtravelreports/mexico.pdf.

## Car rental agencies

You can either rent from the agencies noted in the "Listings" sections of the Yucatán's major towns and resorts, or arrange your rental before your departure.

### In North America

**Avis** US ☎1-800/230-4898, Canada ☎1-800/272-5871, ⊛www.avis.com; ☎1-800/288-8888 in Mexico.
**Budget** US ☎1-800/472-3325, Canada ☎1-800/268-8900, ⊛www.budgetrentacar.com.
**Dollar** ☎1-800/800-4000, ⊛www.dollar.com.
**Hertz** US ☎1-800/654-3001, Canada ☎1-800/263-0600, ⊛www.hertz.com; ☎1-800/709-5000 in Mexico.
**National** ☎1-800/227-7368, ⊛www.nationalcar.com.

**Thrifty** ☎1-800/367-2277, ⊛www.thrifty.com.

### In the UK

**Avis** ☎0870/010 0287, ⊛www.avis.co.uk.
**Budget** ☎0870/153 9170, ⊛www.budget.co.uk.
**Hertz** ☎0870/844 8844, ⊛www.hertz.co.uk.
**Holiday Autos** ☎0870/400 0099, ⊛www.holidayautos.co.uk.
**National** ☎0870/400 4552, ⊛www.nationalcar.co.uk.
**Thrifty** ☎01494/751 600, ⊛www.thrifty.co.uk.

### In Ireland

**Avis** ☎0214/281 111, ⊛www.avis.ie.
**Budget** ☎090/662 7711, ⊛www.budget.ie.
**Hertz** ☎01/676 7476, ⊛www.hertz.ie.
**Holiday Autos** ☎01/872 9366, ⊛www.holidayautos.ie.
**Thrifty** ☎1800/515 800, ⊛www.thrifty.ie.

### In Australia

**Avis** ☎1300/137 498, ⊛www.avis.com.au.
**Budget** ☎1300/794 344, ⊛www.budget.com.au.
**Europcar** ☎1300/131390, ⊛www.deltaeuropcar.com.au.
**Hertz** ☎03/9698 2555, ⊛www.hertz.com.au.
**Holiday Autos** ☎1300/554432, ⊛www.holidayautos.com.au.
**Thrifty** ☎1300/367 227, ⊛www.thrifty.com.au.

### In New Zealand

**Avis** ☎0800/655 111, ⊛www.avis.co.nz.
**Budget** ☎0800/283 438, ⊛www.budget.co.nz.
**National** ☎0800/800115, ⊛www.nationalcar.co.nz.
**Thrifty** ☎0800/737070, ⊛www.thrifty.co.nz.

## Hitching

It's possible **to hitch** your way around the Yucatán, but it's not the ideal strategy. Lifts are relatively scarce, and the roadside often a harsh environment if you get dropped at some obscure turn-off. You may also be harassed by the police. Most drivers expect you to contribute to their expenses, which you may think rather defeats the object.

Apart from all this, the standard risks of hitching still apply: robbery is not unheard of, and women in particular (but also men) are advised **not to hitch alone**. You should wait to know where the driver is going before getting in, rather than stating your own destination first, sit by a door and keep your baggage to hand in case you need to leave in a hurry (feigned carsickness is one way to get a driver to stop).

That said, to get to villages where there's no bus or simply to while away the time spent waiting for one, you may find yourself hitching and you'll probably come across genuine friendliness and certainly meet people you wouldn't otherwise encounter. It does help if your Spanish will stretch to a conversation.

Similarly, hitchhiking is common on the road around Tulum, where you might give a lift to a fellow traveller trying to get back up to Playa. It's also a major form of transport in the interior of the peninsula, where bus service is less frequent, and if you're driving this way, you may want to pick up people who are usually just trying to get to the next town down the road. Riders will always ask how much they should pay as they get out; it's up to you whether to accept any money.

## Local transport

**Public transport** within Mexican towns and cities, usually in the form of buses, is always plentiful and inexpensive, though crowded and, except in Cancún, not particularly user-friendly. Often there's a flat-fare system, but this varies from place to place. Wherever possible we've indicated which **bus** to take and where to catch it, but often only a local will fully understand the intricacies of the system. The main destinations of the bus are usually marked on the windscreen, which helps. In bigger places, **combis** or **colec-**

**tivos** offer a faster and perhaps less crowded alternative for only a little more money. These minibuses or vans run along a fixed route to set destinations; they'll pick you up and drop you off wherever you like along the way, and you simply pay the driver for the distance travelled.

Regular **taxis** can also be good value, but be aware of rip-offs – meters are used only on a few taxis in Mérida, and otherwise drivers apply a zone system. In the latter case, fix a price before you get in. In the big cities, tables of fixed prices are posted at prominent spots, such as hotel lobbies. At almost every airport you'll find a booth selling vouchers for taxis into town at a fixed price depending on the part of town you want to go to – sometimes there's a choice of paying more for a private car or less to share. This will invariably cost less than just hailing a cab outside the terminal. In every case you should know the name of a hotel to head for, or the driver will take you to the one that pays the biggest commission. Never accept a ride in any kind of unofficial or unmarked taxi.

## Ferries

**Ferries** connect islands off the Caribbean coast to the mainland: from Cancún to Isla Mujeres, from Playa del Carmen to Cozumel and from Chiquilá to Isla Holbox. Though not as cheap as they once were, all these services are still pretty reasonable: see the relevant chapters for current fares and schedules.

# Accommodation

Hotels in Mexico can describe themselves as anything from *posadas, hostales* and *casas de huéspedes* to plain *hotels* – terms used more or less interchangeably. Behind the labels, options can range from rustic sand-floor cabañas lit by candles to luxurious pleasure palaces in which all your meals and drinks are prearranged.

Travellers looking for **smaller hotels** have plenty of choice; note, however, that in Cancún's zona hotelera, "small" generally means fewer than three hundred rooms. One agent representing a number of smaller, well-designed resorts, hotels and apartments is the US-based Turquoise Reef (in the US on ☎1-800/538-6802, ⓦwww.mexicoholiday.com). Likewise, enormous **resorts** are a dime a dozen, and if you want a week of unencumbered tanning, with only an occasional sightseeing jaunt, you can usually find very good package deals that may even include airfare.

Finding a room is rarely difficult – in most old and not overly touristy places the cheap hotels are concentrated around the main plaza, with others near the bus station (or where the bus station used to be, before it moved to the outskirts of town). The more modern and expensive places often lie on the outskirts of towns, accessible only by car or taxi. The only times you're likely to have big problems finding somewhere to stay are in coastal resorts over the peak Christmas season, at Easter, on Mexican holidays, and almost anywhere during a local fiesta, when it's well worth trying to reserve ahead.

All rooms should have an **official price** displayed, though price is not always a guide to quality – a filthy fleapit and a beautifully run converted mansion may charge exactly the same, even if they're right next door to each other. To guarantee value, see your room first. You should never pay more than the official rate, and in the low season you can often pay less. The charging system varies: sometimes it's per person, but

## Accommodation price codes

All hotel rooms are subject to a twelve percent **tax**. Some hotels – generally those under US$40/£22 per night – build this into the quoted rate, while most others add it to the bill. Prices listed in this guide are in Mexican pesos, don't include tax, and are typically based on **the cheapest available room for two people sharing in high season** (Jan–April in all of the beach areas, plus July and August in the places that see lots of visitors, such as Tulum). Everywhere puts in an additional price hike for the week between Christmas and New Year and Semana Santa, the week before Easter, a major Mexican holiday period. At smaller hotels, it's worth asking for a discount if you walk in off the street; for larger, chain-owned resorts and hotels, booking ahead is the only way to negotiate something lower than the official, or "rack", rate. All the accommodation listed in this book has been categorized into one of nine **price codes**, as set out below.

❶ less than M$50
❷ M$50–100
❸ M$100–150
❹ M$150–250
❺ M$250–400
❻ M$400–600
❼ M$600–800
❽ M$800–1000
❾ more than M$1000

usually the price quoted will be for the room regardless of how many people occupy it, so sharing can mean big savings. A room with one double bed (*cama matrimonial*) is almost always cheaper than a room with two singles (*doble* or *con dos camas*), and most hotels have large "family" rooms with several beds, which are tremendous value for groups. In the Yucatán, virtually all budget hotel rooms also have **hammock hooks**, so you can often sling up an extra person that way. The big resorts have lots of apartments that sleep six or more and include cooking facilities, for yet more savings. A little gentle haggling rarely goes amiss, and many places will have some rooms that cost less, so just ask (*¿Tiene un cuarto más barato?*).

**Air-conditioning** (*aire acondicionado* or *clima*) inflates prices and is frequently optional; unless it's unbearably hot and humid, a room with a simple **ceiling fan** (*ventilador*) is generally better. Except in the most expensive places, the air-conditioning units are almost always noisy and inefficient, whereas a fan can be left running silently all night and the breeze helps keep insects away.

When looking at a room, always check its **insect-proofing**. Cockroaches and ants are common, and there's not much anyone can do about them, but decent netting will keep mosquitoes and worse out and allow you to sleep. If the mosquitoes are really bad, you'll probably see where previous occupants have splattered them on the walls – it's the same story for bedbugs around the bed.

## All-inclusive resorts

**All-inclusives** are one of the most popular lodging choices in the Yucatán, and the package deals they offer, which include lodging, all meals and gratuities, can be enticing even to travellers who ordinarily wouldn't consider them. For parents with younger children, a package provides a fuss-free programme of activities to keep kids occupied. If you're considering this option, though, don't skimp – cheaper places may seem like a bargain on paper, but the facilities can be run-down and the meals bordering on inedible. Plus, prepaid meals may be a waste if you're enticed into the many excellent restaurants in Playa del Carmen, for instance. To compete with the booming towns on the

Riviera Maya, many resorts in Cancún are moving away from all-inclusive packages to attract a wider range of guests, offering the option of breakfast only or no meals at all (also called a European plan).

## Haciendas

These **grand manors** are one of the great treats of the Yucatán. For the most part ranches or henequen plantations built in the late nineteenth century, many went to ruin during the twentieth century, but in recent years have been restored to varying degrees of their former luxury, complete with long verandahs, intricately tiled floors, lofty ceilings and lush gardens. Most are within an hour's drive of Mérida, though there are a few in Campeche as well. *Hacienda Temozón* (see p.251), for instance, between Mérida and Uxmal, has incorporated many of the typical henequen-processing outbuildings into its layout, and played host to Vicente Fox and Bill Clinton. Even if you're not able to splurge on a US$300 room, you can still enjoy the colonial ambiance of these sprawling places, at *Hacienda Tabi* (see p.256), a former sugarcane plantation, for instance, or the wonderfully rambling and eclectic *Hacienda San Antonio Chalanté* (see p.215) near Izamal, where you can get a room for less than US$30 per night, and you may even have the whole crumbling premises to yourself. In addition to the hacienda hotels mentioned in this book, visit ⓦ www.mayayucatan.com and ⓦ www.yucatantoday.com/culture/eng-hacienda-hotels for listings in Yucatán State.

## Eco-resorts

A growing trend on the Yucatán Peninsula is the so-called **eco-resort**. "Eco-" is a freely used prefix, and often hotels will tout their use of solar panels and wind turbines not because they've chosen this option but because they simply don't have access to the electric grid – as is the case on most of the beach in Tulum. A truly environmentally sound hotel will also have a wastewater treatment system, a composting procedure and a building plan that minimizes impact on plant and animal life – as well as, ideally, an economic and social relationship with the surrounding native culture. *Boca Paila Camps* in the Sian Ka'an Reserve (p.164) is an excellent example, as are *Genesis Ek Balam* near the ruins north of Valladolid (p.205) and *Villas Chimay* on Isla Holbox (p.109). Note it's not necessarily less expensive to run a hotel using wind and solar power; you'll be choosing "eco" because you support the premise, not because you'll be getting a bargain. Visit the International Ecotourism Society at ⓦwww.ecotourism. org for the full list of guidelines, as well as recommended tour operators and lodges.

A network of five Yucatán eco-resorts offers a **package eco-tour** that includes accommodation, car rental, breakfasts and guide service for a week. Each stop on the self-driving tour focuses on a unique bioregion in the peninsula, such as coral reefs or cenotes, and you also hit the big archeological sites of Calakmul, Ek Balam and Uxmal with excellent tour guides. The rate is US$120 per night. *Contact Genesis Ek Balam* (☎985/852-7980, ⓦwww.genesisretreat.com) for details.

## Campsites, hammocks and cabañas

**Camping** is easy enough if you are hiking in the backcountry, or happy simply to crash on a beach, but robberies are common in places with a lot of tourists. There are few organized campsites, and many are first and foremost trailer parks, not particularly pleasant to pitch tents in; however, you can still find a few beach hideaways. Of course, if you have a van or RV you can use these or park just about anywhere else – there are a good number of facilities on the Caribbean coast.

In a lot of campsites, you will be able to rent a **hammock** and a place to sling it for the same price as pitching a tent (around US$5/£3), maybe less, and certainly less if you're packing your own hammock (Mérida is the best place to buy these, though you can find good ones in more touristy towns if you're picky).

Beach huts, or **cabañas**, are found at the more rustic, backpacker-oriented beach resorts, and sometimes inland. Usually just wooden or **palapa** (a palm-frond shack with a cot or hammock – or a place to hang your own), they are frequently without electricity, though as a resort gets more popular, as in Tulum, they tend to trans-

form into sturdier beach bungalows with modern conveniences and higher prices. At backwaters and beaches too untouristed for even cabañas (though this is now quite rare), you should still be able to sling a hammock somewhere, probably the local bar or restaurant, where the palapa serves as shelter and shade.

## Youth hostels

There are three official Hostelling International hostels in the Yucatán, as well as a number of unaffiliated hostels that maintain excellent standards. In very untouristed towns, such as Chetumal, you can find a cheap place to bunk at the community sport centre (*villa deportiva*), where travelling student teams often stay. In the official hostels and those geared towards backpackers, you typically pay around US$10/£5.50 per person for single-sex dorm facilities. A membership card for the HI places isn't necessary, but you may pay more without one. Rules at the *villas deportivas* can be strict (no booze, 11pm curfew, up and out by 9am) but most of the backpackers' favourites are open 24 hours and provide kitchen facilities, laundry, travel advice, Internet and other services. The Hostelling International affiliates are listed at ⓦwww.hostellingmexico.com. You can make online reservations for these and many other popular facilities.

### Youth hostel associations

#### In Mexico

**Hostelling Mexico** Guatemala 4, Colonia Centro, México DF 06020 ☎55/5211-1113, ⓦwww.hostellingmexico.com. This is Mexico's official branch of Hostelling International, with three hostels in the Yucatán.

#### Overseas

**US** ☎301/495-1240, ⓦwww.hiusa.org.
**Canada** ☎1-800/663-5777, ⓦwww.hihostels.ca.
**England and Wales** ☎0870/770 8868, ⓦwww.yha.org.uk.
**Scotland** ☎0870/155 3255, ⓦwww.syha.org.uk.
**Ireland** ☎01/830 4555, ⓦwww.irelandyha.org.
**Northern Ireland** ☎028/9032 4733, ⓦwww.hini.org.uk.
**Australia** ☎02/9261 1111, ⓦwww.yha.com.au.
**New Zealand** ☎0800/278 299, ⓦwww.yha.co.nz.

# Eating and drinking

Whatever your preconceptions about Mexican food, they will almost certainly prove wrong. The cuisine bears very little resemblance to the concoctions served in "Mexican" restaurants or fast-food joints in other parts of the world – certainly you won't find chile con carne outside the tourist spots. Nor, as a rule, is it especially spicy; indeed, a more common complaint from visitors is that after a while it all seems rather bland. For a glossary of what you'll find on local menus, see p.361.

## Where to eat

Basic meals are served at **restaurantes**, but you can get breakfast, snacks and often full meals at cafés, too, and plenty of **take-out** and **fast-food** places serve sandwiches, *tortas* (filled rolls) and tacos (tortillas folded over with a filling), as well as more international-style food. Establishments called **jugerías** are devoted entirely to wonderful juices and fruit salads, while **street stalls** dish out everything from tacos to orange juice to ready-made crisp vegetable salads sprinkled with chile-salt and lime. Just about every city **market** (*mercado*) has a hot-food section, too, invariably the cheapest places to eat. In the big cities and resorts you can get a wider variety of international flavours;

Argentine restaurants are the places to go for well-cooked steaks.

When you're travelling, as often as not the food will come to you; at every stop or even *tope* people clamber onto buses (especially second-class ones) with baskets of home-made foods, local specialities, cold drinks or jugs of coffee. You'll find wonderful things this way that you won't come across in restaurants, but they should be treated with caution, and with an eye to hygiene.

## What to eat

Fresh and varied, the food of the Yucatán Peninsula is a mix of earthy local specialities that have been cooked in some form since the pre-Columbian era alongside dishes from other regions, brought by people who've

## Salsa

Since so much Mexican food is simple, and endlessly repeated in restaurant after restaurant, one way to tell the places apart – and a vital guide to the quality of the establishment – is by their **salsa**. A restaurant with a quality salsa on the table will probably serve up some decent food, whereas a place that takes no pride in its salsa often treats its food in the same manner. To a certain extent you can tell from the **presentation**: a place that has grubby salsa dishes on the table and rarely changes them, probably just refilling them from a supermarket-bought can, will not take the same pride in its food as a *casero* (home-cooking) restaurant that proudly puts its own salsa on the table in a nice bowl.

Frequently, you will be served a variety of salsa and sauces, including bottles of commercial hot sauce (Tapatío, Tabasco, Yucateco), but there should always be at least one home-made salsa concoction. Increasingly this is the **raw**, California-style salsa often called *pico de gallo*: tomato, onion, chile and cilantro (coriander leaves) finely chopped together. More common, though, are the traditional **cooked** salsas: either green or red, and relatively mild (but start with a tiny dab, just in case). The basic ingredients are onion and one or more of the hundreds of varieties of chile, or a base of the tangy tomatillo for green sauces. In Yucatecan places, you will also get a bowl of pickled red onions, which are generally an astounding shade of pink.

moved to this area. And you can choose from an array of international dishes, from sushi in Cancún to delicate handmade pasta and imported prosciutto in the heavily Italian areas of Playa del Carmen and Tulum.

The basic Yucatecan (and Mexican) diet is essentially one of corn and its products, supplemented by beans and chiles. These three things appear in an almost infinite variety of guises. Some dishes are spicy (*picante*), but on the whole you add your own seasoning from the bowls of home-made chile sauce on the table – these are often surprisingly mild, but they can be fiery and should always be approached with caution.

There are at least a hundred different types of **chile**, fresh or dried, in colours ranging from pale green to almost black, and all sorts of different sizes (large, mild *poblanos*, for instance, are often stuffed with meat or cheese to make *chiles rellenos*). Each has a distinct flavour, and by no means are all hot (which is why we don't use the English term "chilli" for them), although the most common, *chiles habañeros*, small and either green or red, are absolutely deadly when eaten straight. You'll always find a chile sauce (salsa, see box p.51) on the table when you eat, and in any decent restaurant it will be home-made; no two are quite alike. Chile is also the basic ingredient of more complex cooked sauces, notably *mole*, a complex spice blend that could be called Mexico's version of curry, traditionally served with turkey or chicken, but also sometimes with enchiladas (rolled, filled tortillas). There are several types of *mole*, the most common being the rich, almost black *mole poblano*, a speciality of Puebla that incorporates bitter chocolate into the mix. Poorly prepared, the sauce can be cloying, but when the scores of ingredients are well balanced, the flavours are clear and brilliant and not to be missed. Another speciality to look out for is *chiles en nogada*, another deadly rich combination featuring *poblano* peppers stuffed with a fruit-laced meat ragout, then covered in a creamy walnut sauce and garnished with red pomegranate seeds. The colours reflect the national flag, and it's served especially in August and September during the build-up to Independence Day, which is also when the walnuts are fresh.

Pinto or black **beans** (*frijoles*), an invariable accompaniment to egg dishes – and with almost everything else too – are frequently served *refritos*, which means not "refried", but "really fried", ideally with a bit of lard for flavouring. They're even better if you can get them whole in some kind of country-style soup or stew, often with pork or bacon, as in *frijoles charros*.

**Corn** (*maíz*), in some form or another, features in virtually everything. In its natural state it is known as *elote* and you can find it boiled or roasted on the cob at street stalls, topped with a deadly combo of mayonnaise, crumbly *cotija* cheese, chile-salt and lime. Hulled kernels (*pozole*) are put in meaty soups and stews and have a pleasant yielding texture. Far more often, though, corn is treated with lye and ground into a paste called *masa*, then formed into tortillas: flat maize pancakes of which you will get a stack to accompany your meal in any Mexican restaurant. In more expensive or touristy places you might get wheatflour ones (*tortillas de harina*), or even bread rolls, known as *bolillos*, but these are considered pretensions to most Mexican diners.

*Masa* forms the basis of a whole category of snack-like Mexican dishes called **antojitos**. Simplest of these are tacos – tortillas filled with anything from grilled beef to the lurid red pork-and-pineapple (called *al pastor* and also known as *arabe*, because the meat is cooked on a shwarma skewer). They're typically served soft, not at all like the baked taco shells you may have had at home (the crisp-shelled version, rarely seen, are called *tacos dorados*). With cheese, either alone or in addition to other fillings, they are called **quesadillas**. **Enchiladas** are rolled, filled tortillas covered in chile sauce and baked; enchiladas *suizas* are the mildest variety, stuffed with chicken and cheese and topped with a green chile sauce. **Tostadas** are flat tortillas toasted crisp and piled with ingredients – usually meat, salad vegetables and cheese (smaller bite-size versions are known as *sopes*). Tortillas torn up and cooked together with meat and (usually hot) sauce are called *chilaquiles*: this is a traditional way of using up leftovers. A thicker oval of *masa* makes the base for *huaraches*, so named because they resemble sandals; the *masa* is lightly fried on a griddle and topped with vegetables or meats and cheese.

*Masa* is also the basis of **tamales**, which are a sort of cornmeal pudding stuffed, flavoured, and cooked in corn or banana leaves. They can be either savoury, with additions like shrimp, shredded pork or corn kernels, or sweet when made with something like coconut and raisins. Steamed tamales (*colados*) are soft, whereas oven-baked ones (*horneados* or *rostados*) have a chewy, crunchy shell and an often molten filling.

Northern Yucatán is cattle country, and the **meat** is delicious as long as you're not looking for a thick, melt-in-your-mouth tender slab of steak. Typical cuts like skirt steak (*arrachera*) are sliced thin, grilled quick and garnished with grilled onions and chiles. For thick American-style steaks, look for a sign saying "Carnes Hereford" or for a "New York Cut" description (only in expensive places or in the north or at fancier resorts). Pork is ubiquitous, though usually cooked to a shreddable consistency and used in small portions as flavouring, rather than as a centrepiece; turkey is also very common in the Yucatán Peninsula. **Eggs** in country areas are genuinely free-range and flavoursome. They feature on every menu as the most basic of meals, and at some time you must try the classic Mexican combinations of *huevos rancheros* (fried eggs on a tortilla with red salsa) or *huevos a la mexicana* (scrambled with onion, tomato and chile).

In the coastal towns, you'll of course enjoy a great deal of wonderfully fresh **fish**, shrimp, rock lobster and conch (*caracol*), which you can order simply grilled, fried with garlic (*en mojo de ajo*) or made into **ceviche** – doused in lime and left to "cook" in the acidic juice with tomato, onion and plenty of coriander. A *coctél* is seafood (usually shrimp) served in a cocktail glass with lime juice, ketchup and chopped onion and chile, usually with a side of Saltines. A beach-restaurant favourite is *tikin xik'* (TIK-in sheek), in which fish fillets are seasoned with rich orange achiote seed, lime and herbs, wrapped in a banana leaf, then baked on the grill. And shrimp tacos – lightly battered fried shrimp seasoned with mayo and chunky *pico de gallo* salsa – are an inexpensive treat.

## Yucatecan specialities

You'll find more typical **Yucatecan dishes** inland, away from the seafood-centric coast: *puchero*, a mutable stew that often includes chicken, beef, pork, squash, cabbage and sweet potato in a delicious broth seasoned with cinnamon and allspice, garnished with radish, coriander and Seville orange; *poc-chuc*, a combination of pork with tomatoes, citrus juice, onions and spices; *sopa de lima*, which is not lime soup exactly, but chicken broth with lime and tortilla chips in it; *pollo* or *cochinita pibil*, chicken or suckling pig wrapped in banana leaves and cooked in a *pib*, basically a pit in the ground, though restaurants cheat on this; *papadzules*, tacos filled with hard-boiled eggs and covered in red and green pumpkin-seed sauce; and anything *en relleno negro*, a black, burnt-chile sauce. Valladolid has its own culinary specialities – one is *longaniza*, a bright-red sausage flavoured with cinnamon – as does Campeche, where chefs use seafood in inventive ways, as in *pan de cazón*, a casserole of tortillas and shredded shark meat, and shrimp fried in a coconut batter.

The most ubiquitous, archetypal Yucatecan treat, however, is the **salbute**, an *antojito* made of a just-crispy corn tortilla topped with shredded turkey (the most traditional Maya meat), bright-pink pickled onions, avocado and radish slices and occasionally a salty tomato sauce. *Panuchos* are nearly identical but for an added dab of refried beans slipped inside the fried tortilla. The Yucatán is also known as "the land of the pheasant and the deer", and in some of the inland villages you can still get venison and other forest **game**, usually smoked and shredded; the *tepezcuintle*, for instance, is a small, delectable rodent that more Maya are raising domestically since it became endangered in its wild form. For breakfast, *huevos motuleños* is an intriguing sweet-savoury mix of fried eggs on a crisp tortilla with beans, topped with mild tomato salsa, ham, cheese, peas and fried banana slices.

For anyone interested in learning how to cook Yucatecan food, the Los Dos **cooking school** (☎999/928-1116, ⓦwww.los-dos .com) in Mérida offers classes starting from US$50 for a half-day, with a guesthouse on site. Several Spanish-language institutes in Mérida and Playa del Carmen also offer culinary classes as part of their curriculum.

## Vegetarian food in Mexico

Vegetarians can eat well in Mexico, although it does take caution to avoid meat altogether. Many Mexican dishes are naturally **meat-free**, and there are always fabulous fruits and vegetables available. Most restaurants serve vegetable soups and rice, and items like quesadillas, *chiles rellenos*, and even tacos and enchiladas often come with non-meat fillings, many of them tasty and exotic, such as cactus leaves (*nopal*), squash blossoms *(flor de calabaza)* and *huitlacoche*, a fungus that grows on corn and is often called the "Mexican truffle" – it even tastes a bit like bacon. Another possibility is *queso fundido*, simply (and literally) melted cheese, served with tortillas and salsa, and perhaps a side of *rajas* (grilled strips of *poblano* peppers). Another boon is the leafy green *chaya*, a highly nutritious plant that grows wild everywhere in the Yucatán and is worked into many traditional dishes. Eggs, too, are served anywhere at any time, and many *jugerías* serve huge mixed salads to which grains and nuts can be added.

However, do bear in mind that vegetarianism, though growing, is not particularly common, and a simple cheese and chile dish may have some meat added to "improve" it. Worse, most of the fat used for frying is animal fat (usually lard), so that even something as unadorned as refried beans may not be strictly vegetarian (especially as a bone or some stock may have been added to the water the beans were originally boiled in). Even so-called **vegetarian restaurants**, which can be found in all the big cities, often include chicken on the menu. You may well have better luck in pizza places and Chinese or other ethnic restaurants.

## Meals

Traditionally, Mexicans eat a light breakfast very early, a snack of tacos or eggs in mid-morning, lunch (the main meal of the day) around two o'clock or later – in theory followed by a siesta, but decreasingly so – and a late, light supper. Eating a large meal at lunchtime can be a great way to save money – almost every restaurant serves a cut-price daily special.

**Breakfast** (*desayuno*) in Mexico can consist simply of coffee (see "Drinking", opposite) and *pan dulce* – sweet rolls and pastries that usually come in a basket; you pay for as many as you eat. More substantial breakfasts consist of eggs in any number of forms (many set breakfasts include *huevos al gusto*: eggs however you like them), and at fruit juice places you can have a simple *licuado* (see "Drinking", opposite) fortified with raw egg (*blanquillo*). Freshly squeezed orange juice (*jugo de naranja*) is always available from street stalls in the early morning.

**Snacks** mostly consist of some variation on the taco/enchilada theme (stalls selling them are called *taquerías*), but *tortas* – rolls heavily filled with meat or cheese or both, garnished with avocado and chile and toasted on request – are also wonderful, and you'll see take-out *torta* stands everywhere. Failing that, you can of course always make your own snacks with bread or tortillas, along with fillings such as avocado or cheese, from shops or markets.

You can eat a full meal in a restaurant at any time of day, but you'll certainly save money by adopting the local habit of taking your main meal at **lunchtime**, when the **comida corrida** or **comida corriente** (set meal, varied daily) is served, from around 1pm to 5pm; in more expensive places the same thing may be known as the *menu del día* or *menu turístico*. You'll usually get a soup, a main dish with a side of beans and a drink or dessert for US$5/£3 or less. More importantly, the *comida* is an affordable alternative to the budget traveller's staples of eggs, tacos and beans. It includes food that doesn't normally appear on menus such as home-made soups, stews, local specialities, puddings and elusive vegetables. You'll find these set lunches at regular restaurants with broader menus, but also at *cocinas económicas*, hole-in-the-wall places open only for the midday meal and catering to neighbourhood workers, who often show up with a lunchbox in hand. Usually managed by local women, they're the best places to sample home-cooked food.

In Tulum, Playa del Carmen and Puerto Morelos in particular, some excellent restaurants serve multicourse gourmet meals for a fraction of what you'd pay in the US, and some of the grand haciendas have exceptionally good restaurants that merit a splurge.

## Drinking

The basic drinks to accompany meals are water, the ubiquitous Coca-Cola or beer. If you're drinking water, stick to bottled stuff – it comes either plain (*sin gas*) or carbonated (*con gas* or *mineral*).

### Refrescos, jugos and licuados

**Soft drinks** (*refrescos*) – including Coke, Pepsi, Squirt (fun to pronounce in Spanish), and Mexican brands such as apple-flavoured Sidral and the mysterious bubblegum-flavoured Pino Negro, made in Mérida – are on sale everywhere. Far more tempting are the real **fruit juices** sold at shops and stalls known as *jugerías* or *licuaderías*. Juices (**jugos**) can be squeezed from anything that will go through the extractor. Orange (*naranja*) and carrot (*zanahoria*) are the staples, but you should also experiment with some of the more obscure and seasonal tropical fruits, most of which are much better than they sound – spiky pink *pitahayas*, for instance, yield a delicate pale drink studded with black seeds, with a flavour like kiwi fruit.

**Licuados** are made of fruit mixed with water (*licuado de agua* or simply *agua de . . .* ) or milk (*licuado de leche*) in a blender, usually with sugar added. A banana-milk *licuado* with generous dashes of vanilla and cinnamon is a popular breakfast drink, and a blend of pineapple and spinach-like *chaya* juice is a surprisingly tasty drink that's supposed to cure practically everything. Beyond that, the combinations get fantastically complex and the names colourful: *el vampiro* often involves beetroot juice, and *el viagra* seems to involve everything in the shop. *Limonada* (fresh lemonade) is also sold in many of these places, as are *aguas frescas* – flavoured cold drinks, of which the most common are *horchata* (rice milk flavoured with cinnamon), home-made birch beer, and *agua de jamaica* (hibiscus or sorrel) or *de tamarindo* (tamarind). These are also often served in restaurants or sold in the streets from great glass jars. Street vendors sell whole green coconuts, into which you can stab a straw, then suck out the clear, faintly sweet juice studded with small chunks of young fruit. Juices and *licuados* are also sold at many ice-cream parlours (*neverías* or *paleterías*); La Flor de Michoacan is a ubiquitous chain operation, with an impressive selection of refreshing cold drinks and ice pops.

### Coffee and tea

A great deal of **coffee** is produced in Mexico, and in you will be served superb strong, black, often sweet (ask for it *sin azúcar* for no sugar) cups of it. In most of the Yucatán, however, weaker *café americano* and *café de olla* (brewed in a clay pot, usually with cinnamon) are more typical, but instant Nescafé is the default. In the Italian-heavy resorts of Tulum and Playa del Carmen, you'll be able to get good espresso and cappuccino. **Tea** (*té*) is often available, too, and you may well be offered a cup at the end of a *comida*. Typically it's some kind of herb tea like *manzanillo* (camomile) or *yerbabuena* (mint), but basic *té negro* is usually available too.

### Alcohol

Though you can get all of the national brands, the standard **beers** in the Yucatán are the light pilsner Sol, the amber León and Montejo, available in light (*clara*) and dark (*oscura*) brews. Look also for fuller-bodied (and more expensive) brews like Bohemia and Negra Modelo. A popular beer treatment is the *michelada*, in which beer is seasoned with lime, hot sauce and Worcestershire sauce and served in a salt-rimmed glass with ice; a *chelada* is just the lime, ice and salt. When ordering, say what type of beer you'd like it made with: a *michelada de Sol*, for example.

You'll normally be drinking in bars, but if you don't feel comfortable – this applies to women, in particular (for more on which, see p.70) – you can also get takeaways from most shops, supermarkets and, cheapest of all, *agencias*, which are normally agents for just one brand. When buying from any of these places, it is normal to pay a **deposit of about 30–40 percent** of the purchase price: keep your receipt and return your bottles to the same store. Instead of buying 330ml bottles, you can go for the 940ml vessels known as *caguamas* (turtles).

Mexican **wine** (*vino* – *tinto* is red, *blanco* is white) is not seen a great deal, though production quality is improving. The best wine-growing region is the Valle de Guadalupe in Baja California, though little from the smaller winemakers makes it to the Yucatán. L.A. Cetto is the largest, and its chardonnay is especially good; also look for smaller producers like Monte Xanic, Adobe Guadalupe and Liceaga (especially its merlot).

**Tequila**, distilled from the cactus-like agave plant and produced in the state of Jalisco, is of course the most famous of Mexican spirits, usually served straight with lime and salt on the side. Lick the salt and bite into the lime, then take a swig of tequila (or the other way round – there's no correct etiquette). The best stuff is what's been around longer: *reposados* are somewhat aged tequilas that have taken on a faint woody taste from their casks – much more complex than your standard José Cuervo. *Añejos* are aged longer; some approach whisky or Scotch in their smoky complexity. In Cancún and the other beach towns, you'll see many shops packed with an overwhelming selection of ritzy varieties, though you can often find inexpensive, very good bottles in the grocery store as well – Cazadores *reposado*, for instance, is smooth and a little sweet, with slightly lower alcohol content than others. In the Yucatán, one distillery is now producing a tequila-like liquor named Sisal, distilled from henequen, another species of agave; it's a little rougher than the best tequilas, but inexpensive.

**Mescal** (often spelled *mezcal*) is basically the same as tequila, but not made in Jalisco; it's usually younger and less refined. The spurious belief that the worm in the mescal bottle is hallucinogenic is based on confusion between the drink and the peyote cactus, which is also called mescal; by the time you've got down as far as the worm, you wouldn't notice hallucinations anyway.

If you want to try other spirits, ask for **nacional** if you want a bargain (and perhaps a bigger headache), as anything imported is fabulously expensive. **Rum** (*ron*), gin (*ginebra*) and **vodka** are made in Mexico, as are some very palatable **brandies** (*brandy* or *coñac* – try San Marcos or Presidente). Most of the **cocktails** for which Mexico is known – margaritas, piñas coladas and so on – are available primarily in tourist areas or hotel bars, and are generally pretty strong. You can wash it all down with **Xtabentun**, a sweet, herb-infused liqueur (anise predominates) that has its roots in ancient Maya techniques. It's often served in coffee, or simply on the rocks as an after-dinner drink.

Whatever you order, if you do it in a more traditional bar or restaurant, you'll be served **botanas** as well. These are complimentary small dishes of snacks, which can be anything from a spicy ground-pumpkin-seed dip (a Yucatecan speciality called *sikilp'aak*) to little morsels of fried fish to Lebanese foods like ground-meat fritters (*quibi*) or hummus. The servings are generous, so you can often make a lunch on the snacks alone, just by ordering beers.

The least heavy drinking atmosphere is in **hotel bars**, tourist areas or anything that describes itself as a "ladies' bar". Traditional **cantinas** are for serious and excessive drinking and have a thoroughly intimidating, macho atmosphere; more often than not, there's a sign above the door prohibiting entry to "women, members of the armed forces, and anyone in uniform". Big-city cantinas are to some extent more liberal, but in small and traditional places they remain exclusively male preserves, full of drunken bonhomie that can suddenly sour into threats and fighting.

# Post, phones and email

Although on the face of it Mexico has reasonably efficient postal and telephone systems, phoning home can be a tricky business, while packages have a tendency to go astray in both directions. One thing to watch is the outrageous cost of international phone calls, faxes and telegrams; call collect or use a calling card wherever possible. Better still, see if you can make your international calls at one of the ubiquitous and inexpensive computer centres.

## Mail

Mexican postal services (*correos*) are reasonably efficient. Airmail to the capital should arrive within a few days, but it may take a couple of weeks to get anywhere at all remote. **Post offices** usually offer a poste restante (general delivery) service: letters should be addressed to Lista de Correos at the Correo Central (main post office) of any town; all mail that arrives for the Lista is noted on a list that's updated daily and displayed in the post office, but is held for only ten days. You may get around that by sending it to "Poste Restante" instead of "Lista de Correos" and having letter-writers put "Favor de retener hasta la llegada" (please hold until arrival) on the envelope; letters addressed thus will not appear on the Lista. Letters are often filed incorrectly, so you should have staff check under all your initials; preferably use only two names on the envelope (in Spanish-speaking countries, the second of people's three names, or the third if they've four names, is the paternal surname and the most important, so if three names are used, your mail will probably be filed under the middle one) and capitalize and underline your surname. To collect, you need your passport or some other official ID with a photograph. There is no fee.

**American Express** operates an efficient mail collection service at offices in Cancún, Mérida, Ciudad del Carmen and Villahermosa (the latter two are operated by partner travel agents). They keep letters for a month and also hold faxes. If you don't carry their card or cheques, you have to pay a fee to collect your mail, although they don't always ask. Given the convenience of communicating via email, though, mail collection is under review and may be cut; check with the company before you leave if you intend to rely on the service.

Sending letters and cards is also easy enough, if slow. Anything sent abroad by air should have an **airmail** (*por avión*) stamp on it or it is liable to go surface. Letters should take around a week to North America and two to Europe or Australasia, but can take much longer (postcards in particular are likely to be slow). Anything at all important should be taken to the post office and preferably registered rather than dropped in a mailbox, although the dedicated airmail boxes in resorts and big cities are supposed to be more reliable than ordinary ones.

Sending **packages** out of the country is drowned in bureaucracy. Regulations about the thickness of brown paper wrapping and the amount of string used vary from state to state, but, most importantly, any package must be checked by customs and have its paperwork stamped by at least three other departments, which may take a while. Take your package (unsealed) to any post office and they'll set you on your way. Many stores will send your purchases home for you, which is a great deal easier. Within the country, you can send a package by bus if there is someone to collect it at the other end.

**Telegram offices** (*telégrafos*) are frequently in the same building as the post office. The service is super-efficient, but international ones are very expensive, even if you use the cheaper overnight service. In most cases, you can get across a short message for less by phone or fax.

## Phones

**Local phone calls** in Mexico are cheap, and some hotels will let you call locally for free. Public phones also charge very little for local calls, but require a phone card. These are available from telephone offices and stores near phones that use them (especially in bus and train stations, airports and major resorts). The hitch: you can use only a Telmex card on a Telmex public phone, and an Avantel card on an Avantel phone. One way to avoid this is by visiting **casetas de teléfono**, phone offices where someone will make the connection for you, for only slightly more per minute than you would pay at a phone box. There are lots of them, as many Mexicans don't have phones of their own; many are specialist phone and fax places displaying a blue-and-white "Larga Distancia" (long-distance) sign. An operator connects you, then presents you with a bill afterwards. There are scores of competing companies, and the new ones, like Computel, tend to be better; many take credit cards. Prices vary,

so if you're making lots of calls it may be worth checking a few out. There are *casetas* at just about every bus station and airport.

Wherever you make them from, **international calls** can be hideously expensive – using a phone card is the easiest option, though even the highest denomination ones won't last long. From a public phone, you pay US$1 per minute to the US or Canada, US$2 to the British Isles or Europe, US$2.50 to Australia or New Zealand. You pay similar rates from a *caseta*, though it's possible to get a better deal there than with pay phones, so shop around. Perhaps the cheapest way to make an international call is using voice-over-IP (VoIP), a service available from a limited but growing number of Internet offices. This can cost as little as US$0.40 per minute to anywhere in the world. Another alternative is to arm yourself in advance with a charge card or calling card that can be used in Mexico; you'll be connected to an English-speaking operator and will be billed at home at a rate that is predictable. The new long-distance provider Yucatel sells cards with

## Useful numbers

To call collect or person-to-person, dial ☎92 for interstate calls within Mexico, ☎96 for the US and Canada, ☎99 for the rest of the world.

### Calling from long-distance public phones
**Mexico interstate** ☎01 + area code + number
**US and Canada** ☎00 + 1 + area code + number
**UK** ☎00 44 + area code (minus initial zero) + number
**Ireland** ☎00 353 + area code (minus initial zero) + number
**Australia** ☎00 61 + area code (minus initial zero) + number
**New Zealand** ☎00 64 + area code (minus initial zero) + number

### Calling Mexico from abroad
**From US and Canada** ☎011 52 + area code + number
**From UK, Ireland and New Zealand** ☎00 52 + area code + number
**From Australia** ☎0011 52 + area code + number

### Calling-card numbers
US and UK calling-card numbers for English-speaking operators and home billing are as follows:
**AT&T** ☎01-800/288-2872 from Telmex or Ladatel phones
**BT** ☎01-800/123-0244 from Telmex phones, ☎1-800/021 6644 from Avantel phones
**Canada Direct** ☎01-800/123-0200 or 1-800/021-1994
**ekit** ☎1-888/206-5546 or 1-877/237-6347
**Sprint** ☎01-800/877-8000

very good per-minute rates in shops and online (🌐www.yucatel.net). You should be able to get through to all toll-free numbers from any working public phone.

It is also possible to **call collect** (*por cobrar*). In theory you should be able to make an international collect call from any public phone by dialling the international operator (☎090) or getting in touch with the person-to-person direct-dial numbers listed in the box opposite, though it can be hard to get through. At a *caseta* there may be a charge for making the connection, even if you don't get through, and a hotel is liable to make an even bigger charge.

**Faxes** can be sent from (and received at) many long-distance telephone *casetas*; again the cost is likely to be a bit steep.

## Mobile phones

If you want to use your **mobile phone** in Mexico, you'll need to check with your phone provider whether it will work there, and how the calls are charged. European mobile phones are unlikely to work in most of Mexico, even though there are two GSM providers, Telcel and Movistar. The Mexican GSM systems operate on 1900MHz, whereas European GSM phones use 900MHz or 1800MHz, so you'll have to have at least a dual-band phone to start with. Additionally, GSM coverage is relatively new in Mexico, and coverage of the country is so far confined largely to urban areas. Telcel has agreements with Cingular and T-Mobile in the US, Microcell in Canada, Hutchison, O$_2$, T-Mobile and Vodafone in the UK, Optus and Telstra in Australia, and MTN in South Africa, among other operators worldwide.

Visitors from the US can roam with Verizon's CDMA service, the older digital net-

work that has much better coverage in the Yucatán. Generally, until GSM coverage is wider, it is better to rent a mobile while you are in the country. This is easy enough, costing around US$4.50–6 per day for a pay-as-you-go phone, with cards available nationwide.

For further information on using your mobile in Mexico, including a coverage map and list of overseas mobile phone companies with roaming agreements for Mexico, see 🌐www.gsmworld.com/roaming/gsminfo/cou_mx. More general information about using your mobile abroad can be found at 🌐 www.telecomsadvice.org.uk/features/using_your_mobile_abroad.

## Email

**Internet** cafés are easy to find in all the larger cities and resort destinations, and the level of service is usually excellent, although servers tend to crash with greater frequency than they do at home. Depending on where you are, access can cost anything from US$0.25 to US$2.50 an hour. Major tourist resorts can be the most expensive places, and it's best there to look for cheaper Internet cafés around the town centre that are frequented by Mexicans.

Most home **email** accounts can be accessed from other computers; if you don't already know how to do this, ask your service provider, or, alternatively, set up a free web-based account with Hotmail (🌐www.hotmail.com) or Yahoo! (🌐mail.yahoo.com), which you can access from anywhere with an Internet connection. Note that Google's free Gmail service is currently not recommended because it requires very recent browsers to function properly, which some Internet cafés in Mexico have not yet installed.

# The media

Few of Mexico's domestic newspapers carry much foreign news, and the majority of international coverage does not extend beyond Latin America. Papers can be lurid scandal sheets, brimming with violent crime depicted in full colour. Each state has its own press, however, and they do vary: while most are little more than government mouthpieces, others can be surprisingly independent.

Probably the best **national paper**, if you read Spanish, is the new *Reforma*, which, although in its infancy, has already established an excellent reputation for its independence and political objectivity. Also worth a read is *La Jornada*: with its unabashedly left-wing agenda, it's quite critical of government policy, especially in Chiapas, and its journalists regularly face death threats as a result. As the press has gradually been asserting its independence since 1995, subjects such as human rights, corruption and drug trafficking are increasingly being tackled, but journalists face great danger if they speak out, not only from shady government groups but also from the drug traffickers. The worst incidents have been confined to northern Mexico and the border cities; Yucatán, by contrast, supports several wide-ranging newspapers, from the conservative, long-established *El Diario* to the more liberal tabloids like *Por Esto*. In Cancún and along the coast, you can also pick up the English-language *Miami Herald Cancún Edition*, but it's mostly a collection of tourism statistics and coverage of ribbon-cutting ceremonies at new hotel developments.

On Mexican **TV** you can watch any number of US shows dubbed into Spanish, but far and away the most popular programmes are the *telenovelas* – soap operas produced in Mexico and elsewhere in Latin America that dominate the screens from 6pm to 10pm and pull in audiences of millions. Cable and satellite are now widespread, and even quite downmarket hotels offer numerous channels, many of them American.

No **radio stations** in the Yucatán and Chiapas have regular English-language programmes. In Chiapas, though, you can tune in to the EZLN's broadcast, Radio Insurgentes, on different FM frequencies depending on the area (see ⓦ www.radioinsurgente.org for details). If you have a short-wave radio, you can pick up the BBC World Service, which is broadcast on various frequencies depending on the time of day. The main ones around Mérida are 15,190KHz, 9525KHz and 5175KHz. Full details of programmes and frequencies can be found on the BBC website at ⓦ www.bbc.co.uk/worldservice. The Voice of America broadcasts 24 hours on a number of frequencies including 5995KHz, 6130KHz, 7405KHz, 9455KHz, 9775KHz, 11,695KHz and 13,790KHz (full details of schedules and frequencies at ⓦ www.voa.gov).

# Opening hours and holidays

It's almost impossible to generalize about opening hours in Mexico; even when times are posted at museums, tourist offices and shops, they're not always adhered to.

The **siesta** is still around, and many shops will close for a couple of hours in the early afternoon, usually from 1pm to 3pm. The strictness of this is very much dependent on the climate; where it's hot – especially on the Caribbean coast outside of the largest resort areas – everything may close for up to four hours in the middle of the day, and then reopen until 8pm or 9pm. Otherwise, though, hours are more like the standard nine-to-five.

**Post offices** set their own hours, but you can count on at least Monday to Friday 9am–3pm. **Banks** are generally open Monday to Friday 9.30am–4pm, though a growing number of HSBC banks are open until 7pm. **Museums and galleries** tend to open from about 9am or 10am to 5pm or 6pm. Many are closed on Monday. Some museums may close for lunch, but archeological sites are open right through the day.

## Fiestas and dances

Stumbling, perhaps accidentally, onto some Yucatecan village **fiesta** may prove the highlight of your travels. Usually, these are devoted to the local saint's day, but many fiestas have pre-Christian origins and any excuse – from harvest celebrations to the coming of the rains – will do. The most famous, spectacular or curious fiestas are mentioned throughout the book, and the main public holidays are listed in the box below.

Traditional **dances** form an essential part of almost every fiesta. The Maya of the Yucatán and Chiapas are not known for ceremonial dancing or the use of masks, so common and colourful in central Mexico. Instead, festive occasions are marked by dances that merge traditional Maya dress with Spanish or other folkloric forms and rhythms – for instance, a variation on the maypole dance is common at rural fiestas. Other dances have more recent inspiration: the *degollete* was a protest dance that came about during the brutal nineteenth-century Caste Wars of the 1800s; it broadly parodies each of the sharply delimited social classes of the time. The most common festive dance is the *jara-*

---

### Public holidays

The main **public holidays**, when virtually everything will be closed, are listed below. Many places also close on January 6 (Twelfth Night/Reyes).

| | |
|---|---|
| **Jan 1** | New Year's Day |
| **Feb 5** | Anniversary of the Constitution |
| **March 21** | Día de Benito Juárez |
| **Good Friday and Easter Saturday** | |
| **May 1** | Labour Day |
| **May 5** | Battle of Puebla |
| **Sept 1** | Presidential address to the nation |
| **Sept 16** | Independence Day |
| **Oct 12** | Día de la Raza/Columbus Day |
| **Nov 1–2** | All Saints/Day of the Dead |
| **Nov 20** | Anniversary of the Revolution |
| **Dec 12** | Día de la Virgen de Guadalupe |
| **Dec 24–26** | Christmas |

*na*, a complex and boisterous rhythm calling for a band of clarinets, a contra-bass and several brass instruments. In Mérida, students perform these dances, but it doesn't compare to seeing the same dances performed by enthusiastic amateurs at a village celebration, who go all-out in their most festive *huipiles* and guayaberas and their best gold jewellery.

**Carnaval**, the week before Lent, is celebrated throughout the Roman Catholic world, and is at its most exuberant in Latin America. Like Easter, its date is not fixed, but it generally falls in February or early March. Carnaval is celebrated with costumes, parades, eating and dancing, most spectacularly in Cozumel and Mérida, and works its way up to a climax on the last day, Mardi Gras (or "Fat Tuesday"). Cancún's festivities attract big-name bands – some of which don't even hit the stage until 5am. Smaller towns, however, often have to wait well into Lent to celebrate because the obligatory travelling carnival rides have to make their way from bigger markets.

The country's biggest holiday, however, is **Semana Santa** – Holy Week – beginning on Palm Sunday and continuing until the following Sunday, Easter Day. Still a deeply religious festival in Mexico, it celebrates the resurrection of Christ, and has also become a veneration of the Virgin, with processions bearing her image a hallmark of the celebrations. In Mérida and the towns of Acanceh and Maní to the south, you can see rather vigorous and elaborate Passion plays (see box, p000) that involve hundreds of people. Many places close for the whole of Semana Santa, and certainly from Thursday to Sunday.

Secular **Independence Day** (Sept 16), in some ways more solemn than the religious festivals, marks the historic day in 1810 when Manuel Hidalgo y Costilla issued *El Grito* (The Cry of Independence) from his parish church in Dolores Hidalgo. It's now marked at midnight on September 15 with a mass, impassioned recitation of the *grito* ("Mexicanos, viva México!") in the town plaza, followed by fireworks, music, dancing and parades. In Cancún, the greater part of the month is given over to festivities.

The Day of the Dead (**Día de los Muertos**) is November 1–2, when offerings are made to ancestors' souls, frequently with picnics and all-night vigils at their graves. People build shrines in their homes to honour their departed relatives, but it's the cemeteries to head for if you want to see the really spectacular stuff. Sweetmeats and papier-mâché statues of dressed-up skeletons give the whole proceedings a rather gothic air. In the Maya areas, the Day of the Dead is called Hanal Pixan. Simple house altars, with white flowers, candles, water and salt, are built on October 30, in preparation for a sunset dinner on October 31 in honour of children who have died; at noon the next day (November 1), bells chime to herald the departure of the children's souls and the arrival of adult spirits, for whom the same meals are prepared until November 2.

**Christmas** is a major holiday, and again a time when people are on the move and transport booked solid for weeks ahead. Gringo influence is heavy nowadays, and after November 20 (the anniversary of the Mexican Revolution, always commemorated with parades of children dressed as Pancho Villa) shop windows and storefronts are crammed with Santa Claus, fake Christmas trees and other Yankee trappings. But the Mexican festival remains distinct in many ways, with a much stronger religious element, beginning around December 16, when people set up Nativity scenes in their homes and perform Las Posadas, re-enactments of the Holy Family's search for lodgings, in town plazas. **New Year** is still largely an occasion to spend with family, the actual hour being celebrated with the eating of grapes, one for each strike of the clock.

# Sport and outdoor activities

The Yucatán is an active traveller's paradise, from scuba diving and snorkelling in reefs and caves to more leisurely exploits like sailing and horseriding. Golf, tennis, jet-skiing and parasailing are staples at all the big resorts. If you're just up for an afternoon's amble to appreciate the wildlife, you can do that too.

## Diving and watersports

Sport **fishing** is enormously popular around Cancún and Cozumel and in Punta Allen, on the flat bays of the Sian Ka'an Biosphere Reserve; there's also good fishing on the Gulf coast. Year-round, you can pick up bonito, barracuda, king fish, grouper and the lively bonefish; April to June is the season for mahi-mahi, wahoo and marlin. You can rent catamarans to **sail** on your own in any of the beach resorts, or take one of a number of yachting day-trips from Cancún. Isla Mujeres is a popular yachting port, as well as the finish line for the biennial Regatta del Sol (mid-May, even-number years) that begins in Pensacola, Florida (when the boats arrive, the island throws a big parade and party). The peninsula, already moderately popular with surfers, is also becoming something of a centre for **kiteboarding**, with dedicated enthusiasts in Playa del Carmen and Tulum, with an annual meet in February.

With the vibrant and complex Meso-american Barrier Reef running directly off the Caribbean coast, the Yucatán Peninsula, particularly around Cozumel, is one of the top **scuba diving** destinations in the world. **Snorkellers** can also enjoy some of the area's undersea wonders – in spots, it's possible to wade to the reef from shore, while a boat trip (with an experienced guide) can make a visit to a more remote coral garden or wall an easy and rewarding experience. With so many dive spots and countless dive shops willing to take you there, it's important to choose an outfit wisely and be clear and honest about your diving skills and experience; a respectable divemaster should not push you to a more advanced dive. It helps if you can find a group of divers of roughly the same level and approach a shop together.

Some old hands dive only with guides who have families, a good indicator that your leaders won't be taking unnecessary risks at your – or their – expense. On Cozumel, would-be snorkellers will want an operator who's willing to travel the distance to the best spots on Colombia and Palancar reefs.

The best coral growth and fish life is around Cozumel, and parts of that are accessible from Playa del Carmen as well. The reef off Puerto Morelos is relatively untouched. Cancún is not known for diving, though some spots are excellent for novices, with sandy floors, little current, easy access and plenty to see. Isla Mujeres has easily accessible snorkelling off the Sac Bajo Peninsula as well as a couple of interesting wreck dives. Along the Gulf coast, as on Isla Holbox, for instance, the water is not nearly as clear, and the reef life not as extravagant.

The Yucatán also offers the unique experience of diving in the freshwater sinkholes called **cenotes**, part of the vast network of underground rivers, caves and caverns that riddle the limestone bedrock that forms the peninsula. The pristine spring water is gin-clear, and the elaborate rock formations otherworldly. Although many dive shops offer cenote diving packages, not all have the experience to back it up, and most of the tragic cave-diving accidents have been the fault of guides who took the sport too lightly. Nonetheless, cavern diving (in which you explore a partially open space, with the entrance in clear view) requires only open-water certification; to go deeper into passageways and closed caves, you'll need excellent buoyancy control. **Snorkelling** can be enjoyed by anyone at a number of cenotes, where the proprietors often rent gear as well. An underwater torch can be a big help. Spelunkers can also explore quite a few **dry caves**.

## Reef behaviour

**Coral reefs** are among the richest and most complex eco-systems on earth, but they are also very fragile. The colonies grow at a rate of only around 5cm per year, so they must be treated with care and respect if they are not to be damaged beyond repair. Remember to follow these **simple rules** while you are snorkelling, diving or in a boat.

**Never** touch or stand on corals, as the living polyps on their surface are easily damaged.

**Avoid** disturbing the sand around corals. Apart from spoiling visibility, the cloud of sand will settle over the corals and smother them.

**Don't** remove shells, sponges or other creatures from the reef, and avoid buying reef products from souvenir shops.

**Don't** use suntan lotion in reef areas, as the oils are pollutants and will stifle coral growth; look for special biodegradable sunscreen for use while snorkelling.

**Don't** anchor boats on the reef: use the permanently secured buoys instead.

**Don't** throw litter overboard.

**Check** ahead of time where you are allowed to go fishing.

**Review** your diving skills away from the reef first if you are an out-of-practice diver.

## Hiking and trekking

The utterly flat Yucatán Peninsula doesn't yield interesting **hiking** or trekking – that you'll have to leave largely for the highlands of Chiapas. But the various types of scrub forest and jungle are filled with dazzling birds and other wildlife. The few trails where you can hike without a guide are mentioned in the relevant sections of the book, and will occupy only an hour or so of your day. In general, you're better off with a guide who can identify local flora and fauna. **Birdwatchers** will benefit from a tour with Mérida-based Ecoturísmo Yucatán (℡999/920-2772, ⓦwww .ecoyuc.com), which also organizes the annual Yucatán Bird Festival. Ecocolors (℡998/884-9214, ⓦwww.ecotravelmexico. com), based in Cancún but operating primarily in the Sian Ka'an Reserve, and Mayan World Adventures (℡983/832-4729, ⓦwww .mayanworldadventures.com), in Chetumal, also offer multiday camping tours with naturalist guides.

Another great experience is **trekking** to remote Maya ruins. You'll need a bit of Spanish, as the tours are usually geared to Mexican students, but if you can manage that, the thrill of chancing upon unexcavated ruins in the midst of the jungle, or getting a behind-the-scenes look at closed sites, is unparalleled. During Mexican holiday seasons, Servidores Turísticos de Calakmul (℡983/871-6064) organizes a four-day hike in the Calakmul Biosphere Reserve taking in the ruins of La Muñeca, which you can reach only on foot; three-day photo safaris; and a truly deluxe five-day outing once a year.

## Spectator sports

Mexico's chief spectator sport is **soccer** (fútbol), and going to a game can still be a thrilling experience, though there are no massive stadiums in the Yucatán. The Mérida team is known by the positively non-violent moniker of Los Venados (the Deer). **Baseball** (béisbol) is also popular, with the Cancún Langosteros and Campeche Piratas among Yucatán's major-league teams. Almost every town has one or two baseball fields where you can while away a summer night – the atmosphere is casual, and entrance fees are nominal or nonexistent.

**Bullfights** (corridas) still take place regularly in Cancún and Mérida, but occur only once a year or so in smaller towns during fiestas, when a bullring complete with stadium seats is erected entirely out of sapling poles. Even if you're leery of the fight itself, these small-town events are boisterous fun, with every man who can muster a matador's costume, however camp and bizarre, allowed to compete, and much drink consumed to bolster courage.

Masked **wrestling** (*lucha libre*) is popular in the Yucatán, though not a major commercial enterprise here in the same way it is in central Mexico. Nonetheless, local matches can incite great passion – keep an eye out for flyers.

# Crafts and markets

**The craft tradition of Mexico, much of it descended directly from arts practised long before the Spanish arrived, is extremely strong in the Yucatán. Regional and highly localized specialities survive, with villages jealously guarding their reputations for particular skills. You can also pick up a considerable amount of Guatemalan weaving and embroidery.**

## Crafts

To buy **crafts**, there is no need these days to visit the place of origin; shops in all the big resorts gather the best and most popular items from around Mexico. On the other hand, it's a great deal more enjoyable to see where the articles come from, and certainly the only way to get any real bargains. The good stuff is rarely cheap wherever you buy it, however, and there is an enormous amount of dross produced specifically for tourists.

**FONART** shops, which you'll come across in major centres throughout Mexico, are run by a government agency devoted to the promotion and preservation of crafts – their wares are always excellent, if expensive, and the shops should be visited to get an idea of what is available and at what price. Among the most popular items are: **silver**, the best of which is wrought in Taxco, although rarely mined there; **embroidery**; **leather**, especially tyre-tread-soled *huaraches* (sandals), sold cheaply wherever you go; **glass** from Jalisco; and **lacquerware**, particularly from Uruapán.

Good buys specific to the Yucatán include men's dapper, Cuban-style **guayabera shirts** and Panama hats (known here as *jipis*). Throughout the peninsula and Chiapas, Maya women wear flower-bedecked embroidered **huipiles**, which vary wildly in quality, from factory-made junk to hand-embroidered, homespun cloth. Even the best, though, rarely compare with the **antique dresses** that can occasionally be found, identical in style (as they have been for hundreds of years) but far better made and very expensive. Silver **jewellery** (genuine sterling should be stamped ".925"), either made into fine filigree or set with colourful semiprecious stones, rich amber or milky Mexican opals, can be elegant and inexpensive.

The most popular souvenir of the Yucatán is a **hammock**, and Mérida is probably the best place to buy one, for both price and selection. If you want something you can realistically sleep in, never buy from street vendors or even a market stall – they're invariably of very poor craftsmanship, with thicker strings woven loosely, so they don't hold their shape. Comfort is measured by the tightness of the weave and the breadth: because you're supposed to lie in a hammock diagonally, to be relatively flat, the distance it stretches sideways is far more crucial than the length (although obviously the woven portion of the hammock, excluding the strings at each end, should be at least as long as you are tall). A good way to judge quality is by weight: a decent-size hammock (*doble* at least, preferably *matrimonial*) with cotton threads (*hilos de algodon*, more comfortable and less likely to go out of shape than artificial fibres) will weigh more than a kilo and set you back about US$25/£13. ("Sisal" hammocks are generally fraudulent; this rough rope material is seldom used today.)

It is illegal to buy or sell antiquities, and even more criminal to try taking them out of the country (moreover, many items sold as valuable antiquities are little more than worthless fakes) – best to just look.

## Markets

For bargain hunters, the **mercado** (market) is the place to head. There's one in every Yucatecan town, which on one day of the week, the traditional market day, will be at its busiest with villagers from the surrounding area bringing their produce for sale or barter. By and large, of course, *mercado*s are mainly dedicated to food and everyday necessities, but most have a section devoted to crafts, and in larger towns you may find a separate crafts bazaar. You can also find a lot of fun smaller gift items, such as Spanish classroom vocabulary **posters**, found in stationers, or local foodstuffs, such as **coffee** in Chiapas, inexpensive but fragrant **vanilla** and Yucatecan **honey.**

Unless you're completely hopeless at bargaining, prices will always be lower in the market than in shops, but shops do have a couple of advantages. First, they exercise a degree of quality control, whereas any old junk can be sold in the market; and second, many established shops will be able to ship purchases home for you, which saves an enormous amount of the frustrating bureaucracy you'll encounter if you attempt to do it yourself.

**Bargaining and haggling** are very much a matter of personal style, highly dependent on your command of Spanish, aggressiveness and to some extent on experience. The standard tricks (never show the least sign of interest, let alone enthusiasm; walking away will always cut the price dramatically) hold true; but most important is to know what you want, its approximate value – and how much you are prepared to pay. Never start negotiating for something you don't intend to buy. In shops there's little chance of significantly altering the official price unless you're buying in bulk, and even in markets most food and simple household goods have a set price. But overall don't let a quibble over a few dollars stop you from buying, and resist the urge to compare prices with fellow shoppers – ten pesos almost certainly means more to the seller than to you, and the best price is the one both you and the seller are happy with.

# Crime and safety

Despite soaring crime rates and dismal-sounding statistics, you are unlikely to run into trouble in Mexico as long as you stick to the well-travelled paths. Indeed, the Yucatán cherishes its very low rate of violent crime and overall graciousness, and it can dismay locals to see travellers clutching their bags tightly in such non-threatening areas as Cancún's zona hotelera or central Mérida.

The precautions to be taken against petty crime are mostly common sense and would be second nature at home. Travelling in the Zapatista-controlled areas of the state of Chiapas you will undoubtedly come across guerrillas and the army, but tourists are a target of neither, and you shouldn't encounter any trouble.

## Avoiding theft

**Petty theft** and **pickpockets** are your biggest worry, so don't wave money around, try not to look too obviously affluent, don't leave cash or cameras in hotel rooms, and do deposit your valuables in your hotel's safe if it has one (make a note of what you've deposited and ask the hotelier to sign it if you're worried). **Crowds**, especially on public city transport, are obvious hot spots: thieves tend to work in groups and target tourists. **Distracting your attention**, especially by pretending to look for something (always be suspicious of anyone who appears to be searching for something near you), or having one or two people pin you while another goes through your pockets, are common ploys, and can be done faster and more easily than you might imagine. **Razoring of bags** and pockets is another gambit, as is the more brutish grabbing of handbags, or anything left unattended even for a split second. When carrying your valuables, keep them out of sight under your clothes. If on the very rare chance that you are held up, however, don't try any heroics: hand over your money and rely on travellers' cheque refunds and credit-card hotlines if appropriate. One trick is to carry a cheap wallet with US$20 and an old identification card, while hiding the bulk of your cash in a money belt.

Use **ATM machines** in shopping malls or enclosed premises and only in daylight when there are plenty of people around.

When travelling, keep an eye on your bags (which are safe enough in the luggage compartments underneath most buses). Drivers are likely to encounter problems if they leave anything in their **car**. The vehicle itself is less likely to be stolen than broken into for the valuables inside. To avoid the worst, always park legally (and preferably off the street) and never leave anything visible inside the car.

## Police

Mexican **police** are, in the ordinary run of events, no better or worse than any other; but they are very badly paid, and graft is an accepted part of the job. This is often difficult for foreign visitors to accept, but it is a system, and in its own way it works well enough. If a policeman accuses you of some violation, explain that you're a tourist, not used to the ways of the country – you may get off scot-free, but more likely the subject of a "fine" will come up. Such on-the-spot fines are open to negotiation, but only if you're confident you've done nothing seriously wrong and have a reasonable command of Spanish. Otherwise pay up and get out. These small bribes, known as **mordidas** (bites), may also be extracted by border officials or bureaucrats (in which case, you could get out of paying by asking for a receipt, but it won't make life easier). In general, it is always wise to back off from any sort of confrontation with the police and to be extremely polite to them at all times.

Far more common than the *mordida* is the **propina**, or tip, a payment that is made entirely on your initiative. There's no need to

## Emergencies

In the event of trouble, dial ☎06 for the police emergency operator. Most phone booths give the number for the local Red Cross (Cruz Roja), but don't expect the phone to be answered promptly.

do this, but it's remarkable how often a few pesos complete paperwork that would otherwise take weeks, open doors that were firmly locked before, or even find a seat on a previously full bus. All such transactions are quite open, and it's up to you to literally put your money on the table.

Should a crime be committed against you – in particular, if you're robbed – your relationship with the police will obviously be different, although even in this eventuality it's worth considering whether the lengthy hassles you'll go through make it worth reporting. **Tourist police** in the resort towns can at least appear more sympathetic, but it doesn't necessarily speed the process along. Some insurance companies will insist on a **police report** if you're to get any refund, but others will be understanding of the situation. The department you need in order to *presentar una denuncia* (report the theft officially) is the **Procuradoría General de Justicia**.

The Mexican **legal system** is based on the Napoleonic code, which assumes your guilt until you can prove otherwise. Should you be jailed, your one phone call should be to your **consulate** – if nothing else, it will arrange an English-speaking lawyer. You can be held for up to 72 hours on suspicion before charges have to be brought. Mexican jails are grim, although lots of money and friends on the outside can ameliorate matters slightly.

## Drugs

**Drug offences** are the most common cause of serious trouble between tourists and the authorities. Under heavy pressure from the US to stamp out the trade, local authorities are particularly happy to throw the book at foreign offenders.

Grown primarily in the Yucatán, Sinaloa, Oaxaca and Michoacán, **marijuana** (known as *mota*) continues to be cultivated in Mexico. It's widely used, particularly along the Caribbean beaches, but it remains strictly illegal, and foreigners caught in possession are dealt with harshly; for quantities reckoned to be for distribution you can wave goodbye to daylight for a long time. For possession of small quantities, you can expect a hefty fine, no sympathy and little help from your consulate.

Other naturally occurring drugs – Mexico has more species of psychoactive plants than anywhere else in the world – still form an important part of many indigenous rituals. In the Yucatán and Chiapas, hallucinogenic mushrooms are the primary item (the **peyote** cactus from the northern deserts is used primarily by the Huichols). The authorities turn a blind eye to traditional use, but use by non-indigenous Mexicans and tourists is as strongly prohibited as that of any other illegal drug, and heavily penalized. Expect searches and hotel raids by police if staying in areas known for peyote.

**Cocaine** trafficking is a national problem, as Mexico is a major staging post on the smuggling route from Colombian supply to American demand. Well-connected gangs involved in the trade are often more powerful than the police and local government. Although the cartels do not exert the social influence in the Yucatán that they do in the northern part of Mexico, stories abound about suspicious packets washed up on the Caribbean beaches, and equally suspicious sorts coming to reclaim them. A very thorough drug checkpoint is set up on the highway out from Mahahual. Cocaine use is also widespread and growing, especially in the beach party towns, but you're advised to steer well clear, considering the legal consequences.

# Travellers with disabilities

Mexico is not well equipped for people with disabilities, but things are improving all the time and, especially at the top end of the market, it shouldn't be too difficult to find accommodation and tour operators that can cater for your particular needs. The important thing is to check beforehand with tour companies, hotels and airlines that they can accommodate you specifically. The list below details organizations that can advise you as to which tour operators and airlines are the most reliable.

If you stick to beach resorts – Cancún in particular – and upmarket tourist hotels, you should certainly be able to find places that are wheelchair-friendly and accustomed to having guests who are disabled. US chains are very good for this, with Leading Hotels of the World, Marriott, Radisson, Sheraton and Westin claiming to have the necessary facilities for at least some disabilities in a number of their hotels.

You'll find that, unless you have your own transport, the best way to travel inside the Yucatán may prove to be by air, since trains and buses rarely cater for disabilities, and certainly not for wheelchairs. Travelling on a lower budget, or getting off the beaten track, you'll find few facilities. Ramps are rare and streets and pavements not in a very good state. Depending on your disability, you may want to find an able-bodied helper to accompany you. If you cannot find anyone suitable among your own friends or family, the organizations listed below may be able to help you get in touch with someone.

## Contacts for travellers with disabilities

### In the US and Canada

**Access-Able** ⓦ www.access-able.com. Online resource for travellers with disabilities.
**Directions Unlimited** 123 Green Lane, Bedford Hills, NY 10507 ☏ 1-800/533-5343 or 914/241-1700. Travel agency specializing in bookings for people with disabilities.
**Mobility International USA** 451 Broadway, Eugene, OR 97401 ☏ 541/343-1284, ⓦ www.miusa.org. Information and referral services, access guides, tours and exchange programmes.

**Society for the Advancement of Travelers with Handicaps (SATH)** 347 5th Ave, New York, NY 10016 ☏ 212/447-7284, ⓦ www.sath.org. Non-profit educational organization that has actively represented travellers with disabilities since 1976.
**Wheels Up!** ☏ 1-888/389-4337, ⓦ www.wheelsup.com. Provides discounted airfare, tour and cruise prices; also publishes a free monthly newsletter and has a comprehensive website.

### In the UK and Ireland

**Disability Action** Portside Business Park, 189 Airport Rd W, Belfast BT3 9ED ☏ 028/9029 7800, ⓦ www.disabilityaction.org. Provides information about access for those travelling abroad.
**Holiday Care** 7th Floor, Sunley House, 4 Bedford Park, Croydon, Surrey CR0 2AP ☏ 0845/124 9971, minicom ☏ 0845/124 9976, ⓦ www.holidaycare.org.uk. Provides free lists of accessible accommodation abroad. Information on financial help for holidays available.
**Tripscope** The Vassall Centre, Gill Ave, Bristol BR6 2QQ ☏ 0845/758 5641, ⓦ www.tripscope.org.uk. This registered charity provides a national telephone information service offering free advice on international transport.

### In Australia and New Zealand

**ACROD (Australian Council for Rehabilitation of the Disabled)** PO Box 60, Curtin, ACT 2605 ☏ 02/6282 4333 (also TTY); 33 Thesiger Ct, Deakin ACT 2600 ⓦ www.acrod.org.au. Provides lists of travel agencies and tour operators accommodating people with disabilities.
**Disabled Persons Assembly** 4/173–175 Victoria St, Wellington ☏ 04/801 9100 (also TTY), ⓦ www.dpa.org.nz. Resource centre with lists of travel agencies and tour operators.

# Women travellers

So many limitations are imposed on women's freedom to travel that any advice or warning seems merely to reinforce the situation. Machismo is certainly a factor in Mexican culture, though it's softened considerably in the Yucatán by the gentler mores of Maya culture.

On the whole, most hassles will be limited to **comments** in the street. They're generally meant as compliments, but you may soon tire of such astute observations as "Guera!" ("Blondie!"), in which case you'll have to simply tune it out – chances are slim that any retorts on your part, in Spanish or otherwise, will reform a sidewalk lecher. *Yucatecos* are on the whole exceptionally gentlemanly and gracious, but, like men anywhere, can be emboldened with a bit of liquor. In the evenings, you're better off **not walking by yourself**.

Any problems are aggravated in the big resort areas, where legendarily "easy" tourists attract droves of would-be gigolos, and the gap between wealthy visitors and the scraping-by population who has built the place is often quite distinct. There are occasional rapes reported in Cancún and Playa del Carmen, but it is hardly the epidemic that some guidebooks make it out to be. Simply be as sensible as you would ordinarily be: drink in moderation and have a plan with friends for extricating yourself from unwanted male attention.

Away from the cities, though, and especially in indigenous areas, there is rarely any problem – you may, as an outsider, be treated as an object of curiosity (or occasionally resentment), but not necessarily with any implied or intended sexual threat. And wherever you come across it, such curiosity can also extend to great friendliness and hospitality.

The restrictions imposed on **drinking** are without a doubt irksome: women are simply and absolutely barred from the vast majority of **cantinas**, and even in so-called Ladies' Bars "unescorted" women may be looked at with suspicion or even refused service. Carrying a bottle is the only answer, since in very small towns the cantina may be the only place that sells alcoholic drinks.

# Gay and lesbian travellers

There are no federal laws governing homosexuality in Mexico, and hence it's legal. Social acceptance of homosexuality is very slowly spreading: Mexico's first "out" congresswoman, the left-wing PRD's Patria Jiménez, was elected in 1997, and 2003 saw the passage of a federal law, forbidding discrimination based on "appearance, mannerism, and expression of one's sexual preference or gender".

There are in fact a large number of **gay groups and publications** in Mexico – we've supplied two contact addresses below. The lesbian scene is not as visible or as large as the gay scene for men, but it's there and growing. There are **gay bars and clubs** in Cancún, Playa del Carmen and Mérida (visit ⓦsergay.com.mx for a basic directory, though it's not entirely up to date; also see nightlife listings in this book). Elsewhere, private parties are where it all happens, and you'll need a contact to find them.

As far as popular attitudes are concerned, religion and machismo are the order of the day, but there's a surprisingly open **subculture** out there once you tap into it. Soft-porn magazines for gay men are sold openly on street stalls and, while you should be careful to avoid upsetting macho sensibilities, you should have few problems if you are discreet. Many Mexicans of both sexes are bisexual, though they do not see themselves as such.

HIV and AIDS (SIDA) are as much a threat in Mexico as anywhere else in the world, and the usual precautions are in order. You can check the latest **gay rights** situation in Mexico on the International Gay and Lesbian Human Rights Commission website at ⓦwww.iglhrc.org, and information on the male gay scene in Mexico (gay bars, meeting places and cruising spots) can be found in the annual *Spartacus Gay Guide*, available in bookshops at home. As for contacts within Mexico: lesbians can get in touch with Grupo Lesbico Patlatonalli, Apartado Postal 1-623, CP 44100, Guadalajara, Jalisco (☎&ⓕ33/3632-0507); while for gay men, CIDHOM (Centro de Información y Documentación de las Homosexualidades

en México), Cerrada Cuaunochtli 11, Col. Pueblo Quieto, Tlalpan, México DF 14040 (☎55/5666-5436, ⓔcidhom@laneta.apc.org), can offer information.

## International gay and lesbian travel contacts

**Arco Iris** US ☎1-800/765-4370 or 619/297-0897, ⓦwww.arcoiristours.com. US-based tour operator specializing in trips to Mexico, usually coinciding with major parties.

**Damron** US ☎1-800/462-6654 or 415/255-0404, ⓦwww.damron.com. Publisher of the *Men's Travel Guide*, a pocket-sized handbook listing hotels, bars, clubs and resources for gay men; the *Women's Traveler*, which provides similar listings for lesbians; and *Damron Accommodations*, which provides detailed listings of over 1000 accommodations for gays and lesbians worldwide. All are offered at a discount on the website.

**Gaytravel.com** US ☎1-800/429-8728, ⓦwww.gaytravel.com. Online travel agent, offering accommodation, cruises, tours and more.

**International Gay & Lesbian Travel Association** US ☎1-800/448-8550 or 954/776-2626, ⓦwww.iglta.org. Trade group that provides a list of gay- and lesbian-owned or -friendly travel agents, accommodation and more.

**Madison Travel** UK ☎01273/202 532, ⓦwww.madisontravel.co.uk. Established travel agents specializing in packages to gay- and lesbian-friendly mainstream destinations.

**Parkside Travel** Australia ☎08/8274 1222, ⓔparkside@harveyworld.com.au. Travel agent associated with local branch of Harvey World Travel; covers all aspects of gay and lesbian travel worldwide.

**Tearaway Travel** Australia ☎1800/664 440 or 03/9827 4232, ⓦwww.tearaway.com. International and domestic travel agency serving the gay community.

# Travelling with children

Travelling with younger kids in this part of Mexico is not uncommon – you will find that most Mexicans dote on children, and youngsters can often help to break the ice with strangers. Although many of the ritziest resort properties on the Caribbean have a **no-kids policy**, you shouldn't have a problem staying at mid-range and budget places.

The biggest concern, especially with small children, is their **vulnerability**. Even more than their parents, they need protecting from the sun, unsafe drinking water, heat and unfamiliar food. Chile in particular may be a problem for kids who are not used to it. Remember too that diarrhoea can be dangerous for younger children; rehydration salts (see p.36) are vital if your child goes down with it. Make sure too, if possible, that your child is aware of the dangers of rabies and other animal-borne illnesses; keep children away from all animals and consider a rabies shot.

For touring, hiking or walking, **child-carrier backpacks** are ideal. They can weigh less than 2kg and start at around US$75/£50. If the child is small enough, a **fold-up buggy** is also well worth packing – especially if they will sleep in it while you have a meal or a drink.

One thing to be aware of, if you try to keep your children away from such things, is the level of on-screen violence typical of the movies shown on buses. You may wish to find seats away from the screen when travelling on long-distance bus journeys to avoid the level of gore that is likely to be shown.

For customized and scheduled travel itineraries geared toward adventurous families, contact the US tour agency Rascals in Paradise (☎415/921-7000, ⓦ www.rascalsinparadise.com).

# Senior travellers

Mexico is not a country that offers any special difficulties – or any special advantages – to older travellers, but the same considerations apply here as to anywhere else in the world. If choosing a package tour, consider one run by an organization such as Saga, Vantage or Elderhostel, specifically designed for over-50s.

If travelling independently, don't choose too punishing a schedule. Remember that in many parts of the Yucatán, Tabasco and Chiapas, tropical humidity can tire you out a lot faster than you might otherwise expect, and especially in such conditions it's wise to take it easy. If you plan on doing a lot of sightseeing, consider setting aside a few days

when you have absolutely nothing specific to do. As far as comfort is concerned, first-class **buses** are generally pretty pleasant, with plenty of legroom, though the movies they show (mostly shoot-'em-up Hollywood action films) may not be entirely to your liking. Second-class buses can be rather more boneshaking, and you won't want to take them for too long a journey if you can avoid it. Rail was always a more tranquil way to travel, but apart from the Expreso Maya tour (see p.45), train travel is alas now a thing of the past.

Most of the **hotels** recommended in this book should more than meet your needs, and in general even relatively low-budget hotels are clean and comfortable. Remember that senior citizens are often entitled to discounts, especially when visiting tourist sights, but also on occasion for accommodation and transport, something which it's always worth asking about.

## Contacts for senior travellers

**Elderhostel** US & Canada ☎1-877/426-8056, ⓦwww.elderhostel.org. Runs an extensive worldwide network of educational and activity programmes, cruises and homestays for people over 60 (companions may be younger). Programmes, including one on the Expreso Maya train service, generally last a week or more and costs are in line with those of commercial tours.

**Saga Holidays** UK ☎0800/096 0089 or 0130/3771 111, ⓦwww.holidays.saga.co.uk. The biggest and most established specialist in tours and holidays aimed at older travellers.

**Vantage Deluxe World Travel** ☎1-800/322-6677, ⓦwww.vantagetravel.com. Specializes in worldwide group tours and cruises for seniors.

# Work and study

There's virtually no chance of finding temporary work in Mexico unless you have some very specialized skill and have arranged the position beforehand. Work permits are almost impossible to get hold of. The few foreigners who manage to find work do so mostly in language schools. It may be possible, though not legal, to earn money as a private English tutor by simply advertising in a local newspaper or on noticeboards at a university.

The best way to extend your time in Mexico is on a **study programme** or **volunteer project**. You may also want to begin or end your trip with a stint of Spanish classes; schools in the Yucatán, which cater to everyone from absolute beginners to teachers looking to freshen up their skills, are marginally more expensive than other popular Mexican study destinations, such as Oaxaca, but the classes are a great way to get to know a city or town, as well as learn the language. Most schools cap class sizes at five students, and you might end up getting one-to-one tutoring for the regular class price if you register during a slow period. Schools will arrange homestays for around US$20 per night, including meals. You can work directly with one of the schools listed on the right, or contact AmeriSpan, a US

organization that selects language schools throughout Latin America, including Mexico, to match the needs and requirements of students, and provides advice and support. For further information, call (from the US or Canada) ☎1-800/879-6640 or 215/751-1100, ⓦwww.amerispan.com.

## Study and work programmes

### Language schools

**El Bosque del Caribe** ☎998/884-1065, ⓦwww.cancun-language.com.mx. Set in a very pleasant neighbourhood in downtown Cancún. Prices are comparable to other locations, at US$187 for 25 hours per week, plus US$160 for a homestay, or you can stay in school housing or an apartment.

**Institute of Modern Spanish** US ☎ 1-877/463-7432, Mexico ☎ 999/927-1505, ⓦ www.modernspanish.com. This Mérida school is one of the busiest and most organized in the city, and runs extra day trips and cultural outings at low rates. Classes start every Monday, and cost about US$300 per week with a homestay.

**International House Riviera Maya** ☎ 984/803-3388, ⓦ www.ihrivieramaya.com. In Playa del Carmen. Very organized curriculum, with options for supplementary classes in cooking or diving. Homestays available, as well as student dorms. Classes from US$185 per week, plus US$155 for homestay.

## From the US and Canada

**AFS Intercultural Programs** ☎ 1-800/237-4636, ⓦ www.usa.afs.org. Runs summer experiential programmes aimed at fostering international understanding for teenagers and adults.

**Association for International Practical Training** ☎ 1-800/994-2443 or 410/997-2200, ⓦ www.aipt.org. Summer internships for students who have completed at least two years of college in science, agriculture, engineering or architecture.

**Bernan Associates** ☎ 1-800/274-4888, ⓦ www.bernan.com. Distributes UNESCO's encyclopedic *Study Abroad* book.

**Experiment in International Living** ☎ 1-800/345-2929 or 802/257-7751, ⓦ www.usexperiment.org. Summer programme for high-school students, focusing on community service, language study, ecology, the arts, and outdoor adventure; students stay with a host family to be part of the local community. The Mexico programme runs for five weeks, starting in the capital and travelling into the Yucatán.

**Global Exchange** ☎ 1-800/497-1994 or 415/255-7296, ⓦ www.globalexchange.org. A non-profit organization that leads "reality tours", giving participants the chance to learn about the country while seeing it. Check out their detailed website for information on "travel seminars" looking at issues such as culture, music, health, religion or agriculture.

**Global Vision International** ☎ 1-888/653-6028, ⓦ www.gviusa.com. Runs volunteer diving programmes to gather data about reefs, with base camps in Mahahual and the Sian Ka'an Biosphere Reserve. Also operates a Mayan cultural education programme in Tulum that grants TEFL certification. From US$2500/£1350 for five weeks.

**Servas** ☎ 212/267-0252, ⓦ www.usservas.org. US arm of a global pacifist network that connects travellers with hosts around the world; especially good for adults. Membership in Servas, by application, is

required to participate. In Canada, apply at ⓦ www.canada.servas.org.

**Studyabroad.com** ☎ 610/499-9200, ⓦ www.studyabroad.com. Good search engine for finding language programmes, semester- and year-long courses, internships and overseas law and business exchanges.

**Volunteers for Peace** ☎ 802/259-2759, ⓦ www.vfp.org. Non-profit organization with links to a huge international network of "workcamps", two- to four-week programmes that bring volunteers from many countries to carry out community projects, a few of which are in Chiapas. Most workcamps take place in summer, with registration in April and May.

**World Learning** ☎ 202/408-5420, ⓦ www.worldlearning.org. Its School for International Training (☎ 1-802/257-7751, ⓦ www.sit.edu) runs accredited college semesters in Oaxaca, comprising language and cultural studies, a homestay and excursions to Chiapas.

## From the UK and Ireland

**British Council** ☎ 020/7930 8466, ⓦ www.britishcouncil.org. Produces free leaflets detailing study-abroad opportunities and gap-year programmes. Also recruits TEFL teachers for posts worldwide.

**BTCV** ☎ 0130/2572244, ⓦ www.btcv.org.uk. One of the largest environmental charities in Britain, with branches across the country, also has a programme of international working holidays (as a paying volunteer), with a comprehensive brochure available.

**Global Vision International** ☎ 0870/668 8898, ⓦ www.gvi.co.uk. Runs volunteer diving programmes to gather data about reefs, with base camps in Mahahual and the Sian Ka'an Biosphere Reserve. Also operates a Maya cultural education programme in Tulum that grants TEFL certification. From US$2500/£1350 for five weeks.

**International House** ☎ 020/7518 6999, ⓦ www.ihlondon.com. Head office of a reputable English-teaching organization which offers TEFL training leading to the award of a Certificate in English Language Teaching to Adults (CELTA), and recruits for teaching positions in Britain and abroad.

**Servas** ⓦ www.servasbritain.u-net.com. UK arm of a global pacifist network that connects travellers with hosts around the world; especially good for adults. Membership in Servas, by application, is required to participate.

**VSO (Voluntary Service Overseas)** ☎ 020/8780 7200, ⓦ www.vso.org.uk. Highly respected charity that sends qualified professionals (in the fields of education, health, community and social work, engineering, information technology, law and media)

## Earthwatch

Earthwatch matches volunteers with scientists working on a particular project. Recent expeditions in Mexico have included scientific monitoring of cacti and orchid growth on the Gulf coast of the Yucatán. Fascinating though this work is, it's not a cheap way to see the country: volunteers must raise US$700–4000 (average about US$2000) for each one- to two-week stint as a contribution to the cost of research. For more information, visit Earthwatch's website (ⓦwww.earthwatch.org), or contact one of the following:

**Earthwatch HQ** 3 Clock Tower Place, Suite 100, PO Box 75, Maynard, MA 01754 ⓣ1-800/776-0188 or 978/461-0081.

**Earthwatch Europe** 267 Banbury Rd, Oxford OX2 7HT, UK ⓣ01865/318838, ⓦwww.earthwatch.org/europe.

**Earthwatch Australia** 126 Bank St, South Melbourne, Vic 3205 ⓣ03/9682 6828, ⓦwww.earthwatch.org/australia.

to spend two years or more working for local wages on projects beneficial to developing countries.
**Willing Workers on Organic Farms** ⓣ020/8780 7200, ⓦwww.wwoof.org. Non-profit organization (open to everyone, not just UK residents) that links volunteers with agricultural projects – you can work where or for however long you like, as long as your paperwork allows. For placement in Mexico, you must pay a US$20 membership to that country's branch organization (ⓦwww.wwoofmexico.com).

# Directory

**Addresses** In Mexico addresses are frequently written with just the street name and number (thus: Madero 125). Calle (C) means Street; Avenida (Av), Bulevar (Blv), Calzada and Paseo are other common terms – most are named after historical figures or dates. An address such as Hidalgo 39 8° 120, means Hidalgo no. 39, 8th floor, room 120 (a ground-floor address would be denoted PB for Planta Baja). Most colonial towns have all their streets laid out in a numbered grid, with odd-numbered streets running east–west, and even ones north–south. The main plaza at the centre of town is usually at a point where all the numbers converge: calles 59, 60, 61 and 62 in Mérida, for example. In such places a suffix – Ote (for Oriente, East), Pte (for Poniente, West), Nte (for Norte, North), or Sur (South) – may be added to the street number to tell you which side of the two central dividing streets it is.

**Airport tax** A departure tax (the equivalent of US$40) is exacted when flying from Mexico. This is included in the price of most air tickets, but be sure to check when buying.

**Alphabetical order** Remember when looking things up in directories that "CH", "LL" and "Ñ" are considered separate letters in Spanish, so CH comes after C, LL after L and Ñ after N.

**Duty-free allowances** Visitors to Mexico are allowed three bottles of liquor (including wine), four hundred cigarettes or fifty cigars or 250g of tobacco, and twelve rolls of camera film or video camera tape. The monetary limit for duty-free goods is US$300. Returning home, note that it is illegal to take antiquities out of the country, and penalties are serious.

**Electricity** Theoretically, 110 volts AC, with simple two-flat-pin rectangular plugs, so most North American appliances can be used as they are. Travellers from the UK, Ireland, Australasia and Europe should bring along a converter and a plug adapter. Cuts in service and fluctuations in the current do occur, and in cheap hotels any sort of appliance that draws a lot of current may blow all the fuses as soon as it's turned on.

**Emergency** General emergency number ☎080; Police ☎060; Fire ☎068; Ambulance ☎065; Green Angels (emergency highway breakdown) ☎55/5250-8221; toll-free tourist advice ☎01-800/903-9200.

**Film and camera equipment** Film is manufactured in Mexico and, if you buy it from a chain store like Woolworth's or Sanborn's rather than at a tourist store, costs no more than at home (if you buy it elsewhere, be sure to check the date on the box, and be suspicious if you can't see it). Up to twelve rolls of film can be brought into Mexico, and spare batteries are also a wise precaution. Any sort of camera hardware, though, will be prohibitively expensive. Slide film is hard to come by too.

**Laundry** *Lavanderías* are ubiquitous in Mexico as the majority of households don't own a washing machine. Most charge by the kilo, and for a few dollars you'll get your clothes back clean, pressed and perfectly folded in less than 24 hours. Many hotels also offer laundry services that, although convenient, tend to charge by the item, adding up to a considerably greater cost.

**Time zones** Mexico has four time zones, but most of the country, including the area from the Yucatán to Chiapas, is on GMT−6 in winter, GMT−5 in summer (first Sunday in April till last Sunday in October), the same as US Central Time.

**Toilets** Public toilets in Mexico can be quite filthy, and sometimes there's no paper, although there will often be someone selling it outside for a couple of pesos (better just to always carry some with you). Toilets are usually known as *baños* (literally bathrooms) or as *excusados* or *sanitarios*. The most common signs are Damas (Ladies) and Caballeros (Gentlemen), though you may find Señoras (Women) and Señores (Men) or, more confusing, the symbols of Moon (Women) and Sun (Men).

# Guide

# Guide

# ① Cancún, Isla Mujeres and Isla Holbox

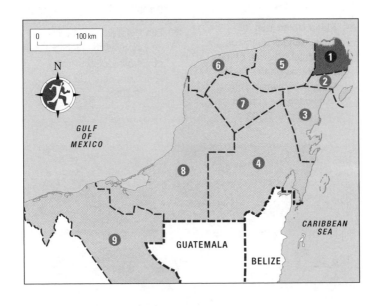

CHAPTER 1 # Highlights

**✱ Parque de las Palapas**
Downtown Cancún's
social centre comes to
life after dark with dancing, craft fairs and ven-
dors selling tasty snacks.
**P.88**

**✱ Playa Delfines** An amazingly beautiful stretch of
sand in Cancún's zona
hotelera. **P.92**

**✱ Playa Norte** This perfectly tranquil beach on
Isla Mujeres is one of the
few places on the Carib-
bean coast where you
can watch the sun set
over the sea. **P.102**

**✱ Isla Contoy** A large
island wildlife sanctuary
that makes the perfect
place for birdwatching or
just playing at castaway.
**P.107**

**✱ Whale sharks** Swim with
these giant, peaceful fish,
some up to 15m long, off
the coast of Isla Holbox.
**P.109**

**✱ Isla Pájaros** This flamingo colony is the highlight
of a small but rich bird
sanctuary near Isla Hol-
box. **P.109**

△ Isla Contoy

# Cancún, Isla Mujeres and Isla Holbox

E asily the largest tourist draw in the Yucatán, the resort city of **Cancún** dominates the northern half of Quintana Roo State and, with its large international airport, is the place where most visitors' tours of the peninsula begin or end. Travellers on package tours and cruiseships pack this place by the thousands, in search of sun and margarita-fuelled fun in an environment that's as welcoming of the American dollar as it is of the Mexican peso.

All concrete and glass hotel towers and shopping plazas, this modern city can seem less than charming at first sight; in reality, however, it's really a dynamic, prosperous place that's lined with 20km of astoundingly beautiful **white-sand beaches** and water so clear you can see your plane's shadow on the seafloor as you arrive. Also, contrary to expectation, Cancún can be a culturally rewarding (and not painfully expensive) place to visit if you know where to look.

**Isla Mujeres**, a tiny island just across the bay from Cancún, affords a slightly more rustic experience, with small, candy-coloured wooden houses lining the narrow streets of the main town. Mujeres is definitely on the tourist route, but there's not a strip mall in sight, and the only entertainment is watching the water lap at the gorgeous beach around the island's northern edge.

Heading inland, you'll see that Cancún and Isla Mujeres are anomalies – the rest of Quintana Roo's northern half is rural and barely touched by tourism. **Isla Holbox**, a dot of land off the northern Gulf coast, is a typical out-of-the-way spot. It has seen increasing boatloads of visitors in the last few years, but remains a friendly, modest beach getaway where birds outnumber humans. While it's just a half-hour ferry hop between Cancún and Isla Mujeres, Isla Holbox is a three-hour bus trip from the airport, followed by a boat ride – precisely what keeps the place quiet.

## Cancún

If nothing else, **CANCÚN** is proof of Mexico's remarkable ability to get things done in a hurry – so long as the political will exists. In the late 1960s, the Mexican government wanted to develop a new resort area to diversify the economy.

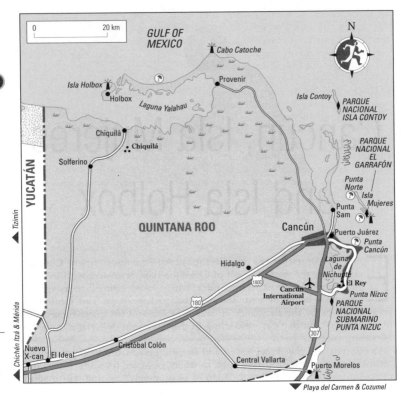

Playa del Carmen & Cozumel

Computers crunched weather data, and surveyors scouted the country's natural attractions to identify a 25-kilometre-long barrier island just off the northern Caribbean coast as the ideal combination of beautiful beaches and sparse population. The largest settlement in the area was the village of Puerto Juárez, with about one hundred residents, and the island that was to become the hotel zone had exactly one small wooden house built on it. Construction on the envisioned resort paradise began in 1970, with the initial task being simply to clear enough jungle on the mainland to build a road and bridge to the barrier island. (Jules Siegel, an American who worked for the Mexican tourism ministry during this period, recounts the early challenges, from impossible deadlines to jaguar attacks, in excellent detail in his *Cancun User's Guide*; see Contexts, p.348.) When the first hotel opened in 1974, it relied on a generator for electricity and trucked-in water.

Today the city has a resident population of half a million and hosts some two million visitors a year, the majority from the US and Canada. The place has never been understated or intimate; it's a high-energy resort destination, relentlessly dedicated to entertainment, with jet skis, top-volume mariachis and wet-T-shirt contests at rowdy megaclubs. Restaurants are elaborate theatre (think toga-clad waiters at trattorias), hotels are fantastical pleasure palaces in a constant state of reinvention, and the crowds range from college kids to families to senior citizens.

Consequently, Cancún has a poor reputation among independent travellers. Prices along the beaches can be steep, and, for anyone who has been out in the rest of the Yucatán or is eager to get there, the abundance of concrete and apparent lack of local culture will be very off-putting. However, a night spent here on the way in or out doesn't have to be wasted time if you appreciate the city as an energetic, wildly successful frontier experiment, rather than lament the lack of historical sights. A closer look reveals lively salsa clubs, barebones beach bars and inexpensive taco stands, all frequented by *cancunenses* who are friendly and proud of the prosperity that the hotels represent.

The city has two quite separate parts: the **zona comercial** or downtown, the shopping and residential centre that, as it gets older, is becoming genuinely earthy; and the **zona hotelera**, the strip of hotels, malls, restaurants and other tourist facilities along a narrow island shaped like a "7" and connected to the mainland at each end by causeways. It encloses a huge lagoon, so there's water on both sides.

In the hotel zone, **Paseo Kukulcán** runs the length of the barrier island, from the airport up to **Punta Cancún** (where the road splits around the convention centre and a warren of nightclubs) and back onto the mainland.

From Punta Cancún it's a half-hour bus ride to **Avenida Tulum**, the main avenue in the downtown area that runs north–south and eventually turns into Hwy-307, the road that follows the length of the Caribbean coast. The central blocks are lined with shops, banks, restaurants and travel agencies, as well as the city's most inexpensive hotels – up side streets, but in view. On either side of Avenida Tulum, divided by intersecting avenues, are the giant city blocks known as *super-manzanas*. The oldest ones, part of the city plan laid out in the 1970s (and soon abandoned as growth outpaced the developers' time and budget), are distinguished by winding and looping streets leading to a central park or market. Each *super-manzana* (abbreviated as SM) is known by a number; SM 22 contains Parque de las Palapas, the main park, along with many of the downtown area's restaurants and bars.

## Arrival and information

Charter flights from Europe and South America, along with direct scheduled flights from dozens of cities in Mexico and North and Central America, land at **Cancún International Airport** (Ⓦ www.cancun-airport.com), 20km south of the centre. Past customs in both the main (B gates) and north (A gates) terminals, you'll find **ATMs** and **currency exchange** desks; the main terminal also has luggage **lockers**.

The best way to the beaches, if your hotel does not provide a pick-up service, is one of the **colectivos** (shared passenger vans) that take you to any part of the hotel zone for a fixed price (M$75 or US$9); they depart when they're full, but it's seldom a long wait. For downtown, take the half-hourly Riviera **bus** (M$15; 5.30am–midnight). Buy tickets for both services from the desks located before and after customs. **Taxis** are available but cost considerably more, starting at M$160 for downtown and M$180 for the part of the hotel zone closest to the airport.

Arriving by bus, whether first or second class, you'll pull in at Cancún's well-organized main **bus station**, conveniently located on a roundabout at the central junction of avenidas Tulum and Uxmal. **Luggage storage** (daily 6am–9.45pm) is upstairs; rates start at M$6 per hour. You can walk to most downtown hotels, and a city bus stops nearby on Avenida Tulum, running either to the hotel zone (southbound side of the avenue) or to the Isla Mujeres ferry (northbound side).

## Addresses in the zona hotelera

Generally addresses here are given as the nearest kilometre marker on Paseo Kuku-lcán; the count starts on the north end, near the bridge over from downtown. It's not an exact science: two sets of markers exist, and are out of sync by about half a kilometre, so addresses are guidelines at best.

The **city tourist office** is half a block south of the bus station, inside the city hall at Avenida Tulum 26 (daily 9am–8pm; ☏ 998/884-8073), and the friendly bilingual staff will help with even the smallest enquiries. They also dish out free maps and leaflets and copies of the numerous promotional listings **magazines**, all of which you can also pick up at just about every travel agency and hotel reception. There are other **tourist information kiosks** on Avenida Tulum and in the zona hotelera; some are genuine, but if you're asked if you want "tourist information" as you pass, it's almost certain you're being selected for a time-share sales pitch. Worth seeking out for local events listings, particularly for the downtown area, is the free flyer *Entérate Cancún*, available at the bookshop La Rana Sabia (Av Uxmal at C Margaritas) or online at ⓦ www.enteratecancun. com. The English-language daily newspaper *Miami Herald Cancún Edition* isn't particularly hard-hitting, but it provides some insight into local politics, along with international news.

## City transport

All the attractions in downtown Cancún are within walking distance, but you need some sort of transport to get to and around the zona hotelera. **Buses** marked "Tulum–Hoteles, Ruta 1" run along Avenida Tulum every few minutes; the fare is M$4.50 for stops within downtown or M$6.50 to or within the hotel zone, and the ride from downtown to Punta Cancún takes about half an hour. (Several other bus routes go to the hotel zone as well – all say "Hoteles" on the front window.) Alternatively, shared VW buses (**combis**) run fixed routes throughout downtown – the handiest is north on Avenida Tulum to the Isla Mujeres ferry dock at Punta Cancún, but otherwise, visitors will have little need for these services, given the frequency of city buses.

**Taxis** are plentiful and can be hailed almost anywhere. Fares are based on a zone system, rather than a meter, and you should agree on the fare before get-ting in. Big hotels in the zona hotelera will have sample rates posted, which reflect a small surcharge; rates are slightly cheaper if you flag a cab in the street. Anywhere in downtown is about M$60, and the trip between downtown and Punta Cancún costs around M$90. **Bicycle** rental isn't really available or advis-able, as distances are too large, and traffic isn't bike-friendly.

## Accommodation

Cancún has plenty of lodging options, much of it very expensive for the casual visitor. **Downtown** holds the only hope of a real budget room, and you're only a short bus ride from the public beaches. Many beachfront palaces of the **zona hotelera** offer exclusive luxury, with extravagant interiors, glitzy restaurants and numerous pools. Prices here range from M$1000 to well above M$5000 per night in the high winter season, with the least costly options being the lagoon-facing properties, which have no beach. All-inclusive deals used to be the norm, but hotels are increasingly catering to all travellers, with everything from room-only pricing to rooms with kitchenettes (see "All-inclusive resorts" in Basics, p.49).

For those on a tight budget, several places downtown offer dorm accommodation; in addition to those hostels recommended below, there is the concrete-block *Villas Juveniles* on Paseo Kukulcán at Km 3.2 in the zona hotelera (T998/883-1337; ❸), but it's exceptionally dirty and run-down – though it's still the only place in the city where you can **camp** (M$40).

## Downtown Cancún

**Alux** Av Uxmal 21 T998/884-6613, Wwww.hotelalux.com.mx. Popular, good-value hotel, if a little dated with its mirror-clad decor; all rooms have a/c, TV and telephone. Travel agency next door and street café on site. ❺

**Cancún Inn El Patio** Av Bonampak 51 T998/884-3500, Wwww.cancuninn.com. A hands-off staff and a location in a residential neighbourhood make this small hotel feel more like a private apartment complex. The thirteen simple rooms ring a quiet garden courtyard. Easy walk to downtown. ❻

**Cancún Rosa** C Margaritas 2 T998/884-0623. Old-fashioned hotel with velvet sofas and plastic flowers in the lobby, a pool and an overgrown garden out the back. Rooms can be a little dark, but there's a huge one with four beds that's good for groups or families. All have a/c. ❻

**Chac Mool** C Gladiolas 18 T998/887-5873, Echacmoolhostel@hotmail.com. Opened in 2004, this tidy hostel has small four-bed dorms as well as a few private rooms, and the option of a/c. The cool rooftop lounge, with a grand view over El Parque de las Palapas, serves M$10 drinks. Free Internet access too. M$100

**Colonial** C Tulipanes 22 T998/884-1535. A decent bargain, in a prime location not far from the bus station and in the middle of downtown's liveliest block. The fifty well-lit rooms are simple and modern, with TV and a choice of a/c or fan, but the place has character, thanks to a small central courtyard. ❺

**Kin Mayab** Av Tulum 75, at Av Uxmal T998/884-2999, Wwww.hotelkinmayab.com. This centrally located hotel is clean and secure, with the most comfortable rooms and best pool in its price range (book ahead). Request the back section, by the pool and away from the street noise. ❼

**Mexico Hostel** C Palmera 30 at Av Uxmal T998/887-0191. The oldest and most popular Cancún hostel with young backpackers, maintaining several dorms and a rooftop terrace where you can hang a hammock. Internet access, bike rental and laundry available. M$90

**Las Palmas** C Palmeras 43 T998/884-2513, Ehotelpalmascancun@hotmail.com. This quiet family operation caters as much to Mexican workers as to backpackers, so there's less of the typical hostel party atmosphere. The real draw are the cheapest a/c beds, in big, clean, single-sex dorms, and a few huge private rooms. Continental breakfast included.

**Punta Allen** C Punta Allen 8 T998/884-0225, Wwww.puntaallen.da.ru. Small but spotless rooms (all with a/c) in an older guesthouse decked out with kitsch. Avenida Yaxchilán is nearby, but the block itself is silent. Continental breakfast is included. ❺

**El Rey del Caribe** Av Uxmal 24, at Av Nader T998/884-2028, Wwww.reycaribe.com. Sunny yellow rooms with kitchenettes, plus a pool and spa services at this casual hacienda-style hotel – the only one in Cancún with an active ecological sensibility, with composting and solar water heaters. Good discounts in the low season. ❼

## Zona hotelera: on the lagoon side

**Grand Royal Lagoon** C Quetzal 8-A T998/883-1270, Wwww.grlagoon.com. You'll find the cheapest rooms in the zona hotelera at this spot, convenient to the main boulevard. Thirty-six small but spotless rooms, done up in cheerful colours, are set around an equally small pool. A few studio rooms have kitchenettes.

**Imperial Laguna** C Quetzal 11 T998/883-4270, Wwww.hotelimperialcancun.com. The best value of the lagoon-side hotels, offering big rooms with kitchens and balconies. There's also a pretty pool, a small garden and a restaurant with a great view of the lagoon. ❽

**Villas Manglar** Paseo Kukulcán Km 20 T998/885-1808, Wwww.villasmanglar.com. A blink-and-you'll-miss-it villa hidden in the wilds of the lagoon-side mangroves. You can lounge by the small pool, but the main draw is the sport-fishing tours run by the experienced owners. Upstairs rooms get better light. Continental breakfast included. ❾

## Zona hotelera: on the beach side

**Ambiance Villas at Kin-Ha** Paseo Kukulcán Km 8.5 T998/883-1100, Wwww.ambiancevillas.com. Big, tastefully furnished double-bed rooms, studios with kitchenettes and full suites with one, two or three bedrooms – all redone in 2003. Every room

# DOWNTOWN CANCÚN

## EATING & DRINKING

| | |
|---|---|
| 100% Natural | 8 |
| Los Almendros | 1 |
| El Café | 17 |
| El Camarote | 5 |
| La Casa 940 | 6 |
| El Chat | 14 |
| Checándole | 12 |
| El D'Pa | 16 |
| Dub | 13 |
| La Habichuela | 7 |
| Los Huaraches de Alcatraces | 18 |
| Karamba | 9 |
| El Pabilo | 10 |
| Pericos | 15 |
| El Rincón Yucateco | 3 |
| Roots | 11 |
| Salus y Chemo's | 2 |
| Ty-Coz | 4 |

## ACCOMMODATION

| | |
|---|---|
| Alux | D |
| Cancún Inn El Patio | B |
| Cancún Rosa | G |
| Chac Mool | J |
| Colonial | I |
| Kin Mayab | H |
| Mexico Hostel | C |
| Las Palmas | A |
| Punta Allen | E |
| El Rey del Caribe | F |

PLAZA BONITA

Mercado 28

La Rana Sabia

Estadio Beto Avila

N

0        200 m

Casa de la Cultura ▼

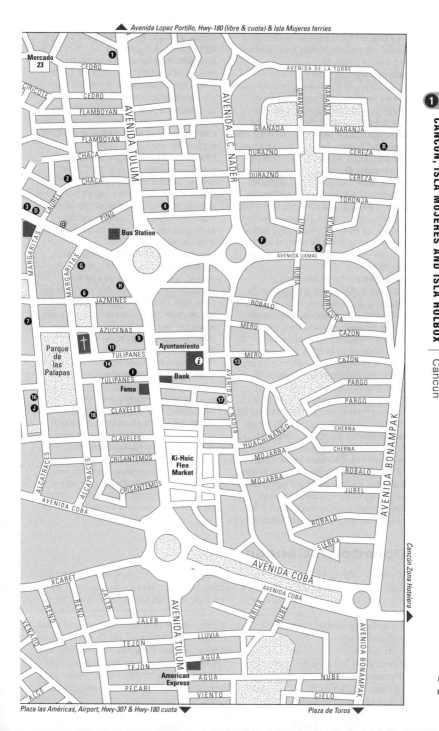

Avenida Lopez Portillo, Hwy-180 (libre & cuota) & Isla Mujeres ferries

Mercado 23

CEDRO
CEDRO
FLAMBOYAN
FLAMBOYAN
CHACA
CHACA
CIRICOTE
LAUREL
PINO
@

AVENIDA TULUM

AVENIDA J.C. NADER

AVENIDA DE LA TORRE
GRANADA
NARANJA
GRANADA
NARANJA
DURAZNO
CEREZA
DURAZNO
CEREZA
TORONJA
LIMA
TORONJA
AVENIDA UXMAL
RUBIA
ROBALO
MERO
MERO
BARRACUDA
CAZON
CAZON
PARGO
PARGO
CHERNA
CHERNA
ROBALO
MOJARRA
MOJARRA
JUREL
ROBALO
SIERRA

Bus Station

MARGARITAS
MARGARITAS
JAZMINES
AZUCENAS
TULIPANES
TULIPANES
CLAVELES
CLAVELES
CRISANTEMOS
CRISANTEMOS
ALCATRACES
ALCATRACES

Parque de las Palapas

Ayuntamiento
Bank

Fama

Ki-Huic Flea Market

AVENIDA J.C. NADER
HUACHINANGO

AVENIDA BONAMPAK

AVENIDA COBA

AVENIDA COBA
AVENIDA COBA

XCARET
HENO
HENO
JALEB
JALEB
TEJON
TEJON
PECARI

AVENIDA TULUM

VENADO
ALCE

LLUVIA
AGUA
AGUA
VIENTO

BRISA
NUBE

NUBE
CIELO

AVENIDA BONAMPAK

American Express

Plaza las Américas, Airport, Hwy-307 & Hwy-180 cuota

Plaza de Toros

Cancún Zona Hotelera

has a terrace or balcony, and the beach is one of the best of those facing the bay. A very good deal for families or groups. ❾

**Aquamarina Beach Hotel** Paseo Kukulcán Km 3.5 ☎ 998/849-4606, ✆ www.aquamarina-beach.com.mx. Relatively small, good-value resort with all the trappings of a larger all-inclusive, such as a pool, volleyball, miniature golf and thrice-weekly theme parties. The beach is a little skimpy, but all rooms have balconies, and some have kitchenettes. All-inclusive and room-only rates available. ❾

**Aristos** Paseo Kukulcán Km 20.5 ☎ 998/885-3333, ✆ www.aristoshotels.com. Far from the action, at the south end of the strip, Aristos has a rather austere feel, with expanses of treeless concrete, but the large rooms do have marble floors and bathtubs, and the beach is nice. European bargain-seekers dominate the guest register. ❽

**Avalon Baccará** Paseo Kukulcán Km 11.5 ☎ 800/713-8170 in Mexico, or in the US on 1-800/261-5014, ✆ www.avalonvacations.com. Small hotel with 27 rooms individually decorated with mosaics and other personal touches; free pre-dinner snacks and tequila add to the personable feel. This hotel was the setting for MTV's *The Real Cancún*, but the usual clientele is older and more business-oriented than their onscreen counterparts. ❾

**Suites Girasol** Paseo Kukulcán Km 9.5 ☎ 998/883-5045. The entry and public areas of this condo high-rise don't look promising, but the rooms are surprisingly large and clean, and all have kitchenettes. The pool is nothing special, but the beach out front is gorgeous. ❽

**Le Meridien** Paseo Kukulcán Km 14 ☎ 998/881-2200, ✆ www.meridiencancun.com.mx. Relatively understated luxury hotel with 213 tasteful country French-style rooms, three pools of different temperatures and rooftop tennis courts. Its Spa del Mar is the best in Cancún, with hydrotherapy

treatments, body wraps and massages from M$750 (open to non-guests). ❾

**El Pueblito** Paseo Kukulcán Km 18 ☎ 998/881-8800, ✆ www.pueblitohotels.com. A rare spot in Cancún that feels more Mexican than American, with big, colourful rooms, an elaborate array of pools and a nice patch of beach. Service is very pleasant too. Note that the low, all-inclusive prices make it appealing to spring-breakers in late March and April. ❾

**Ritz-Carlton Cancún** Retorno del Rey 36, near Paseo Kukulcán Km 14 ☎ 998/881-0808, ✆ www.ritzcarlton.com. The last word in luxury in Cancún, though with utterly no regard for its Mexican location. The trappings are all faux-chateau: chandeliers, tapestries and deep carpeting; service and food are of course up to international standards. ❾

**Sheraton Cancún Resort & Towers** Paseo Kukulcán Km 12 ☎ 998/891-4400, ✆ www.sheraton.com/cancun. Aside from suites with palatial terraces, the rooms at this older resort are nondescript – though well maintained and often very affordable. The beautiful beach here is almost a kilometre long. Guests may also use the more glamorous facilities at the Westin. ❾

**Villas Tacul** Paseo Kukulcán Km 5.5 ☎ 998/883-0000, ✆ www.villastacul.com.mx. An older, smaller resort, refreshingly glitz-free: individual villas, each containing two or three private rooms, are scattered over twelve beautifully landscaped acres, with gardens, tennis courts and a pool. ❾

**Westin Resort & Spa Cancún** Paseo Kukulcán Km 20 ☎ 998/848-7400, ✆ www.westin.com. Striking, minimalist accommodation (Mexican architect Ricardo Legorreta's later style) with pillow-top beds, deluxe showers and impressive views. An additional west-facing beach and pool on the lagoon get afternoon sun. Somewhat isolated, but a free shuttle runs up to the Sheraton. ❾

## Downtown Cancún

With the oldest buildings dating back only thirty years or so, there's no real sightseeing to do in **downtown Cancún**. Whether you're staying here or in the hotel zone, the real attraction is simply strolling around and soaking up the street life, which is best after the sun goes down. The official centre of town is the **ayuntamiento** (town hall), set back from Avenida Tulum with a large plaza in front. Across the avenue is *super-manzana* 22, a block of small streets lined with restaurants and bars, leading to **Parque de las Palapas**, the cultural and recreational hub where crowds gather on weekend evenings, when there's usually some sort of live music or dance performance on the bandstand. Also look for four smaller parks to the north and south, which often host arts and crafts shows and smaller bands.

Heading west from the park, you reach **Avenida Yaxchilán**, the main nightlife strip. A few touts push menus at tourists, but the clientele at the restaurant-bars is mostly Mexican. Entertainment is limited to karaoke inside and serenades by roving *trovadores* on the open terraces (you can hire these musicians for a private performance – they hang out on the corner of Calle Tanchacte).

The evening's other main gathering place is the intersection of Avenida Lopez Portillo and Avenida Tulum, known as **El Crucero**. There's no formal entertainment here; the southwest corner of this busy crossroads is just a place for families and teenagers to hang out, munching *elote* (boiled corn on the cob slathered in mayo, crumbly cheese, lime and chile) or pizza. Head a little bit west on Avenida Portillo and you'll reach a cluster of **market stalls** that cater solely to locals. Although not much of the merchandise may tempt you (meat smokers, underwear and fly-swatters are on offer), it's nice to stroll through a busy shopping area without getting the "Hey, *amigo!*" sales push.

Two daytime markets also give a sense of the city's hum away from the tourist trade. **Mercado 23**, north of the bus station off Avenida Tulum at Calle Cedro, is a small maze of stalls with the flavour of a village market, complete with butchers, vegetable sellers with stacks of local greens and herbalists offering a cure for whatever ails you. Don't miss the store packed with piñatas, party favours and Mexican candies. The bigger **Mercado 28**, west from the park on Avenida Sunyaxchén, was formerly the city's main general market, but now stocks primarily tourist tat. A few traditional vendors hang on, peddling fresh *masa* and wildly coloured sweets. It's best to visit on a Saturday or Sunday afternoon, when families come for big lunches at the food stalls, which cater to Cancún's population of workers from everywhere else in Mexico, dishing up regional specialities.

△ Cancún's coastline

The only true historical attraction in the area, **El Meco** (8am–3pm; M$30) is a small archeological site, recommended only for Maya obsessives or anyone who won't get to any inland ruins; head east on Avenida Lopez Portillo, then 3km north on the coast road. Opened to the public in 1998, the ruins cover less ground than El Rey in the hotel zone (see opposite), but the buildings, including a tall pyramid, are more substantial. Although it was first inhabited in the Early Classic period, it conforms to the Late Post-Classic style of other coastal cities like San Gervasio on Cozumel and Tulum. Not only was the city part of the trade network that flourished on the coast after 1100, but it seems to have been an important religious centre as well. Many of the pieces of jewellery and ceramics found on the site, as well as a full human skeleton with its skull drilled with numerous holes, are now in the Museo INAH in the hotel zone (see below).

## Zona hotelera

Most visitors to Cancún head straight for vacationland: the **zona hotelera** and its clubs, resorts and, of course, **beaches** (see box on p.92). The centre of the action is **Punta Cancún**, the cluster of malls, restaurants and bars around the convention centre at the bend in the "7" formed by the barrier island. East of the main road, on the grounds of the **Dreams Cancun** resort, is Punta Cancún proper, the easternmost point in Mexico, marked by a whimsical circle of purple blocks – the work of Mexican architect Ricardo Legorreta, who designed the hotel. Opened in 1975 as *El Camino Real*, *Dreams Cancun* is still one of the city's most distinctive retreats and worth a jaunt inside, even if you're not a guest, to admire the hallways filled with greenery, and doors and windows framed with vibrant, typically Mexican colours. As an architectural counterpoint, consider the vast **atrium lobby** of the **Gran Meliá Cancún** resort (Paseo Kukulcán Km 16.5), a neo-Mayan pyramid built during the mid-Eighties boom that wins the city's unofficial prize for over-the-top opulence (a distant second: the *Riu Palace*'s super-size, colonial-meets-Classical fantasia at Km 6). From the giant Maya friezes outside to the interior overflowing with cascading plants, koi ponds and waterfalls (as well as dazzled sightseers), it's the pinnacle of Cancún's particular brand of excess.

### The museums

To catch a bit of culture while you're out here, visit **La Casa del Arte Mexicano** in the Embarcadero complex (☎998/849-4332; daily 9am–9pm; M$50), a lively folk-art museum crammed with musical instruments, children's toys and colourful traditional costumes. Although the collection, grouped by craft and filling two large rooms, isn't particularly academic or rigorously presented, it does contain some beautiful pieces, such as intricate tree-of-life sculptures and painted gourds. If you admire an item, chances are you'll find something similar in the **gift shop**, which is stocked with excellent-quality pieces (priced accordingly).

The **Museo INAH** (☎998/883-0305; Mon–Sat 9am–8pm, Sun 10am–7pm; M$30), behind the convention centre, is the national archeology institute's small but absorbing collection of Mayan finds, many from sites along the Caribbean coast. Information, where it's provided at all, is in Spanish, but some of the most fascinating items speak for themselves: delicately wrought clay masks, elaborate zoomorphic incense burners, glowing jade jewellery and skulls sporting filed-down teeth. An English-speaking docent is usually on hand to answer questions.

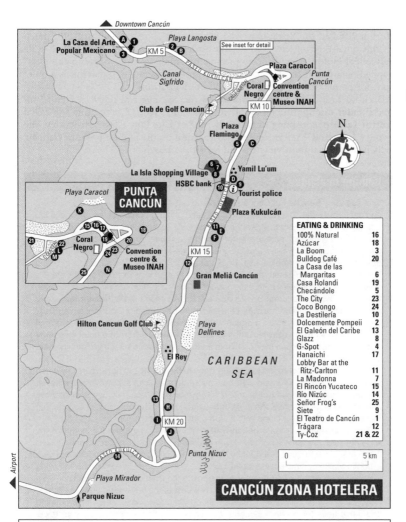

La Casa del Arte
Popular Mexicano
KM 5

Playa Langosta

See inset for detail

Plaza Caracol

Punta
Cancún

Canal
Sigfrido

Coral
Negro

Convention
centre &
Museo INAH

Club de Golf Cancún

KM 10

Plaza
Flamingo

N

La Isla Shopping Village

Yamil Lu'um

HSBC bank

Tourist police

Plaza Kukulcán

PUNTA
CANCÚN

Playa Caracol

Coral
Negro

Convention
centre &
Museo INAH

KM 15

Gran Meliá Cancún

Hilton Cancun Golf Club

Playa
Delfines

El Rey

CARIBBEAN
SEA

KM 20

Punta Nizuc

**EATING & DRINKING**

| | |
|---|---|
| 100% Natural | 16 |
| Azúcar | 18 |
| La Boom | 3 |
| Bulldog Café | 20 |
| La Casa de las Margaritas | 6 |
| Casa Rolandi | 19 |
| Checándole | 5 |
| The City | 23 |
| Coco Bongo | 24 |
| La Destilería | 10 |
| Dolcemente Pompeii | 2 |
| El Galeón del Caribe | 13 |
| Glazz | 8 |
| G-Spot | 4 |
| Hanaichi | 17 |
| Lobby Bar at the Ritz-Carlton | 11 |
| La Madonna | 7 |
| El Rincón Yucateco | 15 |
| Río Nizúc | 14 |
| Señor Frog's | 25 |
| Siete | 9 |
| El Teatro de Cancún | 1 |
| Trágara | 12 |
| Ty-Coz | 21 & 22 |

0 _____ 5 km

**CANCÚN ZONA HOTELERA**

Airport

Playa Mirador

Parque Nizuc

**ACCOMMODATION**

| | | | | | | | |
|---|---|---|---|---|---|---|---|
| Ambiance Villas at Kin-Ha | K | Avalon Baccará | C | Ritz-Carlton Cancún | E | Villas Manglar | I |
| Aquamarina Beach Hotel | A | Grand Royal Lagoon | L | Sheraton Cancún Resort & Towers | D | Villas Tacul | B |
| | | Imperial Laguna | M | | | Westin Resort & Spa Cancún | J |
| Aristos | H | Le Meridien | F | Suites Girasol | N | | |
| | | El Pueblito | G | | | | |

## The ruins

As if to round out the theme park that is Cancún, there are even a few token Maya **ruins**. The largest (which is not saying a lot) are **El Rey** (daily 8am–5pm; M$30), at Km 18, alongside Laguna Nichupté. You will likely find yourself alone, save for the enormous iguana population, when you visit. The Late Post-Classic buildings – contemporary with San Gervasio on Cozumel and Tulum – are strung out on a north–south axis. Objects found during excavation suggest this was a stop on the highly developed sea-trade route around the peninsula, disrupted when the Spanish arrived in the early sixteenth century. Not much of this once-thriving city remains; the ruined structures are mostly small-scale residential buildings, with no impressive pyramids to speak of. With the glass-topped pyramid of the *Hilton* looming in the background, today this is a quiet spot for contemplating the rise and fall of civilizations.

Back north a bit, sandwiched between the *Sheraton* and the *Park Royal Piramides* (enter through the lobby of either hotel) at Km 12, is the tiny site called **Yamil Lu'um**, consisting of two very modest Late Post-Classic structures. The name ("hilly land") refers to the ruins' location on the highest point in Cancún, which provides a good view up and down the beach.

## Cancún beaches

The legendary **beaches** of Cancún are spread out along the barrier island's northern and eastern shores. The north side of the island (the top portion of the "7") faces the tranquil Bahía de Mujeres, where the shallow, pale-green water makes an ideal spot for relaxed swimming, particularly for younger children. Sea grass grows in some places, and though not the ideal scenery, it's no impediment to swimming and is often home to bright tropical fish. Rocks and cliffs break up the sand at Km 6 and Km 8.5 of Paseo Kukulcán, and continue around the point to Km 9.5. The island's scenic east side, where white sand stretches for more than 10km, faces the open Caribbean. While the turquoise waters here appear much more inviting, the waves are sometimes high and currents unpredictable; pay attention to the warning flags and don't swim beyond your comfort zone. In either case, plan to hit the beach in the morning, as many east-facing beaches are in shadow from the hotel towers by late afternoon; the *Westin* (see p.88) has a small west-facing beach for sunning later in the day.

All of Cancún's beaches are technically open to the public, but hotels carefully guard their furniture against interlopers. At beachfront bars and clubs, however, such as *Fat Tuesday* (Paseo Kukulcán Km 6) and *The City* (see p.97), you may use lounge chairs and umbrellas for the price of a drink or an entrance fee. Bear in mind, of course, that these spots on the sand come with a loud party atmosphere.

The ten designated **public beach areas**, at intervals along the full length of the zona hotelera, are quieter but have been encroached on by high-rise neighbours, so that many of the turquoise-and-white Fonatur signs now point to not much more than a public walkway and access point between condo developments. The following worthwhile spots are listed in order of their distance from downtown Cancún:

**Playa Langosta** Paseo Kukulcán Km 5. The best of the bay-facing public beaches, Playa Langosta is a sizeable stretch of sand, with calm, clean water for swimming and a few trees for shade – though it can be hard to find a place to lay your towel at weekends. For refreshments, the adjacent shopping complex is well stocked with bars and convenience stores.

**Playa Delfines** Paseo Kukulcán Km 17.5. The first public beach that you see on the way from the airport is also the largest. Occupying a sizeable break between hotel developments, Playa Delfines is a wide, sloping stretch of powder-fine sand fronted by incredible turquoise waters and offering an impressive view up the coast. Like the other beaches that face the open sea, the waves can be particularly high here, so sunbathing is the main activity, though it's sometimes possible to surf. Occasional strolling fruit vendors provide the only services.

**Playa Mirador** Paseo Kukulcán Km 22.5. For the true isolationist, this long, narrow beach on the mainland, dotted with a few palm trees, is usually deserted. Sea grass grows in patches in the shallow water, but the sand is kept very tidy and clean. Bring everything you need for the day, as there are no shops nearby, nor any services at the beach itself.

## Watersports

Although Cancún isn't known for its stunning undersea life, the reef off **Punta Nizuc** is a passable **snorkelling** spot. Its coral has been damaged by unchecked crowds, but the array of fish is impressive. This area is now a national marine park; if you visit by boat, as most people do, a M$20 entrance fee is charged (though tour operators often don't include this in the quoted price). The typical outing is the so-called **"jungle tour"**, which entails riding two-passenger speedboats through the lagoon mangroves, then out to the reef. Aquaworld is the main purveyor (M$500), though you can book something similar through hotels, or directly at any of the numerous docks on the lagoon side. Less ethically, you can dodge the park fee and reach the reef by land: walk through the *Westin* to the beach, then turn right and walk about twenty minutes down to Punta Nizuc. From there you can cross the rocks and snorkel to your heart's content.

Other reefs off Cancún's coast make good **diving** for beginners, with easy access and little current; contact Manta Divers, at Paseo Kukulcán Km 6.5 (☎998/849-4050, ⓦwww.mantadivers.com). A two-tank dive costs about M$700 and a full PADI open-water certification course is around M$3800. Additionally, both **jet skiing** (M$550 for 30min) and **parasailing** (M$450 for 10min) are very popular in Cancún, with operators dotting the beach at frequent intervals. **Windsurfing** and **kiteboarding** are other options – La Escuela de Tabla Vela, at Paseo Kukulcán Km 3 (☎998/842-9072) is on the flat bay water, away from hotels and therefore away from the crowds. A two-hour introductory course is M$500. Two Much Fun 'n a Boat, at the *Blue Bay* dock, Paseo Kukulcán Km 3.5 (☎998/105-5667, ⓦwww.twomuchfun-n-aboat.com) runs four-hour **catamaran trips** to Isla Mujeres (M$450).

For pure waterfront leisure, head for the winding walkway along **Canal Sigfrido**, opposite El Embarcadero at Paseo Kukulcán Km 4. Especially nice at sunset, you can get an up-close view of the mangroves. Though you might occasionally see kids swimming here, don't be tempted – crocodiles are still plentiful in the lagoon.

## Eating

Cancún's **restaurants** outnumber hotels many times over, and competition for customers is fierce. Downtown, the most popular eating places line Avenida Tulum and its side streets. Though seafood and steak are the mainstay of many menus, you can also eat Middle Eastern, Yucatecan, Italian, Chinese, French, Cajun and Polynesian fare, not to mention international fast food and items from local chains. All the **hotels** in the zona hotelera have at least one formal restaurant, some of which are very elegant indeed, surrounded by tropical foliage with fountains and music. Many also feature a more relaxed beachfront dining room.

For **budget food**, follow the locals and make for the downtown markets. The biggest is **Mercado 28** (see p.89), where two rows of food stalls form a sort of pan-Mexican food court, with specialities from Monterrey, Mexico City, Guadalajara and elsewhere; one restaurant is even dedicated to dishes featuring the health-giving *chaya* plant. **Mercado 23** (see p.89), a few blocks north of the bus station, is much smaller but makes a peaceful venue for a decent Mexican lunch. For dinner, food stalls at **Parque de las Palapas** serve *huaraches* and quesadillas with an array of toppings; they're open until about 11pm.

Almost all of the restaurants in the **zona hotelera** are geared towards one thing only: parting tourists from large amounts of cash. The few recommended here are worth a splurge, or are rare bargains. If you're staying on the beach, you're often better off taking a cab or bus downtown, where you'll find better food at reasonable prices, plus a congenial mix of people.

## Downtown Cancún

### Cafés

**100% Natural** Av Sunyaxchén 26, at Av Yaxchilán. As the name implies, the menu at this largely vegetarian restaurant is decidedly wholesome, with fruit salads, veggie burgers and granola, as well as fresh-tasting Mexican dishes. Breakfasts are especially nice, with inventive combos like poached eggs over nopal leaves with spinach and an almond cream sauce (M$40).

**El Café** Av Nader 5. A buzzing terrace behind the city hall frequented by Cancún's journalists and writers. Good coffee and *pan dulce* for breakfast, plus a simple, reasonably priced lunch and dinner menu with basics like steak and fries (M$80) and enchiladas *de mole*.

**Dub** Av Nader at C Mero. Chilled-out hip café, usually with a DJ providing a live soundtrack. Ice cream, sandwiches and coffee are on the day menu, with wine and light snacks (*jamón serrano*, olives, salads) at night.

**El Pabilo** Av Yaxchilán 31, in the *Xbalamqué* hotel. Mellow literary coffee shop (a "*cafébrería*") with very good cappuccino, espresso and snacks. Live guitar music or readings at night.

**Ty-Coz** Av Tulum behind Comercial Mexicana. A sandwich shop where French and Mexican tastes mix: the warm ham-and-cheese *baguette económico* (M$12.50) is slathered with garlic-herb mayo and studded with pickled jalapenos; smoky chipotles are optional. Tasty coffee and croissants for breakfast (or pop into the takeaway pastry shop in the alley around the corner if you're on the go). Open till 11pm.

### Restaurants

**Los Almendros** Av Tulum 66. The original restaurant in the town of Ticul (see p.258) is credited with inventing the emblematic Yucatecan pork dish *poc-chuc*. The Cancún branch is somewhat stiff, with bright lights and white tablecloths, but the food is well prepared and reasonably priced (mains about M$80). Nightly specials on Mon, Wed, Thurs and Sun.

**Checándole** Av Xpuhil 6. A buzzing, popular restaurant that has been around since the earliest days, with a breezy terrace and a selection of satisfying and fresh-tasting Mexican classics.

Entrees like enchiladas start at M$65; set lunch is M$40. Closed Sun.

**El D'Pa** C Alcatraces at the southwest corner of Parque de las Palapas. Typical French crepes, both sweet and savoury (M$35–75), and decent wine by the glass. Choose a sidewalk table or sit inside among plush furniture – either way, it's very comfortable, and lively at night. Closed Mon.

**La Habichuela** C Margaritas 25 ☎ 998/884-3158, ⓦ www.lahabichuela.com. Long-established, elegant restaurant set in a walled garden in front of the park. The featured *coco-bichuela* (half a coconut filled with lobster and shrimp in a curry sauce, M$325) draws raves, but simpler, less expensive Caribbean concoctions are equally good. The sommelier is attentive and enthusiastic. Neighbouring *Labná* applies the same elegant flair to Yucatecan specialities, with somewhat lower prices.

**Los Huaraches de Alcatraces** C Alcatraces 31 (or enter on C Claveles). This sparkling cafeteria-style restaurant serves up hearty breakfasts and hot lunches for about M$50 and snacks like *huaraches* and quesadillas (M$20). Everything's very fresh, and the staff is happy to explain the various dishes. Closed Mon.

**Pericos** Av Yaxchilán 61 ☎ 998/884-3152, ⓦ www.pericos.com.mx. What opened in 1974 as a four-table *lonchería* is now a phantasmagoria of strolling magicians, crooning mariachis and stilt-walkers. The atmosphere is so over-the-top that even sceptics may be swayed, and the food (tasty steaks and enchiladas, M$140–250) holds its own.

**El Rincón Yucateco** Av Uxmal 24. In business since 1981, this stalwart specializes in simple peninsula cuisine such as *panuchos* (M$40 for four) and *brazo de reina* (M$50), a hearty tamale-like dish, all washed down with cold beers. The busy street out front makes the terrace less than ideal, but the nice staff do much to make up for it. Closed Sun.

**Salus y Chemo's** C Chacá 46. A quiet, cosy neighbourhood restaurant behind the bus station, specializing in hearty *pozole* (spicy hominy stew). The set lunch specials (M$45) are consistently satisfying. Tues–Sun 1pm–9pm.

## Zona hotelera

### Cafés

**100% Natural** Plaza Kukulcán, Paseo Kukulcán Km 13. Plaza Terramar, Paseo Kukulcán Km 8.4 ☎998/883-3636. Like the downtown original, the place to go for a health-food hit. The Terramar location is preferable.

**Ty-Coz** Paseo Kukulcán Km 7 and Paseo Kukulcán Km 7.7. The hotel zone branches of the French sandwich shop have slightly shorter menus, but the *baguette económico* is still the highlight. The small storefront at Km 7.7 closes around 6pm; the other, larger café is open till about 7pm.

### Restaurants

**La Casa de las Margaritas** in La Isla Shopping Village, Paseo Kukulcán 12. Upscale Mexican restaurant with decent regional specialities (such as Oaxacan *tlayudas*, chewy corn cakes with assorted toppings, M$90). It isn't quite as over-decorated as some, and the live music, more than mariachi, doesn't dominate the room. The Sunday buffet (M$140, noon–5pm) is a good deal.

**Casa Rolandi** in Plaza Caracol, Paseo Kukulcán Km 8.5 ☎998/831-1817, ⊛www.rolandi.com. This Cancún fixture serves northern Italian specialities, many done in a wood-burning oven, presented in a candlelit, white-tablecloth setting. Expensive (M$125 to M$530 mains) but suitable for a romantic splurge.

△ La Casa de las Margaritas

**Checándole** in Plaza Flamingo, Paseo Kukulcán Km 11. One of the few spots for satisfying, inexpensive local grub like tacos al pastor in the hotel zone, though the setting, in a mall food court, isn't as nice as its downtown counterpart. Daily 2–8pm.

**La Destilería** Paseo Kukulcán Km 12.5 ☎998/885-1087. The food at this lagoon-side theme restaurant is tasty, varied and not terribly expensive (around M$145 for seafood dishes), but the real draw is the hundred-plus types of tequila, available in tasting flights.

**Dolcemente Pompeii** Pez Volador 7, near Paseo Kukulcán Km 5 ☎998/849-4006. A rare casual restaurant catering to Mexican families and residents in the hotel zone, serving mammoth portions of hearty Italian food, from handmade pastas (M$90 and up) to gelato. Hard to find because it's not affiliated with a mall or hotel: turn north in front of the giant Mexican flag. Closed Mon.

**El Galeón del Caribe** Paseo Kukulcán Km 19.2, across from *Club Solaris* resort. A very rustic restaurant (more like a campsite) off the lagoon side of the road, where fresh fish is grilled over a wood fire for M$100 or so. Just north of bus stop #11, look for a small pull-off and stairs leading down to the water; get your order in before dusk, as there's not enough electricity to keep the place open after the sun sets.

**Hanaichi** Plaza El Parián, Paseo Kukulcán Km 8.7. At this sparkling little sushi joint, Mexican waiters make small talk in Japanese with the visiting business clientele, serving quite decent sashimi (M$20 per piece) and other standards like beef teppanyaki (M$160).

**El Rincón Yucateco** Plaza Maya Fair, Paseo Kukulcán Km 8.5. Branch of a downtown institution, offering big, reasonably priced helpings of peninsula standards. A small taco place 100m east, run by the same people, is equally tasty and affordable.

**Río Nizuc** off Paseo Kukulcán near Km 22. Hidden among the mangroves near the opening to the lagoon is this cheap seafood specialist, where ceviche (M$60) and *tikin-xic* fish (M$60) are popular with locals, who gather on weekends to watch the boats whiz by. Daily 11am–5pm.

**Siete** Paseo Kukulcán Km 13, in the *Fiesta Americana Aqua* hotel ☎998/881-7600. Patricia Quintana, the doyenne of Mexican haute cuisine, opened this high-concept place in Cancún's newest resort in early 2005. The setting is striking (Warhol-esque portraits of Diego Rivera and the wrestler El Santo), as is the food: lobster in hibiscus *mole*, lamb with mescal-orange-garlic sauce. Expensive (mains are between M$250 and M$350), but an excellent taste of the cutting edge, without a trip to Mexico City.

# Entertainment and nightlife

As Cancún's goal is to encourage some two million visitors a year to have fun, the entertainment scene (huge dance clubs, vast theme bars, top-volume everything) in the **zona hotelera** is lavish – or remorseless, depending on how you look at it. **Downtown** offers a less frenetic scene, with several bars with live bands in SM 22 and along Avenida Yaxchilán. Locals dance on weekends to traditional Mexican tunes at Parque de las Palapas. Outside of the bars and clubs listed below, you may find interesting touring bands, as well as the city's chamber orchestra, playing at El Teatro de Cancún (℡998/849-4848) at El Embarcadero.

**Cinemas** show new American releases subtitled in Spanish; the largest one downtown is the multi-screen Cinepolis (✆www.cinepolis.com.mx) in Plaza Las Américas on Avenida Tulum south of Avenida Cobá; tickets are half-price on Wednesday. In the zona hotelera, La Isla Shopping Village, at Paseo Kukulcán Km 12, also has a theatre.

## Bars

Usually embedded in malls or hotels, **bars** can provide a relatively affordable night out, supplementing the usual drinking fare with everything from big-screen sports coverage to romantic piano music in the background. Downtown watering holes often have very good **live musicians** performing at some point in the evening.

### Downtown Cancún

**El Camarote** In the *Plaza Kokai* hotel, Av Uxmal 26 ℡998/884-3218. At this nautical-theme terrace bar, older gentlemen play backgammon and cards. In the back is a small theatre furnished with captains' chairs and a stage – the live music (M$30 cover) tends toward sad ballads.

**La Casa 940** C Margaritas near C Azucenas. Local ska and jam bands play for a mixed clientele of students and assorted bohemians. If the band's not your thing (cover is rarely more than M$20), hang out on the front porch and enjoy some cheap seafood snacks.

**El Chat** C Tulipanes opposite *Roots*. An Internet café by day, *El Chat* draws a crowd of rock-loving youth in the evenings. When a band isn't playing, it's all Nirvana on the stereo. Pool tables too.

**Roots** C Tulipanes 26 ℡998/884-2437. Funky, intimate jazz and blues club that's the main venue for live music in downtown Cancún, and often hosts big-name touring musicians. Also serves dinner. M$30 cover Fri and Sat; closed Sun & Mon.

### Zona hotelera

**Glazz** La Isla Shopping Village, Paseo Kukulcán Km 12 ℡998/883-1881, ✆www.glazz.com.mx. Beautifully designed restaurant-lounge-club space. The lounge offers gigantic cocktails, pillow-filled nooks and hookahs; the small black-and-white club area can get packed after midnight.

**Lobby Bar at the Ritz-Carlton** Retorno del Rey 36, near Paseo Kukulcán Km 14. Soak up the ersatz continental feel while sitting in the overstuffed chairs and listening to the tinkling piano. The giveaway you're in Cancún: the sea view and the tequila menu. Classic cocktails start at M$125.

**La Madonna** La Isla Shopping Village, Paseo Kukulcán Km 12 ℡998/883-4837. A giant reproduction of the Mona Lisa presides over this chic, candlelit bar slinging 150 types of martinis (very loosely defined, obviously).

**Señor Frog's** Paseo Kukulcán Km 5.5 ✆www.senorfrogs.com. Practically synonymous with the name Cancún, the Frog is the first stop off the plane for the spring break hordes. Go for live reggae or karaoke night, or just an anthropological experience.

**Trágara** Paseo Kukulcán Km 15.6 ℡998/885-0267, ✆www.lagunagrill.com.mx. Velvet couches, numerous aquariums and mosaic trim on every surface set a super-cool mood in this breezy lagoon-front lounge – the perfect spot for a sunset drink and a snack from the Asian-fusion finger-food menu.

## Clubs

In Punta Cancún in the zona hotelera, giant **nightclubs** face off across the street, and by about 11pm the road is clogged with meandering, scantily dressed thrill-seekers and touts flogging open-bar deals. The party generally lasts, inside the clubs and out, till 4 or 5am. Most of the clubs charge pricey covers and maintain a "no shorts or sandals" dress code. The music can be generic, though during the big spring break season or other festivals, you can catch some international pop and hip-hop stars performing for less than you'd pay at home. The few downtown clubs – including a very popular gay venue – are a bit cheaper but no less dedicated to serious partying.

### Downtown Cancún

**Karamba** Av Tulum at C Azucenas ⓦwww.karambabar.com. The biggest and busiest gay disco in town, in a breezy, open-sided spot with room for four hundred to dance to pounding house and salsa beats, plus the requisite gay anthems. Most nights see drag acts, strippers and go-go boys galore. M$50 cover; closed Mon.

**Mambo Café** In Plaza Las Américas, Av Tulum south of Av Sayil ⓣ998/887-7894. Cancún's biggest salsa club has a vast wood dancefloor and elaborate jungle decor, complete with a waterfall. The live bands are often touring acts from Cuba and Puerto Rico. M$50 cover; Wed is free. Wed–Sun 10pm–4am.

### Zona hotelera

**Azúcar** At *Dreams Cancun*, Punta Cancún ⓣ998/848-7000. Popular Caribbean club with a ten-piece band that gets the well-dressed crowd grooving to salsa and merengue. M$80 cover; call to reserve a table. Closed Sun.

**La Boom** Paseo Kukulcán Km 3.5, across from El Embarcadero ⓣ998/849-7587, ⓦwww.laboom. com.mx. The only place in the city that begins to approach Ibiza-style decadence, with international house hits on the sound system and an open-air chill-out room. M$185 cover; free on Mon.

**Bulldog Café** At the *Krystal* hotel, Paseo Kukulcán 9 ⓣ998/848-9851, ⓦwww.bulldogcafe.com. Somewhat generic nightclub (complete with a "VIP hot tub"), but it does host touring Mexican rock and pop acts such as Café Tacuba and Molotov. Cover on non-concert nights is M$185.

**The City** Paseo Kukulcán Km 9 ⓣ998/848-8380, ⓦwww.thecitycancun.com. This 24-hour club is a beach party by day (the pool area has a wave machine and a water slide) and a high-tech disco with a mesmerizing laser show by night. During spring break, MTV sets up shop here, and the hip-hop and pop stars du jour are on the bill.

**Coco Bongo** Plaza Forum by the Sea, Paseo Kukulcán 9 ⓣ998/883-0592, ⓦwww. cocobongo.com.mx. Vast state-of-the-art rock and pop disco popular with US college kids, but with more diverse music than competitor *Dady'O* across the road, and a hyper-stimulating floor show involving trapeze acts, Madonna impersonators and stunt bartenders. Cover charge at weekends only.

**G-Spot** Paseo Kukulcán Km 10.5 ⓣ998/883-2180, ⓦwww.gspotdisco.com. The scene is young and the soundtrack trancey at this funky club floating on the lagoon. The semi-open space, filled with plants and curvy, free-form furniture, is refreshingly small compared to the giant party complexes at Punta Cancún. M$150 cover.

## Shopping

When it comes to souvenirs, Cancún's mass-market roots are still strong – meaning you'll find infinite quantities of giant sombreros and vaguely obscene T-shirts but precious little quality craftwork. Vast, air-conditioned **malls** dominate the hotel zone, selling everything from bikinis to Rolexes. La Isla Shopping Village, at Paseo Kukulcán Km 12, is currently the best, offering a great range of international brands plus plenty to occupy the non-shoppers as well. **Prices** are usually fixed, but you can negotiate if you're buying several items at the big clusters of souvenir stalls (confusingly called "**flea markets**"): Coral Negro, at Punta Cancún, has the widest stock of inexpensive Mexicana in the zona hotelera, and the similar Ki-Huic dominates Avenida Tulum downtown. For a **hammock**, El Aguacate in Plaza Bonita, next to Mercado 28 downtown (see p.89), is the only place that stocks quality ones that will hold up to serious travelling.

## Moving on from Cancún

If you're heading west **by car** to Valladolid, Chichén Itzá and Mérida, you have a choice between the speed-bump-filled but scenic free road (*libre*) or the fast new toll highway (*cuota*), running a few kilometres north of the old road for most of its length. From the bus station, drive north on Avenida Tulum about 1km, then turn left to join Avenida López Portillo; after a few kilometres you will have the choice of which road to join. There's another entrance to the *cuota* off Avenida Tulum 1.5km south of the airport. You pay in advance, at the booths on the highway, for the sections you intend to travel along. The trip all the way to Mérida costs M$280.

First- and second-class **buses** go from the terminal on the corner of Avenida Tulum and Avenida Uxmal. Destinations include Mérida, on the ultra-luxe UNO service (8 daily; 3.5hr), first-class (12 daily; 4hr) and second-class (hourly round-the-clock; 6hr); Campeche, on the deluxe ADO GL service (daily 3pm; 9hr) and first-class (6 daily; 7hr); Chetumal on deluxe ADO GL (daily at 4.30pm; 5hr) and second-class (hourly 5am–12.45pm; 6hr); Mexico City on first-class (2 daily at 10am and 1pm; 18hr) and second-class (4 daily; 20hr); Playa del Carmen on first-class (every 10min; 1hr); Tizimín (6 daily; 4hr); Tulum on first-class (9 daily; 2hr) and second-class (3 daily; 2hr); Valladolid (hourly; 3hr).

International **flights** and domestic connections to Mexico City leave regularly from Cancún; from downtown a taxi to the airport costs about M$160; from the zona hotelera, M$180 and up.

### Boats to Isla Mujeres

Two passenger **ferries** (15min; M$35) run to Isla Mujeres. The closest port to downtown is the newer Gran Puerto, at the end of Avenida López Portillo. Departures are nearly every thirty minutes (5.30am–midnight). The slow boat (45min; M$18) still nominally departs five times daily from the older port, Puerto Juárez, about 500m north of Gran Puerto, but it's nothing to count on. To get to either port, catch a bus ("R-13" or "R-1 – Pto Juárez"; M$4.50) or a combi heading north from the stop on Avenida Tulum opposite the bus station (15min), or take a taxi from Avenida Tulum (around M$60). Boats also run from the hotel zone – El Embarcadero and Playa Tortugas are two piers – but tickets start at about M$150 per person, and the crossing takes longer. Alternatively, you can hire a **private launch** at Puerto Juárez to go directly or stop to snorkel along the way. Rates are negotiable, but a typical trip costs about M$600 for the boat, with stops at three reefs and snorkelling equipment provided.

The **car ferry** (M$150 per car, plus M$30 for each passenger) leaves from Punta Sam, 6km north of Gran Puerto, with five departures daily. However, it isn't worth taking a car over to the island, which is quite small and has plenty of bicycles and mopeds for hire.

You may do better at the **craft shows** that take place every few weeks at Parque de las Palapas; vendors, whether local artists or visiting craftspeople from another town, have a more diverse and personal stock and are happy to bargain. For more original **artwork**, check Galería Xaman-Ek in Plaza Caracol and the Casa de la Cultura in downtown Cancún west of the centre on Avenida Yaxchilán (☏998/884-8364), which mounts new art exhibitions every couple of months – it's the best place to meet local artists and get a feel for the scene.

**Film**, **maps** and other basic travel needs are easily purchased at Sanborn's, at the convention centre in the hotel zone and opposite the bus station downtown. Despite the strong American presence, Cancún is short on English-language **books**. Fama, on Avenida Tulum between Calle Tulipanes and Calle Claveles, looks like a basic souvenir shop from the street, but has a few guidebooks and mass-market paperbacks tucked away in the back.

# Sport

In addition to all the usual water activities, Cancún offers plenty of other energetic ways to pass the day. **Golf** is very popular, with two courses offering especially challenging play and fine scenery. The oldest, recently remodelled by Robert Trent Jones Jr, is Club de Golf Cancún (☎998/883-1230, @www .cancungolfclub.com), which straddles both sides of the boulevard at Km 7.5. The Hilton Cancun Golf Club (Paseo Kukulcán Km 17 ☎998/881-8000, @www .hiltoncancun.com) shows particularly creative use of the lagoon setting, with a mangrove trap, a tee on an island and a view of El Rey from the eighteenth hole. Green fees at both are about M$1000.

**Baseball** is a well-attended spectator sport. Root for the local AAA pro team, the Langosteros, at Estadio Beto Ávila, a bit southwest of the centre on Avenida Xcaret. Check the listings flyer *Entérate Cancún* for schedules – there are usually eight or nine evening home games per month during the season, April–Oct. Cheap seats are M$20, and the best ones in the house are only M$80.

Somewhat less authentic, but still entertaining, is the weekly **bullfight** at the Plaza de Toros (☎998/884-8248; Wed at 3.30pm; M$350), at the intersection of avenidas Bonampak and Sayil. To justify the steep entrance price, the *corrida* is preceded by a rather cheesy folk dance show. But the small covered arena has a certain dusty ambiance, and this is the only place in the area with a regular bullfight; otherwise, you'll have to wait for a town fiesta to see one.

On rainy days, **bowling** is a possibility, at Kukulcán Bol in Plaza Kukulcán at Km 13 (daily 10am–1am; M$40 per game; ☎998/885-3425). The place is popular with locals – call ahead in the evenings to make sure some lanes are free.

# Listings

**Airlines** Aviacsa, Av Cobá 37 ☎998/887-4211, at the airport ☎998/886-0093; Aeroméxico ☎998/884-1097; Mexicana ☎998/881-9090; American ☎800/904-6000; Delta ☎800/902-2100; Northwest/KLM ☎800/447-4747.

**American Express** Av Tulum 208, at C Agua (Mon–Fri 9am–5pm; ☎998/884-4000).

**Banks** Most banks (usually Mon–Fri 9.30am–3pm, Sat 9.30am–1pm) are along Av Tulum between Av Uxmal and Av Cobá and in the biggest shopping malls – Kukulcán, Plaza Caracol – in the zona hotelera. The HSBC bank, Av Tulum 192, stays open until 7pm on weekdays.

**Car rental** Available at most hotels and at the airport, or try Buster Rent a Car, Paseo Kukulcán Km 3.5 (☎998/849-7221, @www.busterrentacar.com) or Europcar, Av Nader 27 (☎998/884-4714).

**Consulates** Canada, Plaza Caracol, Paseo Kukulcán 8.5 ☎998/883-3060; UK, *Royal Sands*, Paseo Kukulcán Km 13.5 ☎998/881-0100; US, Plaza Caracol, Paseo Kukulcán Km 8.5 ☎998/883-0272.

**Internet** Immediately across from the bus station and northwest on Av Uxmal are several Internet cafés; some are *casetas* as well. In the zona hotelera, Web access is significantly more expensive; in a pinch, try *Hippo's* in La Isla Shopping Village.

**Laundry** Lavandería Las Palapas, on C Gladiolas,

at the far side of the park (Mon–Sat 7am–8pm, Sun 8am–2pm), or Lavandería Martinez, across the street from *Las Palmas* hotel; in the zona hotelera, ABC Coin Laundry, west of *Aquamarina Beach* at Paseo Kukulcán Km 3.5.

**Medical emergencies** The largest hospital close to the zona hotelera is AmeriMed, Av Tulum Sur 260, behind Plaza las Américas (☎998/881-3400 or 881-3434 for emergencies, @www.amerimedcun.com).

**Post office** Av Sunyaxchén at Av Xel-Ha (Mon–Fri 8am–6pm, Sat 9am–1pm); has a reliable Lista de Correos (postcode 77501).

**Sport-fishing** *Villas Manglar* hotel (p.85) specializes in fishing charters.

**Travel agencies and tours** Most hotels in the zona hotelera have in-house agencies that can arrange day-trips to the chief Maya sites or other attractions along the coast. Otherwise, the student-friendly agency Nómadas has a branch at Avenida Cobá 5 (☎998/892-2320, @www.nomadastravel.com) and leads affordable tours with guides to Chichén Itzá and other nearby attractions. Ecocolors, C Camarón 32, SM 27 (☎998/884-9214, @ww.ecotravelmexico.com), runs single- and multi-day kayaking, birdwatching or bicycling tours.

# Isla Mujeres

Just a few kilometres off the easternmost tip of Mexico in the startlingly clear Caribbean, **ISLA MUJERES** is substantially mellower than Cancún, drawing people for long stays despite the lack of tourist attractions and wild nightlife. A hippie hangout in the 1970s after wealthy Mexican adventurers paved the way for tourism a decade earlier, the eight-kilometre-long island still retains an air of bohemian languor, with wild-haired baby-boomers passing on travel wisdom to a new generation of young backpackers.

Unfortunately, however, Mujeres is no longer the desert island you may have heard about, and its natural attractions have been developed considerably. Several large hotels have sprung up, thousands of day-trippers visit from Cancún, and the once beautiful **Garrafón coral reef** off the southern tip is now almost completely dead and incorporated into a small-scale family-fun park. Inevitably, too, prices have risen. All that said, the island can still seem a respite to those who've been slogging their way from Maya pyramid to Maya pyramid, or to anyone who is overwhelmed by plastic Cancún – the wooden buildings and narrow streets have a genuine Caribbean feel.

The attractions here are simple: first there's the beach, then there's the sea. And when you've tired of those, you can rent a bike, moped or golf cart to carry you around the island to more sea, more beaches and the tiny Mayan temple that the conquistadors chanced upon, full of female figures, which gave the place its name. But you'll eventually want to be back under the palms on **Playa Norte**, the big west-facing beach, by late afternoon: Isla Mujeres is one of

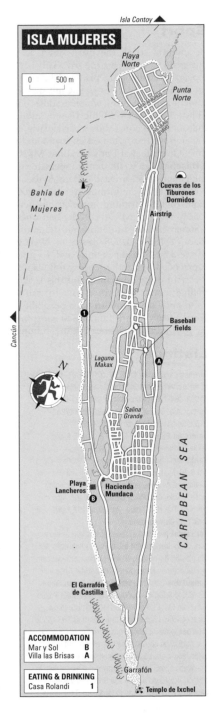

**ACCOMMODATION**
Mar y Sol **B**
Villa las Brisas **A**

**EATING & DRINKING**
Casa Rolandi **1**

the few places along Mexico's eastern shoreline where you can enjoy a glowing sunset over the water, margarita in hand. For a truly secluded beach, you can also take a day-trip to the nearby bird sanctuary of **Isla Contoy**, where you can enjoy empty sand, a seafood lunch and a stroll through the mangroves.

## Arrival, information and island transport

The passenger **ferries** arrive at Isla Mujeres town at two adjacent piers; the car ferry comes in farther south on Avenida Medina, at the end of Calle Bravo. The boats leave from Gran Puerto and Puerto Juárez (10min in a taxi from central Cancún, or 15min on a bus) nearly every half-hour from 5.30am; the last is at midnight. From the pier, it's about a twenty-minute walk to the opposite side of the island and the farthest hotels.

The **tourist office** (Mon–Fri 8am–8pm, Sat & Sun 9am–2pm; Ⓦwww .isla-mujeres-mexico.com) is on Avenida Rueda Medina just west of the passenger ferry piers. Here you can pick up leaflets, maps and copies of the free *Islander* magazine (in Spanish and English).

Two **bus** lines run from Avenida Rueda Medina in the main town down to the southern end of the island (M$3), but you may prefer the flexibility of a **moped** (M$80 per hour) or **bicycle** (M$100 per day), as the island is a very manageable size with few hills; alternatively, hire a **golf cart** (M$140 per hour). Virtually every other storefront rents out all three forms of transport, and prices vary little.

## Accommodation

Isla Mujeres is short on good **budget places to stay**, and, though rates are lower than in Cancún, so is the quality. Most of the reasonably priced options are on the northern edge of the island; the less expensive waterfront views are on the eastern side, where the sea is generally too rough to swim in. There is no official **campsite** on Isla Mujeres, but you can pitch your tent or sling up a hammock in the grounds of the *Poc-Na* **youth hostel**, Calle Matamoros at Calle Carlos Lazo (Ⓣ998/877-0090, Ⓔpocnahostel@yahoo.com.mx; M$60), which opens directly onto a beach. The hostel has other sleeping options, from dorm beds (M$120) to private rooms with a/c (❹–❺), though it can be a little less than spotless and has no public kitchen.

### Isla Mujeres town

**Casa Maya Zazil-Há** C Zazil-Há 129, at Playa Norte Ⓣ998/877-0045, Ⓦwww.kasamaya.com.mx. This offbeat outpost of old-style Isla Mujeres, where faux Olmec heads dot the grounds and hammocks are slung between the trees, is a well-priced option directly on the beach. Free snorkel gear is available for use in the shallow bay out front. ❼–❾

**Francis Arlene** C Guerrero 7, at C Abasolo Ⓣ998/877-0310, Ⓦwww.hotelfrancisarlene.com. Small family-owned hotel with well-tended court-yards and clean, rather brightly painted rooms with frilly bedspreads, plenty of comforts and choice of a/c or fan. ❻

**El Marcianito** C Abasolo 10 Ⓣ998/877-0111. Spotless rooms, if not so well-lit, with new bathroom fixtures. All have a/c and one double bed; an extra bed can be arranged for M$50. ❹

**Posada Isla Mujeres** C Juárez between C Abasolo and C Madero (no tel). Small hotel with sparkling white rooms with fans. If no one's around, enquire with the owners at *Posada Suemi* (also recommended, though not as new) around the corner at Calle Matamoros between Calle Juárez and Avenida Medina. ❹

**Na Balam** C Zazil-Há 118, near Playa Norte Ⓣ998/877-0279, Ⓦwww.nabalam.com. One of the island's most comfortable hotels, with a pool, a tropical garden on the flawless beach, a good restaurant and large rooms that are elegant but not pretentious. Free yoga classes Mon–Fri. ❾

**Playa Secreto** On the northeastern shore Ⓣ998/877-1039, Ⓦwww.hotelsecreto.com. This whitewashed modern hotel looks more Mediterranean than Mexican; details include enormous fluffy beds and a welcoming outdoor lounge by the pool and a partially sheltered cove. For this level of style and service, the ground-floor double rooms are a bargain; continental breakfast included. ❾

**Roca Mar** C Bravo at C Guerrero, behind the church next to the plaza ☎ 998/877-0101. One of the island's oldest hotels, though well maintained. The beach is rocky and the water rough, but there is a pool. ❻–❼

**Suites Los Arcos** C Hidalgo 58, between C Matamoros and C Abasolo ☎ 998/877-1343, ⓦ www .suiteslosarcos.com. Modern rooms with kitchenettes and a/c; the quieter ones in the back have bigger balconies too. Discounts for week-long stays. ❼

**Vistalmar** Av Rueda Medina at C Matamoros ☎ 998/877-0209, ⓕ 998/877-0096. Very pink hotel opposite the ferry piers in central downtown. Good value, especially considering its proximity to the beach. Choice of a/c or fan. ❹

## Elsewhere on the island

**Mar y Sol** 5km south from the ferry, on the bay side ⓦ www.morningsinmexico.com. A hands-off apartment rental, available by the night or the week. The four studios (each with two beds, a/c, a range and a fridge) are basic, but right on the beach. It's a taxi ride from the action on the north end of the island, but walking distance to the nearby village for supplies, or to Playa Lancheros for lunch. ❻

**Villa Las Brisas** 2.5km south from the ferry, on the Caribbean side ☎ 998/888-0342, ⓦ www.villalasbrisas.com. A beautifully designed guesthouse perched above dramatic crashing surf (swim in the pool instead). The five rooms all have king-size beds and fantastic feather pillows; delicious full breakfasts included. ❾

# The Island

The majority of the tourist amenities on Isla Mujeres are on the northern end in the main **town**, which occupies about a third of the island's area. Nonetheless, it's so compact you can take a quick turn around the sixteen or so square blocks of brightly painted houses in just half an hour. The centre third of the island is also built up, a sort of locals-only "suburb" to the main town. Beyond, a single road runs along the west coast towards the southern tip, passing the ruined pirate abode of **Hacienda Mundaca**, tucked amid low, humid forest, and several quiet beaches, the best of which is **Playa Lancheros**. **Garrafón** park occupies the south end, a watery playland for snorkellers that encompasses the island's single, very small Maya ruin, the **Templo de Ixchel**. The road loops around and continues back up the windy, exposed east coast, where the surf crashes incessantly against the rocks. You can complete the circuit in a golf cart or by bicycle in just a few hours, or make a full day of it, taking time out for beach lounging and leisurely lunch.

## Isla Mujeres town and Punta Norte

Narrow, pedestrianized **Avenida Hidalgo**, lined with tequila bars, crochet-bikini vendors and family-friendly restaurants, cuts through the centre of **Isla Mujeres town**. The street's southern end opens onto the central **plaza**, where tamale and *churro* vendors set up shop in the evenings. On one side sits a church that's the site of week-long festivities every December celebrating a legendary statue of the Virgin Mary that's on display inside.

Stretched around **Punta Norte**, the northern lip of the town, the island's major beach, **Playa Norte**, represents the archetypal Caribbean beach, with soft, deep sand, plenty of palm trees and bathtub-warm water stretching out at knee height for nearly a kilometre in some spots. The western side, north of the ferry docks, is cluttered with fishing boats and ceviche stands; this is where *isleños* often swim and set up camp with the family on Sundays. At the northwestern tip, the beach party goes all week long, with a cluster of bars in perpetual happy hour. Across the northern side, the scene gets quieter. Close to the *Avalon Reef Club*, the all-inclusive resort on the promontory (and chief timeshare hawker, you can't help but learn), you can **snorkel** a bit. The small

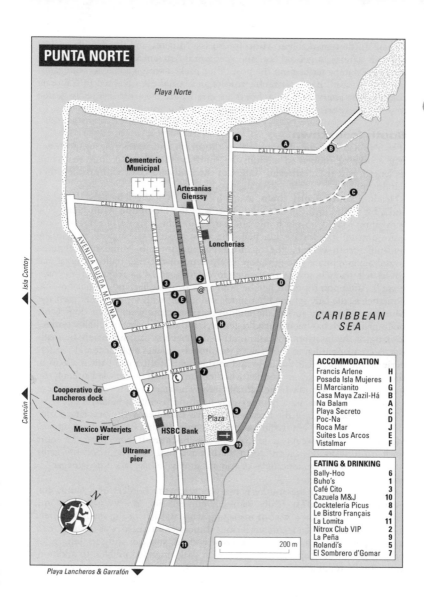

bay in front of *Casa Maya* is particularly calm and a good spot for children to test the waters.

The only other sight to speak of is the town **cemetery**, on Calle Mateos at Avenida Juárez, where you'll find the closing chapter of the saga of Fermín Antonio Mundaca (see p.104). Nestled between shiny new crypts is the pirate's weather-worn grave, half-buried in sand. It's empty, though: the lovelorn man died alone in Mérida. The grim engraving, allegedly carved by the gloomy Mundaca himself, reads, "Como eres, yo fui. Como soy, tu serás" ("As you are, I was. As I am, you will be").

There's little remarkable to **shop** for on Isla Mujeres, and the densely packed souvenir stands can get old fast. An exception is Artesanías Glenssy, a small shed on Calle Mateos across from the post office packed with a collection of exceptionally beautiful **papier-mâché masks** and headdresses painted in elaborate colours and patterns. Opening hours are erratic, and the artist isn't really geared to selling to tourists, but it's worth taking a peek if you can.

## South from town

If you've had enough of lounging on the beach and wandering round town, rent a bike or moped to explore the south of the island. A lone road runs its length, past the dead calm waters of the landward coast and up the other, windswept side.

Heading **south from town**, about halfway down the length of the island and a bit inland lurk the decaying remains of the **Hacienda Mundaca** (daily 9am–5pm; M$10), an old house and garden to which scores of romantic (and quite untrue) legends are attached. The most popular tale reports that in the mid-nineteenth century, the Spaniard Fermín Antonio Mundaca, a reputed swashbuckling pirate (though more likely a run-of-the-mill trader of sugar and slaves), fell madly in love with a young lovely nicknamed La Trigueña ("the brunette"). Attempting to woo her, he built an enormous hacienda in her honour; nonetheless, the lady spurned her suitor and ran off with someone her own age. Mundaca died alone and insane, and his glorious estate went to the dogs. Only one small house has been pieced together, but the entry gate is suitably gothic-looking, as the inscription "La Entrada de la Trigueña" can still barely be made out. A circular garden at the back of the property makes a pleasant and vaguely eerie picnic spot. Near the front and to the right of the main path is a **zoo** of the kind that makes you wonder whether the animals – sprawled sullenly on logs or sunken in pools – are actually alive. The stars are the spider monkeys, quick to pluck food and any other stray items from visitors' hands.

About 100m south of the hacienda is **Playa Lancheros**, the best beach outside of Playa Norte. The white sand is pleasantly shaded by palm trees, and it's virtually deserted except at lunchtime. The **restaurant** here produces some great rustic seafood – according to the battered sign over the wood-fire grills, ingredients in the fantastic *tikin-xic* fish are simply "*adobo*, salt, lime, vinegar . . . and love".

Continuing on to the southern tip, you reach the borders of a family-fun nature park, **Garrafón** (daily 9am–6.30pm; M$165; Ⓦwww.garrafon.com), established in 1999 as a way of managing what was left of the small coral reef just offshore, which had suffered serious damage from decades of unsupervised day-trippers. Though much of the coral is dead, you can still see quite a lot of fish, as visitors keep them well fed with park-provided nibbles. In addition, you'll find kayaking, restaurants and "snuba" set-ups (walk under water while breathing through a long flexible tube). Note that snorkel gear, locker rental and the high-wire zip-line ride from the cliffs down to the water cost extra; an all-inclusive package with meals, towels and gear is an option.

While it is theoretically possible – and recommended by bargain hounds – to reach the reef through the adjacent *Garrafón de Castilla* beach club (M$30, with its own bay for decent snorkelling), you're likely to get nabbed by vigilant park workers who can see you don't have an official life vest; you're also dodging the national park fee that goes to maintaining the reef.

The entrance to the park is almost at the southern end of the island – beyond, the road continues to the old **lighthouse**, which affords a decent view back up the coast. From there you can visit a somewhat gratuitous sculpture park and

△ Zip-line ride at Garrafón

the **Templo de Ixchel** at the southernmost point (daily 9am–6.30pm; M$30; free with Garrafón ticket), where Francisco Hernández de Córdoba first arrived in Mexico in the spring of 1517. The temple was filled with female fertility figures, dedications to the goddess Ixchel, which allegedly inspired the Spaniards to dub the place "the island of women". Today the temple isn't very impressive – it's too much of a ruin, in fact – but it is very dramatically situated on low rocky cliffs, and you can often spot large fish basking below. The striking views continue as you head back north to the main town via the narrow, stark east-coast road, dotted with new holiday villas but still quite wild-feeling compared to the rest of the island.

Offshore, there's plenty of sea life to visit. **Las Cuevas de los Tiburones Dormidos** ("caves of the sleeping sharks"), a few kilometres from the northeast coast, is a popular dive spot where tiger, Caribbean reef, lemon, blue and even bull sharks rest in an oxygen-rich freshwater current that lulls them into stasis. Trips are easily booked through **dive shops** in town, such as Coral at Calle Matamoros 13-A (℡998/877-0763, ⊛www.coralscubadivecenter.com). You can also arrange **snorkelling** trips at the *lancheros* cooperative, north of the passenger ferry landing (M$200; 2hr) at the end of Calle Madero – a popular destination is **El Farolito**, a shallow spot off the tip of the Sac Bajo Peninsula where you're mostly protected from the current.

## Eating

The area along and around Avenida Hidalgo between Morelos and Abasolo, is lined with **restaurants**. For inexpensive, basic Mexican food and great low-priced fruit salads, head for the **loncherías** opposite *Las Palmas* hotel. At night, food vendors set up on the main plaza.

**Café Cito** C Juárez at C Matamoros. Visit this colourful, cheery restaurant for healthy yoghurt-granola breakfasts or more decadent crepes and waffles, along with very good coffee.

**Casa Rolandi** At the *Villa Rolandi* hotel, at the end of the Sac Bajo Peninsula ℡998/877-0500, ⊛www.rolandi.com. The menu at this northern Italian restaurant is the same as at its Cancún counterpart (see p.95), but the setting here is superior, on a covered terrace overlooking the turquoise bay.

**Cazuela M&J** C Bravo at the ocean, past the *Roca Mar* hotel. Enjoy a fine ocean view at this casual café serving inexpensive (mostly Mexican) breakfasts. The signature egg dish is a sort of omelette baked in a *cazuela*, or earthenware casserole. Big glasses of *chaya* juice are another healthful option. Daily 7am–2pm.

**Cocktelería Picus** Av Rueda Medina. Small beachfront hut just north of the ferry landings serving fresh and inexpensive ceviches and shrimp cocktails. Lunch only in the low season.

**Le Bistro Français** C Matamoros 29, at Av Hidalgo. Casual restaurant with an inventive, delicious and reasonably priced menu that's vaguely French-inspired (fish with fennel and capers, for instance). Good breakfasts too. Daily 8am–noon, 6–10pm.

**La Lomita** C Juárez 25-B. Locals line up for a helping of the chef-owner's daily special, anything from bean soup and *chiles rellenos* to pan-fried fish with salsa verde. Fantastic home-cooking that's worth the hike up the small hill two blocks south of the plaza. Lunch only.

**Rolandi's** C Hidalgo between C Madero and C Abasolo. Part of a small family-run chain serving great, reasonably priced wood-oven pizza, lobster, fresh fish and other northern Italian dishes with salads.

**El Sombrero d'Gomar** Av Hidalgo at C Madero. Hearty portions at reasonable prices are the draw at this two-storey palapa-roof restaurant on the main avenue. Stick with Mexican staples – the *chilaquiles* are good for breakfast.

## Drinking and nightlife

Isla Mujeres isn't a big **nightlife** destination – in the off-season, only one or two bars can muster any sort of crowd. Occasionally **bars** on Playa Norte will sponsor big parties, but typically the scene consists of beers and perhaps some Jimmy Buffett renditions by a local guitar player.

**Bally-Hoo** Av Medina near C Abasolo. Swap tales with yachties at this palapa bar on the marina pier; it's the designated hangout for anyone looking to crew a boat.

**Buho's** Playa Norte at C Carlos Lazo, in front of *Cabañas María del Mar*. In high season, this beach bar tends to be the liveliest and most popular, with loud rock music, swinging hammock chairs and a well-attended happy hour in the late afternoon.

**Nitrox Club VIP** C Matamoros between C Guerrero

and C Hidalgo ℡998/887-0568. The only disco in town, drawing both locals and tourists. Wed is ladies night, and Fri has Latin music, with free dance classes from 10pm till midnight. Cover is rarely more than M$20. Closed Mon, Tues.

**La Peña** C Guerrero on the main plaza ℡998/845-7384. An upstairs bar-lounge popular with younger hostel guests, with a view of the Caribbean, cocktails, DJs and a big movie screen.

## Listings

**Banks** HSBC, on Av Rueda Medina opposite the ferry docks, has an ATM; another ATM is between the two docks.
**Internet and books** Cosmic Cosas (C Matamoros at Av Hidalgo) is well maintained and has a cable for laptop hookups; also stocks second-hand books.

**Laundry** Two laundry services, Tim Phó's and Wash Express, are on C Abasolo.
**Post office** C Guerrero at C Mateos (Mon–Thurs 9am–4pm); mail is held at the Lista de Correos for up to ten days (postcode 77400).
**Telephone** A reasonably priced *caseta* is C Madero between C Hidalgo and C Juárez.

## Isla Contoy

Scores of touts on Isla Mujeres devote their efforts to luring you on a boat trip to the island **bird sanctuary** of **CONTOY**, 30km north of Mujeres. Only 8.5km long, it was designated a national park in 1961, and is now home to some 150 bird species, including large colonies of pelicans, cormorants and frigates. The calm western beaches serve as a nesting haven for sea turtles, while the windy eastern coast is a mix of dunes and limestone cliffs. The boat trip out is leisurely, often with stops to snorkel at reefs along the way; by lunchtime you're deposited on a small beach in a lagoon (often with several other groups, which can dampen the isolated spirit) and given the afternoon to either relax in the sun or explore the wild setting, starting at a small welcome centre and observation tower and going along a path into the mangroves that cover the interior of the island.

La Isleña Sea Tours, on Calle Morelos one block back from Avenida Rueda Medina, run a relaxed faux-castaway trip, with lunch caught straight from the sea. Alternatively, you can arrange a similar jaunt through the fishermen's cooperative, at the dock at the end of Calle Madero – preferably on board Capitán Ricardo Gaitan's *Estrella del Norte* (☎998/877-1363, ⓦwww.isla-mujeres.net), the last wooden boat made on the island, some thirty years ago. In all cases, tours last the whole day and include a basic breakfast, grilled fish for lunch, soft drinks and snorkel gear for about M$400 per person. For an additional M$100, payable on the island, you can take a birdwatching tour with one of the resident biologists. Amigos de Isla Contoy (ⓦwww.islacontoy.org), on Avenida Rueda Medina at Calle Maderos or in Cancún in Plaza Bonita, can provide additional information about the wildlife.

# Isla Holbox

A small island off the northeastern point of the peninsula, **ISLA HOLBOX** ("ol-BOSH") is sometimes touted as a new beach paradise to fill the place that Isla Mujeres once had in travellers' affections. The one small village, a hospitable, quiet place with a genuinely warm feel, will seem a relief to anyone who has come from the touristy resorts. The gulf waters here do not have the same glittering clarity as the Caribbean, but they're warm and clean, and the beaches are generally empty. Development is on the rise, of course, but a good part of the island is still very wild, as is the long spit from the mainland that runs east of the island, and all manner of **birds**, including flamingos, thrive here. From July to mid-September, visitors come to see the huge and rare **whale sharks** (see box on p.110) that congregate just off the cape. Sea turtles also nest here during the summer months. Do prepare for the absolutely fearsome mosquitoes that arrive at the end of the summer and stay into October.

The easiest way to reach Holbox is on the daily direct **bus for Chiquilá**, the closest mainland town, which leaves Cancún (3hr) at 7.50am and 1.15pm. Coming from the west is more difficult: buses leave Mérida (6hr) and Valladolid (3hr) in the middle of the night and arrive in time for the 6am ferry. Transferring in Tizimín (3hr) is a little easier, with a choice of three daytime buses. If you are **driving** from Cancún, don't take the toll highway, as there's no convenient exit; turn north off Hwy-180 *libre* at the tiny town of El Ideal.

The **Chiquilá ferry** for Holbox leaves nine times a day, the first run at 6am and the last at 7pm (30min; M$40); you may spot a few dolphins as you cross the lagoon. Holbox is also served by an unreliable **car ferry**, leaving Chiquilá at 8am and 1.30pm daily and returning from Holbox at 11am and 3pm, but there's no sense in taking a car to the tiny island. Secure parking is available near the ferry pier (be certain you've set the price before you leave). If you arrive between ferries, you can hire a private boat (M$250–300), which will take you directly to your hotel if you like. But don't miss the last ferry: Chiquilá is not a place you want to get stranded. There's a restaurant, a basic hotel, a store and a petrol station, but little else. Note also that there's **no ATM** on Holbox, nor in Chiquilá – plan accordingly, particularly if you intend to take a trip to the whale sharks, which is a sizeable investment (M$800 and up).

## Arrival and information

The ferry moors at a dock on the south side of the island, where there's little but the town generator and baseball field. Golf-cart and *triciclo* **taxis** can take you directly to your hotel if you have already made reservations; a ride to *Villas Chimay*, the hotel farthest from town, is about M$50. Otherwise, it's usually M$10 to the plaza, or about a ten-minute walk north on the wide sand street of Avenida Benito Juárez, which also leads on to the beach, two blocks farther. Otherwise, street names are largely irrelevant – all orientation is done from the plaza, as the town stretches for only a few blocks around it.

On the modest main square, called the *parque*, you'll find an **Internet** café, **post office** and **money-exchange** desk, but **no bank or ATM**. About four blocks south (back toward the ferry) is a new **laundry** (Mon–Sat 9am–2pm & 4–8pm), but most hotels have agreements with townspeople to offer inexpensive laundry service. There's no official tourist office, though everything you need to know is in a **free brochure** handed out to ferry passengers. Very few people have cars; locals also use the *triciclos* and electric **golf carts**. The latter are available to rent (M$120 per hour or M$400 for twelve hours) from several outlets near the *parque*, such as Rentadora Monkeys (T 984/875-2029).

## Accommodation

Hotel development stretches east of town for a couple of kilometres; only one property lies to the west. Out of season (early summer and before Christmas), rates for some of the upmarket rooms can fall by almost half; August, however, can be priced as high as Christmas and Easter weeks. All of the hotels on the **beachfront** are mid-range to luxury, but there are a few decent cheaper options in **town**, as well as the excellent *Ida y Vuelta* **campground**, with screened shelters for tents or hammocks, clean bathrooms, a shared kitchen and even a pizza oven (T 984/875-2344, W www.camping-mexico.com; M$60–80). It's east of town, just 200m from the beach, right behind *Xaloc*.

**Faro Viejo** Av Benito Juárez at the beach ☎984/875-2217, ⓦwww.faroviejoholbox.com.mx. Tidy, comfortable rooms directly on the beach (the only stretch in town that's free of fishing boats), plus a few suites ideal for groups, with kitchenettes and porches; full breakfast included. ❼

**Posada d'Ingrid** Two blocks west of the plaza, off the northwest corner ☎984/875-2070. A concrete building around a motel-like yard, this place isn't particularly scenic, but rooms with a/c and TV are quite clean and cheap, and the courtyard fosters a friendly atmosphere. ❺

**Posada Los Arcos** West side of the plaza ☎984/875-2043. ⓦwww.holboxlosarcos.com. Clean, basic rooms, some with kitchenettes, around a small courtyard. Choice of a/c or fan. ❺

**Posada Mawimbi** On the beach several blocks east of town ☎984/875-2003, ⓦwww.mawimbi.com.mx. A great little collection of round, two-storey cabañas, beautifully decorated and tucked among dense greenery. ❻

**Villas Chimay** On the beach 1km west of town ☎984/875-2220, ⓦwww.holbox.info. A wonderful hideaway, and the only lodging on the western beach. Self-sufficient with wind and solar power, and plenty of space between the well-designed bungalows. Delicious home-made bread with breakfast. Rents kayaks and runs jungle tours on the mainland. ❼

**Villas Los Mapaches** On the beach two blocks west of Av Benito Juárez ☎984/875-2090, ⓦwww.losmapaches.com. Spotless, comfortable bungalows with kitchenettes, ideal for longer stays; a larger rental house can accommodate groups or families. ❺–❼

**Xaloc** On the beach east of town ☎984/875-2160 or reservations in the US on 1-800/583-6802, ⓦwww.holbox-xalocresort.com or ⓦwww.mexicoholiday.com. A compact but well-designed property of eighteen cabañas with rough-hewn wooden canopy beds and particularly well-appointed bathrooms; smartly divided into areas for families and adults only, with a pool in each section. Free kayaks and snorkel gear too. ❽

# The island

Uninhabited until the late nineteenth century (locals claim pirates as their forebears), Holbox today is home to only about 2000 people, most engaged in lobster and shrimp fishing or selling lobster and shrimp to hungry visitors. All of the population is concentrated in a **small town** on the north coast. With sand streets, wooden houses and almost no cars, it's tranquil in the extreme. Aside from hanging out on the big grassy plaza, most activities for visitors involve the wildlife on or around the island.

The biggest such natural attraction – literally and figuratively – is the group of **whale sharks** that cluster off the coast in late summer. A boat tour to see the giant fish takes the better part of the day (M$800 per person including lunch and snorkel gear); you may see dolphins, rays and flying fish on the hour-long boat ride out to where the sharks gather, and tours often stop on the way back at Cabo Catoche, the northern cape, where there's a clutch of fishermen's shacks and a tall lighthouse. Mosquitours (☎984/875-2126, ⓔholbox@turismoalternativo.com) has new boats and informed guides who are respectful of the fish and the regulations concerning them.

Other popular tours include **Isla Pájaros**, a very small island wildlife sanctuary inside Laguna Yalahau. A flamingo colony nests here between April and October, along with about 150 other species. Two observation towers give birdwatchers great views at sunset. Also in the lagoon, a freshwater **spring** wells up among the mangroves on the mainland side – a popular swimming hole that's a side destination for many trips. **Isla de Pasión** is a tiny dot of sand off the west end of the island; a big part of the trip is wading through the shallow water to reach it. Visits to all of these places, as well as to a cork-tree swamp near Solferino on the mainland, can be arranged through most hotels, as well as Mosquitours. Any of them can also arrange tours for **fishing**, and a dive shop at *Posada Mawimbi* does **snorkelling** excursions, though the nearby reefs don't compare to those on the Caribbean shore.

## Visiting the whale sharks

The whale shark (*Rhincodon typus*, or *tiburón ballena* in Spanish) is a true shark, but earns its name by its enormous size: the largest known fish, it can reach up to 14m in length, and typical adults are between 7m and 10m long. Another common name, the domino shark, comes from the distinctive black skin covered in rows of white dots. The fish's lifespan is also remarkably long, as it can typically live well into its 70s.

Although whale sharks populate the tropical zone around the globe, the shallow waters off Isla Holbox are the only place in the world where such a large population gathers. The fish typically congregate in pods of ten or twenty, but researchers estimate the Holbox group at more than two hundred – perhaps because the swirling water here, where the Gulf of Mexico meets the Atlantic Ocean, teems with plankton, the whale sharks' primary food. Unlike vicious great whites of the popular imagination, whale sharks are gentle filter-feeders; as they glide slowly in circles, they are simply sucking up whatever small sea life is in front of them. Swimming alongside the passive animals poses no risk, except perhaps of getting tossed about by the current from a turning or diving fish.

Whale shark tourism on Holbox has developed very recently, and regulations for visiting the creatures were applied for the first time in 2003. By law, Isla Holbox is the only departure point for tours. Most of the area in which the fish swim is now a marine park, which requires visitors to be accompanied by trained guides, who should make sure swimmers get no closer than 2m to the sharks. Good captains should never attempt to "steer" the sharks with their boats. Take a hat and biodegradable sunscreen if you have it; regular suntan oil is prohibited by marine-park regulations.

One outfit runs horse-riding tours (2.5hr, M$350) to Punta Ciricote, where there is another cluster of flamingos. Enquire where the horses are tethered on the beach, 100m west of *Los Mapaches*, or at *La Cueva del Pirata* restaurant on the plaza (℡984/875-2183). Kiteboarding is increasingly popular on this breezy island with lots of empty beaches – classes can be arranged at *Casa Tortugas* (next to *Posada Mawimbi*). Marvin Tours (℡984/875-2103), one block off the northwest corner of the plaza, offers aerial tours in a small plane, especially interesting during the whale-shark season, when you can see just how large the population is.

## Eating and drinking

The island's village has several very good **restaurants**, and most hotels have their own offerings as well, though there's very little nightlife to speak of, outside of **hotel bars**. Locals generally lounge around on the plaza, where there might be a traditional Mexican *lotería* runner, or some vendors or musicians.

**Antojitos Dafne Guadalupe** In the centre of the plaza. The local favourite for tasty *panuchos* and *salbutes* in the evenings.

**Azul** One block north of the plaza, off the northeast corner. Tiny blue-lit spot with a range of well-priced items, from thick and meaty lasagna and baguette sandwiches to milkshakes to espresso.

**Carioca's** On the beach just north of the plaza. The only place vaguely resembling a bar, this open-air restaurant occasionally sees some dancing at the weekends.

**La Cueva del Pirata** On the west side of the plaza. Truly wonderful Italian restaurant, complete with hand-made fresh pasta and a charming proprietor. A little expensive compared to other island options, but very much worth the splurge. Dinner only.

**El General Taquitos** North side of plaza. Inexpensive crispy tacos and other typical snacks. Very busy at night, when tables spill out onto the street.

**La Isla de Colibri** On the southwest corner of the plaza. Come for delicious fresh fruit juices and other healthy options, or to meet people and arrange tours, as the place serves as a bit of a community centre. Adjacent, on the side street, the romantic *La Peña de Colibrí* has live music as a complement to dinner.

**Pizzas y Mariscos Edelín** On the east side of the plaza. Basic wood-panelled joint where inexpensive pizzas dominate the menu, but you're better off with the *mariscos* selection, and guacamole.

**Villamar** On the beach at Av Juárez. Good laid-back, local-owned restaurant with inexpensive seafood and other Mexican dishes.

**Viva Zapata** Just west of the northwest corner of the plaza. This relative newcomer serves good basics like pasta, chipotle shrimp and even chop suey. The second-floor palapa is a good place to watch the sun go down. Dinner only.

# Travel details

## Buses

The most useful bus services are those between Cancún and Mérida and those provided by Mayab, which run at least every thirty minutes between Cancún and Playa del Carmen. Second-class service to smaller towns is provided by Centro, Noreste and Cristobal Colón. The following frequencies and times are for both first- and second-class services.

**Cancún** to: Campeche (7 daily; 7hr); Chetumal (hourly 5am–midnight; 6hr); Chiquilá (3 daily; 3–4hr); Izamal (10 daily; 4hr); Mérida (hourly; 4–6hr); Playa del Carmen (every 10min; 1hr); Puerto Morelos (every 10min; 30min); Tizimín (6 daily; 4hr); Tulum (12 daily; 2hr); Valladolid (hourly; 3hr); Villahermosa (14 daily; 12hr).

**Chiquilá** to: Cancún (3 daily at 5.30am, 7.30am & 1.30pm; 3–4hr); Mérida (1 daily at 5.30am; 6hr).

## Ferries

Ferry service runs frequently to **Isla Mujeres** and **Isla Holbox**. Although there are car ferries to both, it's not worth taking a vehicle, as the islands are very small.

**Chiquilá** to: Isla Holbox (9 daily, 6am–7pm; 30min).

**Isla Holbox** to: Chiquilá (9 daily, 5am–6pm; 30min).

**Isla Mujeres** to: Puerto Juárez and Gran Puerto, Cancún (every 30min 5.30am–10pm; 15min).

**Puerto Juárez and Gran Puerto, Cancún** to: Isla Mujeres (every 30min 6am–11.30pm; 15min).

## Flights

Cancún has a busy international airport with daily flights to Mexico City and regular connections to Miami and several other cities in the southern US. Various small companies fly light planes – frequently between Cancún and Cozumel, less often from Cancún to Isla Mujeres, Playa del Carmen and Tulum.

**2**

# Cozumel and the coast

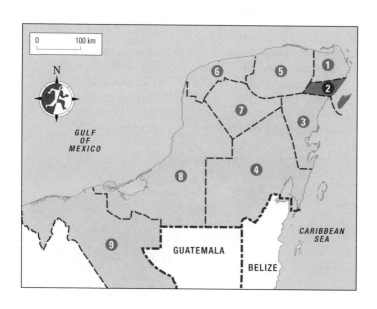

CHAPTER 2　　# Highlights

✳ **Puerto Morelos Reef**
The coral outcroppings
off the coast of Puerto
Morelos are a great place
to learn to dive. **P.119**

✳ **La Ruta de los Cenotes**
Outside Puerto More-
los, this small road cuts
inland through the jungle,
passing several beautiful
swimming holes. **P.121**

✳ **La Quinta** With easily
the best nightlife on the
Caribbean coast, the
central tourist artery
through Playa del Car-
men is an ever-evolving
cosmopolitan party. **P.128**

✳ **Mamita's Beach Club**
Playa del Carmen's best
beach is also its most
stylish social scene.
**P.130**

✳ **Parque Punta Sur** The
nature reserve at the
southern tip of Cozumel
is a must for birdwatch-
ers (look for the Cozumel
vireo), and its beaches
are beautiful too. **P.139**

✳ **Colombia Shallows** This
sandy-floor coral garden
off Cozumel's southwest
coast teems with colour
and life – a mesmerizing
place to snorkel. **P.141**

△ Mezcalito's

# Cozumel and the Caribbean coast

D evelopment along the spectacular white-sand beaches south of Cancún has proceeded furiously over the last few decades, as landowners have raced to cash in on the resort city's popularity. The tourist authorities granted the area south of Cancún the rather grandiose title of the

## The Mesoamerican Barrier Reef

Mexico's Caribbean coast faces the second-longest reef in the world (Australia's Great Barrier Reef comes in first). Stretching from Puerto Morelos, just south of Cancún, to the Bay Islands of Honduras, the **Mesoamerican Barrier Reef** hugs the shoreline for more than 700km. The complex eco-system encompasses not just the main coral outcroppings, but also outlying atolls, such as those around Cozumel, the sea-grass beds close to shore and the mangrove swamps that help feed the coral and filter out pollutants from land. The reef is host to more than five hundred species, including the endangered West Indian manatee and extremely rare and slow-growing **black coral**.

Like most coral systems around the world, the Mesoamerican Barrier Reef has suffered a great deal of damage. Some eighty percent of the oldest hard coral has died just within the past thirty years, and slick algae growth in many spots threatens to smother essential reef organisms. Unsurprisingly, the devastation coincides with the tourism boom onshore. Relatively few building projects have directly attacked the reef (though as recently as 2004, a giant new pier in Playa del Carmen was carved straight through the coral), but careless development has taken its toll, particularly on the mangrove swamps, which have been either torn out or used as dumping grounds. At the same time, hurricanes and other natural disasters have put intense stress on the eco-system.

Compared with other stretches of reef around the Caribbean, however, the Mesoamerican system is relatively healthy, and in 1997, the governments of Mexico, Belize, Honduras and Guatemala forged an agreement ensuring their joint conservation efforts. As part of a larger trend along the coast, Puerto Morelos residents successfully campaigned to have their reef frontage designated a national park in 2000, in order to prevent overfishing and other harmful practices. On land, though, building codes are only slowly being adjusted to be less environmentally harmful, and development is continuing unabated – the hope is that the tourism industry won't kill off one of its most profitable attractions.

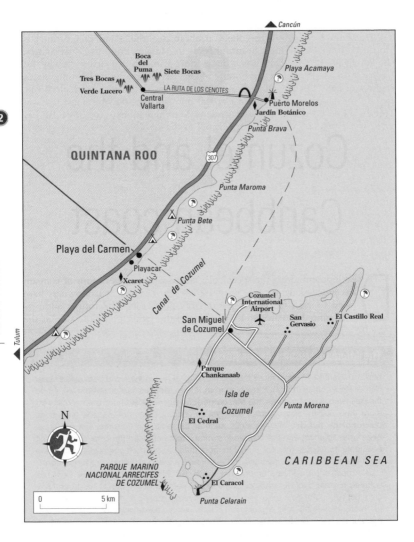

▲ Cancún

Boca del Puma

Siete Bocas

Tres Bocas

Verde Lucero

LA RUTA DE LOS CENOTES

Central Vallarta

Playa Acamaya

Puerto Morelos

Jardín Botánico

Punta Brava

**QUINTANA ROO**

307

Punta Maroma

Punta Bete

Playa del Carmen

Playacar

Xcaret

Canal de Cozumel

Cozumel International Airport

San Miguel de Cozumel

San Gervasio

El Castillo Real

Parque Chankanaab

Isla de Cozumel

Punta Morena

El Cedral

N

PARQUE MARINO NACIONAL ARRECIFES DE COZUMEL

El Caracol

Punta Celarain

CARIBBEAN SEA

0      5 km

**Riviera Maya**, and holidaymakers come in droves to the mammoth gated retreats that dot the coast. That said, finding a relatively deserted stretch of beach is by no means impossible. Immediately south of Cancún, in fact, lies one of the quieter spots: **Puerto Morelos**, a tiny town with clean beaches that has so far avoided unattractive development. (Its other big draw: offshore is the start of the vibrant **Mesoamerican Barrier Reef**, which stretches down to Honduras; the section offshore here is a great, less-visited place to dive and snorkel.) A bit farther south, **Punta Bete** is a little sandy point dotted with a couple of basic hotels. By contrast, the phenomenal growth of **Playa del Carmen**, formerly known only as the place where diving fanatics hopped on the ferry to **Isla Cozumel**, has transformed a fishing camp into a major holiday destination in its own right, renowned for its nightlife and gorgeous beachfront.

A half-hour boat ride across the Caribbean Sea, the island of Cozumel is ringed by some of the most beautiful **reefs** in Mexico. From the early Sixties, the barely populated island was a destination primarily for divers, but in the past two decades, the place has boomed like everywhere else, welcoming direct flights from the US as well as massive **cruiseships** at three separate piers. But despite the crush of visitors, you can still find isolated spots to appreciate the island's rainbow-hued underwater gardens. And there's plenty to see on land as well, from the pretty town of **San Miguel** to the deserted eastern coast, known for its empty beaches and rustic bars, where you can play castaway while enjoying a margarita and some fresh grilled fish.

You can explore the mainland coast easily by car, or take cheap and efficient public transport along Hwy-307: both *colectivos* and second-classes buses will stop anywhere you request. On Cozumel, though, there are no such options, so you'll have to rent a car to see the whole island, or join an organized tour.

# Puerto Morelos

Leaving Cancún behind, **PUERTO MORELOS**, 20km south, is the first town on the coast. Formerly of little interest except as the departure point for the car ferry to Cozumel (see box, p.120), in recent years it has seen a surge in popularity, becoming a base for tours and **dive trips**. With a direct bus service from the airport (11 daily, 9.30am–8.30pm), it's easier for visitors to bypass Cancún altogether, making Puerto Morelos their first stop along the Riviera Maya.

Despite a rash of new hotel and condo construction on the coast to the north, the town itself is the only working fishing village between Cancún and Tulum that hasn't been entirely consumed by tourism, and it's so mellow that the afternoon siesta is still observed by most businesses. Puerto Morelos's **beach** is pretty enough, but not really maintained for sunbathing and often cluttered

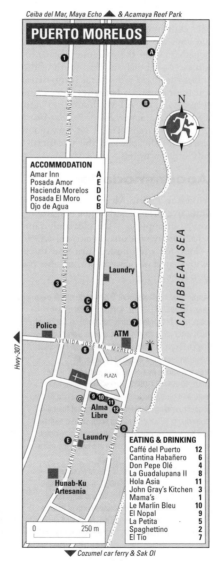

*Ceiba del Mar, Maya Echo ▲ & Acamaya Reef Park*

**PUERTO MORELOS**

N

**ACCOMMODATION**
| | |
|---|---|
| Amar Inn | A |
| Posada Amor | E |
| Hacienda Morelos | D |
| Posada El Moro | C |
| Ojo de Agua | B |

AVENIDA NIÑOS HEROES

AVENIDA NIÑOS HEROES

CARIBBEAN SEA

Laundry

Police

ATM

AVENIDA JOSE MA. MORELOS

Hwy-307

PLAZA

AVENIDA RAJO GOMEZ

@

Alma Libre

AVENIDA MELGAR

Laundry

Hunab-Ku Artesanía

**EATING & DRINKING**
| | |
|---|---|
| Caffé del Puerto | 12 |
| Cantina Habañero | 6 |
| Don Pepe Olé | 4 |
| La Guadalupana II | 8 |
| Hola Asia | 11 |
| John Gray's Kitchen | 3 |
| Mama's | 1 |
| Le Marlin Bleu | 10 |
| El Nopal | 9 |
| La Petita | 5 |
| Spaghettino | 2 |
| El Tío | 7 |

0          250 m

▼ *Cozumel car ferry & Sak Ol*

with fishing boats. Instead, the main draw here is the **reef**, which lies about half a kilometre offshore and is in healthy condition. The town offers a remarkable number of excellent **restaurants** for its population of just 3000, ranging from modern-fusion panache to genre-defining tacos. Inland, on the dirt road to Central Vallarta, are some beautiful **cenotes** that are only just beginning to receive visitors.

## Arrival and information

**Buses** going down the coast leave the station in Cancún every ten minutes and drop you at the highway junction, site of a **tourist information** kiosk with a helpful, enthusiastic staff of one (daily 10am–4pm). Taxis wait here to take you the 2km into town for about M$20, or you might be lucky enough to meet up with the two *colectivos* or one bus that also make the trip, on no discernible schedule. If on the extreme off chance you arrive on the car ferry from Cozumel, you'll be about 1km south of the central plaza.

On the plaza are several **long-distance telephones** by the police station on the corner, an **Internet** café, a supermarket, a couple of **cambios** (7am–10pm) and an **ATM**, though no actual bank. There's a **laundry** just south of the plaza, across from *Posada Amor*, and another to the north, past *Posada El Moro*. Marand Travel (ⓦwww.puertomorelos.com.mx), on the southwest corner of the plaza, is the unofficial tourist info spot, dispensing maps and advising on hotels.

## Accommodation

Hotels in Puerto Morelos are split between those right on the beach, usually a little overpriced, and better bargains a few blocks back. If you want to **camp** your only option is the pleasantly ramshackle *Acamaya Reef Park* (ⓣ987/871-0132, ⓦwww.acamayareef.com; M$90), on the beach 5km north of town – look for a signposted turn near the entrance to the Crococun zoo. Cabañas, with shared or private bath, are also available (❻), and the French owner cooks good food.

**Amar Inn** On the seafront 500m north of the main plaza ⓣ998/871-0026, ⓔamar_inn@hotmail.com. Very bohemian, family-run hotel on the beach with eight large rooms and cabañas; some with high ceilings, loft beds and kitchenettes. Delicious Mexican breakfast included in rates. ❺

**Posada Amor** Av Rojo Gómez just south of the plaza ⓣ998/871-0033, ⓔpos_amor@hotmail.com. Not on the beach, but friendly, and one of the longest-running hotels in town. Some of the quirky, individually decorated rooms (with shared baths) are the least expensive around, while some other, larger ones with private baths are worth the extra money; ask to see a few. ❹–❻

**Ceiba del Mar** 2km north of Puerto Morelos on the coast road ⓣ998/872-8060, ⓦwww.ceibadel-mar.com. Distinctive architecture and large pools make this spa resort, five minutes north of town, a standout. As luxury hotels go, it's not as well appointed as *Maroma* (see p.122) near Punta Bete, but neither is it so isolated. The earth-tone rooms have big

bathtubs with ocean views, and there's a full sauna (open to non-guests by appointment). Rates include continental breakfast and airport transfers. ❾

**Posada El Moro** Av Rojo Gómez 17, just north of the plaza ⓣ987/871-0159, ⓦwww.posadaelmoro.com. Ten clean, relatively new rooms, some with kitchens, in a pretty little garden; rooms off the street are preferable, though, as the neighbouring bar can be noisy at night. Amenities are excellent for the price: there's a small pool, and continental breakfast is included. ❻

**Maya Echo B&B** 3km north of Puerto Morelos on the coast road ⓣ998/871-0136, ⓦwww.mayaecho.com. A longtime Puerto Morelos resident dedicated to sustainable tourism manages this cheerful guesthouse north of town. Each of the three rooms has two twin beds; one has a/c. Rates include a lavish full breakfast. ❻

**Hacienda Morelos** On the waterfront just south of the plaza ⓣ & ⓕ998/871-0015. Huge, bright rooms strung out in a row, motel-style, all with

2

kitchenettes and bathtubs (a rare treat at this price), plus terraces opening right onto the beach. **❼**

**Ojo de Agua** On the seafront 400m north of the plaza ☎ 987/871-0027, 🌐 www.ojo-de-agua.com. Bright, sunny rooms (some have a/c) with colourful decor, most overlooking a giant pool; beyond lies a clean beach. The restaurant bar occasionally hosts a live band. One added perk: ocean-view rooms

don't cost more. **❻**

**Sak Ol** 1km south of the plaza, beyond the car ferry dock ☎ 998/871-0181, 🌐 www.ranchosakol. com. Two-storey thatched cabañas in a tranquil garden setting that leads into a deserted-feeling beach. Rates include large breakfasts with fruit and cereal. Guest kitchen facilities and massage available (M\$450 per hour). **❼**

# The Town

A small, modern plaza sits in the centre of Puerto Morelos. The turn-off from Hwy-307 ends here, and **the town**'s only proper streets lead north and south from it, parallel to the beach. The plaza has a small church, a baseball court and a taxi rank, and hosts a produce market on Wednesdays. It's also home to the wonderful Alma Libre (☎ 998/871-0713, 🌐 www.almalibrebooks.com; Oct–May Tues–Sat 10am–3pm & 6–9pm, Sun 4–9pm), probably Mexico's most extensive second-hand English-language **bookshop**, with some twenty thousand volumes to choose from, including a solid selection of books about the area's natural and archeological attractions. You can pick up a copy of the free *Sac-Be* newspaper here, which reports on the smaller towns in the Riviera Maya, and if you'll be visiting Puerto Morelos for a while, sign up for the owners' exhaustive email newsletter on everything local, from restaurant openings to speed-bump news. They can also transfer the digital photos from your camera to a CD.

Off the east side of the plaza lies the **beach**, a long wooden **dock** and the old **lighthouse**, a squat little concrete structure knocked Tower of Pisa-style by a hurricane. A newer model has been built behind it, but the old one remains as a town icon. Very attractive and reasonably priced **craftwork**, like hammocks and embroidered clothing, can be found at Hunab-Ku Artesanía, two blocks south of the plaza on Avenida Rojo Gómez. Here you can often see the artisans at work making their goods.

With a thriving stretch of the Mesoamerican Barrier Reef only 600m offshore, Puerto Morelos is a great place to **dive** or **snorkel** – and, because the area sees nowhere near the traffic of Cozumel or Playa del Carmen, it's also a good spot for novices to start. A national marine park since 2000, the reef can be visited only with a guide, who will take you to shallow coral gardens or, for more advanced divers, a couple of wreck sites. Long-established Almost Heaven Adventures, on the plaza, offers certification courses and one- and two-tank dives (M\$400–550), as well as **sport-fishing** charters (around M\$2250 for up to four people; 5–6hr) and snorkelling trips (M\$220 per person; 2hr). Dive Puerto Morelos, on Avenida Rojo Gómez just north of the plaza (☎ 998/206-9084, 🌐 www.divepuertomorelos.com), is another reliable, informed outfit, offering trips to the local reef, as well as to inland cenotes and Cozumel.

## Eating and drinking

Most of Puerto Morelos's restaurants and nightlife are on the town plaza, a cheerful spot for dinner, followed by a cold beer or an evening stroll. The bar at the *Hacienda Morelos* hotel occasionally hosts **live music** and parties, as do a few restaurants. Exceptionally cheap and delicious snacks can be found at *La Guadalupana II*, a taco stand on the northwest corner of the plaza, and *El Tío*, just north of the plaza on Avenida Melgar, which does shrimp tacos in the morning and *tortas* and *panuchos* at lunch.

## The ferry to Cozumel

The **car ferry** to Cozumel officially departs from a pier south of Puerto Morelos twice daily (except Sun), at 5am and 2pm, returning from Cozumel at 10am and 6pm; given the price (M$750 per car, plus M$50 per passenger), the time required (at least 1hr wait, 2hr crossing) and the erratic nature of the service (☎998/871-0008 to check if it's running), it's a much better idea to catch the ferry at Playa del Carmen (see p.131) and leave your car on the mainland if necessary.

### Cafés

**Caffé del Puerto** Av Melgar just south of the plaza. Stop off at this casual spot at lunchtime for inexpensive salads and sandwiches (about M$45); an even better deal is the M$100 set menu at dinner, with a daily changing menu that reflects the owners' eclectic tastes. Go early, as they sometimes run out of dishes.

**Le Marlin Bleu** South side of the plaza. French-inspired dishes are on the menu, but this place is best for tacos in all forms, from shrimp to *arrachera*. It's pricier than *La Guadalupana*, but it has a pleasant café atmosphere and is open at lunchtime too. Thurs–Tues 11am–3pm, 6.30–10pm.

**Mama's** Av Niños Héroes three blocks north of the plaza. Homely American-owned breakfast and lunch joint, offering breakfast burritos with veggie chorizo (M$50), oatmeal, fruit smoothies and a wide range of baked goods. Tues–Sat 7.30am–4pm, Sun 8.30am–1pm.

### Restaurants

**Hola Asia** South side of the plaza. Get your fix of General Tso's chicken (M$60) at this nouveau noodle house, or sample other Asian delicacies such as Thai fish with tamarind (M$90) or Indonesian-style coconut shrimp (M$110). The rooftop tiki bar is nice at sunset – and the main expat hangout in town. Mon–Sat 5–11pm, Sun 3–11pm.

**John Gray's Kitchen** Av Niños Héroes north of the plaza ☎998/871-0665. Visitors from Cancún often make the short drive down for dinner at this small, casually elegant restaurant. The owner is an ex-*Ritz-Carlton* chef, and his gourmet background shows: the daily menu features simple, smart combos like pan-roasted duck breast with chipotle, tequila and honey, or mac-and-cheese with shrimp and truffle oil. With most entrées under M$200, it's quite a bargain too. No credit cards. Closed Sun.

**El Nopal** South side of the plaza. This casual, quick-service eatery maintains a small buffet of Mexican and international food, all prepared very well and fresh-tasting. At just M$50 for a main and two sides, it's also a good deal. Closed Sun.

**La Petita** Av Melgar half a block north of the plaza. This small wooden house is a fishermen's hangout and a local favourite for enjoying the catch of the day, sold by the kilo and available fried, grilled or in a ceviche. A whole *pescado frito* and a few beers will set you back about M$100.

**Spaghettino** Av Rojo Gómez north of the plaza. An informal, inexpensive Italian place with a Euro café feel. Pizza, panini and handmade pastas are on the menu.

### Bars

**Don Pepe Olé** Av Rojo Gómez north of the plaza. A sometimes rowdy local bar scene, which starts in the afternoon. Karaoke is the entertainment of choice once the sun goes down, and the Mexican dinner menu is quite good.

**Cantina Habañero** Av Rojo Gómez north of the plaza. Directly across the street from *Don Pepe Olé*, this is the more expat-friendly bar in town, with classic rock on the stereo and plenty of guys telling fish tales.

## Around Puerto Morelos

Although you'll find little to do in the town of Puerto Morelos, the surrounding area contains quite a few natural attractions that you can visit on half- or full-day trips. One great source of knowledge about the area's natural and social history is Maya Echo (☎987/871-0136, ☮www.mayaecho.com), an organization dedicated to the conservation of Maya culture and spirituality. The group leads tailor-made tours (starting at about M$400) into the forest and to local villages, where the Maya will teach you about their way of life and beliefs.

## North of town

Just 2km north of town, across the street from the *Ceiba del Mar* resort, a board-walk runs for about 1km through the **mangroves**. Built and maintained by the hotel, it's a free access point to the swamplands that are home to more than three hundred bird species, such as roseate spoonbills, herons and many migratory songbirds. The boardwalk provides a unique opportunity to explore this eco-system on your own, as the swamps, also home to crocodiles, aren't safe to wade through without a guide. Go early in the morning or late in the afternoon to catch the most bird activity.

Playa Acamaya, 5km north of town, near the *Acamaya Reef Park* campground, is known for **kiteboarding**. Ikarus, the major school in the area, gives most of its classes here, and can lend you one clunky board if you haven't brought your own gear; you can also take lessons and rent equipment from their shop in Playa del Carmen (see p.126). South of town about 2km is another good **beach**; head past the car ferry, following signs for Marina El Cid. The stretch of sand immediately south of the marina, called Punta Brava, is usually clean and empty on weekdays.

## La Ruta de los Cenotes and the Jardín Botánico

On the main highway 1km south of the turn-off to town, a concrete pseudo-Maya arch marks the start of **La Ruta de los Cenotes**, a dirt road that cuts through pristine forest punctuated by swimming holes. Government efforts to attract visitors to the cenotes seem to have begun and ended with the construction of the arch in 2003, so you'll likely have the forest to yourself. Sixteen kilometres along the road past the arch is the very small village of **Central Vallarta**, a former camp for *chicleros* harvesting sap for the chewing-gum industry. The first cenote, which requires a bit of bushwhacking to reach, is **Siete Bocas**, a network of underground caverns often visited by divers; follow the signs at Central Vallarta and hike 25 minutes off the road. If you're just intent on swimming, however, you'll have more fun at **Boca del Puma**, about 1km past the village on the right side of the road, where the owner has installed a long zip-line ride through the trees and an observation tower; mountain bikes are also for rent. **Verde Lucero**, immediately up the road on the left, is also a pretty swimming spot, named for its emerald-green water. At the end of La Ruta you'll reach **Tres Bocas** (look for the surfboard sign), a network of several small cenotes linked by the barest of paths through the forest; a few rustic cabins are for rent here (**❻**). All of the pools charge M$50 admission, and Boca del Puma asks an additional M$50 for its zip-line ride. The road is bumpy but passable by car, or you can hire a taxi at the Puerto Morelos junction (M$400 for 2hr), but you'll get more out of your visit with a guide who's familiar with the local plants and animals that you'll pass en route – Goyo's Info Center, on the north side of the plaza (☎998/871-0189, ⓦwww.mayajungle.com), leads half-day tours (M$400 including lunch); Dive Puerto Morelos (see p.119) also runs **snorkelling** and **diving** trips to the cenotes.

On the east side of the highway, opposite the turn for the cenote route, is the **Jardín Botánico Dr Alfredo Barrera Marín** (also signposted as Yaax Ché; Mon–Sat 9am–5pm; M$70). The 148-acre botanical gardens provide a good introduction to the peninsula's native flora. A three-kilometre path leads through medicinal plants, ferns, palms, some tumbledown Maya ruins and a mock-up *chiclero* camp, where you can see how the sap of the *zapote* (sapodilla) tree is tapped before being used in the production of gum. A longer trail leads through an untended chunk of forest (home to spider monkeys, though they usually keep out of sight) to a viewing platform above the canopy. Anyone particularly interested in botany should hire a guide, either at the site or through one of the several tour operators in Puerto Morelos that run day-trips.

# Punta Bete

The coast between Puerto Morelos and Playa del Carmen is almost solidly occupied by **resorts** large and small. But the sedate beach area of **PUNTA BETE**, some 10km south of Puerto Morelos, with its turn-off signposted just south of the Cristal/Coca-Cola bottling plant around Km 62, is a throwback to less developed times, with little more than a couple of rustic hotels and ramshackle restaurants serving the classic beach meal of ceviche and grilled fish along with ice-cold beers. The beach itself is a bit rocky and nowhere near as beautiful as those in Cancún or Playa del Carmen, though it does have the advantage of being uncrowded.

Punta Bete is about 4km from the highway. About 2km along, the road forks, and to the left you'll find the entrance to the very exclusive *Ikal del Mar* (T984/877-3000, W www.ikaldelmar.com; ❾), an extremely ritzy but unobtrusive hideaway, and then, at the beach, *Los Piños* (T984/873-1506; ❺), a small, somewhat dull concrete block. The best option is a bit back from the sea: charming Swiss-owned *Coco's Cabañas* (T998/874-7056, E marsilhel@hotmail.com; ❻), with five individual cabañas, a small pool and a restaurant serving very good European cuisine.

The right-hand road leads, in roughly the same distance, to Playa Xcalacoco and *Juanito's* (reservations in Cozumel on T987/872-5009; ❺), which has **camping** space (M$45), simple rooms and sun chairs and umbrellas for rent to day-trippers. The **restaurant** dishes up reasonably priced basic Mexican food and fish (daily 8am–8pm). Continuing south past *Juanito's*, at the end of the road, the *Bahía Xcalacoco* hotel (T984/804-5848; ❺) maintains a few very pleasant candlelit rooms. The helpful owners, a local family, can arrange snorkelling and fishing trips and fetch groceries from town. You can also **camp** here (M$40). Second-class buses will drop you at the turn-off to Punta Bete, as will *colectivos* from Playa del Carmen or Cancún, but it's a hike down to the beach. A cab from Playa del Carmen costs about M$100.

About 1km north of Punta Bete proper, the no-fuss resort of *La Posada de Capitán Lafitte* (T984/873-0212, W www.capitanlafitte.com; ❾) is totally relaxing and very welcoming to families. Some repeat guests have been coming since the place opened more than thirty years ago. Rates include breakfast and dinner. Should you be looking to splurge, head 10km south of Punta Bete to one of the finest luxury hotels on the coast, *Maroma* (T998/872-8200, W www.orient-expresshotels.com; ❾). Elegant yet informal, with a strong Mexican style, the hotel has grown almost organically over three decades, developing from the original owners' personal home into a clutch of white-stucco guestrooms tucked amid palm trees. The personal touch is evident in services like the intense *temazcal* sauna ritual, still run by a friend of the former owners, while the excellent haute Latin restaurant meets the highest standards.

# Playa del Carmen and around

Once a soporific fishing village, **PLAYA DEL CARMEN** (known simply as Playa) has mushroomed in recent years, leaving repeat visitors dumbfounded

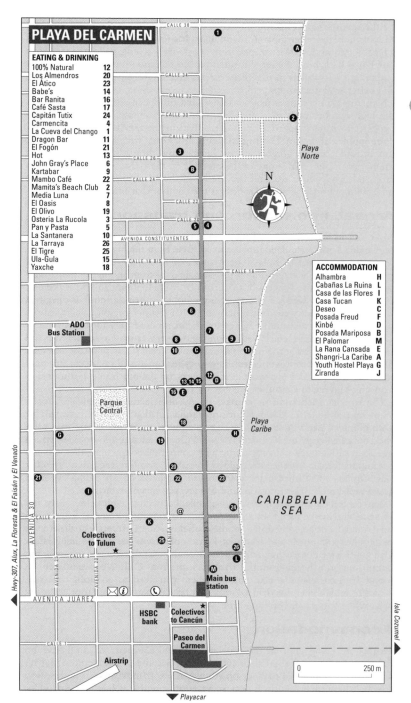

# PLAYA DEL CARMEN

**EATING & DRINKING**

| | |
|---|---|
| 100% Natural | 12 |
| Los Almendros | 20 |
| El Ático | 23 |
| Babe's | 14 |
| Bar Ranita | 16 |
| Café Sasta | 17 |
| Capitán Tutix | 24 |
| Carmencita | 4 |
| La Cueva del Chango | 1 |
| Dragon Bar | 11 |
| El Fogón | 21 |
| Hot | 13 |
| John Gray's Place | 6 |
| Kartabar | 9 |
| Mambo Café | 22 |
| Mamita's Beach Club | 2 |
| Media Luna | 7 |
| El Oasis | 8 |
| El Olivo | 19 |
| Osteria La Rucola | 3 |
| Pan y Pasta | 5 |
| La Santanera | 10 |
| La Tarraya | 26 |
| El Tigre | 25 |
| Ula-Gula | 15 |
| Yaxche | 18 |

**ACCOMMODATION**

| | |
|---|---|
| Alhambra | H |
| Cabañas La Ruina | L |
| Casa de las Flores | I |
| Casa Tucan | K |
| Deseo | C |
| Posada Freud | F |
| Kinbé | D |
| Posada Mariposa | B |
| El Palomar | M |
| La Rana Cansada | E |
| Shangri-La Caribe | A |
| Youth Hostel Playa | G |
| Ziranda | J |

CALLE 38

CALLE 34

CALLE 32

CALLE 30

CALLE 28

CALLE 26

CALLE 24

CALLE 22

CALLE 20

AVENIDA CONSTITUYENTES

CALLE 16 BIS

CALLE 16

CALLE 14 BIS

CALLE 14

ADO Bus Station

CALLE 12

Parque Central

CALLE 10

CALLE 8

Playa Norte

N

Playa Caribe

Playa Caribe

CARIBBEAN SEA

Colectivos to Tulum

CALLE 4

CALLE 2

AVENIDA 30

AVENIDA 25

AVENIDA 20

AVENIDA 15

AVENIDA 14

AVENIDA 1

Colectivos to Cancún

Main bus station

AVENIDA JUÁREZ

HSBC bank

Paseo del Carmen

CALLE 1

Airstrip

0        250 m

Hwy-307, Alux, La Floresta & El Faisán y El Venado

Playacar

Isla Cozumel

by the town's transformation into a high-style party town for Europeans and Mexico City jet-setters. Like Cancún, Playa has few historic underpinnings. It's a bit pricey, and the town's main centre of activity – a long, pedestrianized strip one block back from the sea – is often packed to capacity with visitors rapidly emptying their wallets in pavement cafés, souvenir and silver-jewellery outlets and designer clothes shops.

Nonetheless, Playa does retain a rather chic European atmosphere, owing to the high number of Italian- and French-owned businesses, and, compared to hyperactive, Americanized Cancún just 60km to the north, it seems positively cosmopolitan and calm. The **nightlife** in particular is excellent, and you'll find sophisticated cuisine, hotels for most budgets and diverse shops. The beach at the north end of town is one of the prettiest on the coast, with dazzling white sand and gentle, clear sea, and the stretch of the Mesoamerican Barrier Reef offshore is almost as spectacular here as the coral in Cozumel.

## Arrival, information and transport

Most visitors arrive on short-haul buses at the main **bus station**, at the corner of Avenida 5 and Avenida Juárez, the main street from the highway to the beach. (Another station, on Avenida 20 between calles 12 and 14, handles longer-haul trips on ADO.) If you're heading to Playa directly from the international **airport** in Cancún, the Riviera bus (11 daily, 9.30am–8.30pm; 55min) is the best deal, for M$65 or US$7. Otherwise, any number of private minibus operators will take you directly to your hotel (about M$150 per person). There's also a small **airstrip** on the south edge of town, but it's used only for short hops to Cozumel or Chichén Itzá. If you're coming by **ferry from Cozumel**, you will probably be dropped at the old plaza near Calle 1 Sur. If you're on an Ultramar boat, there's a chance it will be running to its new pier (still under construction in 2005) at the end of Avenida Constituyentes, on the north side. For information on the ferry to Cozumel, see box on p.131.

The **tourist information centre**, on Avenida Juárez at Avenida 15 (daily 9am–9pm; ☎984/873-2804, ✆turismo@solidaridad.gob.mx), is very helpful, with bilingual staff who'll do their best to answer any enquiries you may have. Pick up a free copy of the useful *Playa del Carmen* ad and info booklet, which has hotel and restaurant listings, some with coupons. Look in upmarket bars and restaurants for *La Quinta*, a free glossy magazine detailing the town's trendier side. Online, you can plan for your trip or get news on upcoming events at ⓦwww.playadelcarmeninfo.com and ⓦwww.playamayanews.com.

The central area of town is very walkable, but riding a **bicycle** is easy and pleasant, and a bike path runs along Avenida 10. You can hire **taxis** from stands on Avenida 5, or flag one down on the trafficked streets. To reach smaller towns or beaches just north and south of Playa, **colectivos** are the easiest option: Cancún service departs frequently from Avenida Juárez in front of the main bus station, and vans heading south to Tulum leave from Calle 2 between avenidas 5 and 10. Taxis can also take you anywhere you need to go along the coast – they're more expensive than *colectivos*, but far cheaper than any tour company, even when you pay for waiting time.

## Accommodation

**Hotels** are being built all the time in Playa del Carmen, so you'll have no difficulty finding a room. Prices are dropping because of competition, but it's still virtually impossible to find something for less than M$300 in high season – which here includes the European vacation months of July and August, as well as mid–December through April. In general, the farther from the sea, the cheaper the accommodation; the central beach is currently quite eroded, so waterfront hotels are not good value. The town has several decent budget hotels, and two places with space for **camping** – the beachfront *Cabañas La Ruina* (M$60) and *Youth Hostel Playa* (M$45).

## Hotels

**Alhambra** on the beach at C 8 ☎984/873-0735, ⓦwww.alhambra-hotel.net. With gleaming white a/c rooms and a small pool, this is the strongest beachfront option. The exotic, Moorish-looking building seems a bit out of place, but the pristine palace is a great locale for the daily yoga classes and treatments offered by the resident massage therapist. ❽

**Casa de las Flores** Av 20 no. 150, between C 4 and C 6 ☎984/873-2898, ⓦwww .hotelcasadelasflores.com. Beautiful grounds with colonial-style rooms and a small swimming pool. Very attractive for the price, and worth the four-block walk to the beach. ❻–❼

**Casa Tucan** C 4 between Av 10 and Av 15 ☎984/873-0283, ⓦwww.casatucan.de. A Playa institution, this is still one of its best bargains. Offers spotless rooms (some with palapa roofs and shared bath) and excellent-value studios, a big swimming pool, a friendly restaurant and a generally mellow vibe. Book well in advance. ❹

**Deseo** Av 5 at C 12 ☎984/879-3620, ⓦwww .hoteldeseo.com. Ultra-trendy boutique hotel with loads of high-design details, like mellow electronica piped into the minimalist rooms. Rates include a generous continental breakfast. (Also look for the newer *Básico* hotel, which the same owners opened down the street at Calle 10: equally sharp design, for slightly lower rates.) ❾

**Posada Freud** Av 5 between C 8 and C 10 ☎984/873-0601, ⓦwww.posadafreud.com. Pretty rooms with colourful details smack in the middle of the action at reasonable (and often negotiable) rates. Ground-floor rooms can be a little loud – it may be worth opting for a back, upstairs room or, if you have a big group, the three-bedroom penthouse. ❻–❼

**Kinbé** C 10 between Av 1 and Av 5 ☎984/873-0441, ⓦwww.kinbe.com. Small, friendly Italian-run hotel with comfortable rooms (all with a/c). A small roof deck and a couple of rooms have great views of the water, one block away; guests get discounts at the hip *Mamita's Beach Club* in Playa Norte. ❻

**Posada Mariposa** Av 5 between C 24 and C 26 ☎984/873-3886, ⓦwww.posada-mariposa.com. Quiet hotel filled with overgrown greenery in the Playa Norte area; apartments with balconies and full kitchens are also available. ❻

**La Rana Cansada** C 10 no. 132, between Av 5 and Av 10 ☎984/873-0389, ⓦwww.ranacansada .com. One of the oldest hotels in Playa, *La Rana* is friendly, sparkling clean and laid-back. It has communal kitchen facilities and various room options, including a smart two-level suite with beer delivery by bucket from the bar downstairs. ❻

**Shangri-La Caribe** C 38 on the beach, reservations in the US on ☎1-800/538-6802, ⓦwww .mexicoholiday.com. A small-scale resort, located out of Playa proper but an easy walk down the beach to the action. The rooms are very well laid-out, so the grounds never feel crowded, and the sand here is fine and deep. Rates include breakfast and dinner. ❾

**Ziranda** C 4 between C 15 and C 20 ☎984/873-3929, ⓦwww.hotellaziranda.com. Large rooms with balconies (and some with a/c) overlooking lush greenery and a big, well-groomed backyard. A solid bargain and seldom full. ❺

## Hostels

**Cabañas La Ruina** C 2 on the seafront ☎984/873-0405. Playa's most sociable and economical place to stay, still giving backpackers a slice of the good life on the beach despite large hotels looming all around. That said, the really desirable cabañas are comparable in price to regular hotels; camping and hammock hooks are a good deal, though, at M$60. ❸–❺

**El Palomar** Av 5 between Av Juárez and C 2 ☎984/803-2606, ⓦwww.elpalomarhostel.com. A bit tidier than *La Ruina*, and still close to the beach, this hostel has the advantage of sand-free floors and big, well-ventilated single-sex dorm rooms (M$100). The few private rooms with a shared bath are slightly overpriced, though, at M$300. There's a shared kitchen on the roof deck.

**Youth Hostel Playa** Av 25 at C 8 ☎984/803-3277, ⓦwww.hostelplaya.com. A hike from the beach, but you'll find cheap, comfortable beds and space for camping. Head here if there's no room at *La Ruina* or *El Palomar*, or if you just want a quieter atmosphere. M$90

# The town

**Avenida 5**, called La Quinta, is Playa del Carmen's main tourist thoroughfare. Once a dirt track dotted with a few cabañas, it's now a pedestrian zone stretching 2km north from Avenida Juárez and lined with cocktail lounges, souvenir shops and stylish restaurants.

The big local hangout is the **Parque Central**, completed in early 2004. In front of the equally new town hall on Avenida 20 between calles 8 and 10, it has a small amphitheatre that occasionally hosts theatre and musical performances (check with the tourist office or Ⓦwww.playamayanews.com for schedules). To one side of the park, six stelae are inscribed with the verses of the "Himno de Quintana Roo," an ode to the fledgling state's pioneer spirit and its role as a refuge for the indigenous Maya – very inspiring, but really, all the attention is on the skateboarders who cruise the curving concrete ramps here.

## The beaches

One block east of La Quinta, the main **town beach** has become noticeably eroded in recent years, with a narrowing sandy frontage and rocks popping up in the water and farther back. As the untended sand is particularly sparse, it's worth shelling out a few dollars for chair rental at one of the hotels or beach clubs, some of which also rent kayaks (M$100/hr) and run combo sailing-snorkelling trips (M$300 per person; 2hr). Or simply enjoy a drink at one of the numerous bars and restaurants and take in the lively social scene, which kicks off when happy hour starts, around 5pm.

The better beach, a broad expanse of deep, silky sand that drops into waist-high green water with mid-size swells, lies to the north, past the Ultramar ferry pier at the end of Avenida Constituyentes. This area is the newer, quieter neighbourhood called **Playa Norte** (North Beach), also known as Little Italy. You can check out the several beach clubs that occupy the waterfront, or you can wander farther up the shore and stake out your own spot in the untended areas. If you'd like to take a short **snorkel tour,** the dive shop at *Mamita's Beach Club*, Sealife (Ⓣ984/877-8727, Ⓦwww.sealifedivers.com), runs trips for the very reasonable price of M$200 (1hr 30min); the same operation also specializes in inland **cave diving**.

For anyone interested in **scuba diving**, Tank-Ha, on Avenida 5 between calles 8 and 10 (Ⓣ984/873-0302, Ⓦwww.tankha.com), is a good place to start. The shop offers PADI certification courses (M$3500), one- and two-tank dives (M$400–600) and multiday dive packages (from M$1620) as well as twice-daily snorkelling tours (9am & 1.30pm; M$300; 3hr). **Kiteboarding** specialists Ikarus give basic instructions on the beach in Playa, then take you up the coast near Puerto Morelos for in-water lessons; visit the shop on Av 5 at C 20 (Ⓣ984/803-3490, Ⓦwww.kiteboardmexico.com) for details.

## Playacar

The south side of Playa del Carmen abuts a giant, 880-acre condo development called **Playacar**. Its main road is winding Avenida Xaman-Ha, which makes its way from the entrance off Calle 1 Sur down through the complex, with cul-de-sacs leading to beach properties, tennis courts and more than fifteen remnants of Mayan structures; some are marked with signs off the main artery. Playacar's beaches, if they're not fronting a big resort, are often deserted, and it's a particularly good place for a shady bike ride. On the inland side of Avenida Xaman-Ha is a vast **golf course** (Ⓣ984/873-0624, Ⓦwww.palace-resorts.com). An **aviary**, also on Xaman-Ha (daily 9am–5pm; M$150), is overpriced, but offers an opportunity to check out some sixty species of native birds, including toucans and flamingos, if you won't otherwise have a chance to see them in the southern jungles or on the Gulf coast. If you're staying in Playacar, you can walk up to town in 45 minutes or half an hour, depending on where you're starting from.

## Eating

Playa del Carmen is heaving with **restaurants** of every kind, and even the traditional Mexican places stay open late. The quality of food here is often very good (particularly Italian), but prices are relatively high. The pedestrianized section of **La Quinta** is lined end-to-end with dining tables where you can eat all sorts of cuisine; if you're on a budget, however, you'll need to search out where locals go, like the excellent taco carts on Avenida Juárez in front of the bus station or the inexpensive *comida corrida* and grilled-chicken places starting around Avenida 10 and going farther back from the sea.

### Cafés

**Café Sasta** Av 5 between C 8 and C 10. Pastries and espresso are the main items at this Italian coffeehouse, and the sidewalk tables are an ideal spot for watching the fashion parade along La Quinta.

**Carmencita** Av 5 at C 20. An Argentine café where modern decor belies a traditional kitchen in the back. Empanadas are on the menu, as are hearty sandwiches like grilled steak or chorizo with *chimichurri*.

**La Cueva del Chango** C 38 between Av 5 and the beach. Local favourite for long, late breakfasts or lazy lunches, perfect after a morning stroll up the beach. Good granola, crepes with honey, tasty empanadas and house-roasted coffee served in a big garden. Closes at 2pm Sun.

**La Floresta** West side of Hwy-307, just north of Av Juárez. This big palapa next to the highway is a road-tripper's delight, serving overstuffed *tacos de camarón*, the perfect marriage of batter-fried shrimp, mayo and chunky tomato salsa. Should you need variety, seafood cocktails and ceviches are available too.

**Hot** C 10 between Av 5 and Av 10. Stop by this bakery with a small café for fresh muffins, bagels, brownies and giant cinnamon rolls. Heartier eaters can choose from omelettes and sandwiches, and eggs Benedict on the weekends. Another branch is on C 12 Bis north of Av 5.

**Pan y Pasta** Av 5 at C 20. If you're staying in Playa Norte, head here for excellent European-style pastries and espresso in the morning. They also sell fresh handmade pasta for cooking at home.

### Restaurants

**100% Natural** Av 5 between C 10 and C 12. Like the Cancún branch (see p.95), this link in the local mini-chain serves fresh, often vegetarian Mexican food along with big stuffed sandwiches and fresh fruit juices. Not the cheapest, but reliable and set in a big garden.

**Los Almendros** Av 10 at C 6. No relation to the Ticul classic spot, but tasty food all the same. This traditional Mexican restaurant with an outdoor grill serves delicious tacos and a daily *comida corrida* that's available for both lunch and dinner (M$40). Closed Mon.

**Babe's** C 10 between Av 5 and Av 10. This Swedish-owned Thai noodle house – which also serves a fine Cuban mojito – typifies Playa's international hodgepodge. Dishes like *pad thai* start at M$45.

**El Faisán y El Venado** C 2 just east of Hwy-307. Very well-priced Yucatecan specialities such as *panuchos* and *carne ahumada* (smoked pork in a citrus marinade) are the draw at this sprawling family-friendly restaurant. Lunch only.

**El Fogón** Av 30 at C 6. A basic, brightly lit taco joint that's generally mobbed with locals; anything off the grill is recommended. No booze is served, but you can wash down all the meat with a big selection of *aguas frescas*. There's another branch on Avenida 30 near Calle 28.

**John Gray's Place** C Corazón, north of Av 5 between C 12 and C 14 ☎984/803-3689. An outpost of an excellent restaurant in Puerto Morelos (see p.120), with the same varied, tasty menu (spinach-and-bacon salads, grilled fish with mango salsa) served in the second-floor dining room. In the cosy bar area, try the signature "smoky margarita" made with mescal. Closed Mon.

**Media Luna** Av 5 between C 12 and C 14. Eclectic veggie and seafood restaurant – think *chiles rellenos* presented as a lasagna – with a well-priced lunch special, big healthful sandwiches and delicious breakfasts of fruit salad, French toast and pancakes. Prices look a little steep on paper, but portions are enormous.

**El Oasis** C 12 between Av 5 and Av 10. *El Oasis* earned its reputation selling shrimp tacos out by the highway, but this new branch has a fuller menu of seafood dishes. The tacos aren't quite as good as *La Floresta*'s, but they're the best you can get around La Quinta. Closed Sun.

**El Olivo** Av 10 between C 6 and C 8. A charming and not terribly expensive shoebox-size tapas bar, complete with mini portions of *tortilla española* (potato omelette) as well as savoury seafood snacks, starting at M$30.

**Osteria La Rucola** C 26 between Av 5 and Av 10 ☏ 984/879-3359. A little patch of northern Italy in a quiet Playa Norte block, with excellent dishes like a salad of grilled octopus and arugula (M$70) and

handmade pasta with rosemary, shrimp and black olives (M$90). Closed Wed.

**La Tarraya** On the seafront at C 2. This local institution has been open for more than thirty years, well before Playa was a gleam in a developer's eye. It still serves standard beach fare like ceviches and *pescado frito* (M$90 per kilo) with plenty of cold beer.

**Yaxche** C 8 between Av 5 and Av 10 ☏ 984/873-2502. Haute Maya is the agenda at this gracious restaurant: (very) hot peppers stuffed with *cochinita pibil* (shredded roast pork), a Yucatecan shrimp gratin or lobster flambéed in *xtabentun*, a local liqueur. With entrees between M$120 and M$200, it's very reasonably priced, considering the level of service and presentation.

## Drinking and nightlife

At night, La Quinta becomes a two-kilometre-long street party, and you can wander down the strip of **bars** and **lounges** well into the night, listening to all sorts of music – from salsa and reggae to 1970s classics – and for most people, the night winds up with dancing on the sand at one of the casual beach **clubs**. Drinks aren't cheap, but don't let that stop you from going out, as it's easy to meet people, and plentiful happy-hour specials can ease you into the night without depleting funds too rapidly.

### Bars

**El Ático** C 6 between Av 5 and the beach. This moodily lit, self-titled "art bar" has a very strong Goth sensibility, and equally strong cocktails. A refreshing change from sunny beach culture – or completely pointless, depending on your mood.

**Bar Ranita** C 10 between Av 5 and Av 10. A crew of regulars – mostly expats – hang out at the horseshoe-shaped bar in this snug and mellow wood-panelled spot. A welcome break from Playa's generally top-volume scene.

**Deseo** Av 5 at C 12. The poolside bar at the stylish hotel draws its inspiration from Miami Beach, with beds to lounge on, over-the-top cocktails and bartenders as attractive and ostentatious as the crowd. Drinks are pricey for Mexico (M$80), but this is the pinnacle of Playa style.

**Kartabar** C 12 at Av 1 ☏ 984/873-2228. A stylish lounge, all black and white with enormous candles, offering Lebanese finger food, loads of cocktails and the obligatory belly dancer. The crowd is very high-society Playa.

**El Tigre** Av 10 between C 2 and C 4. Good local spot for beers, ceviches and ridiculously generous *botanas*. Women will probably feel more comfortable accompanied by a man; the billiards area upstairs is men-only. Closes by 5pm.

**Ula-Gula** Av 5 at C 10. This small candlelit bar on a corner of La Quinta is a prime spot for people-

watching, and a DJ usually provides a cool house soundtrack. The restaurant upstairs is uneven, but the simpler dishes, such as the grilled sweetbreads, are delicious.

### Clubs

**Alux** Av Juárez, 400m west of Hwy-307 ☏ 984/803-0713. A trek from the main drag – tell the cab driver "ah-LOOSH" – but worth a visit for its unique setting deep inside a large cave. Dinner of rich, if somewhat overpriced, French-tropical dishes begins at 8pm; a DJ or a floor show of belly dancers and jazz musicians gets started around 10pm. Usually no cover, but drinks are M$70 and up.

**Capitán Tutix** On the beach at C 2. *The* pick-up joint in town; this jam-packed bar and disco has live music every night (10pm–midnight) and a predominantly young party crowd. For the after-party, *Lumpax*, next door, takes over when *Tutix* closes. No cover.

**Dragon Bar** On the beach at C 12 at the *Blue Parrot* hotel. Once legendary, this open-air club isn't too distinct from other places with tables on the sand and swings in lieu of barstools. Nonetheless, it has a popular happy hour, as well as live music in the afternoons and assorted dancers and fire-spinners at night. No cover.

**Mambo Café** C 6 between Av 5 and Av 10 ☏ 984/803-2656. A smaller version of the popular

Cancún club, this space has an excellent sound system and a roster of big-name Cuban and Dominican bands. Wednesday is ladies night, with open bar from 10pm till midnight. Cover is usually M$50. Closed Mon.

**Mamita's Beach Club** On the beach at C 28. The single coolest place to be during the day, with plenty of room to spread out and a hip but not overbearing party atmosphere, complete with a live DJ. Chairs and umbrellas are for rent, but you can spread a towel at the water's edge and still get waiter service for drinks if you like; the food is very good (if a tad pricey). The smaller bar on the northern edge often stays open into the evening, and the club occasionally hosts blowout nighttime dance parties.

**La Santanera** C 14 between Av 5 and Av 10. Super-stylish club with international DJ cred (Rob Garza of global mixmasters Thievery Corporation is a partner), a comfortable, breezy lounge area, diverse music and good strong drinks. The scantily clad party crowd – equal parts visitors and residents – usually staggers out around 5am. No cover.

## Shopping

Of all the beach towns, Playa offers the most stylish **shopping**, from folk art to designer flip-flops, though very little of it is cheap. You'll also find numerous pharmacies and giant souvenir marts. Prices are fixed at glossier places on La Quinta, but sometimes you can bargain in smaller shops on side streets.

**Ambar Mexicano** Av 5 between C 4 and C 6. Rich chunks of amber in distinctive, modern silver settings, ranging in price from relatively low to stratospheric (for the largest pieces with insects preserved inside). The sales environment is blessedly low-pressure, compared to many of the big jewellery stores on the strip.

**La Calaca** Av 5 between C 12 and C 14. A well-stocked folk-art shop specializing in carved wood masks. Smaller souvenir items include skeleton dioramas, punched-tin lanterns and painted gourds.

**Casita de la Música** Av 5 between Av Juárez and C 2. Pick up the latest Mexican pop hits here, or choose from a decent selection of more traditional Yucatecan *trova* ballads and folk music from elsewhere in Mexico.

**Idé** Av 5 at C 16. Very creative, modern jewellery incorporating semiprecious stones, particularly opals. Pricier than other silver vendors, but the intricate work is unique and done on the premises.

**Juan's Hammocks** Av 10 between Av Juárez and C 2, next to the Roger's Boots storefront. At first glance this small shack doesn't look promising (it doubles as a money exchange), but it's a great source for well-priced, good-quality hammocks, available in a rainbow of tightly woven colourful nylon threads. (Avoid the thick-string cheapies – they're uncomfortable and won't hold their shape.)

**Mayan Arts** Av 5 between C 6 and C 8. Tucked in a small garden courtyard (look for the stained-glass "El Jardín de Marieta" sign), this excellent gallery is packed with comical and grotesque wood masks, folk paintings and beautiful antique *huipiles*, the intricately embroidered Maya women's smocks. The latter are expensive, but a good piece shows a level of craftsmanship that you can no longer buy new at any price.

**Paseo del Carmen** Av 5 at C 1 Sur. Major attractions at this stylish open-air mall include hip Euro labels such as Custo Barcelona and Bershka, as well as a few cool bars and lounges like Havana import *La Bodeguita del Medio*, which specializes in mojitos.

**Pygmees** Av 5 between C 8 and C 10. A funky clothing, accessories and houseware store featuring whimsical kids' outfits from French label Poudre de Perlimpinpin and bright asymmetrical cotton clothing for men and women.

**Qué Pequeño es el Mundo** C 1 Sur between Av 20 and Av 25. The friendly and informed staff are quick to make recommendations on English and Spanish titles alike. Come here to stock up on Maya and Mexican history, or just good beach novels. Closed Sun.

## Listings

**Airport** The small airstrip just south of town handles short jaunts, chiefly to Cozumel, but also to Chichén Itzá and other key Maya sites; operators include Aeroferinco (☎984/873-0636) and Aeroméxico (☎984/873-0350, ⓦwww.aeromexico.com).

**Banks** HSBC, Av Juárez between Av 10 and Av 15 (Mon–Fri 9am–7pm); Bancomer, Av Juárez between Av 25 and Av 30 (Mon–Fri 9am–4pm). Both have ATMs.

**Buses** The distinction between Playa's two bus

△ Mamita's Beach Club

## The ferry to Cozumel

Two competing **ferry** services depart from Playa del Carmen to San Miguel in Cozumel nearly every hour between 6am and 11pm. Mexico Waterjets is marginally preferable for the 45-minute crossing, as its air-conditioned boats are more comfortable and a tad faster; the company operates from the pier at Calle 1 Sur, two blocks from the main bus station. The newer Ultramar service, which leaves from the same place (but scheduled to move to a pier on the north side in 2006) for some reason has slower boats. As the price from both companies is the same (M$90, or M$125 for a same-day round-trip ticket), your best bet is to head for a Mexico Waterjets booth and the old pier on the south side – which is also only two blocks from the main bus station. If you have a car, you can leave it in the secure lot behind the bus station for about M$90 per day.

stations is somewhat fluid; typically, long-haul ADO-run trips go from Av 20 between C 12 and C 14, and short-haul services, including Riviera and Mayab buses, leave from the central station, Av Juárez at Av 5. Either way, you can buy tickets for all routes at the central station – just ask which terminal the bus will leave from.

**Car and bike rental** All the large car rental companies have outlets in Playa – most are situated on the main coastal highway at the turn-off into town or in Plaza Marina near the Cozumel ferry pier at C 1 Sur. Try Localiza, Av Juárez between Av 5 and Av 10 (☎984/873-0580). Playa Bike, Av 1 Norte between C 10 and C 12 (☎984/806-0398), rents motorbikes (M$400 per day), bicycles (M$120 per

day) and beach equipment like snorkels and boogie boards.

**Cinema** Cines Hollywood in Plaza Pelicanos, Av 10 at C 10.

**Internet and phone** The streets off Av 5 hold numerous Internet cafés; one on C 4 between Av 5 and Av 10 doubles as a *caseta*. There's also a Telmex *caseta* on Av Juárez between Av 10 and Av 15.

**Laundry** Giracaribe Laundry, Av 10 between C 12 and C 14; Lavandería del Carmen, C 2 between Av 10 and Av 15.

**Post office** Av Juárez between Av 15 and Av 20 (Mon–Fri 8am–2pm); geared to dealing with tourists. The Lista de Correos (postcode 77710) keeps mail for ten days.

## Xcaret

The huge, surprisingly pleasant and wild theme park of **XCARET** (Mon–Sat 8.30am–9.45pm, Sun 8.30am–6pm; M$500; ⓦ www.xcaretcancun.com) is 6km south of Playa del Carmen. Budget travellers and anyone on a longer trip can pass it up, but if your time is limited or you have children to entertain, the park is an opportunity to experience in one place all of the natural attractions of the Yucatán, such as snorkelling through underground caverns or in a fish-filled bay. There's also a vast butterfly habitat, a cave full of bats, a high-tech aquarium and a sea turtle reserve and education centre. You can also catch a live dance performance or visit a "Maya village," complete with artisans working on traditional crafts. An open-air chapel on the park's highest hill offers respite from the crowds, as well as a fine view. Bus-and-entrance packages are available through every big hotel in Cancún and Playa del Carmen. All Mayab buses will stop near Xcaret on Hwy-307 (M$17 for the ten-minute ride from Playa).

# Isla Cozumel

A forty-kilometre-long island directly off the coast from Playa del Carmen, **ISLA COZUMEL** is far larger than Mujeres (see p.100) and, unfortunately, has grown to cater primarily to the mainstream tastes of the cruiseship passengers that put ashore here. During the high season (Nov–April), up to twenty liners a week, each with several thousand passengers, dock at one of the island's three piers, all just south of the main town of **San Miguel** (often called just Cozumel).

Don't be put off by the hordes, though: the huge, diverse reefs that ring much of the coast offer the best diving in Mexico and have been dazzling visitors since Jacques Cousteau first brought them to international attention in the early 1960s. The island, which the Maya dubbed *cuzamil* ("land of the swallows"), is also a destination for birdwatchers, as it's a stopover on migration routes and has several endemic species or variants; Parque Punta Sur, a nature park on the southern tip of the island, is a haven for many of the rarest ones. And the windswept eastern coast, with its deserted beaches and pounding waves, provides a beautiful respite from crowds.

### Some history

In the Terminal Classic period, the few centuries before the Spanish arrived in 1518, the island was a major Maya centre, carrying on sea trade around the coasts of Mexico and as far south as Honduras and perhaps Panama. While this community – one of several along the Yucatán coast that survived the collapse of Classic Maya civilization after 1200 – has long been dismissed by archeologists as the decadent remnant of a moribund society, that theory is now being revised. The community's architecture might have declined in the years between 1200 and the Conquest, but large-scale trade, city specialization in particular crafts and even a degree of mass production are all in evidence at the site of **San Gervasio**, the only extensively excavated ruins on the island. Cozumel's later Maya rulers did not enjoy the same grand style as their forebears, but the rest of an increasingly commercialized population was probably better off. The island itself may even have been an early free-trade zone, where merchants from competing cities could trade peaceably. Whatever the truth, you get little opportunity to judge for yourself – an American air base, built here during World War II, erased all trace of Cozumel's largest ancient city, and the lesser ruins scattered across the roadless interior are mostly unrestored and inaccessible. (The airfield, converted to civilian use, remains the means by which most visitors arrive.)

After about 1600, Cozumel was virtually deserted, more the territory of pirates than any settled population. In the mid-nineteenth century, though, as the bitter Caste Wars (see p.330) between the rebel Maya and the Spanish colonists made life on the peninsula highly dangerous and unstable, the island became a place of refuge, and by the 1880s, the town of **San Miguel** was established as a home for the growing population. Over the years, island culture has developed distinct from that of the mainland, with *cozumeleños* relishing their lifestyle, which is somehow even more easy-going than on the rest of the coast. San Miguel hosts a particularly colourful celebration of **Carnaval**, the decadent week prior to Lent, celebrated with elaborate costumes, colourful parades and exuberant bands and parties.

### Arrival, information and transport

**Arriving by ferry**, you'll be right in the centre of San Miguel, with the plaza just across the street from the pier. From the **airport**, a VW combi service (around M$40) makes the short drive into town. If you've come in on a **cruise-ship**, you are either on the southern edge of town (at the Punta Langosta pier), or a four-kilometre walk or M$40 taxi ride away (from both the international and Puerta Maya piers). The handiest branch of the **tourist office** (Mon–Sat 8.30am–5pm; ☎987/869-0212, ✉turismoczm@yahoo.com.mx) is in a kiosk

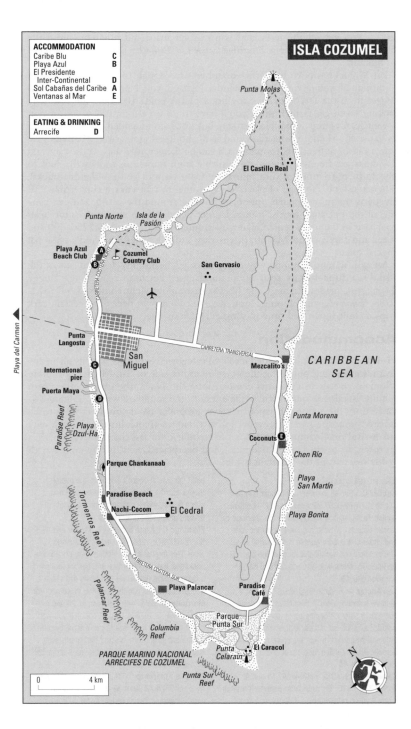

ISLA COZUMEL

**ACCOMMODATION**
| | |
|---|---|
| Caribe Blu | **C** |
| Playa Azul | **B** |
| El Presidente Inter-Continental | **D** |
| Sol Cabañas del Caribe | **A** |
| Ventanas al Mar | **E** |

**EATING & DRINKING**
| | |
|---|---|
| Arrecife | **D** |

Punta Molas

El Castillo Real

Punta Norte

Isla de la Pasión

Playa Azul Beach Club

Cozumel Country Club

San Gervasio

Playa del Carmen

Punta Langosta

San Miguel

CARRETERA TRANSVERSAL

Mezcalito's

CARIBBEAN SEA

International pier

Puerta Maya

Paradise Reef

Playa Dzul-Ha

Punta Morena

Coconuts

Chen Río

Parque Chankanaab

Paradise Beach

Nachi-Cocom

El Cedral

Playa San Martín

Tormentos Reef

Playa Bonita

CARRETERA COSTERA SUR

Playa Palancar

Paradise Café

Palancar Reef

Columbia Reef

Parque Punta Sur

PARQUE MARINO NACIONAL ARRECIFES DE COZUMEL

Punta Celarain

El Caracol

Punta Sur Reef

0        4 km

N

just as you get off the ferry, and you can get maps and brochures from the helpful staff; the ubiquitous *Free Blue Guide to Cozumel* is the most useful piece of literature.

San Miguel has been modernized and is easy enough to get around on foot – though if you're carrying substantial luggage, you'll probably want a **taxi** to get from the ferry dock to any hotel past Avenida 10. Buses are distinctly lacking, so to get farther afield you'll have to go on a tour, take a taxi or rent a vehicle. **Cycling** is feasible in town, but not recommended for any distance, as car traffic is fast and heedless, and hard shoulders are narrow. **Mopeds** give you a bit more freedom, though roads can be dangerously slick in the rain, and accidents are frequent; **jeeps** are available from numerous outlets (be sure to check the restrictions of your insurance if you want to go onto the dirt tracks). There's also no shortage of places on Cozumel to rent **cars**; a convertible VW Beetle is the most popular option for tooling around the island, and can handle all the principal tourist routes. To rent per day from any of the numerous *rentadoras* in the town centre, bikes cost around M$90, mopeds M$250–300 and jeeps and cars around M$450. Prices vary little, but you may find occasional special offers.

An exhilarating, if bumpy, way to see the wild, beautifully deserted side of the island is a **dune-buggy tour** of the uninhabited northeast coast. Jungle Buggy Tours, at Rentadora Isleña, Calle 7 between avenidas Melgar and 5 (☎987/872-0788, ⓦwww.cozumelhomes.com), has built their own fleet of all-terrain cars; trips include lunch and time to snorkel (M$900; 8hr).

## Accommodation

**Hotels** in Cozumel are divided into two categories: expensive, usually all-inclusive resorts strung out along the coast on either side of San Miguel, and more affordable places in the town centre. Along the beach, the ones to the north require a taxi ride into town, while a few to the south are within walking distance from the action. The spots in town are preferable if you don't want to be isolated from the social scene or are on a budget. (Note, however, that there's **no hostel** on Cozumel, nor any room to be had for less than M$200 a night.) In town, an ocean view is overrated, and overpriced, as it usually comes with traffic noise from the malecón below.

### San Miguel

**Aguilar** C 3 Sur 98, between Av Melgar and Av 5 Sur ☎987/872-0307, ⓦwww.cozumel-hotels.net/aguilar. Quiet, slightly kitsch rooms (no shortage of plastic flowers), all with a/c, away from the road and situated around a garden with a small pool. The location just two blocks south of the plaza is particularly convenient, and scooter and car hire are available. ⑥

**Las Anclas** Av 5 Sur 325 ☎987/872-5476, ⓦwww.lasanclas.com. A handful of well-designed two-storey suites (sleeping up to four) with kitchenettes, all spotless and perfectly maintained. A little shared garden makes the place feel extra homely. Rough Guides readers receive a ten percent discount. ⑧

**Caribe** C 2 Norte 332, between Av 15 and Av 20 ☎987/872-0325, ⓔmanuelbrito_estrella@hotmail.com. If you can take the shocking-pink exterior

paint job (which doesn't extend to the pastel rooms, luckily), this is a pleasant enough mid-range option, with a swimming pool and lots of flowers around the grounds. ⑥

**Flamingo** C 6 Norte between Av Melgar and Av 5 Sur ☎987/872-1264, ⓦwww.hotelflamingo.com. This fun hotel, which offers well-priced dive packages, has a roof terrace and bar, as well as a Cuban-fusion restaurant that hosts live salsa bands. Guests can use the beach at Playa Azul. ⑦

**Marruang** Av Salas 440, between Av 20 and Av 25 ☎987/872-1678. A bargain option if you want to get well away from San Miguel's tourist centre. Rooms are clean, with TVs and firm mattresses, and you can pick up snacks at the market directly across the street. ④

**Palapas Amaranto** C 5 Sur between Av 15 and Av 20 ☎987/872-3219, ⓦwww.amarantobb.com. Fanciful architecture and tasteful furnishings distinguish these three round stucco palapas and two apartments stacked in a tile-trimmed tower. Rooms – all with fridge and microwave, most with a/c – are clustered around a cosy courtyard and small pool. If arriving in the afternoon, check in or enquire at *Tamarindo*, as there's staff on the premises only in the morning. ❻

**Palma Dorada** Av Salas 44, between Av Melgar and Av 5 ☎987/872-0330, ✉pdinn@prodigy.net .mx. Friendly management complements the cheery, tidy rooms, and a few suites with kitch-enettes are also available. An airy rooftop lounge provides a nice spot to relax. ❺

**Pepita** Av 15 Sur 120, at C 1 Sur ☎987/872-0098. By far the best of the budget options (such as they are in this town), with clean, attractive rooms with a/c and TV, a pretty courtyard and complimentary coffee in the morning. ❺

**Tamarindo B&B** C 4 Norte 421, between Av 20 and Av 25 ☎987/872-6190, ⊛www.tamarindobb. com. Run by a friendly French-Mexican couple who take good care of the five pretty rooms with whim-sical details; two of the rooms share a kitchen, and a/c is available in two others. You can also use the outdoor grill in the huge yard, and a full breakfast is included. ❻

### Elsewhere on the island

**Caribe Blu** Carretera Costera Sur Km 2.2 ☎987/872-0188, ⊛www.caribeblu.net. Very close to town with an excellent dive shop, Blue Angel, and shallow dive training right off the hotel's small beach. All rooms have sea views and private balco-nies; there's also a pool. ❼

**Playa Azul** Carretera Costera Norte Km 4 ☎987/872-0043, ⊛www.playa-azul.com. Swanky

little resort on the best stretch of beach north of town, with fifty elegant ocean-view rooms. Guests have access to a spa and gym, and several bars and restaurants; the pool is a bit small, however. Golf and dive packages are available, and rates dip significantly in low season. ❾

**El Presidente Inter-Continental** Carretera Costera Sur Km 6.5 ☎987/872-9500, ⊛www .cozumel.interconti.com. The sharp-edged modern-ist design of Cozumel's first luxury hotel, built in 1969, can feel a little severe, but the setting is flawless, with a very pretty protected beach and accessible snorkelling from the very long pier. All rooms have ocean views, and the new spa, opened in late 2004, offers lavish treatments. ❾

**Sol Cabañas del Caribe** Carretera Costera Norte Km 5.1 ☎987/872-0017, ⊛www.solmelia.com. This small resort is showing its age in its dated decor, but it's very mellow and quiet, with just 39 rooms and nine private cottages facing the water. You can snorkel right off the dock. ❽

**Ventanas al Mar** On the east coast, 5km south of *Mezcalito's* beach bar and the intersection with the Carretera Transversal ⊛www.cozumel-hotels .net/ventanas-al-mar. For those seeking a truly remote getaway, this full-service hotel, the only one on the eastern coast and powered entirely by wind turbines, opened in 2004. It offers gigantic rooms with terraces overlooking the crashing surf, and an empty beach stretching off from the north side. Rates include a full breakfast, and discounts are offered at *Coconuts* beach club next door. If you plan to stay a while, however, it's great value to stock up on groceries (there are no shops on this side of the island) and use the kitchenette in your room. ❼

# San Miguel

The only major population centre on the island, **SAN MIGUEL** is home to about 85,000 people. It's clean and cheerful and a bit sprawling, with long blocks and low buildings, a few of which are little Caribbean-style clapboard houses that have somehow resisted decades of heavy weather. The primary drawback is that the wide seafront avenue, **Avenida Rafael Melgar**, is all too often a throng of day visitors traipsing from one duty-free diamond shop to the next, and you may be hassled by aggressive salespeople. The weekends, though, are blissfully quiet – no cruiseships generally stop on Cozumel on Sunday, and only a couple arrive on Saturday and Monday.

The town's large main square, the **Plaza del Sol**, stands directly opposite the ferry dock dominated by a tall clock tower. The plaza is the hub of activity for tourists, though *cozumeleños* come out on Sunday evenings, when there's live music. It's also popular to stroll the **malecón** (Avenida Melgar), which is graced with grand bronze statues commemorating Cozumel's Maya cultural heritage and long tradition of fishing.

On the malecón between avenidas 4 and 6, the attractive **Museo de la Isla de Cozumel** (daily 9am–5pm; M$50) has small exhibits on the flora and fauna of the island, its famous reef systems and its history from the Maya era to the present. You'll also see a good collection of Maya artefacts and old photos showing the colourful culture of Cozumel. In the back on the ground floor a traditional Maya hut is staffed by a friendly and informative local who

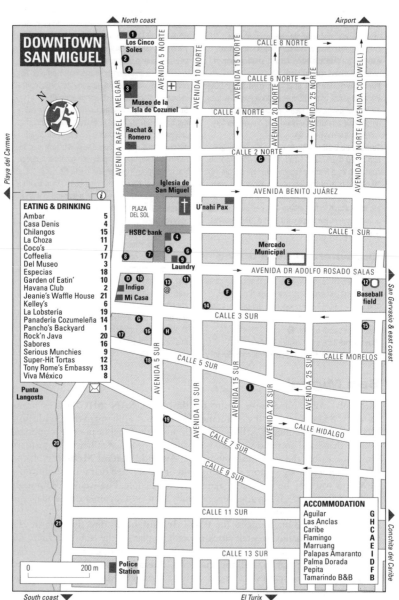

DOWNTOWN SAN MIGUEL

**EATING & DRINKING**

| | |
|---|---|
| Ambar | 5 |
| Casa Denis | 4 |
| Chilangos | 15 |
| La Choza | 11 |
| Coco's | 7 |
| Coffeelia | 17 |
| Del Museo | 3 |
| Especias | 18 |
| Garden of Eatin' | 10 |
| Havana Club | 2 |
| Jeanie's Waffle House | 21 |
| Kelley's | 6 |
| La Lobstería | 19 |
| Panadería Cozumeleña | 14 |
| Pancho's Backyard | 1 |
| Rock'n Java | 20 |
| Sabores | 16 |
| Serious Munchies | 9 |
| Super-Hit Tortas | 12 |
| Tony Rome's Embassy | 13 |
| Viva México | 8 |

**ACCOMMODATION**

| | |
|---|---|
| Aguilar | G |
| Las Anclas | H |
| Caribe | C |
| Flamingo | A |
| Marruang | E |
| Palapas Amaranto | I |
| Palma Dorada | D |
| Pepita | F |
| Tamarindo B&B | B |

Los Cinco Soles

Museo de la Isla de Cozumel

Rachat & Romero

Iglesia de San Miguel

PLAZA DEL SOL

U'nahi Pax

HSBC bank

Mercado Municipal

Laundry

Indigo

Mi Casa

Baseball field

AVENIDA RAFAEL E. MELGAR

AVENIDA 5 NORTE

AVENIDA 10 NORTE

AVENIDA 15 NORTE

AVENIDA 20 NORTE

AVENIDA 25 NORTE

AVENIDA 30 NORTE (AVENIDA COLDWELL)

CALLE 8 NORTE

CALLE 6 NORTE

CALLE 4 NORTE

CALLE 2 NORTE

AVENIDA BENITO JUÁREZ

CALLE 1 SUR

AVENIDA DR ADOLFO ROSADO SALAS

CALLE 3 SUR

CALLE MORELOS

CALLE 5 SUR

AVENIDA 5 SUR

AVENIDA 10 SUR

AVENIDA 15 SUR

AVENIDA 20 SUR

AVENIDA 25 SUR

CALLE 7 SUR

CALLE HIDALGO

CALLE 9 SUR

CALLE 11 SUR

CALLE 13 SUR

Police Station

0     200 m

Punta Langosta

Playa del Carmen

North coast

Airport

San Gervasio & east coast

Conchita del Caribe

South coast

El Turix

will explain (primarily in Spanish) the uses of the various foodstuffs, herbs and accoutrements lying about. Overall, the place is a concise introduction to the primary points of Yucatán history, and everything is labelled in both English and Spanish. It occasionally hosts live music and theatre events; check with the tourist office.

San Miguel's name was chosen in the late 1800s, when workers unearthed a large, richly adorned statue of Saint Michael. Research suggests that it dates from the early sixteenth century, when Spanish explorer Juan de Grijalva likely brought it to the island as a gift for the native Maya. The discovery inspired townspeople to take San Miguel as their patron saint, and to build the **Iglesia de San Miguel** (Sun Mass at 7am, 9am, 6pm, 8pm) on the site where the statue was found, one block off the plaza at the corner of Avenida Juárez and Avenida 10. The statue of the winged archangel brandishing his sword is still on display on the church altar.

Continuing inland past the church, the town gets more diverse – and afford-able. Avenida Coldwell (Avenida 30) is lined with a number of inexpensive restaurants and bars, as well as the main town **baseball field** (at Avenida Salas), which hosts games throughout the summer. The **central market**, on Avenida Salas between avenidas 20 and 25, is another outlying sight, where the orderly produce and butcher stalls tucked under a high tin roof seem to be in a com-pletely different town from the T-shirt shops and tequila bars around Plaza del Sol. You can also find colourful, inexpensive kitchen equipment and bargain lunch counters and juice bars.

# The rest of the island

Beyond San Miguel, only a few roads extend across the island. Immediately to the **north** is a small hotel zone, with pleasant sandy **beaches** and the best place to go swimming close to town. On the coast road heading **south** from San Miguel, you pass additional hotels; the reef comes very close to shore here, making for easy and scenic **snorkelling** but no natural beaches. About 9km south of town the sand returns, and a number of **beach clubs** offer various activities for every kind of visitor. Just east of the highway, the small village of **El Cedral** is the only other population centre on the island. The south coast road then bends inland, marking the boundary of **Parque Punta Sur**, a nature reserve that encompasses some beautiful beaches and lagoons.

Head east from San Miguel on the dead-straight, cross-island highway (called the Carretera Transversal) to reach **San Gervasio**, the island's only excavated Maya ruins, and, after 15km, the **east coast**. Spend time here if you want a very isolated day lounging in a hammock – the farther south you go on the slightly potholed route along the water, the fewer people you'll see. You can seldom swim, however, as the water is rough on this side. And appealing as all this is, of course just offshore is the whole rich world of the **coral reefs**, which are more heavily visited than anything the island has to offer above the waterline.

### The northern coast

The coast road **north out of San Miguel** leads to a short strip of hotels and one nice **beach club**, Playa Azul (adjacent to the eponymous resort, 4km north of town; daily 10am–5pm), a small patch of clean sand, calm water and a few rocky spots for snorkelling. It's all but empty on weekdays, but on Sunday afternoons it's the place to come if you want to hang out with locals, as the restaurant and playground get packed with families on their day off. The paved road continues 3km past Playa Azul, then bears slightly inland to end near the

Cozumel Country Club (☎987/872-9570, Ⓦ www.cozumelcountryclub.com.mx), a lush **golf course** set around a large lake.

## The southern coast

Heading south of San Miguel, Avenida Melgar turns into a small highway that passes several more hotels, all catering to divers. There's accessible **snorkelling** off the pier at *Hotel Caribe Blu*, where you can drift along a nice stretch of reef; the hotel's dive shop rents masks and fins. The next good place to snorkel is

△ Endangered sea turtle

Playa Dzul-Ha (Mon–Sat 8am–5pm, Sun 9am–5pm), a popular but not totally mobbed spot where you can wade out to the coral gardens from shore. The beach bar rents gear, and has a full dive centre. For actual swimming and lounging, you may want to pay the M$50 drink minimum to use the pool, but there's no charge for regular beach access.

Two kilometres farther, **Parque Chankanaab** (daily 7am–5pm; M$100) is the island's main tourist destination, though you'll probably want to skip it unless you have children. It's a bit overdeveloped, complete with mini-golf and dolphin pens, and can get very crowded on cruiseship days, but it's a good option for kids because its lagoon, which teems with vivid fish, is very calm. **Playa Corona**, the public beach immediately past Chankanaab, was an excellent place to swim and snorkel till an asphalt spill damaged some of the reef (and, less visibly, part of Chankanaab); if cleanup, slated for completion at the end of 2006, is successful, this could still be a great destination. In the meantime, try Paradise Beach (ⓦ www.paradise-beach-cozumel.net; daily 9am–6pm), at Km 14.5; it can get crowded, but the amenities include free use of beach chairs, kayaks, snorkel gear and floating water-toys moored offshore. For those willing to pay (M$100 minimum at the restaurant), **Nachi-Cocom**, at Km 16.5, offers a more serene beach experience, as it's barely known among cruiseshippers. It has a beautiful beach with shallow water, and very well-kept facilities, such as an enormous swimming pool and Jacuzzi, though there's no snorkelling here.

A large arch on the inland side of the road at Km 17.5 marks the turn for the village of **El Cedral**, founded in 1847 and now primarily a vacation spot for San Miguel's better-off residents. There's little more here than a small Maya site and a modern Spanish church filled with folk art, but several small cenotes – best reached on horseback (2hr, M$250) – are nearby; enquire at the church. In late April and early May, the village hosts the ten-day-long Fiesta de la Santa Cruz, a huge fair commemorating the meeting of Maya and Spanish cultures, with bullfights, prize-winning livestock and dancing.

The least crowded of the leeward beaches, with a laid-back atmosphere to match, is **Playa Palancar** (daily 9am–6pm), at Km 19. There's no entertainment other than the restaurant, which serves seafood specialities like *tikin-xic*. You can also arrange a boat ride out to snorkel at the Palancar Reef just offshore.

## Parque Punta Sur

At the southern end of the island, **Parque Punta Sur** (daily 9am–5pm; M$100) encompasses 2750 acres, including several lovely beaches, the Punta Celarain **lighthouse** and the **Templo El Caracol** – which may have been built by the Maya as an ancient lighthouse, and is worth visiting to hear the sounds produced when the wind whistles through the conch shells embedded in its walls. You can climb to the top of the lighthouse for amazing views over the coast or visit the adjacent **museum of navigation** (daily 10am–4pm; same ticket), which has a series of interesting displays on maritime history. A creaking wood-sided truck transports visitors between various sites (or you can rent bicycles or electric buggies), including viewing towers over a large network of lagoons and a beach restaurant serving good fried fish.

Parque Punta Sur is also a prime spot for **birdwatching**, as the mangroves host a number of migratory species, such as roseate spoonbills, giant frigates and various herons, as well as four endemic ones, including the vibrant Cozumel emerald, the widespread Cozumel vireo and the Cozumel thrasher, until recently thought to be extinct. For additional fees, you can arrange a small-group night tour of the **crocodile** or **sea turtle reserve** areas and scientific monitoring stations in the park (M$300–350; reservations on ☎987/872-0914, or ask at the park entrance).

## San Gervasio

Midway across the island, 6km north of the Carretera Transversal, **San Gervasio** (daily 7am–5pm; M$50) is the largest excavated Maya site on the island. The city was built to honour **Ixchel**, goddess of fertility and weaving, and was one of the many independent city-states that survived the fall of Chichén Itzá; it was also part of a larger trading community on the Yucatán coast, along with Tulum and El Rey in Cancún. Today the ruins are not very impressive to a casual visitor, but, as they are part of a larger nature reserve, they're worth a trip for their scenic setting in the jungle. An early-morning or late-afternoon visit will reveal numerous bird species, butterflies and other wildlife.

Portions of San Gervasio were modelled on Chichén Itzá, with several small plazas connected by *sacbeob*, the limestone-paved white roads that the Maya built. One of the first buildings you reach, the **Manitas** structure, is a small residential room with red handprints all over it. The significance of this somewhat common motif, found at several other Mayan sites, is still not understood. Off to the right stands the Chichan Nah, a dwarfish building probably used for ceremonial purposes, as it is similar in scale to the miniature temples at Tulum. By contrast, Structure 31, closer to the main plaza, is a relatively large residential building with a front portico, a style used primarily by the Chontal Maya of lowland Mexico and Guatemala. In the later centuries, it was likely the seat of the *halach winik*, the leader of Cozumel. The main cluster of buildings, arranged around a compact plaza, formed the central administrative area; the principal shrine to Ixchel, the **Ka'na Nah**, lies 500m to the northwest along a *sacbé*. The tallest pyramid on the site (though still not particularly towering compared to some mainland structures), it shows a few remnants of painted stucco. Down the northeast *sacbé*, which is marked by a delicate arch, you'll find the Post-Classic Nohoch Nah temple and the much older Casa de los Murciélagos ("house of bats"), a residential building started in 700 AD.

## The east coast

Often impressively wild, Cozumel's **eastern shoreline** remains undeveloped because it faces the open sea and in most places is too rough for swimming. Nonetheless, the twenty-kilometre drive along the island's southeastern side is a refreshing contrast to the bustle of San Miguel and the western coast. You'll pass loads of empty **beaches** (tantalizing – but swim only where you see others, and be wary of strong currents) and the occasional no-frills **beach bar**, open only till sundown because there's no electricity.

The first of these as you arrive via the cross-island road, and generally the most crowded and rowdy as it's right at the intersection, is *Mezcalito's*, a simple cluster of thatch roofing and plastic chairs in front of a sprawling white beach. From here, you can also join an ATV tour to the unremarkable ruins of **El Castillo Real**, 18km north on a very rough track. Local legend has it that each potential Maya leader went here, alone, for 365 days and nights to test his fortitude and strength of character. For the contemporary traveller, however, the hideously potholed and unmaintained road is a trial – or an adventure, if you like an off-road outing. The ruins themselves are not scenic enough to merit the damage you would surely do to a rental car.

Heading south along the eastern coast highway, you pass a number of variations on the rustic beach-bar theme. They're all fairly interchangeable – where you land simply depends on at what point you care to stretch your legs. Except on Sundays, when locals come out, there's never enough of a crowd to fill all of the bars, and the farther you drive, the fewer people you'll see. About a third of the way down the east coast road, **Punta Morena** is home to a bit of a surfer scene and another bar-restaurant that also rents bleak concrete cabins (❸). The more preferable *Coconuts* bar follows, with a striking view from a tall bluff; and a beach that is usually empty. *Chen Río*, a little farther on, has a protected cove where you can swim and snorkel (bring your own gear), and the bar serves great margaritas. The relatively serene **Playa San Martín**, just south, is for the true misanthrope – no services and usually no people, though flags mark the day's swimming conditions. Past a rocky point lies *Playa Bonita*, another beach club that's best for all-day lounging; the water is shallow and you can rent umbrellas for the day. Finally, the road turns inland at the entrance to Parque Punta Sur and the *Paradise Café*, known for its all-reggae soundtrack and great shrimp quesadillas.

## The reefs

The beaches and reefs encircling the southern half of the island are a designated nature reserve called the **Parque Marino Nacional Arrecifes de Cozumel**. The coral growth is diverse, with spectacular drop-offs, walls and swim-throughs, some beautiful coral gardens and a number of remote reefs where you can see larger pelagic fish and occasionally dolphins. Regulations require that you be accompanied by a licensed dive guide (see p.144); a M$50 park fee should be tacked on to any organized diving or snorkelling trip you make.

On the west side, a steady current typically runs south to north, making for easy drift dives and snorkelling. Dozens of dive spots cater to all skill levels. Perhaps the best spot for both **diving** and **snorkelling** is **Palancar Shallows**, about 2km off the southwest coast. The area ranges from five-metre-deep gardens to a mini-wall dropping 18m. The main strip reef is riddled with fissures and caves. You'll see Cozumel's famous **black coral** as well as giant stove-pipe sponges that harbour brilliant fish. The other sections of the five-kilometre-long Palancar Reef are accessible to divers only, but are equally fascinating – Palancar Deep in particular stands up to repeat visits. North of Palancar, the walls at El Cedral and Las Palmas are two excellent spots for **advanced divers**.

Just to the south, **Colombia Shallows** is the farthest trip most day boats make from San Miguel. Although it's only 10m at its deepest, this sprawling coral garden can still dazzle seasoned divers as well as snorkellers. Sediment-rich run-off from the mangroves that edge the shore help create a thriving eco-system: tall coral towers studded with vibrant sponges and anemones punctuate the floor, and meadows of sea grass are spawning grounds for a dazzling variety of fish. Rays frequent the area, as do nurse sharks and eels. At **Punta Sur**, directly south from Laguna Colombia, strong currents (and an hour-long boat ride) deter all but the strongest divers. Those who make the trip are rewarded with a dramatic network of deep caverns and fissures, completely encrusted with vibrant corals and sea fans.

## Eating

Many of San Miguel's **restaurants** are overpriced tourist traps catering to a rather bland palate, but beyond the plasticky chain spots and dull steakhouses coasting on their prime plaza frontage, you can find some excellent bargains, as well as a few places worthy of throwing down a chunk of change. In general, you're better off wandering several blocks back from the seafront for good food and local flavour and sticking to the large array of casual cafés, rather than the more formal restaurants. The cheapest snacks of all can be at the city **market**, on Avenida Salas between avenidas 20 and 25. For a more laid-back atmosphere you can enjoy long, lazy lunches in the palapas dotted every few kilometres along the southwestern and eastern coasts.

## Cafés

**Chilangos** Av 30 (Coldwell) between C 3 Sur and C Morelos. *Huaraches* (big, open-face quesadillas) are the house speciality at this popular snack bar, open only in the evenings; select your own combination of toppings, such as cheese and *nopales* (cactus strips). Closed Sun.

**Coco's** Av 5 no. 180, between C 1 and Av Salas. At this Cozumel institution, you get American diner-style breakfast from the early hour of 6am till noon – complete with chatty waitresses, free coffee refills and Formica tables – blended with Mexican standards like eggs with *mole* (M$45). The cinnamon rolls are delightfully gooey. Closed Mon.

**Coffeelia** C 5 Sur 85, between Av Melgar and Av 5. A proud local owner presides over breakfast and lunch from her homely kitchen in this sweet café with room to lounge outdoors. The menu mixes fresh Mexican dishes, fruit smoothies and huge Dutch-style pancakes. Breakfast is served all day; in the evening, you might see a singer or a storyteller.

**Del Museo** Av Melgar between C 4 and C 6, at the Museo de la Isla de Cozumel. Enjoy a quiet breakfast or early lunch on the upstairs balcony of the city museum. The view of the sea is impressive, the coffee is spiked with cinnamon and the food – from *huevos rancheros* to club sandwiches – is fresh and filling. Closed Sun.

**Garden of Eatin'** Av Salas between Av Melgar and Av 5. Vegetarians will rejoice at the sprawling, sparkling-clean salad bar and the tasty sandwiches (about M$50), ranging from falafel to imaginative combos involving pesto and sprouts.

**Jeanie's Waffle House** Av Melgar at C 11 Sur. "La Casa del Waffle" is a popular breakfast and lunch spot, with not just waffles but also sandwiches and substantial fruit salads, served at tables on the sand.

**Panadería Cozumeleña** C 3 at Av 10. Stop by this sweet-smelling bakery (entrance on Calle 3) to pick up *pan dulce* to go, or, for a more leisurely light breakfast, settle in at the adjacent coffee shop, a neighbourhood hangout (entrance on the corner).

**Rock'n Java** Av Melgar 602, between C 7 and C 11 ☎987/872-4405. Healthy sandwiches, salads and veggie chile (all between M$40 and M$80) are balanced out by fantastically rich and delicious desserts, such as German chocolate cake, at this American-owned seafront diner. Delivery is

available to hotels south of town. Sat 7am–2pm, closed Sun.

**Serious Munchies** Av Salas between Av 5 and Av 10. Giant sandwiches (M$30–50) are the main menu item, ranging from cheese and avocado to big and messy meatball, or you can opt for a veggie-heavy stir-fry. A good place to stock up for a day-trip or picnic. Daily noon–11pm.

**Super-Hit Tortas** Av 30 (Coldwell) at Av Salas. Meaty Mexican-style sandwiches with plenty of toppings for just M$15; in the summer, they make an ideal snack before going to a baseball game at the field behind. There's another branch at Avenida 30 and Calle 15.

## Restaurants

**Casa Denis** C 1 between Av 5 and Av 10. Open since 1945, *Casa Denis* occupies a little wood-frame house just off the plaza. Bigger meals like chicken enchiladas (M$80 and up) can be bland, though far better than at any other restaurant around here; it's best to stick with a beer and some *panuchos* (M$35) as you watch the action from your sidewalk table.

**La Choza** Av Salas at Av 10. Busy and popular palapa-roof restaurant known for its Mexican home-cooking, though it has become a little inconsistent. It's best for the daily lunch special, which isn't on the menu; ask the waiter, and you could get a rib-sticking meal for about M$50.

**Conchita del Caribe** Av 65 between C 21 and C 23. Though in an unpromising-looking converted garage, this locally famous seafood spot well off the tourist track serves inexpensive and delicious food. The ceviches, served in generous portions, are particularly good. Closes at 6pm.

**Especias** C 5 Sur at Av 10 ☎987/876-1558. Inexpensive Argentine, Mexican and even occasionally Thai meals (from about M$30 to M$70), served by an exceptionally friendly husband and wife team. The breezy dining room looks onto a small garden and is also a pleasant stop for an end-of-the-day beer. Beware of occasionally erratic opening hours, but the place generally serves every evening but Sunday from 5pm on.

**La Lobstería** Av 5 at C 7. As the name suggests, lobster *al gusto* (choose from several classic preparations) is the main draw at this restaurant, located in a hundred-year-old palapa house. But the rest of the menu is equally appetizing, with each dish receiving a special touch, like fish in a lively

△ La Lobsteria

cilantro-mint salsa verde (M$100) and tamarind dressing on the big green salad. Excellent service too. Closed Sun.

**Pancho's Backyard** Av Melgar 27 at C 8 Norte ☎987/872-2141. By no means an "authentic" Mexican dining experience – especially at lunch, when it's a favourite with cruiseship passengers – but easily the best service on the island. Very good margaritas, tortilla chips hot out of the fryer, and fresh-tasting, slightly dressed-up Mexican entrees (M$100 and up for mains like shrimp with poblano peppers); the vegetarian selection is strong too. Closed for lunch Sat & Sun.

**Sabores** Av 5 between C 3 Sur and C 5 Sur. Real home-cooking at this lunch-only *cocina económica*, which is run out of the chef-owner's house. Just walk through the living room and kitchen and out to the huge shady garden, where you can choose from several entrees (M$45, or a few dollars more for shrimp dishes). The set price includes soup and an all-you-can-drink jug of *agua de jamaica*. Everything is prepared individually and with care – don't miss it.

**El Turix** Av 20 between C 17 and C 19, across from Corpus Christi church. Chef Rafael Ponce, originally from Mérida, has cooked as far afield as Montréal but returned to Mexico to recreate traditional Yucatecan dishes like *cochinita pibil* (pit-roasted pork) as well as a great coconut pie. The restaurant is simple, with big wooden tables, and the prices are low; everything's less than M$100. Closed Sun.

## Drinking and nightlife

Evening entertainment centres on the Plaza del Sol, which is ringed with party-hearty **bars** blasting classic rock and dance hits and featuring choreographed dancing barmen, lurid cheap cocktails and the like. On Sunday evenings the crowd is a little more mellow and mixed, as local families come out to chat and listen to strolling musicians. As with everything else on the island, drinks can be a little pricey, at least in San Miguel, and happy hours hard to come by.

**Ambar** Av 5 no. 141, between C 1 and Av Salas ☎987/869-1955. A little slice of Playa style in Cozumel, this candlelit lounge serves up cocktails with live DJ accompaniment. It's also a dinner option, with refined, if slightly expensive, northern Italian food, such as spinach-and-ricotta ravioli in brandy sauce for M$110. Closed Sun.

**Arrecife** Carretera Costera Sur Km 6.5, at *El Presidente Inter-Continental*. The verandah bar at the island's ritziest hotel is an ideal spot for a sunset piña colada, usually to the accompaniment of mellow piano music.

**Havana Club** Av Melgar between C 6 and C 8 (enter through the Diamonds International store) t987/872-2098. About the only place in town where you can sit on a balcony and watch the sunset. The clientele is cigar-puffing, old-hand divers with tales to tell, and the mojitos are ridiculously expensive but tasty.

**Kelley's** Av 10 between Av Salas and C 1 Sur. A big open-air bar where you might see your divemaster or tour guide in their off-hours. Very friendly, with a pool table and live music on Fri. Serves big, tasty portions of American food during the day.

**Tony Rome's Embassy** Av 5 between Av Salas and C 3 Sur. Karaoke venue where the larger-than-life proprietor, a cheery showman and a consummate host, entertains the crowds nightly. Loads of campy fun, but better for drinks than dinner.

**Viva México** Av Melgar at Av Salas. The one big nightclub in town where locals and tourists meet, offering a very loud and lively mix of hip-hop with Latin and club hits, all in a second-floor palapa fronting the sea. Two-for-one drink specials to those who arrive on the early side (don't expect much of a scene before 11pm).

## Dive shops

Of the dozens of **dive shops** in town, Deep Blue, Avenida Salas at Avenida 10 (☎987/872-5653, ⓦwww.deepbluecozumel.com), is one of the best, offering tailor-made small-group tours to some of the most interesting and remote reefs off the island; a two-tank dive is M$700. The shop also runs a full range of certification courses. If you want to **snorkel** you'll need to organize a boat ride out to the reef – all of the dive shops in town should be able to take you (approximately M$250 for several hours in the water). The best spots, like Palancar and Colombia, are a little farther south, but you'll know you have a good tour operator if it's willing to make the extra effort without complaint. **Sport-fishing** tours are also readily available – the season runs from March to July; Albatros Charters (☎987/872-7904, ⓦwww.gocozumel.com/albatros) can take up to six passengers on full- and half-day trips (from M$4000), or contact the experienced guides at fly-fishing operation Pesca Mexicana (in the US on ☎1-713/816-0228, ⓦwww.pescamexicana.com), who run trips for two starting at M$3250.

## Shopping

**Shopping** in Cozumel is not particularly rewarding outside of the market (see p.137), as the whole seafront has been given over to gem merchants and giant souvenir marts. In these two categories, however, Rachat & Romero (Av Melgar at C 2) has a good selection of **loose gems**, and Los Cinco Soles (☎987/872-0132, ⓦwww.loscincosoles.com.), on the seafront at Calle 8, is a vast handicrafts superstore. Its smaller, standard-issue souvenirs are overpriced, but the selection of **jewellery** and **housewares** – including elegant, modern pewter serving bowls and lead-free ceramic dishes – is excellent. More distinctive Indigo, at Av Melgar between C 3 and Av Salas, is a tiny but richly stocked storefront selling **antique embroidery** from around Latin America, as well as Cuban cigars. U'nahi Pax, at Av Juárez and Av 15 (☎987/872-5269), special-

### Black coral

If you do shop in Cozumel, don't buy **black coral**, an endangered and beautiful type of sea life that is unfortunately sold everywhere. The island used to have one of the largest colonies of this rare, slow-growing species, but it has been severely depleted since the tourist trade started here in the 1960s. Don't, under any circumstances, go breaking it off the reefs.

izes in Mexican **musical instruments,** from pre-Columbian drums and rattles to elaborate harps and big-bellied guitars, along with a good selection of folk **music** on CD.

## Listings

**Airlines** Aeroméxico ☎987/872-3454; Continental, at the airport ☎987/872-0847; Iberia, Av Melgar 17 ☎987/872-3456; Mexicana, Av Melgar 17 ☎987/872-2945.

**Banks** HSBC (Mon–Fri 9am–7pm) is on Av 5 at C 1 Sur.

**Car rental** Try Rentadora Isleña, C 7 between Av Melgar and Av 5 (☎987/872-0788, ⊛www .cozumelhomes.com), or Aguilar, in the lobby of the *Hotel Aguilar*, C 3 Sur 98 (☎987/872-0307), which also rents scooters and bicycles.

**Cinema** Cinépolis at Av Melgar 1001, between C 15 and C 17.

**Consulate** US, Plaza Villamar ☎987/872-4574.

**Internet and telephone** The Crew Office, Av 5 no. 201-A between Av Salas and C 3 Sur, has excellent service and can also download images from digital cameras.

**Laundry** Lavandería Express, C Salas between Av 5 and Av 10.

**Medical emergencies** Visit the walk-in clinic on C 6 at Av 15 (☎987/872-0103) or the 24-hour Centro de Salud, at Av 20 and C 11 (☎987/872-0140). Most doctors are accustomed to dealing with English-speaking patients, and those with diving-related issues.

**Post office** A fifteen-minute walk south from the centre, on Av Melgar at the corner with C 7 Sur (Mon–Fri 9am–4pm, Sat 9am–1pm); for Lista de Correos use postcode 77600.

# Travel details

### Buses and colectivos

First-class **buses** run every ten minutes between Cancún and Playa del Carmen, stopping at the turn to Puerto Morelos on request (hand luggage only), and less frequently from Cancún airport on the same route. Note that buses in Playa del Carmen depart from two stations; one handles largely coastal destinations, while the other has inland and long-distance service. For destinations in between the main towns on the coast, second-class buses will stop anywhere on request, as will **colectivos,** the white, shared passenger vans that depart Playa very frequently from Avenida Juárez in front of the main bus station (toward Cancún) and on Calle 2 between avenidas 5 and 10 (Tulum-bound). In Cancún, colectivos to Playa depart from the parking lot across Avenida Tulum from the bus station. You can also flag down a colectivo or second-class bus anywhere along the highway – both will stop if they have vacant seats.

**Playa del Carmen** to: Cancún (every 10min; 1hr); Cancún airport (hourly 8am–6.15pm; 55min); Chetumal (hourly 6am–midnight; 4hr); Cobá (2 daily; 2hr); Mérida (hourly; 5hr); Palenque and San Cristóbal de las Casas (5 daily; 11–17hr); Tulum (frequently; 1–2hr); Tuxtla Gutiérrez (4 daily; 18–19hr); Valladolid (5 daily; 3hr); Villahermosa (10 daily; 12hr).

**Puerto Morelos** to: Cancún (every 10min; 30min); Cancún airport (hourly 8.30am–6.45pm; 20min); Playa del Carmen (every 10min; 30min).

### Ferries

**Cozumel** to: Playa del Carmen (every hour from 5am–10pm; 30min).

**Playa del Carmen** to: Cozumel (every hour from 6am–11pm; 30min).

**Puerto Morelos** to: Cozumel, cars only – erratic and not recommended (3 daily; 2hr 30min).

### Flights

Several US airlines fly direct to **Cozumel** from cities such as Houston, Dallas and Minneapolis, and internal flights connect Cozumel to Mexico City.

**Playa del Carmen** has an airstrip for small planes running on-demand tourist jaunts to Chichén Itzá and Cozumel.

# ③

# Tulum and the Sian Ka'an Biosphere Reserve

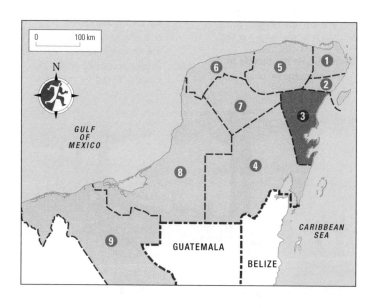

0    100 km

N

GULF
OF
MEXICO

⑥    ⑤    ①
②
⑦    ③
④
⑧

⑨

GUATEMALA

CARIBBEAN
SEA

BELIZE

CHAPTER 3  # Highlights

✱ **Playa Xcacel** This beautiful, empty beach is a research station and protected area for nesting sea turtles. **P.151**

✱ **Hidden Worlds** Experienced guides lead tours through some of the most scenic cenotes and caverns on the peninsula. **P.152**

✱ **Tulum** See the stirring seafront ruins (with their own tiny beach) or lounge at a cabaña along the equally gorgeous sand to the south. **P.153**

✱ **Cobá** Rent a bicycle to explore these ruins, buried in dense jungle filled with wildlife, then climb the main pyramid for a stupendous view of green in every direction. **P.161**

✱ **Reserva de Monos Arañas de Punta Laguna** This reserve boasts a large population of spider monkeys as well as a tranquil lake great for canoeing. **P.162**

✱ **Sian Ka'an Biosphere Reserve** Boasting tropical forest, mangroves and unspoilt beaches, the reserve is one of the largest protected areas in Mexico. **P.162**

△ La Vita è Bella

# 3

# Tulum and the Sian Ka'an Biosphere Reserve

The heavily built-up **Riviera Maya**, as the tourism ministry has dubbed this whole stretch of the Caribbean coast, continues south of Playa del Carmen along Hwy-307, with all manner of grand resorts and condo villages lining the flawless sand – interspersed with the occasional empty beach. The farther south you go (and the greater the distance from Cancún's airport), the beach properties thin out and tend to cater to people willing to make a little extra drive for a less expensive, more isolated beach experience, culminating in the candle-lit, hippie-inflected cabañas of **Tulum**. On the inland side, the limestone shelf is riddled with some of the peninsula's most impressive **cenotes**, beautiful water-filled caves that are refreshing and fascinating whether you want to swim, snorkel or scuba dive. Tulum, with its scenic Maya **ruins** and mellow beach-party scene, marks the southern border of Quintana Roo's tourist development. If you're not content just to lie on the beach, you can take a trip northwest to the grand ruins of **Cobá**, a vast Maya city buried in the forest.

After Tulum, the jungle thickens and Hwy-307 narrows and heads inland a bit, skirting more than a million acres of wilderness that have been set aside in the **Sian Ka'an Biosphere Reserve**. The area forms a rich haven for marine and bird life, as well as larger forest mammals. The only village inside the reserve, the tiny **Punta Allen**, is a destination for travellers looking for quiet isolation and great fishing. On the edge of the reserve, just off Hwy-307, the rambling ruins of **Chunyaxché** are often empty, plus the ancient roads and canals the Maya built here are a great place to spot wildlife. Bus service south of Tulum is not as frequent and flexible as along the Riviera Maya, though certainly still manageable; numerous tour operators will take you into the reserve for a reasonable price.

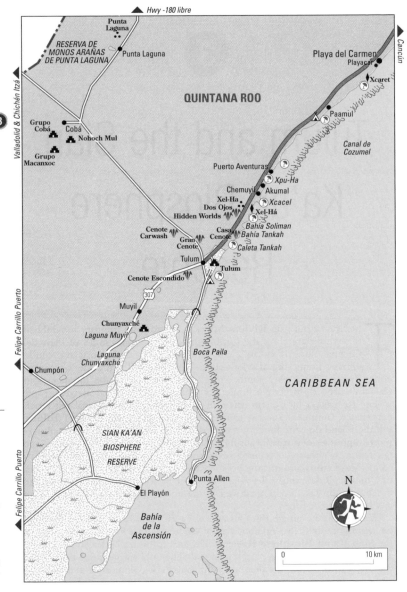

# From Playa del Carmen to Tulum

Almost the entire 60-kilometre stretch of coast between Playa del Carmen and Tulum has been transformed into resorts or condominium "villages" with gated entrances and little or no access for non-residents to the sea; the most egregious of these is the expensive, sterile **Puerto Aventuras**, 20km south of Playa, which feels like a theme park minus the rides. But amid the slick developments are a few less formal spots, such as **Paamul** and **Akumal**, and hidden beaches (**Xpu-ha**, **Xcacel**, **Caleta Tankah**) that are easy to reach from Hwy-307 even if you're travelling by one of the frequent second-class buses or *colectivos*; the latter run almost constantly between Playa and Tulum and will stop anywhere along the highway. For more structured fun, you can stop off at **Xel-Ha**, a semi-natural water park that's nice for kids, or take a cenote tour at **Hidden Worlds**, both just north of Tulum.

## Paamul, Xpu-ha and Akumal

The first community south of Playa, **PAAMUL** is a tidy RV park with a good **restaurant** that serves all the standard ceviches and quesadillas, but with more care than at typical beach seafood joints. The reef runs very close to shore here, making for some of the best wade-in **snorkelling** within the vicinity of Playa. The community also operates two overnight **lodging** options directly on the water – concrete rooms or sturdy wooden bungalows with porches (T984/875-1051, Wwww.paamulcabanas.com; ❻) – to take advantage of the quiet half-moon beach.

Twenty-five kilometres further south, **XPU-HA** is an especially lovely piece of beach, perfectly white and curving around in a large, gentle arc, that's gradually becoming more developed but still retains an air of peace and quiet. An all-inclusive resort, the *Copacabana*, breaks up the view, but serves as a landmark for several smaller, more interesting **overnight** options. Just north of the *Copacabana* a narrow road marked "X-5" leads to *Villas del Caribe* (T984/873-2194, Wwww.xpuhahotel.com; ❻), a small hotel adjacent to the excellent *Café del Mar* **restaurant** and bar (closed Mon), which serves healthy breakfasts and diverse lunch and dinner items, such as gazpacho and Greek-style octopus. At the next turn to the north ("X-2"), *Esencia* (in the US on T1-877/528-3490, Wwww.hotelesencia.com; ❾), with 29 beautifully designed rooms, plunge pools and a spa, offers intimate luxury of the most elite kind; rare for similar beach properties, kids are welcome. Just next door, the somewhat more afford-able *Al Cielo* (T984/840-9012, Wwww.alcielohotel.com; ❾) has four beautiful rooms and a pleasantly empty plot of sand out front. Even if the rooms are not in your price range, you can rent equipment from the beach bar and lounge on the chairs for the price of a drink. If you're on a budget you can stay in basic cabañas or **camp** (M$40) on the beach at *Bonanza Xpu-ha* (no tel; ❶–❹); look for a sign and the second narrow dirt road south of the *Copacabana*, marked "X-7".

Further on about 10km (turn at "Playa Akumal"), **AKUMAL** is primarily a condo community, but it does harbour simple **rooms** maintained by the dedi-cated Centro Ecológico de Akumal (T984/875-9095, Wwww.ceakumal.org; ❸); they're located behind the chummy *Turtle Bay* **restaurant** and not far from the large beach, which centres on a quiet bay. For more entertainment, head up the coast road to *La Buena Vida* beach **bar**, a funky place bedecked with fish skel-etons. Aquatech Divers (T984/875-9020, Wwww.cenotes.com), one of the most respected **cave-diving** operations in the Yucatán, also has its offices in Akumal.

Directly south of the town of Chemuyil, a few kilometres past Akumal, you'll find an exceptionally quiet beach at **Xcacel**, a sea turtle research station and sanctuary where the animals come to lay their eggs; visitors are welcome between 8am and 6pm. There are no services at all – the attraction is the pristine bay with good waves for body-surfing, plus it's only 500m from the highway, if you're walking.

## Xel-Há and Hidden Worlds

A water park in the rough, **XEL-HÁ** (daily 9am–6pm; Mon–Fri M$275, Sat–Sun M$198; ⓦ www.xelha.com), 13km north of Tulum, is a popular tourist attraction built around a natural formation of lagoons, inlets and underground caves. The entrance fee is steep (and doesn't include locker and snorkel rental), but if you have children and want to explore the natural features of the peninsula in a somewhat controlled environment, this is the place to go. Across the road, the small and only partly excavated Xel Há **ruins** (daily 8am–5pm; M$30) are notable for the extant stucco paintings in the Grupo Pájaros, on the east side of the site near the highway; on the west edge, you'll find miniature, chest-high temples that resemble ones found at Tulum, as well as a couple of cenotes, linked by a ruined *sacbé*.

Just south of the ruins, **HIDDEN WORLDS** (tours daily 9am–3pm; ⓣ 984/877-8535, ⓦ www.hiddenworlds.com.mx) comprises a cluster of outstanding cenotes and caverns. Guided group snorkelling (M$250–450) and diving (M$500 for one tank) trips run several times a day; you pile into a jeep with a handful of other visitors and trundle through the forest to the enormous Tak Be Ha cavern, the glimmering, sunlit Dos Ojos cenote and the Dreamgate, an awe-inspiring 200-foot-wide cavern. You can also visit some of these spots on your own, for a M$50 entry fee paid at Dos Ojos, but if this is your first visit to a cenote, the tours add a great deal to the experience, as guides know quite a lot about the geology and eco-systems in the cenotes.

Several kilometres south of Hidden Worlds, at **Bahía Soliman**, you can **camp** (M$50) at the *Oscar y Lalo* **restaurant**, immediately to the north from the beach access road. The kitchen serves super-fresh seafood amid dense palms overlooking an isolated inlet, where you can also snorkel and kayak. The southern part of the pretty bay is called **Tankah**, where the **Casa Cenote** (in front of the eponymous hotel; free) is a great place to snorkel – a network of seven pools that wind through the trees and eventually into the bay. Or you can rent kayaks (M$80/hr) at the adjacent *Tankah Inn* and paddle out to a very good reef. Immediately south of the well-priced and family-friendly *Sunscape Tulum*

---

### Exploring the cenotes

The area north and west of Tulum has one of the largest concentrations of **cenotes** on the peninsula, including Nohoch Nah Chich, the longest water-filled cave system in the world. First-time visitors – especially those who might be leery of tight spaces and dark water – are strongly encouraged to stop off at Hidden Worlds, a cluster of cenotes and caverns managed by a crew of cave-diving experts who were among the first to explore the Yucatán's underground attractions in the early 1980s. Group tours depart several times a day, led by guides who explain the geological processes by which the caves were formed, as well as put tentative snorkellers at ease. If you'd prefer to explore on your own, you can just rent gear here or at a number of the other cenotes that see a lot of visitors, such as those on the Tulum–Cobá road. **Divers** must have open-water certification for **cavern diving** (in which you explore within the reach of daylight), while **cave diving** (in which you venture into closed passageways and halls) requires rigorous special training. While local development threatens the cenotes and the fresh groundwater in the long term, inexperienced and clumsy visitors can do more damage in the short term: wear only **biodegradable sunscreen**; **do not touch** the surprisingly delicate stalactites; never break off anything as a souvenir; **mind your flippers**, as it's easy to kick up silt or knock into the rocks; and be very careful climbing in and out of the water – use the provided paths and ladders.

resort (☎984/871-3333, Ⓦwww.sunscaperesorts.com; ❾), the **Caleta Tankah Beach Club** (M$30; Ⓦwww.tankah.com.mx) capitalizes on a protected cove with palm trees for shade; between the colourful fish in the sea and a cenote just inland, there's plenty to explore, and few crowds.

# Tulum and around

One of the most picturesque of all the Maya sites, **TULUM**, 130km south of Cancún, is small but exquisitely poised on fifteen-metre-high cliffs above the impossibly blue Caribbean. When the Spanish first set eyes on the place in 1518, they considered it as large and beautiful a city as Seville. They were, perhaps, misled by their dreams of El Dorado, the glory of the setting and the brightly painted facades of the buildings – as Tulum is no match for the great Maya cities in terms of architectural grandeur and finesse. Nevertheless, on account of its location, it sticks in the memory like no other, and draws crowds second only to Chichén Itzá. It is also still an important Maya spiritual and cultural centre.

Tulum's beautiful **seafront** has been an equally powerful attraction, but, as happened in Playa, its status as a backpacker hangout par excellence is rapidly passing into history as the area develops its infrastructure, both for tourism and new Mexican residents. A few candle-lit, cold-water cabañas still cater to young international travellers, but a larger set of visitors value the more luxurious sensibility of the newer resorts. The actual **town** of Tulum is also growing rapidly, with a new campus of the Universidad de Quintana Roo in the planning stages; a desperately needed 2004 facelift, complete with topiary and mini-roundabouts, has made it a somewhat pleasant source of all the basic services. It's also the easiest place to line up a tour of the Sian Ka'an Biosphere Reserve (see p.162), or a diving or snorkelling excursion to one of the nearby cenotes (see opposite) – several of the best in the Yucatán are just a few kilometres away.

△ The beach at Tulum

## Arrival and information

Arriving in Tulum by bus or private transport can be confusing because there are three distinct parts to the community: the ruins, the town and the beaches. Coming in from the north, Hwy-307 turns slightly inland to reach a traffic light and the well-marked pedestrian and bus entrances to the **ruins** – though the site itself is on the water, 1km east. If you plan to head directly to the ruins, get off the bus here, rather than at the Tulum town station, 1.5km ahead.

Another kilometre south along the highway is the beginning of the **town** proper, strung along either side of the road (called Avenida Tulum) for a further kilometre or so. Most of the local accommodation, however, is a few kilometres east, right on the **beach** – all of it connected by a narrow road running north–south along the water. To reach the hotels (accessible only

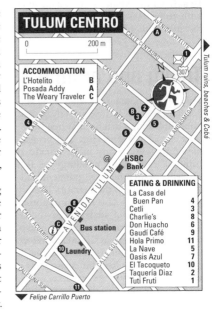

**TULUM CENTRO**

0              200 m

**ACCOMMODATION**
L'Hotelito    B
Posada Addy    A
The Weary Traveler    C

**HSBC Bank**

**EATING & DRINKING**
La Casa del
   Buen Pan    4
Cetli    3
Charlie's    8
Don Huacho    6
Gaudí Café    9
Hola Primo    11
La Nave    5
Oasis Azul    7
El Tacoqueto    10
Taquería Diaz    2
Tuti Fruti    1

**Bus station**

**Laundry**

*Felipe Carrillo Puerto*

by car or taxi), first turn left at the second traffic light after the ruins (a San Francisco de Asis supermarket is on one corner of the intersection), following signs for "Boca Paila–Punta Allen"; the drive is about 3km out to the beach road, where the intersection is dominated by a new all-inclusive resort, the first of its kind here. Turning left on the beach road leads to most of the cheaper cabañas, and the road dead-ends at the southern edge of the ruins. Heading right from the intersection will take you past some of the nicer resorts, though after about 2km the paving gives way to severely rutted dirt (it's passable in a rental car, though). Continuing down this road leads to the most convenient entrance to the Sian Ka'an Biosphere Reserve and, eventually, the village of Punta Allen.

The **bus** station, open 24 hours, is at the southern end of town; luggage storage is available, but expensive (M$10/hr). To get to the beach hotels, you must hire a taxi from here (starting at M$35), as there's no public transport (though plans for bus services are being considered). Tulum's taxi drivers have a reputation for denying the existence of hotels that don't pay them commission; if you want to get to a particular hotel, insist on being taken there. **Colectivos** north to Playa or south to Felipe Carrillo Puerto depart from in front of the bus station.

Almost opposite the bus station is *The Weary Traveler* hostel and **information** centre (see Accommodation). The owners publish good free maps and maintain another info office 1km along the road between town and the beach (8am–8pm).

## Accommodation

Although Tulum's beach is an obvious draw, you may want to stay in **town** if you arrive late in the day, have a limited amount of time or just prefer hot water round-the-clock. Hotel owners in the *zona hotelera* along the **beach road** do not have permanent electricity, relying instead on varying combinations of solar panels, windmills and diesel generators; most have power for only about six hours in the evening.

Depending on your point of view, the candle-lit ambiance is rustic charm or expensive primitivism. Either way, the resulting calm – save for the crash of the surf – helps disguise the increasing development. The hotels closest to the ruins (turn left on the beach road) are some of the cheapest, and the ones that made this area famous with hippie backpackers; they provide sand-floor **cabañas** with shared bathrooms and often little to no security – though this seems to be improving. To the south (right), you'll find some ritzier boutique **resorts**, with jet-set guests and prices to match.

For budget **hostel** accommodation, *The Weary Traveler* (☎984/871-2389, ⓦwww.thewearytraveler.info; M$90), opposite the bus station, is the most convenient, if very party-centric; you don't get breakfast, but you do get a free shuttle to the beach. In the hotel zone, *Tribal Village* (☎984/745-3587, ⓦwww .tribalvillagetulum.com; M$120) has slightly pricier dorm beds. Alternatively, you can **camp** at some of the cheaper cabaña spots very close to the ruins, or at *Camping Oasis Piedra del Sol* (M$70), 4km south of the junction with the road in from town.

## In town

**El Crucero** East side of Hwy-307, at the first stoplight in town, by the pedestrian entrance to the ruins ☎984/871-2610, ⓦwww.el-crucero .com. Fun, friendly hotel convenient for visiting the archeological site. Choose very affordable dorm beds (M$85), standard rooms or deluxe rooms with a/c and distinctive murals painted by a local artist, who has a gallery on site. The bar-restaurant, with its outgoing bartenders, is extremely hospitable. ❷–❺

**L'Hotelito** West side of Av Tulum between C Orion and C Beta ☎984/871-2061, ⓔhotelito@tulumabc.com. This tiny, Italian-run hotel, with its palapa roofs and garden courtyard, has a country feel despite its location in the middle of town. The upstairs rooms have high ceilings with fans; downstairs rooms have a/c. ❻

**Posada Addy** C Polar Oriente between C Satelite and C Centauro ☎984/871-2423. The very clean rooms in this bright-green concrete building are basic Mexican modern, with limestone floors and polyester bedspreads; one giant room has four beds. Parking available. ❺

## On the beach

**Azulik** 800m south of the junction with the road to Tulum town; reservations in the US on ☎1-877/532-6737, ⓦwww.azulik.com. The most romantic option in the area. Deluxe wood cabins, shielded by trees, are done up with fine linens, and soaking tubs carved from tree trunks perch on cliffs over the crashing surf. A quiet beach lies just to the south. No kids allowed, and no electricity. ❾

**Cabañas Copal** 700m south of the junction; reservations in the US on ☎1-877/532-6737, ⓦwww .cabanascopal.com. The round, wood-floor cabañas are packed in pretty close here, but they're a decent mid-range option nonetheless. There's no electricity but plenty of hot water, and a clothing-optional beach. Services include bike rental and spa treatments, such as a ritual Maya *temazcal* sauna. ❻

**Dos Ceibas** 5.5km south of the junction ☎984/877-6024, ⓦwww.dosceibas.com. Small, attractive hotel with a variety of spacious, colourful cabañas in front of a turtle-hatching beach. Yoga and meditation classes offered on site. ❻–❾

**Cabañas El Mirador** 2.6km north of the junction ☎998/845-7689, ⓦwww.hotelstulum.com. Just south of where the coast road dead-ends against the ruins, this old backpackers' standby offers basic sand-floor cabañas with beds or hammocks and shared bathrooms with cold water. The restaurant sits atop a cliff, with a wonderful view and cooling breezes. ❹

**Nueva Vida de Ramiro** 4.5km south of the junction ☎984/877-8512, ⓦwww.tulumnv.com. Peaceful, slightly quirky eco-hotel that relies entirely on wind turbines for power. Attractive wood cabins on stilts (all with front decks) are carefully built over and around untamed greenery. The beach is splendid here, and the restaurant serves tasty seafood, fruit shakes and great espresso. ❽

**Papaya Playa** 400m south of the junction ☎984/804-6444, ⓦwww.papayaplaya.com. The various accommodation options here range from spacious cottages with private bath and hot water to clean, simple cabañas. A small restaurant and bar, set on a cliff above the beach, plays chilled-out lounge beats to encourage the overall backpacker party scene. ❻–❾

**El Paraiso** 1.9km north of the junction ☎984/871-2007, ⓦwww.elparaisotulum.com. The whimsically painted tile-floor rooms, with porches and two double beds, are set back from the action that's going on at the eponymous beach club. A few cabañas are closer to the water, and advisable only if you plan to join the party at the bar. No hot water. ❹–❼

**La Posada del Sol** 1km south of the junction ☎984/876-6206, ⓔlaposadadelsol@hotmail.com. The four artfully designed, high-ceiling "jungle" rooms on the wooded side of the road are exceptionally well priced for their size and attractiveness; three beachfront rooms cost a bit more, but are equally beautiful. There's an excellent jewellery shop in the lobby. ❼

**Cabañas Punta Piedra** 2km south of the junction ☎984/876-9167. One deluxe cabaña takes up the beach view, but the five fairly basic cabins farther back – the cheapest available on the strip with private bath – are the real draw; bike rental and dive shop too. ❹–❻

**Las Ranitas** 5.4km south of the junction ☎984/877-8554, ⓦwww.lasranitas.com. This understated but comfortable French-owned hotel has fourteen well-designed breezy rooms and two family suites, plus tennis courts, a pool and an excellent library. The biggest perk, however, is 24-hour electricity. ❾

**Zamas** 1.2km south of the junction; reservations in the US on ☎1-415/387-9806, ⓦwww.zamas .com. Enormous, comfortable rooms, some right on one of the prettiest stretches of beach in Tulum. Hot water and electricity are plentiful, but the style remains bohemian – though don't expect yoga, like at other similarly priced resorts. Good restaurant on site (see p.159). ❽

**Cabañas Zazil-Kin** 2.4km north of the junction ☎no tel, ⓦwww.hotelstulum.com/zazilkin .htm. The sturdy, sand-floor cabañas with shared baths were recently spruced up, following a change of ownership in 2004 (this was formerly the popular *Don Armando's*). It's still one of the most reliable of the inexpensive places near the ruins – arrive as early in the day as possible, as rooms go fast. ❹

# The town and the beach

Tulum **town** is in the midst of a growth spurt, with a well-groomed central Avenida Tulum giving way to muddy potholes in the back streets. It offers all the basic services and an increasing number of good dinner restaurants and bars, but it's utterly devoid of typical attractions. The place is generally empty of visitors by day because they've all decamped to the **beach**, one of the longest stretches of impeccable white sand along the Caribbean coast. The most popular spot is **El Paraiso Beach Club**, about 2km north from the junction with the road to town. The draw here is not just the sand itself, but the fully stocked bar and friendly hippie vibe. If you're looking for more solitude, head immediately north to Playa Maya, a public beach that's generally empty, though you'll have to bring your own towel and refreshments. It's followed by **Mar Caribe Beach Club**, which is more of a locals' hangout where you can get super-fresh ceviche and a somewhat rowdy scene at weekends. You can also pop into the sea anywhere along the stretch north or south of here, as long as you don't camp out on the lounge chairs maintained by hotels.

For something more energetic than hammock-lounging, head for one of several dive shops along the beach. The one at *Cabañas Punta Piedra* also runs **hiking** trips into the jungle (M$300; 6hr) and rents **bicycles** (M$80/day). Back in town, the Aktún Dive Center, at the intersection with the beach road and the road to Cobá (☎984/871-2311, ⓦwww.aktundive.com), organizes **cavern snorkelling** tours (M$300) as well as PADI scuba-diving and specialized **cave diving** courses (M$3000–11,000). On the north edge of town, near the entrance to the ruins and *El Crucero* hotel, Sian Ka'an Info Tours (☎984/871-2499, ⓦwww.siankaan.org) offers a variety of **nature tours** into the Sian Ka'an Biosphere Reserve; you can choose from a straightforward walking and boat tour, or a kayaking, snorkelling, fishing or cycling trip.

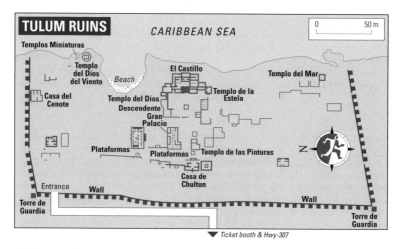

## The ruins

On a sunny day, with the turquoise sea glittering behind the weather-beaten grey stones, the first view of the **Tulum ruins** (Nov–April daily 7am–5pm, May–Oct 8am–6pm; M$37) can be quite breathtaking, despite the small scale of its buildings, all clustered in a compact mass within fortified walls. The city was built in the Late Post-Classic period, after 1200 AD, and was still thriving when the Spanish arrived in the early sixteenth century. The entire site seems a bit haphazard because walls flare outward and doorways taper inward – not the effect of time, but rather an intentional design, and one that is echoed in other sites along the coast like El Rey in Cancún and San Gervasio on Cozumel. On the whole, the buildings appear less than grand when compared to the majestic Castillo at Chichén Itzá.

Tickets are sold at the site entrance, about 1km from the main highway and parking lot, where there's also an enormous warren of souvenir shops; a shuttle bus (M$20) is available for those who don't want to walk. The area is less than 500m long and takes only an hour or so to see, though you may want to allow time to **swim** at the tiny, perfect beach that punctuates the cliffs. Arrive in the early morning or late afternoon to avoid the worst crowds.

You're admitted to the site through a breach in the wall that surrounded the city on three sides (the fourth faced the sea). This **wall**, some 5m high with a walkway along the top, may have had a defensive purpose, but more likely it delineated the ceremonial and administrative precinct – the site you see today – from nearby residential enclaves. Archeologists believe the towers that mark the corners of the wall were small temples rather than military structures, owing to the altars installed in them. In any case, the walls did take on a defensive role around 1890, in the waning years of the Caste Wars. Maya followers of the Talking Cross liberation movement (see box, p.175) reoccupied the site, where they practised rituals and held out against Mexican armies for more than 25 years.

Walking straight towards the sea from the entrance, you reach the **Casa del Cenote**, a square structure straddling a water-filled cave; a small tomb occupies its central portion. On the bluff above and to the right are the **Templos Miniaturas**, several scale-model temples, complete with tiny lintels and mouldings, which were probably shrines. Up the hill stands the **Templo del Díos del**

**Viento** (Temple of the Wind God), a small, single-room structure. It's set on a round platform, a rare design for this region. This building finds its twin in a similar chamber, the **Templo del Mar**, which overlooks the water at the southern edge of the site.

Skirt the small beach to get to the north side of the main promontory and the **Templo del Díos Descendente**, in which the flared walls of the small temple at the top of a long staircase are emphasized by an additional level of moulding that juts out at an opposite angle. The diving (or descending) god, carved in stone above the narrow entrance of the temple, is one of Tulum's quirks: the small, upside-down winged figure appears all over the city, but in only a handful of places elsewhere in the Maya world. His exact meaning is unclear – he may represent the setting sun, or rain or lightning, or he may be the bee god, since honey was one of the Maya's most important exports. Immediately adjacent to the temple, the imposing **Castillo**, on the highest part of the site, commands fine views in every direction, but to protect the worn stones, visitors may now only look up at the building from the plaza at its base. The fortress-like pyramid, flanked by steep staircases, may have served not just as a temple, but also as a beacon or lighthouse; even without a light, however, it would have been an important landmark for mariners along an otherwise featureless coastline. Just south of the Castillo, the squat, barely restored **Templo de la Estela** (Temple of the Stele) was named for a commemorative stone tablet found inside; it bears a date well before the foundation of the city, so was presumably brought here from elsewhere.

Turning away from the sea, you face a cluster of buildings arranged on a city-like grid, with the chief structures set on stone platforms along parallel streets. The most fascinating of these – and what used to be the main attraction here, before it was closed to visitors – is the colonnaded **Templo de las Pinturas** (Temple of the Paintings). The murals, actually painted on the exterior of an older temple, have been preserved by the surrounding gallery you see now, decorated with masks of the rain god Chac. The predominant images are of Maya gods and symbols of nature's fertility: rain, maize and fish. One remarkable piece, done at a later date than the others, shows Chac seated on a four-legged animal – clearly inspired by the conquistadors with their horses.

## Eating

Because the accommodation in Tulum is spread over 10km and the town is so far from the beach, almost every hotel in the area has its own restaurant – ranging from cheap and grungy to very chic. Guests tend to stick to the restaurants in their own hotels, but a few **places to eat** along the coast road merit a special trip. In the village, a number of inexpensive **cafés** serve *comida corriente* and rotisserie chicken, and there's an increasing number of cheerful, mid-range places run by European expats.

### Cafés

**Los Cántaros** East side of Hwy-307, in front of *El Crucero* hotel. Tasty *nevería* (ice cream shop) serving numerous fruity flavours of sorbet – a refreshing treat after touring the ruins.

**La Casa del Buen Pan** Tulum town, C Sagitario Poniente at C Alfa. Savour the a/c along with organic coffee and a perfectly flaky croissant at this European-style bakery; there's an adjacent garden where you can enjoy your light meal. Baking starts early, so ring the bell if the door isn't yet unlocked.

**Gaudí Café** Tulum town, west side of Av Tulum, opposite the bus station. Good for inexpensive set-price breakfast specials, Spanish sandwiches and really strong coffee.

**Tuti Fruti** Tulum town, west side of Av Tulum between Av Satelite and C Centauro. The "Tortas Gigantes" sign is more prominent than the proper name on this small shack, and they're not kidding:

massive sandwiches, starting at M$20, are served along with a full range of juices and *licuados*. Open 24hr.

## Restaurants

**Cetli** Tulum town, west side of Av Tulum between C Orion and C Beta, at *L'Hotelito* ☎984/745-9001. Chef Claudia trained in Mexico City's premier culinary academy, and at her tiny, surprisingly inexpensive restaurant she serves refined versions of Mexican classics, such as a delicate peanut-based *mole de cacahuete*. Closed Sun.

**Don Huacho** Tulum town, west side of Av Tulum between C Beta and C Osiris. The town's longtime Mexican seafood specialist features the mysteriously spiced *pescado a la Don Huacho*, very fresh ceviche and tasty shark empanadas, which are great with beer.

**Hechizo** On the coast road, 7.5km south of the junction with the road to Tulum town (turn at "Rancho San Eric", the last driveway on the left before the Sian Ka'an entrance) ☎984/100-0170, ⊕hechizo@bigfoot.com. A gem of a restaurant owned by a former *Ritz-Carlton* chef. The short, sophisticated international menu (watermelon-and-goat-cheese salad, lobster *pozole*) changes daily; appetizers cost about M$50, mains around M$180. Call or email to reserve one of the eight tables. Closed Mon and parts of the low season.

**Hola Primo** Tulum town, two blocks east of Av Tulum on C Acuario. This palapa-roof kitchen on the "Cancha Maya" (the plaza around the ceiba tree where the town was founded) caters to locals with *sopa de lima*, *panuchos* and *salbutes*. You can fill up on savoury snacks for just a few pesos.

**La Vita è Bella** On the coast road, 1.6km north of the junction. Reasonably priced sandwiches and wood-oven pizzas are served until 11pm; a cocktail bar opens at 9.30pm, and a European party crowd often gets dancing later under the big palapa.

**La Nave** Tulum town, east side of Av Tulum between C Orion and C Beta. A busy town hangout with fresh-fruit breakfasts, inexpensive pizza from a wood-fired oven (M$45 and up) and Italian staples like fresh gnocchi (M$65 and up).

**Posada Margherita** On the coast road, 2.5km south of the junction at *Posada Margherita* hotel☎984/100-3780. Fantastic beachfront Italian restaurant with dishes like fresh taglierini with shrimp and zucchini and fish poached in sea water. The antipasto platter, served on a slice of a tree trunk, is a bounty of piquant cheeses, cured meats and olives. Prices are higher than the informal setting might suggest (around M$140 for entrees), but the food is worth it.

**Qué Fresco** On the coast road, 1.2km south of the junction, at *Zamas*. A good mid-range Italian restaurant with fresh pastas and a wood-fired pizza oven. Its beachside setting makes it a great way to start the day too – try the Caribbean French toast.

**El Tacoqueto** Tulum town, east side of Av Tulum at C Acuario. A dependable *lonchería* with gut-busting daily specials for about M$40 or delicious hot-off-the-grill tacos for even less.

**Taquería Diaz** Tulum town, west side of Av Tulum between C Orion and C Beta. Vying for the title of best taquería in town, this place specializes in assorted grilled meat fillings. Dinner only; closed Wed.

# Nightlife

Although many visitors tell tales of the ultimate beach party in Tulum, tracking down that elusive revel in the sand can be a little difficult. Look for flyers in town, or ask around at cabaña camps like *Tribal Village* and *Zazil-Kin*; there's often some kind of beachfront bongo jam and DJ fest around the full moon. Otherwise, most people stick to their hotel **bars** for an evening's entertainment.

**Charlie's** Tulum town, west side of Av Tulum between C Alfa and C Jupiter. This long-standing hangout with a Mexican menu (good guacamole) also hosts art shows and features live music under its big palapa.

**Mezzanine** On the beach 1.5km north of the junction with the road to Tulum town. Opened in late 2004, this super-cool bar-lounge channels Ibiza style; it's the only place on the beach where you can regularly find a dance scene.

**Oasis Azul** Tulum town, east side of Av Tulum between C Beta and C Osiris. Blue lights, a disco ball and a soundtrack of international techno and house hits set the party tone at this hip bar. Sit out front on the sidewalk and sip a drink, or pack onto the small dance floor in the back.

**El Paraiso Beach Club** On the beach 1.9km north of the junction. This very hospitable beach bar has plenty of room for dancing on the sand. A big screen shows movies, or trippy visuals during the occasional massive parties.

## Listings

**Bank** An HSBC with an ATM is in the middle of town, about 300m north of the bus station on the east side of Av Tulum; you can change money at one of several cambios on the main street.

**Buses** The main bus station is at the southern end of Tulum town,

**Car rental** Ana y José, on Av Tulum just south of the post office ☎984/871-2030, ⓦwww.anayjose.com.

**Colectivos** gather in front of the main bus station, offering service to Playa del Carmen (frequently) and Felipe Carrillo Puerto (every 1–2hr).

**Internet** *The Weary Traveler*, opposite the bus station, offers Internet access, including a wireless hub. Praetorian, on the east side of Av Tulum across from the HSBC bank, is reliable and you can also get your photos downloaded from your digital camera.

**Laundry** Lavandería Burbujas, two blocks east of the main drag on C Jupiter, the street just south of the bus station.

**Post office** On the west side of Av Tulum just after the first town intersection (marked by a small obelisk).

**Tours** Sian Ka'an Info Tours, in front of *El Crucero* hotel by the ruins entrance (☎984/871-2499, ⓦwww.siankaan.org), runs **nature tours** into the reserve. Aktún Dive Center, on Av Tulum at the intersection with the beach road and the road to Cobá (☎984/871-2311, ⓦwww.aktundive.com), organizes **cavern snorkelling** tours and **cave diving** courses.

## Cenotes near Tulum

As an alternative to the beach, there are a large number of **cenotes** very close to Tulum; a couple of them are the most impressive in the area. In addition to Hidden Worlds (see p.152) north of town, you can also check out **Gran Cenote** (M$50), just 4km west from Tulum on the road to Cobá (turn inland at the intersection with the San Francisco de Asis market). A collapsed cavern that's good for swimming and snorkelling, the pool can get very busy in the middle of the day, as it's a popular stop for tours, but the dramatic stalagmites and stalactites are well worth braving crowds for. **Cenote Carwash** (also called Aktun-Ha; M$30), 4km further west, is less impressive on the surface – it's simply a big pond, without any rock structure above – but strap on a snorkel mask or dive tanks and you'll be astounded by the underwater rock formations, touted as among the best on the peninsula. Divers have an advantage here, as they can reach the spectacular **Room of Tears cave**, dripping with stalactites, and go below the algae bloom that thrives March through October, making snorkelling impossible. Both the Gran Cenote and Carwash are easily accessible by second-class bus or a taxi. You may have trouble carrying on by bus from the cenotes to Cobá (see opposite), however, because coaches are infrequent and often full.

For more solitude, you may want to go instead about 3km south of Tulum on Hwy-307, where a small ranch road leads 1km east to **Cenote Escondido** (also called Mayan Blue). This is a secluded spot that's good for snorkelling and rarely crowded; pay the entrance fee (M$30) at a small kiosk on the west side of Hwy-307, opposite the ranch road.

# Cobá and Punta Laguna

About 50km northwest of Tulum lies the wonderfully isolated Maya site of **Cobá**, a fascinating place to visit for its jungle setting and the added fun of getting around the far-flung pyramids by rented bicycle, if you like. Although the ruins aren't as well restored as those at Tulum, their scale is much more impressive, and the dense greenery and wildlife make a good counterpoint to the coast. Moreover, they're not difficult to reach – the narrow but well-paved road out of Tulum leads past the Gran Cenote and Carwash about 48km to a large roundabout, and the village of Cobá and the ruins are just a few kilometres farther. Approximately 20km east of the ruins, the **Reserva de Monos Arañas de Punta Laguna** is home to the northernmost community of spider monkeys in Mexico; even if you don't see the critters, the lake here is a beautiful place to canoe. Buses run regularly to Cobá from Tulum, but there's no public transport at all to the monkey reserve. If you don't have a car and would like to visit everything in a day outing, including a stop at Gran Cenote or Cenote Carwash (see opposite), ask at your Tulum hotel about tours, which are typically informal and cost not much more than a taxi fare.

## Cobá

Set in the dense, muggy inland forest amid several lakes, the crumbling ancient city of **COBÁ** (daily 7am–6pm; M$37) is a fascinating and increasingly popular site, but as the clusters of buildings are spread out over several kilometres, the site can absorb a high number of visitors without feeling crowded, and you can ramble through the forest in peace, looking out for its toucans, egrets, coatis and myriad tropical butterflies, including the giant iridescent blue morpho. A visit here requires at least a couple of hours to see everything; renting a bicycle just inside the site entrance is highly recommended.

Occupied from about 100 AD until the arrival of the Spanish, the site was so long established and legendary that it was mentioned in the *Chilam Balam* of Chumayel, the book of Mayan prophecy and ritual lore written in the eighteenth century, well after the city had been abandoned. The city's zenith was in the Late Classic period, around 800 AD, when most of the larger pyramids were built, and its wealth grew from close links with the great cities of Petén, in lowland Mexico and Guatemala. These cities influenced Cobá's architecture and its use of stelae, typically seen only in the southern Mayan regions. Cobá also prospered later through its connections with coastal cities like Tulum, and several structures, built around 1200, reflect the style found at those sites.

The first cluster of buildings you reach is the compact **Grupo Cobá**, with a large central pyramid known as the Iglesia (church), used for Mayan ceremonies even after the city ceased to function. Claustrophobic corbel-vault passages lead a little way inside to tiny rooms. Up the main path, at a fork, the **Conjunto Pinturas**, named for the paintings inside the temple that tops the main building, is a complex assembled with recycled stones in the Late Post-Classic era, after 1200. Along the left path is a small **ball-court**, only one side of which has been excavated – the stone skull carving set in the ground is a marker found in most courts. Just behind the playing field is the **Xaibé** (Crossroads) pyramid, so named for its position at a major junction of *sacbeob*, the limestone-paved highways the Maya built to connect cities; the pyramid's rounded, stepped design is typical lowlands building style.

The path ends at the looming **Nohoch Mul**, taller than El Castillo at Chichén Itzá and, in its narrow and precipitous stairway, resembling the pyramid at Tikal in Guatemala; at the top, a small temple, similar to structures at Tulum, dates from around 1200 AD. The view takes in nearby lakes, as well as the jungle stretching uninterrupted to the horizon.

Retrace your steps to the central fork, where another path leads 1km down a shady *sacbé* to **Grupo Macanxoc**, a cluster of some twenty stelae, most carved during the seventh century AD. Stele 1 shows part of the Maya creation myth and the oldest date recorded in the Maya Long Count calendar system, which tracks the days since the moment of creation. Other stelae depict an atypically high number of women, suggesting that Cobá may have had female rulers. Clambering between the carvings, you're crossing not natural hills, but unreconstructed pyramids; in a way, these offer a more palpable sense of the civilization that thrived here than some of the more immaculately rebuilt structures.

### Practicalities

Four **buses** (M$25) a day run to Cobá from Tulum and continue on to Valladolid. The first one leaves Tulum at 7am (arriving at 7.30am) and the next, which continues to Chichén Itzá after stopping in Valladolid, arrives in Cobá at 9.30am – you could therefore theoretically cover both sites via public transport from Tulum, though you would be very rushed. Five buses run back to Tulum from Cobá, the last leaving at 6.30pm. A taxi from Tulum to Cobá costs M$200 each way. At the site, you can catch a breeze and speed up your tour by **renting a bike** for M$25, or hire a *triciclo* cab for M$75 (M$100 with a guide).

The **village** of Cobá, where the bus stops, is little more than a cluster of houses and cabañas a few hundred metres from the site entrance, which fronts a small lake (filled with crocodiles; don't be tempted to swim). **Hotels** are few, but two are quite comfortable: *Villas Arqueológicas* (℡985/858-1527, ⓦwww .clubmed.com; ➐), overlooking the lake, offers a wonderful bit of tropical luxury, complete with a swimming pool and an archeological library; the relatively new *Hotelito Sac-bé* (℡984/879-9340; ➌-➎), on the left side of the main street through the village, is the better of two budget options, with five clean rooms offering various amenities (one has a/c). Enquire at the post office across from the bus stop if no one's at the hotel. There's a good **restaurant** in front of the lake, *La Pirámide*, which serves Yucatecan specialities like *cochinita pibil*, as well as other Mexican dishes. Additionally, you'll find several no-frills **cafés** adjacent to the entrance to the site.

## Reserva de Monos Arañas de Punta Laguna

From the roundabout just southeast of the Cobá ruins, continue northeast 18km (following signs for Nuevo X-Can) to reach the **Reserva de Monos Arañas de Punta Laguna**, at the small village of the same name. From the entrance kiosk, you're required to hike with a guide (M$30 per person, plus M$150 for a guide for a group of up to ten people) to where the spider monkeys usually congregate – there's no guarantee you'll see them, but they're at their liveliest in the early morning and the late afternoon. The trail winds past unrestored ruins and a cenote, and in the middle of the reserve is a big brackish lake where you can rent canoes (M$50) and paddle around looking for herons and crocodiles. To reach the area you'll need a car, though some Cobá tours from Tulum (enquire at your hotel) and Valladolid (through *La Candelaria* hostel; see p.200) include a visit to the reserve. Pack food as well as snorkel gear for the cenote, since there are no concessions nearby.

# The Sian Ka'an Biosphere Reserve

**SIAN KA'AN** means "the place where the sky is born" in Maya, which seems appropriate when you experience the sunrise in this stunningly beautiful part of the peninsula. The nature reserve is a huge, sparsely populated region sprawling along the coast south of Tulum, with only about a thousand permanent inhabitants, mainly fishermen and subsistence farmers, gathered in the village of **Punta Allen** and in an experimental agricultural settlement called El Ramonal.

Created by presidential decree in 1986 and made a World Heritage Site in 1987, the Sian Ka'an Biosphere Reserve is one of the largest protected areas in Mexico, covering 1.3 million acres. It contains all of the principal eco-systems found in the Yucatán Peninsula and the Caribbean: approximately one-third of the area is **tropical forest**, one-third fresh- and saltwater marshes and **mangroves**, and one-third marine environment, including a section of the Mesoamerican Barrier Reef. The variety of flora and fauna is astonishing. All five species of Mexican **wild cat** – jaguar, puma, ocelot, margay and jaguarundi – live in the forest, along with spider and howler monkeys, tapir and deer. More than three hundred species of **birds** have been recorded

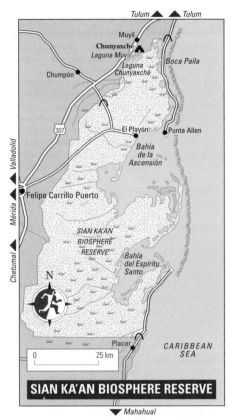

(including fifteen types of heron and the endangered wood stork, the largest wading bird that breeds in North America), and the coastal forests and wetlands are important feeding and wintering areas for North American migratory birds. The Caribbean beaches provide nesting grounds for four endangered species of **marine turtle**, while some extremely rare West Indian manatees have been seen offshore. Morelets and mangrove **crocodiles** lurk in the swamps and lagoons.

Although you can enter the park unaccompanied (M$20), either on the Punta Allen road south from Tulum's *zona hotelera* or west off Hwy-307, south of the village of Muyil, you will benefit more from an organized tour, which is easily arranged in Tulum. One of the best operators is Sian Ka'an Info Tours, part of a non-profit group called Centro Ecológico de Sian Ka'an, which funds its research and educational programmes with two principal **tours**: a day-trip (M$700) and a sunset excursion (Nov–April; M$450) inside the reserve. Both begin with an instructive walk through mangroves and diverse eco-systems to a large cenote, followed by a boat ride across the lagoons and the ancient Maya canals that crisscross the marshy areas here. It's a beautiful trip around the fringes of the reserve's vast open spaces, with excellent opportunities for birdwatching, especially on the sunset tour. You can reserve a place on either trip at the office in Tulum (see p.160). Alternatively, a visitors' centre a few kilometres inside

## The UNESCO biosphere concept

Established in 1968 by UNESCO (United Nations Educational, Scientific and Cultural Organization), the biosphere project is an ambitious attempt to combine the protection of natural areas and the conservation of their genetic diversity with scientific research and sustainable development for local peoples. Biosphere reserves consist of a strictly protected **core area** in which human activity is kept to a bare minimum and the land is typically public property; a designated **buffer zone** used for non-destructive activities such as experimental research; and an outer **transition zone**, merging with unprotected land, where traditional land-use and human settlements are permitted, as is private or community land-ownership.

The success of a biosphere reserve depends to a great extent on the co-operation and involvement of **local people** – the Sian Ka'an management plan, for instance, incorporates several income-generating projects, such as fishing (using low-impact techniques), ornamental plant nurseries and low-impact tourism. But although Sian Ka'an has a relatively large uninhabited core area, the reserve's transition zone is under heavy pressure from the spread of tourism in Tulum – the beach property in this area is particularly valuable, and large plots have been sold off in recent years to wealthy Mexicans and Americans, raising serious concerns that the reserve is being compromised. At the same time, however, nature conservancy groups have been able to purchase plots to maintain untouched areas.

Mexico's biosphere programme, after a lull in the 1990s, has regained focus since 2000. Including Sian Ka'an, five of the country's fourteen biosphere reserves are in the Yucatán. Calakmul, the largest in the peninsula, was established in 1993 in Campeche State and contains the vast ruined city of the same name. Off the Caribbean coast, the enormous coral atoll named Banco Chinchorro, established in 2003, is a sanctuary for marine life. And the peninsula's sizeable flamingo population is protected in two separate reserves: Ría Celestún, stretching along much of the west Gulf coast, and Ría Lagartos, along the northern coast. Both were natural parks that earned biosphere status in 2004.

For further **information** on the Sian Ka'an biosphere, contact the Amigos de Sian Ka'an, a non-profit organization formed to promote the aims for which the reserve was established. The Amigos support scientific research and produce a series of guide and reference books on the natural history of Sian Ka'an. Their main office is in Cancún (☎998/880-6024, ⓦwww.amigosdesiankaan.org).

---

the reserve, operated by Ecocolors (☎998/884-3667, ⓦwww.ecotravelmexico .com), rents kayaks, bicycles and snorkel gear.

**Accommodation** is available at Punta Allen (see opposite), or at the rigorously eco-friendly *Boca Paila Camps* (☎984/871-2499, ⓦwww.cesiak.org; ❺–❼), run by Centro Ecológico de Sian Ka'an. The camp's sturdy tents are hidden among the trees in a prime location near the beach; guests share bathrooms (with composting toilets), but there is hot water, heated with solar and wind power. The staff is very informed about the reserve, and the inexpensive **restaurant** is worth the long drive from Tulum for its sunset view across the jungle. Note that although there are many enticing stretches of sand along the road south from the Tulum hotel zone, biosphere regulations **prohibit camping** on the beach to control erosion – which is not to say it's not done, unfortunately.

## Punta Allen

Right at the tip of a narrow spit of land, with a lighthouse guarding the northern entrance to the **Bahía de la Ascensión**, the remote fishing village of **PUNTA ALLEN** is not the kind of place you stumble across by accident.

With a population of just five hundred, it's the largest village inside the reserve and a focus of initiatives by both government departments and non-profit organizations promoting sustainable development. Bonefish and tarpon in the bay are a draw for active travellers; layabouts will appreciate the mellow, timeless atmosphere that pervades the sand streets. Telecommunications are almost completely absent, and the most noise you'll hear is the creak of your hammock and the rustle of palm fronds in the breeze. The road south from Tulum's *zona hotelera* has helped maintain Punta Allen's special quality: it's famously rutted, almost rollercoaster-like, in the rainy season, and is still slow going during the dry months, typically requiring at least three hours for the 50km drive.

An **alternate route** from south of Tulum is equally tedious, but less affected by wet weather and more convenient if you'll be continuing south later: a narrow road runs straight east from Hwy-307 to a small dock in the middle of the reserve. Turn off the highway 46km south of Tulum, after Km 181; look for a small hand-painted white sign for "Playón" (or "Vigia Chico", if coming from the south). Several kilometres in, you pay the reserve entrance fee, then continue straight on for 42km more. At the dock, you can get a launch across the bay to Punta Allen (M$50 for 2–3 people); allow about two and a half hours for the drive, keeping in mind that the last boat leaves at 6pm. If you don't have a car, the only option is a **colectivo** from Felipe Carrillo Puerto (see p.175), which is relatively fast, but at the expense of your teeth rattling out of your head on the bumpy track. It's also often packed over capacity. In any case, the trip is so time-consuming that you will use half a day just getting there, so take plenty of cash and plan to spend at least a couple of nights to recover from the jarring trip and prepare for the return.

Entering Punta Allen from the north, past the tiny naval station on the right and beached fishing boats on the left, the first and cheapest of the **accommodation** options is the bohemian *Posada Sirena* (☎984/877-8521, ⓦwww .casasirena.com; ❺) but, if you can afford it, *Cuzan Guesthouse* (☎983/834-0358, ⓦwww.flyfishmx.com; ❼), the next hotel south, is far preferable – it specializes in **bonefish tours** and rents wood cabañas and tepees, some with

△ Sian Ka'an Biosphere Reserve

hot water. In the off season, prices are cut by almost half. The bar and restaurant are great, though you'll need to book meals if you're not staying there. *Serenidad Shardon* (reservations in the US on ☎1-248/628-7217, ⓦwww.shardon.com; ❸–❾) offers everything from camping space and dorm beds to all or parts of a big beach house; it's also the only place in the village that takes credit cards.

A couple of **restaurants**, such as *Xoken* at the north end of the beach, serve basic seafood, but, as very few of the locals eat out, *Cuzan* is the most reliable and consistent. A **mobile shop** in a truck travels the length of the peninsula on Thursdays and Saturdays, selling meat, bread, fruit and vegetables, reaching Punta Allen about 2pm. Although there's no dive shop, the hotels generally have some form of **watersports equipment** for their guests and allow non-residents to rent. Fishermen can be persuaded to take you into the reserve for a fee: for instance, a three-hour snorkelling tour, during which you might see some of the local loggerhead turtle population, runs to about M$1200 for a boat. Victor Barrera is a recommended local guide who takes people **fishing** in the flat waters of Bahía de la Ascensión and organizes **ecotours** (☎984/879-8040, ⓦwww.macabimarch.com).

On land, for a great view over the bay you can simply follow the trail south from the village to the **lighthouse**, 2km away. On the way, you'll pass the Sendero de Laguna Negra, a loop of well-tended hiking **trails** through the woods, punctuated by viewing platforms.

If you're **leaving** by launch and *colectivo* to Carrillo Puerto, boats depart at 6am and 3pm – sign up beforehand at Tienda Caamal to reserve your space. The last launch leaves around 5pm.

# Chunyaxché

Heading south from Tulum, the highway narrows as it runs along the west edge of the Sian Ka'an reserve. After about 20km, you reach the ruins of **CHUNYAXCHÉ** (daily 8am–5pm; M$24), at the village of **Muyil**. Catch any second-class **bus** from Tulum to Chetumal and ask to be dropped at the gate to the ruins. A sign on the west side of the highway points to the modest entrance, with just a ticket booth and restrooms. Despite the size of the site – probably the largest on the Quintana Roo coast – and its proximity to Hwy-307, you're likely to have the place to yourself, as most visitors to the Yucatán don't travel farther south than Tulum.

Archeological evidence indicates that Muyil was continuously occupied from the Pre-Classic period until after the arrival of the Spanish in the sixteenth century. There is no record of the inhabitants coming into direct contact with the conquistadors, but they were probably victims of depopulation caused by European-introduced diseases. Most of the buildings you see today date from the Post-Classic period, between 1200 and 1500 AD. The tops of the tallest structures, just visible from the road, rise 17m from the forest floor. There are more than one hundred mounds and temples, none of them completely clear of vegetation, and it's easy to wander around and find dozens of buildings buried in the jungle; climbing them is forbidden, however.

The centre of the site is connected by a *sacbé* to the small **Muyil lagoon** 500m away. This is joined to the large Chunyaxché lagoon and ultimately to the sea at **Boca Paila** by an amazing **canalized river** – the route used by ancient Maya traders. At the end of the boardwalk leading through the mangroves to the lagoon, you might find a fisherman offering a boat tour down the river, where you'll come across even less explored sites, some of which appear to be connected to the lagoon or river by **underwater caves**.

**Leaving the site**, particularly if you're making your way up to Tulum, should be easy enough, provided you don't leave too late; continuing south could prove a little more difficult, as buses to Chetumal run only every two hours, and *colectivos* are often full when they pass.

# Travel details

## Buses

Bus service in this area is provided primarily by first-class ADO and Mayab, and supplemented by second-class Oriente and ATS. The second-class buses will stop anywhere on the highway on request, but run infrequently – in this case, you're better off in a **colectivo**.

**Cobá** to: Cancún (3 daily via Playa del Carmen; 3hr); Chichén Itzá (9.30am via Valladolid; 1.5hr); Tulum (5 daily; 30min); Valladolid (4 daily; 1hr)

**Tulum** to: Cancún (frequently; 2hr); Chetumal (5 daily first-class, 11 daily second-class, all via Bacalar; 3–4hr); Chichén Itzá (2 daily via Valladolid; 2hr); Cobá (4 daily; 30min); Felipe Carrillo Puerto (3 daily; 1hr); Mérida (3 daily first-class, 6 daily second-class; 4–7hr); Playa del Carmen (frequently; 1hr); San Cristóbal de las Casas (2 daily via Palenque; 13hr); Valladolid (5 daily; 1.5hr); Villahermosa (3 daily; 10hr)

## Colectivos

White shared vans line up in front of Tulum's bus station and depart whenever they are full – every ten or fifteen minutes for Playa del Carmen, and every hour or so for Felipe Carrillo Puerto. They will stop anywhere on request. You can also flag them down from the roadside, and they will stop if they have an empty seat. Pay as you get out.

## Boats

Launches to Punta Allen from El Playón in the Sian Ka'an reserve run on request throughout the day, with the last one leaving at 6pm – but try to be there earlier, in case there's a crowd, as boats hold only six people.

# The Costa Maya and the Río Bec

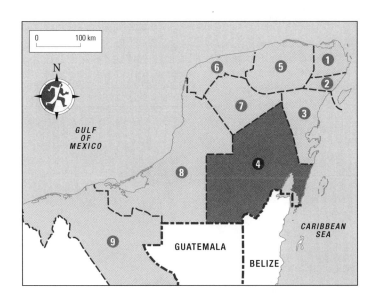

CHAPTER 4    # Highlights

* **Mahahual** A beach bum's fantasy, with a string of cabaña camps and a few friendly restaurants. **P.176**

* **Banco Chinchorro** Scores of ships have dashed against this large coral atoll 30km off the coast, making a vast playground for scuba divers. **P.178**

* **Laguna Bacalar** As clear and gloriously coloured as the Caribbean, this 45-kilometre-long freshwater lake is home to a huge variety of birds and fish. **P.179**

* **Río Hondo** Team up with a tour operator in Chetumal to go rafting along this seldom-visited river, which forms Mexico's border with Belize. **P.185**

* **Kohunlich** Giant monster masks, a sprawling palace complex with fantastic views, and parrots swinging among the enormous fan palms are the main draws at this archeological site. **P.187**

* **Calakmul** The largest, most remote ruined Maya city in the Yucatán. **P.191**

△ Banco Chinchorro

# The Costa Maya
# and the Río Bec

South of Tulum, Quintana Roo State noticeably changes character: the jungle creeps up flush against the narrow highway, now just two lanes with the merest whisper of a hard shoulder, and margaritas are in very short supply. With the exception of an isolated beach-bum community on the **Costa Maya**, south of the Sian Ka'an Biosphere Reserve, the real personality of this part of the peninsula is found in the inland towns and villages. This region was the centre of the **Zona Maya**, the semi-independent area established by Maya guerrillas during the decades-long Caste Wars, the bitter battles that marked the second half of the nineteenth century. Decades of grand campaigns and small uprisings finally succeeded in earning the Maya some measure of autonomy, and a lessening of the exploitation they had suffered at the hands of Spanish colonists and Mexican hacienda-owners.

Ancient Maya history, too, is everywhere in evidence along the southern border of Mexico, reached by heading due west out of Chetumal via Hwy-186. The jungle to the south of this narrow road, which was laid down only in the latter half of the twentieth century, is some of the densest and richest in the country, and it contains fantastic Maya ruins, collectively known as the **Río Bec sites**. These tumbledown cities dot either side of the highway well into Campeche State, making for a fascinating archeological tour in an area that's still very unaffected by tourism, and barely populated. With mostly older, rickety second-class buses plying the roads and very few places to bunk, the Río Bec is a difficult and sometimes pricey place to explore (taxis provide the only transport to many ruins), but very rewarding if you make the effort.

The first settlement of any size beyond Tulum – a good 100km south – is **Felipe Carrillo Puerto**, a crossroads on the way to Valladolid and Mérida with strong Maya roots. Carrillo makes a good base for excursions into Sian Ka'an (see p.174) and smaller Maya communities inland. The main highway continues through the village of Limones, where a turn-off leads to the Costa Maya towns of **Mahahual** and **Xcalak**; their isolated beachfronts have become the next logical camping place for those who've deemed Tulum too crowded.

Back on Hwy-307 and continuing south, you pass the seldom-visited Maya ruins of **Chacchoben**, followed by the beautiful **Laguna Bacalar**, an important destination for birds and the people who love them. The impeccably clear lake is also popular with Mexican vacationers. The road ends in **Chetumal**, the

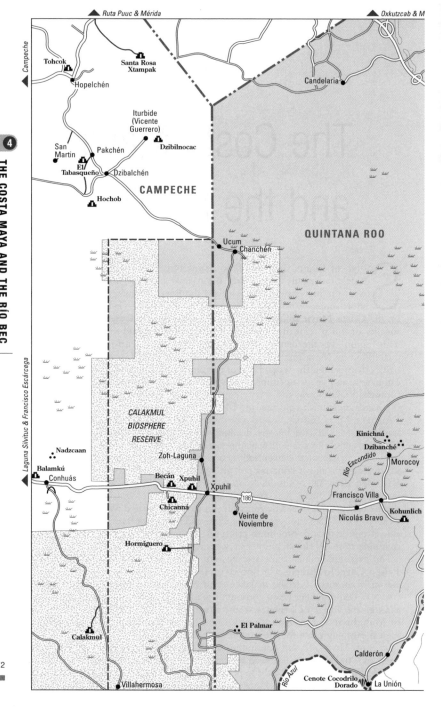

Campeche

Tohcok
Hopelchén
Santa Rosa Xtampak

Candelaria

Iturbide (Vicente Guerrero)
Dzibilnocac

San Martin
Pakchén
El Tabasqueño
Dzibalchén

Hochob

CAMPECHE

QUINTANA ROO

Ucum
Chanchén

CALAKMUL BIOSPHERE RESERVE

Laguna Silvituc & Francisco Escárcega

Nadzcaan

Kinichná
Dzibanché
Morocoy

Río Escondido

Balamkú
Conhuás

Zoh-Laguna

Becán  Xpuhil
Xpuhil
186

Chicanná

Francisco Villa

Veinte de Noviembre

Nicolás Bravo
Kohunlich

Hormiguero

El Palmar

Calakmul

Calderón

Villahermosa
Río Azul
Cenote Cocodrilo Dorado
La Unión

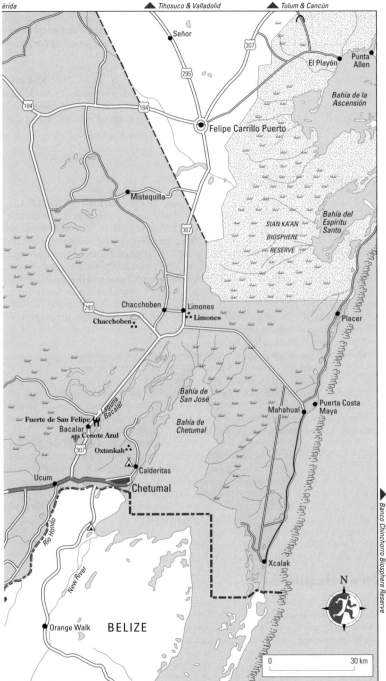

Señor

307

El Playón • Punta Allen •

295

*Bahía de la Ascensión*

184

184

⊙ Felipe Carrillo Puerto

Mistequilla •

307

*SIAN KA'AN*

*BIOSPHERE*

*Bahía del Espíritu Santo*

*RESERVE*

293

Chacchoben • Limones • Limones

**Chacchoben** • Placer •

*Bahía de San José*

*Laguna Bacalar*

*Bahía de Chetumal*

Mahahual • Puerta Costa Maya •

**Fuerte de San Felipe**

Bacalar • **Cenote Azul**

307 Oxtankah • •

Calderitas

Ucum • **Chetumal**

*Río Hondo*

*New River*

Xcalak •

N

• Orange Walk **BELIZE**

0 _____ 30 km

state capital and the gateway to Belize. A small, pleasant enough city, situated on a wide bay with a multicultural border-town feel, Chetumal is a good point from which to explore the **Río Hondo**, the wide river that serves as Mexico's southern border.

From Chetumal, Hwy-186 runs west through the **Río Bec** zone, which includes recently excavated and beautifully adorned ruins like **Kohunlich**, though most travellers use the town of Xpuhil, just over the border in Campeche State, as a base because it's closer to the Yucatán's largest ruined city, **Calakmul** – awe-inspiring not only for its size but also for its setting at the centre of an enormous biosphere reserve.

# Felipe Carrillo Puerto

A modest town with a population of about 15,000, **FELIPE CARRILLO PUERTO** is home to an organic honey operation and the largest greenhouse system in Mexico. Life is very slow-paced here, and visitors (of which there are very few) will find little to do aside from hanging out on the town plaza in the evenings with the locals. And as a jumping-off point for excursions into the wilderness or to smaller Maya villages, it's a very pleasant place to spend a night or two. More intriguing, but less visible, is the town's history as the capital of the Zona Maya in the nineteenth and early twentieth centuries. Chan Santa Cruz, as the town was first known, began as a stronghold for Maya following the cult of the Talking Cross in the 1850s (see box, opposite). Although the town was all but destroyed during the wars, the cultural pride fostered by its period of independence is still evident today.

Along with its original name, much of the town's historical trappings are gone, though you can still visit the **Santuario de la Cruz Parlante**, built on the site of the Talking Cross. Turn west off the main street at the Pemex, and the complex is four long blocks down on the right. The remnants of the cross are now kept in a smaller village nearby, but the sanctuary retains an air of mystic power (remove your shoes when you enter), with the altar topped with several crosses "dressed" in *huipiles*, in the distinctive Yucatec Maya way.

The other, more imposing relic of the religion is the **Iglesia de Balam Na**, which dominates the main plaza in front of the bus station. In a tidy bit of tables-turning, the Cruzob forced white interlopers they'd captured in the jungle to build the first Maya temple of the post-Columbus era, beginning in 1851. Despite its pagan roots, it nonetheless resembles a Franciscan church, with its arched roof and single-nave layout. After the Caste Wars ended in the early twentieth century, the building, and the rest of the town, was abandoned. Though Chan Santa Cruz was resettled and renamed in the 1930s, the Balam Na was consecrated as a Catholic church only in 1948; its governing order is Irish, as the local population would not accept Spanish priests.

## Practicalities

There is a rudimentary **tourist office** (Mon–Fri 8am–2pm, 6–9pm), six blocks south of the **bus station** and one block east. On the main north–south street (Hwy-307) you'll find a **petrol station** and an adjacent **ATM**. Across the street, an **Internet café** and **caseta** provides inexpensive service. Although you can visit nearby natural spots and villages on your own (see p.176), you'll learn more about the environment and have greater interaction with the local Maya if you travel with the small **tour operator** here. Carlos Meade of Yaxche Arbol de la Vida, a nonprofit organization, works with Xiimbal Tours (☎983/834-1073, Ⓦwww.xiimbal.com) to promote sustainable tourism through trips to small Maya communities and hikes to the barely excavated ruins near Mistequilla. The group also runs jaunts to the ruins of Chunyaxché and around the lake at the nearby Maya village of Señor, and maintains the portal **website** Ⓦwww .carrillopuerto.net. For a relaxing day out a bit closer to town, visit Rancho El Angel (☎983/834-0358, Ⓦwww.birdwatchmexico.com), a beautiful and tranquil patch of forested land just twenty minutes south of town, owned by the proprietors of *Cuzan Guest House* in Punta Allen; a typical tour includes **birdwatching**, hiking several botanical trails, swimming and enjoying lunch cooked over a wood-fired grill (M$250). You can also catch a **colectivo to Punta Allen** here (3hr): it leaves at 10am and 3pm from the first block east out of the central traffic circle.

If you **stay overnight**, try the cheery *Hotel Esquivel* (☎ & Ⓕ983/834-0313; ❺), on the plaza and only 100m from the bus station, with a good and reasonably priced restaurant attached. Several other enjoyable **restaurants** serve inexpensive fare: *Los Tucanes*, two blocks east of the petrol station, is a big, breezy seafood place popular in the afternoons. In the evenings, the cosy, colourful *La Placita Maya*, two blocks south of the bus station, is the best spot for tacos. About 1km out of the centre on the road to Valladolid, *El Jardín* serves delicious home-cooked lunches in its pretty outdoor setting. Also, don't miss the bargain *panuchos* and *salbutes* sold all day at the bus station – even if you're just

---

## The Talking Cross movement

In 1850, after the first wave of the Caste Wars ended in the Maya's defeat at Mérida, a group of rebels led by **José María Barrera** (himself a mestizo) retreated into the forest of Quintana Roo. The story goes that they set up camp near a cenote and discovered a cross, embedded in a tree, that spoke to the group and encouraged them to fight against their oppressors.

The apparition was not unique – such talking crosses and statues, known as *way'ob*, are common in Maya mythology as conduits through which disincarnate spirits speak. While contemporary scholarship is of course a bit sceptical, the Maya were inspired enough by the phenomenon and galvanized for further fighting. Following the cross's directions (with the help of a "translator", Manuel Nahuat) and armed with weapons supplied by the British via neighbouring British Honduras, the **Cruzob**, as the fighters soon called themselves, began conducting raids against Franciscan missions and Spanish forts around the central peninsula. The encampment by the cenote grew into a formal town named **Chan Santa Cruz** ("little holy cross"), which functioned as the Cruzob's capital. They established control of territory as far north as Tulum and well inland, and they enforced it ruthlessly: light-skinned non-Maya were typically shot on sight or captured and enslaved.

After the rest of the peninsula was subdued, the Cruzob continued their guerrilla struggle; even after 1901, when the British withdrew support and Mexican armies occupied and gutted Chan Santa Cruz, the rebel Maya held a large patch of the jungle, later negotiating with the Wrigley's chewing-gum company to grant access to *chicle* trees and making a good bit of money in the process. In 1935 they finally signed a treaty, carefully worded to emphasize that they were not conceding, only allowing the Mexican government to rule them. Around the same time, Chan Santa Cruz was resettled and given an innocuous new name, **Felipe Carrillo Puerto**, after a former governor of the Yucatán who was assassinated in 1924. Though they've since stowed the guns, many of the Maya in this area maintain the syncretic religious practices – which meld Catholic elements such as baptism with ancient healing and prayer rituals – that were born out of this violent era.

passing through, it's worth hopping off the bus to savour these quintessential Yucatecan snacks.

## Towards Valladolid and Mérida

Heading northwest from Carrillo, a well-paved road leads into the densely forested interior and eventually to Valladolid. Along the way you may want to stop off at the scenic lake at the edge of the traditional Maya village of **Señor**, or in **Tihosuco**, where the small but engaging **Museo de la Guerra Castas** (Tues–Sun 10am–6pm; M$5) tells the story of the Maya rebellion (in Spanish). A botanical garden grows at the back, and the gift shop sells locally made herbal treatments. The Franciscan church here is particularly dramatic, its crumbling nave open to the sky and overgrown with vines and weeds; it was torched during one of the many battles in this town between 1848 and 1865, and until recently stood empty, still blackened by the fires that destroyed it. Now a good part of the interior has been whitewashed and reclaimed for regular church services. At the front on the plaza stands a weathered monument to native son Jacinto Pat, one of the Caste Wars' great leaders.

**Colectivos** provide the most frequent service to Señor, Tihosuco and Valladolid, departing every hour or so from the Carrillo market, on the northwest corner of the central traffic circle. But you may find it difficult to hop from village to village, as the shared vans are often packed full – hence the particularly high number of locals thumbing a ride along this route. Keep a sharp eye out for people on the roadside if you're driving.

# The Costa Maya

The beaches that line the 250km of coast between the southern edge of the Sian Ka'an reserve and the Belize border, while not as scenic as those in Tulum, are quite beautiful in their sheer emptiness. Because of this, the **COSTA MAYA**, as this area is known, has recently become the object of fascination among those seeking a truly remote getaway, and for people hoping to make some money on this relatively untouched patch of Caribbean-front property (the latter group includes investors in a lavish and bizarrely out-of-place cruise-ship pier, the Puerta Costa Maya). At the same time, the government has finally invested in basic services like electricity and a petrol station. Nonetheless, the two towns in the region, **Mahahual** and **Xcalak**, have a very end-of-the-world feel, and those looking for solitude will certainly find it here. Watersports enthusiasts will also want to make the trek to **Banco Chinchorro**, a divers' playground that was designated a biosphere reserve in 2003.

Infrequent transport has helped keep the tourist droves at bay. **Buses** to Mahahual and Xcalak leave Chetumal at 6am and 4pm daily from the main bus terminal; an additional bus runs at 11am on weekends. Service goes first to Mahahual, then 15km south past the hotels and camping spots on the coast road, then back inland and down to Xcalak. Coming from Tulum, you can connect with this service at the town of Limones if you're there by 8am and 5pm respectively, and 1pm for the added weekend service.

## Mahahual

**MAHAHUAL**, 60km east of Hwy-307 via a fast, dead-straight highway, is a tiny town of wood shacks along a narrow beach. Even though the glitzy pier looms a few kilometres north, the pace is still more akin to Playa of twenty years past than to Cozumel, and has attracted a small European expat community. So far the area has yet to be radically developed: phone lines reached here in mid-2004, electricity can be sporadic, and there's still **no bank, ATM** or **Internet** café. Ships dock at the pier about four times a week in high season, and on those days the seemingly abandoned community springs to life to accommodate the handful of vacationers who escape the pier's walled compound – souvenir stands are set up, and a few jet skis buzz in the shallow, pale-green water off the beach. The town also grows festive during Semana Santa (the week before Easter) and Christmas, when Mexican families pack the beaches. Check out the website Ⓦ www.mahahual.biz for details on local services.

The main tourist activity in Mahahual is **snorkelling** or **diving** around the pristine offshore reef. Dreamtime Dive Centre, at Km 2.7 on the coast road south of town (Ⓦ www.dreamtimediving.com), is a reliable, dedicated shop, though only the *Maya Palms* resort (reservations in the US on ☏ 1-888/843-3483, Ⓦ www.2dive.com; ❾), 10km south of town, has a licence for diving inside the borders of the Banco Chinchorro reserve.

For **food**, the usual selection of ceviche restaurants line the beach; *Cocina Económica Mari*, one block back from the water, serves cheap, home-cooked lunch. At the southern end of town, *Casa del Mar* offers delicious, well-priced breakfasts and beer-batter shrimp tacos, as well as occasional full-moon parties, while *Luna de Plata*, across the road, is an excellent Italian restaurant (with a few rooms to rent: ☏ 998/102-6459; ❺).

### Practicalities

**Accommodation** is basic and generally less expensive than what you'd find in Tulum. The priciest option (but well worth the splurge) is 15km north of town, along the road to Placer and Tampalam: *KaiLuumcito* (☏ 800/538-6802 in the US, Ⓦ www.mexicoholiday.com; ❾), a tiny, deluxe-rustic resort (no electricity, but plenty of hot water, and booze at the honour-system bar) has ten spacious palapa-protected tents and a flawless beach-bum vibe, honed from three decades of experience along the coast. Rates include excellent breakfast and dinner. The cheapest option is in town – the basic shared-bath cabañas at *Coco Ha* (no tel; ❹) – though you'll do better to press on to *Travel In'* (see below). Additionally, *Los 40 Cañones* (Ⓦ www.los40canones.com; ❺–❻) is a very friendly and tidy place for a bit more.

The unpaved coast road leading **south from town** contains several other options, easily reached by the bus that runs through twice a day. Note, though, that the beaches here are nothing like the bare white sands at Tulum; they're often shaded with pine trees, not palms, and there's lots of sea grass in the water. Just south of town, *La Cabaña de Tío Phil* (☏ 983/835-7166, Ⓔ tiophilhome@hotmail.com; ❺) has comfortable rooms and can organize snorkelling and boat trips, while around Km 5.5, *Balamku* (☏ 983/838-0083, Ⓦ www.balamku.com; ❼) has an eco-friendly outlook, recycling greywater and keeping natural landscaping around its attractive white stucco, thatch-roof cottages. *Travel In'*, at Km 6, offers **camping** (M$60) on the beach or two simple rooms with shared bath (Ⓔ adam.denning@planet_interkom.de; ❹). Its **restaurant**, a hangout for many expat residents, serves home-made bread and inexpensive, internationally flavoured meals in the evenings, except on Sunday, when it's closed. A bit farther, *Kabah-Na* (☏ 983/838-2195, Ⓔ kabahna@yahoo.com, Ⓦ www.kabahna.com; ❺) has attractive cabañas and can provide meals on request. Much farther south (Km 29), wind-powered *Xahuayxol* (☏ 983/837-

0732, @ www.xahuayxol.com; ❽) offers a few festively painted wood cabins on stilts and a much nicer beach (and charges accordingly).

**Leaving** Mahahual, it's faster to take the morning *colectivo* to Chetumal (departs around 10am) than to take the bus, which goes through Xcalak. Note that on the way out on the main highway from Mahahual, a military **checkpoint** conducts very thorough searches for drugs and other contraband – but as long as you haven't got any of that stuff, the police are perfectly pleasant.

# Xcalak

You can theoretically carry on 10km farther south to **XCALAK**, the only other community in the area, but the coast road becomes virtually impassable. Instead, turn back inland after *Xahuayxol* to join the paved route that runs diagonally down from the main east–west highway (or, to bypass Mahahual entirely, turn south off the latter road after 50km). At the tip of the isthmus that stretches like a finger towards Belize, Xcalak was once the largest town in Quintana Roo, but is today a desolate village that still hasn't got over being flattened by a hurricane in 1955; steady electricity was restored only in 2004.

As Xcalak has no real beaches to speak of, the main reason to visit is its superb snorkelling, diving and fishing. **Banco Chinchorro**, an atoll littered with more than a hundred shipwrecks and encrusted with rainbow-hued coral, is easy to visit via Xcalak, or simply enjoy the clean reef closer to shore. The other local "sport" seems to be trawling for kilos of cocaine washed up on the beach (aka *pez cuadro*, or "square fish"), as smuggling operations occasionally go awry offshore and the cargo is dumped overboard. The same is true in Mahahual, but here it only enhances the generally sketchy feel of the town. For more information on Xcalak, check out the good website, @ www.xcalak.info, maintained by the few relocated American and Canadian residents.

### Practicalities

In town proper, at the northern edge, *Marina Mike's* (☎ 983/831-0063, @ www .hotelinxcalak.com; ❼–❽) has its own very tiny beach as well as a handful of gorgeous **rooms** with full kitchens and huge balconies overlooking the sea. For those on a budget, the *Maya Village* (no tel, @ www.mayavillage.com, ask around town for Alan, the owner; ❶–❹), just over the bridge on the north side of town, has basic palapas and **campsites** (M$60), but try to confirm ahead of time via email that it's open – it has been unreliable in the past.

Further north, past a small bridge in what is sometimes grandly referred to as the *zona hotelera*, lie a few more lodging options. The best one is *Costa de Cocos* (☎ 983/831-0110, @ www.costadecocos.com; ❼), a laid-back spot with its own fishing boats and dive instructor, plus good snorkelling right off the dock; rates include a continental breakfast buffet, and their **restaurant**, which is the only place to eat regularly in the area, is excellent and reasonably priced. (*The Leaky Palapa*, in town, serves lunch and dinner Sat–Mon.) A bit more beachfront-luxe are *Tierra Maya*, 2km from Xcalak (☎ 983/831-0404, @ www.tierramaya.net; ❼), and the charming *Sin Duda Villas*, 8km further north (☎ 983/831-0006, @ www.sindudavillas.com; ❼–❾). Back in town, the PADI dive shop XTC (☎ 983/831-0461, @ www.xcalak.com.mx) runs **snorkelling trips** (M$265; 2hr), offers open-water certification courses (M$3500) and has a licence to dive at Banco Chinchorro.

# Laguna Bacalar and around

Glimpsed through the trees to the east as you continue south along Hwy-307, the gorgeous **LAGUNA BACALAR** resembles the Caribbean Sea, sparkling clear and ranging in colour from palest aqua to deep indigo. The reeds and trees around the water host a variety of **birdlife**, and in the lake you'll find fresh-water snails and huge fish that reach nearly 2m in length. At 45km long and, on average, 1km wide, Laguna Bacalar is the second largest lake in Mexico (after Lago de Chapala, south of Guadalajara), linking with a series of other lakes and eventually the Río Hondo and the sea.

Near the northern end of the lake, about 15km south of Limones, a rather grand intersection (built for the benefit of cruiseship passengers) marks the way to the ruins of **Chacchoben** (8am–5pm; M$33), 9km west of the highway. The "place of red corn", as its name means, is open to visitors while undergoing heavy excavation. There's virtually no explanatory signage for the exposed buildings, but the archeological work in progress reveals the real physical labour required to reassemble any ruin. A visit is recommended only if you have your own car, however, as bus transport past this spot, off the main highway and not near any large town, is so difficult to negotiate as to make the trip not worthwhile.

The site, which flourished in the Early Classic period (250–600 AD), is usually deserted, and you can explore amid the palms and dripping Spanish moss in peace. Its core is a huge raised plaza, dominated by a stepped pyramid with rounded corners, similar to those found at Uxmal, though much smaller. Palapa thatch protects a few extant stucco decorations. Leaving the site, you can continue inland on the back road to explore the Ruta Puuc or head straight to Mérida.

More Maya remains dot the southern end of the lakeshore, around the town of **Bacalar**, which was a key point on the pre-Columbian trade route. The

△ Laguna Bacalar

*Chilam Balam* of Chumayel, one of the Maya's sacred books, mentions it as the first settlement of the Itzá, the tribe that occupied Chichén Itzá. Now it's a quiet place to stop for a day or two, preferred by naturalists as a base for bird-watching and kayaking on the glassy lake. The town clusters on a hill above the water, with a long road running along the shoreline below. On the plaza is an **ATM** and an **Internet** café, and the **bus stop** is just off the southwest corner.

In the centre of the town, just down the hill from the plaza, **Fuerte de San Felipe** was built by the Spanish in the 1730s for protection against British pirates from Belize (then British Honduras). The fort became a Maya strong-hold during the Caste Wars and, in 1901, was the last place to be subdued by the government. Today it is a small **museum** (Tues–Sun 9am–7pm; M$50) that displays some of the Maya relics found here, as well as trappings of pirate days. At the north end of town there's a **public beach** (*balneario ejidal*) with a restaurant and palapas for lounging (M$5). About 1.5km out along the far southern end of the lakeshore road you can have more watery fun at the inky-blue "bottomless" (well, 140m) **Cenote Azul** (8am–8pm; free), which is busy with swimmers, dive-bombing teens and live musicians at weekends. Several **restaurants** capitalize on the lake view, but more reliable is the basic yet satisfying *Orizabas*, off the northwest corner of the town's plaza.

If you want to **stay overnight**, check out a number of options strung out along the water. In town, on the lakeshore road, *Casita Carolina* (☎983/834-2334, ⓦwww.casitacarolina.com; ❺) is an American-owned guesthouse with five rooms, a spacious back garden and a shared kitchen. At the south end of the road, past Cenote Azul, the wonderfully kitsch and comfortable *Hotel Laguna* (☎983/834-2206, ⓕ983/834-2205; ❺) is done up with seashell-encrusted lacquer countertops and plaster pillars galore. Two places outside of town, particularly good for birdwatchers, offer a somewhat wilder setting: *Villas Ecotucan* (☎983/834-2516, ⓦwww.villasecotucan.com; ❻), 5km north, has comfortable cabañas on attractively landscaped grounds between the lake and acres of uncleared forest. Ten kilometres south of Bacalar, an excellent budget nature hideaway is *Botadero San Pastor* (☎983/831-3494, ⓔbotadero@yahoo.com; ❷), with a few fixed tents and space for **camping**, as well as kayaks for guests' use. *Colectivos* and second-class buses can drop you on the highway near the entrances to both places.

# Chetumal and around

If you're heading south to Belize or Guatemala, you can't avoid **CHETU-MAL**, 15km from the Belize border and capital of the state of Quintana Roo. Until 1898, when the Mexican Navy established the frontier outpost of **Payo Obispo** (Bishop's Point) on this spot, no official border ran through the Bahía de Chetumal, which forms the city's southern edge; today elements of the neighbouring country's culture still linger in the little clapboard houses and the residents' often British-sounding names. After being obliterated by Hurricane Janet in 1955, the city has taken decades to reassert itself, but it still has very few notable "sights" to speak of. Indeed, it's largely oblivious to tourists and dedicated almost entirely to unglamorous cross-border commerce – which can be refreshing after the rustic hedonism of the Caribbean beach resorts. Mexicans come to visit the **duty-free zone** between the two countries, a dilapidated mini-mall area accessible by bus where shops flog an odd assortment of goods:

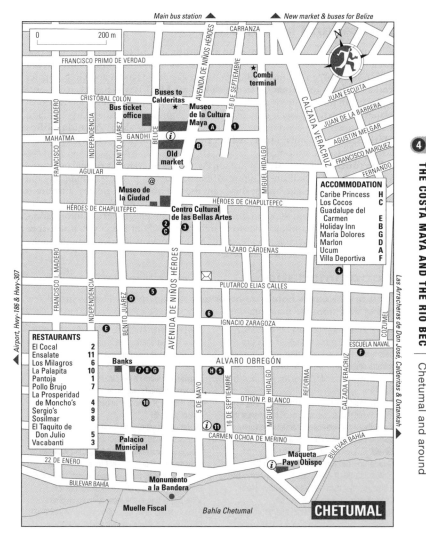

Main bus station ▲     ▲ New market & buses for Belize

CARRANZA

0    200 m

FRANCISCO PRIMO DE VERDAD

AVENIDA DE NIÑOS HÉROES

16 DE SEPTIEMBRE

★ Combi terminal

CRISTÓBAL COLÓN

CALZADA VERACRUZ

JUAN ESCUTIA

Buses to Calderitas
★

Bus ticket office

Museo de la Cultura Maya Ⓐ ❶

JUAN DE LA BARRERA

AGUSTIN MELGAR

I. MADERO

INDEPENDENCIA

BENITO JUAREZ

GANDHI

BELICE

ⓘ

FRANCISCO MARQUEZ

MAHATMA

FRANCISCO

Old market

Ⓑ

MIGUEL HIDALGO

FERNANDO

AGUILAR

@

Museo de la Ciudad

ACCOMMODATION
Caribe Princess   H
Los Cocos   C
Guadalupe del Carmen   E
Holiday Inn   B
María Dolores   G
Marlon   D
Ucum   A
Villa Deportiva   F

HÉROES DE CHAPULTEPEC

Centro Cultural de las Bellas Artes

HÉROES DE CHAPULTEPEC

❷ Ⓒ ❸

LÁZARO CÁRDENAS

FRANCISCO I. MADERO

Airport, Hwy-186 & Hwy-307

INDEPENDENCIA

BENITO JUAREZ

AVENIDA DE NIÑOS HÉROES

✉

PLUTARCO ELIAS CALLES

Ⓓ ❺

❻

IGNACIO ZARAGOZA

Ⓔ

❹

ESCUELA NAVAL

Ⓕ

Las Arracheras de Don José, Calderitas & Oxtankah

COZUMEL

RESTAURANTS
El Cocal   2
Ensalate   11
Los Milagros   6
La Palapita   10
Pantoja   1
Pollo Brujo   7
La Prosperidad de Moncho's   4
Sergio's   9
Sosilmar   8
El Taquito de Don Julio   5
Vacabanti   3

Banks
❼❽Ⓖ

ALVARO OBREGÓN

Ⓗ❾

REFORMA

CALZADA VERACRUZ

5 DE MAYO

16 DE SEPTIEMBRE

MIGUEL HIDALGO

OTHON P. BLANCO

❿

ⓘ❶❶

CARMEN OCHOA DE MERINO

Palacio Municipal

22 DE ENERO

Máqueta Payo Obispo
ⓘ

BULEVAR BAHÍA

BULEVAR BAHÍA

Monumento a la Bandera

Muelle Fiscal    Bahía Chetumal

**CHETUMAL**

Dutch cheese, Taiwanese hi-fis, American peanuts, reproduction Levi's from the Far East, Scotch whisky, and more. Likewise, vendors of appliances and cheap lingerie line the main avenue, but despite these modern details, Chetumal retains a certain old-fashioned graciousness, especially palpable in the evenings, when the bay boulevard is filled with lovers and families.

Although it can't really be praised as a destination for its own sake, Chetumal does make a decent one- or two-day stop for resting and restocking; everything from food to Internet access is significantly cheaper here. From the city, you can also make day or overnight trips to the Río Bec archeological sites or to the little-visited Río Hondo area, both to the west. Be warned, though, that car rental (see p.184) is the one thing in Chetumal that's not a great deal.

# Arrival and information

Chetumal's main **bus station** is on the north side of town, a short taxi ride from the centre (about M$18); locker rental costs M$5 per hour. A **bus ticket office** in town, on Avenida Belice between avenidas Gandhi and Colón, spares you a trip back to the station to buy tickets for ADO, Riviera and Caribe services. The **airport** – rumoured to be under development to receive international planes but currently open only for the daily flight from Mexico City – is 2km west of town. The central part of Chetumal is strung along **Avenida Niños Héroes**, the town's main street, which runs south from a big electricity-generating plant to the waterfront.

The **tourist information** office, on Avenida 5 de Mayo at Avenida Carmen Ochoa (Mon–Fri 8.30am–4.30pm; ☎983/835-0500), provides helpful bus and hotel information, plus maps; they can also fill you in on nearby attractions in Belize. A smaller kiosk on the malecón at Avenida Hidalgo maintains later hours (Mon–Fri 9am–8.30pm, Sat 9am–3pm). For pre-departure information, ⓦwww.chetumal.com provides basic information about the city. A **bookstore** at the corner of avenidas Héroes and Ochoa stocks primarily Spanish books, but does have a few English guides.

# Accommodation

Most of Chetumal's **hotels** are on or near Avenida Niños Héroes in the few blocks back from the malecón.

**Caribe Princess** Av Obregon 168 ☎983/832-0900, ©caribe_princess@hotmail.com. One of the best examples of the city's time-warp ritz; smoky mirrors and shades of pink dominate the decor. Rooms are clean and all have a/c; free parking too. ❻

**Los Cocos** Av Héroes 134 ☎983/832-0544, ⓦwww.hotelloscocos.com.mx. A better deal than the *Holiday Inn*, with large, comfortable rooms, a pool and a sprawling terrace bar and restaurant. ❼–❾

**Guadalupe del Carmen** Av Zaragoza 226 ☎983/832-8649. Clean and tidy two-storey hotel, a little roomier than budget competitor *María Dolores*; some rooms have a/c. ❹

**Holiday Inn** Av Héroes 171 ☎983/835-0400, ©hotel@holidayinnmaya.com.mx. This luxury option has all the comforts of a chain hotel, plus an onsite travel agency. Compared to the giant suites at *Los Cocos*, though, you're paying for the name. ❾

**María Dolores** Av Obrégon 206 ☎983/832-0508. Basic budget offering that's popular with backpackers. Rooms are cramped but very clean, and there's a good restaurant onsite. ❹

**Marlon** Av Juárez 87 ☎983/832-9411, ©hotel-marlon@hotmail.com. Quiet, modern business hotel with well-kept rooms arranged around a freeform indoor pool. ❻

**Ucum** Av Mahatma Gandhi 167 ☎983/832-0711, ⓕ983/832-6185. One of Chetumal's better deals, though it looks unpromising from the motel-like front section. If possible, opt for rooms in the back building, by the huge pool, which are a little brighter and have a choice of a/c or fan. ❺

**Villa Deportiva** in the local sporting club on C Escuela Naval at Av Calzada Veracruz ☎983/832-0525, ext. 23. Clean enough hostel with basic rooms (M$30) and very small beds (four to a room). You'll probably have the place to yourself unless a travelling sports team is in town.

# The city

Chetumal is a hotchpotch of modern concrete buildings erected after 1955 (some even exuding a bit of 1960s flair) and a few old wood houses with porches that remain from the settlement's earliest days. The only tourist attraction, on Avenida Niños Héroes at the northern edge of the city centre, is the large, modern **Museo de la Cultura Maya** (Tues–Thurs, Sun 9am–7pm, Fri & Sat 9am–8pm; M$50). Numerous interactive displays and models – including a full-scale replica of the mural-filled room at Bonampak (see p.314) – provide insight into the natural world of the Yucatán as well as the ins and outs of ancient Maya society, mathematics and cosmology. The explanations (in Spanish and English) are a bit flowery, but overall it's a quality survey of the peninsula's culture. The auditorium shows foreign art and independent films every week for free. On the street in front of the museum, the *Alegoría del Mestizaje* **sculpture** is one of the most striking depictions of the popular theme of the intermingling of Spanish and indigenous cultures, showing modern Mexico born of a conquistador and a Maya woman. Immediately south is a little warren of shops and *loncherías* – what's called the "old" **market** (the newer, larger one, where most of the fresh produce is sold and buses for Belize gather, is 1km northwest along Avenida Héroes).

A few blocks south of the old market on Avenida Héroes, the **Centro Cultural de las Bellas Artes**, in a striking 1936 neo-Maya-style school, now houses the **city museum** (Tues–Sun 9am–7pm; M$10), with a collection of romantic memorabilia – from locally made Raleigh bicycles to ladies' hand fans – reminiscent of Chetumal's swashbuckling days, when it was a city of *vaqueros sin caballos* ("cowboys without horses"). The state schools for the performing arts are also located here, offering free live performances several evenings a week.

Avenida Héroes continues down to the bay and the spic-and-span **malecón**, popular for fishing and evening strolls. A few blocks east, behind the modern Palacio Legislativo, a small Caribbean-style wooden house contains the fascinating **Maqueta Payo Obispo** (Tues–Sat 9am–8pm, Sun 10–3; free), a scale model of the town as it looked in the 1920s, hand-carved in 1985 by an elderly resident named Luis Reinhardt McLiberty, with the help of local students. The small adjacent museum tells the story of the lighthouse barge *Chetumal*, with which the Mexican army helped establish the town and the country's border with then British Honduras, in order to stop the flow of arms in to the rebels defending the Zona Maya. The town was renamed after the barge (itself named after a Maya lord of the sixteenth century) in 1936.

## Eating and drinking

The intersection of Avenida Héroes and Avenida Obregón has the highest concentration of restaurants, while the **market stalls** south of the Museo de la Cultura Maya have good, inexpensive fare at lunch. **Nightlife** isn't particularly vibrant, but on weekend evenings, when a double-decker shark-shaped party bus cruises up and down the malecón, the plaza is busy with food stalls, and residents flock to the bar-restaurants (and the drive-through liquor store) strung along the seafront east of the plaza.

**Las Arracheras de Don José** East on malecón, where the boulevard turns north. The speciality of this sprawling terrace restaurant, very popular on weekend nights, is meat tacos, from plain old pork to ostrich (*avestruz*), served with a fantastic array of fresh salsas. Want more meat? Steaks are also well priced.

**El Cocal** in *Los Cocos* hotel. Not the cheapest food in town (entrees range from M$40 to M$150), but Mexican dishes at this open terrace restaurant are served with more care; breakfast is good too. The mix of tourists and dressed-up locals makes for a convivial atmosphere, and evenings often see the live keyboard stylings of some crooner or other. Open till 1am Fri and Sat.

**Ensalate** Av Ochoa between Av 5 de Mayo and Av 16

Septiembre. This lunch café specializes in baguette sandwiches, with a good range of vegetarian choices.

**Los Milagros** Av Zaragoza between Av Héroes and Av 5 de Mayo. Enjoy tasty, inexpensive breakfasts at this little sidewalk café popular with local journalists.

**La Palapita** Av Blanco between Av Héroes and Av Juárez. A sweet, very local *lonchería* in a little wooden house. One of several bargain options on this block.

**Pantoja** Av Gandhi at Av 16 de Septiembre. Good *comida corrida* (M$45), a favourite with the locals, and hearty dishes like *mondongo* and *chilaquiles* for breakfast. Closed Sun.

**Pollo Brujo** Av Obregón between Av Juárez and Av Héroes. Roasted chicken and nothing else, served fast and hot.

**La Prosperidad de Moncho's** Av Calzada Veracruz between Av Calles and Av Cardenas. A sprawling, casual *restaurante familiar* under a tent, with live bands on weekend afternoons; in the evening, attention turns more seriously to drinking, and the clientele is typically all-male.

**Sergio's** Av Obregón 182. This upmarket but reasonably priced restaurant (most entrees are less than M$100) has a few veggie options, such as soups, pizzas and salads, as well as inexpensive, well-prepared steak.

**Sosilmar** Av Obregón, in the *María Dolores* hotel. One of the best budget options in town, with good meat and fish and a few splurgy items like *camarones al diablo* for M$90. Closed Sun.

**El Taquito de Don Julio** Av Calles between Av Héroes and Av Juárez. A good choice for an evening snack if you don't want to walk out to *Don José's*. Make a meal of overstuffed grilled-meat tacos and some *queso fundido* on the fluorescent-lit terrace.

**Vacabanti** Av Héroes opposite *Los Cocos* hotel. Chetumal's only contemporary "bistro-lounge", frequented by members of the city's very small youth subculture, who sip cocktails and watch MTV.

## Listings

**Airlines** Aerocaribe, Aviacsa and Mexicana run daily flights to Mexico City. Mexicana and Aerocaribe reps are located in the tourist kiosk in front of the Mayan culture museum (Mon–Sat 9am–2.30pm); Aviacsa is on Av 5 de Mayo at Av Cardenas (☎983/832-7676).

**Buses** Long-haul buses leave from the main bus station. Services include: Mahahual and Xcalak (daily at 6am & 3.15pm, plus Sat & Sun at 11am; 3hr 30min–4hr 30min); Xpuhil (14 daily; 2hr); Francisco Escárcega (12 daily; 4–5hr); Cancún (hourly 4.45am–midnight via Tulum, Playa Del Carmen; 4–6hr); Mérida (12 daily; 8–9hr); Campeche (3 daily via Escárcega and Xpuhil; 7hr); Villahermosa (6 daily; 9–11hr); Palenque and San Cristóbal (3 daily; 7–10hr); Mexico City (4 daily; 24hr). Buses to Flores in Guatemala (1 daily; 12hr) also leave from here. For Bacalar (hourly), it's easier to catch *combis* in town, at the Terminal de Combis on Av Hidalgo at Av Primo de Verdad. For Belize, see box, below.

**Car rental** Sacbe Tours (see "Tour operators", right) has a few cars for rent.

**Combis** leave from the station on Av Primo de Verdad at Av Hidalgo, making them an easier option than buses for nearby destinations, such as Bacalar (every 30min; 30min), Ucum (hourly from 7am), La Unión (5 daily; 2.5hr) or Nicolas Bravo (4 daily; 1hr 15min).

**Internet** *Arba* Internet café, in the central market just south of the Museo de la Cultura Maya, is cheap and has fast connections.

**Medical services** The hospital on Av Juárez between Av Aguilar and Av Héroes de Chapultepec is the most centrally located.

**Post office** on C Plutarco Elias Calles at Av 5 de Mayo (Mon–Fri 8am–6pm, Sat & Sun 9am–12.30pm).

**Tour operators** are not plentiful in Chetumal, and often need several days' advance notice to arrange something for you. On the plus side, because there are not yet many fixed routes, you can often tailor a trip precisely to your tastes. Sacbe Tours (☎983/833-2080, ⊛www.sacbetours.com) runs day-trips to Kohunlich and the Río Hondo area. Ernesto Parra Calderón, with Mayan World Adventures (☎983/832-4729, ⊛www.mayanworldadventures.com), is another excellent guide, specializing in eco-tourism.

---

### Moving on to Belize

Buses run frequently between Chetumal and **Corozal** (1hr), the closest town on the Belize side, though you must get off the bus and walk across the bridge at the official border at Subteniente Lopez, 8km west of Chetumal. Citizens of the UK, US, Canada, Australia and New Zealand do not need a visa. The cheapest, very rattle-trap buses leave from Lázaro Cárdenas market (called the "mercado nuevo"), on the north side of town on Avenida Calzada Veracruz, between 10am and noon; you can get over the border for about M$20, and a few of these continue on to **Orange Walk** (2hr 30min) and **Belize City** (5hr). First-class service on better-outfitted vehicles departs from the main bus station (5 daily; 3hr to Belize City). Note that cars rented in Mexico cannot typically be driven into Belize. Likewise, there's no air travel straight from Chetumal; you have to cross to Corozal, twenty minutes inside the border, and take an internal flight.

# Around Chetumal

On weekends, the town descends en masse on **Calderitas**, a small seaside resort just 6km north around the bay; there's only one **place to stay**, the *Yax-Há* RV park (℡983/834-4127, ✉yax_ha1@yahoo.com; ❻), which has nice, breezy rooms and a large picturesque garden with a swimming pool right on the seafront. You can hire a **boat** at the adjacent *Cahuamo II* bar (℡983/834-4220) for various day outings: to the beaches on the nearby empty island of Tamalcab (M$300 for 6–8 people); a tour around the bay to look for manatees (3hr; M$1500); or to several other nature spots. **Buses** to Calderitas leave frequently from Avenida Cristóbal Colón west of Avenida Héroes, behind the museum.

Seven kilometres north of Calderitas, **Oxtankah** (8am–5pm; Mon–Sat M$22) is a small Maya site with the remains of a maritime city that was occupied in the Early Classic period (250–600 AD) and developed to exploit ocean resources – specifically salt. You'll find the ruins of several buildings around two squares, with an architectural style similar to that of the Petén to the southwest. In the middle of it all is a Franciscan chapel built by the Spanish. Oxtankah is also allegedly the site of the original **mestizaje**, the intermixing of Spanish and Indian races that literally gave birth to modern Mexico. The legendary first couple were Gonzalo Guerrero, whose ship was wrecked off the coast in 1511, and Za'azil, a high-ranking woman in the Maya tribe that took Guerrero in. Guerrero assimilated, had three children – the first mestizos – and even fought against the Spaniards who arrived a few years later intent on conquering the peninsula. The site is peaceful and wooded, with the flora neatly labelled, including one fantastically huge ficus tree just west of the chapel. You'll need your own transport to get to Oxtankah (follow the shoreline north through Calderitas) or a taxi from Chetumal (M$130 round-trip with waiting time), as there's no bus.

West and south of Chetumal, the winding, deep-green **Río Hondo**, which forms the border between Mexico and Belize, is an area rich in wildlife, from furry capybaras to massive numbers of bats. A couple of tour operators in Chetumal offer guided day-trips to the area, which are preferable to visiting on your own, as there are only a few villages and no hotels or other services if you get stranded. If you just want to get a glimpse of the area, you can take a long and bumpy trip via car or an early *combi* bound for La Unión; departures are from the station on Avenida Primo de Verdad at Avenida Hidalgo in Chetumal. You can't linger, though, as the last bus returns from La Unión around 5pm.

The closest, most accessible point on the river is the family-friendly *balneario* at **El Palmar** (just south of the town of Ucum and the turn from Hwy-186), with a nicely maintained beach area on the bank, as well as a large spring-fed swimming pool and a small restaurant. About halfway along the river road, near the village of Calderón, an eco-tourism centre called El Aventurero has cut tidy labelled trails through the forest and down along the water. Admission is a bit pricey at M$80, however, and the staff speaks only Spanish. Finally, at the end of the line, about 1km beyond where the bus turns around in La Unión, the emerald-green Cocodrilo Dorado cenote is another refreshing place to swim. The person who owns the land will allow **camping** (M$40) nearby, but you shouldn't count on this option, as there's often no one around to let you through the fencing.

# The Río Bec and Calakmul

The road that runs across **the south** of the peninsula, Hwy-186 from Chetumal to Francisco Escárcega, passes through some of the emptiest areas of the Yucatán. Many trees have been cleared through subsistence farming practices, or felled for logging or cattle-ranching, but the forest becomes thicker as you travel west toward Campeche State, where a vast chunk of land north and south of the highway is given over to the **Calakmul Biosphere Reserve**, which encompasses the densest jungle on the peninsula.

The area is rich in Maya remains, most of which have been open to the public only since the mid-1990s, and constitutes what's known as the **RÍO BEC**. Populated during the Classic era, this land forged a link between the Petén cities to the south and the younger settlements just being established in the Chenes area to the north. The enormous site of **CALAKMUL**, located west of the other sites – in Campeche State and deep in the wilderness near the border with Guatemala – is the highlight of this area; the view from its main pyramid, the largest in the Maya world, takes in a pure sea of green from horizon to horizon. Travellers typically get accommodation and arrange tours to all of the ruins at **Xpuhil** (see box, below), a village named after the nearby archeological site, on the border between Campeche and Quintana Roo states. Tourist services are rudimentary in this area, and people can be baffled by the appearance of foreigners, but you will often be able to enjoy the ruins and the untamed forest in complete solitude, the antithesis of a visit to Chichén Itzá.

## Visiting the Río Bec sites

The typical strategy for visiting this string of ruins is to spend the night in Xpuhil, hire an early-morning taxi to visit Calakmul and Balamkú, and return to Xpuhil to see the ruins in town in the late afternoon. You can then take a late bus to Chetumal or Campeche (see p.193). If you have the time, though, it will be a more rewarding and relaxing visit if you take at least two days and allow yourself to see more. Renting a car in Campeche or Chetumal affords the most flexibility, but taking taxis can cost about the same amount, leaving you the option of continuing on a loop route rather than returning your car. (Also, the drive down the one-lane road to Calakmul is tedious, requiring frequent braking for wild turkeys – it can be a treat to leave the driving to someone else.)

Using Xpuhil as a base, **taxis** can be arranged from either of the tourist hotels, though you can usually get a better rate if you deal directly with the drivers gathered at the crossroads in town. Expect to pay at most M$600 per head to go to Calakmul and Balamkú or to Kohunlich and Dzibanché, and M$300 for Chicanná, Becán and Xpuhil, including waiting time; all prices go down significantly if you have more people in the car. If you're not in a hurry, it's also possible to start off sightseeing from Chetumal by taking a *combi* to the town of Nicolas Bravo, then hiring a taxi from there to visit Dzibanché and Kohunlich (about M$400), ending by flagging down a second-class bus to Xpuhil.

Alternatively, you could take an organized **tour** to Calakmul from Campeche for M$750 per person (see "Listings", p.279, for details) or, if your Spanish is up to it, with the experienced team at Servidores Turísticos de Calakmul (℡983/871-6064, ©ciitcalakmul@prodigy.net.mx), which runs the tourist office in Xpuhil; tours may cost more, but a good guide can really make the area come alive, as many of the more recently opened sites still have no signage.

## Dzibanché and Kinichná

About 65km out of Chetumal, the first sites you reach are Dzibanché and Kinichná, both 15km north of the highway, 5km past the town of Morocoy and accessible under the same hours and entrance fee (8am–5pm; M$33). If you're travelling by taxi, specify that you'll be visiting both sets of ruins, as they're about a ten-minute drive apart. It takes less than an hour to tour everything.

**DZIBANCHÉ** is the earliest city in the area, thought to be the base for the influential Snake Kingdom (Kaan) clan before it ascended to rule in Calakmul in the early seventh century. Because of its early date, the city is not truly a Río Bec site – the buildings are relatively simple and show none of the later ornate detail. It's a good place to start, though, as the plain buildings, sparse trees and dry soil make a sharp contrast to the sites farther down the road and deeper in the jungle. The most completely restored structure is Edificio 6, or the **Edificio de los Dinteles**, named for the original wood lintels that were found in the two rooms at the top of the pyramid. The northern one has been replaced, but the southern wood remains, dating from the 700s. In the plaza at the back of the site, the stairs of **Edificio 13** are carved with the figures of war prisoners.

At **KINICHNÁ**, the centrepiece of the small site, and the only excavated structure is a hulking **pyramid**, built layer upon layer by succeeding leaders, each of the three levels representing a different era and style. Only completists will make the climb up the exceedingly tall steps, some up to a metre high; despite the building's seeming height, however, it barely clears the trees.

## Kohunlich

The ruins of **KOHUN-LICH** (daily 8am–5pm; M$40) are beautifully situated a few kilometres past the turn for Dzibanché, then 9km south from the village of Francisco Villa, in a dense jungle of near-pre-historic proportions that's home to green parrots and enormous lurid butterflies. Allow about an hour and a half to visit all of the buildings, spread out among the towering fan palms and linked by a loop trail. The buildings range from the Late Pre-Classic to the Classic periods (100–900 AD), and the majority are in the Río Bec architectural style (see box, p.188). But, to quote the early writer and adventurer John L. Stephens, the site is a perfect example of "a strong and vigorous nature . . . struggling for mastery over art",

△ Stucco mask at Kohunlich

as even the buildings that have been excavated in the last few decades are once again being consumed by the creeping foliage and moss.

The best-preserved structure here, the **Templo de los Mascarones**, is named after the five two-metre-high stucco masks that decorate its facade. Disturbing enough now, these wide-eyed, open-mouthed gods once stared out from a background of smooth, bright-red-painted stucco. Other structures, following recent reconstruction efforts, include a ball-court, the moss-covered Pixa'an palace and an elite residential area called the **27 Escalones**, worth the detour to see the great views over the jungle canopy from the cliff edge on which it is built (prime real estate was just as valuable 1400 years ago, it seems).

In a pinch, *Cabañas Kohunlich* (no tel; ❸), just east of the junction with the road to the ruins, has very provisional **cabins** with private baths, but stop in first if you want your room made ready, as they don't see a lot of guests. Otherwise, the intimate honeymoon-luxe *Explorean* resort (☎ 800/366-6666, ⓦ www .theexplorean.com; ❾), halfway up the winding road to the site, provides quite a different experience, complete with an infinity pool perched on the hillside. Its **restaurant** is open to non-guests, and the view over the jungle canopy can be worth the price of a post-ruins drink.

## Río Bec

Despite giving its name to the entire region, the scattered buildings of the city of **RÍO BEC**, 10km east of Xpuhil and south of the *ejido* of 20 de Noviembre, are frustratingly inaccessible. The area is still under excavation and usually closed to visitors, though some years it opens for a few months in the spring. Ask in the tourist office in Xpuhil about arranging an expedition on horseback, perhaps, as otherwise only four-wheel-drive vehicles can tackle the dirt tracks here. If you do visit, you will see the most extreme example of the Río Bec false-pyramid style: as at Xpuhil, the "steps" on the twin towers were never meant to be climbed: the risers actually angle outwards.

---

### The Río Bec style

While Río Bec is the name of a specific archeological site, it also refers to a characteristic **architectural style** common to all of the sites found in this area. Río Bec buildings, most built around 600 AD, were influenced by neighbouring Petén, which was noted for its massive pyramids with rounded corners, and commemorative stelae dotting the plazas.

The Río Bec style's most distinctive feature is a dramatic distortion of the great early pyramids of the Petén. In the Río Bec, the shape of the steep Gran Pirámide at Tikal, for instance, is further elongated to form a tall, slender tower with an unclimbable steep-stepped facade. These are usually built in pairs and topped with temples that are impossible to reach and generally filled in with solid rock; narrow roofcombs add another level of ornamentation to these purely decorative structures. In the lower register, the central doorway is often adorned with the gaping mouth of a god – typically thought to be the ancient deity **Itzamná**, the god of night and day – whose teeth frame the opening. The remaining surfaces of Río Bec buildings are covered with smaller masks of other gods (look for the distinctive curled nose of **Chac**, the rain god, who often appears in stacks on corners), all curling tongues and rolling eyes, alternating with intersecting crosses and inset stone squares forming checkerboard patterns, another distinctive motif of the region. Tour all the Río Bec sites in a day or two, and you'll come away dizzy from the intertwining grotesquery.

# Xpuhil

Thanks solely to its location halfway between Chetumal and Escárcega, the one-street village of **XPUHIL** (also spelled Xpujil), straddling Hwy-186 at the border of Campeche and Quintana Roo states, is the de facto base for exploring the Río Bec region. The best resource in the area is an unofficial **tourist information** office (☎983/871-6064; daily 9am–2pm, 9am–8pm during Aug and Semana Santa) at the east end of Xpuhil, maintained by a dedicated ecotourism group that also operates a campsite near Calakmul (see p.192). It can arrange hiking, mountain-biking, horse-riding **tours** (M$1000 to Río Bec) and birdwatching trips, combined with expert archeological knowledge – though it's best to email ahead to give the organizers warning outside of the busy Mexican holiday seasons.

Xpuhil has only a few perfunctory **places to stay**. Your best bets are the *Posada Victoria*, above the bus station, where the passable rooms have a/c and TV (no tel; ❺), and *El Mirador Maya* (☎983/871-6005, ✉mirador_maya@hotmail.com; ❺), which has decent cabañas with porches, but the noise of trucks struggling to crest the hill on which the hotel sits, 1km west of the bus station, is noticeable at night. This place is geared to foreign guests, with a money **exchange** counter and a decent, only mildly overpriced **restaurant**. You'll also find a very touch-and-go **Internet** café (two blocks south of the highway at the western end of town – look for signs for "La Selva Ciber Estancia"), several Ladatel **phones** and a small **post office**. A **petrol station** lies several kilometres east of town.

A far better lodging option is 10km north of Xpuhil, in the tranquil village of **Zoh-Laguna**, where *Cabañas and Restaurant Mercedes* (☎983/871-6054, 🖷983/871-6055; ❹) offers spotless cabins with private baths, and the kindly owners will provide tasty meals on request. If you don't have your own car, you can hire a taxi from Xpuhil for M$30 one way, or hop on a *colectivo* if your timing is right – though this will drop you about 700m from the hotel itself.

**Leaving Xpuhil**, there are three ADO and three Sur **buses** a day to Chetumal, and eight in total to Escárcega and onward, though you may not always be able to secure a seat because these first-class buses can be packed with through travellers. The schedule board in the station does not include several second-class Caribe buses – enquire about these if you're in a pinch. **Colectivos** gather in front of the station, but don't run frequently. It's also possible to catch a series of second-class buses through to the Chenes sites or to Mérida via Dzibalchén, Hopelchén and the Ruta Puuc, passing through the northern half of the Calakmul Biosphere Reserve on a reasonably well-maintained road.

## The ruins

The smallest of all the sites in the area, the Xpuhil **ruins** are less than 1km west along the highway from the bus stop in Xpuhil village (8am–5pm; M$30). Much of the stone carving at this ancient settlement, which was probably a satellite of Becán to the west, is in excellent shape, and you need about half an hour to see it all. The path leads first past a small residential complex, then to the main building, a long, low structure studded with three striking towers (unusual, as other Río Bec buildings have only two). The stairs up the ersatz pyramids are purely decorative, as they are almost vertical. A narrow staircase leads partway up the inside of the south tower, providing a bit of a view over the neatly cleared grassy plaza that fronts the structure.

## Hormiguero

Only the most dedicated Mayaphiles make the effort to reach **HORMIGUE-RO** (8am–5pm; M$25), a small site with excellently preserved decoration. It's a bumpy 22km drive south from the crossroads in Xpuhil (no buses run this way; the forty-minute taxi ride costs M$150 round-trip with waiting time), but the beautifully preserved stone decoration is quite remarkable. Tucked in deep forest, only two of its buildings have been completely excavated. Both show a combination of the distinctive monster mouths, later used extensively in the Chenes sites (see p.279), and the towers typical of Río Bec buildings – although here the temples at the tops of the impossibly steep towers are actually functional, unlike those at Xpuhil. Keep your eyes on the forest floor here as you explore – Hormiguero has its name ("anthill") for good reason.

## Becán

Though it covers a relatively small area, **BECÁN** (daily 8am–5pm; M$33), 6km west of Xpuhil then 500m north on a signed track, is a site with several details that set it apart from its neighbours; allow about an hour and a half for a basic tour. The most remarkable feature is the dry **moat**, 16m wide and 5m deep, which surrounds the site entirely. This moat and the wall on its outer edge form one of the oldest known defensive systems in Mexico and are unique among Maya sites. The structure has led some to believe that this, rather than present-day Flores in Guatemala, was the site of Tayasal, early capital of the Itzá. Becán was first occupied in 600 BC and reached its peak between 600 and 1000 AD, when it apparently functioned as a regional capital and trade centre.

Unlike many of the excavated sites in the northern Yucatán, most of the buildings here seem to have been residential rather than ceremonial; in fact, the tightly packed buildings – with rooms stacked up and linked with corridors and unusual, winding internal staircases – create a strong sense of dense urbanism, akin to modern apartment blocks.

Enter the ruins through a break in the east wall, and you face an alleyway overhung with a typically Maya narrow vaulted arch; passing through, you reach the **Plaza Central**, dominated by the massive 32-metre-high **Structure IX** and the complex temple-palace **Structure X**, topped with the gaping mouth of Itzamná. At its far south end, a glass box protects a beautiful stucco **mask** of the sun god, Kinichná. Though it's nowhere near as large as the Kohunlich masks, the work is marvellously intricate, with much of the original pigment still in place.

Whereas the area around the Plaza Central feels crowded, the raised **Plaza Oriente** exudes a more orderly grandness and is clearly an elite residential area. **Structure I** sports some of the tallest, steepest towers of all the Río Bec sites, topped with small galleries probably used as observatories, and **Structure II** exhibits another typical decorative technique: small limestone cubes inset to form checkerboard patterns and crosses, which represent the cardinal points. Because much of the site was excavated only in the last few decades, the restoration process is meticulously marked throughout: small chips of stone set in the plaster walls mark the edges of the buildings as they were first found; everything above this line is recent restoration. You can climb several of the buildings, and from the tops of the tallest ones, you can see the towers of Xpuhil to the east.

## Chicanná

Two kilometres west of Becán, **CHICANNÁ** (daily 8am–5pm; M$30) is south of the highway, across from the *Chicanná Ecovillage Resort*. Entering the site, you

4

first reach the large **Structure XX**, topped with a second tier made of stacks of heads of the rain god, Chac. You can walk inside some of the rooms to see some surviving stucco details, such as small human faces. Following the path around, you eventually come to the impressive **Structure II**, the design of which gives the site its name ("House of the Serpent Mouth"). Its massive square doorway forms a face and gaping mouth, complete with spiky teeth, thought to be the god Itzamná due to his distinctive crossed eyes and round earrings. The rest of the building is covered in smaller masks of hook-nosed Chac, made up of intricately carved mosaic pieces of limestone, many still painted with red stucco, in a style that was developed in this area and the adjacent Chenes cities, then picked up and refined by later builders in the Puuc region to the north.

After visiting the site, you can stop for a drink and a dip in the pool at *Chicanná Ecovillage Resort* (☎983/871-6075, 📧chicanna@campeche.sureste.com; ⑨), which also offers nicely manicured grounds and a/c comfort at a reasonable price. Continuing west on the highway, you reach *Rio Bec Dreams* (☎983/834-2516, 🌐www.riobecdreams.com; ⑤), a small budget **lodging** option (cosy wood cabins with shared bath, or larger private-bath cabañas for families) and a good travellers' resource, as the owners are archeology buffs who can advise on the latest site openings and arrange good guided tours; the gift shop is stocked with excellent titles from Mérida's Dante bookshops. Non-guests can stop in at the **restaurant**, with its varied (non-Mexican) menu, to have a cold beer and the like.

## Calakmul

The ruined city of **CALAKMUL** (daily 8am–5pm; M$38, plus M$20 for the biosphere reserve) is one of the best Maya ruins for quiet contemplation of the culture's architectural legacy. Though the site is only partially restored and a tedious sixty-kilometre drive south off Hwy-186, 58km west of Xpuhil, its sheer size and location in the heart of the **Calakmul Biosphere Reserve**, which encompasses more than 1.7 million acres of jungle, make this Classic-era city irresistible. Arrive at 7am, when the reserve's entrance gate on the highway opens (it takes more than an hour to reach the ruins), and look for **wildlife** on the ride down – ocellated turkeys, white-tailed deer, peccaries and toucans are common, and jaguars roam the forest by night. Even if you don't see anything, you'll certainly hear the jungle life: in the morning, booming howler monkeys and raucous frogs make the pristine forest as noisy as midtown Manhattan.

Although the ruins were uncovered in the 1930s, excavation has been going on only in the past two decades; every year new discoveries yield more revelations about the city's historical significance, and it was designated a UNESCO World Heritage Site in 2002. At the very least, Calakmul is probably the biggest archeological zone in Mesoamerica, extending for some 70 square kilometres; at its peak, it was home to about 200,000 people. The central area alone contains nearly seven thousand buildings and more stelae and pyramids than any other Maya city. The treasures of Calakmul are on display in the **Museo Fuerte de San Miguel** in Campeche (see p.277) and include two hauntingly beautiful jade masks. Another was found in a tomb in the main pyramid as recently as January 1998. Also at the museum, you can see the first mummified body to be found in Mesoamerica, from inside Structure XV, which was unearthed in 1995.

Because its architectural style adheres more purely to the plainer Petén tradition, Calakmul is not considered a true part of the Río Bec; unlike the neighbouring cities, which interacted with the Chenes settlements to the north, it looked to the south for trade and culture. Calakmul's primary influence was

Tikal, with which it had an often violent rivalry as the two cities' rulers angled for control of lucrative trade routes. Calakmul was the mighty Snake Kingdom, a powerful clan that was first based at Dzibanché. Once established at Calakmul, the leaders were referred to with fear and awe in records found in other ruins such as Palenque. Recent hieroglyphic translations reveal how its greatest leader, Yuknoom Ch'een, who reigned between 636 and 686 AD, controlled many smaller cities and outposts through puppet kings. Decades of struggle finally led to a bloody rout of Tikal in 657, but this only led to recrimination, and Yuknoom's son, Yich'ak Ka'k' (also known as Jaguar Paw), suffered his own staggering defeat in 695, which all but ruined Calakmul; by the middle of the ninth century, the city was basically abandoned.

Several paths wind through the excavated areas, with the shortest loop taking a couple of hours (it's a twenty-minute walk just from the car park to the first set of buildings), though you could easily spend the better part of the day here if you're stocked with bug repellent, snacks and water. The shortest route heads directly for the jackpot: the main plaza, where the **Gran Pirámide** (Structure II) dwarfs everything around it. It is the largest Maya building in existence, with a base covering almost five acres, and from the ground it's difficult to see the top, as it recedes in stacked layers of construction, each one added by a new leader. Two giant monster masks flank the central stairway, and one of the temples contained the tomb of Jaguar Paw. Daunting as it may be, the climb yields an awe-inspiring view of nothing but jungle, though on a crystal-clear day, you may be able to glimpse the tip of the Danta pyramid, at El Mirador in Guatemala.

After this, the rest of the site can seem a bit anticlimactic, as the level of decoration is unremarkable and the buildings are smaller. Seek out the **residential section** to the east, where a tight warren of private rooms is built against a section of a large defensive wall that enclosed this elite district of the city. Also look for a huge interior stucco **frieze**, substantially larger and more ornate than the one at Balamkú (see below), which was scheduled to open to the public in mid-2005.

A few kilometres inside the reserve, Servidores Turísticos Calakmul, an excellent eco-tourism organization, maintains *Yaxche* (☎983/871-6064, Ⓔciitcalakmul@prodigy.net.mx; M$160), a **campsite** with a few basic cabins. It also rents tents, hammocks and hiking gear, and will point you to **nature trails** within the reserve. You can try stopping for a **meal**, but as the kitchen uses all local products, it may not have provisions on hand in slow seasons. Otherwise, there's a basic café at *Puerta Calakmul*, very poorly signposted east off the road immediately inside the park entrance; it's also a **hotel**, featuring cabins decorated with pretty, nature-inspired touches (☎984/803-2696, Ⓔpuertacalakmul@hotmail.com; ❼).

## Balamkú and Nadzcaan

Most organized tours to Calakmul stop at **BALAMKÚ** (daily 8am–5pm; M$32), just 5km west of the turn-off to the larger city and 3km north of the highway. The main draw at this small site is a beautifully preserved seventeen-metre-long stucco **frieze**, located in a cluster of buildings farthest from the entrance and protected in a concrete shed embedded inside the central palace; ask the caretaker to let you in. The embellished wall, crawling with toads, crocodiles and jaguars, seems to undulate in the dim light, and the rolling eyes of the red-painted monster masks, though smaller than those at Kohunlich, are perhaps more alarming here. The elaborate iconography establishes a parallel between the rising and setting sun, as it dips into the underworld, and the dynastic cycle, as kings ascend to the throne, then die and settle in the maw of the earth. Likewise, the frieze's very location inside and under a public space is suggestive of the underworld.

Less than 1km west of the Calakmul turn, immediately before the town of Conhuas, a dirt road leads 15km north to a sizeable collection of pyramids (some 50m tall), plazas and ball-courts: the city of **NADZCAAN**, which once linked the Petén cities with Edzná farther north (see p.280). Stelae found inside the temples are dated around 650 AD. The perimeter of the area contains caves and quarries where limestone was excavated for building. Serious archeological work began here only around 1999, and there are still no services, signage or even entry fee – you're free to thrash around on your own in the untamed undergrowth. The solitude is fantastic, but a visit is advisable only for those with sturdy cars.

If you're continuing on to Escárcega, *La Laguna* **restaurant**, trimmed all over with seashells, makes a good rest stop, just off the highway and overlooking the small but scenic Laguna Silvituc.

# Travel details

## Buses

Bus service is not as convenient in this corner of the Yucatán as elsewhere; Chetumal is the main hub, especially for long-distance services to other states and into Belize.

**Chetumal** to: Bacalar (hourly; 30min); Belize City via Corozal and Orange Walk (5 daily; 3hr); Campeche (3 daily via Escárcega and Xpuhil; 7hr); Cancún (hourly 4.45am–midnight via Tulum and Playa del Carmen; 4–6hr); Flores, Guatemala (1 daily; 12hr); Francisco Escárcega (12 daily; 4–5hr); Mahahual and Xcalak (2 Mon–Fri, 3 Sat–Sun; 3hr 30min–4hr 30min); Mérida (12 daily; 8–9hr); Mexico City (4 daily; 24hr); Palenque and San Cristóbal (3 daily; 7–10hr); Villahermosa (6 daily; 9–11hr); Xpuhil (14 daily; 2hr).

**Felipe Carrillo Puerto** to: Chetumal (4 daily; 2hr); Mérida (8 daily; 5hr).
**Mahahual** to: Chetumal (2 Mon–Fri, 3 Sat–Sun; 4hr 30min).
**Xpuhil** to: Chetumal (8 daily; 2hr); Dzibalchén (1 daily at 4am; 1hr 30min); Escárcega (8 daily; 2hr)

## Colectivos

**Felipe Carrillo Puerto** to: Punta Allen (10am & 3pm; 3hr); Valladolid (hourly; 2hr); Chetumal (hourly; 2hr)

## Flights

Aerocaribe, Aviacsa and Mexicana run daily flights between Chetumal and Mexico City.

# 5

# Valladolid and Chichén Itzá

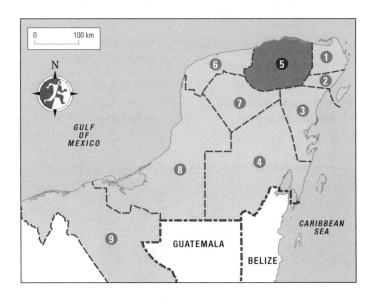

# CHAPTER 5

# Highlights

* **Iglesia de San Bernardino de Siena** Valladolid's Franciscan mission is the oldest permanent church in the Yucatán. **P.201**

* **Cenote Dzitnup** See the transfixing beam of sunlight that shines down through the cave ceiling onto the glowing blue water. **P.203**

* **Ek-Balam** Some of the best-preserved stucco decoration in the Maya world is on display here. **P.204**

* **Ría Lagartos Biosphere Reserve** Three small towns inside this strip of marshes along the coast are bases for fishing and birdwatching trips, or simply lazing on the empty beaches. **P.205**

* **El Castillo** The giant pyramid that towers over the ruined city of Chichén Itzá is the very symbol of Maya power in the Yucatán Peninsula. **P.210**

* **Convento de San Francisco de Padua** This massive monastery looms over the plaza in the small, scenic town of Izamal. **P.214**

△ Ek-Balam

# 5

# Valladolid and Chichén Itzá

S
econd only to the beaches around Cancún, the biggest tourist draw
in the Yucatán Peninsula is the ruined city of **Chichén Itzá**, a beeline
west from the coast along Hwy-180 towards Mérida. The vast, well-
excavated and fascinating archeological site is dominated by the towering Castillo, perhaps the most iconic of all the Maya pyramids. While it's not
impossible to visit the entire site in a day-trip, the area is huge, and you'll be
unnecessarily rushed, not to mention crammed in with the busloads of visitors
who pack the place from late morning on. Better to plan instead on staying
overnight, either at one of the luxury hotels near the site or in the adjacent
village of **Pisté**, which provides budget tourist amenities. An early start will
not only help you avoid the worst crowds, but also give you a chance to see
some of the diverse and colourful birds that flourish in the forests growing up
around the ruins.

If you're as interested in contemporary Maya culture as in the ancient remains,
however, you can't do better than to stay in **Valladolid**, just 40km east of
Chichén Itzá and connected by frequent bus or *colectivo* service. Unfortunately,
many visitors in their haste miss this charming, predominantly Maya city that
exemplifies the distinct atmosphere and structure of the inland towns built
during the Spanish colonial period. Here you'll see the basic plan of a central
plaza dominated by a cathedral (plus vendors, strolling lovers, taxi drivers and
stray dogs) that's endlessly repeated, at varying scales, in the villages and cities
throughout the rest of Yucatán State.

A fascinating counterpoint to Chichén Itzá, the Maya ruins of **Ek-Balam**
lie north of Valladolid. The place is distinct from its neighbour in its decorative style, with rare and perfectly preserved stucco adorning the main building;
the setting – a swath of rolling grasslands that covers the northeastern part of
the state – is a change, too, as is the complete lack of crowds. From Valladolid,
Hwy-295 continues north towards the Gulf coast, running through the travel
hub of **Tizimín**, a larger city than Valladolid but less scenic. If you're getting
around by bus, you'll have to change here to carry on to the **Ría Lagartos
Biosphere Reserve**, a sixty-kilometre-long strip of marshland that harbours
more than 330 species of birds, including a large flamingo population; the
raucous pink creatures are most easily visited from the town of **Río Lagartos**,
directly north from Tizimín. Beach-lovers can get their fix at the remote towns

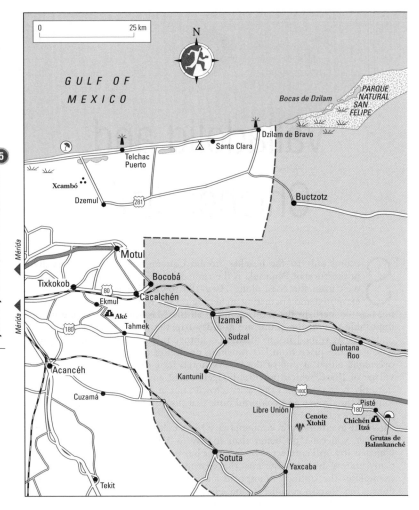

of **San Felipe**, west on a narrow road along the coast from Río Lagartos, and **El Cuyo**, twice the distance to the east. From Chichén Itzá or Valladolid, Hwy-180 continues west, with the free and toll roads merging at the town of Kantunil. At this point, you can carry straight on to Mérida, or you can make the very worthwhile detour north to **Izamal**, one of the region's most beautiful small towns, notable for its glowing egg-yolk-yellow buildings and its enormous Franciscan mission church.

If you're driving to Chichén Itzá from the coast, the old highway is more scenic, but slower (about three hours, compared to two and a quarter on the *cuota*). It's also perhaps the most heavily travelled tourist route on the peninsula; brace yourself for the occasionally aggressive souvenir vendor who will besiege your car mid-speed bump.

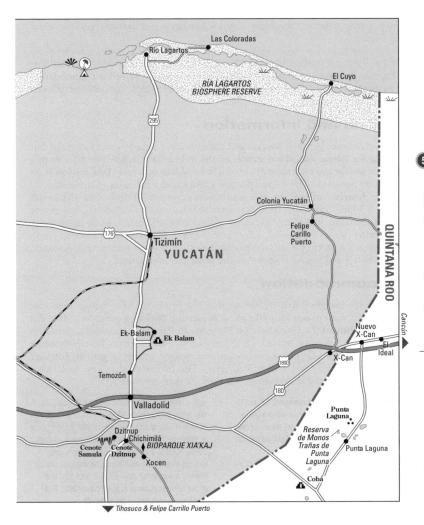

Tihosuco & Felipe Carrillo Puerto

# Valladolid and around

The second town of Yucatán State (after Mérida), about 160km west of Cancún, **VALLADOLID** took a severe bashing when the Caste Wars began here in 1847, but has retained a strong colonial feel, with towering churches dotting the city grid. Unlike Mérida, with its cosmopolitan bustle, or Campeche's museum-piece, multicoloured centre, Valladolid exudes the quieter, less pretentious attitude of a rural capital, catering to the farmers and ranchers who live in the surrounding counties, while village women gather in the plaza to sell their hand-embroidered huipiles and other craftwork. The slow pace may not be to every traveller's liking, but Valladolid offers a slice of Mexican life that is entirely different from that found in the beachfront towns. The main recreation

199

here is swimming in the nearby cenotes, **Dzitnup** and **Samula**, easily reached by bicycle.

Another reason to work Valladolid into your itinerary is its location about 40km east of Chichén Itzá, which makes it close enough that you can beat the crowds there on an early bus. Also, the reasonably priced accommodation ranges from a particularly nice youth hostel to surprisingly inexpensive colonial charmers on the plaza.

## Arrival and information

First-class buses between Mérida and Cancún don't actually enter Valladolid, but stop at **La Isleta**, a small bus station on the toll highway, where you transfer to a shuttle bus for the ten-minute ride into town; Valladolid's main **bus station** is on Calle 39 between calles 44 and 46, just a block and a half west of the plaza.

The **tourist office**, on the southeastern corner of the plaza (Mon–Sat 9am–8.30pm, Sun 9am–1pm; ⓦ www.chichen.com.mx/valladolid), has plenty of information, including free maps of Valladolid and details of in-house **tour operator** Viajes Valladolid (ⓣ 985/856-1857, ⓦ www.viajesvalladolid.com), though it's a pretty casual set-up, and the office is often unattended; however, most hotels and souvenir shops on the plaza also have **maps**.

## Accommodation

Valladolid's budget hotels are serviceable, but prices are low enough here that you might want to opt for perks like a swimming pool or a mansion setting. An excellent **hostel**, *La Candelaria*, on the edge of Parque la Candelaria, on Calle 35 between calles 44 and 42 (ⓣ 985/856-2267, ⓔ candelaria_hostel@hotmail .com; M$80), offers spotless dorms and private rooms, a garden, Internet access, bike rental and well-priced tours. The owner of the Rey de Béisbol sports shop (see p.202) also rents out very inexpensive rooms.

**Hotel Lily** C 44 no. 192, between C 37 and C 39 ⓣ 985/856-2163. One block off the plaza, this small, homely hotel rents 21 basic rooms (upstairs ones get a little more light) at reasonable rates. ❹

**María de la Luz** C 42 on the plaza ⓣ 985/856-2071, ⓦ www.mariadelaluzhotel.com. The best value on the plaza, *María de la Luz* offers clean, comfortable rooms with (somewhat noisy) a/c, all arranged around a small pool. ❺

**María Guadalupe** C 44 no. 198, between C 39 and C 41 ⓣ 985/856-2068. The best of Valladolid's cheapies, with well-kept rooms featuring private baths and a/c in a small two-storey 1960s building

with a little curvy flair. Colectivos for Cenote Dzitnup leave from outside. ❹

**El Mesón del Marqués** C 39 no. 203, on the plaza ⓣ 985/856-2073, ⓦ www.mesondelmarques.com. Lovely hotel in a former colonial mansion, overlooking a courtyard with fountains and lush plants. There's a wonderful palm-fringed pool, and one of the best restaurants in town (see p.202). Full breakfast is included in the price. ❻

**Zací** C 44 no. 193, between C 39 and C 37 ⓣ 985/856-2167. Pleasant, modern, three-storey hotel with a quiet courtyard and a small pool; the big rooms have either a fan, or, for a few dollars more, a/c and TV. ❹–❺

## The city

Valladolid's sedate social scene centres on the **Parque Principal**, bounded by calles 39, 40, 41 and 42. The pretty, peaceful plaza is at its finest at dusk, when the curving love seats are filled with chatting couples, and the bubbling fountain, topped with a statue of a woman in a traditional Yucatecan huipil, is lit from below.

Each of the town's seven central neighbourhoods is named after an elegant church; the two white towers of one, the usually closed eighteenth-century

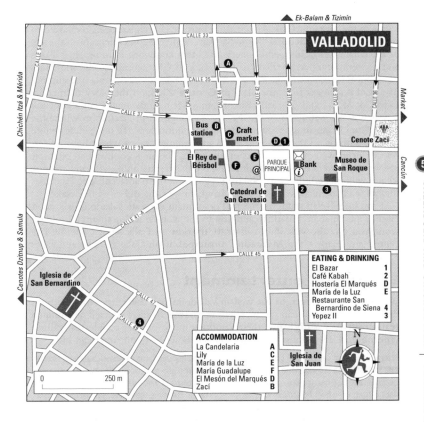

Map labels:

Ek-Balam & Tizimín

VALLADOLID

CALLE 33
CALLE 35
CALLE 37
CALLE 39
CALLE 41
CALLE 43
CALLE 45
CALLE 47
CALLE 49
CALLE 41-A

CALLE 54
CALLE 50
CALLE 48
CALLE 46
CALLE 44
CALLE 42
CALLE 40
CALLE 38
CALLE 36

Chichén Itzá & Mérida
Cenotes Dzitnup & Samula
Market
Cancún

Bus station
Craft market
Cenote Zací
El Rey de Béisbol
PARQUE PRINCIPAL
Bank
Museo de San Roque
Catedral de San Gervasio
Iglesia de San Bernardino
Iglesia de San Juan

0    250 m
N

**EATING & DRINKING**
| | |
|---|---|
| El Bazar | 1 |
| Café Kabah | 2 |
| Hostería El Marqués | D |
| María de la Luz | E |
| Restaurante San Bernardino de Siena | 4 |
| Yepez II | 3 |

**ACCOMMODATION**
| | |
|---|---|
| La Candelaria | A |
| Lily | C |
| María de la Luz | E |
| María Guadalupe | F |
| El Mesón del Marqués | D |
| Zací | B |

**Catedral de San Gervasio**, rise gracefully over the south side of the plaza. The sixteenth-century **Iglesia de San Bernardino de Siena**, 1km southwest of the plaza (Wed–Mon 9am–8pm; Mass daily at 6pm), is the oldest church in town, and in the Yucatán. Franciscan missionaries began work on it shortly after the Spanish established Valladolid as an outpost in 1545. The church buildings, which include a large monastery, were once on the very edge of town, so the Franciscans could minister to both the Spanish city residents and the Maya villagers in the surrounding countryside. In 1848, Maya rebels briefly took control of the city and drove the terrified Spaniards out, sacking the church (and much of the rest of the town) in the process; despite this, a fine Baroque altarpiece from the eighteenth century remains, as do some striking seventeenth-century paintings on the side walls. The **monastery** (usually closed to visitors), on the north side, was built over a cenote, so resident monks were self-sufficient, with their own water and food grown on surrounding farmland. For a brief period in the seventeenth century, one of the monk's cells was used as a lock-up for the infamous pirate Lorencillo (legend has it he was lured inland by a beautiful Valladolid resident who had been a passenger on a ship he attacked); Lorencillo's crew rescued him in a raid before he could be executed. To reach the complex, take scenic Calle 41-A, which runs diagonally southwest from two blocks west of the plaza. While you're down this way, you can also see the seventeenth-century **San Juan** church, with its twin spires, on Calle 40 at Calle 49.

East of the plaza on Calle 41, a smaller historic church has been converted to the **Museo de San Roque** (Mon–Sat 9am–9pm; M$20). Objects from the site of Ek-Balam (see p.204), embroidery and other craftwork from nearby villages and contemporary Maya altars to the rain god Chac comprise the museum's small but diverse collection. For a refreshing break, especially on a hot summer day, head northwest from the plaza to **Cenote Zací**, on the block formed by calles 34, 36, 37 and 39 (daily 8am–6pm; M$10). Right in the middle of the city, it was the water source for the Maya stronghold of Zací, from where the fierce Cupul clan fought against the first conquistadors. It's the easiest cenote to visit, with broad stairs leading down into a huge cavern where light reflects off the green water and glimmers on the walls. The air is cool, and an open-air restaurant affords a fine view. Swimming is possible, but, unlike at many cenotes, it's not encouraged (there are no changing facilities). An adjacent "zoo" includes the noble chicken, as well as a white hawk, or *zací*, the old city's namesake.

As the huipil-clad statue in the plaza's fountain suggests, Valladolid is a good place to purchase craftwork; in addition to the women selling their embroidery work, you can also visit the main **craft market** on Calle 44 at Calle 39. The central city market, the **Mercado Municipal**, is on Calle 32 between calles 35 and 37.

## Eating and entertainment

Whatever your budget, to eat well in Valladolid you don't have to stray from the plaza, where you can get inexpensive **snacks** or treat yourself at a refined **restaurant**. As for **nightlife**, there's nothing much beyond people-watching; a **cinema** on Calle 40 just south of Calle 41 shows first-run American hits.

**El Bazar** Northeast corner of the plaza. Houses a dizzying selection of inexpensive, always busy *loncherías* and pizzerias. It's also about the only place in town aside from *Hostería El Marqués* where you can eat after 9pm.

**Café Kabah** Southeast corner of the plaza. This second-floor pastry, ice cream and coffee shop with rickety old-fashioned furniture has a view over the square.

**María de la Luz** C 42, on the plaza. This popular terrace restaurant has a basic Mexican and Yucatecan menu, including local dishes like the bright-red *longaniza* pork sausage. Good-value (M$45) breakfast buffet with American and Mexican dishes offered daily.

**Hostería El Marqués** C 39 no. 203, in *El Mesón del Marqués*. Valladolid's best restaurant is set in a tranquil interior courtyard on the plaza, though it is occasionally packed with tour groups. The menu features Yucatecan classics such as *sopa de lima* and *poc-chuc*, along with city specialities like *escabeche de Valladolid* (chicken in a spicy vinegar broth). Prices are reasonable, starting at just M$60 for mains.

**Restaurante San Bernardino de Siena** C 49 no. 227. Locally known as *Don Juanito's* and frequented mostly by Mexicans, this family-run, mid-price restaurant is a great place for a lazy lunch or dinner away from the hustle and bustle of the town centre, two blocks behind Iglesia de San Bernardino. Grilled fish and meat are the specialities.

**Yepez II** C 41 between C 38 and C 40. Friendly open-air bar and restaurant opposite the Museo de San Roque with live music after 9.30pm, as well as very cheap Mexican snacks (*queso fundido* for M$20). Families come for dinner, but the crowd becomes predominantly male (not too rowdy, though) once the music starts. Open daily till 2am.

## Listings

**Banks** Bancomer, which changes travellers' cheques and has an ATM, is next door to the post office on the plaza.

**Bicycle rental** from the Rey de Béisbol sports shop, C 44 no. 195, between C 39 and C 41, owned by Antonio "Negro" Aguilar, a one-time professional baseball star who is also a great source of local information.

**Buses** The main station is on C 39 between C 44 and C 46. You can buy tickets for first- and second-class service, but first-class long-distance trips require a change on Hwy-180 just outside of the city.

**Colectivos** depart for Tizimín, Ek-Balam, Cenote Dzitnup and Chichén Itzá from designated meeting points along C 44, one block off the plaza. Chichén Itzá service is comparable in price to buses (M$15), and may depart more frequently, especially early in the morning.

**Laundry** in Supermaz, a shopping plaza on C 39 between C 48 and C 50.

**Post office** on the plaza, C 40 near the corner of C 39 (Mon–Fri 9am–3pm).

**Telephone and Internet** A Ladatel *caseta* on the plaza also has computers (daily 7am–10pm).

## Cenotes around Valladolid

Perhaps the most photogenic swimming hole in the Yucatán, the remarkable **Cenote Dzitnup**, also called X'Keken ("pig") cenote (daily 7am–6pm; M$20), is 7km west of Valladolid on Hwy-180 *libre*. Visitors descend through a cramped tunnel into a huge vaulted cave, where a nearly circular pool of crystal-clear turquoise water glows under a shaft of light from an opening in the ceiling. Bleacher seats and lots of electric lights have been added to accommodate everyone who pops in as part of a bus tour. A dip in the ice-cold water is a fantastic experience, but take a sweater to warm up afterwards, as the temperature in the cave is noticeably cooler than outside. Across the road, at the equally impressive (but smaller and less developed) **Cenote Samula** (daily 8am–5pm; M$20), the roots of a huge tree stretch down into the pool. While Dzitnup is frequently crowded and plagued by small children asking for tips, you may well find yourself alone at Samula.

**Colectivos** run direct to Dzitnup from outside the *Hotel María Guadalupe* in Valladolid (M$10; see p.200). Alternatively, any westbound second-class **bus** will drop you at the turn-off, 5km from town; then it's a 2km walk down a signed track. You could also take a taxi or, best of all, **cycle** on the paved bike path; the most scenic route is down Calle 41-A to San Bernardino, then along Calle 49, which eventually connects to Avenida de los Frailes, then the old highway and the *ciclopista*.

If you have your own car, you may want to make the longer trip to **Bioparque Xla'kaj** (M$5), 5km south of town, then 2.2km east on the road to

△ Cenote near Valladolid

5

VALLADOLID AND CHICHÉN ITZÁ | Valladolid and around

Xocen. Despite the grand name, the destination is simply a huge, open-air cenote with easy access on stone stairs. The surrounding grounds, maintained by the nearby farm community of Chichimilá, are a bit enthusiastically manicured, but there are also refreshments for sale, as well as several nice palapas for **overnight** guests (no tel; ❸), tentatively set to open in early 2006. Cycling here is not recommended, as the last 2.2km are along a very narrow, hilly road with no hard shoulder.

# From Ek-Balam to the Gulf coast

From Valladolid the vast majority of traffic heads straight on to Mérida or back to Cancún and the Caribbean beaches. A few places north, however, merit exploring – especially if you're looking for wildlife or less-visited Maya ruins. You can easily visit the small but flawless site of **Ek-Balam** 25km north; travel via Tizimín to see the flamingo colony on the coast at **Río Lagartos**; or go to the beach at **San Felipe** or **El Cuyo**. If you want to go all the way to the coast as a day-trip, you'll need to make an early start – the last bus from Río Lagartos for Tizimín leaves at 5pm. You'll have to return at least to Tizimín to continue on to Mérida, and all the way back to Valladolid for buses to the Caribbean coast.

## Ek-Balam

Little visited but well excavated, **EK-BALAM** (daily 8am–5pm; M$32) is notable for the high quality and unique details of its sculpture. Plans for a bus service from Valladolid to the site were in the works in 2005; enquire at the tourist office, or catch a **colectivo** on Calle 44 just west of the plaza.

Enclosed by a series of defensive walls, the compact site is really only the ceremonial centre; the entire city, which was occupied from the Pre-Classic period through the Spanish Conquest, spreads out over a very wide area, punctuated by *sacbeob* leading out in all directions. The entrance is along one of these ancient roads, leading through a freestanding four-sided arch. Beyond are two identical temples, called **Las Gemelas** (the Twins), and a long **ball-court**. The principal building, on the far side of the plaza, is the massive **Acrópolis**, the stones along its two-hundred-metre-long base adorned with bas-relief. Thatched awnings protect the site's finest treasure, an elaborate stucco frieze fully uncovered only around 2000; 85 percent of what you see is original plaster from the ninth century that didn't even require retouching once the dirt was brushed away.

A staircase leads up the centre of the building. On the first level, two doorways flanking the steps display near-matching designs of twisted serpents and tongues; in the right-hand carving, the snake's tongue is emblazoned with a glyph thought to represent the city of Ek-Balam. Just below the summit, a **Chenes-style doorway** in the form of a giant gaping mouth is studded with protruding teeth. This is the **entrance to the tomb** of Ukit-Kan-Lek-Tok, the city's powerful king in the mid-ninth century. The lower jaw forms the floor, while the skulls, lilies, fish and other symbols of the underworld carved below reinforce its function as a tomb gateway. Of the detailed human figures that surround the door, one's disproportionate limbs and deformed hands and feet suggest it is a portrait of a real person – one theory holds that this deformity was a result of inbreeding in the royal class. The figure at the top centre of the mouth is thought to be the king himself. Back on the ground, in the plaza, an exceptionally well-preserved **stele** depicts a king receiving the objects of power from Ukit-Kan-Lek-Tok, the smaller figure at the top of the stele, seated with one leg folded under. Given the rich detail at the site, it's worth hiring a **guide** for about M$250 for a small group. Juan Canul, who has worked on many excavations, is recommended; ask for him at the ticket desk.

## Practicalities

In the nearby village (turn left just before the gate to the site), the highly recommended *Genesis Ek Balam* (☎985/858-9375, Ⓦwww.genesisretreat.com; ❸–❻) is a beautiful, bargain-priced **eco-lodge** with a big garden and a bio-filtered pool; the hospitable Canadian owner, who built the place herself, can arrange tours and activities, such as tortilla-making or language lessons, with the local Maya. You can also rent bicycles here – perhaps to visit **Cenote Xcanché** (daily 9am–6pm; M$80), 1.5km from the ruins, where you can rappel down a limestone cliff into the water.

The **café** at *Genesis*, *Chaya's Natural Restaurant*, makes a great stop after the ruins, with treats like avocado ice cream, chocolate-chile cookies and rich, savoury *chaya* crepes.

# Tizimín and Río Lagartos

Travelling by bus from Valladolid north to see the flamingos at Río Lagartos, you have to transfer 51km from Valladolid in **TIZIMÍN**, the unofficial capital of Yucatán's cattle country. It's a pleasant enough city, but of very little interest to travellers except during Epiphany in early January, when the Feria de los Tres Reyes draws both Catholic pilgrims and cowboys, who like to show off their barbecue skills. The rest of the year you can savour the local beef served at the excellent *Tres Reyes* restaurant; prices are a little higher than you might expect, hovering around the M$100 mark, but you get free appetizers, and service is very good. It's located on the plaza, on calles 50, 51, 52 and 53 – an easy walk from the two bus stations, around the corner from each other at Calle 46 and Calle 47, very near the **market**. If you do find yourself here overnight, the best of the modest **hotels** in the centre is *Hotel San Carlos*, on Calle 54 between calles 51 and 53 (☎986/863-2094; ❺), while *Posada Maria Antonia*, on C 50 between C 53 and C 51, just off the plaza (☎986/863-2384; ❹) is a good cheap choice. Tizimín also has direct **bus** services to and from Mérida and Cancún.

The village of **RÍO LAGARTOS**, 100km north of Valladolid, is protected from the Gulf of Mexico by a long barrier island; it's set on a small spit, surrounded on three sides by water inhabited much of the year by tens of thousands of **pink flamingos** (Nov–March most migrate to Celestún on the west coast). Spanish explorers mistook this shallow inlet (*ría*) for a river (*río*), and resident crocodiles for alligators (*lagartos*). The former error, at least, has been corrected, and now the area of marshy flatland along the water in either direction from the town is the **Ría Lagartos Biosphere Reserve** – a popular destination with naturalists, as it's home to almost four hundred bird species. Despite talk of turning the area into a new tourist centre, shameless graft has rendered Río Lagartos itself a rather depressed fishing village, so it's the flamingos alone that make a visit worthwhile. A day-trip from Valladolid is manageable, but if you want to **stay the night**, *Posada Leyli* (☎986/862-0106; ❸), on Calle 14 near the north end of town, is about the only option; if possible, push on to San Felipe, a short drive east (see p.206).

You're likely to be swamped by offers to take you out to see the birds as soon as you arrive at the bus station (on Calle 19 just east of the main north–south street through town) or get out of your car. If not, one convenient place to go to is *Restaurante Isla Contoy*, on the waterfront on the west side of town, where you can arrange a **boat** trip to some of the many flamingo feeding sites, subject to endless variations in price and length; an hour-long tour usually costs about M$350, with a maximum of seven people. (There is **no bank or ATM** in town, so plan accordingly.) Make sure your guide understands that you don't want to harass the flamingos, as some will get too close if they think their passengers would prefer to see some action. If you want a longer trip, it's worth tracking down the amiable Marcel Flores (known as "Leches"), who may be able to take you as far as **Las Coloradas**, often the most spectacular flamingo colony, about 16km east of Río Lagartos. Ask for him at *Los Negritos* restaurant, on the main street as you drive into town. As well as flamingos, you're likely to see fish eagles, spoonbills and, if you're lucky, one of the very few remaining crocodiles for which Río Lagartos was (mis)named.

## San Felipe and El Cuyo

If it's **beaches** you're after, head either west 12km along the coast to San Felipe, or to El Cuyo, about 50km east of Río Lagartos. Both are generally cheerier places all around, with **SAN FELIPE** sporting especially clean streets lined with tidy little painted houses. The bay here, which is thick with tarpon, is also popular for **fly-fishing**. Most of the buses from Tizimín to Río Lagartos come out here as well; the last one leaves from Río Lagartos at 5pm if you want to carry on from there.

There are a couple of good seafood **restaurants** (*Pescadería Danilu*, on the main street, is popular) and one very pleasant waterfront **hotel** in town, *Hotel San Felipe de Jesus,* Calle 9 between calles 14 and 16 (☎986/862-2027, ✉sanfelip@prodigy.net.mx; ❺), which also has a decent restaurant and offers fishing trips and free boat service to the beaches on the offshore spit. Otherwise it's about M$50 for a boat from the pier at the east end of the malecón (where you can also get **tourist information**), and you can set up **camp** on the beach. At Mexican holiday times – July, August and Easter week – these spots are crowded; the rest of the year, quite deserted. If you do camp, be sure to bring protection against mosquitoes; otherwise, it's easy enough to arrange for the boat to collect you in the evening.

Another pleasant beach hideaway, **EL CUYO** lies east of Río Lagartos, but the coast road does not go through in this direction; instead, head east 50km from Tizimín to Colonia Yucatán, then north 38km through rolling farmland to the water. Noreste **buses** make the hour-long trip six times daily from Tizimín. The small barrier island is connected to the mainland by a long causeway across a rather sinister-looking lagoon, its water muddy red and foamy from the high salt content. The town itself is tidy and pleasant, with broad, wild-feeling beaches that are busy only during the Mexican holidays. The *Aida Luz* **hotel** (no tel; ❺), one block back from the beach, is a spic-and-span motel-like arrangement; *Flamingos Cabins* (☎999/943-7141, ⓦwww.flamingoscabins.com; ❻) has a more rustic style, and can arrange birdwatching and kayaking tours. Fish is of course the order of the day, and *La Conchita* **restaurant**, one block west of the main plaza, does it best.

# Chichén Itzá and around

The most famous, the most extensively restored and by far the most visited of all Maya sites, **CHICHÉN ITZÁ** lies conveniently along the main road from

Cancún to Mérida, a little more than 200km from the coast. A fast and frequent bus service runs all along this road, making it feasible to visit as a day's excursion from Cancún, as many tour buses do, or en route from the coast to Mérida. The site, though, deserves better, and to do the ruins justice and see them when they're not entirely thronged with tourists, an overnight stop is highly recommended – either at the site itself or, less extravagantly, in the nearby village of **Pisté** or in Valladolid (see p.199). The eerie **Grutas de Balankanché**, a few kilometres east of the ruins, make an intriguing side visit for the relics the ancient Maya left in these caves.

## Arrival and information

Arriving at Chichén Itzá, the highway curves around the site to the north, making an arc that merges with the site-access road (once the original highway straight through) on both ends. If you're on a through bus, it may drop you at the junction of the bypass and the access road on the west side, about ten-minutes' walk from the entrance; most **buses**, though, now drive right up to the site entrance and also stop in the neighbouring town of Pisté to the west. The rather grandly named Chichén Itzá International Airport, north of the ruins, is in fact a small **airstrip** that receives charter tour flights from the Caribbean coast.

The main **entry to the site** (daily 8am–5pm, though the process of getting everyone out starts at least an hour earlier; M$88) is on the west side. A huge **visitor centre** (open until 10pm) houses a museum, restaurant, **ATM** and shops selling souvenirs, film, maps and guides. **Guided tours** of the ruins can be arranged here: group tours in one of four languages (Spanish, English, German or Italian) for up to twenty people cost approximately M$300 and last ninety minutes; private tours (1–2 people) cost a little more. You can also buy tickets and get in at the **smaller eastern gate** by the *Hotel Mayaland* (see p.209), where there are fewer facilities. Book at the hotel reception area for two-hour **horse-riding trips** around the wilder, southern part of the site, Chichén Viejo (M$500 with guide).

A **sound-and-light show** runs nightly in Spanish (7pm in winter, 8pm in summer; M$30, or included in price of day entrance ticket); it's a bit of a yawn, but it does recreate the shadow-serpent effect (see p.210) on the stairs of El Castillo. It's worth seeing only if you're staying nearby, as there's nothing else to do in the evening.

About a half-hour walk west from Chichén Itzá, **Pisté** is an unattractive village straddling the road between Mérida and Valladolid. Its main function is providing visitors hotel rooms (see p.209), so they can get up early enough to beat the buses that arrive at the ruins around 10.30am. You'll also find an **Internet** café here, opposite the **bus station**, at the east end of town.

## Accommodation

Visitors to Chichén Itzá have a choice of staying in a handful of more expensive **hotels** immediately to the east of the ruins – all but one are on the short access road off Hwy-180 (signposted "zona hotelera") – or along the main street in the town of Pisté, to the west of the site. In Pisté, most hotels are on the main road, between the village and the ruins, so it's easy to shop around for the best deal – though quality can be low and occupancy high; the few reliable *posadas* have only a few rooms apiece. You can **camp** or sling up a hammock at the *Pirámide Inn* (M$50). On page 209, the Pisté hotels are listed in order from east to west, beginning with those nearest the ruins (and the bus station).

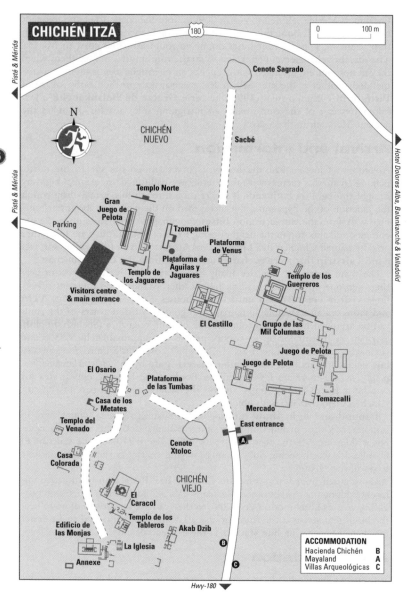

CHICHÉN ITZÁ

180

0          100 m

N

CHICHÉN
NUEVO

Cenote Sagrado

Sacbé

Pisté & Mérida

Pisté & Mérida

Hotel Dolores Alba, Balankanché & Valladolid

Parking

Templo Norte

Gran
Juego de
Pelota

Tzompantli

Plataforma
de Venus

Plataforma de
Águilas y
Jaguares

Templo de
los Jaguares

Templo de los
Guerreros

Visitors centre
& main entrance

El Castillo

Grupo de las
Mil Columnas

Juego de Pelota

Juego de Pelota

El Osario

Plataforma
de las Tumbas

Casa de los
Metates

Templo del
Venado

Mercado

Temazcalli

East entrance

A

Casa
Colorada

Cenote
Xtoloc

CHICHÉN
VIEJO

El
Caracol

Edificio de
las Monjas

Templo de los
Tableros

Akab Dzib

La Iglesia

B

Annexe

C

Hwy-180

ACCOMMODATION
Hacienda Chichén        B
Mayaland                    A
Villas Arqueológicas   C

## Near the ruins

**Dolores Alba** Hwy-180 *libre* Km 122, 2km east of Chichén Itzá east entrance ☎999/928-5650, ⓦwww.doloresalba.com. The best-value hotel on either side of the ruins, with clean, colourful rooms, a good restaurant (see p.213) and two swimming pools, one built out of a natural spring. Transport is provided to the site (but not back). ❺

**Hacienda Chichén** Off Hwy-180, near the east entrance to the ruins ☎985/924-2150, ⓦwww. yucatanadventure.com.mx. This place has a gracious old-colonial feel, with wrought-iron furniture and plenty of greenery, as well as a couple of small ruins within its grounds. Rooms, in individual cottages that housed Carnegie Institute archeologists in the 1920s, aren't quite as attractive as the public spaces, though. ❾

**Mayaland** Off Hwy-180, at the east entrance to the ruins ☎985/851-0100, ⓦwww.mayaland.com. High-end resort with a gorgeous hacienda-style dining room and luxurious thatched-hut suites dotted about the gardens. ❾

**Villas Arqueológicas** Off Hwy-180, near the east entrance to the ruins ☎985/851-0034, ⓦwww .clubmed.com. Not as lavish as its neighbours, but certainly comfortable (it's run by Club Med). Rooms are set round a patio enclosing a pool and cocktail bar. By night, its library full of archeological tomes doubles as a disco, which is usually empty. ❼

### In Pisté

**Pirámide Inn** Hwy-180 *libre* at the west end of town, next to the bus station ☎985/851-0115, ⓦwww.chichen.com. Conveniently situated near

the main entrance to the ruins, with a pool, *temazcal* sauna, extensive gardens and a somewhat New Age clientele. ❻

**Posada Flamboyanes** 200m west of the *Stardust Inn* no tel. Check availability at this newer option (opened in 2004) first, as it's the best budget spot in Pisté. But with only three rooms, all with private baths and fans and overlooking a garden, the place is likely to be full (in which case, head for *Posada Chac-Mool*, next door). ❹

**Posada Chac-Mool** Just west of *Posada Flamboyanes* ☎985/851-0270. No frills, just nine small, sparkling-clean rooms, with choice of fan or a/c. ❹–❺

**Posada Olalde** On C 6, south of the main road; coming from the bus stop, turn left across from *Posada Carrousel* ☎985/851-0078. The basic rooms, with fans and hot water, can be a bit dim, but they're very clean. This is one of the quieter spots, since it's off the main road. ❹

## The site

Though in most minds the ruins of **Chichén Itzá** represent the very image of the Maya, in fact it's the city's divergence from Maya tradition that makes it so archeologically intriguing. Experts are fairly certain that the city was established around 300 AD, and began to flourish in the Terminal Classic period (between 800 and 925 AD); the rest of its history, however, as well as the roots of the Itzá clan that consolidated power in the peninsula here after 925, remain hotly disputed. The old highway that used to pass through the site is now a path dividing the ruins in two: the Itzá-era **Chichén Nuevo** (New or "Toltec" Chichén) to the north and Terminal Classic **Chichén Viejo** (Old Chichén) to the south.

### Chichén Nuevo

Entering from the main entrance on the west side of the site, you're deposited near the centre of Chichén Nuevo, the newer, northern half of the city, all very well excavated and restored. Most buildings here, including the central **Castillo**

---

### The Toltec debate

At Chichén Itzá, the emphasis on human sacrifice, the presence of a huge ball-court and the glorification of military activity (in the form of distinctive soldiers' portraits) all point to a strong influence of the **Toltec culture** in central Mexico. For decades researchers guessed this was the result of the city's defeat by the Toltecs, a belief reinforced by the resemblance of the Templo de los Guerreros to the colonnade at Tula, near Mexico City, along with Toltec-style pottery remains and numerous depictions of the Toltec god-king, the feathered serpent Quetzalcoatl (Kukulcán to the Maya).

Work since the 1980s, however, supports a theory that the Itzá people were not Toltec invaders, but fellow Maya who had migrated from the south (an explanation for their subjects referring to them as "foreigners" in texts). The Toltec artefacts, this view holds, arrived in central Yucatán via the Itzás' chief trading partners, the **Chontal Maya**, who maintained allegiances with Toltecs of central Mexico and Oaxaca.

pyramid, the **Templo de los Guerreros** and an enormous **ball-court**, date from the city's peak, sometime during the Post-Classic period, between 925 and 1200 AD.

## El Castillo

If you arrive reasonably early, head first to **El Castillo** (also called the Pyramid of Kukulcán), the structure that sits alone in the centre of a great grassy plaza. At 25 metres high, it doesn't compare to larger structures at Cobá and Calakmul, but the climb up will give you a good overview of the entire area. The pyramid is a simple, relatively unadorned square building, with a monumental stairway ascending each face (though only two are restored), rising in nine receding terraces to a temple at the top.

The simplicity is deceptive, however, as the building is in fact the **Maya calendar** rendered in stone: each staircase has 91 steps, which, added to the single step at the main entrance to the temple, amounts to 365; the number of stone panels on each face is 52, a deeply symbolic number representing the number of years required for the two Maya calendar systems (the solar year and the 260-day year) to align and repeat; and other numbers relevant to the Maya calendar recur throughout the construction. Most remarkably, near sunset on the spring and autumn equinoxes, the great serpents' heads at the foot of the main staircase are joined to their tails (at the top of the building) by an undulating body of shadow – an event that lasts just a few hours and draws spectators, and awed worshippers, by the thousands.

Inside El Castillo an **earlier pyramid** survives almost wholly intact. An entrance has been opened at the bottom, through which you reach a narrow, dank and claustrophobic stairway (formerly the outside of the inner pyramid) that leads steeply to a temple on the top. In the temple's inner sanctuary, now railed off, stands one of the greatest finds at the site: an **altar**, or perhaps a throne, in the form of a jaguar, painted bright red and inset with jade "spots" and eyes. The inner stairs are open from 11am to 3pm, and from 4pm to 5pm (last entrance at 4:45pm).

## The "Toltec" plaza

El Castillo marks one edge of a **plaza** that formed the focus of Chichén Nuevo, and all its most important buildings are here, many displaying a strong Toltec influence in their structure and decoration. The **Templo de los Guerreros** (Temple of the Warriors), lined on two sides by the **Grupo de las Mil Columnas** (Group of the Thousand Columns), forms the eastern edge of the plaza. These are the structures that most recall the great Toltec site of Tula, both in design and in detail – in particular the colonnaded courtyard (which would have been roofed with some form of thatch) and the use of Atlantean columns, representing warriors in armour, their arms raised above their heads. The temple is richly decorated on its north and south sides with carvings and sculptures (originally with paintings too) of jaguars and eagles devouring human hearts, feathered serpents, warriors and, the one undeniably Maya feature, masks of the rain god Chac, with his curling snout. On top (now visible only at a distance, as you can no longer climb the structure) are two superb examples of figurines called **Chac-mools**, thought to be introduced by the Toltecs: offerings were placed on the stomachs of these reclining figures, which are thought to represent the messengers who would take the sacrifice to the gods, or perhaps the divinities themselves.

As with El Castillo, the Templo de los Guerreros was built over an earlier temple, in which some remnants of faded **murals** can be made out (the interior of

△ Groupo de las Mil Columnas

the temple is very often closed to the public, however). The "thousand" columns alongside originally formed a square, on the far side of which is the building known as the **Mercado**, although there's no evidence that this actually was a marketplace. Near here, to the south, is a small, dilapidated ball-court.

Walking west across the plaza towards the main ball-court, you pass the **Plataforma de Venus**, a raised, square block with a stairway up each side guarded by feathered serpents. Here, rites associated with Quetzalcoatl when he took the form of Venus, the morning star, would have been carried out. Slightly smaller, but otherwise identical in design, the adjacent **Plataforma de Águilas y Jaguares** features reliefs of eagles and jaguars holding human hearts. Human sacrifices may even have been carried out here, judging by the proximity of a third platform, the **Tzompantli**, where victims' heads likely were hung on display. This is carved on every side with grotesquely grinning stone skulls.

### The Gran Juego de Pelota and the Templo de los Jaguares

Chichén Itzá's **Gran Juego de Pelota**, on the west side of the plaza, is the largest known ball-court in Mesoamerica – with walls some 90m long and an overall field 149m in length. Its design is a capital "I" surrounded by temples, with the goals, or target rings, halfway along each side. Along the bottom of each side runs a sloping **panel** decorated in low relief with scenes of the game and its players. Although the rules and full significance of the game remain a mystery, it was clearly not a Saturday afternoon kick-about in the park. On the panel, the players are shown processing from either side towards a central circle, the symbol of death, and one player, just right of the centre (whether it's the winning captain or the losing one is up for debate) has been decapitated, while another (to the left) holds his head and a ritual knife. Along the top runs the stone body of a snake, whose heads stick out at either end of this "bench". Throughout the court is a whispering-gallery effect that enables you to be heard clearly at the far end of the court, and to hear what's going on there.

The **Templo de los Jaguares** overlooks the playing area from the east side. At the bottom – effectively the outer wall of the ball-court – is a little portico supported by two pillars, between which a stone jaguar stands sentinel. The outer wall panels, the left and the right of the interior space, are carved with the images of Pawahtuns, the gods who supported the sky and who are thought to be the patrons of the Itzá people. Inside are some worn but elaborate relief carvings of the Itzá ancestors inserted in the Maya creation myth – a powerful demonstration of their entitlement to rule.

### Cenote Sagrado

The **Cenote Sagrado** lies at the end of the *sacbé* that leads about 300m off from the north side of the plaza. It's an almost perfectly round hole in the limestone surface of the earth, some 60m in diameter and more than 30m deep, the bottom third full of water. It was thanks to this natural well (and perhaps another in the southern half of the site) that the city could survive at all, and it gives Chichén Itzá its name (literally "at the edge of the well of the Itzá"). This well was regarded as a portal to the "other world", called Xibalba, and the Maya would throw offerings into it – incense, statues, jade and especially metal disks (a few of them gold) engraved and embossed with figures and glyphs – as well as human sacrificial victims. People who were thrown in and survived were believed to emerge with the power of prophecy, having spoken with the gods.

### Chichén Viejo

The **southern half of the site** is the most sacred part for contemporary Maya, though the buildings here are not, on the whole, in such good condition. They were built for the most part prior to 925 AD, in the indigenous architectural styles used in the Puuc and Chenes regions. A path leads from the south side of El Castillo to the major structures, passing first the pyramid **El Osario** (the Ossuary, also called the High Priest's Grave), the only building in this section that shows any Toltec-style detail. Externally it is very similar to El Castillo, including the serpent carvings lining the staircase, but inside, most unusually, a series of **tombs** was discovered. A shaft, first explored at the end of the nineteenth century, drops down from the top through five crypts, in each of which was found a skeleton and a trap door leading to the next. The fifth is at ground level, but here too was a trap door, and steps cut through the rock to a sixth chamber that opens onto a huge underground cavern: the burial place of the high priest.

Follow the main path and you arrive at **El Caracol** (the Snail, for its shape; also called the Observatory), a circular, domed tower standing on two rectangular platforms and looking remarkably like a modern-day observatory in outline. No telescope, however, was mounted in the roof, which instead has slits aligned with various points of astronomical significance. Four doors at the cardinal points lead into the tower and a circular chamber. A spiral staircase leads to the upper level, where observations were made.

Immediately to the south, the so-called **Monjas** (Nunnery) is a palace complex showing several stages of construction. Part of the facade was blasted away by a nineteenth-century explorer, but it is nonetheless a building of grand proportions. Its **annexe**, on the east end, has an elaborate facade in the Chenes style, covered in small heads of Chac that combine to make one giant mask, with the door as a mouth. By contrast, **La Iglesia**, a small building standing beside the convent, is a clear demonstration of Puuc design, its low band of unadorned masonry around the bottom surmounted by an elaborate mosaic frieze and roofcomb. Hook-nosed masks of Chac again predominate, but above the doorway are also the figures of the four mythological creatures that held up the sky – a snail and a turtle on one side, an armadillo and a crab on the other.

South of Las Monjas, a path leads in about ten minutes to a further group of ruins that are among the oldest on the site, but unrestored; this is also a good area for birdwatching, with few people around to disturb the wildlife. Nearer at hand, to the east, is the **Akab Dzib**, a relatively plain block of palace rooms that takes its name ("Obscure Writings") from undeciphered hieroglyphs found inside. Red palm prints – frequently found in Mayan buildings – adorn the walls of some of the chambers. Backtrack along the main path to the building opposite El Osorio, the **Plataforma de las Tumbas**, a funerary structure topped with small columns; behind it is a jungle path that heads back to the main east–west road via the site's other water source, Cenote Xtoloc.

## Eating and entertainment

For refreshment after the ruins, the **restaurant** at the *Hotel Dolores Alba* is good and affordable, with basics from hamburgers to tacos. Across the road is the package-tour stop *Parque Ikkil* (8am–6pm; M$40), the centrepiece of which is the large Sagrado Azul **cenote**, well appointed with changing facilities and easy-access stairs (skip the unappetizing buffet restaurant, though). In Pisté, the best dining options are *El Carrousel*, for cheap beers and snacks, and *Las Mestizas*, which does some good regional cuisine, such as *poc-chuc* and *brazo de reina*. The pricier hotels all have their own restaurants. At the west end of town, in front of the small plaza, a short row of *loncherías* serve *comida corrida* for about M$30, and are also open in the evenings, dishing up standard snacks. There's also a bakery, *Pan del Mayab*, near the west end as well. The only thing to do in the evening is hang out on the plaza, where entertainment consists of watching the local dogs run around.

## Grutas de Balankanché

Just 1.6km east of the *Dolores Alba* hotel (see p.208), the **Grutas de Balankanché** are a somewhat creepy complement to Chichén Itzá's sunlit grandiosity, and a cool and clammy way to pass an hour. These caverns were reopened in 1959, when a sealed passageway was discovered, revealing a path to an underground altar to the rain god, Chac. "Guided tours" (in English daily 11am, 1pm & 3pm; M$50) – in reality, a taped commentary broadcast over loudspeakers – lead you past an underground pool and stalagmites and stalactites to a huge rock formation that resembles a ceiba, the Maya tree of life. Around its base lie many of the original Maya offerings, mostly Chac-faced incense burners and other pottery. Be warned that in places the caves can be cold, damp and thoroughly claustrophobic, despite the rather heavy-handed use of coloured lights. Charles Gallenkamp's book *Maya* (see p.345) has an excellent chapter devoted to the discovery of the caves, and to the ritual of exorcism that a local traditional priest insisted on carrying out to placate the ancient gods and disturbed spirits.

Second-class **buses** between Valladolid and Mérida will drop you at *las grutas*, or you can catch a **colectivo** from Calle 44 in Valladolid.

# West to Mérida

Moving on from Chichén Itzá and Pisté, the most direct route to Mérida (see p.220) is along Hwy-180. If you're driving via the *libre* road, you can stop off at **Cenote Xtohil**, 2km south from the highway after the town of Libre Unión (allegedly named for its high number of couples cohabiting out of wedlock), then 1km east on a narrow track. It's the perfect swimming hole: free, isolated and empty on weekdays. If you continue on the southbound road, you reach the village of **Yaxcaba**, the centrepiece of which is a grand Franciscan church topped with three towers, the only one of its kind in Mexico.

North of Hwy-180, the small town of **Izamal**, dominated by a beautifully maintained sixteenth-century Franciscan mission, is the centre of a vibrant Catholic tradition, while farther along the back road to Mérida, the ancient Maya ruins of **Aké** meld with a working henequen plantation.

# Izamal

The exceptionally scenic small town of **IZAMAL** makes a fine day visit or overnight stop for both its historic monuments and gracious feel. From Pisté, head west on Hwy-180 to Kantunil (where the *cuota* and the free road merge), then 18km north. By bus from the Chichén Itzá area, you will have to back-track to Valladolid, where you can catch one of the four Izamal-bound Oriente buses a day. It's also a very easy day-trip from Mérida, with buses leaving every 45 minutes or so from the Noreste terminal at Calle 50 and Calle 67. Arriving at the **bus station**, on Calle 32 at Calle 33, you're one block back from (and within view of) one of two plazas set corner-to-corner, the main one at the front of a Franciscan convent and another on the building's north side.

The most immediately striking thing about Izamal is that the convent and all of its buildings are painted a rich ochre colour, which positively glows in the setting sun. The paint job is the byproduct of the most exciting event in this quiet town's recent history: Pope John Paul II's visit in 1993. More recently, the town's artisans – master wood-carvers, papier-mâché artists and embroiderers – have received a great deal of encouragement from Banamex, thanks in part to billionaire tastemaker Roberto Hernandex, the bank's ex-president, buying a home on the main plaza; rumour has it he'll eventually build a luxury hotel here, along the lines of the splendid *Temozón* (see p.251) south of Mérida.

Ancient Izamal was an important religious centre for the Maya, where they worshipped **Itzamná**, mythical founder of the ancient city and one of the gods of creation, at a series of huge pyramid-temples of the same name. Most are now no more than low mounds in the surrounding country, but several survive in the town itself and are fascinating to see rising up right in the middle of the residential grid; a couple of businesses on the main plaza have pyramids literally in their backyards. The largest pile, **Kinich Kakmó** (daily 8am–8pm; free), dedicated to the sun god, has been partly restored. It's just a couple of blocks north of the two central plazas; the helpful brown-clad tourist police roaming the squares have a knack for offering directions the moment you look remotely confused.

Very early in the colonial period, the Franciscans sought to establish Izamal as the centre of their religious leadership. In 1552 Fray Diego de Landa (later responsible for a vicious inquisition and auto-da-fé in Maní) lopped the top off a pyramid and began building the grand **Convento de San Antonio de Padua** (daily; free), which now anchors the main squares. It's impressive not only because it looms above the town, but also because its expansive porticoed yard occupies some 24,000 square metres.

When the complex was completed in 1561, de Landa consecrated it with one of two statues of the Virgin that he had brought back from Guatemala. Several years later, when church leaders from Valladolid attempted to claim the statue, it is said to have become impossibly heavy, and they were forced to leave it in Izamal. In light of this and numerous other presumed miracles, a cult developed that still draws pilgrims from all over the peninsula, even though the original statue burned in 1829 and had to be replaced by its twin. Today Nuestra Señora de Izamal is the official Patroness of Yucatán, and during the **fiesta** dedicated to her in August, penitents climb the monastery's broad front staircase on their knees. The statue is usually on view in the *camarín*, a special chapel around the back of the main altar, reached by a long hall that runs adjacent to the nave, also a good place to admire the flying buttresses supporting the structure. Next to the small chapel is the small **Museo Sanctuario de Nuestra Señora** (Tues–Sat 10am–1pm & 3–6pm, Sun 9am–4pm; M$5 donation), which includes the statue's elaborate gowns, a meticulous chronological display that's reminiscent of Elvis's Graceland museum – particularly when you get to the silver lamé number from 1974. A few evenings a week, a **sound-and-light show** (Tues, Thurs & Sat at 8.30pm; M$45) is projected on the front facade of the main church. Fray Diego looks on from his post on a pedestal in the plaza on the north side of the monastery.

### Practicalities

In the north plaza you'll find a Banorte **bank** with ATM. On the main plaza is a **post office** (Mon–Fri 8am–2.30pm) and the **tourist office** (9am–6pm; ☏988/954-0096), should you for some reason not have found someone eager to help; ask here for a free Banamex-produced **map** of the town that identifies artisans' workshops, as well as other local treasures, like the home of Izamal's most respected elderly resident (a font of stories, for those who speak Spanish). **Horse-drawn buggies** lined up around the plaza will take you for a pleasant *paseo* around the town (20min; M$40) and the pyramids, as well as out to the old wooden **train station**, which will supposedly be put back into use for day runs to Mérida by 2007.

Of the very few **hotels** in town, *Posada Flory*, on C 30 at C 27 just off the plaza (☏988/954-0562; ❸–❹), is a bargain, with ten homely rooms (some with a/c), operated by a chatty, hospitable woman. For a bit more, *Macan Ché B&B* (☏988/954-0287, ⓦwww.macanche.com; ❺–❼), is an assortment of comfortable cottages tucked among rambling gardens a few blocks east of the main plaza, on Calle 22 between calles 33 and 35. A few kilometres south, near the town of Sudzal, and well worth the drive if you have your own transport, is the rambling, artfully decorated *Hacienda San Antonio Chalanté* (☏999/908-0726, ⓦwww .haciendachalante.com; ❻); the owner is a champion horsewoman, and offers riding around the expansive grounds.

Back in town, *Restaurante Portales*, facing the southwest corner of the convent, serves good basic local **food** and snacks, as well as hamburgers and the like; the more formal *El Toro*, on Calle 30 just east of the convent, has a Spanish colour scheme but a strong Yucatecan menu, with hearty *chaya* tamales and *queso relleno*. Hecho a Mano, a particularly good craft and folk-art **shop**, on Calle 31 facing the park, is stocked with everything from Mexican wrestling masks to Huichol yarn paintings from Nayarit, as well as excellent photography by one of the owners (10am–2pm, 4–7pm, closed Sun).

# Aké

Midway between Izamal and Mérida on the back road via Cacalchén, the **AKÉ** (9am–5pm; M$24) **ruins** are partially integrated into an inhabited village. Aké was probably in alliance with the old city of Izamal, as it is linked to it by one of the peninsula's largest *sacbeob* (Maya roads). The most impressive building here is the **Edificio de las Pilastras**, a large platform topped with more than twenty stone pillars, resembling something from central Mexico or even Greece more than anything typical of the Yucatán. A working henequen **hacienda**, San Lorenzo de Aké, a bit tumbledown but a fine example of neo-French architecture from the end of the nineteenth century, intermingles with the Maya rubble, and you're welcome to wander through the machinery to see the fibre-making process. North of the henequen plant, a church has been built on top of one of the old Maya temples. You'll need a car to visit the site, as there's no bus service (though a second-class bus runs the scenic Hwy-80 between Izamal and Mérida six times daily). To reach the ruins, turn south off the main road just before Tixkokob; the smaller side road peters out after 10.5km, a little way past the village of Ekmul, and the entrance is to the far right, beyond an overgrown plaza and the main hacienda building.

Also along this route, 6km west of the village of Cacalchén and 10km east of the turn to Aké, *Hacienda San José* (T 999/910-4617, W www.starwood.com; ❾) is good for a splurgy **lunch** and time to take in the very good bird life in this area; as one of the very tastefully restored Starwood properties, it's also a gorgeous place to **lodge**.

# Travel details

## Buses

Tizimín is a handy transport hub for northeastern Yucatán – you can go straight from there to Mérida or Cancún, for instance, without returning to Valladolid. Improved bus service at the Chichén Itzá ruins now spares travellers the hike to Pisté for transport. To make your way back to the Caribbean coast from Chichén Itzá, it's best to take any bus you can as far as Valladolid, and if necessary change there for first-class service. You can bypass Cancún by taking a second-class bus to Tulum via Cobá.

**Chichén Itzá** or **Pisté** to: Cancún (hourly, 8am–4.30pm; 2hr 30 min–4hr); Mérida (hourly 6am–5pm; 2–4hr); Playa del Carmen (2 daily; 3hr 30min); Tulum (3 daily; 2hr); Valladolid (hourly 8am–5.30pm; 45min).

**Izamal** to: Cancún via Valladolid (hourly; 5hr); Tizimín (3 daily; 1hr); Mérida (approx every 30min 5.30am–7.15pm; 1–2hr).

**Tizimín** to: Cancún (6 daily; 2hr 30min–4hr); Chetumal (2 daily; 9hr); Chiquilá, for Holbox (4 daily; 2hr); El Cuyo (6 daily; 1hr); Mérida via Izamal (hourly; 2–4hr); San Felipe via Río Lagartos (9 daily; 1hr 30min); Valladolid (hourly 5.30am–7.30pm; 1hr).

**Valladolid** to: Campeche (1 daily; 6hr); Cancún (every 45min; 2hr–3hr 30min); Chetumal (3 daily; 8hr); Chichén Itzá (hourly 7.15am–5.30pm; 45min); Mérida (approx every 30min; 2hr 30 min–4hr); Playa del Carmen (8 daily; 3hr); Tizimín (approx hourly 5.30am–8pm; 1hr); Tulum (8 daily; 2hr).

## Flights

Charter small-plane tours run from Playa del Carmen to a small airstrip near Chichén Itzá.

# Mérida and around

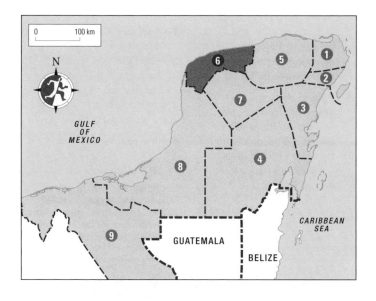

0    100 km

N

GULF
OF
MEXICO

GUATEMALA

BELIZE

CARIBBEAN
SEA

# CHAPTER 6

# Highlights

**∗ Plaza de la Constitución** On Mérida's main square, you can take in everything from crooning *trovadores* to hippie drummers. **P.228**

**∗ Catedral de San Ildefonso** The first cathedral built in the Americas is the site of a major pilgrimage in September and October. **P.228**

**∗ Palacio de Gobierno** Inside the Yucatán governor's offices in Mérida, Fernando Castro Pacheco's stirring modernist murals depict local history. **P.229**

**∗ Dzibilchaltún** The temple at this Maya ruin north of Mérida aligns perfectly with the sunrise on the equinoxes; be sure to also see the site's excellent museum of Maya culture. **P.237**

**∗ Progreso** All of Mérida decamps to this Gulf coast town in July and August, but the rest of the year you may have the broad beach entirely to yourself. **P.238**

**∗ Celestún** Visitors flock here mainly to see the 30,000 flamingos that congregate during the peak winter season. **P.240**

△ Palacio Cantón

# Mérida and around

I f you want to truly appreciate the melding of Spanish and Mayan culture that's the cornerstone of local heritage, Mérida, the next most popular stop in the area after Cancún and Chichén Itzá, is the place to come. The capital of Yucatán State is modern and prosperous but also distinctly proud of its past, boasting a rich historical core filled with beautifully decaying mansions, a very good archeology museum, a teeming market and the oldest cathedral in the Americas. It's the region's cultural centre, with a busy schedule of traditional music and dance, as well as the best weekend street party – *every* weekend – anywhere on the peninsula.

A far more sedate and relaxing city than the Mexican metropolis of popular imagination, Mérida has enough to occupy you for several days and serves as a great base for a handful of easy day- or weekend trips thanks to its location, non-stop flow of buses in and out and ready availability of inexpensive and lovely accommodation (some of those crumbling old homes in the centre have been put to very good use). Outside of the city, where the landscape was once a vista of spiky, grey-green henequen plants, many of the former plantation **haciendas** have also been converted into striking hotels.

Though most use Mérida as a base for visiting the great Maya sites of Uxmal and Chichén Itzá (see p.247 and p.206) as well as the scenic Maya ruins along the Ruta Puuc that loops south of the city (see p.252), it's also near the beach. About a half-hour's drive straight north from the city, the resort town of **Progreso** functions as Mérida's collective patio in the summertime and during Semana Santa. Otherwise, it's virtually a ghost town, with green water lapping at the shore and only a few travellers lolling on the sand; some "snowbird" Americans maintain winter homes here, but mostly this is not a heavily touristed area.

The whole Gulf coast, a bit to the west but largely to the east, is dotted with vacation homes, interspersed with older fishing villages as well as much older Maya ruins like **Xcambó**. The Maya used this low-lying, marshy strip of land to mine salt, one of the great treasures of their time. The *salinas*, or salt flats, harbour diverse birdlife; travelling along the coast highway in the evening, you can often see flamingos and great herons winging home. You'll see even more flamingos if you go west of Mérida to the **Ría Celestún Biosphere Reserve**, a long strip along the Gulf waters where pink birds roost year-round. There's not much else to do but go swimming or ogle these and hundreds of other types of birds, but those alone could keep you busy for years. Closest to the city, the Maya ruins of **Dzibilchaltún**, best known for their impressive alignment with the rising equinox sun, host a very sophisticated museum, which, with its collection of Maya and Spanish art and artefacts, presents a powerful picture of the interaction between the two peoples from the Conquest to the present.

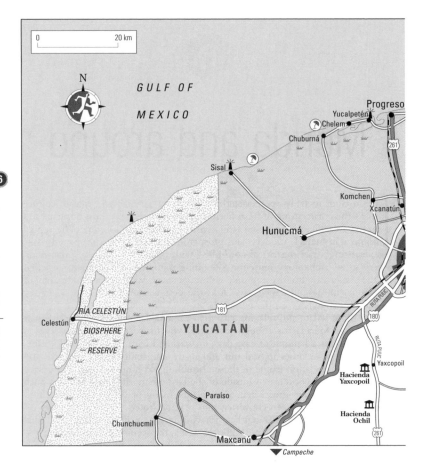

Campeche

# Mérida

In every sense the leading city of the peninsula, **MÉRIDA** still bears the nickname "La Ciudad Blanca" (the white city) even though its sprawl of two-storey buildings, once bare white limestone, are now covered in peeling layers of gem-coloured paint. Bus traffic rumbles down its stone streets, but it remains a wonderfully calm and likable place, with a small-town geniality despite its population of nearly one million. Come dusk, the curving loveseats (*confidenciales*) that dot the numerous parks fill with pairs of lovers, young and old. But don't mistake Mérida for a sleepy backwater: the cultural scene ranges from free traditional entertainment every night of the week (all well attended by older folk in Mérida's version of formalwear – the huipil for ladies and the white guayabera for gents) to avant-garde dance festivals, foreign films and lively theatre performances.

This all draws thousands of visitors, both Mexican and foreign, and since 2000, the city has welcomed a rash of expat residents, bent on renovating the crum-

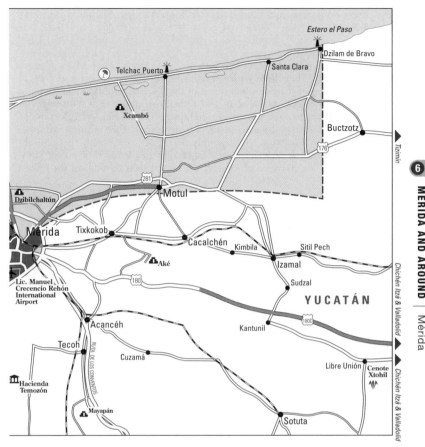

*Tizimín*

*Chichén Itzá & Valladolid*

*Chichén Itzá & Valladolid* ▶

bling **historic mansions** that dot the centre. Because of the city's prosperity and rich cultural life, people have been quick to name Mérida the next hot spot for artsy gringo investment. But even as the trendiness rises, the city retains its grace and manners of the past: every street in the centre boasts a well-maintained colonial church or museum, and locals still ride in the little horse-drawn taxis that gather by the plaza in the evenings.

## Some history

Founded on January 6, 1542, by conquistador **Francisco de Montejo the Younger** (who also established Campeche), Mérida was the product of a bloody, stubborn struggle between the Spanish and the local Maya. It was built over, and partly from, the ruins of a Maya city known as **Tihó** or Ich-cansihó, and intended from the start as the Spanish capital in the Yucatán. Despite some initial impressive construction around the plaza, however, the city never was a jewel in Spain's crown, largely because the Yucatán contained no gold or other natural wealth, so colonists struggled along with what resources they had: land and forced Maya labour. They established sugarcane and maize plantations outside the city, and looked longingly back to Europe for influence.

It was the *meridanos'* desperate squeezing of the Maya people that sparked the **Caste Wars**, beginning with small uprisings in 1847 and gaining momentum in the spring of 1849, when, in a surprise attack, rebel Maya armies besieged Mérida. They were within a hair's breadth of capturing it and thus regaining control of the peninsula (most of the Spanish populace fled to Sisal on the coast, hoping to board ships and return to Europe), but with victory in reach, the Maya peasant fighters decided they could no longer neglect their fields and left the siege lines to plant corn in hopes of an autumn harvest. Thus spared, the Yucatecan elite quickly arranged a deal with the central Mexican government ceding the peninsula's independence in exchange for support against the Maya rebellions, which nonetheless ground on for some fifty years.

In the meantime, the *haciendados* (plantation owners) discovered "green gold": the henequen plant, which produced valuable fibre for rope, in demand all over the world (see box, p.252). By 1900, Mérida had become an extraordinarily wealthy city. Much of this wealth was poured into the grandiose mansions of what was then the outskirts of town, along the Paseo de Montejo, and into European educations for the children of the upper classes. The city's wealthy fancied themselves living in "the Paris of Mexico".

Today, even with the henequen trade all but dead (it petered out around World War II, when nylon became the material of choice), the city remains elegant, bustling, prosperous and intellectual – Mérida is said to have the highest number of PhDs per capita in Mexico. Its streets are filled with a vibrant mix of Maya, mestizos, Lebanese (who emigrated here in the early twentieth century) and more recent transplants from Mexico City and abroad, drawn by Mérida's tranquil urbanity.

## Arrival

Even if practically every road in the peninsula didn't lead to Mérida, it would still be an inevitable stop. The Lic. Manuel Crecencio Rejón **airport** (T999/946-1372) is 7km southwest of the city and has a **tourist office** (daily 8am–8pm) and post office, plus long-distance phones and car rental desks. To get downtown, take a colectivo (buy a ticket at the desk), a taxi from the rank at the front (about M$50 to the centre) or bus #79 ("Aviación"), which drops off at the corner of calles 67 and 60, near the market, about fifteen minutes' walk from the central Plaza de la Constitución.

Mérida sees a dizzying amount of **bus** traffic and maintains several small second-class terminals, but visitors are most likely to arrive at one of two main stations, which lie next to each other on the southwest side of town. In no case do city buses provide direct service to the plaza; you'll have to walk (about 20 minutes from any of the stations) or take a **taxi**. Most taxis work on a zone system, so a ride to the plaza or a nearby hotel should cost no more than M$30; to hotels on Paseo de Montejo will cost M$40. Drivers will expect a small tip if they handle your luggage. Don't worry too much about arriving **at night** – only the Noreste bus terminal, near the market, is in an area that's relatively deserted in the evening.

The **Terminal CAME**, reserved for express and first-class service from ADO, ADO GL, Maya de Oro and UNO, is on Calle 70 between calles 69 and 71. You'll arrive here if you're coming directly from Cancún, Campeche or Chichén Itzá. The **Terminal de Segunda Clase**, across the street on Calle 69

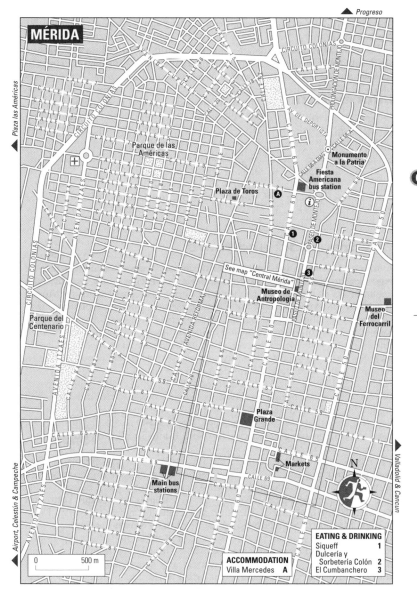

MÉRIDA

Progreso

Plaza las Américas

Parque de las Américas

Plaza de Toros

Monumento a la Patria

Fiesta Americana bus station

See map "Central Mérida"

Museo de Antropología

Museo del Ferrocarril

Parque del Centenario

Plaza Grande

Markets

Main bus stations

N

Airport, Celestún & Campeche

Valladolid & Cancún

0          500 m

ACCOMMODATION
Villa Mercedes    A

EATING & DRINKING
Siqueff                          1
Dulcería y
  Sorbetería Colón      2
El Cumbanchero        3

between calles 68 and 70, deals with Mayab, ATS, TRP, TRT and some Oriente buses. The latter station has a **luggage storage** service. Some ADO GL and UNO services from Cancún arrive at the **Fiesta Americana** hotel, north of the centre off Paseo de Montejo at Avenida Colón. This station is convenient only if you're staying at that hotel or at the *Villa Mercedes*, as it's a slightly longer hike to the centre.

Southeast of the plaza is the **Noreste** terminal, on Calle 67 at Calle 50. Noreste buses arrive here, but so do those operated by Occidente, Oriente and Lineas Unidas del Sur (LUS). AutoProgreso buses from Progreso and the northern beaches arrive at the dedicated **Terminal de Autobuses a Progreso** on Calle 62 between calles 65 and 67.

## Information

In addition to the tourist bureau at the airport (see p.222), Mérida's main **tourist office** is in Teatro Peón Contreras, on the corner of calles 60 and 57-A (daily 8am–8pm; ☎999/924-9290, ❾www.merida.gob.mx/turismo). Pick up a free copy of the excellent *Yucatán Today* magazine (❾www.yucatantoday.com), in English and Spanish, to find out what's going on around town and in the rest of the state. There are also plenty of leaflets available, and you'll usually find some English-speaking staff. **Tourist information booths** are in the Palacio de Gobierno on the main plaza and on Paseo de Montejo at Avenida Colón, just south of the *Fiesta Americana* hotel.

## City transport and tours

As most of the places of interest in Mérida are within walking distance of one another, it really isn't worth the bother of having a **car**, nor of using public **buses** to get around. To visit some of the less central sites (the **Museo Regional de Antropología** on Paseo de Montejo, for example), you may want to catch a bus, but be warned that the system is remarkably convoluted, with numerous competing companies and overlapping routes, and often on the brink of being completely revamped. As of last check, many buses and *combis* leave from Calle 54 and Calle 65-A, near the market; northbound buses often run up Calle 56. For Paseo de Montejo, look for bus #17 on Calle 59 between calles 56 and 58, or #18 on Calle 56 at Calle 59. You can flag buses down at any corner; fares are posted on the doors – usually M$4. **Taxis** can be hailed all around town and from ranks at Parque Hidalgo, the post office, Parque de San Juan and the airport. Most use zone fares (M$30, M$40 or M$50 depending on the distance), but some newer cars (marked "Radio Taxi") use metres, so they can be cheaper for short trips.

For basic orientation, Mérida's tourism bureau gives an informative **free walking tour** of the centre every day but Sunday, at 9.30am; make reservations at the office located inside the Palacio de Gobierno on the plaza. Better, though, is to get a peek inside some of Mérida's grand mansions on a **garden tour** with the Mérida English Library, Calle 53 between calles 66 and 68 (Nov–April Wed 9.30am; M$200; ☎999/924-8401). A tour by **horse–drawn carriage** (*calesa*) is slow-paced but relaxing; typical rates are M$150 for an hour-long trip around the centre and up Paseo de Montejo, or M$250 for a longer tour that also visits the out-of-the-way Parque de las Américas and many old houses. Two **bus tours** cover similar routes, going much farther afield than you'd ever walk: better to avoid the eyesore red double-deckers and go instead for the festive little open-sided number that departs from Parque Santa Lucía (Sun 10am and 1pm, Mon–Sat 10am, 1pm, 4pm and 7pm; M$75; ☎999/927-6119).

## Accommodation

Of Mérida's numerous **hotels**, many are housed in lovely colonial buildings and are also very reasonably priced. Although the city can get crowded at peak times, you should always be able to find a room. The cheapest hotels are concentrated **next to the main bus station**, a noisy and grimy part of town relatively far from the centre, while a string of upmarket hotels lies along **Paseo de Montejo**, just north of the centre, most of them ultramodern and lacking in charm. The best-value hotels are in between, both geographically and in terms of price – there's a glut of excellent B&Bs and smaller inns in the blocks around the plaza, all housed in converted old homes, complete with vintage tile floors and lofty ceilings. A glamorous but more rural alternative is to stay outside town in a **hacienda**. The closest one is listed here, but if you're happy to go further afield, check the state tourism website (ⓦwww.mayayucatan.com) for a full list of estates, ranging from ramshackle ruins to ultra-deluxe resorts.

Mérida's **hostel** scene is booming, with a number of well-designed places scattered about. You can **camp** outside of town, to the northwest just past Caucel, in the big grassy garden at *Ecoquinta Ucu* (☎999/953-0104, Ⓔecoquintaucu@yahoo.com.mx; M$60). This country retreat also has a pool and a couple of private rooms.

## Hotels

**Caribe** C 59 no. 500, Parque Hidalgo ☎999/924-9022, ⓦwww.hotelcaribe.com.mx. Mérida's best mid-range hotel is just a block from the Plaza de la Constitución, on a pretty, small square of its own. Rooms don't have any particular flair, but the patio restaurant is lovely, as are the views of the cathedral and plaza from the rooftop pool. There's parking and an onsite travel agency as well. ❻

**Casa Lucía** C 60 no. 474-A, between C 63 and C 65 ☎999/928-0740, ⓦwww.casalucia.com.mx. A small, artfully restored hotel across from Parque Santa Lucía that conjures old European style (Venetian tiles in the pool), while still displaying some typically Méridan details, like the heavy wood doors from the original building. The Latin American artwork throughout is excellent. ❾

**Dolores Alba** C 63 no. 464, between C 52 and C 54 ☎999/928-5650, ⓦwww.doloresalba.com. Popular mid-range hotel situated around two courtyards and a large swimming pool. Rooms have TV, telephone and a/c, and there's a restaurant and parking onsite. You get a lot for your money, but the place is a bit out of the way. ❺

**El Español** C 69 no. 543-C, at 70 ☎999/923-2854, ⓦwww.hotelelespanol.com.mx. An upmarket alternative to the adjacent dives, located directly across from the main bus stations. Has a small pool and clean, quiet rooms with powerful a/c. ❻

**Maison Lafitte** C 60 no. 472, between C 53 and C 55 ☎999/928-1246, or reservations in the US on 1-800/538-6802, ⓦwww.maisonlafitte.com.mx. An excellent, relatively new colonial-style hotel on the main drag, with comfortable, contemporary rooms and a lush courtyard and pool area. Rates include full breakfast. Spa services are available and a travel agency is onsite. ❼

**La Misión de Fray Diego** C 61 no. 524, between C 64 and C 66 ☎999/924-1111, ⓦwww

.lamisiondefraydiego.com. Very elegant colonial hotel with twenty minimalist, monastery-chic rooms and a good Spanish restaurant inside the pretty courtyard. ❽

**Trinidad Galería** C 60 no. 456, at C 51 ☎999/923-2463, ⓦwww.www.hotelestrinidad .com. Wonderfully eccentric hotel crammed full of bizarre artefacts, odd sculptures and paintings. Rooms upstairs are lighter and more spacious, but all are individually decorated (some have a/c). Also has a pool, a small breakfast café and two art galleries. The *Trinidad* (C 62 at C 55), under the same ownership, has several cheaper rooms, and guests can use the pool at the *Galería*. ❺

**Villa Mercedes** Av Colón no. 500, between C 60 and C 62 ☎999/942-9000, ⓦwww .hotelvillamercedes.com.mx. A luxury hotel in a converted Art Nouveau mansion, with more individual charm than others in its price range; photos found during the late-1990s renovation decorate the tasteful rooms. Offers all standard perks for business travellers. ❾

**Hacienda Xcanatun** 12km north of Mérida on the road to Progreso ☎999/941-0213, ⓦwww .xcanatun.com. This eighteenth-century plantation house on lush grounds has been remade as a small, exclusive hotel featuring luxurious suites – some with baths hewn from local rock, some with hot tubs. There's also a full spa and a very good restaurant (see p.233). ❾

## B&Bs and inns

**Las Arecas** C 59 no. 541, between C 66 and C 68 ☎999/928-3626, ⓦwww.lasarecas.com. This small, colonial-style guesthouse, owned and managed by a local, is a fantastic bargain. Of the four tidy, modestly furnished rooms, two have kitchenettes and one has a/c. All have access to the small central garden and fountain. No kids. ❹–❺

**Casa Bowen** C 66 no. 521-B, between C 65 and C 67 ☎ and ℻ 999/928-6109. A budget travellers' favourite for years, this pretty, old building midway between the bus station and the plaza is centred on a bright courtyard. Spare but perfectly pleasant rooms have high ceilings (some with a/c, or the occasional dusty chandelier), and there are two apartments with kitchens. ❹

**Casa Mexilio** C 68 no. 495, between C 59 and C 57 ☎ 999/928-2505, or reservations in the US on 1-800/583-6802, ⓦ www.mexicoholiday.com. One of Mérida's real treasures. This very attractive B&B, in a restored colonial townhouse, is a fascinating labyrinth of individually decorated rooms, tranquil gardens, sun terraces and a pool. The full breakfast (included) is delicious. ❻–❾

**Casa San Juan** C 62 no. 545-A, between C 69 and C 71 ☎ 999/923-6823, ⓦ www.casasanjuan.com. A variety of reasonably priced rooms, some with a/c and all furnished in a very homely style, are located in a landmark house midway between the bus station and the plaza. Its owner, a knowledgeable Cuban expat, can arrange tours with archeologists working in the field. Reserve ahead (two-night minimum), as it's often booked with longer-term residents. Prices include continental breakfast. ❺

**Luz En Yucatán** C 55 no. 499, between C 58 and C 60 ☎ 999/924-0035, ⓦ www.luzenyucatan .com. Delightful studio rooms and apartments in a rambling house, all done in rich, quirky colours, plus a pool and plenty of comfortable public space. The owner can arrange spa services, Spanish lessons and more. Rates are negotiable for longer stays. ❺–❼

**Medio Mundo** C 55 no. 533, between C 64 and C 66 ☎ 999/924-5472, ⓦ www.hotelmediomundo .com. Well-travelled owners have created this hospitable guesthouse, distinguished by eclectic furnishings from all over the world and a better-than-average book exchange shelf. Ten sunny tile-floor rooms (fan or a/c) have pillow-top beds and huge bathrooms.

### Hostels

**Hostal del Peregrino** C 51 no. 488, between C 54 and C 56 ☎ 999/924-5491, ⓦ www.hostaldelper-egrino.com. Beds are a bit on the pricey side here, but the setting in a beautifully redone house – with an especially nice outdoor kitchen – can be a relief from the backpacking grind. Private rooms are also available, for not much more per person than the dorms. Bikes for rent too. M$120

**The Nest** C 67 no. 547-B, between C 68 and C 70 ☎ 999/928-8365, ⓦ www.nesthostel.com. The go-to hostel for younger travellers. Colourful, modern dorm rooms are named after the schools in the Harry Potter books, it's only a block from the bus station, and there are tons of perks (such as free lockers). Try to avoid top bunks in fan-only dorms, though – they can be very stuffy. M$75–95

**Nómadas** C 62 no. 433 at C 51 ☎ 999/924-5223, ⓦ www.nomadastravel.com. The longest estab-lished of Mérida's hostels, and still the best bal-ance of price and amenities. Rooms (including six private ones) are clean, and there's space to camp; you also get a pool, live music and plenty of helpful advice from the in-house travel agency. Student discounts available. M$65

## The city

Like the rest of the peninsula, Mérida had little effective contact with central Mexico until the completion of road and rail links in the 1960s, but trade with Europe brought wealth well before then: in the early 1900s, a standard French ship route was Marseilles to New York via Havana and Mérida's port

---

### Mérida's corners

As you walk around the centre of the city, notice the small red-and-white plaster **plaques** embedded in the walls at many street corners: originally, the corners were marked not by a written name, but by a statue of the given symbol – most commonly animals, but also objects such as a clenched fist or a flower – mounted on top of the building, clearing up language confusion in the Spanish–Maya city with a universally identifiable "elephant corner" or "cat corner", for example. Today, the illustrated plaques have replaced the original figures, but many of the surrounding business names still reflect the old corner designation. And a few of the plaques, such as "La Ermita" (the hermitage), are the last remaining evidence of major buildings that used to serve as landmarks.

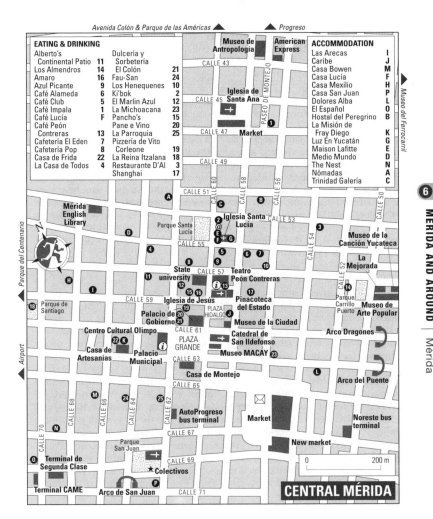

Avenida Colón & Parque de las Américas ▲ ▲ Progreso

**EATING & DRINKING**

| | |
|---|---|
| Alberto's Continental Patio | 11 |
| Los Almendros | 14 |
| Amaro | 16 |
| Azul Picante | 9 |
| Café Alameda | 6 |
| Café Club | 5 |
| Café Impala | 1 |
| Café Lucía | F |
| Café Peón Contreras | 13 |
| Cafetería El Eden | 7 |
| Cafetería Pop | 8 |
| Casa de Frida | 22 |
| La Casa de Todos | 4 |
| Dulcería y Sorbetería El Colón | 21 |
| Fau-San | 24 |
| Los Henequenes | 10 |
| Ki'bok | 2 |
| El Marlin Azul | 12 |
| La Michoacana | 23 |
| Pancho's | 15 |
| Pane e Vino | 20 |
| La Parroquia | 25 |
| Pizzería de Vito Corleone | 19 |
| La Reina Itzalana | 18 |
| Restaurante D'Al | 3 |
| Shanghai | 17 |

**ACCOMMODATION**

| | |
|---|---|
| Las Arecas | I |
| Caribe | J |
| Casa Bowen | M |
| Casa Lucía | F |
| Casa Mexilio | H |
| Casa San Juan | P |
| Dolores Alba | L |
| El Español | O |
| Hostal del Peregrino | B |
| La Misión de Fray Diego | K |
| Luz En Yucatán | G |
| Maison Lafitte | E |
| Medio Mundo | D |
| The Nest | N |
| Nómadas | A |
| Trinidad Galería | C |

Museo de Antropología · American Express · Museo del Ferrocarril · CALLE 43 · PASEO DE MONTEJO · Iglesia de Santa Ana · CALLE 45 · CALLE 47 · Market · CALLE 49 · Mérida English Library · Parque Santa Lucía · Iglesia Santa Lucía · Museo de la Canción Yucateca · La Mejorada · State university · Teatro Peón Contreras · Parque de Santiago · Iglesia de Jesús · Palacio de Gobierno · Pinacoteca del Estado · Museo de la Ciudad · Parque Carrillo Puerto · Museo de Arte Popular · Centro Cultural Olimpo · Catedral de San Ildefonso · Arco Dragones · Casa de Artesanías · Palacio Municipal · PLAZA GRANDE · Museo MACAY · Casa de Montejo · Arco del Puente · AutoProgreso bus terminal · Market · Noreste bus terminal · Parque San Juan · New market · Terminal de Segunda Clase · Colectivos · Terminal CAME · Arco de San Juan · **CENTRAL MÉRIDA** · 0 200 m

**MÉRIDA AND AROUND | Mérida**

227

at Sisal. As a consequence the city looks more European than almost any other in Mexico – many of the houses built in the nineteenth century use French bricks and tiles, brought over as tradable ballast in ships that exported henequen.

Mérida's colonial centre (*centro histórico*) is laid out on a simple **grid** of numbered streets: even numbers run north-south, odd from east to west. The city now sprawls much farther than most visitors will ever see – particularly up **Paseo de Montejo** (called Prolongación de Montejo in its northern stretch), where chain stores and slick restaurants start to appear – but the rich and vibrant centre, which radiates out from the main **Plaza de la Constitución**, is dense with historic attractions and other entertainment. Most sights, from the main market on the south side to the broad boulevard of Paseo de Montejo to the north, are easily reached on foot from the plaza.

## The Plaza de la Constitución

The **Plaza de la Constitución,** often called the Plaza Grande or the Plaza Mayor, formed by calles 60, 61, 62 and 63, acts as the hub of the city's life, particularly in the evenings, when couples meet on the park benches and bands of *trovadores* in white guayaberas wait to be hired for serenades. The plaza is ringed by some of Mérida's oldest buildings, dominated by the **Catedral de San Ildefonso** (daily 6am–noon & 5–8pm). Construction on the building began in 1562 and finished before the end of the sixteenth century, making it the oldest cathedral in the Americas. Singularly vast and white, it is almost severe in its simplicity, reflecting the trend toward crisper Renaissance design and away from the manically ornate Spanish Plateresque style, inspired by Gothic forms. On its facade, the entwined eagle and snake, symbol of the Mexican republic, is a later addition, replacing the Spanish empire's two-headed Hapsburg eagle, which was removed in 1822. Most of the church's valuables, including its eighteenth-century gilt altar, were looted and burned on one particularly violent night in 1915, fuelled by the anticlerical movement during the Mexican Revolution. One object that was lost has been recreated: the **Cristo de las Ampollas** (Christ of the Blisters), which is in a chapel to the left of the main altar. According to legend, the original statue of Christ on the cross was carved from a tree in the village of Ichmul that burned for a whole night without showing the least sign of damage; later, in 1645, the parish church at Ichmul burned down, and the crucifix survived, though blackened and blistered. Though the statue was ultimately destroyed during the purge of 1915, the reconstructed image is the focal point of a local **fiesta** from mid-September through mid-October, when each day a different professional group, or *gremio* (taxi drivers, bakers and so on), pays its respects at the church, then parades on the plaza.

Beside the cathedral, separated from it by the Pasaje San Alvarado, the old bishop's palace has been converted into shops, offices and the **Museo MACAY** (Museo de Arte Contemporáneo Ateneo de Yucatán; Wed–Mon 10am–6pm; M$20), which has the best modern art collection in the state, with permanent displays featuring the work of internationally acclaimed Yucatecan painters Fernando Castro Pacheco, Gabriel Ramírez Aznar and Fernando García Ponce. Ponce's enormous, multilayered collage paintings are particularly striking; one covers the entire wall behind the double staircase at the entrance to the exhibition halls. Temporary exhibitions range from local photographers to European masters on loan from Mexico City museums.

On the south side of the plaza, the **Casa de Montejo** was built in 1549 by Francisco de Montejo, a captain under Hernán Cortés and the first conquistador to attempt to bring the peninsula under the charge of Spain. His first effort, in 1527, failed, as did several later forays; his son, Francisco de Montejo the Younger, did what the father could not, securing the northern part of the peninsula in the 1540s. But soon after the father built his triumphant palace, he was stripped of his titles and recalled to Spain; his son moved in, and his family occupied the place until 1828. The building now belongs to Banamex, and most of the interior is used as office space for the bank. Visitors are welcome to see the lavishly restored wood-panelled dining room, off the back right corner of the Moorish-feeling courtyard. Above a staid doorway of Classical columns, the facade, in sharp contrast to the cathedral, is richly decorated in the Plateresque style (probably the first instance of it in the New World), with conquistadors depicted trampling savages underfoot. The woolly men with clubs hearken from Spain as well; similar figures can be seen on the Colegio de San Gregorio in Valladolid, Spain, where the Montejos hailed from.

Opposite the cathedral, the **Palacio Municipal** is another impressive piece of sixteenth-century design, with a fine clock tower and a large painting upstairs depicting the *mestizaje*. Next door, the gleaming modern **Centro Cultural Olimpo** contains an auditorium and an art gallery showing local works and travelling exhibits. In the basement, a fancy new **planetarium** has shows about astronomy and science (Tues–Sat 10am, noon, 5pm, 7pm, Sun 5pm & 7pm; M$30); narration is in Spanish, but the imagery is impressive, and the a/c can be a treat on a hot day.

Completing the square, the nineteenth-century **Palacio de Gobierno** (daily 8am–10pm) is a must-see; enormous modernist murals by Fernando Castro Pacheco cover the walls on the ground floor and in the large front room on the second floor. They powerfully depict the violent history of the Yucatán, particularly the trials of the indigenous people, though it's interesting to note that the images are sometimes at odds with the accompanying explanatory texts in Spanish, English and Maya. One block east on Calle 61, the small but informative **Museo de la Ciudad** (Tues–Fri 10am–2pm & 4–8pm, Sat & Sun 10am–2pm; free) traces city history from ancient Maya times through the henequen boom; texts are in Spanish and English.

## North of the Plaza de la Constitución

Most of the remaining monuments in Mérida lie north of the plaza, bordering Calle 60 and the Paseo de Montejo. Calle 60 is one of the city's main commercial streets, lined with its fancier hotels and restaurants. It also boasts a lovely series of colonial buildings, starting one block north of the plaza with the seventeenth-century Jesuit **Iglesia de Jesús**, on the corner with Calle 59, between Parque Hidalgo and Parque de la Madre; if the doors are open, peek inside – the lavish chandeliers and frescoes are an opulent surprise in such a spare church. The building is made of stones from the original Maya city of Tihó, and a few pieces of decorative carving are visible in the wall on Calle 59.

On the same block of Calle 59, the **Pinacoteca del Estado Juan Gamboa Guzmán** (Tues–Sat 8am–8pm, Sun 8am–2pm; M$28) houses a collection of nineteenth-century portraits of prominent Yucatecans and Mexican leaders – Austrian-French Emperor Ferdinand Maximilian, who was executed less than three years into his reign, looks particularly hapless among the crowd of presidents. Back on Calle 60 and continuing north, you reach **Teatro Peón Contreras**, a grandiose Neoclassical edifice built by Italian architects between 1900 and 1908, in the heady days of Porfirio Díaz, the Mexican dictator whose decadence inspired the Revolution. Across the street stands the **state university** (Universidad Autónoma de Yucatán), a highly respected institution that has existed, under various names, since 1624.

One block north of Teatro Peón Contreras, the sixteenth-century **Iglesia Santa Lucía** stands facing the elegant plaza of the same name – a small colonnaded square that used to be the town's stagecoach terminus. Three blocks further on is the **Plaza Santa Ana**, a modern open space, bordered by a small cluster of market stalls, where you turn right, then take the second left to reach the Paseo de Montejo.

## Paseo de Montejo

Running north from Plaza Santa Ana (Calle 58 at Calle 45), **Paseo de Montejo** is a broad boulevard designed for strolling, its sidewalks dotted with trees and modern sculptures by Yucatecan and foreign artists. It's also lined with the magnificent, pompous mansions of the henequen-rich grandees who strove to outdo each other's high-European style around the end of the nineteenth century. One of the most striking, the Palacio Cantón, at the corner of Calle 43, houses Mérida's **Museo Regional de Antropología** (Tues–Sat 8am–8pm, Sun 8am–2pm; M$32). The Beaux Arts palace, grandly trimmed in wrought-iron and marble, was built at the beginning of the twentieth century for General Francisco Cantón, a railway tycoon and the former state governor, and set off a competitive building boom along the avenue. The walk out **to the museum** from the plaza takes about half an hour, but you can also get there on a "Paseo de Montejo" bus running up Calle 56, or in a horse-drawn **calesa** (about M$100 from the centre to the museum, or pay M$150 for the full hour tour, then get dropped off here).

△ Monumento a la Patria

Given the archeological riches found near Mérida, the collection itself is perhaps something of a disappointment, but it's a useful introduction to the surrounding sites nonetheless, with displays covering everything from prehistoric stone tools to modern Maya religious practice. The museum is gradually being revamped with more modern displays and text in English, as well as Spanish. Not surprisingly, you'll find sculptures and other objects from Chichén Itzá and elsewhere, but more interesting are the attempts to give some idea of what it was like to live in a Maya city. Topographic maps of the peninsula, for example, explain how cenotes are formed and their importance to the ancient population, while a collection of skulls demonstrates the habits of lengthening skulls and filing teeth and filling them with turquoise inlay. Other displays cover jewellery, ritual offerings and burial practices, as well as the workings of the Maya calendar. Upstairs, temporary exhibits examine Mérida's history and specific archeological sites. The **bookshop** offers leaflets and guidebooks in English to dozens of ruins in the Yucatán and the rest of Mexico.

Another fifteen minutes' walk north on Paseo de Montejo, past scores of other old mansions that now contain banks and insurance companies, brings you to the 1956 **Monumento a la Patria**, about ten long blocks beyond the museum. It is a titan, covered in neo-Maya sculptures relating to Mexican history. Beyond the monument, the street continues under the name Prolongación de Montejo and leads into "new" Mérida, the district of glossy shops and chain restaurants frequented by the younger, wealthier population.

### East of the Plaza de la Constitución

If you want to flesh out your impressions of the *centro histórico*, head several blocks east of the plaza where you'll find the former monastery of **La Mejorada**, at Calle 59 between calles 48 and 50; it housed the city's devout Franciscan community along with Las Monjas (a convent) on Calle 63 and the now destroyed San Francisco de Mérida monastery (the old market and post office are built on its ruins). Today it's home to the **Museo de Arte Popular** (Tues–Sat 9am–8pm, Sun 8am–2pm; free) and displays a fine collection of indigenous dress found throughout Mexico; rich wood and glass cases show huipiles, jewellery and household items, while old black-and-white photos provide glimpses of village life and ceremonies. (The museum was closed for renovation in 2005, however, so confirm with the tourist office that it has reopened before you make the trek.)

Just around the corner on Calle 57, the **Museo de la Canción Yucateca** (daily 9am–5pm; M$15, free on Sun) details the diverse musical influences on the local *trovadores*, from pre-Columbian traditions to Afro-Cuban styles. The presentation, except for one "interactive" room with music clips, is very old-school, with hall upon hall full of vitrines of memorabilia and walls hung with oil portraits of the great composers and singers of the *trova* tradition. The gift shop is an excellent place to pick up some romantic tunes.

A few blocks south of this area and just east of Calle 50, you can also spy two of the old city's entrance **arches** (thirteen of them once studded Mérida's walls from the sixteenth to the early nineteenth century). The Arco del Puente, at Calle 61, sports an adjacent walkway, a four-foot-tall tunnel for single-file pedestrians. (A third arch, the most elegant, stands on the south side of town, on Calle 64 by the Parque de San Juan, marking the former Camino Real to Campeche.)

## Out of the centre

The very dedicated museum-goer can head east of Paseo de Montejo to the **Museo del Ferrocarril**, at Calle 43 and between calles 44 and 46 (Mon–Fri 9am–4pm, Sat & Sun 9am–2pm; M$20), to visit the collection of old engines from the Chiapas-Mayab railway line; sadly, passenger trains are a thing of the past in the Yucatán, as bus service has proven more efficient. For a taste of modern architecture, you could head to the **Parque de las Américas**, west from Paseo de Montejo on Avenida Colón. The park, inaugurated in 1946, is planted with a tree from every country on the American continent, while the bandstand, library and curving pergolas all display a distinctive neo-Maya style, incorporating motifs from Chichén Itzá and other ancient sites.

Nearby, at the corner of Avenida Reforma (C 72) and Calle 25, the **Plaza de Toros** hosts a bullfight once a month or so on Sunday at 3.30pm (M$20–60). To the west of the plaza (head straight out on Calle 59 to Avenida Itzáes), the sprawling green space of **Parque del Centenario** contains a **zoo** (free admission), with a very full aviary. The park is not particularly lush, but it is a nice place to see modern Mérida at leisure, if you want a break from the historic centre; children will like the miniature train that runs through the zoo area.

## Markets and craft shops

Mérida's main **market**, a huge place between calles 67, 69, 54 and 56, is for most visitors a major attraction, a scrum of consumer goods, from freshly hacked-up beef to hand-tooled leather belts to more varieties of bananas than you can count on one hand. Arrive before noon to see the most bountiful foodstuffs; **craft shops** (many in a separate wing on Calle 60 at Calle 65) are open all day. A contested reorganization plan recently moved most market vendors to this new building, which houses more than 2000 stalls, from an older, crumbling maze just to the north (where some vendors are still holding out). The new place is cleaner and more orderly, if not quite so exotic-feeling to the visitor.

As far as quality craftwork goes, though, you're almost always better off buying in a shop – prices in the market are no great shakes, either, unless you're an unusually skilful and determined haggler. Before buying anything, head down Calle 63 two blocks west of the plaza to the **Casa de Artesanías** (Tues–Sat 9am–8pm, Sun 9am–1.30pm), run by the government-sponsored Fonapas organization. The shop sells consistently high-quality crafts from the peninsula, as well as a selection of delicate silver filigree jewellery; the clothing options are somewhat limited, though.

The most popular souvenir of Mexico is a **hammock** – and Mérida is probably the best place in the country to buy one. Head to Tejidos y Cordeles Nacionales, a top specialist very near the market at Calle 56 no. 516-B, just north of Calle 65. More a warehouse than a shop, it has hundreds of the things stacked against every wall; buy several and you can enter into serious negotiations over the price. Similar stores nearby include the highly respected El Aguacate, on Calle 58 near Calle 73, and La Poblana at Calle 65 no. 492, near Calle 60. The latter also sells **ahulado**, the bright, flower-patterned oilcloth popular all over Mexico.

Men will want to look for **guayaberas**, the traditional pleated, embroidered dress shirt that both Cubans and *meridanos* claim to have invented; Filipino traders, who visited both places, probably deserve some credit too. Since the Revolution put a halt to Cuban guayabera exports, factories in Mérida have flourished, and you can choose from a huge range of colours, and long or short sleeves. Guayaberas Cab, Calle 60 between calles 65 and 67, does very upmarket versions in pure linen; you can find less expensive designs, in polyester-blend fabrics, in shops around the market.

Women's **huipiles** are also on sale everywhere, varying wildly in quality, from factory-made, machine-stitched junk to hand-embroidered, homespun cloth. Even the best, though, rarely compare with the antique dresses that can occasionally be found – identical in style (as they have been for hundreds of years) but far better made and very expensive; Retro Style, a shop on Calle 60 between calles 47 and 49, occasionally has a few, along with other local **antiques**.

Also look for fun smaller gifts such as Spanish classroom vocabulary **posters** (Papelería El Estudiante, on Calle 63 between calles 62 and 64, has a good selection) or local foodstuffs, such as **coffee** and **honey**. Mérida's distinctive *trova* **music** is available in many gift shops on CD; it's especially cheap at the weekly serenade on Parque Santa Lucía, where vendors sell remastered classics or newer songs they've written themselves. You can also try the gift shop at the Museo de la Canción Yucateca (see p.231).

## Eating

Good **restaurants** are plentiful in the centre of Mérida, though the best (and some of the least expensive) are open only for lunch. Dinner restaurants are typically operated by hotels, and frequented by out-of-towners; prices are high and most menus verge on international-bland. Nonetheless, evening is the perfect time to visit the bustling sidewalk cafés on the **Plaza Hidalgo**, along Calle 60 between calles 61 and 59, and on **Paseo de Montejo**, where businesses tend to be open later, with some slicker places popular with young locals.

A number of less-expensive spots surround the intersection of calles 62 and 61, at the northwest corner of the plaza, but cheapest of all are the *loncherías* in the **market**, where you can get good, filling *comidas corridas*. Around the Plaza de la Constitución several wonderful **juice bars** – notably *Jugos California*, on the southwest corner, and *La Michoacana*, on calles 61 and 56 – serve all the regular juices and *licuados*, as well as more unusual local concoctions such as home-made root beer. Combine these with something from the **bakery** Pan Montejo, at the corner of calles 62 and 63, to make a great breakfast.

## Cafés

**Café Alameda** C 58 between C 55 and C 57. While away an afternoon with coffee and backgammon at this lunch-only café with a sleepy, old-fashioned feel. It's a popular Lebanese hangout, and the Middle Eastern snacks are quite tasty.

**Dulcería y Sorbetería El Colón** C 61 on the north side of the plaza. Popular spot for exotic fruit sorbets, especially coconut; try a *champola*, a big scoop in a tall glass of milk. There's another branch on Paseo de Montejo, between C 39 and C 41, which is a good place to stop after visiting the archeology museum.

**Cafetería El Eden** C 55 between C 56 and C 58. Bohemian, candlelit hangout with trees growing through the roof and benches made of coffee-bean sacks. Coffee is of course available, along with beer and wine and a basic menu of inexpensive snacks. Daily 5–10pm.

**Café Impala** Paseo de Montejo at C 47. Sidewalk dining until late, with basic sandwiches, burgers and Yucatecan standards, but it's best just for coffee, sweets and people-watching. Daily 6pm–2am.

**La Parroquia** C 62 no. 507, between C 65 and C 67. *Lechería* serving blended milk drinks, yoghurt and fruit plates. Great for a bargain breakfast or a late-night treat (try the cinnamon-laced chocolate milk).

**Café Peón Contreras** C 60 adjacent to the Teatro Peón Contreras. One of the most pleasant outdoor spots in the city, right in the midst of Calle 60's bustle. Serves passable Mexican food and pizza.

**Cafetería Pop** C 57 between C 60 and C 62. A good breakfast joint, with vintage 1960s decor that also serves hamburgers, spaghetti and Mexican snacks. Close to the university, it's a favoured hangout for students and older intellectuals. Daily 7am–midnight.

## Restaurants

**Alberto's Continental Patio** C 64 no. 482, at C 57 ☎999/928-5367. A slice of old-world Mérida, with a beautiful interior courtyard and courtly service. The food, which blends Mexican and Middle Eastern flavours, is erratic and ungodly expensive, however; better to go just for light snacks and a drink, and a chat with the charming Lebanese owner.

**Los Almendros** C 50 between C 57 and C 59, in the Plaza Mejorada. One of Mérida's most renowned restaurants is marred by inconsistency, but when it's on, it serves delicious, moderately priced Yucatecan food, such as *poc-chuc*, which the original *Los Almendros*, in Ticul (see p.258), claims to have invented. Dressier *Gran Almendros*, around the corner, has slightly higher prices, but can be fun on a Sunday afternoon, when it's bustling with families.

**Amaro** C 59 no. 507, between C 60 and C 62. Set in a lovely tree-shaded courtyard with a fountain and a romantic guitarist Wed–Sat. A little overpriced, but interesting veggie options, such as *crepas de chaya*, offer a welcome change for non-meat-eaters tired of quesadillas.

**Café Club** C 55 between C 58 and C 60. Small, very friendly restaurant specializing in natural and mostly vegetarian foods, with a bargain set lunch for M$40. Daily 7am–5pm.

**Café Lucía** in the *Casa Lucía* hotel, C 60 no. 474-A. The good Italian and international menu isn't too outrageously priced, considering the upmarket clientele of local politicos and excellent collection of modern Latin American art on the walls (go at least for a drink to admire this).

**Casa de Frida** C 61 no. 526, at C 66 ☎999/928-2311. Inventive Mexican-French dishes (try the roast duck *in mole poblano* or the bone-marrow *gorditas*) distinguish the menu of this eclectic little restaurant, painted in candy colours, with a cosy back patio. Entrees are about M$100 – not expensive, considering the care and presentation put into the food. Tues–Sat 6pm–midnight.

**Casa de Piedra** in *Hacienda Xcanatun* ☎999/941-0213. Yucatecan-French fusion is the speciality at this elegant place 12km north of town. Dishes like duck glazed with bitter orange and *xtabentun* are not cheap, but the setting, in the hacienda's old machine-house, is dramatic, and warmed by the glow of candles. Mon–Sat 1.30–11pm, Sun 1–6pm.

**Restaurante D'Al** C 54 at C 53. A typical *cocina económica* serving hearty, stick-to-your-ribs daily specials (about M$30) on flowered tablecloths, but open into the evenings. Also, a rarity at this type of hole-in-the-wall restaurant: beer is served.

**Ki'bok** C 60 no. 468, between C 53 and C 55. Modern, stylish coffee bar and restaurant serving large breakfasts and a varied dinner menu, which includes delicate treats like crepes with squash blossoms. Open until midnight; 2am on Fri and Sat.

**El Marlin Azul** C 62 between C 57 and C 59. Longtime local favourite for excellent but inexpensive seafood (trucked in every morning from

Celestún), including tasty fish tacos and perfectly fresh ceviche. Note that it closes at 4.30pm, however, and there's no sign on the blue awning. Also serves breakfast.

**Pane e Vino** C 62 between C 59 and C 61. This wood-panelled restaurant serves workhorse Italian: simple but satisfying dishes like big cheesy lasagne and large helpings of fresh pasta in creamy sauces. Entrees are all under M$100. Closed Mon.

**Pizzería de Vito Corleone** C 59 no. 508, at C 62. Inexpensive pizza joint that also does takeaway. Head for tables on the upstairs balcony if you don't want to get roasted by the wood-burning oven.

**La Reina Itzalana** Parque de Santiago, C 59 between C 70 and C 72. This and a couple of other basic restaurants in the same market are some of the few places in town to get a casual, super-cheap dinner of *panuchos, salbutes* and *sopa de lima*. Packed with families until 10 or 11pm; also open for lunch.

**Shanghai** C 59 between C 56 and C 58. The slick Chinese buffet is nothing exotic or remarkable, but the food is inexpensive and fresh-tasting and a nice break from *panuchos* and *salbutes* if you've been hoofing around on a budget.

**Siqueff** C 60 at C 35. One of the longest-running Lebanese haunts in town is quite a way out of the centre, but merits a visit to its small Moorish-style garden courtyard for *kafta*, *kibi* (fried balls of bulgur and meat) and hummus, with guacamole on the side. Venison (*venado*) is an occasional special, and this is also where the signature Yucatecan egg dish *huevos motuleños* was invented in the 1920s. Entrees M$60–100. Lunch only.

## Drinking, entertainment and nightlife

Mérida is a lively city, and every evening you'll find the streets buzzing with revellers enjoying a variety of **free entertainment**. To find out what's happening on any particular night, pick up a free copy of the monthly *Mérida...en la cultura* schedule from the tourist office or bigger hotels. **Venues** include the plazas, the garden behind the Palacio Municipal, Teatro Peón Contreras (next to the tourist office) and the Casa de la Cultura, Calle 63 between calles 64 and 66. Typical performances include energetic **jaranas**, vibrant Yucatecan folk dances to a distinctive local rhythm (Palacio Municipal, Mon); Glen Miller-style **big band** music (Parque de Santiago, Tues); and the very popular **Serenata Yucateca**, a performance of traditional *trova* songs at the Parque Santa Lucía (Thurs). More free culture – often with an international bent – can be sampled at the **Centro Olimpo de Cultura** on the northwest corner of the plaza; the schedule of lectures, films and performances is posted outside.

Perhaps the best time to see the Plaza de la Constitución and the surrounding streets is Sunday, when vehicles are banned from the area and day-long music, dancing, markets and festivities take over – a real pleasure after the usual traffic rumble. Street markets are set up along Calle 60 as far as the Plaza Santa Ana, and there's a **flea market** in the Parque Santa Lucía. Saturday nights are quite lively as well, with marimba bands and more, though not so many of the streets are closed to traffic.

There's plenty to do of a more commercial nature, too, from **mariachi nights** in hotel bars to **salsa dancing** in nightclubs. By far the best of the more tourist-oriented events is the **Ballet Folklórico de la Universidad de Yucatán**, a wonderful dance interpretation of traditional Mexican and Maya ceremonies at the Centro Cultural Universitario, Calle 60 at Calle 57 (Fri 9pm; M$30).

Should you want to see a **film**, first check the schedule at Teatro Mérida on Calle 62 just north of the plaza; its small upstairs cinema is often running art films. Cines Hollywood, on Parque de Santiago (C 59 between C 70 and C 72), shows first-run films, usually American. Otherwise, head out to the Plaza las Américas mall, which has a multi-screen Cinépolis (Ⓦ www.cinepolis.com.mx).

Apart from the hard-drinking cantinas (and there are plenty of these all over the city, including a couple on Calle 62, just south of the plaza), many of Mérida's **bars** double as restaurants, with early closing times to match.

## Bars, discos and live music

**Azul Picante** C 60 between C 55 and C 57. This small salsa club caters more to tourists than other ones listed here do, but it offers free lessons early in the evenings, as well as Mexican- and Caribbean-themed nights.

**La Casa de Todos** C 64 at C 55. This very small student bar has a strong leftist bent. Some nights there's a rousing folksinger or two on the tiny stage; other nights, young punk bands.

**El Cumbanchero** Paseo de Montejo at C 37. More convenient than *Mambo Café*, this small salsa bar is owned by the son of the late Rubén González, of Buena Vista Social Club. Dancing starts around dinnertime, with an older crowd at first, then giving way to younger dancers around 10pm. Also open for brunch on Sundays.

**Fau-San** C 64 between C 65 and C 67. Those who want to get a taste of a cantina without the serious boozing can visit this little bar-restaurant, which emphasizes food slightly more than drink. Order with restraint, as the *botanas* that come with your drinks are very generous.

**Los Henequenes** C 56 at C 57. A modern reinvention of a traditional *botana* bar, set in a restored old house. Despite its slightly too-slick atmosphere, go anyway for the two-for-one beer specials, live music and local clientele.

**Mambo Café** In the Plaza Las Américas mall. Worth the cab ride (about M$40) if you're looking to mingle with salsa-mad locals in what's considered the city's best nightclub. Touring Dominican and Cuban bands often play here. Free on Wed; otherwise, cover is about M$50. Wed–Sat 10am–3am.

**Pancho's** C 59 between C 60 and C 62. A steak restaurant with a pricey Tex-Mex menu and a lively, if tiny, dancefloor, *Pancho's* is a magnet for hip young Méridans and Americans homesick for "Mexican" food. The fun theme, with bandolier-draped waiters in sombreros and giant portraits of Señor Villa, is ridiculously over-the-top. Try to hit the happy hour, 6–9pm.

# Listings

**Airlines and flights** Flights depart from Lic. Manuel Crecencio Rejón airport (☎999/946-1372) for Mexico City, Cancún, Ciudad del Carmen and Villahermosa, as well as some international destinations; to get to the airport, catch bus #79 ("Aviación") going east on C 67. A taxi from the centre costs about M$50. Aerocaribe/Mexicana Internacional, Paseo de Montejo 500 ☎999/928-6790; Aeroméxico, Plaza Americana, *Hotel Fiesta Americana* ☎999/920-1260, at the airport ☎946-1400; American at Nice Trip travel agency, C 62 no. 309-D at Av Colón ☎999/925-9643; Continental, Paseo de Montejo 437 at C 29 ☎999/926-3100; Mexicana, C 56 no. 493 ☎999/924-7421.

**American Express** Paseo de Montejo 492, between C 41 and C 43 (Mon–Fri 9am–5pm, Sat 9am–noon; ☎999/942-8200, ℱ942-8210).

**Banks** Most banks are around C 65 between C 60 and C 64, have ATMs and are open 9am–4pm. The most centrally located is Banamex in the Casa de Montejo on the south side of the plaza; it also has an ATM.

**Books** Librería Burrel, C 59 between C 60 and C 62, is good for maps; Librería Dante across the street sells guidebooks (another Dante branch is on the west side of the plaza). The Conaculta bookstore adjacent to Teatro Daniel Ayala, C 60 just north of the plaza, carries a good stock of art books, guides and music. Alternatively, borrow English-language books from the extensive Mérida English Library, C 53 between C 66 and C 68,

which also functions as a meeting point for the city's expat community.

**Car rental** Family-run Mexico Rent a Car, with offices at C 57-A between C 58 and C 60, and at C 62 no. 483-A, is friendly, with very good rates that include all types of insurance (☎999/927-4916, ℮mexicorentacar@hotmail.com). Otherwise, try the international agencies, all of which have offices at the *Fiesta Americana* (☎925-7595), allowing you to compare quotes easily.

**Colectivos and combis** Shared taxis and small buses congregate at Parque de San Juan, C 62 at C 69. Destinations include Dzibilchaltún, Oxcutzcab and Ticul. For Progreso, colectivos leave from the east side of C 60 between C 65 and C 67.

**Consulates** Opening hours are likely to be fairly limited, so it's best to phone ahead. Belize, C 53 no. 498, at C 58 (☎999/928-6152, ℮dutton@sureste .com); Cuba, C 1-D no. 320, at C 42 (☎999/944-4216, ℮consulcuba@yuc1.telmex.net.mx); USA, Paseo de Montejo no. 453, at Av Colón (☎999/925-5011).

**Internet and telephone** There are Internet cafés on every street in central Mérida; try Maya Site, C 60 between C 53 and C 55, which also has fax and long-distance services, or Chandler's, in the shopping complex on the north side of the plaza. A small *caseta* in the *Fiesta Americana* mall has better-than-usual prices for calls to the US and Europe.

**Laundry** If your hotel doesn't do laundry, try Lavandería Agua Azul, C 70 no. 505, at C 61,

## Moving on from Mérida

As the biggest travel hub in the Yucatán, Mérida has a profusion of **bus stations**, each theoretically dedicated to certain bus companies and regions; in practice, however, different terminals do duplicate routes and services. Typically, if you want the fastest long-distance service, head for ADO and luxury ADO GL and UNO service at the first-class **Terminal CAME**; you might, however, be able to find a comparably fast trip at a lower price at the **Terminal Segunda Clase** across the street. Very slow buses to small towns leave from the **Noreste** terminal: visit here for coastal towns east and west of Progreso (such as Chelem, San Felipe, Dzilam de Bravo) and some points on the Ruta de los Conventos southeast of Mérida (such as Mayapán; see p.260). Dzibilchaltún and Progreso service runs from the **AutoProgreso** bus station on Calle 62 between calles 65 and 67. Additionally, **colectivos** often provide more frequent service to destinations an hour or two outside of the city, and to smaller villages. For service to Dzibilchaltún, Oxcutzcab and Ticul, shared taxis and small buses congregate on Parque de San Juan (Calle 62 at Calle 69). For Progreso, *colectivos* leave from the east side of Calle 60 between calles 65 and 67. Principal destinations and the corresponding bus stations and services can be found in "Travel details", p.242.

### The Ruta Puuc bus

Infrequent buses make the more out-of-the-way ruins on the **Ruta Puuc** (see p.245) difficult to visit without your own car, but the Autotransportes del Sur (ATS) company offers a day-trip service for tourists that's budget-friendly, if a bit rushed. The trip costs M$130 and leaves at 8am every day from the Terminal de Segunda Clase, visiting Uxmal, Sayil, Kabáh and Xlapak. You get just long enough at each site to form a general impression, and there's no guide or lunch included in the price. To go to Uxmal only, it's M$70.

which offers full-service washes, stain removal and ironing.

**Medical care** Clinica de Mérida Hospital, Av Itzáes 242 at Av Colón (☎999/920-0411, ⓦwww .clinicademerida.com.mx), is accustomed to dealing with foreigners.

**Post office** C 65 between C 56 and C 56-A (Mon–Fri 8am–4.30pm, Sat 9am–1pm), but may be turned into a museum; use of the Lista de Correos is currently not recommended.

**Tourist police** This special squad, dressed in white shirts and brown trousers, roams the plaza, giving directions and otherwise helping visitors (☎999/925-2555 ext. 260).

**Travel agencies and tours** For out-of-town trips, student travel agency Nómadas (☎999/948-1187, ⓦwww.nomadastravel.com) has good-value excursions to Uxmal and Chichén Itzá, as well as excellent plane fares to Mexico City. For a natural outing, Ecoturísmo Yucatán (☎999/920-2772, ⓦwww.ecoyuc.com) runs a day trip to three nearby cenotes. Otherwise try Yucatan Trails, C 62 no. 482, between C 57 and C 59 (☎999/928-2582, ⒺYucatantrails@hotmail.com), where tours include a handy one-way Mérida–Chichén Itzá–Cancún package; Cuba trips are also available. The knowledgeable Canadian owner offers luggage storage for M$10/day.

# The Gulf coast

The distance between Mérida and the port of **Progreso**, the closest point on the coast, is just 36km (thirty minutes to the north by bus). About halfway between the two, a few kilometres east of the main road, lie the ancient ruins of **Dzibilchaltún**, with a **cenote** at the very middle of the site that's fed with a constant supply of fresh water from a small spring. The drive out of Mérida follows Paseo de Montejo through miles of wealthy suburbs and shopping malls before reaching the flat countryside.

It's easy enough to visit Dzibilchaltún on the way to Progreso from Mérida: **combis** for Chablecal, which leave from Parque de San Juan (calles 62 and 69) about every half hour, stop at the ruins; leaving, you can walk or hitch a ride back to the main highway, where you can flag down a Progreso bus. Combis return to Mérida from the corner of calles 80 and 31 near the post office, on the north side of Progreso's Parque Central (note that leaving on Sunday evenings in the summer, with the rest of the weekender crowds, means that you'll have a very long wait). To go straight to the coast from Mérida, **buses** leave from the terminal dedicated to Progreso service on Calle 62 between calles 65 and 67.

## Dzibilchaltún

The archeological importance of the ruins of the ancient city of **DZIBIL-CHALTÚN** (daily 8am–5pm; M$58) is hardly reflected in what you see. The area was settled from 1000 BC right through to the Conquest – the longest continuous occupation of any known Maya site. More than eight thousand structures have been mapped, but unfortunately, little has survived, in particular because the ready-dressed stones were a handy building material and therefore used in several local towns and in paving the Mérida–Progreso road. In addition, there is virtually no descriptive labelling on the buildings, so it's worth hiring a **guide** (M$200 for up to six people) at the main entrance. Dzibilchaltún features an excellent museum, and the area is part of an **eco-archeological park**, where birders can catch the rough-winged swallow and the Yucatán woodpecker. Allow about two hours to see everything.

Just past the site entrance, the small but smartly done **Museo del Pueblo Maya** (Tues–Sun 8am–4pm) provides an overview of Maya culture and the history of the region up to the present. The exhibits place special emphasis on the continuity of Maya culture and art under Spanish rule, with some beautiful examples of colonial-era wood carvings (including a *retablo* salvaged from Mérida's cathedral after the Revolution-era fire), as well as samples of huipiles from across the Maya world.

From the museum, a meandering nature trail leads to the **Templo de las Siete Muñecas** (Temple of the Seven Dolls). The temple was originally a simple square pyramid, subsequently built over with a more complex structure. Later still, a passageway was cut through to the original building and seven deformed clay figurines (dolls) were buried, with a tube through which their spirits were meant to commune with the priests. The structure is remarkable for being the only known Maya temple to have windows, and for having a tower in place of the usual roofcomb. A great time to visit is on the **equinoxes**, when the sun shines straight through the tower doors, in a display of ancient astronomical savvy that draws crowds of tourists. In conjunction with the buildings that surround it, the temple is also aligned with other astronomical points and must have served in some form as an observatory.

One of the ancient causeways that linked the city's major points runs dead-straight from the temple to another cluster of ruins arrayed around a plaza. The centre of the grassy field is dominated by the shell of a Franciscan chapel built around 1600, and the gates of a cattle ranch from the next century are still standing to the west. A little farther west, **Cenote Xlacah**, in addition to providing the ancient city with water, was of ritual importance to the Maya: more than six thousand offerings – including human remains – have been discovered in its deeper end (44m down, and connecting to an underground river system). It's also home to a species of spiny fish found only in the Yucatán.

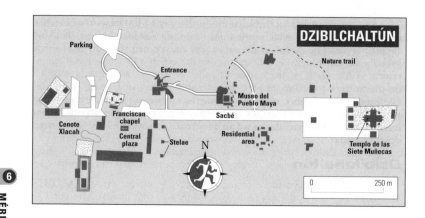

## Progreso and around

First impressions of **PROGRESO** – a working port with a six-kilometre-long concrete pier – are unprepossessing, especially at the end of a summer weekend when crowds of day-trippers have just pulled out, leaving beer bottles and food wrappers in their wake. But the beach, really the only reason to visit, is long and broad, with fine white sand (though the water's not too clear), and it makes for a pleasant, non-touristy day out from Mérida. If you're there in the winter, the beach will be empty, except perhaps for a handful of intrepid tourists from one of the cruiseships that docks here occasionally.

If you stray from the beach, you'll discover Progreso is a small place, and it's not difficult to find your way around. The **bus station** is on Calle 29 (running east–west, four blocks south of the water) at the corner of Calle 82. Calle 80, one block east, is the main street, running north–south and dead-ending at the beach. You'll find the **tourist office** (Mon–Fri 8am–2pm, Sat 8am–1pm; ☎969/935-0114) here, in the Casa de la Cultura at Calle 27; it has only a free map and a couple of flyers, though. On cruiseship days, the courtyard out the front hosts a craft market. Also on Calle 80 is the lively city **market** (the fruit-and-veg vendors are usually shut by 2pm), along with a few **banks** with ATMs, and a couple of Internet cafés.

**Hotels** in town range from very seedy to somewhat overpriced; but because Progreso is a popular family destination, many have large rooms ideal for groups. The high season is July and August and Semana Santa; outside of that, prices drop considerably. Best bets include the *Hotel Progreso,* Calle 29 no. 142, at Calle 78 (☎969/935-0039, ℗935-2019; ❺), which is several blocks back from the beach but has clean rooms and a choice of a/c or fan, and *Casa Isidora,* on Calle 21 between calles 58 and 60 (☎969/935-4595, ⓦwww.casaisidora.com; ❻). The latter is in a grand old house a little east of the centre and has a small pool. The spic-and-span *Hotel Embajadores,* on C 64 at C 21 (☎969/935-5673, ⓦwww.progresohotel.com; ❷–❹), is a blessed option on the bargain end, with dorm beds (M$80) as well as tidy rooms, and a communal kitchen. It's run by a veteran of the hostel scene who always has a hot pot of coffee and a story to tell; you can rent bikes and arrange boat trips here too.

For **eating**, try the lively *Eladio's,* on the malecón at Calle 80, where you can make a good meal of the tasty *botanas* that come free with beers. Also popular is *Sol y Mar,* across the street, for seafood snacks, and *Le Saint Bonnet,* a family restaurant on calles 19 and 78 that serves more elaborate local seafood specialities and has a pool for guests. All of these places set out tables on the beach across the road as well. For cheap *comida corriente,* the town's small, friendly market has several good lunch stalls.

## East of Progreso

The beach road stretches **east from Progreso** for some 85km, first on a big new highway that runs parallel to the shore a couple of kilometres inland, then, as the summer villas give way to wilder coast, on a narrow, barely two-lane road right up against the water. On the way you pass a couple of smaller fishing villages, and some minor Maya ruins, ending at **Dzilam de Bravo**, a small fishing town on the edge of a coastal nature reserve. From there, you can loop back to Mérida on inland roads via Motul.

The shorefront behind the beach is built up from Progreso all the way to the fishing village of **Chicxulub Puerto** some 5km east, and a walk between the two takes you past the crumbling mansions of the old henequen exporters, interspersed with modern holiday villas and condominiums. You'd never guess that this area is where a massive meteor crashed 65 million years ago, permanently altering the Earth's atmosphere; today there's no sign, and the most remarkable thing about Chicxulub Puerto is the excellent *Restaurante Moctezuma* (aka *Los Barriles,* for the giant wood barrels that form its front entrance), just east of the small plaza. A sprawling seafood specialist, it's a favourite destination for a late **lunch**.

Continuing east, you're soon shunted away from the beach and onto the new highway, which runs parallel to the shore about 1km south of the water. The land in between was formerly occupied by coconut plantations, but the tallest tree varieties were highly susceptible to a blight called lethal yellowing disease that spread in the 1980s; now the real estate is given over to holiday homes. At Km 15 on the highway, a smart **viewing platform** (free; follow signs for the *mirador turística*) over the Uaymitún inlet is a great place to see flocks of **flamingos** – not in such great numbers as at Celestún (see p.240), but impressive considering their proximity to the highway. Go at sunset, but before the 6pm closing time, for your best chance of spotting them; the caretakers will rent binoculars for M$10.

If you're driving, you can detour south following signs for Dzemul, passing another flamingo-filled inlet, then to **Xcambó** (9am–sunset), the grass-covered ruins of an Early Classic Maya salt-trading outpost. A thatch-roof chapel, built from the ruins' stones in the 1950s following a reported apparition of the Virgin, sits astride some old foundations, and a huipil-dressed cross stands atop the tallest building. Entrance is free, but you should tip the watchman, who may also show you some human bones allegedly dug up at the site. Continue south on this road to reach *Rancho Komchen,* a private bird sanctuary and casual eco-lodge (T999/743-9533, Wwww.komchen.org; ❹) and *Hacienda San Juan de Lizárraga* (T999/996-8621, Esanjuandelizarraga@hotmail.com; ❻), a huge property with a pool, beautiful gardens and very reasonable rates for the big, antiques-filled rooms; a resident naturalist leads tours.

Back on the coast road, you reach **Telchac Puerto** after another 10km. This laid-back seaside village is also popular in the summer with escapees from the city heat of Mérida. A couple of nice small hotels, *Posada Liz* (T991/917-4125, Eposadaliz_telchac@hotmail.com; ❹) and *Hotel Principe Negro* (T991/917-4004; ❺), are west of the plaza (note that they're a bit of a hike if you're coming from the bus stop). The plaza has several good seafood **restaurants** and *Dulcería Chay,* specializing in traditional coconut and lime sweets.

With more time, it's possible to get even further east along an ever-narrowing road, passing a few remaining coconut plantations not killed by the yellowing blight. After Chabihau, 15km from Telchac Puerto, the holiday homes peter out, and the coast reverts to its wild state. In the village of **Santa Clara** (really just a few buildings stuck between the sea and the salt flats), *La Morena* restaurant serves excellent fresh fish that's worth stopping for; the beach here is tranquil.

At the end of the road, **Dzilam de Bravo** is a remote fishing village with a sea-defence wall that precludes a beach; the real draw is **Bocas de Dzilam**, 40km away in the Parque Natural San Felipe, a state nature reserve. Set in 620 square kilometres of coastal forests, marshes and dunes, the *bocas* (Spanish for "mouths") are freshwater springs on the seabed; the nutrients they provide encourage the wide biological diversity found here. The wildlife you may see is superb, including turtles, tortoises, crocodiles, spider monkeys and dozens of bird species. To visit, you'll need to track down local guide Javier Nadar, better known as Chacate (ask around for him in the main square). He charges M$850 for a boat and a ceviche lunch (4–5hr; up to five people), M$350 for shorter trips (3–4hr). A more direct way to get to the town of Dzilam de Bravo is to catch a second-class **bus** in Mérida from the Autobuses del Noreste terminal at the corner of calles 50 and 67. Three buses daily pass through on their way to and from Tizimín and Progreso, and four buses daily leave for Izamal.

### West of Progreso

Venturing **west from Progreso** is not as promising as heading east, though in the 19km of coast road, you will find a couple more beach villages, all but deserted during the off season. To reach them, you must go back inland and around the naval base and commercial port at **Yucalpetén**. Further west, the small resorts of **Chelem** and **Chuburná**, respectively fifteen and thirty minutes from Progreso and easy day-trips from Mérida, have clean, wide beaches and some **accommodation** and restaurants. *Hotel Sian Ka'an* (☎969/935-4017, ⓦwww.hotelsiankaan.com; ❽), in Chelem, is one good option, offering big oceanfront rooms ideal for groups or families, with balconies and kitchenettes, as well as a good fish **restaurant**.

Beyond Chuburná, the coast road, which was damaged by Hurricane Isidore in 2002, is no longer negotiable, and you'll have to turn inland again. It's not worth making a detour back to the coast at **Sisal**, however; unbelievably, it was Mérida's chief port in colonial times (and gave its name to the henequen fibre that was exported from here), but now it's quite shabby and practically deserted.

# Celestún

Were it not for its amazing bird-filled lagoon that boasts a large flock of flamingos, **CELESTÚN** – which lies 93km west of Mérida, at the end of a sandbar on the peninsula's northwest coast – would be little more than a one-boat fishing village. Instead, a flotilla of small boats waits to take visitors on short outings up the broad, uninhabited inlet, dense with greenery on either side and noisy with bird calls. Along with all manner of herons, you may also see the blue-winged teals and shovellers that migrate here in the winter to take advantage of the plentiful fish in these warm, shallow waters.

To visit the **flamingos**, hire a guide at the official *parador turística*, just past the bridge on the main road into Celestún. When arriving in town by bus, ask the

△ Flamingos in Celestún

driver to drop you off, as otherwise it's a twenty-minute walk back from the main square. You'll need to purchase a group ticket (M$400) from the ticket booth, then individual tickets (M$40, maximum six people per boat) for an 80-minute tour, stopping at the flamingo feeding grounds and a cluster of freshwater springs (bring your bathing suit). A 2hr 20min trip, which heads farther up the lagoon and may give you time to swim in the rich red waters among the mangroves, is M$800 for the boat plus M$40 per person. If you're already in town and don't feel like trekking back out to the *parador*, you could arrange a trip from Celestún's beach with personable local guide Filiberto Couoh Cavich (also known as Ruso), which takes in seven different ecological sites of interest (2hr 30min–3hr; M$1500 for eight people); ask at *Restaurant Celestún* on the beachfront.

Protected by inclusion in the 146,000-acre **Ría Celestún Biosphere Reserve**, the flamingos are nevertheless occasionally harassed by boats approaching closer than the mandated 50m in order to give visitors a spectacular flying display. If your boatman looks as if he might want to drive too close, you should make it clear that you don't wish to interrupt the birds' natural behaviour; you will still get good photos from a respectful distance.

## Practicalities

Celestún has half a dozen **places to stay**, all on Calle 12, the main street that runs along behind the beach, one block toward the water from where the bus drops you on the plaza. The *Hotel Maria del Carmen*, Calle 12 no. 111, at Calle 15 (☎988/916-2170; ❺), has rooms with balconies, and some with a/c; *Hotel San Julio*, on Calle 12 at Calle 9 (☎988/916-2170; ❹), is more basic, but still on the beach; and the *Ría Celestún* **hostel**, also on Calle 12, at Calle 13 (☎988/916-2219, ✉hostelriacelestun@hotmail.com; M$80), offers decent dorm beds. Ten kilometres north of the town, the remote and lovely *Eco Paraíso Xixim* (☎988/916-2100, ⓦwww.ecoparaiso.com; ❾) operates primarily on wind and solar power and offers well-appointed cabañas, excellent showers and miles of deserted beach and wildlife-filled scrub to explore, as well as many organized tours around the area; rates include breakfast and dinner.

Several **seafood restaurants** can be found on the dusty main street and on the beach – the ceviche in Celestún is invariably good. For cheap home-cooking, visit *La Abuelita Mulix*, on Calle 12 at the main intersection, or the *loncherías* by the small market (just off the inland side of the plaza). There's also a bakery, a bank (but **no ATM**) and a gas station.

If you are travelling by car, you can avoid retracing your route completely by taking a series of small roads back to Hwy-180 south of Mérida. Leaving Celestún, turn south 23km east of town, then east in Chunchucmil. This village and those that follow are all former henequen haciendas – the ruins of the old buildings stand on every central plaza, strikingly similar in layout and architecture. One of these, *Hacienda Santa Rosa* (℡999/910-4852, ⓦwww.starwood.com; ❾), has been beautifully renovated as a hotel (see p.268). You will rejoin the highway at **Maxcanú**, either returning to Mérida (about 50km) or continuing south to Campeche.

# Travel details

## Buses

Wherever you go in this corner of the Yucatán, you'll have to pass through Mérida, but bus service from there is more frequent than any other city in the region.

**Celestún** to: Mérida (10 daily; 2hr)

**Mérida** (C=Terminal CAME; SC=Terminal Segunda Clase; N=Noreste; AP=AutoProgreso; FA=Fiesta Americana) to: Celestún (N, 10 daily; 2hr); Campeche (C, hourly on ADO, 3 daily on ADO GL; FA, 1 daily at midnight; SC, hourly; 2hr 30min); Cancún (C, hourly on ADO, 6 daily on ADO GL, 1 daily at 5.45pm; FA, 11 daily; SC, hourly via Chichén Itzá and Valladolid, 8 daily; 4–8hr); Celestún (N, 10 daily, 2hr); Chetumal (C, 4 daily, SC, 11 daily; 6–8hr); Chichén Itzá (C, 3 daily, N, hourly; 1hr 30min–2hr); Chicxulub Puerto (N, 5 daily; 1hr 30min); Chiquilá/Holbox (SC, 1 daily at 11.30pm; 6hr); Ciudad del Carmen (C, 17 daily, SC, 10 daily; 5hr 30min–7hr); Dzibilchaltún (AP, hourly; 30min); Dzilam de Bravo (N, 7 daily; 4hr); Escárcega (C, 5 daily, SC, 8 daily; 4hr 30min–6hr); Felipe Carrillo Puerto (SC, 15 daily; 2hr 30min); Izamal (N, every 45min; 1hr); Mayapán (N, 2 daily; 1hr); Mexico City (C, 5 daily; 20hr); Oxcutzcab (SC, 11 daily, N, 6 daily; 2hr); Palenque (C, 4 daily; 7hr); Playa del Carmen (C, 12 daily, SC, 1 daily via Cobá at 5am; 5–7hr); Progreso (AP, every 30min; 45min); Río Lagartos (N, 3 daily; 6hr); San Felipe (N, 1 daily at 5.30pm; 6hr 30min); Santa Elena (SC, 5 daily; 1hr); Sisal (N, 3 daily; 2hr); Telchac Puerto (N, 7 daily; 1hr 30min); Tizimín (N, 16 daily; 4hr); Tulum (C, 3 daily, SC, 1 daily via Cobá at 5am; 6hr); Uxmal (SC, 6 daily; 45min–1hr 15min); Valladolid (C, 10 daily, N, hourly; 2–3hr); Villahermosa (C, 17 daily, SC, 9 daily; 8–10hr); Yaxcaba (N, 1 Sat–Mon at 6.15pm; 3hr)

**Progreso** to: Tizimín (3 daily via Telchac Puerto and Dzilam de Bravo; 2hr); Mérida (every 30min; 45min)

## Flights

Flights depart daily from Mérida's airport for Mexico City, Cancún, Ciudad del Carmen and Villahermosa, as well as for Miami and Houston, Texas.

# 7

# Uxmal and the Ruta Puuc

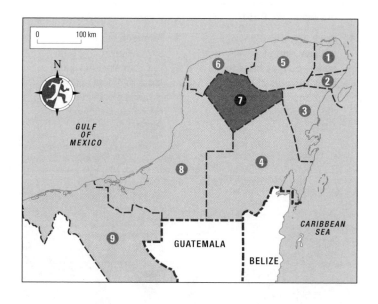

# CHAPTER 7

# Highlights

* **Uxmal** Along with Chichén Itzá and Palenque, this is one of Mexico's three greatest ancient Maya sites, boasting some of the region's finest architecture. **P.247**

* **Haciendas** Stay at a restored nineteenth-century hacienda and get a sense of henequen plantation life. **P.251**

* **Sayil** If you can get to the vast site of Sayil early, you may have the ruins to yourself – and the birds that teem in the surrounding forest. **P.254**

* **Grutas de Loltún** Visit these spectacular caverns, which trace their geologic history from the Stone Age. **P.257**

* **Fortress churches** Designed to awe the native population, the fortified churches along the Ruta de los Conventos are still impressive for their enormity. **P.258**

* **Acanceh** Virtually unknown, this rural town's main square juxtaposes a hefty ancient pyramid alongside a huge colonial church. **P.259**

△ Casa de las Tortugas

# 7

# Uxmal and the Ruta Puuc

A bout 80km south of Mérida in the Puuc hills lies a group of the peninsula's most important archeological sites. Chief among them is **Uxmal**, second only to Chichén Itzá in size and historical significance, yet perhaps greater in its initial impact and certainly in the beauty and harmony of its unique architectural style. The **Ruta Puuc** itself heads down from Mérida to Uxmal and then, along Hwy-261, on to **Kabáh**, not far beyond, before turning east along a minor road past **Sayil**, **Xlapak** and **Labná**. Though Uxmal is firmly established on the tourist trail, and perpetually crowded, these lesser Maya sites are surprisingly little visited. If these places or their equivalent were in Europe or the United States, you wouldn't be able to move for tourists: here, however, if you time your excursion right, you may get a vast site covering several square kilometres entirely to yourself. The Ruta Puuc sites themselves are not only rather accessible – particularly if you are coming from Mérida, the main city in Yucatán State – but they are also very well restored, in comparison with many of the other ancient Maya cities.

Though the Puuc sites are the undoubted highlight, there are plenty of other attractions to blend into the mix when touring this area. The Ruta Puuc takes in contrasting **haciendas** at Yaxcopoil, Ochil and Temozón on the way to Uxmal, while beyond Labná it passes the crumbling Hacienda Tabi as well as

---

## The Ruta Puuc bus

All the Ruta Puuc sites are far enough apart that it's impractical to visit more than a fraction of them by bus, unless you're prepared to spend several days and endure a lot of waiting around. If you are reliant on public transportation, the simplest way to visit the main Maya sites is to take the **"Ruta Puuc" day-trip bus** (M$130), run by Autotransportes del Sur from the second-class bus station in Mérida. This departs daily at 8am, returning to Mérida at 3.45pm, and stops for 20 minutes at Xlapak, 30 minutes each at Labná and Sayil, 50 minutes at Kabáh and two hours at Uxmal. Though very rushed at every site, since Uxmal is the last visited it's possible to stay here longer and pay for a later bus back. Alternatively, almost every travel agency in Mérida offers some kind of Ruta Puuc or Ruta de los Conventos trip that includes meals and a guide, with prices starting from around M$400 per person.

the impressive caverns of the **Grutas de Loltún**. These are just outside **Oxkut-zcab**, on the old main road from Mérida to Quintana Roo, and from here you can return to Mérida via **Ticul** and Muna, or take the fast new road past the Maya ruins of **Mayapán**.

The latter route, known as the **Ruta de los Conventos**, bypasses a string of villages with gigantic fortified churches, relics of the early years of the Spanish occupation. The most impressive of these is the Franciscan monastery of San Miguel in **Maní**, and while the other villages en route are far less visited, many of them offer other attractions in the form of minor ruins, caves or **cenotes**, the latter especially impressive at Cuzamá, where a horse-drawn rail cart will take you to Los Tres Cenotes.

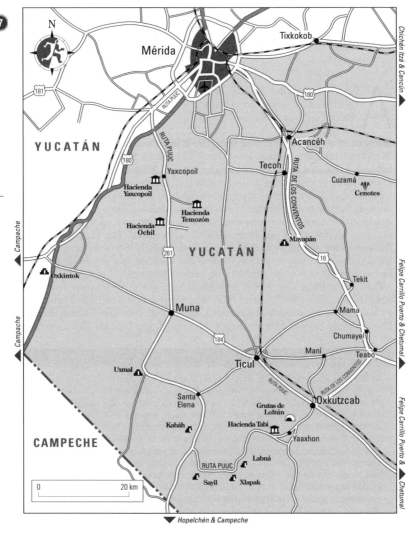

If you **rent a car,** in two days (three would be more relaxed) you can explore all of the key sites, either returning to Mérida by evening or finding a **room** around Uxmal or in Santa Elena, Oxkutzcab or Ticul. For details of car rental agencies in Mérida, see p.235.

# Uxmal and around

Meaning "thrice-built", **UXMAL** (pronounced OOSH-mal) represents the finest achievement of the Puuc culture before it fell into its ultimate decline. Little is known of the city's history, but what is clear is that the chief monuments, and the city's peaks of power and population, fall into the Terminal Classic period, around 800–1000 AD. Though there are indications of settlement long before this, most of the buildings that you see date from this time. After 900 AD the city began to decline, and by 1200 Uxmal and all the Puuc sites, together with Chichén Itzá, were all but abandoned. The reasons are unknown, although political infighting, ecological problems and loss of trade with the Toltec site of Tula, near Mexico City, may have played a part. Later, the **Xiu Dynasty** settled at Uxmal, which, along with Chichén Itzá and Mayapán, became part of the League of Mayapán (see p.260). From here, in 1441, the rebellion originated that finally overthrew the power of Mayapán and put an end to any form of centralized Maya authority over the Yucatán.

A UNESCO world heritage site, Uxmal is second in popularity only to Chichén Itzá. Even if you stay over the night before, it's hard to steal a march on the inevitable crowds, as the first coaches draw up at opening time, but as ever it's best to visit early or late to escape the worst of both heat and crowds. There's an extensive cleared and restored area, so at least there's plenty of space for people to disperse once inside.

## Arrival, information and accommodation

Several **buses** a day run direct from Mérida to Uxmal, and any bus heading down the main road towards Hopelchén (or between Mérida and Campeche via Hopelchén) will drop you just a short walk from the entrance. There's a pay car park at the modern **entrance to the site** (daily 8am–5pm; M$78, M$40 on Sun), where the **tourist centre** includes a small museum, a shop with guides to the site, a snack bar, phones and an ATM. Uxmal's **sound-and-light** show (daily; M$30, reduced if combined with entry ticket) starts at 7pm in winter and 8pm in summer: the commentary is in Spanish (translation equipment is available for M$25) and of dubious historical accuracy, but the lighting effects highlight the relief decorations on the walls beautifully, and the bats, fireflies and shooting stars will entertain you once the novelty has worn off. Note that no buses run late enough to get you back to Mérida after the hour-long show – a taxi from Mérida costs around M$500 for a round-trip with waiting time, or there are plenty of organized tours.

Several **hotels** can be found very close to the site, none of them in the budget category. All are subject to sudden arrivals of huge tour groups, which can make quality of service and food dip rapidly, and all are likely to offer good-value inclusive deals when not full. Two are right at the site's entrance: Club Med's *Villas Arqueológicas* (☎997/974-6020, 🌐 www.clubmedvillas.com; ❼) is probably the best value here, with a pool and tennis courts, though the a/c rooms are tiny; *The Lodge at Uxmal* (☎997/976-2010, 🌐www.mayaland.com; ❾) is much more spacious and has a pool and tennis, as well as a breezy restaurant and bar,

*La Palapa*, that offers a convenient spot for a cool drink. Across the main road from the site entrance, the colonial-style *Hacienda Uxmal* (T997/976-2012, Wwww.mayaland.com; ❾) is a sister hotel to *The Lodge*, and also very comfortable and marginally less expensive. Other accommodation nearby but not within walking distance includes budget options in Santa Elena (see p.254) or the ultra-luxury of *Hacienda Temozón* (see p.251).

## The site

It's worth remembering that Uxmal, among the most spectacular of all Maya sites, looks this way in part because there has been a huge amount of **reconstruction**. Some scholars claim that this has been at the expense of proper archeology, and even that the shape of the famous Pyramid of the Magician is unique only because it has been wrongly rebuilt. But most visitors will probably feel that the mix of accessibility and preservation has been judged about right (even if the number of visitors sometimes suggests it's a little too accessible), and it's certainly an easy site to visit, and a hard one not to enjoy. The main restored buildings are set out on a roughly north–south axis in a large cleared site; the alignment of individual buildings often has astrological significance, usually connected with Venus or the Sun.

### The Pirámide del Adivino

Entering the site, you'll see the back of the great **Pirámide del Adivino** (Pyramid of the Magician) rise before you. The most remarkable looking of all Mexican pyramids, it soars at a startling angle from its oval base to a temple some 30m above the ground, with a broad but steep stairway up either side. The legend of the pyramid's creation tells that an old sorceress, who lived in a hut where the pyramid now stands, hatched a dwarf son from an egg and encouraged him to challenge the king to a series of tests – all of which the dwarf won, thanks to a little magic. Finally the king challenged him to build a pyramid overnight: the dwarf succeeded, and became ruler of Uxmal. Despite the legend, however, archeological evidence shows at least five separate stages of construction – six if you count the modern restoration, which may not correspond exactly to any of its earlier incarnations.

Visitors are no longer permitted to climb the pyramid, but from the base of the rear (east) stairway you can see a tunnel that reveals **Templo III**, one of the earlier levels. At the top, surrounded by a platform, the temple at the summit has a facade decorated with interlocking geometric motifs. On the west face of the pyramid, the stairway runs down either side of a second, earlier sanctuary in a distinctly different style. Known as the **Edificio Chenes** (or Templo IV), it does indeed reflect the architecture of the Chenes region (see p.282), the entire front forming a giant mask of Chac. At the bottom of the west face, divided in half by the stairway, you'll find yet another earlier stage of construction (the first) – the long, low facade of a structure apparently similar to the so-called "Nunnery" (see below).

### The Quadrángulo de las Monjas and the Casa de las Tortugas

Directly behind the pyramid, the **Quadrángulo de las Monjas** (Nunnery Quadrangle), a beautiful complex of four buildings enclosing a plaza, is one of many named quite erroneously here by the Spanish, to whom it resembled a convent. Whatever it may have been, it *wasn't* a convent; theories range from a military academy to a sort of earthly paradise, where intended sacrificial victims

△ Quadrángulo de las Monjas

would spend their final months in debauchery. The four buildings, probably all constructed between 895 and 906 AD, are each set on a slightly different level, possibly representing the four main levels of the Maya universe. The facade of each is decorated with complex patterns of stone reliefs, full of complex religious symbolism – the quadrangle itself is a slightly irregular shape, apparently to align with Venus.

All four sides display Maya architectural skills at their finest – the false Maya vaults of the interiors are taken about as wide as they can go without collapsing (wooden crossbeams provided further support), and the frontages are slightly bowed in order to maintain a proper horizontal perspective. The **north building**, raised higher than the others and even more richly ornamented, is probably also the oldest. Approached via a broad stairway between two colonnaded porches, it has a strip of plain stone facade (from which doors lead into vaulted chambers) surmounted by a slightly raised panel of mosaics, featuring geometric patterns and human and animal figures, with representations of Maya huts above the doorways. The **west building**, which has been heavily reconstructed, boasts even more varied themes, and the whole of its ornamentation is surrounded by a coiling, feathered rattlesnake with the face of a warrior emerging from its jaws. The **east building** is almost a reflection of the west across the courtyard, with similar decoration and an equal number of rooms inside.

An arched passageway through the middle of the **south building**, the lowest of the four, provided the square with a monumental entrance directly aligned with the **ball-court** outside. Today a path leads through here, between the ruined side walls of the court and up onto the levelled terrace on which stand the Palacio del Gobernador (see p.250) and the **Casa de las Tortugas** (House of the Turtles). This very simple, elegant building, named after the stone turtles carved around the cornice, ably demonstrates another constant theme of Puuc architecture: stone facades carved to appear like rows of narrow columns. These probably represent the building style of the Maya huts still in use today, consisting of walls of bamboo or thin branches lashed together. The plain bands of masonry that often surround them mirror the cords that tie the hut walls in place.

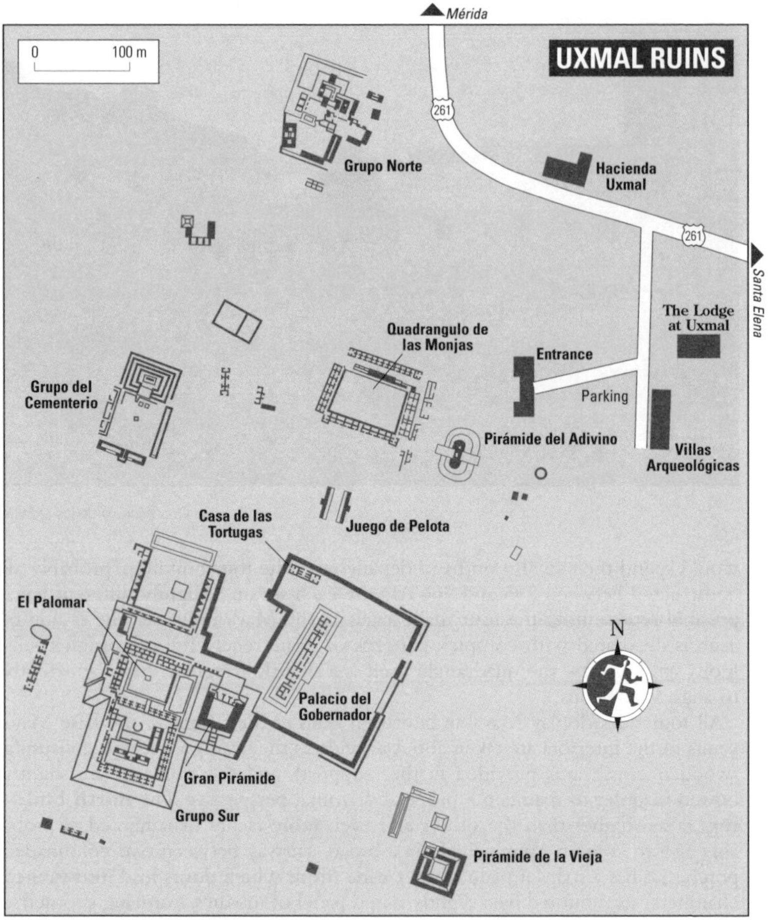
Mérida
UXMAL RUINS
0
100 m
261
261
Santa Elena
Grupo Norte
Hacienda Uxmal
The Lodge at Uxmal
Quadrangulo de las Monjas
Entrance
Parking
Grupo del Cementerio
Pirámide del Adivino
Villas Arqueológicas
Casa de las Tortugas
Juego de Pelota
El Palomar
N
Palacio del Gobernador
Gran Pirámide
Grupo Sur
Pirámide de la Vieja

## The Palacio del Gobernador and the Grupo Sur

It is the **Palacio del Gobernador** (Governor's Palace) that marks the finest achievement of Uxmal's builders. Explorer and writer John L. Stephens, arriving at the then virtually unknown site in June 1840, had no doubts as to its significance: "If it stood this day on its grand artificial terrace in Hyde Park or the Garden of the Tuileries," he later wrote, "it would form a new order . . . not unworthy to stand side by side with the remains of the Egyptian, Grecian and Roman art". The palace faces east, away from the buildings around it, probably for astronomical reasons – its central doorway aligns with the column of the altar outside and the point where Venus rises. Long and low, it is lent a remarkable harmony by the use of light and shade on the facade, and by the strong diagonals that run right through its broad band of mosaic decorations, particularly in the steeply vaulted archways that divide the two wings from the central mass, like giant arrowheads aimed at the sky. Close up, the mosaic is equally impressive, featuring masks of Chac alternating with grid-and-key patterns and highly stylized snakes. Inside, the chambers are narrow, gloomy and unadorned;

but at least the great central room, 20m long and entered by the three closer-set openings in the facade, is bigger than most. At the back, the rooms have no natural light source at all.

Behind the palace stand the ruinous buildings of the **Grupo Sur** (South Group), with the partly restored Gran Pirámide (Great Pyramid), and El Palomar (Dovecote, or Quadrangle of the Doves). You can climb the rebuilt staircase of the **Gran Pirámide** to see the temple on top, decorated with macaws and more masks of Chac, and look across at the rest of the site. **El Palomar** was originally part of a quadrangle like that of the Nunnery, but the only building to retain any form is this, topped with the great wavy, latticed roofcomb that gives it its name.

After you've taken in the main site, the outlying structures are rather anti-climactic. The **Pirámide de la Vieja** (Pyramid of the Old Woman), probably the earliest surviving building at Uxmal, is now little more than a grassy mound with a clearly man-made outline, while the **Grupo del Cementerio** (Cemetery Group) is also not restored. Nevertheless, traces of carved hieroglyphs and human skulls are visible in the low altars in the middle of this square.

## Eating

If you're looking for lunch after your visit and you don't fancy the snack bar of the hotels at the site entrance, numerous **restaurants** can be found along Hwy-261 towards Mérida, many of them catering mainly to tour groups. One good option is *Restaurante Cana-nah*, in the otherwise dumpy *Rancho Uxmal* hotel, about 1.5km from the site. The food is tasty and inexpensive, and diners are welcome to use the swimming pool.

## Northeast towards Mérida

Between Uxmal and Mérida, there are few towns of any note, and with new roads being built and the old ones improved, it's possible to bypass virtually all the settlements en route. However, several restored haciendas offer compelling reasons to break your journey and even spend a night.

Just west off Hwy-261, about 30km north of Uxmal, the refurbished **Hacienda Ochil** operates as a restaurant (standard meals for M$70) with a small henequen **museum** displaying old photos and henequen at various stages of processing as well as a group of excellent *artesanía* stores and workshops. Some of the old railway lines along which carts of henequen were transported have been restored to working order, and you can also see the plant being grown; occasionally there are demonstrations of the entire production process. For more sybaritic luxury, **Hacienda Temozón** (☎999/923-8089, ⊛www.starwoodhotels.com; ❾), about 8km off Hwy-261 to the east, is one of the grandest of the haciendas that have been converted into luxury hotels; on its sprawling grounds you'll find two cenotes, a dramatic swimming pool and a gym in the old machine room. There is also a pricey international restaurant on the premises.

Some 10km further north, **Hacienda Yaxcopoil** (Mon–Sat 8am–6pm, Sun 9am–1pm; M$40, kids free) lies on the edge of the village of the same name. The main house here stands in a state of picturesque disrepair – peeling walls, sagging ceilings and rooms full of mildewed tablecloths and faded pictures. There's a Maya room with a few ancient carved stones, *metates* (used for grinding corn) and pots, but the main draw is wandering around the place, which is full of poignant corners: there's a water tank/swimming pool with crumbling changing rooms, a beautifully preserved old pumping engine by a well, and lush

## Haciendas and henequen

The country all around Mérida is liberally dotted with the crumbling remains of old **haciendas**, an increasing number of which are being restored as luxury hotels, restaurants or tourist attractions in one form or another. The oldest of them had their origins as early as the seventeenth century, when Spanish colonists were granted vast landholdings on which they raised cattle or practised other forms of agriculture. The heyday of the haciendas, however, was the end of the nineteenth century and the beginning of the twentieth, when the henequen boom brought vast wealth to their owners.

A type of agave cactus from which fibres can be extracted for use, above all, in the manufacture of rope and twine, **henequen** is also known as sisal, after the port on the Yucatán coast from which it was originally shipped (though technically, sisal and henequen are slightly different plants). The great, spiky leaves are harvested by hand, taking just a few from each plant every year to prolong the plant's life. The collected leaves are transported to the **machine house**, crushed and shredded to extract the individual fibres; the introduction of steam-powered machinery to do this initiated the boom, and at some of the haciendas you can see the original nineteenth-century equipment.

Henequen still grows throughout the area, but is now processed only in small quantities: the market for the "green gold" that paid for so many of Mérida's grandiose mansions collapsed in the 1940s with the invention of artificial fibres, though by then the haciendas were already in decline from their high point between the turn of the century and the end of World War I – foreign competition and redistribution of land following the Revolution having dealt the first blows.

At their height, the bigger haciendas were virtually self-sufficient and self-ruling fiefdoms. Each had a grand house at the centre, where the owner or his overseer would live, with the machine room for processing nearby. Surrounding these are the workers' one-room homes, the company store (where many workers and their families were kept permanently in debt, from generation to generation) and other outbuildings including a chapel, pump room, stables, jail and, at the more enlightened places, a hospital and school. Some even had their own station on the main railway line, connected by narrow gauge lines on which the henequen and the processed fibres would be transported by horse-drawn cart.

gardens that you're free to wander, still watered by the original irrigation system. Note the old machine rooms in a separate block – though beware of rocky floors and unprotected drops. If you really want to escape the crowds, there's one **room to rent** here, a huge, tiled, high-ceilinged space with two double beds, a fridge, coffeemaker, bathroom and terrace. You can cook over a fire or they'll bring meals in for you (☎999/927-2606, ⓦ www.yaxcopoil.com; ❻).

If you're travelling by bus, *Yaxcopoil* and *Ochil* lie right beside the road, so it's easy enough to be dropped here and flag down another to continue your journey; buses to Muna, many to Ticul and any that pass Uxmal roll by.

# The Ruta Puuc

From Uxmal, the **RUTA PUUC** continues south through the town of Santa Elena, a handy base for exploring this region, to the site of Kabáh, and shortly afterwards turns left (east) along a minor road to the market town of Oxkutzcab. The Maya sites of Sayil, Xlapak and Labná are all along this road, as are the Grutas ("caves") de Loltún and, with a bit of a detour, Hacienda Tabi.

## The Puuc style

As with Chichén Itzá, the **Puuc sites** were once thought to be the product of invading Toltecs from central Mexico, but are now accepted as being as authentically Maya as Tikal or Palenque. Though Uxmal is easily the best-known today, the less celebrated sites were originally more important. The earliest significant examples of Puuc style are found at sites like Oxkintok (p.266) and Edzná (p.280), but at the height of the Classic era it was the area around Kabáh and Sayil that dominated the region. Sayil at its height had a population of some 17,000 and the whole region, now barely inhabited, may have supported hundreds of thousands. Uxmal rose to dominance only at the end of the Classic period, around 800–900 AD, perhaps thanks to the city's relationship with the **Chontal Maya** of the Gulf coast lowlands, who became the Yucatán's most important trading partner by the Terminal Classic period (800–1000 AD). The Chontal Maya themselves traded extensively with Oaxaca and central Mexico and are thought to have passed on their architectural styles and themes to the Yucatán.

Each Puuc site has its unique characteristics, but there are also marked continuities in architectural and artistic technique, religious symbolism, hieroglyphic writing and settlement patterns – scarcely surprising since there were also great causeways (*sacbeob*) linking the main centres. **Puuc architectural style** is characterized by buildings of amazingly classical proportions, decorated with broad stone mosaic friezes of geometric patterns, or designs so stylized and endlessly repeated as to become almost abstract. The face of **Chac**, the rain god, is everywhere. He must have been more crucial here than almost anywhere, for Uxmal and the other Puuc sites have no cenote or other natural source of **water**, relying instead on artificially created underground cisterns known as **chultunes**, jug-shaped and coated with lime, to collect and store rainwater. In recent years almost all of these have been filled in, to prevent mosquitoes breeding.

If you're on a day-trip from Mérida, you can get from the caves onto the fast new highway via Mayapán (see p.260) without even entering the town of **Oxkutzcab**. However, if you're taking things at a more leisurely pace, want somewhere to stop over, or are reliant on public transportation, then either Oxkutzcab or the larger, livelier alternative of **Ticul** are the places to head.

Many of the organized **tours** cover this route in the opposite direction, starting with a visit to the Grutas de Loltún and ending up at Uxmal in the late afternoon in time for a tour followed by the sound-and-light show. If you're staying at Uxmal or nearby and start early, there's a good chance of seeing the smaller Puuc sites when very few others are around.

Two things seem particularly striking when visiting the Puuc sites today. First, though each has its unique features, the overall impression is of a consistent **style** – the geometric patterns of Xlapak are echoed at Labná; the Chac masks that abound at Kabáh are also seen – in slightly less profusion – at Uxmal and all the other sites. The other striking factor is the extraordinary change in **population**. Today, along the entire route from Uxmal to Labná you'll see just one small town at Santa Elena; 1200 years ago, there were several hundred thousand people living here.

## Santa Elena

The village of **SANTA ELENA**, sixteen kilometres south of Uxmal, and just seven from Kabáh, is worth visiting mainly for the magnificent view from its large **church,** which dominates the skyline for miles around from a position atop a small hill. Ask for the sacristan, who will open the door to the spiral staircase that leads to the roof. Beside the church is a morbidly interesting small **museum** (daily 8am–6pm; free) with displays on local funerary practices, including the 200-year-old mummified remains of four children that were discovered under the church floor in 1980.

Two exceptionally pleasant (and popular, so book ahead) **places to stay**, both on Hwy-261 as it bypasses the village centre, make it particularly enticing. The *Flycatcher Inn* (no phone, Ⓦ www.geocities.com/flycatcherinn; ❻, breakfast included) is the first you reach, a B&B with one suite and three rooms decorated with local craftwork. It's about a five-minute walk south from the main square, or through-buses from Mérida will drop you on the highway very nearby. A little further south is *Sacbe Bungalows* (Ⓣ 985/858-1281, Ⓦ www .sacbebungalows.com.mx; ❹), where a hospitable Mexican-French couple offer basic but spotless bungalow rooms, all with porches, dotted about their spacious, lovingly planted grounds. There is also a very pleasant **camping** area (M$40 per person). For a small additional charge the owners will cook you a delicious breakfast and supper. In between the two hotels is a small **restaurant**, *El Chac Mool*, which does decent, inexpensive local food (closes at 8pm); *La Central*, slightly further away in the village's main square, also offers good simple meals. Note as well that, after the sound-and-light show at Uxmal, you may be able to hitch a ride back to Santa Elena with Uxmal's workers – check with your hotel, who may also be able to arrange some kind of shared transport.

## Kabáh

The extensive site of **KABÁH** (daily 9am–5pm; M$30), meaning "Mighty Hand", stretches across the highway some 25km from Uxmal. Much of it remains unexplored, but the one great building, the **Codz Poop**, or Palace of Masks, lies not far off the highway to the east, near the main entrance. The facade of this amazing structure is covered all over, in ludicrous profusion, with goggle-eyed, trunk-nosed masks of Chac – to get into the doorways you need to tread over the masks's noses. Even in its present state – with most of the long, curved noses broken off – this remains the strangest and most striking of all Maya buildings, decorated so obsessively, intricately and repetitively that it almost seems insane. A couple of lesser buildings are grouped around the Codz Poop, directly in front of which stands a rare, working *chultun* with a concave stone floor gathering water into the underground chamber.

The other main buildings of the site lie across the highway. At first almost invisible through the trees, **La Gran Pirámide** is an unusual circular pyramid – now simply a green conical mound that, once you spot it, is so large you can't believe you missed it. It is thought that this Great Temple, erected on a natural elevation, functioned as a "house of the gods", where priests offered sacrifices or interpreted divine messages. Just beyond, a sort of triumphal arch marks the point where the ancient thirty-kilometre causeway, or *sacbe*, from Uxmal entered the city. Though only traces have been found, it is believed that such causeways once linked all the major sites here.

**Leaving Kabáh**, you may have to virtually lie down in the road to persuade a bus to stop for you – ask the guards at the site for the bus times. Getting a ride with other visitors, though, is pretty easy, and with luck you may even meet someone touring all the local sites.

## Sayil

A sober, restrained contrast to the excesses of Kabáh, the site of **SAYIL** (daily 8am–5pm; M$30) lies some 5km along a smaller road heading east off the high-

way, from a junction 5km beyond Kabáh. Once one of the most densely populated areas in the Puuc region, it is estimated that up to 17,000 people inhabited
Sayil from 700 AD to 1000 AD. In the early part of that period, before the
ascendancy of Uxmal, Sayil was probably the foremost centre of the region.

Today the site is dominated by one major structure, the extensively restored,
eighty-metre-long **Gran Palacio** (Great Palace), built on three storeys, each
smaller than the one below. Although several large masks of Chac adorn a frieze
around the top of the middle level, the decoration mostly takes the form of
bamboo-effect stone pillaring – seen here more extensively than at any other
Puuc site. The interiors of the middle level, too, are lighter and airier than usual,
thanks to the use of broad openings, their lintels supported on fat columns. The
upper and lower storeys are almost entirely unadorned, featuring plain stone
surfaces with narrow openings. Water for the palace's inhabitants was once provided by eight *chultunes*, or underground cisterns.

Few other structures have been cleared, and those that have are widely scattered in the forest. The distances between cleared sites not only give a strong
impression of how big Sayil once was – it's a brisk, sticky, fifteen-minute walk
from the Gran Palacio to the Palacio Sur (see below) – but also mean there's
plenty of surviving tropical forest here, and plenty of wildlife. You'll see birds
of all sorts, including hummingbirds, and there's a chance of spotting monkeys
and other larger animals, such as the racoon-like coati. From the Gran Palacio
a path leads through the forest, past the piled stones of unexcavated remains,
to **El Mirador**, a small temple with a roofcomb, and a large stele carved with
the phallic figure of Yum Keep, god of fertility, now protected by a thatched
roof. A signed turn-off, this path leads to a group of buildings dominated by
the Palacio Sur as well as the **Templo de las Jambas Jeroglíficas**, named
for the uninterpreted glyphs carved all around one half-buried doorway. The
**Palacio Sur**, when you finally reach it, is a large, little-restored structure with
another characteristic bamboo facade, overlooking a ball-court, some unrestored mounds that make up the rest of the Grupo Sur, and the end of the
ceremonial *sacbe* through the site. You've actually been following this *sacbe* for
much of your walk through Sayil, though there's little evidence of that fact to
the amateur eye.

## Xlapak and Labná

It's around ten kilometres from Sayil to Labná, and just over halfway lies
**XLAPAK** (daily 8am–5pm; M$24). Maya for "old walls", Xlapak is the small-
est and least-visited of the Puuc sites, dominated by just one restored building,
a small, elegant palace with huge Chac masks above its doorways and at the
corners. Between the masks, the walls are adorned with geometric patterns. The
remains of a *chultun* can be seen on the far side. There's almost no signage at all
at Xlapak, and from the palace unmarked trails lead through the forest to other
nameless, half-uncovered mounds, again characterized by geometric patterns.

The ancient city of **LABNÁ** (daily 8am–5pm; M$30), historically far smaller
and less important than Sayil, is in many ways a more impressive site. There has
been more clearance and reconstruction here, so that the main buildings – the
Palacio, the Edificio de las Columnas, El Mirador and the Arco de Labná – can
all be seen as part of a harmonious whole. The **Palacio**, near the entrance, is
similar to, though less impressive than, that of Sayil. Traces of sculpture include
the inevitable Chac, and a crocodile-snake figure with a human face emerging
from its mouth – thought to symbolize a god escaping from the jaws of the
underworld.

The main sites are clearly joined by the remnants of a raised *sacbe*, the best-preserved portion of which leads from the Palacio to the **Arco de Labná**. Originally part of a complex linking two great squares, like the Nunnery at Uxmal, it now stands alone as a sort of triumphal arch. Both sides are richly decorated: on the east with geometric patterns; on the west (the back) with more of these and niches in the form of Maya huts or temples. Nearby **El Mirador** is a barely restored temple mound topped by the well-preserved remains of a tall, elaborate roofcomb. An inner passageway at one time led to the site's principal temple. Many of Labná's buildings were originally adorned with human figures; you can still see the lower half of one standing by the roofcomb of El Mirador as well as painted stucco remnants inside the "huts" atop the Arco. The last of the main structures, the **Edificio de las Columnas**, is a long, low building, its facade punctuated by five doors, characterised by the classic Puuc-style bamboo column decoration from which it takes its name.

## Hacienda Tabi

Between Labná and the Grutas de Loltún (see opposite) there's a sudden dramatic change in the countryside from tropical forest to farmland. If you're travelling by car and can afford the time, it's worth taking a detour to the extraordinary **Hacienda Tabi** (M$15), an abandoned sugar plantation that once covered 35,000 acres, about a tenth of which was declared a protected ecological reserve by the Mexican government in 1995 and is currently being restored. Note that it's poorly signed and the final couple of kilometres are along a deeply rutted mud track through citrus groves – nearly impassable if it has recently rained. To get there, follow the small road that offers a shortcut from Labná to Loltún via Yaaxhon; the 3km track to Tabi turns off this road.

At the end of the track you're confronted by the spectacular, Neoclassical facade of the vast Casa Principal, or main house, the rooms behind which are very much a perpetual work in progress. Facing the house across a large cleared lawn are the semi-ruinous remains of a chapel, sugar mill and rum distillery— little else remains, and the only activity here is to explore the solitude

△ Hacienda Tabi

and isolation of the forest, which encroaches on the rest of the old buildings or to sit and watch for wildlife. You can make advance arrangements to **stay the night** in one of the enormous, high-ceilinged, barren, tiled bedrooms upstairs (**❻**, including dinner and breakfast), and you're likely to have the place to yourself as it's off the beaten track. There are also dorm beds and space to **camp**; indeed most people who stay here are school or study groups, and that is the level of luxury you should expect. For further information contact the Fundación Cultural Yucatán in Mérida, Calle 58 no. 429-D (☎999/923-9453, ⓦwww.fcy.org.mx).

## Grutas de Loltún

The **GRUTAS DE LOLTÚN** (daily 9am–5pm, accessible only with guided tours, at 9.30am, 11am, 12.30pm, 2pm, 3pm & 4pm; M$20, plus M$30 for tour) are the most impressive easily accessible caves in the Yucatán. The hour-long tours, most in good English, concentrate on strange rock formations and the patterns seen in giant stalactites and stalagmites (including the inevitable Virgin), but there's also plenty of fascinating history and some spectacular caverns. Mammoth bones discovered here attest to prehistoric periods of climate change, and the caves were revered by the Maya as a source of water long before they built their cities. At the entrance, a huge bas-relief warrior guards the opening to the underworld, and throughout are traces of ancient paintings and carvings on the walls. The surrounding jungle is visible through the collapsed floor of the last gallery and ten-metre-long tree roots find an anchor on the cavern floor.

Outside you'll find two decent, if slightly pricey, **restaurants**: *El Guerrero* has its tables set out right by the exit from the caves (reached down the side road beside the caves); *Los Aluxes de Loltún* is on the main road directly opposite the entrance. Both have fairly standard Mexican menus, with tasty *panuchos* and the like. **From Oxkutzcab** (see below) the short taxi ride to the caves will cost you approximately M$50, or **colectivos** and trucks that pass the caves leave from Calle 51 next to the market. If you get there by 8.30am you may be able to catch the truck taking the cave employees to work. Getting back is more difficult, as the trucks are full of workers and produce, but if you wait something will turn up.

## Oxkutzcab

**OXKUTZCAB** has all the facilities you might need, but not a great deal else; its main claim to fame is the huge daily **fruit market**, bustling and lively in the mornings, where local produce, notably citrus, is sold, mostly by the crate or sack. The centre of town is around the junction of calles 51 and 50 where the main plaza and the *mercado* are separated by a hefty Franciscan church.

For **accommodation**, there are a number of basic hotels around the market area, of which the best is *Hospedaje Trujeque* (☎997/975-0568; **❹**, a/c and TV available), centrally located on Calle 48 opposite the plaza, with simple rooms round an internal courtyard. The newly expanded *Hotel Puuc*, however, at Calle 55 and Calle 44 on the way out of town towards Labná (☎997/975-0103; **❹**), is much more preferable and only marginally more expensive, with bright, clean rooms with a/c and TV. The Banamex **bank** on Calle 50, opposite the plaza, has an ATM, and there's an **Internet café** (M$13 per hour) at the corner of calles 51 and 52. Basic **restaurants** and *loncherías* skirt the market area; for something slightly more upmarket try the *Restaurante El Peregrino* at the *Hotel Puuc* or, in the evening, *Caffe Centro* on Calle 51 by the market.

## Ticul

Located 80km south of Mérida on Hwy-184, **TICUL** is a substantially larger town, than Oxkutzcab and historically an important centre of Maya shamanism as well as a pottery- and shoe-producing centre. The streets are full of shoe shops and stores selling reproduction Maya antiquities, most too big to carry home; visitors are welcome to watch the ceramic manufacturing process at the *fábricas*. Thanks to its position on what used to be the main road between Mérida and the Quintana Roo coast (the newly upgraded highway via Mayapán now takes much of the traffic), Ticul is also an important transport centre, well served by **buses** to and from Mérida and with services to Cancún and the east coast.

All this can make Ticul a noisy place, though surprisingly life manages to continue at a pretty slow pace, with as many bicycles (and passenger-carrying *triciclos*) as cars. The centre of town is around the junction of calles 25 and 26; there's a large plaza to either side of this junction, plus the usual massive church and several **hotels** in the immediate vicinity. Simplest of them is the friendly *Sierra Sosa*, Calle 26 no. 199-A, between calles 23 and 21 (T/F997/972-0008; ❹), whose basic rooms have a shower and fan (upstairs is better), though a/c and TV are available. Smarter alternatives are the *Hotel Plaza,* Calle 23 no. 201 between calles 26 and 26A (T997/972-0484, Wwww.hotelplazayucatan .com; ❺), with TV, telephone and a/c in all rooms, or the newly refurbished, double-glazed *Hotel San Antonio*, with similar facilities, facing the other plaza at calles 25A and 26 (T997/972-1893; ❺). Only slightly further afield, the *Posada Jardín* at Calle 27 no. 216 between calles 28 and 30 (T997/972-0401, Wwww .posadajardin.com; ❺) has four excellent-value, individually furnished cabins with separate sleeping and sitting areas, a/c, TV, fridge and coffeemaker, set in a lovely, bright garden with a small pool.

Ticul's best-known **restaurant,** *Los Almendros*, is the original branch of what is now a small chain and claims to have invented *poc-chuc* and other Yucatecan dishes. It recently moved to a big new site, complete with a pool, on the edge of town as you head out towards Oxkutzcab. It's packed with families at weekends, and periodically with tour groups at other times. Back in the centre, there's a good pizzeria, *La Gondola*, at the corner of calles 23 and 28. For an inexpensive *comida*, try the *Lonchería Carmelita*, at the corner of calles 23 and 26, or, as usual, least expensive of all are the *loncherías* near the bus station. For night-time dining, don't miss the tortas at the front of the market on Calle 23 between calles 28 and 30.

**Buses** from Mérida and elsewhere use a station directly behind the church at the corner of calles 24 and 25-A. **Colectivos and trucks** for Mérida as well as Santa Elena, Oxkutzcab and surrounding villages set off when they're full from various points in the immediate vicinity of the bus station; for Mérida around the corner of calles 24 and 25, other destinations mainly from Calle 25A alongside the church. Other practicalities are also central – the *Banamex* **bank** facing the plaza on Calle 26 just off Calle 25 has an ATM; directly opposite is a good **Internet café**, next to the (closed) *Ciné Lopez*. A small, locally run **tourist information office** (T997/972-2350) can be found on the corner of calles 23 and 26, above the *Lonchería Carmelita*.

# The Ruta de los Conventos

The **Ruta de los Conventos** can easily be followed from Mérida or from Ticul or Oxkutzcab, as part of a two-day or longer tour. The route itself is something of a recent invention of the tourist authorities, for although it's true that almost all the villages along the way do have impressive, fortified churches or monasteries – above all at **Maní** – the same can be said of towns and villages throughout the Yucatán. Nevertheless it's a worthwhile and enjoyable excursion, with a fascinating and wholly Mexican mix of churches, minor Maya ruins, caves and cenotes, set against a background of small towns and villages that see relatively few tourists. If you follow Hwy-18 you can turn off to almost any town en route and find a vast, ancient church, but the highlights of the route are **Acanceh**, with its remarkable blend of ancient and modern; **Los Tres Cenotes** where, as the name suggests, three cenotes lie along the tracks of a hacienda's old rail system, and the journey itself is much of the attraction; and the late Maya site of **Mayapán**.

The **churches** themselves date mainly from the seventeenth century or even earlier, as the Spanish were trying to establish their control. They were built so huge partly to impress, as a sign of the domination of Christianity over traditional gods (often on the site of Maya temples, using the stone from the older buildings), and partly as fortresses and places of refuge in times of trouble; windows are few, high and narrow, and interiors are relatively plain.

Leaving Mérida by car, the easiest route is to take Calle 69 to the Periferico, and then follow signs to Mayapán. The improved highway – **Hwy-18** – that this takes you to bypasses all of the towns and villages mentioned below, but on the whole they're well signposted and only a short way from the new road.

## Acanceh

**ACANCEH** (pronounced Akanké) is somewhere that could exist only in Mexico. Just over 20 kilometres from Mérida, this town, with its extraordinary mix of Maya, modern and colonial in a setting almost entirely ignored by tourism, is in many ways a perfect introduction to the route. Penetrating through the scrappy outskirts of what is a sizeable town, you arrive suddenly at the central plaza where, beside the church – a sixteenth-century Franciscan construction dedicated to Nuestra Señora de la Natividad that in any other setting would be impressive – is a large Mayan **pyramid** (daily 8am–5pm; M$24). Behind this is a second smaller pyramid, and nearby there's a third – all of them surrounded by people's backyards and the everyday life of the town. At the top of the large pyramid, protected under thatched shades, are four huge stucco masks, all of them defaced but still very clear to see. It's not known exactly whom they represent, but they are old (Early Classic or before) and some of the finest of their kind that survive: some say that the features show Olmec influence. Acanceh was an important Maya centre before many of its better-known neighbours were, reaching its high point in the Early Classic period (300–600 AD) before gradually declining in the face of the rising power of nearby Mayapán.

The **Palacio de los Stuccos** is about four blocks away, behind the market (get directions from the booth at the main pyramid). Though fenced, it seems to be open all day and is usually deserted save for some truly huge iguanas. A long, low building, the palace may have been an elite residential complex as its name suggests, or possibly an administrative centre. At the top is a corbel-arched passageway and, under cover, the stuccos from which the palace takes its name. These are far from complete, but there are plenty of easily identifiable figures, animals and glyphs.

## Los Tres Cenotes

The trip to **LOS TRES CENOTES** ("The Three Cenotes") at **Cuzamá** is a significant diversion from the Ruta de los Conventos, and a time-consuming one likely to take at least three hours. For locals it's usually a Sunday afternoon jaunt; busy at weekends, the area is practically deserted during the week, though transport is always available. The starting point is the **Hacienda Chankanaan**, which you'll find by following signs to Cuzamá, beyond Acanceh. Almost nothing survives of the hacienda buildings, but the cenotes lie among the semi-abandoned henequen fields, reached by the hacienda's old narrow gauge rail lines. Arriving at the hacienda you'll be hailed by locals offering *carritos* (or *truks*), the rickety, individual horse-drawn wooden rail carriages in which you take the trip (about M$130 per *carrito*). These can seat four or five in some discomfort, with no brakes, suspension or proper seats. The journey is roughly 45 minutes each way, plus as long as you choose to spend at the cenotes. Uncomfortable or not, you get a real sense of journeying back in time as you leave the road behind and head off along the wobbly tracks through the fields.

The first cenote, **Chelentun**, is the easiest to access, with a concrete stairway down to the water, but also the least appealing. The second, **Chansinic'che**, and third, **Bolonchoojol**, are much more attractive, but reached by steep, terrifyingly rusty metal ladders, repaired in places with any materials that came to hand. It's well worth it, though, for the cool, clear water at the bottom – plenty of small fish testify to its cleanliness – and the spectacular views as sunlight spears through the narrow openings above. Bolonchoojol, in particular, is famously photogenic. To enjoy the trip to the full, do as the locals do and bring along a picnic, as well as swimming gear and towels.

## Tecoh

Next stop along the Ruta proper, **TECOH** has another vast, fortified church on its plaza, but its main claim to fame is an extensive cave system, the **Grutas de Tzabnah** (Mon–Fri 10am–5pm, Sat & Sun 8am–5pm; M$30), containing no less than thirteen cenotes. This is a trip only for the cave enthusiast, however: there's no lighting except for the flashlights you and your guide will carry, and the caves are slippery, dark, low-ceilinged and full of bats. Taking the full tour involves crawling through tight, muddy passageways as well as various steep inclines where you need a rope. There are some impressive caverns along the way, and at the far end a welcome swim in the tenth cenote, but you'll get muddy and sweaty again on the way out – at least until plans to put in a staircase and lighting are realized. Not surprisingly, perhaps, there are few visitors except at weekends, when locals descend.

## Mayapán

Roughly halfway from Mérida to Maní, the ruins of **MAYAPÁN** (daily 8am–5pm; M$24) lie right beside the road. The most powerful city in the Yucatán from the thirteenth to the fifteenth century, Mayapán's history is in some dispute. According to Maya chronicles it was one of the three cities (the others being Chichén Itzá and Uxmal) that made up the **League of Mayapán**, which exercised control over the entire peninsula from around 987 to 1185. The league broke up when the **Cocom Dynasty** of Mayapán attacked and overwhelmed the rulers of an already declining Chichén Itzá, establishing itself as sole controller of the peninsula. However, archeological evidence suggests that the Maya chronicles must be wrong, as Mayapán does not appear to have been a significant settlement until the thirteenth century. The rival theory has Mayapán founded around 1263, after the fall of Chichén Itzá.

Whatever its history, Mayapán became a huge city by the standards of the day, with a population of some fifteen thousand (rulers of subject cities were forced to live here, perhaps even as hostages, so they could be kept under control), on a site covering five square kilometres, in which traces of more than four thousand buildings have been found. Its hegemony was maintained until 1441, when Ah Xupan, a Xiu leader from Uxmal, finally led a rebellion that succeeded in overthrowing the Cocom and destroying their city, thus paving the way for the fractured tribalism that the Spanish found on their arrival, which made their conquest considerably easier.

What can be seen today is in some ways a disappointment, and certainly no match for the Classic Maya sites. The buildings, by Maya standards, were relatively crude and small – at best poor copies of what had gone before – and only a small proportion of them have been restored (a visit doesn't take long). This has led to the widespread dismissal of the Mayapán society as "decadent" and failing, but a powerful case can be made for the fact that it was merely a changing one. As the priests no longer dominated here, hence the lack of great ceremonial centres, what developed instead was a more genuinely urban society: highly militaristic, no doubt, but also far more centralized and more reliant on trade than any previous Maya culture.

The site has its undeniable attractions, too. Scattered throughout are numerous frescoes, carvings and stuccos (look for the thatched shelters), many with their original colours still visible. Keep an eye out also for the cenote, shadowed by banana palms (there were no less than 26 small cenotes scattered across the ancient city, but this is the only one in the central cleared area). At the main structure, the so-called **Castillo de Kukulkan**, steep, narrow steps lead to an unshaded platform from where there's a seemingly infinite view across the surrounding plains. Low down at the rear of the building are stucco reliefs of decapitated warriors – there's a niche where their heads would have been, where perhaps the heads or skulls of real enemies were displayed.

## Maní and around

Continuing south from Mayapán along Hwy–18, there's a string of villages distinguished by their huge fortress-like churches; most see few tourists and have no facilities apart from the odd general store. Many of the women here still dress daily in elaborately embroidered *huipiles*, and there's a real sense of traditional rural life. The churches are generally open during the day, though there's no guarantee of this.

Before reaching Maní, you'll pass a number of other small villages whose mammoth churches are pretty plain on the inside, though enlivened somewhat by a few naive carvings of saints. **Tekit**, a village otherwise devoted to farming, has some good examples of these, while at **Mama**, the vast, crumbling fortress of a church is cathedral-like in scale, and probably the oldest on the route. Dating originally from the sixteenth century, it was much altered and added to during the following centuries, yet the cloister-style garden courtyard around a well at the back merits a look if you can get in, though the church is often locked. In **Chumayel** the rather smaller Templo de la Purisima Concepcion has a brightly gilded altar set off by whitewashed walls, and at **Teabo** there's another monster, albeit not quite on the scale of Mama. Beyond Teabo, an entirely new section of road extends towards Peto on the way to Felipe Carrillo Puerto and Chetumal, so take care not to miss the turn (by a giant Pemex station) for Oxkutzcab and Maní.

**MANÍ**, just twelve kilometres north of Oxkutzcab, is the most historic of the towns along the Ruta de los Conventos. Founded by the Xiu after they abandoned Uxmal, it was, at the time of the Conquest, the largest city the Spanish encountered in the Yucatán, though almost no trace now survives. Avoiding a major confrontation, Maní's ruler, Ah Kukum Xiu, converted to Christianity and became an ally of the Spanish. In 1548, one of the earliest and largest **Franciscan monasteries** in the Yucatán was founded here; this still stands, surrounded now by Maya huts, and just about the only evidence of Maní's past glories are the ancient stones used in its construction, and in walls around the town. In front of the church, in 1562, Bishop Diego de Landa held an infamous auto-da-fé, in which he burned the city's ancient records (because they "contained nothing in which there was not to be seen the superstitions and lies of the devil"), destroying virtually all surviving original Maya literature. The monastery itself offers an enjoyable wander through courtyards and cloisters full of plants, flowers and old wells, while the church has some fine, elaborately carved altars and saints in niches. Maní has little else to offer beyond an entrancingly slow pace of life, though Méridans often come down here on day-trips to dine at *El Príncipe Tutul-Xiu* (Calle 26 between 25 and 27, open Tues–Sun 11am–7pm), a festive palapa-roof **restaurant** that has been serving Yucatecan standards for more than thirty years.

# Travel details

## Buses

Few major buses originate in this region, as they tend to pass through on their way from Mérida to Chetumal or Campeche, while most of the local buses originate in Mérida.

**Mérida** (C=Terminal CAME; SC=Terminal Segunda Clase; N=Noreste; AP=AutoProgreso) to: Mayapán (N, 2 daily; 1hr); Oxkutzcab (SC, 11 daily, N, 6 daily; 2hr) Santa Elena (SC, 5 daily; 1hr); Uxmal (SC, 6 daily; 1hr 15min).

**Ticul** to: Mérida (at least 20; 1 hr 45 min)

## Combis and colectivos

**Mérida** to: Ticul (1 hr 45 min), Oxkutzcab (2hr), Santa Elena (1 hr 15min)

**Santa Elena** to: Campeche (5 daily; 2hr 45min); Merida (8 daily; 1hr 30)

# 8

# Campeche

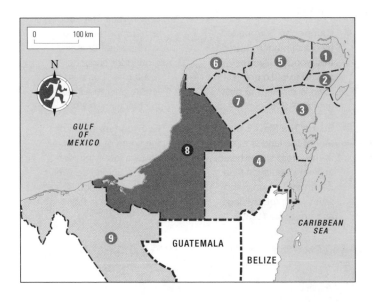

CHAPTER 8 # Highlights

* **Caves and cenotes** Riddled with cenotes and interconnected cave systems, the area includes two of the Yucatán's largest at Calcehtok and Xtacumbilxunaan. **P.268 & p.283**

* **Campeche** Surrounded by brash modern Mexico, this wonderfully preserved fortified colonial town is redolent of past glories. **P.270**

* **Edzná** The Maya's mastery of the land is evident at this great site, whose ancient population was dependent on an elaborate system of drainage and irrigation. **P.280**

* **Chenes sites** Home to a wildly decorative architectural style whose buildings become monsters or gods with doorways that appear as their gaping mouths. **P.282**

* **Sea Turtles** The southern Campeche coast is an important breeding ground for endangered sea turtles; come in July and August to witness the hatching. **P.284**

* **Eco-tourism** Much of the south of Campeche State is low-lying wetland, draining into vast river systems and abundant in wildlife. **P.287**

△ Dzibilnocac

# 8

# Campeche

The third of the states that make up the Yucatán Peninsula, Campeche is far less visited than its neighbours, even though its capital city is a UNESCO world heritage site and the importance of the area in Maya times grows ever clearer with time. The ruins of **Edzná**, **Oxkintok** and the **Chenes sites**, notably **Hochob**, are indeed magnificent, but it is the city

265

of **Campeche** that is the region's highlight – a place whose heart evokes an era when pirates were a constant threat, and the wealth of the Americas flowed through on its way to Spain. Today it combines the feel of Old Spain in its superbly preserved colonial centre, the frantic chaos of modern Mexico in its raucous outskirts, and the hot, heady atmosphere of a tropical port that's half-asleep in the mid-afternoon.

Campeche State is located on the southwest part of the Yucatán Peninsula, where the coastline with the Gulf of Mexico curves from a north-south direction to east-west. The **main route** through the area is Hwy-180, which heads down from Mérida to Campeche and then around the coast via Ciudad del Carmen to Villahermosa. Hwy-261 takes a more leisurely course from Mérida towards Campeche, heading inland via Uxmal and Hopelchén, and giving access to the Chenes sites along the way. At Hopelchén a minor road heads south through barely inhabited forest to Xpuhil. Hwy-261 joins up with Hwy-180 just south of Campeche, but then turns inland again towards the dusty junction town of Escárcega. Here it meets Hwy-186, which runs right across the south of the state – east via Xpuhil and the Río Bec sites to Chetumal, west and south towards Palenque and Villahermosa. There is a good **bus service** on all these major highways, with Campeche as the hub, but away from these routes the country is sparsely inhabited, and there's barely any transport at all, and, for that matter, very few roads.

# Mérida to Campeche along Hwy-180

The direct road from Mérida to Campeche, taken by first-class buses and all *directo* services, is **Hwy-180**, which follows the line of the old colonial Camino Real. This is a fast, flat drive of 160km or so, especially quick if you take the toll superhighway for the first half of the journey. The toll road bypasses the most interesting stops on the journey, however, at the Maya site of **Oxkintok** and the hat-producing town of **Becal**. Entering the state of Campeche the superhighway ends, and there's a further worthwhile detour to **Hecelchakán**. Here a road heads down to the coast at Isla de Jaina, and there's a small archeology museum with figures from Jaina and objects from other nearby sites.

The longer route follows **Hwy-261** for almost 250km past Uxmal and Kabah, entering Campeche state near **Bolonchén de Rejón**. Much slower as it winds through the hills inland, this is also a far prettier route with a number of possible stops if you're driving. Uxmal and Kabah themselves could take the best part of a day, while several of the smaller Chenes sites are reached from **Hopelchén**. As you approach Campeche, Edzná is also not far off this road. Many second-class buses follow this route, and with an early start you should be able to go this way, take in at least one site, and continue the same day. Only Uxmal and Kabah, though, actually lie right on the road.

## Oxkintok

Only recently excavated, **OXKINTOK** (daily 8am–5pm; M$30), in Yucatán State, is a large and beautifully maintained site, relatively little visited. The ruins are signed off Hwy-180, a few kilometres along a minor road that leads to Muna and Uxmal and then a dusty white track to the site itself. They are not easily reached by bus – you'd have to get to Maxcanú and take a *triciclo* taxi for several kilometres from there. Similarly, there are no facilities or shops of any kind nearby, so be sure to bring some water and perhaps pack a lunch;

there are picnic tables under palapa shades near the entrance and further into the site.

Oxkintok was probably the dominant city in the region during the Early Classic period (c250-600 AD), thanks in part to a strategic position among low hills which command the route from the coast at Celestún to Uxmal and Sayil, and also to Dzibilchaltún and the salt lagoons to the north and west. It is among the earliest of the Puuc sites, and although power later passed to the better-known cities further south, Oxkintok continued to be inhabited right through the Classic Maya era.

The site features three main groups of buildings: Ah Dzib, to the right as you enter; Ah Canul, to the left; and Ah May, directly ahead of you. Tzat Tun Tzat, the so-called "**Maya labyrinth**", is behind the Ah Dzib group, to the right of Ah May. All of the structures here are old – older than most you'll see at other Puuc sites – and for that reason on the whole smaller, less decorated and perhaps a little cruder than those at the great sites. Nonetheless this proto-Puuc style contains many of the seeds of the architectural forms that would reach their height at Uxmal. The **Ah Dzib** group is the oldest of all, dating mainly from the pre-Classic era (c300 BC–250 AD). The small ball-court here was equipped with a *temazcal* – a steam-bath similar to those still used by the Maya today – where players would undergo ritual purification before a game.

Sadly, the labyrinth – El Laberinto or **Tzat Tun Tzat** – the most famous individual structure here, is closed to the public so you can no longer explore the numerous dimly lit passageways and sixteen rooms on three levels from which it takes its name. It is a highly unusual building for this era, with its tiny windows and many small rooms: locals claim that there are tunnels, as yet undiscovered, linking the labyrinth to other buildings here, or even to nearby caves. This fits neatly with ancient myths that at Oxkintok there was an opening to Xibalba, the Maya underworld.

Between the labyrinth and the Ah May group, a damp depression, alive with plants, cacti and butterflies, marks the site of an ancient cistern or *aguada* – scattered around the site are also numerous underground *chultunes*, their openings usually blocked with flat stones or metal discs. The **Ah May group** itself, also known as the Plaza Suroeste, offers great views of the surrounding countryside, studded with unexplored mounds. The Palacio Junquillos (building MA-9) was built later than most at the site: its dressed-stone walls with simple bamboo-column decoration overlook a large plaza, very reminiscent of the style of other Puuc sites.

The **Ah Canul** group is the largest and perhaps most impressive of all. Most of the facade of El Palacio Ch'ich (CA-7) has crumbled, but a couple of columns survive, carved with human figures that still stand sentinel over the plaza in front of them. In the centre of the plaza, you can make out the opening to a large *chultun*, while adjacent to it lies the Palacio del Diablo, of which almost nothing remains save the column from which it takes its name, carved with a figure with two holes in the top of its head. The Spanish thought that horns had sprouted from these – hence the name. There were once many other human figures adorning these buildings, but neglect and easy access mean this site has been very heavily looted. The Palacio Pop (CA-3) is among the oldest structures at the site: on its floor, remnants of a painted palm mat design have been found (a palm mat, "Pop" in Maya, was a symbol of authority).

### Around Oxkintok

More than twenty **cave systems** are found in the countryside around Oxkintok – some are single caverns, others huge interconnecting areas. It is suspected that many of them are further connected to each other in ways not yet discovered. Their presence is perhaps the basis of the Oxkintok myth of an opening to the underworld, and there's plenty of evidence that they have been used by the local population since pre-history, as a place to live, a place of refuge (including as recently as the nineteenth-century, during the Caste Wars; see p.330), or a place of worship. You may well be accosted at the entrance to Oxkintok by a local guide offering to take you to one of these caves, and if you have the time and are prepared for a bit of walking over rough ground, it's an opportunity worth taking (the guide will almost certainly speak no English though).

One local cave, **Aktun Usil**, with its entrance in the middle of a field not far from Oxkintok, is a short drive on a rough track followed by a little clambering over rocks. It is named Ak (tortoise) Tun (stone) because the domed cavern roof is shaped like the inside of a tortoise shell. It seems that this cave was used purely for ritual purposes: no sign of habitation has been found, but there were burials, possibly of priests, symbols painted on the ceiling, and found items including dozens of stingray spines, used for ritual blood-letting.

The best known of the local caves, though, are the **Grutas de Calcehtok**, which some claim to be the largest cave system in the Yucatán; they're near the village of Calcehtok, signed off the road from Hwy-180 to Muna not far beyond Oxkintok. You'll usually find someone to guide you at the entrance, and you are strongly advised not to go in without a guide, as there are no paths or lighting. The basic tour of less than an hour will show you some impressively large vaulted caverns, in whose stalactites and stalagmites you'll find faces and shapes of deer and other animals. It will also probably leave you pretty dirty (the guides love to claim that the mud you are covered in is, in fact, bat guano, which may be, in part, true). Longer trips are real explorations and for pot-holing enthusiasts only, involving as they do a great deal of climbing, sliding and squeezing through narrow gaps.

Inside the caves all sorts of pre-Hispanic objects have been found, including obsidian knives, ceramics, sculptures and lots of bones, some from human burials. Anything of any value has long since been removed, but in some of the deepest caverns the guides still offer to show you human skeletons. There are also numerous *haltunes* – water-collecting basins carved out by the Maya.

## Maxcanú, Becal and Hecelchakán

The old highway has been routed around all the towns it used to pass through, so you'll need to turn off to visit any of the following. Although there are motels and the odd restaurant along the highway, you'll find far more characterful places away from it. **MAXCANÚ**, the nearest town to Oxkintok, is a sizeable rural centre, but something of a backwater now that the highway bypasses it. There's little going on here – you'd probably only stop in to break up your journey or get something to eat – but you could take a look at the recently renovated church of San Miguel on the main plaza. Directly opposite the church's main doors is an incongruously fancy bar where locals enjoy good home-made **food**; alternatively, try the reliable *Restaurante San Valentin*, not far off the plaza beyond the market. If you want to **stay** in this region, just about the only option is the ultra-luxury on offer at the gorgeous *Hacienda Santa Rosa* (☏999/910-4875, ⓦwww.starwoodhotels.com/luxury; ❾). Some of the eleven rooms here have their own private garden and plunge pool, and there are extensive grounds with native plants, as well as a beautiful main pool. You could also call in here for a meal, though since it's so small it would be wise to phone in advance to let them know. The hacienda, in the village of Santa Rosa,

## The Jaina figurines

The **Isla de Jaina** (which means "the place of the house on the water" in Maya) is the source of thousands of beautiful, detailed **clay figurines** that now grace the collections of museums throughout the world as well as at Hecelchakán and Mexico City. Typically just 10–20cm tall, the figures depict ordinary Maya as well as priests, lords, warriors and ball players, and they have provided a huge proportion of what is known today about everyday Maya life – what people wore, what they looked like, how they entertained themselves. The figures were placed in the graves of the people they depicted, often held in their hands or laid on their chests. Many of them also work as rattles or whistles, and clearly they were meant to accompany their owners to the underworld, perhaps as offerings or companions, or to make a noise to attract attention or ward off evil spirits.

Over 20,000 tombs have been counted on the island, and though some archeologists argue that they were the burial sites of local residents, it seems far more likely that Jaina was some kind of necropolis where people from all over the region were buried. Its western location may have been symbolic of the setting sun, or the island may have marked an entrance to **Xibalba**, the Maya underworld. Initially, perhaps, this was an elite burial place: early interments have few figurines, but of very high quality. As the burial location gained in popularity, the quality of the figures declined – increasingly they were made in moulds rather than entirely by hand, and they began to feature ordinary people as well as members of the upper class.

In many ways, however, it is these lesser figurines that are of most interest: they depict people going about their daily activities – weavers with their waist-looms, ball players at the doors of temples, dwarfs, musicians, the sick, the blind – and show clothing in great detail, revealing clearly that what people wore was dependent on their social status. They also record ancient Maya physical characteristics – short stature, hooked noses and straight hair – as well as artificial features like intentionally deformed skulls, ornamentation of the teeth and crossed eyes.

The island was occupied throughout the Classic Maya period, from as early as 250 AD to as late as 1000 AD, though whether it was purely a ritual centre or a city in its own right is again a matter of some disagreement. In order to build here, the ancient Maya were forced to transport materials from the mainland: they did so in sufficient quantity to construct two substantial pyramids, as well as many lesser buildings.

is extremely hard to find; it's off Hwy-180, near Maxcanú, about 10km down unmarked roads, past Granada.

About 20km further, **BECAL**, just across the border in Campeche State, is famous for the manufacture of baskets and, above all, the ubiquitous Yucatecan **jipis**, or "Panama" hats (genuine Panama hats, confusingly, come from Ecuador). Like Maxcanú, this is a hot, slow-moving place where little seems to happen, but it's interesting to see a village so consumed with a single cottage industry – a fountain made of concrete hats even graces the town square. If you pull over here you're likely to be approached by a friendly local offering to show you round, which basically means being taken to a nearby hat shop – though you may get a short tour in the back of a *triciclo* thrown in, with a stop at one of the town's many *cuevas* (the cellars in which the villagers traditionally make and store their hats, the damp, cool conditions keeping the fibres soft and flexible). Ask your guide to point out a *jipi* too, the fibrous plant from which the hat-making material is extracted. There doesn't seem to be a great deal to choose from between the many hat shops; they all sell similar products at prices ranging from around M$120 to M$1200, depending on quality, which is mainly determined by the fineness of the fibres and tightness of the weave. The best hats can supposedly be crumpled into a ball and will spring back into shape.

A little under halfway from Becal to Campeche, **HECELCHAKÁN** lies just off the highway, where a road to the **Isla de Jaina** turns off. Despite the tempting signs, there's little point following the dusty road to the sea, as there's no access to the archeological site or the island itself, and the surrounding coast is windswept and entirely lacking in facilities. You can, though, view some fine examples of the Jaina figurines (see box, p.269), as well as many other objects from local sites, in Hecelchakán's small and recently refurbished **Museo Arqueológico del Camino Real** (Tues–Sat 10am–1pm & 4–7pm; about M$25), housed in an elegant old mansion on the main plaza. The other side of the vast, colonial square that marks the centre of town is presided over by the impressive church of San Francisco de Asís, a sixteenth-century foundation whose dome and towers are later additions.

On the plaza itself, among wonderful topiary hedges in animal and geometric shapes, a couple of *loncherías* serve tacos, *tortas* and juices for a quick lunch. If you're looking for **accommodation** around here, the *Hacienda Blanca Flor*, a short way north of Hecelchakán near the village of Poc-Buc (at Km 85.5 on the highway, ☎999/925-8042, ⓦwww.mexonline.com/blancaflor.htm; ❽) has sixteen large, comfortable rooms with a/c in a converted seventeenth-century hacienda. It was one of the first hacienda hotels (opened in 1988) and occasionally shows its age a little, especially in the decor, but it's set on a beautiful working ranch, complete with a nice pool and live animals, such as lambs, goats and horses. Simple but excellent meals are available.

# Campeche

Capital of the state that bears its name, startlingly beautiful **CAMPECHE** is one of Mexico's finest colonial gems. At its heart, relatively intact, lies a historical port town still surrounded by hefty defensive **walls and fortresses**; within them, interspersed with the occasional grand Baroque church, are elegant eighteenth- and nineteenth-century houses painted in pastel shades, hundreds of which have been restored to their former glory. Around the old **centre** are the trappings of a modern city that is once again becoming wealthy, while the **seafront** is a bizarre mixture of centuries-old and twentieth-century modern.

In the past, few travellers have stopped here, preferring to sweep by en route to Palenque or Villahermosa. Though more visitors are beginning to discover the immaculately preserved and tranquil streets which compare favourably with Mérida's, for the moment at least, Campeche remains unblighted by tourist overkill.

## Some history

In 1517 a crew of Spanish explorers under Francisco Hernández landed outside the Maya town of Ah Kin Pech, only to beat a hasty retreat on seeing the forces lined up to greet them. Not until 1540 did the second-generation conquistador **Francisco de Montejo the Younger** found the modern town – which he named Villa de San Francisco de Campeche – and from here set out on his mission to subjugate the Yucatán. From then until the nineteenth century, Campeche was the chief port on the peninsula, exporting goods from throughout the region, but above all **logwood** (*Haematoxylum campechianum*, a tree also known as *palo de campeche* or *palo de tinte*), the source of a red dye

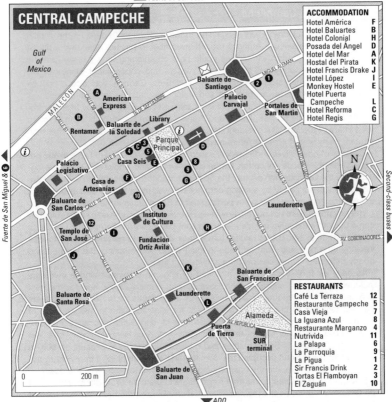

**CENTRAL CAMPECHE**

Fuerte de San José

Gulf of Mexico

MALECÓN

American Express

Baluarte de Santiago

Palacio Carvajal

Portales de San Martín

Rentamar

Baluarte de la Soledad

Library

Parque Principal

Casa Seis

Palácio Legislativo

Casa de Artesanías

Baluarte de San Carlos

Templo de San José

Instituto de Cultura

Fundación Ortiz Avila

Launderette

Baluarte de San Francisco

Baluarte de Santa Rosa

Launderette

Puerta de Tierra

Alameda

SUR terminal

Baluarte de San Juan

Fuerte de San Miguel 5 & 6

Second-class buses

AV. GOBERNADORES

0  200 m

ADO

| ACCOMMODATION | |
|---|---|
| Hotel América | F |
| Hotel Baluartes | B |
| Hotel Colonial | H |
| Posada del Ángel | D |
| Hotel del Mar | A |
| Hostal del Pirata | K |
| Hotel Francis Drake | J |
| Hotel López | I |
| Monkey Hostel | E |
| Hotel Puerta Campeche | L |
| Hotel Reforma | C |
| Hotel Regis | G |

| RESTAURANTS | |
|---|---|
| Café La Terraza | 12 |
| Restaurante Campeche | 5 |
| Casa Vieja | 7 |
| La Iguana Azul | 8 |
| Restaurante Marganzo | 4 |
| Nutrivida | 11 |
| La Palapa | 6 |
| La Parroquia | 9 |
| La Pigua | 1 |
| Sir Francis Drink | 2 |
| Tortas El Flamboyan | 3 |
| El Zaguán | 10 |

called hematein, which attracted huge prices in Europe. Although logwood was planted – and still grows – throughout the Caribbean, the finest is said to be that from Campeche. Rapidly accruing wealth made Campeche an irresistible target for **pirates** (see box, p.272) until locals finally prevailed upon the Spanish authorities to fortify the city. Construction of the **walls**, with their eight massive *baluartes* (bulwarks), began in 1686 after a particularly brutal massacre of the local population, and the original defences were completed in 1704. Much of the wall has been demolished and replaced by a ring road, but two substantial sections survive, along with seven of the eight original *baluartes*.

## Arrival and information

To get to or from the **airport** (☎981/816-6656), about 10km southeast of town, you'll have to take a **taxi** (M$80). Campeche has two **bus stations**, for first- and second-class services, as well as a separate minor terminus for local and rural buses, including those to Edzná (see p.281). The **first-class** station is a very long way (probably around 5km) from the centre on Avenida Central; there are taxis outside, or buses and *colectivos* (almost any one immediately outside on Avenida Central should take you into town – look for "Mercado" or "Centro". The **second-class** terminal is about 2km out on Avenida Goberna-

## The pirates of Campeche

For about three hundred years, beginning in the mid-sixteenth century, the wealth of the Spanish colonies in America proved irresistible to **pirates**. Many were based in the West Indies, from where they could prey on shipping as it passed, but the Campeche coast, above all the sheltered waters and unpopulated islands of the Laguna de Términos around modern-day Ciudad del Carmen, was also a popular hideout. Despite their swashbuckling and violent reputation – far from undeserved – the majority of pirates were in fact at least semi-official, authorized by their governments (primarily the English, Dutch and French) to seize Spanish shipping in return for a share of the loot. Such raiders described themselves as **privateers** rather than pirates; many were former or future naval officers.

Cargoes of gold, silver and jewellery sailed from Campeche, as did less exotic but equally valuable goods like cotton, feathers, hardwoods and, above all, Campeche logwood. By the late sixteenth century the Spanish authorities had begun to take effective measures against piracy by sending cargoes in fewer, more heavily armed ships and assembling convoys in Caribbean ports to sail to Spain under armed escort.

The privateers were not put off, however: as their prey became less vulnerable they came up with alternative tactics – which meant bad news for Campeche. Unable to ply their trade at sea, the privateers turned their attention to **raiding coastal towns**. Wealthy as a port and from its trade in local wood and tobacco, the isolated and poorly defended Campeche became a favourite target.

As early as 1568 the port was attacked by a group of pirates whose members included the English captains John Hawkins and Francis Drake, and for the next hundred years the frequency and severity of the **attacks** increased, as privateers banded together to create formidable fleets for joint assaults. In 1663 a force of as many as twelve ships and 1500 English, French and Dutch buccaneers – commanded by Christopher Myngs and including the notorious Henry Morgan – attacked Campeche, seizing 14 Spanish ships and over 150,000 pesos in treasure. In 1667 a band under Lewis Scott occupied the town for three days, stripping it of almost everything that could move and then demanding a ransom not to burn the place down.

Finally, in 1685, a force under the French pirate Laurent de Graff, along with Michel de Grammont, invaded the town silently by night. Ringing the bells of the church of San Francisco, they gathered the population of Campeche – for whom this was a signal to assemble – and imprisoned virtually everyone inside the church. Then they systematically and savagely sacked the town. The following year, the Spanish began to fortify the city and, though raids on shipping continued into the nineteenth century (when privateers operated under the flag of the Texan navy), Campeche itself was never seriously threatened again.

dores; to get to the centre, cross Avenida Gobernadores and take a city bus, also marked "Centro" or "Mercado". Virtually all of these buses and *combis* will head down to the market, outside the city wall on the landward side, where they may wait awhile before continuing round the line of the city walls to the post office, near the Parque Principal. These are also the points of departure to get back to the bus stations; for first-class look for "Av Central" or "ADO", for second class "Gobernadores", "Universidad", "ISSTE" or "Terminal Sur". Buses from **Edzná** and other local destinations such as Champotón use Sur's local terminal on Avenida Republica, by the Alameda a block from the Puerta de Tierra. For drivers, the main **routes in and out of town** are Avenida Gobernadores, which heads to Hwy-180 from Mérida, and Avenida Central, which joins with Hwy-180 heading south and is also the route to Edzná and Hwy-261, and the inland route to Mérida. Alternatively, and perhaps more easily, if you follow the seafront road in either direction, it will eventually take you to Hwy-180.

Campeche's **state tourist office** (daily 8am–4pm & 6–9pm; ☎981/811-9229 or 1-800/900-2267, ⊛www.campechetravel.com), in the tent-like building on Plaza Moch Couoh, on the seaward side of the imposing Palacio de Gobierno, is helpful and there's usually someone there who speaks English. You can pick up brochures on attractions throughout the state, though specifics on activities outside the city are somewhat limited. They also have a list of independent **guides** (speaking various languages) who lead tours of the city and archeological sites, though you might be expected to provide the transport; Betty Mena Pacheco (☎981/811-0733) is particularly friendly and knowledgeable. The **city tourist office** is right on the Parque Principal, on Calle 55 alongside the cathedral (see p.275). Though rather less organized and with fewer brochures, they're also extremely helpful. Smaller **information booths** at the bus stations, in the Baluarte de San Pedro and in the Casa Seis are not always manned, but have leaflets, maps and details of activities and tours.

## City tours

For a concise overview of the city, take the **tranvía tour** on one of two open-sided buses that depart from the Parque Principal. The city route (daily, hourly, on the hour, 9am–1pm & 5–9pm; M$70, children M$15) is a 45-minute trundle around all the main sights and *barrios*, including outlying areas you'd be unlikely to walk to, while the other bus runs south along the seafront and up to Fuerte de San Miguel (daily, hourly on the hour 10am–1pm & 6–9pm; same prices), or north to the Fuerte de San José (daily 9am & 5pm; same price). The excellent live commentary is in Spanish and English.

## Accommodation

Because Campeche is not yet fully on the tourist circuit, it still boasts plenty of reasonably priced **hotels**, though, for the same reason, the cheapest ones can be depressingly shabby. Avoid rooms overlooking the street, as the city's narrow lanes magnify traffic noise. Most of the budget hotels are within a couple of blocks of the Parque Principal; a couple more upmarket, business-style choices are outside the old city walls facing the sea. There are also two excellent backpacker **hostels** and one new super-luxury hotel: if you're looking in this category, you might also want to check out the *Hacienda Uayamón* (see p.282), 21km out of town on the way to Edzná.

**América** C 10 no. 252, between C 59 and C 61 ☎981/816-4588, ⊛www.hotelamericacampeche .com. Probably the best of the mid-price options, set in an elegant colonial building. Good value if slightly threadbare rooms have TV and fan or a/c; most overlook a small, pleasant courtyard. Fast, free Internet and small continental breakfast are included. ❺
**Baluartes** Av 16 de Septiembre 128, between C 59 and C 61 ☎981/816-3911, ⊛www.baluartes .com.mx. This bland modern hotel has the best position in town, on the seaward side of the walls. Spacious rooms feature a/c and TV, plus there's a large outdoor pool and a café with an international menu. Go for a sea-view room, which is bigger and costs the same. Can be full when there's a congress in town. ❼

**Colonial** C 14 no. 122, between C 55 and C 57 ☎981/816-2222. Best of the budget options, with simple but immaculately tidy rooms set in a charming old building. Optional a/c in a couple of the rooms. ❹
**Posada del Ángel** C 10 no. 309, between C 53 and C 55 ☎981/816-7718. Good location alongside the cathedral but not great value – rooms are rather small and dark. Option of TV and fan or a/c. ❺
**Hostal del Pirata** C 59 no. 47 between C 14 and C 16 ☎981/811-1757, ✉piratehostel@hotmail .com. The new kid on the block, this very friendly place tries to keep its prices just below those at the *Monkey Hostel*. Additionally, it offers discounts to IYHF members and student-card holders. It has a quieter location than its rival does and similar facilities, including a roof terrace, a café-bar and

bike rental. Single-sex and mixed dorm beds begin at M$70 (with card); private rooms are also available.

**Francis Drake** C 12 no. 207, between C 63 and C 65 ☎981/811-5626, 🌐 www.hotelfrancisdrake .com. Opened in late 2002, this small hotel in a renovated colonial building has plush rooms (and some suites) and a helpful staff; there's no pool, but far more character than the two oceanfront options. **❻**

**López** C 12 no. 189, between C 61 and C 63 ☎/🖷 981/816-3344, 🄴 hotelpez@prodigy.net. mx. A standard Mexican hotel with clean rooms (a/c and TV) around a central passageway. Minimal continental breakfast included. **❺**

**Del Mar** Av Ruíz Cortines 51, between C 57 and C 59 ☎981/811-9191, 🌐 www.delmarhotel.com.mx. Bland, concrete building in a great location with all facilities. A slight step up in class from its near neighbour the *Baluartes*, but only good value if you go for a city view. **❼**

**Monkey Hostel** C 57 at corner of C 10 ☎1-800/ CAMPECHE, 🌐 www.hostalcampeche.com. Fabulous location on the west side of the plaza for this long-established backpacker haven with a helpful staff and clean rooms. Offers a roof terrace, laundry, bike rental, transportation to nearby archeological sites, a book exchange and more. Breakfast is included. Beds in single-sex dorms begin at M$80; basic double rooms are also available.

**Puerta Campeche** C 59 no.61, between C 16 and C 18 ☎981/816-7508, 🌐 www.starwoodhotels .com/luxury. Located just inside the Puerta de Tierra, this extraordinary hotel occupies most of a block of restored colonial houses. The rooms are in these small houses, with some suites occupying an entire two-storey home. There's a pool built around the rooms of a ruined house, a fancy restaurant, and every other facility you might expect (including in-room DVD players) in what is – by some way – Campeche's most expensive and luxurious hotel.

**Reforma** C 8 no. 257, between C 57 and C 59 ☎981/816-4464. A very basic, very central hotel with rooms around a courtyard, and a couple with balconies overlooking the city walls. Most rooms have just a bed and a fan, though for double the price there are a couple with a/c and TV. The place is clean and friendly, but faded splendour would be the polite description of the decor (chipped and broken would be the less so). The nearby *Hotel Campeche* and *Hotel Castelmar* offer similar prices and facilities, perhaps still more run-down. **❸**

**Regis** C 12 no. 148, between C 55 and C 57 ☎981/816-3175. Seven very large rooms, all with a/c, are arranged around a small patio. This is a reasonable alternative to the *Colonial* or the *América*, and about halfway between the two in price. Often full. **❺**

# The city

Perhaps the greatest pleasure to be had in Campeche is simply wandering around the old streets or seafront – especially in the early evening, as the heat lessens, the lights come on behind the grilled windows of the old homes and locals come out to stroll, or to jog or blade along the waterfront **malecón**. Along the way plenty of museums, churches, mansions and fortresses repay consideration, though none, with the possible exception of the **archeological museum** in the Fuerte de San Miguel, that could really be described as a "must-see".

As you explore, it's worth remembering that even-numbered **streets** run parallel to the sea, starting inside the ramparts with Calle 8; odd-numbered streets run inland. The plaza, **Parque Principal**, is bordered by calles 8, 10, 55 and 57. Outside the ring of the old city wall, the grid system is less strictly adhered to; the **market**, immediately outside the wall on the landward side, is as far as you're likely to need to venture into the modern city except when you arrive or leave. Much of the city wall itself has been demolished and replaced by a ring road – the **Avenida Circuito Baluartes** – but two substantial sections survive, along with seven of the eight original *baluartes* (bulwarks). The city defences were completed by two large fortresses, overlooking the city from hills along the coast in either direction: the **Fuerte de San José** to the northwest, and the **Fuerte de San Miguel** to the southeast. Both now house museums – in the case of the Fuerte de San Miguel, the finest in the city. With the exception of the forts, everything that follows is in easy walking distance.

## The Parque Principal

The obvious starting point for exploring Campeche is the **Parque Principal**, the city's main plaza, and the fine colonial buildings that surround it. Chief among these is **La Catedral de Nuestra Señora de la Concepcion**, founded in 1540, the year the town was established, and one of the oldest churches on the peninsula. The bulk of the construction, though, took place much later, and what you see today is a relatively ordinary Baroque structure. Look inside for the chapel museum (daily 10am–2pm & 5–7pm; free) where the cathedral's relics and treasures are stored. Many of these are statues of saints that are paraded through the streets on their name-days. The centrepiece and highlight here is an amazing body of Christ, interred in a dark-wood and silver catafalque and attended by angels. It is not known where this came from, but it has been in the cathedral since at least the seventeenth century, and was probably made locally. Every Good Friday, it is carried through the streets by forty men.

Directly across the plaza, the **Centro Cultural Casa Seis** (daily 9am–9pm; free) is a mansion that has been restored to something approaching its nineteenth-century glory, with fine furnishings and paintings. The central patio is a giant cistern: rain that fell on the house was collected underneath, and could be drawn up from the well-like structure in the centre. Today Casa Seis hosts art exhibits and cultural performances, including musical *serenatas* most Thursday evenings, and there's a good café onsite. Around Casa Seis, less grand mansions in not as good repair house hotels, restaurants and offices.

On the seaward side of the plaza, in front of the city wall, a beautiful building contains the well-used public **library** (with a good reference section that's open to anyone). Formerly the city's main barracks, this structure comprised government offices before it was destroyed by Hurricane Isidore and rebuilt as a library. On the fourth, inland side of the square, elegant *portales* shelter a row of not very elegant shops.

## Around the plaza

Leaving the plaza to wander the old city streets, there are a number of other grand old houses that you can see inside – many converted to schools, hotels or offices. Two notable ones as you pass are the **Palacio Carvajal**, on Calle 10 between 51 and 53, an elaborate Moorish-style colonial house that was formerly the city home of the fabulously wealthy owners of Hacienda Uayamón (p.282), and the **Fundación José Ortiz Ávila**, in the former home of an ex-governor of the state at Calle 59 between 12 and 14. The former now houses government offices and has recently been closed for restoration, but can normally be visited informally; the latter contains Ávila's library and a huge collection of guns – opening hours are a bit erratic, but entry is free and it remains open till late in the evening.

There are plenty of colonial churches, too, most of them open sporadically for services. Among the finest is the **Templo de San José**, at the corner of calles 63 and 10. Though it was begun in the mid-seventeenth century, many of the church's most striking features date from the end of the eighteenth, in particular the wonderful tiled facade. One of the mismatching towers also incorporates Campeche's original lighthouse. The church is now part of the Instituto Campechano, so you can get in during school hours; you'll often find temporary exhibitions here. Another elegant sight is the church and monastery of **San Roque**, also known as San Francisquito, on Calle 12 between 59 and 61. Now housing the **Instituto Cultural**, it's open Monday to Friday 8am to 9pm and at weekends for special events and church services. There are richly decorated altars in the church as well as a beautiful courtyard where occasional art displays and concerts are staged.

## The city wall and museums

Immediately off the Parque Principal, behind the library, you'll find one of the best-preserved sections of the **city wall**. Here, on Calle 8 between calles 55 and 57, the **Museo de las Estelas** (Tues–Sat 8am–8pm, Sun 8am–6pm, Mon 8am–2pm; M$24) is housed in the Baluarte de la Soledad. The small but interesting collection of columns and faded stelae from Edzná and other local Maya sites here depict religious and civil ceremonies amongst other things; explanations are in Spanish only. From the battlements above there's an excellent view of the ruination of the seafront; the land outside the wall, reclaimed from the sea in the 1970s, is cluttered with ugly concrete hotels and stadia. Heading southwest along the line of the wall here takes you past the bizarre, flying-saucer-like Palacio Legislativo to the **Baluarte de San Carlos**, which has cannons on the battlemented roof and, underneath, the beginnings of a network of ancient tunnels that runs under much of the town. Mostly sealed off now, the tunnels provided refuge for the populace from pirate raids, and before that were probably used by the Maya. The *baluarte* houses Campeche's **Museo de la Ciudad** (daily 9am–8pm; M$24), a tiny but rather lovely collection of local memorabilia that includes excellent silver, models of ships, an ancient ship's compass and the like.

From here you could walk right around the old centre following the line of the wall, but in practice it's much more interesting to cut through the old streets. Those on this southwest side of town, calles 57, 59 and 61 for example, are far less commercial than those around the plaza, with more of a sense of history. Calle 59 will lead you eventually to the **Puerta de Tierra** (daily 8am–9pm; M$5 for access to wall), the main gate on the landward side, which now sits in the middle of another well-preserved stretch of wall. The elaborate defences here include a hole for pouring boiling oil straight down onto any attackers below. On a quiet day, you may have to ring the bell here for someone to come and let you out again. From the Puerta de Tierra you can walk along the top of the walls in either direction, to the Baluarte de San Juan or the Baluarte de San Francisco. It's shadeless and exposed on top of the wall, but there's an interesting contrast in views. From the **Baluarte de San Francisco** you can look out over the Alameda and market and some of the busiest parts of the new town; head towards the **Baluarte de San Juan** and turn in the other direction and you can gaze down over the neatly restored colonial facades to see just how much lies derelict behind them. Every Tuesday, Friday and Saturday this section of the wall hosts an enjoyable **sound-and-light show** (8.30pm; free), starting from the Puerta de Tierra which includes a walk along the wall in the company of the "soldiers" guarding it.

## Beyond the city wall

If you take the city *tranvía* tour you'll see much of what's interesting outside the city wall. Perhaps most striking is the way that, to the east especially, the *barrios* of San Martín, San Francisco and Guadalupe look little different from the city centre, their streets lined with low colonial houses, albeit here in a much less glamorous state of repair. Indeed these are some of the oldest parts of the city. There are good places to eat out here, including a number of *loncherías* under the arcades of the **Portales San Martín**, not far beyond the wall. Nearby, another of the city bulwarks, the Baluarte de Santiago, has been not very accurately reconstructed to house the **Jardín Botánico Xmuch'haltún** (Mon–Fri

8am–2pm & 5–8pm, Sat & Sun 8am–2pm), with a small collection of native plants.

Substantially further from the centre, the two outlying **forts**, in opposite directions along the coast, require transport to get to. Each is wonderfully preserved, with a dry moat and cannons among the battlements that still look ready to blast approaching ships out of the water. The **Fuerte de San Miguel**, on a height overlooking the coast some 4km to the southwest of the centre, is in fact one of the city's chief attractions – or at least the impressive **Museo Arqueológico** (Tues–Sun 9am–7.30pm; M$24) that it houses is. Though the information provided is in Spanish only, the beautiful relics, from all over the peninsula, speak for themselves. Maya artefacts from Edzná and Jaina predominate, including delicate Jaina figurines, many of which are cross-eyed (a feature that the Maya considered a mark of beauty). There's also some fine sculpture and pre-Hispanic gold, but the highlight is the treasure from the tombs at Calakmul. The most important of the burials is identified here (though the identification doesn't seem to be widely accepted) as that of the Calakmul ruler Jaguar Paw (see p.192); the jade death masks are mesmerizing and the jewellery and other objects that accompanied the dead fascinating. Take a look at the views over the ramparts, too, which are wonderful at sunset. To get here you can take a city bus along the coast road (look for "Lerma" or "Playa Bonita") but that will leave you with a stiff climb up the hill to the fort. An easier alternative is to take the *tranvía* or a taxi on the way out here and walk down to the road to get a bus back into town.

The **Fuerte de San José** (Tues–Sun 8am–8pm; M$24) occupies a similarly superb defensive position on a hill on the opposite side of the city. Another fine example of Spanish military architecture, completed in 1792, it houses a museum of armaments and assorted sundry items from the colonial era. Look out for the vast modern statue of Juárez on the ridge nearby. Getting here, the tactics are the same as for San Miguel, though if anything it's an even worse walk up; buses to look for are marked "Morelos" or "Bellavista."

Originally the city defences dropped straight into the sea, but now they face a reclaimed strip of land on which stand the spectacular (spectacularly ugly in most eyes) concrete Palacio de Gobierno and state legislature building, a series of striking **sculptures** representing various aspects of the city – piracy, warfare at sea, fishing – and several big hotels.

If you're desperate for **beaches**, take one of the buses along the waterfront marked "Playa Bonita" or "Lerma", two seaside destinations not far beyond San Miguel, south of the city. Playa Bonita is the better of the two, with palapas for shade or to hang your hammock under. Busy with locals at weekends and holiday times, it's likely to be empty and faintly depressing during the week.

## Eating and drinking

Restaurants abound in the centre of Campeche, especially along Calle 8 and Calle 10. **Seafood**, served almost everywhere, is a good bet; try the *pan de cazón* (a kind of lasagne made with layers of tortillas and shredded shark meat) or shrimps (*camarónes*) in spicy sauce. The café in the centre of the plaza serves excellent coffee and home-made ice cream, and Campeche's **market**, just north of the walled city, is surrounded by simple *comedores* offering cheap and tasty *comidas corridas*.

**Café La Terraza** C 63 between C 10 and C 12. Tiny place opposite the Church of San José serving sandwiches, juices, cakes and coffee in a cool interior courtyard.

**Restaurante Campeche** C 57 on the Parque Principal. Large, unfussy restaurant next door to the *Hotel Campeche*, with an extensive menu of Yucatecan specialities and Mexican food in general,

△ Sculptures near the seafront

all at reasonable prices.

**Casa Vieja** C 10 no. 319 on the Parque Principal. Cuban-owned and -themed restaurant with tables on a balcony overlooking the main square. Tasty food, but prices match the classy setting – you can just have a cocktail, however, and the rum is excellent.

**La Iguana Azul** C 55 no. 11. Gorgeously decorated colonial house opposite *La Parroquia*, with a warren of rooms. Up front is a large wooden bar; farther back, a lush courtyard. The reasonably priced menu includes local and Creole dishes.

**Restaurante Marganzo** C 8 no. 267 between C 57 and C 59. Rather touristy, but very pleasant and less expensive than it looks. The varied menu includes plenty of fish – try the *quesadillas de jaíba* (crab). Excellent breakfasts too.

**Nutrivida** C 12 no.157, between C 57 and C 59. Health-food store serving vegetarian and wholefood snacks, sandwiches, juices and the like. Mon–Fri 8am–2pm & 5.30–8.30pm, Sat 8am–2pm.

**La Palapa** Av Resurgimiento. Delicious *botanas* (bite-size snacks) are served with every drink at this large bar, a 30min walk south along the malecón from the city centre. There are plenty of other spots on the seafront in this direction, but most are on the opposite side of the street.

**La Parroquia** C 55 no. 8, between C 10 and C 12.

Traditional, family-run restaurant with high ceilings and a café atmosphere. Look for the excellent-value *pan de cazón* and other local dishes. Very popular with locals. Open 24hr.

**La Pigua** Av Miguel Alemán 179-A. One of the city's most traditional restaurants – and a favourite of local businessmen – this pretty, somewhat elegant lunch spot serves delicious seafood that can be enjoyed in an air-conditioned palapa. Not cheap, but certainly better value than many in the centre. Follow C 8 northeast beyond the wall. Daily 12.30–6pm.

**Sir Francis Drink** Av Miguel Alemán 143. Next door to *La Pigua* and under the same management, *Sir Francis Drink* is slightly cheaper and more touristy, with a thoroughly cheesy pirate theme, but the food is good, with seafood as the speciality. Daily 8am–6pm.

**Tortas El Flamboyan** C 8 between C 57 and C 59. Just half a block from the Parque Principal, this is a good place for a cheap sandwich lunch at a tiled counter.

**El Zaguán** C 59 no. 6, between C 10 and C 12. Small, friendly restaurant-bar, with tables in wooden booths, serving inexpensive but good local and Mexican specialities, including *pan de cazón* and *mole poblano*.

## Listings

**Airlines** Aeroméxico (☎1-800/021-4010 or 981/816-3109) operates a variety of internal flights.

**American Express** Inside the VI-PS travel agency, C 59 between Av Ruíz Cortines and Av 16 de Septiembre near the *Hotel del Mar*. Mon–Fri 9am–8pm, Sat 9am–1pm; ☎981/811-1100, ⊕816-8333.

**Banks** Banks and ATMs throughout the centre, for example at: C 8, corner C 59; C 8 between C 59 and C 57; C 8 in the government building opposite the Palacio Legislativo and Baluarte San Carlos; C 10, corner C 55 on the main square; C 10 at C 53 (Banamex); C 10 between C 53 and C 55.

**Bike rental** Rentamar (☎981/811-6461, ⊕rentamar@aol.com), C 59 opposite the American Express office, by *Hotel Baluartes*, rents bicycles (from M$40/hr) and motorbikes and mopeds (from M$100/hr).

**Buses** Separate terminals for first-class services from ADO, Sur and others, and second-class Autobuses del Sur, ATP and TRP (see p.271). For stopping buses on Hwy-180, or for Escárcega, Hopelchén, Bolonchén de Rejón and Iturbide (for the Chenes sites), you'll need the second-class terminal. For Edzná there are departures from the local terminal (see pp.272 & 281) at 7am, 8am, 9am and 10am.

**Car rental** Maya Car Rental (☎981/816-0670) in the *Hotel del Mar*, Localiza in the *Hotel Baluartes* (☎981/811-3187) or through one of the travel agencies listed below.

**Internet and phone facilities** There are Internet cafés on almost every street in the centre of Campeche, charging around M$10 per hour. Good ones for example on C 12 at C 61 and C 12 at C 59; the place on C 57 between C 10 and C 12 has long-distance phones and fax as well as Internet, and at C 55 between C10 and C 12 is one that stays open to 2am on weekends.

**Laundromats** Good ones include Klar, C 16 no. 305 at C 61, and Lave Klin, Av Circuito Baluartes Norte between C 14 and C 16. They charge by weight

– around M$10 per kilo.

**Post office** Av 16 de Septiembre at C 53, in the Palacio del Gobierno Federal (Mon–Fri 8.30am–3.30pm).

**Shopping** Casa de Artesanias Tukulná, C 10 no. 333 between C 59 and C 61, is a particularly well-stocked craft shop, with the added advantage of occupying a fine colonial house. The Librería Levante, C 12 between C 59 and C 61 next to the Instituto Cultural, is a wonderful place to browse glossy art books, though almost everything is in Spanish. Excellent hammocks made by inmates are sold for reasonable prices at stalls outside the local prison, about 12km north of town on the highway.

**Taxis** Taxis within the city are inexpensive. They're usually waiting at the bus stations, and there are taxi-stands throughout the centre. To call a cab try ☎981/816-2363, 816-2359 or 816-2355.

**Tours and travel agencies** Servicio Turístico Xtampak at C 57 no.14, between C 10 and C 12 (Mon–Sat 8am–3pm & 5–9pm; ☎981/811-6473) runs day-trips to Edzná (M$20 half-day transport only, from M$750 with guide, lunch and other excursions). Other tours include Calakmul, the Chenes sites, kayaking on the rivers around Champotón and birdwatching. Other operators include the *Monkey Hostel* (see Accommodation), Corazón Maya, located in the Baluarte San Pedro, C 18 and C 51 (☎981/816-8086, ⊛www.corazonmaya.cjb .net), and IMC, in the lobby of the *Hotel Baluartes* (☎981/811 7263, ⊛www.travel2mexico.com). For regular travel services, airline tickets and the like, try VI-PS (see American Express above) or the agencies in the lobbies of the hotels *del Mar* or *Baluartes*. The "pirate ship" *Lorencillo* sails twice daily (Tues–Sun noon and 5pm; M$50) on a 90-minute trip into the Gulf from the port at Lerma. Transport from the city centre (M$20) meets each sailing, leaving 45 minutes earlier from Av 16 de Septiembre at the bottom of C 59.

# Edzná and the Chenes sites

Some 50km from Campeche lie the ruins of **Edzná**; beyond them, Hwy-261 leads towards Hopelchén and the main **Chenes sites** of Hochob, Dzibilnocac, El Tabasqueño and Santa Rosa Xtampak. Edzná is the biggest, the best known and the most easily accessible of these sites, though it is far from a pure example of the Chenes style, as it also features elements of Río Bec, Puuc and Classic Maya design. The other sites are tough to get to unless you have your own transport, and often have just one important structure. However, the buildings are spectacular and there's a real sense of adventure in getting there – especially as you may well be the only visitor.

## The Chenes style

Chenes **architecture** is characterized by highly decorative facades, often on relatively small buildings. Above all it features buildings whose doorways form the mouth of a giant mask, created out of stone reliefs, that often takes up the entire front of the building. Most frequently the mask represents Itzamná, the Maya creator god, in the form of a giant serpent. *Chen* means "well" in local Maya and is a fairly common suffix to place names in this region, where towns have grown up around these sources of water. The Maya cities were no doubt equally dependent on wells, but they're not in evidence at any of the sites.

## Edzná

Yet another Maya site that's far more impressive than its relative obscurity might suggest, **EDZNÁ** (daily 8am–5pm; M\$33) reached the height of its power very early, in the pre-Classic period from around 250 BC to about 150 AD. At this time, the flood-prone, marshy valley in which Edzná lies was transformed by a drainage system of canals, aqueducts (one stretching 12km) and reservoirs into highly productive, terraced agricultural land supporting a population of thousands. Handily located on major trade routes between the coast and the Maya highlands, Edzná became the dominant power in the region. After 150 AD, however, possibly as a result of war, the city declined and there was virtually no more building until the height of the Classic era, from 600 AD onwards. Most of what you see now dates from around 700–900 AD; you'll need a minimum of an hour to visit.

The main plaza of Edzná is dominated by the raised **Gran Acrópolis**, atop which stands the site's largest and most famous structure, the great **Templo de los Cinco Pisos** (Temple of the Five Storeys). A stepped palace-pyramid more than 30m high, each of its storeys contains chambered "palace" rooms: while solid temple pyramids and multi-storey "apartment" complexes are relatively common, it is rare to see the two combined in one building. At the front, a steep monumental staircase leads to a three-room temple, topped by a roofcomb. It's a hot climb, but the view from the temple is one of the most impressive in the Yucatán. On the way up, notice the hieroglyphic inscriptions (as yet undeciphered) on the first four steps and, halfway, three giant, much-ruined masks. At the top, looking out over two plazas, the farthest of which must have been capable of holding tens of thousands of people, it is easy to imagine the power that the high priest or king commanded. Beyond lie the unexcavated remains of other large pyramids, and behind them, the vast flat expanse of the Yucatán plain. Inside the west-facing temple a stele of the god of maize was illuminated by the setting sun twice a year, on the dates for the planting and harvesting of maize.

Descend back to the Gran Acrópolis, where the **Templo del Norte** demonstrates two separate stages of construction; an original pyramid with stepped sides, and a later one faced with sloping stone. Behind it, the **Patio Puuc** has the characteristic columnar decoration of the Puuc style. Down in the main plaza itself, the clear line of two ceremonial *sacbeob* can be seen leading away from the Gran Acrópolis. The **Nohochná** (Casa Grande or Big House), across from the Gran Acrópolis, is some 55m long and includes a room used as a *temazcal* (sauna), with stone benches and hearths over which water could be boiled. The steps on its front may have been used as seating for events and rituals in the plaza – the acoustics at the site allow you to hear clearly announcements made from the top of the Templo de los Cinco Pisos. The buildings around the

**Pequeña Acrópolis** are rather older and smaller, but impressively decorated, above all the **Templo de los Mascarones**, where two haunting stucco masks represent the Sun god – rising on the east (left-hand) side, setting on the west. If you walk beyond this main, cleared area, following the signs to the **Vieja Hechicera**, you'll get a better idea of the scale of the original city, and also of the tasks faced by its builders – there's a great deal of water and marshy ground here. At the end of the path, some five minutes' walk, is another large plaza, with the partially restored pyramid rising from it.

## Practicalities

It's relatively easy to get here by **bus** from Campeche. There are departures from the Sur terminal on Avenida Republica (see p.272) at 7am, 8am, 9am and 10am which will drop you at the entrance; check with the driver for return or onward options. The last ride back to Campeche is at 3.30pm. Alternatively, there are plenty of **organized trips** from Campeche (see p.279) and going further afield.

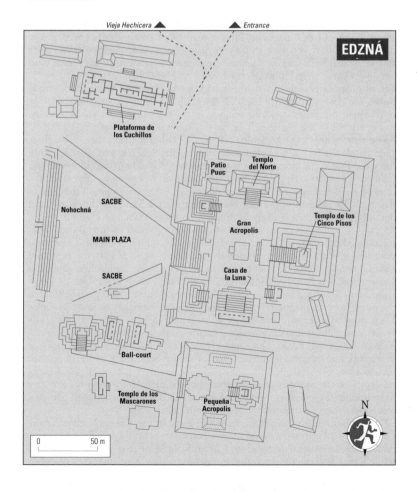

Vieja Hechicera ▲          ▲ Entrance

**EDZNÁ**

Plataforma de los Cuchillos

Patio Puuc

Templo del Norte

SACBE

Nohochná

Templo de los Cinco Pisos

Gran Acropolis

MAIN PLAZA

Casa de la Luna

SACBE

Ball-court

Templo de los Mascarones

Pequeña Acropolis

N

0          50 m

The only **accommodation** closer than what's in Campeche is at the wonderful and congenial *Hacienda Uayamón* (☎981/829-7257, ⒲www .starwoodhotels.com/luxury; ❾), off the old Campeche-Edzná road (via China). Certainly the hacienda was one of the grandest of all in its day. Founded as a cattle ranch as early as the sixteenth century, its vast lands were raided by pirates in the seventeenth, but it reached its height in the nineteenth century, when its production of sugar, logwood and, above all, henequen made it one of the largest, wealthiest and most famous haciendas in the country, with its own station on the main line from Mexico City. Most of the rooms – each individual, and many with a private outdoor terrace and plunge pool – are in the old workers' housing scattered through the extensive grounds. There's exuberant birdlife here, and armadillos and other small animals are often seen around the rooms. The roofless old machine room now contains a pool, there's a restaurant in the *casa principal*, and amenities from horse-riding to massage are on offer.

## The Chenes sites

Examples of true **Chenes** style are accessible only with a car or exceptional determination. The chief sites are reached from the village of **Hopelchén**, about 90km east of Campeche. Here a road heads south, newly paved all the way to Xpuhil; if you take it, be sure to fill your tank at Hopelchén, as it's almost 200km with very few services, especially as you get further south onto the newly paved stretch through tropical forest. Hopelchén itself has basic facilities, including a branch of Bancomer with an ATM on the plaza, and a simple **hotel**, *Los Arcos* (☎01996/822-0123; ❸), Calle 23 on the corner of the plaza, near where the buses stop. You might also want to check out the interesting woodcarvings in the eighteenth-century Church of San Antonio de Padua.

The first of the local archeological sites is **Tohcok** (daily 8am–5pm, free), right beside the highway, immediately outside Hopelchén as you approach from the west. This is no more than a single unrestored building, but it's worth five minutes as you drive past; the friendly site guardian will point out the main features in rapid-fire Spanish. The more significant Chenes sites lie off the road to the south. **El Tabasqueño** (daily 8am–5pm, free), reached by a 4km track from the village of Pakchén, and about 30km from Hopelchén, has a temple with a doorway in the form of the mouth of a monster (typical of the Chenes style) surrounded by masks of Chac as well as a tower, which is unusual. The most beautiful of the Chenes sites, **Hochob** (daily 8am–5pm, M$24), can be found 15km down a paved side road that turns off just outside Dzibalchén. Even this is very small – it basically consists of a lovely little hilltop plaza with one very elaborately decorated building; other structures are buried, barely perceptibly, in the jungly forest all around. That main building (romantically named "Structure 1") is amazingly beautiful, however – a three-room temple (low and fairly small, as are most Chenes buildings) with a facade entirely covered in richly carved, stylized snakes and masks. The central chamber is surmounted by a crumbling roofcomb, and its decoration takes the form of a huge mask of Itzamná, with the doorway in the shape of a gaping mouth: to either side are hooked fangs, while above are the eyes and to either side elaborate decoration on the ears. Surrounding the plaza are other small structures (including one with part of a roofcomb), their facades softly carpeted with green moss.

**Dzibilnocac** (daily 8am–5pm, free), the Place of the Painted Vault or of the Great Painted Turtle, is something of a contrast – a very large, flat site that is undergoing substantial restoration. Currently, little of it is open to view, but while there's nothing to match the beauty of Hochob there are plenty of elaborate facades and masks typical of the Chenes style, and one very pretty little pyramid with an elaborate temple on top. Dzibilnocac is also the one Chenes site that's relatively easily accessible by bus. It lies on the edge of the small town of Iturbide (or Vicente Guerrero, as many of the road signs and buses know it), 18km down a badly potholed road from Dzibalchén, which has a frequent second-class service from Hopelchén and Campeche. To be on the safe side, arrive early and check return times on arrival.

In the other direction from Hopelchén, Hwy-261 north towards Mérida passes one other Chenes site at **Santa Rosa Xtampak** (daily 8am–5pm, M$24), 32km off the highway on a rough paved road. Only recently rediscovered and partly restored, this site mirrors Edzná in history (it was developed very early – Xtampak means "old walls"), style (predominantly Chenes, but with Puuc and a variety of other influences), size and importance. In its heyday there were no less than ten ceremonial plazas here, built across a naturally raised but artificially levelled platform. Numerous semi-ruined structures can still be explored, the most important of them being the three-storey palace. As at all of these sites, masks of Chac and doorways in the form of mouths are constant motifs.

Back on the main highway, you pass the **Grutas de Xtacumbilxunaan** (daily 9am–5pm, M$30) shortly before Bolonchén de Rejón. This cave system is another that claims to be the largest in the peninsula, and certainly it's an impressively vast hole, some 350m deep, into which you descend. At times there are tours, but normally you simply head down on your own: although there's electric light and concrete paths this can be unnerving if you're here alone, as during the week you probably will be. At weekends Mexican families arrive to use the picnic area at the entrance and swim in the underground cenotes. **Bolonchén** itself is an attractive little town, with nine decorative wells outside its church (Bolonchén in fact means "nine wells"), but offers no compelling reason to stop.

△ Hochob

# South from Campeche

South of Campeche, Hwy-180 splits again into free (*libre*) and toll (*cuota*) roads. The old seafront route is winding and scenic, alternating between rolling hills fuzzy with sea grass and reeds, and striking vistas onto the green Gulf waters; the only flaw is that it can be very slow, especially given the likelihood of tailing an underpowered delivery truck servicing the small towns along the way. The toll highway, however unremarkable, is straight, fast and easy. It ends just outside **Champotón**, a sleepy port at the mouth of the Champotón River that's famous for its seafood cocktails. Here, Hwy-261 heads due south towards Francisco **Escárcega**, where it meets cross-country Hwy-186: to the east this will take you past the Río Bec sites to Chetumal and the Riviera Maya; west it heads towards Palenque and Villahermosa, with the opportunity to turn off for **Candelaria** and the site of **El Tigre**, both in the wildlife-rich, little visited valley of the Candelaria river. Hwy-180 meanwhile heads southwest to the Isla del Carmen and the steamy oil port of **Ciudad del Carmen**, en route to Villahermosa via the coast.

## Along the coast

Leaving Campeche on the free **coastal road** you head first through **Lerma**, the city's port, with major oil facilities and a sizeable fishing fleet. There are some good fish restaurants here, but it's not an even remotely attractive place. Immediately afterwards you hit the town beaches at Playa Bonita (see p.277) before a long, winding inland stretch of road eventually ends on the coast at **Seybaplaya**. A torpid place, stretching for miles along the coast, Seybaplaya is home to dozens of small fishing boats and thousands of pelicans and other seabirds. From here on, southern Campeche State is low, flat, hot and monotonous; along the coast the white sand **beaches** frequently look tempting, but they're generally less attractive close up, with coarse sand and shallow water that smells none too clean. There are usually thousands of shells, though, and the beaches along this stretch of coast, from Campeche all the way down to Ciudad del Carmen, are important breeding grounds for green and endangered Kemp's Ridley and hawksbill **turtles**. There are a number of places where the turtles are protected and where, in nesting season (May to September, but busiest in July and August), you may be able to witness the young turtles making their way to the sea. There are reserves at Seybaplaya, for example, and at Isla Aguada right by the northern end of the Puente la Unidad; visits, though, are probably best arranged as a tour from Campeche, as there may well be no one around if you just turn up.

The free and toll roads come together again near **Champotón**, a growing fishing village at the mouth of the broad Río Champotón. Here in 1517 a Spanish force under Francisco Hernández de Cordoba landed – having been driven away from Campeche and caught in a storm – to replenish their stocks of fresh water. They were surprised by a Maya force and heavily defeated; Hernández de Cordoba died of his wounds a few days later, and the place became known as the Bay of the Bad Fight. Today it's more famous for delicious and fabulously cheap shrimp cocktails and *ceviche*, served up at *coctelerías* all along the surrounding beaches. Trips upstream, where there's kayaking, fishing and a chance to visit a couple of crumbling haciendas, can also be organized, most easily at one of the tour agencies in Campeche. If you do want to arrange one locally, enquire at one of the local **hotels**, the *Snook Inn* (☎982/828-0018, ✉snookinnchampoton@hotmail.com; ❺), a modern, motel-style place with a pool and TV and

a/c in all rooms, or the *Hotel Geminis* (☎982/828-0008, ✉marcastl@yahoo
.com.mx; ❹–❺), somewhat older, simpler and cheaper, but also with a pool and
optional a/c and TV. Both are on Calle 30 close to the main road and the mouth
of the river, and right by the bus station and market.

Most visitors heading in this direction turn inland at Champotón, on their
way southeast towards Escárcega for Chetumal or Palenque. If you're heading
to Villahermosa, however, opt for the improved highway south of Champotón
en route to **Ciudad del Carmen**. Although this isn't really a compelling destination, the drive down the coast is fast and pretty, passing along some lovely
stretches of beach. At **Isla Aguada**, the Puenta de la Unidad (M$42 toll) crosses
the eastern entrance to the Laguna de Terminos, joining the Isla del Carmen
to the mainland. If you're driving be careful not to exceed the 50-kph speed
limit; traffic cops posted at either end of the bridge are notorious for demanding heavy fines on the spot. Locals fish off the bridge, and in the evening you'll
often see kids holding up strings of fish for sale.

# Ciudad del Carmen

The only town of any size on the 35-kilometre-long Isla del Carmen, **CIU-
DAD DEL CARMEN** doesn't merit a special trip except perhaps during its
lively **fiesta** in the second half of July, celebrating the town's namesake, Our
Lady of Carmen. If you do wind up here, you'll find a place that offers occasionally bizarre contrasts. Sprawling for miles around is evidence of new-found
wealth (from oil, and from it being the home port of one of Mexico's largest
fishing fleets), such as traffic-jammed outskirts full of shopping malls, Holiday
Inns and motels. One traffic circle sports an enormous bronze shrimp (giant
shrimp and prawns for export are the fishing fleet's chief catch).

Penetrate as far as the seafront **Plaza Central** (bounded by Calles 24 and 22,
parallel to the shore, and by Calles 31 and 33), however, and there's a small-town
Mexican feel, hot and crowded. A renovated malecón runs along the seafront,
and from here the source of the town's growth is immediately apparent – there
are oil rigs just yards offshore. In this seafront area are the few relics of the
town's colonial past too. The conquistadors landed here in 1518, but the first
permanent settlers were pirates (see p.272), for whom the isolated island made
an ideal base from which to prey on shipping in the Gulf. To see what little of
the old town survives, head south from the plaza to calles 22 and 25, where the
pretty Iglesia de Jesús presides over the **Parque Juárez**, a beautifully preserved
colonial square. North on Calle 22, a small **museum** (daily 8am–8pm; M$15)
has an imaginative display charting the history of the city.

## Practicalities

Modern Ciudad del Carmen is a very big place, but once you've found your
way to the central plaza there's no need to stray more than a few blocks – if
you've negotiated the traffic, you probably won't want to. ADO (first-class) and
Sur (second-class) **buses** use the same station on Avenida Periférica Oriente,
a very long way out. To get to the centre, take a taxi or colectivo (5am–11pm;
about 20min). There's a downtown ADO ticket office on Calle 24, next to
the *Hotel Zacarias*. There's also a surprisingly busy little **airport**, not far off
the highway east of town. From here, a taxi will be your only option. The
**tourist desk** (Mon–Sat 9am–9pm) in the modern government offices on
the malecón, in front of the central plaza, is helpful but not always manned
and, though they have plenty of information on Campeche State, there's little
about Ciudad del Carmen itself apart from an incomprehensible map. You'll

find several **banks** on Calle 24 just south of the plaza: Banamex and Bancomer, both at the junction with Calle 29-B, have **ATMs**, and there's another in the Ayuntamiento building, on the seaward side of the plaza. The **post office** (Mon–Fri 9am–3pm) is on the corner of Calle 22 and Calle 27. There's a handy **Internet café** in the Plaza Delfin, on Calle 20 across from the Plaza de Artesanías y Restaurantes.

Most of the accessible budget **accommodation** in town is around the plaza near the waterfront. At fiesta time places fill up, so book ahead. The big, basic *Hotel Zacarias* (T 938/382-3506; ❹), on the plaza at the corner of Calle 24 and Calle 31, has rooms with a choice of a/c or fan; *Hotel Victoria* (T 938/382-9301; ❺), at Calle 24 and Calle 27, is a little more comfortable but not great value. More luxurious is the *Hotel del Parque*, on Calle 33 between the plaza and the waterfront (T 938/382-3046; ❻), where all rooms have a/c, TV and a phone. **Food** in Ciudad del Carmen is a mixture of specialities from the Yucatán Peninsula and the more spicy flavours of the state of Tabasco, with a stress on shellfish. Immediately north of the plaza, a huge new white footbridge crosses to the malecón. At the landward end of this is the Plaza de Artesanías y Restaurantes, with more than a dozen small restaurants, cafés and *neverías* (though not much sign of *artesanías*); beyond this lies the market area and the town's more commercial streets. Other options include *Portal Regis*, in the pedestrianized section of Calle 33 by the main church, with tables right on the plaza and a good-value lunchtime *comida*; and *La Fuente,* Calle 20 and Calle 29, on the waterfront, a traditional Mexican café serving simple food round the clock. More upmarket hangouts favoured by expat oilmen include *Los Pelicanos,* Calle 24 between calles 29 and 29-A, with a Tex-Mex menu and a well-stocked bar that's a popular early evening hangout, and *Il Giglio*, a pricey pizzeria/Italian restaurant nearby on Calle 24, opposite the *Hotel Victoria*.

## Francisco Escárcega

Hot as hell and not a great deal more pleasant, the dusty town of **FRAN-CISCO ESCÁRCEGA** (always referred to as Escárcega), which straggles along the road and old train tracks for a couple of kilometres, is not somewhere to hang out longer than you have to – though it's likely you will put in some time here, given its status as a major junction of bus routes. If you're heading to or from Xpuhil and Calakmul along the Río Bec (see p.186), or by direct road to Chetumal, or to Palenque, this could be the spot where you'll have to make a transfer.

Heading south from Champotón on the inland route, Hwy-261 meets the east–west Hwy-186 at Escárcega. The ADO bus station is on the edge of town at the junction with the highway; from there, it's 1500m straight up what becomes the town's main drag – a long walk or a short cab ride – to the centre and the Sur second-class bus station (this too may move to the outskirts soon). In the **centre** there's a branch of Bancomer with an **ATM** on Calle 27, more or less opposite the Sur terminal, and there are numerous basic places to eat and some very grungey hotels nearby. There are rather better **food and lodging** options near the ADO. Of the cluster of restaurants around the road junction, try *La Teja*. The garishly painted *Hotel Escárcega* (Av. Justo Sierra no.86; T 982/824-0186; ❹) is the pick of the largely unappealing hotels on the town's main drag, with modern rooms with a/c (at a substantial premium) or fan. It's not particularly close to either bus station, though walkable from ADO if you're not too laden down – otherwise take a taxi or *triciclo*. There's a little **tourist office** on the highway at the western edge of town.

# El Tigre and Candelaria

The site of **EL TIGRE** (daily 8am–5pm, M$24) is 75km from the highway via a road that is very badly potholed in places – it's a diversion that, even with your own vehicle, will take at least three hours plus time spent at the site. Not surprisingly, many people don't make it down here – if you do, yours may be the first name in the visitors' book for days.

El Tigre is often identified as Itzamkanac, which is where Cortés had the last Aztec emperor, Cuauhtemoc, executed in 1524; he also found extensive cocoa plantations here, and supposedly built many bridges. Certainly there's plenty of water: from the high ground the site occupies there are wonderful views over the Río Candelaria and its wetlands, and the ancient city had an important river port that gave it widespread trade connections – the port is being excavated, but is not part of the site you see. The part you do see consists primarily of a small plaza with a ball-court below it. The main pyramid here has a huge stucco mask, and there are two more, similar to those at Edzná, on the smaller pyramid nearby. They're easily spotted because of their thatched protective roofs. Major excavation is ongoing here, with dozens of workers frequently on site and lots of clearance work being carried out. This new work involves relatively little reconstruction, and what there is uses different coloured materials so that it is immediately apparent what is original and what's new.

The drive down here from the highway is an interesting one, through land that has been relatively recently settled and cleared of forest. In an attempt to help preserve what is left, the state government is promoting eco-tourism in the region, and you can get numerous glossy leaflets at tourist offices or in various hotels. Their efforts centre on the town of **CANDELARIA**, where there's an impressive bridge over the equally impressive Río Candelaria. This is a pleasant small town, and the river nearby offers waterfalls and wonderful opportunities for observing bird and animal life. To date, however, there's almost no infrastructure to support the eco-tourism claims, apart from the ability to hire a *lancha* for a trip on the river through one of the **hotels**. If you do want **to stay** here, the *Hotel Itzamkanac*, on the main road through town (℡982/826-0127; ❺) has very pleasant rooms with a/c, or the *Hotel del Bosque* (℡982/826-0395; ❹), signed just off the road as you come into town, is a simpler place with fan-cooled or a/c rooms. *Restaurante Lupita*, next to the *Hotel Itzamkanac*, is a friendly spot serving excellent plain meals and an inexpensive lunchtime *comida*.

# Travel details

## Buses

**Campeche** to: Mérida (daily, hourly first class; at least 50 daily second-class); Escárcega (daily, hourly); Iturbide (12 daily); Ciudad del Carmen (6 daily); Xpuhil (4 daily); Santa Elena/Uxmal (5 daily); Hopelchén and Bolonchén de Rejón (daily, hourly); Cancún (5 daily); Ciudad del Carmen (12 daily); Escárcega (daily, hourly); Villahermosa (15 daily); Chetumal (12 daily), Santa Elena/Uxmal (4 daily), Hopelchén and Bolonchén de Rejón (10 daily); Palenque/San Cristóbal de las Casas/Tuxtla Gutiérrez (2 daily).

**Escárcega** to: Mérida (at least 9 first-class daily); Cancún (7 first-class daily; most at night); Villahermosa (12 first-class, 5 second-class daily); Chetumal (12 first-class, 4 second-class daily); Campeche (12 first-class, 22 second-class, daily); Palenque (3 first-class daily; two are in the middle of the night); Ciudad del Carmen (8 second-class daily); Xpuhil (4 second-class daily).

## Flights

Perhaps because it is so close to Mérida, **Campeche**'s "international airport", currently has no international flights and only a few domestic ones, though AeroMexico does fly to Mexico City three times a day. Surprisingly, **Ciudad del Carmen**'s airport is busier, with daily flights to Houston on Continental, occasional direct flights to other US cities, and at least twice-daily service to both Villahermosa and Mexico City with Mexicana.

# 9

# Palenque and Villahermosa

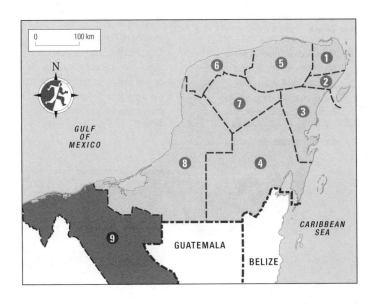

# CHAPTER 9

# Highlights

**✳ Parque La Venta** Don't miss the giant stone heads at this reconstructed Olmec site in the heart of Villahermosa. **P.296**

**✳ Palenque** Among the greatest achievements of the Maya, Palenque has a setting dramatic enough to more than do justice to its architecture. **P.303**

**✳ Wildlife** You don't have to travel far for exotic wildlife, but there are fabulous spotting opportunities above all in the protected wetlands of the Pantanos de Centla and in the unspoilt tropical forests that crowd the Guatemalan border. **P.302 & P.317**

**✳ Waterfalls** West of Palenque, a series of rivers running off the mountains forms a string of spectacular waterfalls, most famously at Agua Azul and Misol-Há. **P.311**

**✳ Yaxchilán** Set on the riverbank in the midst of thick forest, and accessible only by boat, there's a real sense of adventure about a journey to the Maya site of Yaxchilán. **P.317**

△ Agua Azul

# Palenque and Villahermosa

Though not technically part of the Yucatán, **Palenque** and **Villaher-mosa**, across the state borders in Chiapas and Tabasco respectively, are culturally and historically bound to the peninsula. There's no doubt that the great Maya site of Palenque, which sits on the very edge of the vast plain of the Yucatán, where the land starts to rise towards the Chiapas highlands, is intimately connected to the sites of the Yucatán Maya. The entire region, in fact, with its slow-moving **tropical rivers** making their way to the Gulf, was a vital trade highway for the ancient Maya, as it was for the Olmec before them. In addition to Palenque, the region boasts important Maya sites at **Bonampak** and **Yaxchilán**, on the banks of the mighty **Río Usumacinta**, as well as at **Toniná**, higher in the mountains near the town of **Ocosingo**. All of these, as well as the magnificent **waterfalls** that tumble down alongside the road from Ocosingo to Palenque, can easily be visited on day-trips if you're based at Palenque.

**Villahermosa**, capital of the state of Tabasco, is by far the largest city in the region, and a virtually unavoidable road junction, especially if you're travelling by bus. At its supreme attraction, the Parque La Venta, you'll find the most important objects from the Olmec site of La Venta (including the giant basalt heads for which the Olmec culture is primarily known) displayed in a steamy jungle setting. This is one of the very few opportunities to witness anything of the Olmec culture.

Not far from Villahermosa, the Maya site of **Comalcalco** lies en route to the coast. Here, almost uniquely, an abundance of clay and shortage of stone meant that the Maya constructed their pyramids from bricks, making for an extraordinary and unexpected site. The **coast** itself, with alternating estuaries and sand bars, salt marshes and lagoons, is well off the beaten track. A road runs very close to the shore, however, enabling you to reach the deserted beaches. As yet these have somewhat limited facilities – even the main coastal town, **Paraíso**, is a tiny place.

This area is also exceptionally rich in **wildlife**, and you'll experience this above all if you visit Bonampak or Yaxchilán, off the Frontier Highway at the edge of Mexico's last unspoilt tropical forests. Though development is making inroads at a frightening pace, vast tracts of forest are protected, and a little adventure will guarantee some exotic sightings. Monkeys are common at many

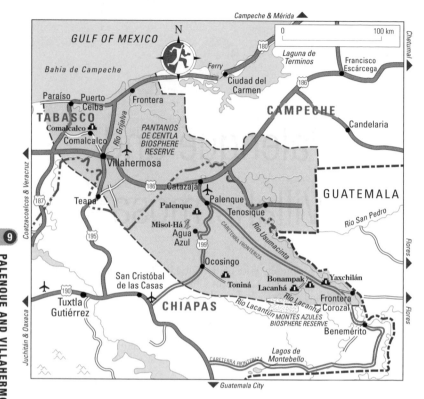

of the sites, as are birds of every description and crocodiles basking on the banks of the Río Usumacinta. As they approach the sea, the rivers come together to form vast flood plains where again natural reserves have been created, most accessibly at the Pantanos de Centla Biosphere Reserve, to protect the unique flora and fauna.

# Villahermosa

At first sight, **VILLAHERMOSA** – or "Beautiful Town" – certainly doesn't live up to its name. Sprawling and crowded, traffic-choked and manic, it feels far more like a big city than Mérida or anywhere else in the Yucatán. Stay a while longer, though, and the place can start to grow on you, with its spacious parks and revitalized downtown, where sudden vistas of the broad sweep of the **Río Grijalva** appear amid attractive plazas, and ancient streets are interspersed with impressive ultramodern buildings, art galleries and museums. In the evening, as the traffic disperses and the city cools down, its appeal is heightened further.

Most visitors rightly confine their explorations to a relatively small area downtown and to the essential **Parque La Venta**. This outdoor archeological exhibition and zoo, on the bank of a lagoon some 3km from the centre, is beyond doubt the highlight of any visit. It provides one of the few accessible glimpses of the ancient **Olmec** civilization, set in a surprisingly authentic jungle atmosphere. Downtown, the focus of interest lies in the pedestrianized streets of the **Zona Remodelada** (also known as Zona Luz or simply La Zona), where the Río Grijalva flows alongside the oldest part of the city. This lively area is bordered by two main squares, the **Parque Juárez** to the north and the **Plaza de Armas**, or zócalo, to the south. Everything here is in easy walking distance and you can also walk, or take a short bus or taxi ride, to the riverside **CICOM** complex, with its major archeological museum. One final trip you might want to make is to the ambitious **Yumká** safari park, in the outskirts near the airport.

## Arrival and information

Villahermosa's busy regional **airport**, the Aeropuerto Carlos A. Rovirosa, lies about 13km east of the centre on the main road towards Escárcega and Palenque. No buses run to the centre from here; a taxi will set you back around M$170. Arriving at one of the **bus stations**, you'll find things are pretty hectic as the highway thunders past through the concrete outskirts. The **first-class** terminal (known simply as ADO) is an efficient modern building just off the main highway through town on Javiér Mina. There's a *guardería* here (daily 7am–8pm; M$5 per item) and a small tourist information booth. To get to the centre there are reasonably priced taxis or a number of *combis* passing outside the terminal – look for those labelled "Parque Juárez" or "Malecón". Otherwise, it's at least twenty minutes' walk to town: head up Merino or Fuentes, opposite the station, for six or seven long blocks, and then turn right at Madero, which will eventually get you to the zócalo (Plaza de Armas), past most of the cheap hotels.

To get from ADO to the **second-class terminal**, turn left on Mina, walk three blocks down to the highway, Bulevar Adolfo Ruíz Cortines, turn right and cross it on the overpass. Not all second-class buses actually use the main terminal, but they all stop within a block or so – as ever, it's thoroughly crowded and chaotic. To get from here to the centre, head east along Ruíz Cortines towards the river, then turn right to follow Madero towards the centre. Outside the second-class terminal, **combis** are plentiful – look for "Madero", for example, or "CICOM" – but it's sometimes difficult to know where they're going. **Taxis** are around, too, but not as easy to find as at ADO. If you drive in, be warned that parking can be elusive near the centre.

Despite the growth in visitor numbers, there's no really handy **tourist office** in Villahermosa. The small booths at the airport, ADO, history museum and Parque La Venta have a jumble of leaflets (more on the state than the city, and also available at many hotels), but nothing very useful. The main state and federal office (Mon–Fri 8am–6pm, Sat 8am–1pm; ☎993/316-2889, ext 217) is in government buildings at the junction of Paseo Tabasco and Avenida de los Ríos, near the Tabasco 2000 shopping centre and modern hotel area, and too far away from the centre to be of much use.

## Accommodation

**Hotels** in Villahermosa don't come cheap, though you will find some reasonable-value hotels in the centre if you look hard enough. Some of the best **budget** options are on Madero or Lerdo de Tejada, close to the heart of things. There are a couple of business hotels near the zócalo, but more **upmarket** hotels are generally further out, particularly in the modern hotel area around Tabasco 2000 (see p.298), not far from La Venta but well away from the centre.

Most of the big chains have a place here, but even so rooms can be hard to come by when there's a conference on.

**Cencali** Paseo Tabasco and Juárez ☎ 993/315-1999, 🌐 www.cencali.com.mx. The best-value spot in the Tabasco 2000 area. Set in quiet, luxuriant gardens on the shore of a lagoon, the *Cencali* has an inviting pool, comfortable, well-furnished rooms with a/c, and suites with beautiful tiled bathrooms; upstairs rooms have balconies. ❾

**Del Centro** Madero 411 ☎ no tel. Simple apartments with bath, TV and separate sitting room – excellent value for longer stays.

**Howard Johnson** Aldama 404 ☎/🖷 993/314-4645, 🌐 www.hojo.com.mx. Just what you'd expect from the chain: comfortable, modern a/c rooms and suites with great bathrooms, TV and phone. Refurbished rooms on the upper floors are better. Free parking. ❼

**Miraflores** Reforma 304 ☎ 993/312-0022, 🌐 www.miraflores.com.mx. One of the better-value business class options in La Zona with all of the amenities that you would expect at this price, including a couple of bars. Parking. ❻

**Oriente** Madero 425 ☎ 993/312-0121, 🖷 312-1101. Offers clean, tiled rooms with TV and modern, private bathrooms. Fan ❹ a/c ❺

**Palomino Palace** Javier Mina at corner of Fuentes, across from ADO terminal ☎ 993/312-8431. Conveniently located for late arrivals and usually has rooms available, but overpriced for what you get. Rooms, some with a/c, all have private shower and TV. Bar and restaurant. ❺

**Plaza Independencia** Independencia 123 ☎ 993/312-1299, 🌐 www.hotelesplaza.com.mx. Well-furnished, comfortable rooms and suites in a quiet area just off the zócalo and handy for CICOM. There's a lift, a pool, a good restaurant, a bar with live music and free off-street parking. ❼

**Provincia Express** Lerdo de Tejada 303 ☎ 993/314-5376, 🖷 314-5442. Cramped rooms in this budget business hotel all have a/c, private bath, TV and phone. ❻

**San Miguel** Lerdo de Tejada 315 ☎ 993/312-1426. The cheapest option in the area. Rooms are very basic (despite the fact that some have a/c, TV and private bath), but at least the sheets are clean. ❹

**Tabasco** Lerdo de Tejada 317 ☎/🖷 993/312-0077. Spartan but functional place similar to adjacent *San Miguel*. In a good location in the Zona Luz. ❹

## The city

The Parque La Venta, whose forest setting offers an accessible glimpse of the Olmec civilization as well as a fine zoo, is Villahermosa's must-see attraction. Downtown, everything of interest is confined to a relatively small area between the two main squares, the Parque Juárez to the north and the Plaza de Armas, or zócalo, in the south. Here the attractive plazas and quiet ancient streets, interspersed with impressive ultramodern buildings, art galleries and museums, offer unexpected vistas of the broad sweep of the Río Grijalva. In the evening, as the traffic disperses and the city cools down, its appeal is heightened; everything is open late and people enjoy strolling the pedestrianized streets around this Zona Remodelada. On the outskirts near the airport, you'll find the entertaining Yumká, an expertly run safari park that allows you to step out into the African wild.

## Downtown

The oldest part of Villahermosa can be found **downtown**, in the **Zona Remodelada**, where vestiges of the nineteenth-century city (the original colonial buildings were built mostly of wood and have perished) survive on streets busy with shoppers and commerce. Many of the main shopping blocks are now pedestrianized, and the buildings along them are gradually being cleaned up and restored. At the northern end of the Zona the Parque Juárez, at the junction of Madero and Zaragoza, is bustling in the evenings, as crowds swirl around watching the street entertainers. Opposite, on Madero, the futuristic glass **Centro Cultural de Villahermosa** (Tues–Sun 10am–8pm; free) presents changing exhibitions of art, photography, and costume, as well as film screenings and concerts, plus a good café. Works in the exhibitions are usually for sale.

△ Casa de Azulejos

In the centre of the Zona, on the corner of Sáenz and Lerdo, the distinctive pink and purple paintwork of **La Casa Siempreviva**, dating from the early twentieth century, immediately catches the eye. Now a free gallery with a small café, it's one of the few fully restored houses from that era, with tiled floors, arched stained-glass windows, and some later Art Deco features. In the 1930s, it was home to journalist and women's rights activist Isabel Rullan, and in the 1940s it became Villahermosa's first hotel with private bathrooms. Just a couple of doors down at Sáenz 203 is another old mansion turned into a museum – the **Casa Museo Carlos Pellicer** (Tues–Sat 10am–7pm, Sun 10am–5pm; free). The former home of the man chiefly responsible for La Venta (see p.296), this is filled with bits and bobs related to his life, including some of his old shirts and his bed. In the side streets roundabout are a number of other small **art galleries** – look around for signs of current exhibitions. The steps at the far end of Lerdo lead up to the small, tree-shaded **Parque Los Pájaros**, where budgerigars sing in a large, globe-shaped cage and water flows through a series of blue-tiled fountains and pools.

Heading on south, Villahermosa's small **Museo de Historia de Tabasco**, at the corner of 27 de Febrero and Juárez (Tues–Sun 10am–8pm; M$15), gives a quirky, detailed account of Tabasco's history (almost entirely in Spanish), illustrated by such diverse objects as an early TV, the printing press for *El Disidente* (a newspaper from 1863), archeological pieces from Comalcalco, and information on other local Mayan sites. The main attraction, however, is the museum building itself (c1900); popularly known as the **Casa de Azulejos**, it is tiled from top to bottom with patterns from all over Europe and the Middle East, forming an optical illusion on the lobby floor. Look up to see the statues of nymphs and classical figures perched on the railings around the roof.

The zócalo, the **Plaza de Armas**, with its river views, is a pleasant place to while away some time, especially in the cool of the evening when there may also be some music on offer. Here, the imposing white-painted **Palacio del Gobierno** hosts regular temporary exhibitions. Its classical columns, turreted corners and clock tower face the pretty little **Templo de la Concepción**. The first church was built here in 1799, but this and its successor were each demolished twice over – the present building dates from 1945. On the corner of the plaza the **Puente Solidaridad** footbridge over the Río Grijalva has a vast concrete *mirador* in the form of a lighthouse, though currently this is closed to the public. Nearby, new jetties on the riverbank offer trips on the river.

Don't be tempted, incidentally, by the impressive-looking spires of Villahermosa's **Catedral del Señor de Tabasco**, which can be seen from much of the city. This is a long way from downtown, at the corner of Paseo Tabasco and 27 de Febrero, and if you actually get there you'll find that the spires are just about all that exists – the rest of the building has never been completed.

## The CICOM complex

An easy walk along the riverbank from the Zona Remodelada, or a short *combi* ride along the Malecón, brings you to Villahermosa's cultural centre, **CICOM** – the Centro de Investigaciones de las Culturas Olmeca y Maya. The complex includes a museum, concert hall, a beautiful theatre, a research library and a fine restaurant, along with the **Centro de Estudios e Investigación de las Bellas Artes** (daily 10am–2pm & 6–9pm; free), which hosts art and costume displays.

The highlight for most visitors to CICOM, though, is the **Museo Regional de Antropología Carlos Pellicer Cámara** (Tues–Sun 9am–5pm; M$25), where original pieces and models are displayed on four levels, proceeding chronologically from prehistoric times on the top floor to the Olmecs on the ground floor. In addition to the exhibits of Olmec and Maya ceramics and other artefacts (including a fascinating toy jaguar with wheels), you can also view a full-size reproduction of the famous Bonampak murals (see p.314). Carlos Pellicer, a poet and anthropologist born in Villahermosa and the driving force behind the rescue of the stone carvings from the original La Venta as well as this museum, is commemorated by a bronze statue outside the museum.

## Parque La Venta and around

A visit to Villahermosa's **Parque La Venta** (daily 8am–4pm, zoo closed Mon; M$40) could easily fill half a day. The most important artefacts from the Olmec site of La Venta, some 120km west of Villahermosa at the border with Veracruz State, were transferred here in the late 1950s, when they were threatened by Pemex oil explorations. Little is known about the **Olmec culture**, referred to by many archeologists as the mother culture of Mesoamerica. Its legacy, which included the Long Count calendar, glyphic writing, a rain deity and most likely the concept of zero and the ball-game, influenced all subsequent civilizations in ancient Mexico, and the fact that it developed and flourished in the unpromising environment of the Gulf coast swamps 3200 years ago only adds to its mystery.

Although hardly the exact reproduction it claims to be, the Parque La Venta does give you a chance to see a superb collection of artefacts from the earliest Mexican civilization. The **museum**, housed under an enormous thatched roof just inside the entrance, familiarizes you with what known facts there are about the Olmecs, as well as the history of the discovery of La Venta. The most significant and famous items in the park are the four gigantic **basalt heads**, which present such a curious puzzle with their African features. There's a whole series of other Olmec stone sculptures; follow the numbers as the path winds through the park. In their zeal to recreate an authentic jungle setting, the designers have included monkeys and coatis (members of the racoon family), which wander around freely, while crocodiles, jaguars and other animals from the region are

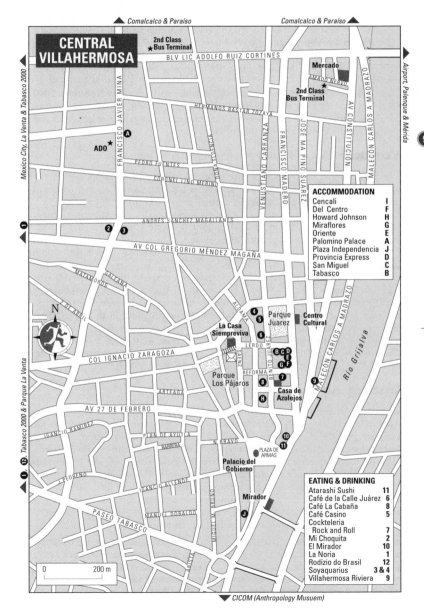

CENTRAL VILLAHERMOSA

▲ Comalcalco & Paraíso    Comalcalco & Paraíso ▲

BLV LIC ADOLFO RUIZ CORTINES

2nd Class ★ Bus Terminal

Mercado

2nd Class Bus Terminal

ADO ★

**ACCOMMODATION**

| | |
|---|---|
| Cencali | I |
| Del Centro | F |
| Howard Johnson | H |
| Miraflores | G |
| Oriente | E |
| Palomino Palace | A |
| Plaza Independencia | J |
| Provincia Express | D |
| San Miguel | C |
| Tabasco | B |

Parque Juárez

Centro Cultural

La Casa Siempreviva

Parque Los Pájaros

Casa de Azulejos

AV 27 DE FEBRERO

PLAZA DE ARMAS

Palacio del Gobierno

Mirador

Río Grijalva

MALECÓN CARLOS A MADRAZO

**EATING & DRINKING**

| | |
|---|---|
| Atarashi Sushi | 11 |
| Café de la Calle Juárez | 6 |
| Café La Cabaña | 8 |
| Café Casino | 5 |
| Cockteleria Rock and Roll | 7 |
| Mi Choquita | 2 |
| El Mirador | 10 |
| La Noria | 1 |
| Rodizio do Brasil | 12 |
| Soyaquarius | 3 & 4 |
| Villahermosa Riviera | 9 |

0    200 m

N

Mexico City, La Venta & Tabasco 2000

Tabasco 2000 & Parque La Venta

Airport, Palenque & Mérida

▼ CICOM (Anthropology Musuem)

9

**PALENQUE AND VILLAHERMOSA** | Villahermosa

297

displayed in the zoo's sizeable enclosures. The mosquitoes add an unplanned touch of reality.

Parque La Venta is set inside the much larger **Parque Tomás Garrido Canabal**, which stretches along the shore of an extensive lake, the **Laguna de Ilusiones**. There are walking trails here and boats for hire, or you can climb the Mirador de los Águilas, a tower in the middle of the lake. Also in the park, opposite the La Venta entrance, the small **Museo de Historia Natural** (Tues–Sun 9am–5pm; M$15) features displays on the geography, geology, animals and plants of Tabasco, focusing on the interaction between humans and the environment.

**To get to La Venta,** take a taxi or hop on one of the *combis* that run along Madero in the city centre ("Tabasco 2000", "Circuito 1", "Parque Linda Vista" among others); they also run along the highway from the second-class bus terminal.

Beyond La Venta, many of the *combis* continue to the nearby **Tabasco 2000** area. This extension of the city is an impressive, if soulless, example of modern Mexican architecture, with concrete shopping malls, government buildings and a planetarium, as well as a number of large hotels.

## Yumká

Villahermosa's newest ecological attraction, **Yumká** (daily 9am–5pm, last entry 4pm; M$50, children M$25), is an enjoyable combination of a safari park and an environmental studies centre. Its formal name, Centro de Interpretación y Convivencia con la Naturaleza, is a bit of a mouthful, so most people simply call it Yumká, after the Chontal Maya god, a dwarf who looks after forests. The park is large, covering more than six square kilometres, so after a guided walking tour of the Tabasco jungle, complete with monkeys, you board a train for a tour round enormous paddocks representing the savannas of Africa and Asia. Elephants, rhinos, giraffes and antelopes are rarely displayed in Mexico and almost never in such spacious surroundings. After a stop at the **restaurant** (which serves the green-fleshed *pejelagarto* – alligator gar, a pike-like fish), you can take a boat tour of the lagoon (M$20), where, in addition to hippos, there are good birdwatching opportunities.

Yumká is 14km from the centre of Villahermosa, very close to the airport. **Combis** leave regularly from along Amado Nervo behind the market at the top end of Avenida Constitución. A taxi will set you back M$170.

## Eating and drinking

There are surprisingly few decent **places to eat** in central Villahermosa. Although there are plenty of food joints and juice bars around the bus station, for the most part the Zona Remodelada boasts only **fast food** or bland hotel fare. For the former, head for Calle Aldama, north of its junction with Lerdo de Tejada: right on this junction there's a *Flor de Michoacan* ice-cream place, and heading up Aldama you'll find half a dozen taco and pizza joints. For a wider choice, better quality and more cosmopolitan flavours you're best off travelling out towards Tabasco 2000, where the hotel **restaurants** are amongst the best in the city. As ever, the **market** is good for fruit, bread, and cheap tacos: you'll find it several blocks northeast of the Zona Remodelada, at the top end of Av Constitución.

**Atarashi Sushi** Vazquez Norte 203. Characterful sushi restaurant with the usual Japanese fare along with a selection of steaks. Rather pricey, but the *sushi combinación especial* allows you to sample ten different types of sushi without breaking the bank.

**Caminito** Paseo Tabasco 1017 ☎993/315-8735. Argentine restaurant in Tabasco 2000 area. If it's steak you crave, this is the place.

**Cockteleria Rock and Roll** Reforma 307 ☎993/312-0593. Directly opposite the *Hotel*

*Miraflores*, a bustling, lively place with excellent seafood cocktails, *ceviche* and prawns.

**Café La Cabaña** Juárez opposite the Casa de los Azulejos. Thoroughly traditional café where local gents linger over their coffees and conduct their business. Food is served, though it's rather pricey – you may be better off eating at one of two similar cafés further up the street: *Café Casino*, near the corner of Zaragoza, or *Café de la Calle Juárez*, between the two. Both have decent breakfasts and *comidas*.

**Mi Choquita** Javiér Mina 304A. Good, inexpensive breakfasts and regional dishes prepared in a typical Tabascan style as well as an excellent value lunch-time *comida*. It's located a few blocks south of the bus station and opposite a branch of *Soyaquarius* (see right).

**El Mirador** Madero 105 ☎ 993/314-3495. Excellent seafood restaurant with river views, and not unreasonable prices. Try the delicious *róbalo* (bass).

**La Noria** Av Gregorio Méndez 1008 ☎ 993/314-1659. Lebanese and Middle Eastern restaurant with very cheap prices and a menu containing items you are unlikely to find anywhere else in the state.

**Rodizio do Brasil** Paseo Tabasco 1102 in Tabasco 2000 ☎ 993/316 28 95. Brazilian-style restaurant with an attentive staff, serving up plenty of grilled meats.

**Soyaquarius** Branches at Fidencia 100 and Javiér Mina 309. This vegetarian- and health-food shop bizarrely also sells hamburgers and fried chicken. Good for delicious, fresh sandwiches and daily specials. Open daily 8.30am–5.30pm.

**Villahermosa Riviera** Constitución 104, fourth floor. Luxurious and expensive – with main courses starting around M$130 – but the food is fantastic. Views along the river at sunset are magical and there's often live music.

## Listings

**Banks** There are branches of all major banks at the airport, throughout the centre and at Tabasco 2000, and you can easily change cash and travellers' cheques. Most banks have ATMs.

**Buses** To get to the first-class terminal take a "Central" or "Chedraui" *combi* (the latter go to a huge department store behind the terminal); most of these also go past the second-class terminal. Between them, ADO and Cristóbal Colón operate dozens of services to all the main destinations.

**Internet access** Internet cafés are widespread in the Zona Luz. Good ones include *Naveghalia*, open until 3am at Lerdo 608, up the steps past the Casa Siempreviva; a nameless place (look for Internet sign) at Aldama 621C just below Zaragoza; and *Clubcafé*, corner of Zaragoza and Doña Fidencia. All charge around M$10 an hour.

**Laundry** Top Klean on Madero, near 20 de Noviembre, charges about M$30 per kilo.

**Post office** The main post office is at the corner of Sáenz and Lerdo opposite Casa Siempreviva (Mon–Fri 9am–3pm, Sat 9am–1pm).

**Travel agents and tour operators** There's no shortage of travel agencies in the Zona Luz, and all the big hotels have a tour desk to arrange domestic flights and trips to Palenque. *Creatur*, Paseo Tabasco 1404 in Tabasco 2000 (☎ 993/310-9900, ⓦ www.creaturviajes.com), is particularly helpful, with multilingual staff.

# Around Villahermosa

Despite the best efforts of the state tourist board, few visitors to Tabasco venture beyond Villahermosa except to head towards Palenque. There are a couple of worthwhile excursions, though, especially if you're heading to or from the city of Campeche via **the coast**. This is a beautiful drive where it's never hard to find deserted beaches and lagoons; there's also a spectacular wildlife area, the **Pantanos de Centla Biosphere Reserve**, though little in the way of infra-structure to visit it. On the way, the unique ruins of **Comalcalco** make a more than worthwhile stop, especially if you combine them with a jaunt to one of the local **cacao haciendas**.

## Comalcalco and the cacao region

On the road north from Villahermosa to Comalcalco, you wind through the heart of the **cocoa-growing region**. It's a slow journey through a populous area where every village protects its peace with axle-breaking *topes*. Around thirty kilometres from Villahermosa, the main road passes through **Cupilco**, notable for the exuberantly decorated **Templo de la Virgen de Asunción**. Architecturally this is nothing special, but the paint-job – gold and blue with floral patterns – is certainly eye-catching. **Comalcalco** itself, a surprisingly large town with ruins on its northern fringe, lies twenty-eight kilometres further on.

Built in the Classic period, **COMALCALCO** (daily 10am–4pm; M$33, including museum) is the westernmost Maya site known. It was occupied around the same time as Palenque (250–900 AD), with which it shares some features, and it may have been ruled by some of the same kings. The area's lack of building stone forced the Chontal Maya to adopt a distinctive, almost unique, form of construction: kiln-fired brick. As if the brick-built pyramids themselves were not sufficient to mark this site, the builders added mystery to technology – each brick was stamped or moulded with a geometric or representational design before firing, with the design face deliberately placed facing inwards, so that it could not be seen in the finished building.

You can see the astonishing designs on the bricks in Comalcalco's excellent little **museum**, though the labels are in Spanish only. Animals depicted include crocodiles, turtles, frogs, lizards, dogs and mice, while those portraying the sculpted faces of rulers display an advanced level of artistic development. The most amazing figure, however, is of a skeleton that appears to be leaping out at you from the surface of the brick.

The abundant clay that provided such a versatile medium for architects and artists here also formed the basis for many more mundane artefacts. Comalcalco means "place of the *comales*" – fired clay griddles for cooking tortillas – and these and other clay vessels have been excavated in great numbers. Some of the largest jars were used as **funerary urns** and several are on display here, including one with an intact skeleton.

Though there are dozens of buildings at Comalcalco, only around ten or so of the larger ones have been restored. Owing to the fragile nature of the brickwork you're not allowed to enter or climb on many of them, but you can follow a path up to Structure 3 and around the Palacio. Entering the site, you first come to **Temple I**, the main structure of the **North Plaza Cluster**, a tiered pyramid with a massive central stairway. Originally, the whole building (like all of the structures here) would have been covered with stucco made from oyster shells, sculpted into masks and reliefs of rulers and deities, and brightly painted. Only a few of these features remain – the exposed ones protected from further erosion by shelters, while others have been deliberately left buried. Facing Temple I at the opposite end of the site is the **Gran Acrópolis**, a complex of buildings, some still being excavated, raised above the plaza. Here you can climb up to **El Palacio** for some excellent close-up views of the brickwork, including a series of massive brick piers and arches that once formed an enormous double corbelled vault, 80m long and over 8m wide – one of the largest enclosed spaces the Maya ever built. There's a fine stucco mask of Kinich Ahau, the Maya sun god, too and at the side of **Temple V** a small, corbel-arched room contains stucco reliefs of nine, richly dressed, half-life-size figures apparently in conversation or even argument – they may represent the **Lords of Xibalba**, the Maya underworld.

Three kilometres beyond the ruins, **Hacienda Cholula** (☎933/334-3815) is a small cacao hacienda where they're attempting to sustain a small business producing organic chocolate in a traditional way; there are guided tours (daily 9am–5pm, M$100 per group, English-speaking guides usually available) and a small shop where the end product is for sale – this is traditional Mexican drinking chocolate, sold in solid blocks that you crumble into hot milk and water and whisk to produce a drink. The tour is short but fascinating, with a brief overview of the entire process, from the young cacao plants to the final production of chocolate. It's also something of a nature trek – there's a large troupe of howler monkeys here as well as innumerable birds (and thousands of mosquitoes), and alongside the cacao grow coffee, cinnamon and bananas.

## Practicalities

It's easy enough to get to Comalcalco by **bus from Villahermosa** in around an hour and a quarter: ADO has two departures a day, and Transportes Somellera runs an hourly service from the second-class station. Faster and more frequent are the red, white and blue **combis** (M$8) that leave from the terminal one block behind the ADO. Once in Comalcalco you'll probably be dropped off at or near the ADO terminal. Green *combis* (M$5), found a block further, ply the route to the ruins, or any bus heading north will pass by. Ask the driver for *ruinas* or get off after about five minutes, when you see the sign. The ruins are on the right along a long straight paved road; some *combis* go all the way there, otherwise it's a fifteen-minute walk. For drivers, the ruins are signed off the main road on the northern edge of town.

There are no official **guides** at Comalcalco, but Eugenio Martinez Torres is often to be found at the entrance, or you can call in advance to arrange a tour (T 933/327-4629; around M$220 per group). He speaks a reasonable amount of English and knows a great deal about the site, having collaborated on a book about Comalcalco's bricks. There's a small **café** and toilets at the site, and plenty of buses back to Villahermosa and on to Paraíso, running along the main road. It's hot and humid here, so water and insect repellent are both necessities.

# The north coast

Skirting the coast and passing through areas of wetland teeming with wildlife, the little-travelled, minor **north coast** road is a treat. Mangrove swamps and lagoons formed by the deltas of the great Usumacinta and Grijalva rivers are covered with flocks of feeding waterbirds, and if you look hard enough you may spot the odd crocodile. However, if it's beaches you've come for, you are likely to be disappointed – the sand is grey-brown and, though generally clean, you're rarely out of sight of the refinery or other oil installations. There are few hotels along this stretch, but plenty of spaces for **camping** – amid swarms of mosquitoes and sandflies. With your own transport you could pretty much pick your spot; on public transport the coast is harder to get to, though many local villages are well served, and from any one of them a *triciclo* (which are abundant, and many of which here are motorized) can take you wherever you wish.

# Paraíso

If you want to travel the coastal route, continue north on the road past the Comalcalco ruins to **PARAÍSO**, 17km away on the banks of the Río Seco. It's a pleasant place, with some beaches nearby and a sleepy atmosphere if you need to wind down, and if you're looking for somewhere to spend the night it's preferable to Frontera. There are plenty of buses heading this way, though Paraíso's **bus stations** are not too central. ADO is 1km south of the centre along Benito Juárez, the main road: turn right out of the station and keep walking – eventually you'll see the town's most distinctive monument across the river up ahead, the twin-towered colonial church that dominates the modern plaza. The main second-class station, with departures for points along the coast, is fifteen minutes' walk north of the centre; to get into town head south (left) and aim for the church towers. *Combis* from Villahermosa or Comalcalco are handier – they'll drop you on the town side of the main bridge over the river, just off Juárez and a short walk from the centre. The best-value **hotel** in town is the *Buganvilias* (Juárez 1, ☎933/333-0037; ❺), a motel-style place on the river right by the bridge at the entrance to town, with good, clean a/c rooms with TV, private bathrooms and drinking water. A slightly more expensive alternative is the comfortable *Solimar* (☎933/333-2872; ❻), a block north of the plaza at Ocampo 114; this business-style accommodation is where the oil men stay when they are in town. The *Solimar* has a pricey **restaurant**, *Costacarey*, with a standard Mexican menu, or there are some more moderately priced alternatives, as well as plenty of juice bars, on and around the zócalo: *Real de la Costa* on the east side is perhaps the best, with a wide selection of Mexican food, meats, pastas, and seafood dishes; *El Parillan*, on Juárez near the bridge, serves excellent charcoal-grilled chicken and other meats. On the west side of the plaza you'll find several Internet cafés, including *Compucentro*. Local **beaches** at Playa Limón or Playa Paraíso are an easy twenty-minute *combi* ride north of Paraíso; busy at weekends, they're entirely deserted during the week.

### Puerto Ceiba and around

Ten kilometres east of Paraíso, the road passes through **PUERTO CEIBA** on the shores of the **Laguna de Mecoacán**. There's a *parador turístico* here offering ferry trips and outdoor activities, and dozens of palapa seafood restaurants serving fish straight out of the lake, many of them concentrated at El Bellote, just outside Puerto Ceiba by the bridge across the lagoon. All of these are busy with locals at weekends and holiday times, but virtually deserted during the week. Continuing on past Puerto Ceiba, the road crosses **Laguna Santa** to the east, and there are turn-offs for several beaches before it meets Hwy-180, 50km or so north of Villahermosa. **Playa Azul**, a favourite for watersports enthusiasts, and quieter **Playa Pico de Oro** are two of the most obvious to head for, both several kilometres from the main road. They look magnificent – seemingly endless fine sand strands backed by palms, with palapa shelters for shade – but in practice, except at local holiday times, they can be deserted and windswept, the facilities all closed and the sand littered with plastic bottles and palm fronds.

## Frontera and the Pantanos de Centla Biosphere Reserve

Baking and half-asleep, the town and working port of **FRONTERA**, about 50km east of Paraíso, seems unchanged since Graham Greene visited in 1938 and immortalized it in *The Lawless Roads*: "Shark fins glided like periscopes at the mouth of the Grijalva River . . . three or four aerials stuck up into the blazing sky from among the banana groves and the palm-leaf huts; it was like Africa seeing itself in a mirror across the Atlantic. Little islands of lily plants came floating down from the interior, and the carcasses of old stranded steamers held up the banks. And then around a bend in the river Frontera . . . the Presidencia and a big warehouse and a white blanched street running off between wooden shacks".

The sole reason for staying in Frontera these days is to visit the **PANTANOS DE CENTLA BIOSPHERE RESRVE**, an unspoilt wetland area positively teeming with wildlife. Among the more exotic species here (few of which you are likely to encounter) are jaguar and tapir, osprey and tiger heron, and, in the water, manatee and crocodile; the mangrove forests are also full of rare orchids and bromeliads. The Desarrollo Ecoturístico Punta Manglar (☎913/398-1688; open daily, but most activities available only at weekends), on the banks of the Usumacinta 10km south of Frontera, offers guided walks, canoe and ferry trips, and other educational **activities** in the reserve, plus it has a small **restaurant** for refreshment. To get there you'll need your own transport – head back along the highway towards Villahermosa then take the Jonuta road, right by the huge bridge over the river. Just a few kilometres further down this road, the Centro de Interpretación Uyotot-Ja (☎913/313-9362; Tues–Sun 9am–5pm; M$20 admission includes a guided tour) is a rather larger tourist centre with an observation tower, restaurant, boat trips (from about M$400 for up to ten people) and walkways over the marshy riverbanks; again, you may find that most of the activities are available only at weekends.

### Practicalities

Frontera offers little in the way of excitement – with time on your hands the best thing to do is head to the mouth of the Río Grijalva and the picturesque, palm-filled **Playa del Bosque**, easily accessible by local bus or *combi*. Virtually everything you'll need in town is around the zócalo, including banks and a couple of nondescript **hotels**; the *Marmor Plaza* (☎913/332-0001; ❺) on Juárez is the best option, with reasonable-value, bland a/c rooms. For tasty shrimp or an inexpensive *comida*, try *El Conquistador*, in a crumbling colonial building in the same block at Juárez 8. The **bus stations** are pretty handy: arriving by second-class bus, turn left out of the terminus and walk two blocks along Madero to get to the zócalo; from first-class head left along Zaragoza, then right, and walk three blocks down Madero to approach from the other direction. There are frequent services to Villahermosa and Ciudad del Carmen.

# Palenque

Set in thick jungle screeching with insects and overlooking the endless Yucatán plains from the foothills of the Chiapas mountains, **PALENQUE** is hauntingly beautiful. For many, it is the finest of Mexico's Maya sites: less crowded than Chichén Itzá, larger than Uxmal, and with a far more spectacular setting than either. Although more structures are being excavated every year, it is not a huge site – you can see everything in a morning – but it is a fascinating one, strongly linked to the lost cities of Guatemala while keeping its own distinctive style.

The town of **Santo Domingo de Palenque** (9km from the ruins and always known simply as Palenque) is a large and rapidly growing place with every facility you might need. An excellent base for exploring the ruins and the waterfalls in the nearby hills, it is lively enough – there's music in the turquoise-painted zócalo most evenings - but of almost no intrinsic interest. Since there are a number of excellent camping sites, cabañas and hotels near the ruins, you may prefer not to stay in town at all.

## Arrival and information

Arriving at any of the **bus terminals**, you'll be on Juárez, just off the main highway through town. If you know when you're leaving it's worth buying your onward ticket as soon as you arrive – or at any rate as soon as possible – as buses out of Palenque can be very crowded, particularly the more popular first-class

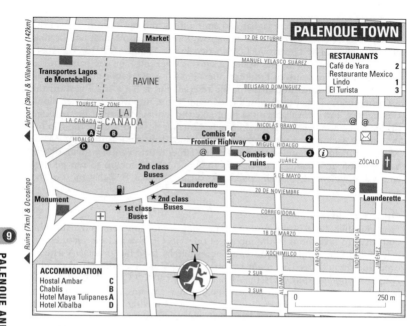

services towards Mérida or San Cristóbal. Palenque's three main streets, avenidas Juárez, 5 de Mayo and Hidalgo, all run parallel to each other and lead straight up to the **zócalo**, the Parque Central. There is a **tourist office** (Mon–Sat 9am–9pm, Sun 9am–1pm; ☎916/345-0356) in the Plaza de Artesanías on Juárez at the corner of Abasolo, a block below the zócalo, but all you're likely to get is a street map and some tour leaflets. You'll generally get better **information** from local tour operators (see listings) or at your hotel.

## Accommodation

Palenque has seen a massive boom in **hotel** construction in recent years. There are plenty of places on the streets leading from the bus stations to the zócalo, especially Hidalgo (though the traffic noise makes these best avoided) and 20 de Noviembre. The most attractive area to stay in is in **La Cañada** "rainforest" area, a short walk from the town centre among the relative quiet of the remaining trees. Surrounded by the growing town, this is hardly rainforest, though howler monkeys and exotic birds can often be seen; generally hotels here are more upmarket, though with some excellent budget options. You'll also find a host of great places lining the **road to the ruins**, in every category from luxury hotel to campsite. Additionally, on this road is **El Panchan** (Wwww.elpanchan.com), a small complex of inexpensive accommodation options sharing various facilities. Note that some places will try to charge up to fifty percent more during peak times – July and August, Semana Santa and Christmas.

### In town

**Posada Canek** 20 de Noviembre 43 ☎916/345-0150. One of several along this road, the *Canek* describes itself as a youth hostel and is great-value if you're travelling alone, as they offer dorm beds in shared rooms (M$70) as well as huge double rooms, some with private bath. Luggage storage is available and there are views of the surrounding hills from the balconies. ❸

**Hotel Chan Kah** at the corner of Juárez and Inde-pendencia ☎916/345-0489. The most upmarket accommodation in town (and the only one with a lift), this very comfortable spot has big rooms with a/c, many with balconies overlooking the garish zócalo. Can be noisy though. ❻

**Posada San Vicente** Hidalgo 100A ☎916/345-0856. A remarkably cheap budget option halfway between the zócalo and La Cañada. Rooms are clean and comfortable and have en-suite bath-rooms. ❸

**Posada Shalom** Corregidora ☎916/345-2641. Clean rooms have cable TV and tiled private bath-rooms. Luggage storage and laundry service are available. There's a place with the same name at Juárez 158 (☎916/345-0944); it's also clean and convenient and has laundry service, but it offers less amenities for exactly the same price. ❹

## In La Cañada

**Hostal Ambar** Hidalgo and C 6 Pte Nte ☎916/345-1008, ✉ambarhostel@hotmail.com. This popular backpacker hangout is the cheapest option in La Cañada. Dorm beds (M$70), basic, fan-cooled doubles (❸) and fancier rooms with TV and a/c are available (❺).

**Chablís** Merle Green 7 ☎916/345-0870, ☏345-0365. Large, modern and spacious whitewashed rooms have a/c and private bath; some have a balcony. No TV, but there's a video bar. ❺

**Hotel Maya Tulipanes** Cañada 6 ☎916/345-0201, ⊛www.mayatulipanes.com.mx. Opposite *Ambar*, this rather bland but very comfortable hotel has a/c rooms, shady grounds, a small pool and a good restaurant. ❽

**Hotel Xibalba** Merle Green 9 ☎916/345-0411, ⊛www.palenquemx.com/shivalva. Friendly place in an A-frame building with a wooden deck. Refur-bished rooms feature private baths, cable TV and a/c. There's a good if rather pricey restaurant and a helpful travel agency. ❺

## On the road to the ruins

**Camping Chaac** at the roadside 2km from the site entrance ☎916/348-0707 ✉vtdeviaje@starmedia .com. Rustic, thatched, screened cabañas (❸, includes breakfast), plus camping (from M$50) and a small restaurant on the banks of two streams. The shared showers are clean, there's a river pool to bathe in and also a *temazcal* (sweat bath) built by the friendly owner.

**Chan Kah Resort Village** 4.5km from town on

the left ☎916/345-1100, ⊛www.chan-kah .com.mx. Luxury brick and stone cabañas, rather tightly packed in a lovely forest and river setting, humming with birdlife. Amenities include three stone-lined swimming pools and a restaurant. ❾

**Mayabell Camping and Trailer Park** at the road-side 2km from the site entrance ☎916/345-0597, ✉mayabell82@hotmail.com. There's something for everyone at this favourite spot of backpackers and adventure-tour groups. In addition to palapa shelters for hammocks and tents, *Mayabell* has vehicle pads with electricity and water, and some very comfortable private cabañas with hot water. The tiled, shared showers have hot water as well, and there's a restaurant, Internet access and a *temazcal*. The site is rarely crowded, though it can be rowdy. Hammock space from M$30 (rent a hammock for an additional M$15), tent from M$50, RV from M$130, cabaña ❺

**Cabañas Safari** 1.5km from town, on the left ☎916/345-0026, ✉safarihotel@hotmail.com. Very comfortable, thatched cabañas and suites are beautifully decorated inside. The spacious grounds feature a deck and hammocks, and include organic cocoa bushes and a small rubber plantation. ❺

**Hotel Villas Kin-Ha** 4km from town on the right ☎916/345-0954, ⊛www.villas-kinha.com. One of the newest places along the road, with comfortable a/c thatched cabañas, a pool and a restaurant. ❼

## El Panchan

**Beto's Cabins and camping** The least expensive place here, with shelters for hammocks (with lockers, from M$40) and very basic shared-bath cabins. ❷

**Chato's Cabañas** ☎916/341-3486, ✉info@elpanchan.com. Closest to the El Panchan entrance. Offers neat, thatched cabañas and two-storey houses, some with private bath. ❸

**Margarita and Ed's** Probably the most comfort-able and best-value of the places here, with thatched cabins (❸) or a building with conven-tional double rooms featuring a/c and private baths (❹).

**Rakshita's** ✉rakshita@yahoo.com. Brightly painted, cosy cabañas, some with private bath, plus a deck with hammocks, surrounded by a lovely garden with a maze. There's a great vegetar-ian restaurant onsite, and massage and meditation are offered. ❸

# The ruins

The **ruins of Palenque** occupy the top of an escarpment marking the north-western limit of the Chiapas highlands. Superficially, the site bears a closer resemblance to the Maya sites of Guatemala than to those of the Yucatán, but ultimately it's unique – the **towered palace** and **pyramid tomb** are like nothing else, as is the abundance of reliefs and inscriptions. The setting, too, is remarkable. Surrounded by hills covered in jungle, Palenque is at the same time right at the edge of the great Yucatán plain – climb to the top of any of the structures and you look out across the dark green of the hills, over an endless stretch of low, pale-green flatland.

Founded around 100 BC as a farming village, it was four hundred years before Palenque began to flourish, during the Classic period (300–900 AD). Towards the end of this time the city ruled over a large part of modern-day Chiapas and Tabasco, but its peak came during a relatively short period of the seventh century, under two rulers: **Hanab Pakal (Jaguar Shield)** and **Chan Bahlum (Jaguar Serpent)**. Almost everything you can see (and that's only a tiny, central part of the original city) dates from this era.

## Ruin practicalities

Getting to the ruins of Palenque, nine kilometres from town, is no problem. Two **combi** services, Chambalu and Otolum, run at least every fifteen minutes (6am–6pm; M$7 one-way) from their termini on Allende, either side of Juárez, and will stop anywhere along the road – useful if you're staying at one of the hotels or campsites near the ruins. After 6pm, you'll have to either walk or take a **taxi**. There are also plenty of organized **tours** from town (see p.310).

The ruins (daily 8am–5pm, last entry 4.30pm; M$38 including museum, plus M$10 to enter park) are in the **Parque Nacional de Palenque** and guided tours are available from the entrance, costing around M$350 for groups of up to seven people and lasting about two hours. Arrive early and climb the temples in the morning mist if you want to avoid the worst of the heat and the crowds.

By the entrance there's a small **café** and numerous souvenir stalls selling drinks, as well as toilets and some expensive lockers. Usually you'll also find a group of Lacandón (see box, p.315) in white robes – or merely people in white robes imitating Lacandón – selling arrows and other artefacts. Signs inside the site are in English, Spanish and Tzeltal, though Chol is the language spoken by most modern Maya in this part of Chiapas.

## El Palacio and around

As you enter the site, **El Palacio**, with its extraordinary watchtower, stands ahead of you. The centrepiece of the site, El Palacio is in fact a complex of buildings constructed at different times to form a rambling administrative and residential block. Its square **tower** (whose top floor was reconstructed in 1930) is unique, and no one knows exactly what its purpose was – perhaps a lookout post or an astronomical observatory. Bizarrely, the narrow staircase that winds up inside it starts only at the second level, though you're no longer allowed to climb it. Throughout you'll find delicately executed **relief carvings**, the most remarkable of which are the giant human figures on stone panels in the grassy courtyard, depicting rulers of defeated cities in poses of humiliation. An arcade overlooking the courtyard held a portrait gallery of Palenque's rulers, though many of these have been removed.

To the right of the entrance, at the end of a row of smaller structures, stands the **Templo de las Inscripciones**, an eight-stepped pyramid, 26m high, built up against a thickly overgrown hillside. You are no longer permitted to climb the pyramid, which is a shame as the sanctuary on top contains a series of stone panels carved with hieroglyphic inscriptions relating to Palenque's dynastic history. Inside the pyramid is the **tomb of Hanab Pakal**, or Pakal the Great (615–683 AD). Discovered in 1952, this was the first such pyramid burial found in the Americas, and is still the most important and impressive. Sadly, the huge numbers of visitors took a toll on the tomb, and it is now closed to the general public. Some of the smaller objects found inside – the skeleton and the jade death mask – are on display at the Museo Nacional de Antropología in Mexico City, but the massive, intricately carved stone **sarcophagus** is still inside. One of the most renowned iconographic monuments in the Maya world, the sarcophagus lid depicts Pakal at the moment of his death, falling into Xibalba, the underworld, symbolized by a monster's jaws. Above the dead king rises the **Wakah Kan** – the World Tree and the centre of the universe – with **Itzam-Ye**, the Celestial Bird, perched on top representing the heavens. In order that the deified king buried here should not be cut off from the world of the living, a psychoduct – a hollow tube in the form of a snake – runs up the side of the staircase, from the tomb to the temple. For now, though, you will have to be satisfied with the replica in the site museum.

In June 1994, another remarkable tomb was discovered in **Templo XIII**, a pyramid next to the Templo de las Inscripciones. This burial, currently the only one open to the public, is considered by archeologists to date from a similar period to that of Pakal, and its sarcophagus contains a number of jade and obsidian grave goods, and food and drink vessels to sustain the deceased on his or her way to Xibalba.

### The Grupo de la Cruz and around
More recent excavations in the south of the site have revealed a painted tomb and a stone throne at **Templo XX**, inscribed with over two hundred glyphs, among other rich grave goods, but there are no plans to open it for public viewing (details of this ongoing project, and dozens of pictures, can be seen at ⓦ www.mesoweb.com). In **Templo XIX**, next door, the same archeological project discovered some magnificent reliefs, a couple of which have been replaced with reproductions giving a very clear idea of the colour and magnificence of the many carvings found at Palenque.

These two buildings lie on higher ground on the far side of the Río Otulúm, one of several streams that cascade through the site. As it passed through the city in its heyday, the Otulúm was lined with stone and used as an aqueduct. Also on this far bank are the **Templo del Sol**, the **Templo de la Cruz** and the **Templo de la Cruz Foliada** – together known as the Grupo de la Cruz (Group of the Cross) – half-obscured by the dense vegetation around them. Each is a tall, narrow pyramid surmounted by a temple with an elaborate stone roofcomb. All, too, contain carved panels representing sacred rites – the cross found here is as important an image in Maya iconography as it is in Christian, representing the meeting of the heavens and the underworld with the land of the living. On the right-hand side of the Templo de la Cruz, God L, one of the gods of the underworld, is depicted smoking tobacco.

The **Templo del Bello Relieve** (**Templo del Jaguar**) is reached by a small path that follows the brook upstream from behind the Templo de las Inscripciones – a delightful shaded walk. Almost as soon as you step out of the cleared area you're in thick jungle, with only the sound of the rushing water to disturb

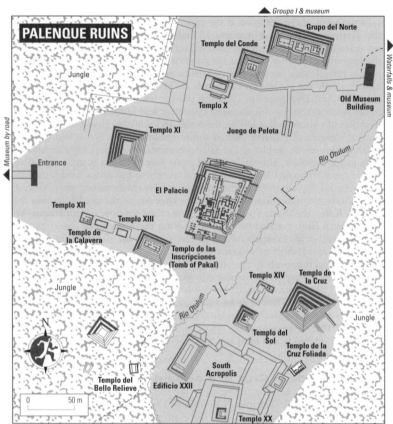

▲ Groupo I & museum

**PALENQUE RUINS**

Grupo del Norte

Templo del Conde

Jungle

Waterfalls & museum

Old Museum Building

Templo X

Museum by road

Templo XI

Juego de Pelota

Río Otulum

Entrance

El Palacio

Templo XII

Templo XIII

Templo de la Calavera

Templo de las Inscripciones (Tomb of Pakal)

Templo XIV

Templo de la Cruz

Jungle

Río Otulum

Templo del Sol

Templo de la Cruz Foliada

Jungle

N

South Acropolis

Templo del Bello Relieve

Edificio XXII

Templo XX

0    50 m

you. More temples are being wrested from the jungle beyond, but the paths are closed, and if you want to penetrate further you won't be permitted to pass without a guide. The path leads eventually to the *ejido* of Naranjo, a little over an hour's walk away, and while you're on it it's easy to believe you're walking over unexcavated pyramids: the ground is very rocky and some of the stones certainly don't look naturally formed.

### The Grupo del Norte and around

On the northern edge of the cleared site, the lesser buildings of the **Grupo del Norte** and the **Juego de Pelota** (ball-court) are on lower ground across a grassy area from El Palacio. Beyond them, two **paths** lead downhill towards the museum, following the stream as it cascades through the forest and flows over beautiful limestone curtains and terraces into a series of gorgeous pools. Either way, you should leave most of the crowds behind. The smaller path immediately behind the Grupo del Norte leads down via the buildings of Grupo I and Grupo II – the larger one by the old museum building is a slightly easier walk. It skirts first close to **Grupo C**, a small cluster of buildings minimally restored and cleared. **Grupo B** is a small residential complex right on the path, exquisitely located between the aptly named **Baño de la Reina (Bathing Pool of**

**the Queen**) and a small waterfall on a second stream, the Arroyo Murcielagos. Beyond this, the **Grupo de los Murcielagos** is another residential area where you can see remnants of the original drainage systems as well as benches and stairways. The paths join again where the river is crossed by a suspension bridge, eventually emerging on the main road opposite the museum.

## The museum

Palenque's spanking new **museum** (Tues–Sun 8am–4.45pm, included in site entry), on the road 1.5km from the site entrance, will give you a good idea of the scale of Palenque, and a look at some of its treasures. There are fine displays of many of the glyphs and carved relief panels found at the site, as well as examples of the giant ceramic censers (incense-burners) in the form of gods or mythological creatures, a number of which were found in extraordinarily good condition. An intricate model of El Palacio reveals how it would have appeared in the Classic period – with the tops of the buildings adorned with roofcombs – and there's a map of the entire site showing that only around a quarter of the structures have been excavated (at its height, the population may have reached 100,000). There's also a copy of Pakal's famous sarcophagus lid from the Templo de las Inscripciones.

If you already have a ticket, you can re-enter the site by the gateway opposite and climb back up the paths to the top, but since there's no ticket office here, you can't enter for the first time. *Combis* pass in both directions, and if you're heading for the site entrance you may consider it worth paying M$50 to avoid the stiff, hot climb up the road.

# Eating and drinking

**Food** in Palenque town is fairly basic, and most restaurants serve up similar dishes, often just pasta and pizza, to customers who've really only come for the ruins; there are several places along the road to the site – some of which cater mainly to tour groups – including a couple in El Panchan (see "Accommodation", p.305). The hotels in La Cañada invariably have a restaurant attached and, though standards are generally fine, prices are higher than in town. Bargains can be found among the set menus posted on boards outside most restaurants. **Avenida Juárez** also has several budget options between the bus stations and the zócalo, while **Avenida Hidalgo** has more Mexican-style food, with several taco places and even a couple of seafood restaurants. There's a good Mexican **bakery**, *Flor de Palenque*, on Allende next to the Chambalu *colectivo* terminal.

**Coctelería Rocamar** at the corner of Independencia and 5 de Mayo. Seafood is the speciality at this place, which is hugely popular with locals. Known for generous portions and reasonable prices.

**Don Mucho** El Panchan. Excellent Mexican/Italian restaurant in the El Panchan complex. A prime spot for breakfast or a leisurely lunch after visiting the ruins, though sometimes busy with small tour groups.

**Hotel Chan Kah** at the corner of Juárez and Independencia. First-floor terrace bar/restaurant with great views over the action on the zócalo. Prices reflect the location, but this is a good place for an early evening drink.

**Restaurante Maya** at the corner of Hidalgo and Independencia on the zócalo. The central location

and extensive menu make this spot popular with tourists, and, therefore, rather pricey. Set meals from around M$35 are better value.

**Restaurante Mexico Lindo** Hidalgo between Aldama and Allende. Reasonably priced restaurant with a wide-ranging Mexican menu, salads and good-value *comidas*.

**Na Chan Kan** at the corner of Hidalgo and Jiménez. Offers good-value breakfasts and set meals, and an enjoyable situation on the zócalo for coffee and people-watching.

**Rakshita's** El Panchan. Airy vegetarian restaurant. The stir-frys and vegetarian specials are a welcome change of diet; also breakfasts and juices.

Las Tinajas at the corner of 20 de Noviembre and Abasolo. Pleasant, family-run restaurant with a wide menu of meats, fish, chicken and pasta in addition to the usual Mexican fare. No alcohol. El Turista at the corner of Juárez and Abasolo oppo-site the tourist office. Excellent *jugos* and *licuados*. Café de Yara at the corner of Hidalgo and Abasolo. Café culture comes to Palenque – try the cappuccinos (from a proper espresso machine) and breakfasts especially.

## Listings

Banks Several along Juárez have ATMs and will change travellers' cheques; the best exchange rates are at Banco Azteca/Western Union, at the back of the giant Elektra electrical and furniture store on Juárez, not far up from the bus stations. Internet Internet cafés are plentiful. They include Ciber-konqueror and Cafeteria Internet, both just past the post office at the corner of Independencia and Nicolas Bravo; RedMay@, Juárez near the Elektra store; and Cibernet, Independencia near 20 de Noviembre.

Laundry Several in town, including a good one on 5 de Mayo at the corner of Allende.

Post office On Independencia, a block from the plaza (Mon–Fri 9am–6pm, Sat & Sun 9am–1pm).

Tours Walk the streets of Palenque and you'll be accosted by touts offering a huge variety of tours to local attractions, above all the waterfalls at Agua Azul and Misol-Há (see opposite) and the ruins of Bonampak and Yaxchilán (p.314 & p.317). There are also trips to Tikal in Guatemala or to Toniná, and adventure tours, including kayaking and horse-riding. Prices vary according to season (and even time of day if there's one seat left to fill) but start from around M$120 for the waterfalls, M$450 for a day trip to Bonampak and Yaxchilán. Be sure to check what's included – entrance fees, meals and English-speaking guides most importantly. The agents listed below are consistently reliable.

Travel Agents/Tour Operators Two of the best for tours are Na Chan Kan (⊤916/345-0263, ℮nachan@tnet.net.mx), with a small office on Juárez just up from the bus station and a main office at the corner of Hidalgo and Jiménez where they meet the zócalo, and Viajes Shivalva, based at the *Hotel Xibalba* in La Cañada (⊤916/345-0411, ⊛www.palenquemx.com/shivalva).

## Around Palenque

Any of the following destinations can easily be visited as a day-trip from Palenque, and each can also be made part of a longer excursion, with plenty of accommodation options along the way. The easiest way to do this is with a **tour**, and there are dozens to choose from (see Listings, above), or if you have your **own transport**. However there are also good bus and *combi* connections in every direction.

To the south, a series of stunningly beautiful **waterfalls** is the chief attraction on the winding mountain road that heads from Palenque towards **Ocosingo**. The awesome cascades on the Río Shumulhá at **Agua Azul** and the exquisite waterfall at **Misol-Há** are usually visited on a day-trip from Palenque, but it's perfectly possible to visit them independently and stay nearby, or to make this part of a more extended excursion to take in Ocosingo itself and the nearby ruins of **Toniná**. There are several places to stay in Ocosingo, and it's an opportunity to experience something of the atmosphere of the Chiapas highlands, though the ruins are the real reason to visit.

Heading slightly further east will take you to the Usumacinta river and the spectacular Maya sites of **Bonampak** and **Yaxchilán**. Impressive ruins aside, this is an opportunity to experience something of the remaining tropical forest and the teeming wildlife around the banks of the river.

Moving on from Palenque towards Villahermosa or Escárcega and the heart of the Yucatán, there's little to detain you once you get onto the fast Hwy-186. At the junction with the Palenque road is **Catazajá**, where a huge lake is a popular weekend outing for locals. *Combis* from Palenque run here (look for "Playas"), or you can easily walk into the village from the junction a couple of hundred metres away. Down at the waterfront there are numerous restaurants – try *El Pelicano* or *El Manati* – and *lanchas* available for trips on the lake with its abundant birdlife.

## Misol-Há

Just 18km from Palenque, **MISOL-HÁ** (M$10 entry), a 25-metre waterfall, provides a stunning backdrop to a pool that's safe for **swimming**. A fern-lined trail leads along a ledge behind the wide cascade – refreshing from the spray and mist even if you don't swim – and the air of the lush rainforest is filled with bird calls. Most tours arrive here early (around 9.30am) or at lunchtime and spend no more than half an hour, so if you can visit mid-morning or mid-afternoon you'll find things much quieter. There's inexpensive **accommodation** in beautifully situated wooden cabañas (☎0155/5329-0995 ext 7006; ❺), where the roar of the waterfall will lull you to sleep. The cabins, the **restaurant** (mainly catering to tour groups), and the **craft shop** on site are owned and run by the San Miguel *ejido*; each cabin has a private bathroom and electricity, and some are family-size, with kitchens. With your own car, this is a potential alternative to staying at Palenque; if you're relying on public transport, the falls are an easy 1500-metre walk from the road.

## Agua Azul and Agua Clara

The whole area around the cascades of **AGUA AZUL**, 64km from Palenque, 4km down a track from the main road in the Parque Nacional Agua Azul, is exceptionally beautiful, with dozens of lesser falls found both up- and downstream. If it's safe to walk upstream (it may not be in the rainy season) you'll come across a perilous-looking bridge over the river and eventually you'll reach an impressive gorge where the **Río Shumulhá** explodes out of the jungle-covered mountain. At the right time of year, the river is alive with butterflies. Higher up, the swimming is safer, too – though watch out for signs warning of dangerous currents, as there are several tempting but extremely perilous spots, and people drown here every year.

Agua Azul is a major tour-bus destination, so don't expect to have it to yourself. If you come **by bus** (not on a tour), you'll be dropped at the crossroads, where there are usually taxis (M$10) waiting to take you to the base of the falls. Otherwise it's a 45-minute walk downhill to the waterfall and at least an hour's sweaty hike back up. Local villagers have set up two tariff stations along the road, at each of which (if they're manned) you'll be charged M$10. At the bottom, where the tour buses park, there are several basic **restaurants**, souvenir shops and a **campsite** with hammock space. Simple **cabañas** (☎0155/5329-0995 ext 7002; ❹) are also available for rent – enquire at the Modulo de Información near the car park. Make sure to keep a close eye on your belongings, though, and be warned that **violent attacks** on tourists have occurred away from the main area.

Not far from Agua Azul – 8km back towards Palenque – **AGUA CLARA** is a more recently developed river attraction that also features on the itinerary of many tours. Here the water is calmer and you can rent kayaks and small boats to explore the river or trek a couple of kilometres through the forest to a quiet natural pool where the Tulijá and Shumulhá rivers join; there's also horse riding here. Again there have been reports of attacks on tourists around Agua Clara, so ideally you should have a guide, and certainly not venture away from the main areas alone.

## Ocosingo

Though a fair-sized town in its own right, **OCOSINGO**, its streets lined with single-storey, red-tiled houses and the air thick with the scent of wood smoke, makes a complete contrast to tourist-crowded Palenque. It's a place that has stayed close to its country roots – with farmers in from the ranches wearing cowboy hats and local women selling *maíz* from great bubbling vats – and it's also the base for visiting the amazing Maya site of **Toniná**. The **zócalo**, surrounded by *portales*, a big old country church on the east side, and the *ayuntamiento*, with its thoroughly incongruous tinted glass, opposite, is central to town life.

The area around Ocosingo was something of a **Zapatista** stronghold, and as recently as 2003 the nearby Rancho Esmeralda (see below) was seized by the rebels. You'll see plenty of signs proclaiming Zapatista control in the region ("Pueblo Zapatista . . . el pueblo manda y el gobierno obedece" – the people command, the government obeys), and there are army checkpoints on the roads, but for the most part the uprising has died down, and for tourists it's entirely safe.

## Practicalities

**Buses** stop on Ocosingo's main road or at a makeshift terminal nearby. To get to the zócalo turn left out of the terminal and walk down the hill for about four blocks until you reach Calle Central, then turn left for a further two blocks. You'll find pretty much everything you need within a block or two of here.

**Accommodation** options are plentiful, including the *Hotel Central* (T919/673-0024; **④**), on the north side of the plaza, where good-size rooms have fans and TV, and *Hotel San José*, just off the northeast corner of the plaza along Calle 1 Ote Nte (T919/673-0039), with clean, comfortable budget rooms (**③**) as well as some fancier ones with cable TV and a/c (**⑤**). The best of the lot, however, is the colourful *Hospedaje Esmeralda* (T919/673-0014, Wwww .ranchoesmeralda.net; **④**), a traveller's meeting place at Calle Central Norte 14 half a block north of the plaza, which has a range of en-suite and shared-bath rooms for one to four people; if you're travelling alone they can sometimes arrange shares, plus the place doubles as a **tourist information** office. The friendly staff can advise on *combis* to the ruins of Toniná, help book light aircraft flights over them or to Tikal (around M$4250 for four people; T961/675-5798) and organize horse-riding expeditions (around M$200 per day) or visits to attractions farther afield. The *hospedaje* started life as the *Rancho Esmeralda*, a hotel and campsite in a rural setting near Toniná, and there's a folder of newspaper reports documenting the seizure of the *Rancho* by the Zapatistas, as well as plenty of other reading material to borrow.

The *Esmeralda* also has a good **restaurant**, and there are several other budget **places to eat** surrounding the square, most serving a standard Mexican menu of tacos and tortilla dishes. *El Campanario* on the north side is very friendly and has a rack of tourist information leaflets on the region; the bright-yellow *El Desván*, on the opposite side of the zócalo, is a slightly fancier place that serves pizza as well as the usuals. In the **food market**, or *tianguis*, indigenous women sell fruit and vegetables and locally produced cheeses, including the round waxy *queso de bola* and the delicious creamy *queso botanero*. To get there turn right at the church for one block, then left along Calle 2 Sur Oriente for another four.

There are a couple of **ATM**s, one at Banamex on the plaza, and another at Banco Santander opposite *Hospedaje Esmeralda* on Calle Central Norte. A few **Internet** cafés can be found along this road as well, including Compuchat near the zócalo and Xanav (9am–2pm & 4–10pm; T919/673-1334) at 40C, which doubles as a travel agent for domestic flights.

**Leaving Ocosingo** by road is easy enough until mid-evening, with frequent buses and *combis* to San Cristóbal (12 daily; 2hr) and buses to Palenque (16 daily; 3hr 30 min). The last Autotransportes Tuxtla-Gutiérrez (ATG) buses in either direction officially leave at 7.30pm – though they're *de paso* and so are likely to be later. Cristóbal Colón services continue after midnight, with buses to Palenque at 3am and 4am, and San Cristóbal at 12.30am and 1.30am. There is a 24-hour **left luggage** service at the Cristóbal Colón terminal (M$5).

## Toniná

Some 14km east of Ocosingo, the Classic-period Maya site of **TONINÁ** (museum daily 8am–5pm, site daily 9am–3.30pm; M$33 including museum) is large and impressive, and yet it sees few visitors. At its height, Toniná was a great regional power: the city defeated Palenque and captured its ruler in 699 AD, and from then until after 900 AD, when it became the last of the great Maya centres to fall victim to whatever disaster led to them all being abandoned, it was probably the greatest power in the Usumacinta basin.

To reach Toniná **from Ocosingo**, you can take one of the frequent *combis* (M$10) that leave from the market area, heading either for the site itself or the large army base by the turn-off to the site – look for "Predio" or "Ruinas". A taxi will cost around M$70 one-way. At the entrance to the site, the *Restaurante Toniná* serves simple food, cold beer and soft drinks, and also sells quality T-shirts and postcards.

When approaching Toniná, you'll see its stunning modern **museum**, which is well worth a look before heading off to the ruins. Designed in an angular, pyramidal style to resemble a ruin itself, the museum has an impressive collection, including a helpful model of the site and many sculptures and relief carvings found here. In ancient times Toniná was known as "the place of (celestial) captives" and there are numerous representations of bound prisoners, most of whom were later decapitated, a process also shown in many reliefs. Glyphs on the panels record the place where the prisoners were captured, while those on

△ Toniná

the loincloths of the captives may tell who they were. There's extensive explanation of how to decipher Maya dates and glyphs, too, though the labelling throughout is in Spanish only.

The **ruins** of Toniná, a five-minute walk from the entrance, centre on an enormous grassy plaza, once surrounded by buildings, with a series of seven artificial terraces climbing the hillside above it. At the bottom are two restored ball-courts and an overgrown pyramid mound. **Ball-court 1** exemplifies Toniná's obsession with prisoners; built around 699, possibly to celebrate the great victory over Palenque, it had representations of bound captives instead of the usual rings for the balls to pass through.

Occupying the entire hillside and including dozens of temples and other buildings on its various levels, the main structure, the **Acrópolis**, is quite vast. A flashlight is useful to explore the labyrinthine interiors – there are warrens of small rooms and even internal staircases ascending from one terrace to the next. As you climb the hill there's plenty to explore, but look out above all for the reliefs and stucco masks that survive in situ – easily spotted under their protective thatch or corrugated-iron roofs. The most extraordinary of these is the enormous (16m x 4m) **Mural of the Four Suns**, on the sixth platform. This amazingly well-preserved stucco codex tells the story of Maya cosmology by following the four suns (or eras of the world) as they were created and destroyed. The worlds are depicted as decapitated heads surrounded by flowers. A grinning, skeletal Lord of Death presents a particularly graphic image as he grasps a defleshed human head.

The final two levels are crowded with temples, and the climb to the very summit – the **Temple of the Smoking Mirror** – is by steep, narrow steps. At the top, though, you are rewarded with awesome views, especially if the guard usually posted there lends you his powerful binoculars. In the foreground, the pasture-land that surrounds the cleared site is studded with unexcavated mounds.

## Bonampak

The outside world first heard of **Bonampak** (Painted Walls) in 1946, when Charles Frey, an American conscientious objector taking refuge deep in the forest, was shown the site (though not its famous **murals**) by the Lacandón, who apparently still worshipped at the ancient temples. The first non-Maya ever to see these murals – astonishing examples of Classic Maya art – was the American photographer Giles Healey, who arrived shortly after Frey's visit, sparking a long and bitter dispute over exactly who was responsible for their discovery. Bonampak's ruins are small and not the most spectacular, but the murals definitely make it worth the visit.

Bonampak lies in a small national park controlled by and for the Lacandón Indians, on the fringe of the much larger Montes Azules Biosphere Reserve. However you get here, you'll have to leave your transport at the turn-off from the highway and continue in a Lacandón *combi* (M$100 round trip) down the dirt road into the park – many of them are in an alarming state of disrepair, but no other vehicles are allowed in. This will take you to the **entrance to the site** (daily 8am–4pm; M$33), where you are usually closely supervised, especially near the Temple of the Frescoes. No flash photography of the frescoes is allowed and, as usual, you will be charged extra to use a video camera.

## The site

After crossing the airstrip (barely used now that the road has been improved), you enter the site at the northwest corner of the main plaza, which is bounded by low walls – the remains of some palace-style buildings. In the centre of the plaza **Stele 1** shows a larger-than-life **Chan Muan**, the last king of Bonampak, dressed for battle. Standing at 20m, it is one of the tallest in the Maya world; you'll encounter other images of him throughout the site. Ahead, atop several steep flights of steps, lies the **Acrópolis**. On the lower steps more well-preserved stelae show Chan Muan preparing himself for blood-letting and apparently about to sacrifice a prisoner. From the highest point of the acropolis there's an impressive sense that you're surrounded by primeval forest – the Selva Lacandona – with just a small cleared space in front of you.

Splendid though these scenes are, the highlight of the site is the famed **Temple of the Frescoes**. Inside, in three separate chambers, on the temple walls and roof, the renowned **Bonampak murals** depict vivid scenes of haughty Maya lords, splendidly attired in jaguar-skin robes and quetzal-plume head-dresses; their equally well-dressed ladies; and bound prisoners, one with his fingernails ripped out, spurting blood. Musicians play drums, pipes and trumpets in what is clearly a celebration of victory.

Dated to around 790 AD, the murals show the Bonampak elite at the height of their power: unknown to them, however, the collapse of the Classic Maya civilization was imminent. Some details were never finished and Bonampak was abandoned shortly after the scenes in the temple were painted. Though time and early cleaning attempts have taken their toll on the murals, work in the 1990s restored some of their glory. No more than three people are permitted to enter each chamber at any one time (strictly enforced) so you may have to queue to see them.

**Room 2**, in the centre, is the heart of the scene: it contains a vivid, even gruesome depiction of battle and the defeat of Bonampak's enemies: tortured prisoners lie on temple steps, while above them lords in jaguar robes are indifferent to their agony. A severed head has rolled down the stairs and Chan Muan grasps a prisoner (who appears to be pleading for mercy) by the hair – clearly about to deal him the same fate. The chambers to either side continue the story with celebrations of the victory and the arrival of rulers of vassal states to pay tribute. In **Room 1** an infant wrapped in white cloth (the heir apparent?) is presented to assembled nobility under the supervision of the lord of Yaxchilán, while musi-

---

## The Lacandón

You may already have encountered the impressively wild-looking **Lacandón Maya** selling exquisite (and apparently effective) bows and arrows at Palenque. Though the wearing of their simple, hanging white robes and uncut hair is today mainly for the benefit of tourists, the Lacandón were until recently the most isolated of all the Mexican tribes. The ancestors of today's Lacandón are believed to have migrated to Chiapas from the Petén region of Guatemala during the eighteenth century. Prior to that the Spanish had enslaved, killed or relocated the original inhabitants of the forest.

The Lacandón refer to themselves as "Hach Winik" (true people); "Lacandón" was a label used by the Spanish to describe any native group living in the Usumacinta Valley and western Petén outside colonial control. Appearances notwithstanding, some Lacandón families are (or have been) quite wealthy, having sold timber rights in the jungle, though most of the timber money has now gone. This change has led to a division in their society, and most live in one of two main communities: **Lacanhá Chansayab**, near Bonampak, a village predominantly made up of evangelical Protestants, some of whom are keenly developing low-impact tourist facilities (see p.316); and **Nahá**, where a small group still attempt to live a traditional life.

cians play trumpets in the background. **Room 3** shows more celebration and the execution of captives, while Chan Muan's wife, **Lady Rabbit**, accompanied by noblewomen, prepares to prick her tongue to let blood fall onto the paper in a clay pot in front of her. The smoke from burning the blood-soaked paper will carry messages to ancestor-gods. Other gorgeously dressed figures, their senses probably heightened by hallucinogenic drugs, dance on the temple steps.

## Practicalities

If you want to spend the night, the same Lacandón drivers can take you to the village of **Lacanhá Chansayab** where there are several **places to stay**, though none currently has a phone. The turn-off for the paved road to Lacanhá is actually at San Javier (blink and you'll miss it), a few kilometres before the Bonampak turning. Four kilometres down the side road you'll find *Camping Margarito* (from M$40, tents available), run by the friendly Chan Kayun family who also have a small **restaurant**. This is where most tours camp for the night; a turning to Bonampak branches off left here.

Lacanhá village itself is very spread out; *Camping Carmelo* (from M$40) is the first place you pass, and then entering the more inhabited area at the airstrip you'll see signs pointing to several purpose-built **campsites**, **cabins** and **hammock shelters**, none of them charging more than around M$100 for their basic facilities. *Campamento Lacanhá* is to the left and others are a kilometre ahead, in the main part of the village. A few places also have simple dorm **rooms** (❷), with mosquito-netted beds and electric light. The best, in a grassy area on the bank of a clear, fast-flowing river, is run by Vicente Kin Paniagua. Don Vicente and his family produce some of the best *artesanía* in the village – clay and wood figurines and drums in addition to beautifully crafted bow-and-arrow sets. The villagers are eager to show you the gorgeous rivers and waterfalls in the forest, and you can reach the **Lacanhá ruins** in under two hours from here. Ask for Kin Bor or Carlos Chan Bor, at the house where the paved road enters the village; either of them will be able to fix you up with knowledgeable Lacandón guides to lead you. There's also a **hiking trail** to Bonampak (with some interpretive labels) and, though you can do this on your own, you'll have a less apprehensive trip through the forest if you have a guide. The hike is wonderful in the dry season (Jan to late April) – be prepared for mud at other times.

### Frontera Corozal

The settlement of **FRONTERA COROZAL** lies on the Mexican bank of the Usumacinta, 19km off the highway down a paved side road. From here you take a boat to get to the ruins and jungle of **Yaxchilán**. There's a Mexican **immigration post** in Frontera, and visitors are frequently asked to show their passports even if they have no intention of leaving Mexico. The small, new community **museum** here is also on the itinerary of most tours: it showcases the history of the settlement, founded only in 1976, and the relationships between the Chol, Lacandón and Tzeltal people; local archeology (there are a few large stelae); and flora and fauna. Should you want **to stay**, the best option is to head for the thatched and brightly painted **cabañas** of *Escudo Jaguar* (☎0155/5329-0995 ext 8057; ❸ shared bathroom, ❺ en suite), named after Shield Jaguar, a king of Yaxchilán. The spacious rooms have comfortable beds with mosquito nets, hot water in the tiled bathrooms, and full-length windows opening onto the porch – a touch of luxury at a bargain price. There's also a good **restaurant** here, and you can **camp** nearby for M$40. More basic accommodation is available at the *Nueva Alianza* **posada** (☎0155/5329-0995 ext 8061; M$50 per person), near to the immigration post, which also has a decent *comedor*.

To reach **Yaxchilán**, you need to get a ride in a *lancha* – a narrow riverboat with benches along the side and a tin roof for shade. Several companies now compete for business. Tickets are sold at the Tikal Chilan boat co-operative office next to the museum or at *Escudo Jaguar:* you will also have to pay your entrance fee for the site here, as cash is no longer kept at the isolated ruins. Fares vary with group size, with one to four people paying M$500 between them, and little or no scope for bargaining. The **river trip** is fabulous in itself, down a broad, fast-flowing river with Mexico on one bank, Guatemala on the other, and usually a great deal of wildlife including crocodiles to help pass the time; depending on the state of the river the journey downstream to Yaxchilán takes around half an hour; the return more than twice as long. If you're heading back after visiting the site, the last buses and *combis* leave Frontera around 4pm.

## Yaxchilán

A large and impressive site, accessible only via the river on whose bank it lies, **Yaxchilán** (daily 8am–4pm; M$25) was an important Classic-period centre. From around 680 to 760 AD, the city's most famous kings, Escudo Jaguar (Shield Jaguar) and his son Pájaro Jaguar IV (Bird Jaguar), led a campaign of conquest that extended Yaxchilán's sphere of influence over the other Usumacinta centres and made possible alliances with Tikal and Palenque. The buildings occupy a natural terrace above the river, with others climbing steep hills behind – a superb natural setting. It's hot and sticky here, but the site repays the effort with its dramatic location – the difficulty of the journey heightens the feeling of isolation – and its jungle setting, the trees alive with birds and frequently with monkeys too.

From the entrance, the main path leads straight ahead to the **main plaza**. The temples here bear massive honeycombed roofs, and everywhere there are superb, well-preserved relief and stucco carvings. These panels, on lintels above doorways and on stelae, depict rulers performing ritual events, often involving blood-letting to conjure up spirit visions of ancestors. Some of the very best lintels were removed in the nineteenth century and are now in the British Museum in London, but the number and quality of the remaining panels is unequalled at any other Maya site in Mexico. **Stele 1**, the largest, stands right in the middle of the plaza near the base of the staircase ascending to Edificio 33. This depicts Pájaro Jaguar IV in a particularly eye-watering blood-letting ceremony, ritually perforating his penis. **Stele 2,** originally sited at Edificio 41, has survived several attempts to remove it from the site and now lies at the west side of the plaza, where it shows the transfer of power from Escudo Jaguar to Pájaro Jaguar IV. When the water is low here, you can see a structure built on a rock shelf on the riverbed. Some archeologists suggest this was a bridge support, and there is a similar, smaller pile on the opposite bank; alternatively it may have been a jetty, or some kind of toll booth for river traffic, or simply an altar for religious rituals.

Steep stairs climb from the plaza towards the **Gran Acrópolis** and to **Edificio 33**, the most famous building at the site, also know as El Palacio. This is what you imagine a pyramid lost in the jungle should look like, especially if you've been brought up on Tintin: in ancient times the building was a political court; more recently it has been used in religious rituals by the Lacandón Maya, and even today you may well find incense burning here. There are more superb carvings including wonderfully preserved lintels and, inside one of the alcoves, a headless statue of Pájaro Jaguar IV. According to local legend the present Creation will end when the head is reattached to his body.

**PALENQUE AND VILLAHERMOSA** | Palenque

A slippery, sometimes steep path continues through the forest, over several unrestored mounds, towards the Pequeña Acrópolis, from where you can head back to the site entrance and your boat. A detour off this path climbs steeply again towards **Edificios 39–41**, 90m above the river level – buildings that probably had some kind of astronomical significance and may have been observatories. Here and at the **Pequeña Acrópolis** the buildings are smaller and less impressive than those around the main plaza, but again they are rich in carvings. **Edificio 44** was erected by Escudo Jaguar to celebrate his victories - there were many stelae here depicting the battles, and on the lintels the king himself can be seen, grasping his prisoners by the hair. A lintel on **Edificio 42** depicts Pájaro Jaguar IV with one of his warriors.

## The Frontier Highway and transport to the sites

The **Carretera Fronteriza** (Frontier Highway) provides access to the Usumacinta Valley and the Lacandón forest – Mexico's last frontier. Along the way it passes Bonampak and Frontera Corozal, the embarkation point for the river trip to Yaxchilán. Following the line of the river and the Guatemalan frontier, the highway is now paved all the way round to Comitán de Dominguez, though the middle sections (well beyond Frontera Corozal) are still through wild, uninhabited forest where there remains the risk of armed robbery. Army checkpoints are frequent, so be sure to carry your passport. The **destruction of the forest** brought about by the construction of the road and the settlement that has followed it are palpable: en route you'll see signs to new attractions, waterfalls in the forest, tourist centres, and everywhere smoke rising as forest is cleared for farmland.

The good news is that large areas are protected, above all in the Montes Azules Biosphere Reserve, and that for the moment **wildlife** remains abundant – toucans and macaws fly across the road, howler and other monkeys are frequent visitors to the archeological sites, and on the riverbanks alarmingly large crocodiles and giant iguanas will watch your boat speed past.

By far the easiest way to visit Bonampak and Yaxchilán is with a **tour** from Palenque (see p.310); make sure that meals and site entry fees are included. Day-trips give you about an hour at Bonampak and two at Yaxchilán, which is just time to see the sites with no hanging around. The chief disadvantage of the day-trips is that you tend to arrive and leave at exactly the same time as everyone else, so these isolated places can seem almost crowded. Overnight tours, usually with accommodation at the Lacandón Maya community of Lacanhá Chansayab, allow for much more relaxed visits. Alternatively it's easy enough, and usually substantially cheaper, to **organize your own trip**, although the final cost will depend on finding people to share the boat trip from Frontera Corozal to Yaxchilán. The starting point for DIY trips is either the Río Chancala *combi* office on Hidalgo near the corner of Allende in Palenque, or Transportes Lagos de Montebello on Avenida Manuel Velasco Suarez, who have buses heading along the Frontier Highway. The first departures are around 4.30am: *combis* charge M$40 to Frontera Corozal or any point en route (San Javier for Lacanhá or the Bonampak turn-off); buses are cheaper, but for Frontera Corozal they will leave you on the highway, a M$30 taxi ride into town. For details of local accommodation and transport to the sites see Lacanhá Chansayab or Frontera Corozal (p.316).

# Travel details

## Flights

Villahermosa has a major airport with frequent daily flights to Mexico City and many other domestic destinations including Ciudad del Carmen, Mérida and Cancún, as well as a daily connection to Houston with Continental.

## Buses

**Villahermosa**: Villahermosa is a major transport hub, with a constant stream of both second- and first-class services heading out on Hwy-180 towards central Mexico (and even as far as the US border) as well as south towards Chiapas and east towards Campeche and Mérida. Main **first-class** services are as follows: Campeche (15 daily; 6hr); Cancún (11 daily; 12hr); Chetumal (9 daily; 7hr); Mérida (18 daily; 9hr); Mexico City (27 daily; 12hr); Oaxaca (3 daily; 9hr); Palenque (12 daily; 2hr 30min); Tenosique (12 daily; 3hr); Tuxtla (10 daily; 7hr); Veracruz (15 daily; 7hr). **Second-class** buses also run to most of these places – especially Palenque with stops en route – but are particularly useful for destinations within Tabasco state such as Comalcalco, Paraíso and Frontera.

**Palenque**: At peak times there are not enough buses serving Palenque – you may find you have to head to Villahermosa (12 first-class and at least 6 second daily; 2hr 30min) and pick up a connection there. Main **first-class** services are: Chetumal (3 daily; 7hr); Mérida via Campeche (4 daily; 9hr); Mexico City (4 daily; 17hr); Oaxaca (1 daily at 5.30pm; 14hr); Tulum, Playa del Carmen and Cancún (3 daily; 10/11/12hr); Tuxtla via Ocosingo and San Cristóbal de las Casas (9 daily; 3/5/7hr). **Second-class** main services are to Cancún via Campeche and Mérida (2 daily); Cancún via Chetumal and Playa del Carmen (1 daily, more at weekends); Tuxtla via Ocosingo and San Cristóbal (15 daily).

**Transportes Lagos de Montebello** has services along the Frontier Highway for Bonampak, Frontera Corozal (for Yaxchilán) and Comitán. **Combis Río Chancala** also has services along the Usumacinta Valley as far as **Benemérito**.

# Contexts

# Contexts

# History

The history of the Yucatán is inextricably linked with that of the surrounding territories. The indigenous Yucatec Maya, whose extraordinarily advanced culture and sphere of influence extended as far south as present-day Honduras, lived in a constantly changing pattern of local allegiances until the arrival of the Spanish in the early sixteenth century. Subsequently part of a loose political entity controlled from Spain – at times under the power of Mexico, sometimes thrown in with Guatemala and Central America – the Yucatán was, very briefly, an independent state before being subsumed into the newly formed Mexico in the 1820s.

## Prehistory

The exact date when human beings first crossed the Bering Strait into the Americas is debatable, but the earliest widely accepted figure is around 15,000 years ago. Successive waves of nomadic, Stone Age hunters continued to arrive until around 6000 BC, pushing their predecessors gradually further south. Some of the earliest signs of human presence in the Yucatán can be found in the peninsula's many caves – prehistoric paintings in the Grutas de Loltún, for example.

The first signs of settled habitation – the cultivation of corn, followed by the emergence of crude pottery, stone tools and even of trade between the regions – come from the **Archaic** period, around 5000–2000 BC. Thereafter, similar patterns of settlement start to appear throughout **Mesoamerica**, an area stretching from the mid-north of modern Mexico right the way to the heart of Central America. The first established civilization does not appear until the **pre-Classic** or Formative era (2500 BC to 250 AD), with the rise of the Olmecs.

Still the least known of all the ancient societies, the **Olmecs** are regarded as the "mother culture" of Mesoamerica, inventors of the calendar, glyphic writing, a rain deity – and probably also the concept of zero and the ball-game. What you see of them in museums today – or above all at the **Parque La Venta** in Villahermosa – is a magnificent artistic style, exemplified in their sculpture and in the famous colossal heads. These, with their puzzling "baby-faced" features, were carved from monolithic blocks of basalt and somehow transported over ninety kilometres from the quarries to their final settings – proof in itself of a hierarchical society commanding a sizeable workforce.

By the end of the pre-Classic period, Olmec civilization was already in decline – La Venta, the most important cultural centre, seems to have been abandoned around 400 BC, and the other towns followed over the next few hundred years. As the Olmec weakened, new civilizations grew in strength and numbers, establishing cities throughout central Mexico at sites such as Monte Albán, near Oaxaca, Cuicuilco, in the great Valley of México where Mexico City now stands, and above all **Teotihuacán**, the first truly urban society in Mesoamerica, whose architectural and religious influences reached as far south as the Maya heartlands of Guatemala.

# The Pre-Classic Maya

The first identifiably **Maya** settlements appeared in the Guatemalan highlands from around 1500 BC. From here, over the next few hundred years, the Maya spread in all directions, including to the lowlands of the Yucatán Peninsula. Early villages were little more than temporary encampments, but gradually the cultivation of corn, beans, squash and chile allowed for the development of larger settlements – always near a source of water, which in central Yucatán usually meant a cenote. The **spread of agriculture** allowed the population to grow and with population growth came a society that was increasingly hierarchical and specialized, with pottery replacing stone implements, woven cloth in place of animal fur, and writing, art and science beginning to flourish. Thatched, oval or rectangular Maya huts– recognizable to today's inhabitants of the Yucatán – formed the basis of these early villages, but buildings of increasing size and complexity were soon constructed specifically for religious purposes.

Recent discoveries suggest that by the late pre-Classic period some Maya settlements, above all in the Guatemalan highlands, were becoming very sophisticated indeed, and that previous assumptions about the timing of the development of Maya civilization may have to be brought forward. In the Yucatán development lagged behind, but even here cities of substantial size were beginning. Among the **early sites** are Edzná, where a system of canals and moats helped drain agricultural land and defend the city, Dzibilchaltún and Oxkintok, all of which lie on routes from the highlands to the Gulf coast, with its salt pans and trading opportunities.

# The Classic era

It was in the **Classic period**, however, from around 250 AD to 900 AD, that the Maya reached their peak of power and achievement. While in Europe the Roman Empire was in decline and the Dark Ages beginning, the Maya were embarking on six-and-a-half centuries of extraordinary technological, architectural, artistic and scientific advance. Without the use of metal tools, draught animals or the wheel, they built **city-states** that controlled hundreds of thousands of people, created intricate **statuary** and sculpture, and devised a **mathematical and calendar system** far more advanced than those known in the "civilized" world. For more on Maya achievements, see p.336.

Again, the first great centres of the Classic period were not in the Yucatán but in the highlands further south – cities such as Tikal, Copán and Kaminaljuyú. The most celebrated cities of the Yucatán, on the whole, were latecomers: Palenque, Yaxchilán, Uxmal and Chichén Itzá all flourished towards the end of the Classic era. Which is not to say that Yucatán was not thriving, just that important sites like Calakmul or Sayil lived to some extent in the shade of still greater powers further south.

## Conflict and downfall

There was never a single Maya empire, but rather a series of independent – yet interdependent – city-states in an almost constant state of shifting **alliances, rivalry and war**. War was necessary not just for control over rivals and access to their resources, but also for the prestige of the ruler and to provide captives, preferably high-born, for ransom and sacrifice. Some, such as Calakmul and Tikal or Yaxchilán and Palenque, seem to have been traditional rivals; others, like Yaxchilán and Bonampak or Sayil and its Puuc neighbours, enjoyed long-standing alliances.

Among the major conflicts that we know about – mainly from carvings or even paintings (such as the famous Bonampak murals) created to celebrate the victory – the battles between Tikal and Calakmul stand out. In 562 AD **Calakmul** succeeded in putting together an alliance with Yaxchilán and others that inflicted a major and lasting defeat on Tikal; it was only when this alliance fell apart that Tikal was able to take its revenge – humiliating Calakmul and its ruler, Jaguar Paw, in battle in 695. Further west, **Palenque**, under its great rulers Hanab Pakal (Jaguar Shield) and Chan Bahlum (Jaguar Serpent), spent much of the seventh century asserting its authority over the Usumacinta Basin region, forcing Yaxchilán into subservience. A hundred years later, the roles were reversed as **Yaxchilán** became the greater power – again under two kings, Escudo Jaguar (Shield Jaguar) and his son Pájaro Jaguar IV (Bird Jaguar) – and Palenque the subject. Similar swings of power affected central and northern Yucatán too, where **Uxmal** and later Chichén Itzá rose to dominance at the very end of the Classic era.

Quite what caused the **downfall of Classic Maya civilization** remains the subject of fierce debate, yet what is certain is that societies throughout Meso-america suffered a similar fate at similar times. Teotihuacán, the great power of central Mexico, was abandoned as early as 750 AD (at the end of a long decline), and within a hundred years many of the great Maya centres – in particular those in the highlands – followed suit. Maya societies in the Yucatán were among the last to retain their authority, but by around 950 AD they too were in terminal decline, if not abandoned altogether. Only Chichén Itzá continued to thrive.

Numerous theories attempt to explain the Maya collapse, among them the notion that it was caused by invaders from the north, occupying a vacuum left by the fall of Teotihuacán. Certainly Teotihuacán's demise must have severely affected its trading partners throughout Mexico and perhaps started a **chain of disasters** that had a knock-on effect. More likely than invasion, though, the causes were natural, with the Maya paying the price of their suc-cess: overpopulation exacerbated by the failure of harvests, perhaps resulting from overexploitation of the land. Such events can easily be imagined spilling over into the political sphere in a rigorously structured society, with a loss of faith in rulers and priests, perhaps even rebellion.

# Post-Classic society

If the Yucatán saw the final flourish of Classic Maya civilization at sites like Uxmal, it also saw the most powerful surviving **post-Classic societies** (900–1500 AD), above all at **Chichén Itzá**. This was the one city in the entire Maya lands – or at least the only one we know of – that not only revived its former glory from around 1000 AD on but may even have surpassed it. For many years it was believed that the revival of Chichén Itzá was the result of an invasion by the **Toltecs**, whose capital was at Tula in central Mexico. Certainly there are many apparent links between the two cities, not just in architecture, but in a new obsession with war and sacrifice, and with the legendary feathered-serpent god **Quetzalcoatl** (Kukulcán to the Maya). These days, though, most archeologists believe that Chichén Itzá remained under Maya control, albeit with strong trading and cultural links with the Toltecs. This theory sees not an invasion by a foreign power, rather the arrival of a new Maya clan, the **Itzá**, driven north by the collapse of their cities in Guatemala.

Whatever their origins, the Itzá consolidated their influence, and Chichén Itzá remained the dominant power in the peninsula until it was abandoned in the first half of the thirteenth century. Shortly afterwards, around 1263 AD, the Itzá ruler Kukulcán II founded a new city, **Mayapán**. A walled city with some 10,000 inhabitants, it led a broad alliance of small city-states that united the Yucatán for some two hundred years. Some of these were based at the great old centres like Uxmal and Chichén Itzá, others were newly prosperous towns, especially on the Caribbean coast, such as Tulum, Xel-Ha and Cozumel. What Mayapán lacked, however, was the great architecture and vast ceremonial centres of its predecessors – signs, perhaps, of a less hierarchical, more trade-based society. **Maritime trade** certainly flourished in the late post-Classic age – Christopher Columbus himself (though he never got to Mexico) encountered a heavily laden boat of Maya traders, plying the sea between the Yucatán and Honduras.

Mayapán's supremacy ended in 1441 after an attack by the Xiu people, based at Uxmal. From then until the arrival of the Spanish, the Yucatán's city-states continued to form alliances and enmities, and apparently to prosper, but they remained disparate, with no central authority or dominant group.

# The Spanish Conquest

Having heard tales of gold and empires to be claimed in the new territories ever since Columbus's accidental discovery of the Americas in 1492, the Spanish started to probe the Mexican coast from their bases in Cuba. The first expedition to land in the Yucatán was led by **Francisco Hernández de Cordoba** in 1517. Cordoba discovered Isla Mujeres, but after being driven away from Ah-Kin-Pech (Campeche) by hostile natives and caught in a storm, his team landed at the mouth of the Río Champotón to replenish their stocks of freshwater. There they were surprised by a Maya force under Moch Cuouh and heavily defeated. Cordoba died of his wounds a few days later, and the place became known as the Bay of the Bad Fight. The following year, **Juan de Grijalva** sailed round the Yucatán and up the coast as far as present-day Tampico, reporting back on the wealth of central Mexico.

The most notable Spanish invasion, of course, began with **Hernán Cortés's** landing on the coast near modern Veracruz on April 21, 1519 (Good Friday). With him were just 550 men, a few horses, dogs and a cannon, yet in less than three years they had defeated the Aztecs and effectively established control over most of Mexico. Mopping up the rest of the Aztec Empire was a relatively straightforward task for the conquistadors, but it took twenty more years to overcome the Maya.

## The defeat of the Maya

Almost immediately after their campaigns in central Mexico, the Spanish turned their eyes south. During the 1520s Pedro de Alvarado and his brother Gonzalo conquered most of what is now Guatemala and the southern Mexican highlands of Chiapas. In 1526, **Francisco de Montejo**, a veteran of the Grijalva and Cortés expeditions, travelled to Spain to petition the king for the right to conquer the Yucatán. The following year he landed at Cozumel with about 200 men, and from there crossed to the mainland. At first, his task seemed an easy one: most local chiefs, aware of the conquests elsewhere, swore loyalty to the Spanish Crown. However, as he advanced inland he found towns already deserted, and his troops began to suffer ambushes and attacks. In a pitched battle at **Aké** (near modern Tizimín) 1200 Maya warriors were killed, but Montejo also lost nearly half his force and the Maya refused to surrender. Leaving behind a small garrison, Montejo retreated to Veracruz to gather a larger army.

In 1531 Montejo returned with his son – **Francisco de Montejo the Younger** – and defeated the Maya at Campeche and set up a base there. Montejo the Younger waged a successful campaign in northern Yucatán, making alliances and declaring Chichén Itzá his capital. Meanwhile his father had travelled to Maní, where he established friendly relations with **the Xiu**, who a century earlier had brought about the downfall of Mayapán. Again, however, many Maya allies turned on the Spanish, and by 1535 the Montejos had again been forced to withdraw from the Yucatán, their troops demoralized by the fierceness of the resistance and the lack of financial reward for their efforts.

The final chapter in the conquest of the Yucatán began in 1540, when Montejo the Younger returned to Campeche with a yet larger force, founding Mérida two years later. What really tipped the scales this time was the support of the Xiu, whose leader in **Maní** converted to Christianity. The Xiu dominated much of western and northern Yucatán and most of their subject cities either followed their lead or were easily subdued. The east continued to resist, but armies led by Montejo's cousin (another Francisco de Montejo) gradually established control. By 1546, the Yucatán was firmly under Spanish control.

# Colonial rule

Cortés was appointed governor of **Nueva España** (New Spain) in 1522, and there followed three hundred years of direct Spanish rule, under a succession of 61 viceroys personally responsible to the Spanish king. The boundaries of the new territory initially stretched from Panama to the western states of the US, although it wasn't long before internal struggles erupted over their control. In 1542, the state of **Guatemala** was formed, whose territory included the Yucatán. In 1565, the capital of the new state was moved to Panama, and the Yucatán and Guatemala reverted to New Spain. In 1570, the state of Guatemala was re-established, but this time the Yucatán was attached to Mexico, and there it remained throughout the colonial era, albeit never wholly absorbed thanks to the difficulties of communication with the centre.

For the Spanish, the initial colonial concerns were reconstruction, pacification and conversion. To this end they began building grand towns (to a plan, with a plaza surrounded by a grid of streets, laid down in Spain) and constructing **churches**, often in areas that had been sacred to the Maya or on top of their pyramids. The cathedral in Mérida was built in 1561, on the ruins of a Maya temple; in Maní, the stones of the old temples were used in construction of the monastery. Churches were built like fortresses, to awe the Maya population and to serve as refuge for the white population if necessary. Moreover, they were built in places sacred to the Maya, to encourage them to worship there and prove the superiority of the new god; mass conversions were the order of the day.

The most dramatic and immediate consequence of the Spanish Conquest and colonization, however, was the **decimation of the Maya population**, not through war or famine (though some died that way) but as a result of successive epidemics of infectious **diseases**, including smallpox, measles and influenza, to which the New World had no natural immunity. It has been estimated that within a century, the native population of Mesoamerica was reduced by as much as ninety percent. Not surprisingly, the effects were catastrophic, and not only for the Indians themselves. The few survivors were treated more and more like slaves.

The Spanish Crown theoretically offered some protection to the native population – outright slavery was outlawed for example – but in practice Spanish authority was very distant from the ordinary people of the Yucatán. Indeed, many Maya were overseen by Maya chiefs, who collected tax and tribute on behalf of the colonial authorities. Some priests, too, attempted to champion indigenous rights, notably **Bartolomé de las Casas** in Chiapas, but they were few and far between. In the Yucatán, it was a Franciscan friar, **Diego de Landa**, later bishop of Mérida, who was responsible for one of the most notorious acts of all. In 1562, he held an auto-da-fé on behalf of the Inquisition, at which forty-two local Indians were tortured and executed for heresy, and over twenty Maya codices – hieroglyphic books recording Maya history and beliefs – were burnt. This constituted virtually every known written Maya record at the time. Ironically it is Landa, whose acts had been condemned in Spain, who is responsible for much of what we do know of the ancient Yucatecan Maya. Perhaps as an act of contrition, he later gathered all the information he could discover about the Maya, and compiled it in his famous book, *Relación de las Cosas de Yucatán*.

For much of the Yucatán, the colonial era settled into a pattern of semi-enslavement for the Maya population on vast landholdings granted to Spanish colonists. The region was far from the centre of Mexico, and outside the mainstream of its politics; since it had few natural resources, it was largely left to itself. The exception was around the coasts, where persistent **piracy** led much of the population to flee inland. From bases in the uninhabited areas around the Laguna de Términos (near modern Ciudad del Carmen), pirates and privateers, many of them British, operated with impunity throughout the seventeenth century. They preyed on vessels plying between Veracruz and Cuba, exploited local resources of logwood and mahogany, and frequently raided coastal towns, above all Campeche. Finally driven out at the beginning of the eighteenth century, they moved round the coast and, in 1763, with official support from Britain and following numerous battles with Spanish fleets, **British Honduras** (now Belize) was founded with the old pirate population as its basis.

What wealth there was in colonial Yucatán – and indeed throughout Mexico – was concentrated in the hands of a tiny local elite and the imperialists in Spain. The governing philosophy was that "what's good for Spain is good for Mexico", and towards that end all **trade**, industry and profit was exclusively aimed. No local trade or agriculture that would compete with Spain was allowed, so the cultivation of vines or the production of silk was banned; heavy taxes on other products – coffee, sugar, tobacco, cochineal and silver and other metals – went directly to Spain. This didn't prevent the growth of a small class of extraordinarily wealthy **hacendados** (owners of massive estates or haciendas) whose money funded the architectural development of colonial towns like Mérida and Campeche, from fortress-like huddles at the beginning of the colonial era to the full flowering of Baroque extravagance by its end – but it did stop the development of any kind of realistic economic infrastructure, even of decent roads linking the towns. There was no practical overland route from the Yucatán to central Mexico throughout the colonial era, for example.

Even among the wealthy there was growing **resentment**, fuelled by the status of Mexicans: only "**gachupines**", Spaniards born in Spain, could hold high office in the government or Church. Such people of course constituted a tiny percentage of the population – the rest were **criollos** (creoles, born in Mexico of Spanish blood) who were in general educated, wealthy and aristocratic, and **mestizos** (of mixed race) who dominated the lower ranks of the Church, army and civil service, or lived as anything from shopkeepers and small ranchers to bandits and beggars. At the bottom of the pile were the surviving Maya.

# Independence

By the beginning of the nineteenth century, Spain's status as a world power was in severe decline, while new political ideas, realized with the French Revolution and the American War of Independence, were transforming the world. Although the works of such political philosophers as Rousseau, Voltaire and Paine were banned in Mexico, the opening of the ports made it inevitable that their ideas would spread – especially as it was traders from the new United States who most took advantage of the opportunities. Literary societies set up to discuss these books quickly became centres of **political dissent**.

The spark, though, was provided by the French invasion of Spain, as colonies throughout Latin America refused to recognize the Bonaparte regime, and the campaigns of Bolívar and others in South America began. In Mexico, the "gachupine" rulers proclaimed their loyalty to Ferdinand VII (the deposed king) and hoped to carry on much as before, but creole discontent was not to be so easily assuaged. The literary societies continued to meet, and from one, in Querétaro, emerged the first leaders of the Independence movement: **Father Miguel Hidalgo y Costilla**, a creole priest, and **Ignacio Allende**, a disaffected junior army officer.

When their plans for a coup were discovered, the conspirators were forced into premature action, with Hidalgo issuing the famous Grito (cry) of Independence – ¡"Méxicanos, viva México!" – from the steps of his parish church in Dolores on September 16, 1810. The mob of Indians and mestizos who gathered behind the banner swiftly took the major towns of San Miguel, Guanajuato and others to the north of the capital, but their behaviour – seizing land and property, slaughtering the Spanish – horrified the wealthy creoles who had initially supported the movement. In 1811, Hidalgo's army, huge but undisciplined, moved on the capital, but at the crucial moment Hidalgo decided to retreat, and his forces broke up as quickly as they had been assembled. Within months, Hidalgo, Allende and the other ringleaders had been captured and executed.

By this time most creoles, frightened at what had been unleashed, had rejoined the ranks of the royalists. But many *mestizos* and much of the indigenous population remained in a state of revolt, with a new leader in the *mestizo* priest **José María Morelos**. Morelos was not only a far better tactician than Hidalgo – instituting a highly successful series of guerrilla campaigns – he was also a genuine radical. By 1813, he controlled virtually the whole of central and northern Mexico, with the exception of the capital and the route from there to Veracruz, and at the **Congress of Chilpancingo** he declared the abolition of slavery and the equality of all races. However, the royalists fought back with a series of crushing victories, Morelos was executed in 1815, and his forces were reduced to carrying out the occasional minor raid.

Ironically, it was the introduction of liberal reforms in Spain, of just the type feared by the Mexican ruling classes, which finally brought about **Mexican Independence**. Worried that such reforms might spread across the Atlantic, many creoles pre-empted a true revolution by assuming a "revolutionary" guise themselves. In 1820 **Agustín de Iturbide**, a royalist general but himself a *mestizo*, threw in his lot with Guerrero; in 1821 he proposed the **Iguala Plan** to the Spanish authorities, who were hardly in a position to fight, and Mexico was granted Independence.

# The Yucatán declares independence

Always culturally, as well as physically, separate from the rest of Mexico, the Yucatán briefly attempted to go it alone as a nation. This was not as radical a notion as perhaps it sounds – Chiapas was in a similar situation, while Guatemala and the territories of Central America, though invited to join Mexico, chose to go their separate ways. Yucatán's independence initially lasted a matter of months, however, before both the Yucatán and Chiapas joined the new nation of Mexico.

The post-independence years were chaotic to say the least, with constant changes of government, and in 1835 a new regime in Mexico City under General Santa Ana attempted to impose far more central control on the regions. Local discontent culminated in the **Mérida Congress** approving a declaration of independence for the Yucatán. At first, Governor Santiago Méndez blocked it, saying that the Yucatán would recognize the rule of the central government if the old constitution were reinstated. Promises were made but swiftly broken by President Santa Ana, and the Yucatán formally declared independence in 1841. Mexican flags were replaced by the flag of the **Republic of Yucatán** – five stars, two red stripes and one white one, on a green field.

Soon the Yucatán was suffering from loss of trade as Mexico blockaded its ports, yet more significantly the Caste Wars broke out in 1847. Desperate for help, Méndez offered sovereignty over the Yucatán to any nation that helped defeat the rebellion. Although the US considered the offer seriously, it was the newly wealthy Mexican government that took it up following the end of the Mexican-American War, and Yucatán was again reunited with Mexico on August 17, 1848.

# The Caste Wars

The **Caste Wars** were one of the most successful indigenous uprisings in history – creating an autonomous Maya state that survived for over fifty years – and yet its origins were at least as much political, over land and labour rights, as they were racial. Initially, at least, the uprising was supported by poor mestizos as well as the Maya.

For all its promises, the effect of Independence on most people in Mexico was simply a change of ruler, from the Spanish to locally born Creoles. Indeed for the lowest rungs of the population, this development actually made things worse – the protection of the Spanish Crown disappeared, and the liberalization of **land** laws allowed the privatization of previously communal land. Meanwhile the power of the Church was barely diminished, but with a reduction of funds from the government the burden of tribute on the poor became even greater. At the same time, the loss of Spanish trade meant major changes to agriculture: **henequen** was first planted in the 1830s, and by 1845 had become the Yucatán's chief export (see box, p.252); sugarcane was also widely introduced. As a result, forestland that had previously been communal was taken over by the great haciendas and cleared – these supposedly unexploited forest areas were often sacred to the Maya, homes to their gods. Water, too, was sold off, with cenotes and springs that had been in communal use for centuries handed over to private owners.

In the battles for independence, and also in internal struggles which had pitted Campeche against Mérida in a reflection of the wider struggles between liberals and conservatives taking place throughout Mexico (Campeche eventually became a separate state in 1862), many Maya had been recruited to **armed militia**, often with promises of land or freedom for their service. Such promises were rarely honoured, but the participants had learnt the use of arms, and military organization – a training the white elite of the Yucatán would regret.

The spark that ignited the Caste War is generally taken to be the execution, in July 1847, of rebel leader **Manual Antonio Ay** in Valladolid. That same year Valladolid itself, Tepich and Tabi were sacked by the rebels, and much of their white population slaughtered. By May 1848 a loose alliance of Maya forces, led by **Cecilio Chi** and **Jacinto Pat**, had occupied almost the entire peninsula and advanced to within 24km of Mérida and 8km of Campeche, where the white population had taken refuge. Allegedly, the only reason the governor had not issued orders for a complete evacuation of the Yucatán was the shortage of paper in the besieged city. At the very point of victory, however, the spring rains came, and the Maya army evaporated as its soldiers went back to their fields to plant corn.

Within months, the Mexican-American War ended, the Yucatán accepted Mexican sovereignty, and well-equipped **Mexican troops** poured in to suppress the rebellion. The rebels were pushed back into the southeastern corner of the state – what today would be southern Quintana Roo – and both Chi and Pat were assassinated in 1849. The fighting had left perhaps 200,000 people dead or displaced in the Yucatán, and over the next ten years as many as 2000 Maya were arrested and sold as slaves in Cuba.

## Chan Santa Cruz

In 1850 the **Talking Cross** appeared to a group of Maya (see box, p.175). Through it, their gods spoke to them and urged them to fight for independence. The same year, the town of Chan Santa Cruz (later Felipe Carrillo Puerto) was founded, to become the cultural, military and political capital of the ongoing Maya rebellion. From here the Maya administered a growing state, supplied with arms and other necessities from British Honduras, and launching occasional guerrilla attacks into Mexican territory. At its peak the **Maya nation of Chan Santa Cruz** controlled all the land from modern Playa del Carmen to the border of British Honduras, and inland as far as Tepich and Tihosuco; it was recognized by Britain (which benefited from the trade) as a de facto independent nation.

Chan Santa Cruz was never allowed to live at peace, however, and the Mexican government fomented rivalries with other Maya groups, supplying them with weapons and promising land rights. By the 1890s, the people and their leaders were becoming weary, and with the dictator Porfirio Díaz in power in Mexico City, British relations with Mexico improved. Partly to protect their huge new investments (in rail construction for example), the British government recognized the sovereignty of Mexico and closed the border between Chan Santa Cruz and British Honduras, cutting off the Maya nation's main line of supply. In 1901, Mexican general Ignacio Bravo occupied the town of Chan Santa Cruz, destroying the Talking Cross and officially ending the war. The final battle was anti-climactic, with the Maya short of arms and their army crippled by diseases that the Mexicans brought with them. Quintana Roo was made a territory of Mexico in 1902 (finally achieving statehood in 1975).

Isolated resistance to the Mexican republic continued for many years, with major incidents in 1917 in Vigia Chico and 1933 in Dzula, and outbreaks of rebellion reported even in the 1950s. Many of the original causes of the war, however, disappeared (at least in theory) when the victorious revolutionary armies marched into the Yucatán in 1915, bringing with them promises of land reform and the cancellation of debt labour.

# Dictatorship and revolution

Distracted by the Caste Wars and as physically isolated as ever, the Yucatán was largely a spectator during the long years of Reform wars that tore apart central Mexico from 1855 to 1876. The liberal reforms that resulted, above all the reduction of the power of the Church, reached the Yucatán late, and watered down. In 1876 a new radical liberal leader, **Porfirio Díaz**, overthrew the elected government and proclaimed his own candidate president. The following year he assumed the presidency himself, and was to rule as dictator for the next 34 years. At first his platform was a radical one but it was soon dropped in favour of a brutal policy of **modernization**.

In many ways the achievements of his dictatorship were remarkable: some 16,000km of railway were built (including the line from Mexico City to Mérida), industry boomed, telephones and telegraph were installed, and major towns, reached at last by reasonable roads, entered the modern era. In the countryside, Díaz established a police force – the notorious *rurales* – that stamped out much of the banditry (though later, their corruption became almost as bad as the bandits). But the costs were high: rapid development was achieved by handing over huge swaths of the country and its people to foreign investors, who owned the vast majority of the oil, mining rights, railways and natural resources. Corruption was rife.

This was also the era when the vast **haciendas** of the Yucatán reached their peak of power, wealth and privilege. Able to rely on the forced labour of a landless peasantry, whose serfdom was ensured by wages so low that they were permanently in debt to their employers, they had little interest in efficiency, or in production for domestic consumption. By 1900, the entire land was owned by some three to four percent of its population. The rich became very rich indeed; Yucatán's poor had lower incomes and fewer prospects than they had a century earlier.

With the onset of the **twentieth century**, opposition was growing to Díaz, not just among the poor but also the young, educated middle classes, concerned above all by the racist policies of their government (which favoured foreign investors above native ones) and by the lack of opportunity for themselves. In 1910, **Francisco Madero** ran against Díaz for president, and, when he was imprisoned and the election awarded to Díaz, Revolutionary forces took up arms. In the northern state of Chihuahua, **Pancho Villa** and **Pascual Orozco** won several minor battles, and in the southwest, **Emiliano Zapata** began to arm Indian guerrilla forces. After numerous Revolutionary successes, Díaz fled into exile, and on October 2, 1911, Madero was elected president.

Like the originators of Independence before him, Madero had no conception of the forces he had unleashed. He freed the press, encouraged the formation of unions and introduced genuine **democracy**, but failed to do anything about the condition of the peasantry or the redistribution of land. The renewed fighting between Revolutionary factions continued, on and off, for nearly ten years – and even after that there were sporadic attempts at a Catholic counter-revolution in the 1920s and 1930s.

Again, the Yucatán was only peripherally involved, with all the major battles taking place in northern and central Mexico. When **Salvador Alvarado** marched into Yucatán at the head of a Revolutionary army in 1915, the resistance of the conservative local elite was swiftly overcome.

# The Yucatán in modern Mexico

The first president who was in a secure enough position to start to make real progress towards the Revolutionary ideals was **Plutarco Elías Calles**, elected in 1924. Work on large public works schemes began – roads, irrigation systems, village schools – and about eight million acres of land throughout Mexico were given back to the villages as communal holdings, *ejidos*. At the same time Calles instituted a policy of virulent **anticlericalism**, closing churches and monasteries, and forcing priests to flee the country or go underground. Through the 1930s, Calles continued to control his successors from behind the scenes, steering national politics to the right in the bleak years of the Depression.

**Lázaro Cárdenas**, elected in 1934, revived the Revolutionary momentum. As the spokesman of a younger generation, Cárdenas set up the single broad-based party that was to rule Mexico for the rest of the twentieth century, the **PRI** (Party of the Institutionalized Revolution). He set about an unprecedented programme of reform, redistributing land on a huge scale (170,000 square kilometres during his six-year term), creating peasant and worker organizations to represent their interests at national level, and incorporating them into the governing party. He also relaxed controls on the Church to appease internal and international opposition.

In 1938, he nationalized the **oil companies**, an act that has proved one of the most significant in shaping modern Mexico and bringing about its industrial miracle. For a time it seemed as if yet more foreign intervention might follow, but a boycott of Mexican oil by the major consumers crumbled with the onset of **World War II**, and was followed by a massive influx of money and a huge boost for Mexican industry as a result of the war.

In the Yucatán, the so-called Mexican miracle was slower to take hold, and the fifty years following the Revolution were ones, on the whole, of gradual decline. Though the lot of the peasantry improved hugely thanks to land distribution and the break-up of the haciendas, in economic terms the region went backwards. Many of the haciendas had been damaged during the Revolution, and henequen production was also hampered by the confusion following land redistribution and the loss of much of the workforce to work their own fields. At the same time new sources of henequen in Asia and South America were becoming available. With the widespread replacement of henequen products by artificial fibres in the 1940s, Yucatecan agriculture lost its final overseas markets. It was not until the 1970s that the modern world started to catch up with the Yucatán. There were two chief drivers: the selection of **Cancún** for massive government investment in tourism, and the exploitation of **oil** reserves off the Gulf coast of Campeche. Suddenly the area was wealthy again and development since, above all in tourism, has been unrelenting.

The final decades of the twentieth century were traumatic for Mexico. Vast oil revenues and a one-party state proved an ideal breeding ground for **corruption**, which permeated every level of government. Despite the country's wealth, a huge foreign debt had been built up, and in the 1980s falling oil prices and rising interest rates provoked a major **economic crisis**. Public faith in the governing party was further shaken by the 1985 **earthquake** that devastated Mexico City and again revealed widespread corruption – both in the distribution of aid and in the contracts that had been awarded to erect sub-standard buildings in the first place. The governing party was further damaged by the outbreak, in 1994, of the **Zapatista** rebellion in Chiapas, a revolt that, though currently quiet, is still not entirely resolved. Finally there were **drugs**, with cartels smuggling vast quantities across the border into the US, protected by corrupt police and government officials. Their wealth and ruthless use of violence for many years made the cartels inviolate, and even today the government struggles to contain them.

All these crises, and the loss of their traditional support (even though they could still rely on the party machine to deliver election victories, earned or not) forced the PRI into ever more **radical change**, and in the 1990s much of the old party ideology was torn up in the name of economic reform. Above all the NAFTA free trade treaty was signed with the US, and the *ejido* system (see box) was reformed. At the same time, the electoral system was cleaned up. For the first time, the PRI started to lose elections.

## The end of the ejido?

Land reform was one of the great promises of the Mexican Revolution, and its most cherished legacy. Land redistributed after the Revolution was parcelled out in communal holdings, known as **ejidos**, which could not be sold as they belonged to the state. At a local level the land was held communally, divided up by the communities themselves, following the pre-Hispanic and colonial tradition. In the 1990s, however, the constitution was amended to allow the sale of *ejido* lands. Many peasants and indigenous communities feared that their landholdings were now vulnerable to speculators or corrupt officials, especially as many poor communities exist in a state of almost permanent debt, and believed that their land would be seized to cover outstanding loans, worsening their economic plight still further. All too often they have been proved right.

# Into the new millennium

On July 2, 2000, **Vicente Fox Quesada**, the candidate of the right-wing PAN party, was voted in as president and inaugurated in December that year. It was a landmark event. Not only was he the first opposition candidate ever to have been democratically placed in power, it was also the first peaceful transition between opposing governments since Independence. Furthermore, it was the end of seven decades of PRI rule and of the world's longest-surviving one-party dynasty.

Though his power is compromised by the continuing influence of the PRI in Congress and in local governments throughout the country, the president retains his popularity amongst most Mexicans, who still look to him with optimism. It remains to be seen what will happen in the presidential elections of 2006, but if the Yucatán is any guide, PRI influence continues to wane. The area had been known by Mexican political commentators as "The Land of the Dinosaurs" for the continuing grip that the PRI party machine maintained here. But even here that grip is slipping, with PAN providing the governor of Yucatán state (Edgar Ramírez Pech, elected in 2001) as well as the mayor of Mérida (Manuel Fuentes Alcocer) and other mayors across the state elected in a series of surprise results in 2004. The PRI did win the majority of elections in Campeche (in 2003) and Quintana Roo (2005), but clearly, times are changing.

## Drug-running in the Yucatán

The Yucatán was not exempt from the worst excesses of **corruption and drugs** – indeed as a stronghold of the PRI's old guard, it witnessed one of the most extreme cases. **Mario Villanueva**, governor of Quintana Roo from 1993 to 1999, disappeared a few days before his term of office – and his immunity from prosecution – ran out. He spent two years on the run before being arrested in Cancún in 2001. Villanueva is still in jail awaiting trial, but the allegations against him are breathtakingly broad.

On the one hand he is alleged to have taken millions of dollars in bribes from developers of the Riviera Maya coast, riding roughshod over ecological considerations and the rights of *ejido* landholders. At the same time, it is claimed that, with his direct involvement, Cancún and the surrounding area became one of the major shipment points used by Colombian drug cartels moving their products to the US. Although serious damage was done to this trade by his arrest and that of many associates, the war against drugs continues. In 2004, following the murder of three federal agents, the Cancún attorney general's office was occupied by the Mexican army, and over twenty senior local government and police officials arrested, suspected of involvement in the continuing drug trade.

# The Maya belief system

L
ike so many ancient cultures, the Maya have been subject to the fantastical theories of explorers as well as the imaginings of armchair spir-
itualists: "The Maya were not aided by extraterrestrial beings", a sign at
several archeological sights clarifies. "What they accomplished was due
to their ingenuity and hard work". It doesn't help, though, that the archeological record is so spotty, partially due to the fragile limestone in which the Maya
predominantly built, but more the fault of the Spanish conquerors who were
not content just to destroy the physical symbols of the Maya but also bent on
systematically replacing the pagan culture with Catholicism.

Much of our knowledge of the ancient Maya, then, is derived from the
surviving traditions, handed down through the generations, often in secret to
protect them from Spanish depredations. The **Chilam Balam**, for instance, are
cumulative records of lore and prophecy recorded in various villages in Latin
script in the late seventeenth and early eighteenth centuries. Experts also draw
on various Spanish contemporary accounts, as well as the sculpture, pottery and
jewellery retrieved from tombs. Images carved into the ruins of buildings offer
clues, while the breakthrough in decoding the hieroglyphic system, a success of
just the past few decades, has contributed greatly to the historical record. Further hints come from other Mesoamerican cultures, as the Maya share a great
deal with the Aztecs and Toltecs, as well as the earliest culture with a strong
archeological record, the Olmecs.

## The Olmec influence

The cities of the **Olmecs**, the first great Mesoamerican civilization, formed
a template that was traced by subsequent cultures, including the Maya. They
were the first Mesoamerican civilization literally to set their cosmology in
stone, making a permanent record of their rulers, and the gods and spirits with
whom they communed. The Olmec place of creation was the mighty volcano
of **San Martín**, in the south of modern Veracruz State, and they built a replica
– a sacred artificial mountain, complete with fluted sides – in their city at **La
Venta** in Tabasco. This was the original Mesoamerican **pyramid**, a feature
that recurs in virtually every subsequent culture. Into the base of their volcano
pyramid the Olmecs embedded huge **stelae**, flat carved stones portraying ruling dignitaries communicating with gods and spirits. These were the first stelae
in Mesoamerica, and later versions fill the plazas of ruined cities in the Maya
world and all over Central America.

One stele at La Venta depicts a **World Tree**, a symbol of the "axis mundi" at the
centre of the Mesoamerican universe – its roots in the earth, its branches in the
heavens, linking the underworld of the dead with the earth and sky. Though this
was perhaps the first such representation, World Trees have been found in cities all
over Mesoamerica. Among the Maya, the World Tree is specifically the spreading
boughs of the silk-cotton (ceiba) tree. At Palenque there are several images of the
ceiba, including one on the lid of a ruler's sarcophagus, where the ruler is shown
falling through a World Tree inscribed in the night sky – the Milky Way.

Opposite Mexico's first pyramid, the Olmecs built a **gateway** to the spirit
world, home to a pantheon of gods, spirits and the souls of dead ancestors, in

the form of a sunken, court-shaped plaza with an enormous pavement of blocks made of the mineral serpentine. They added two large platforms topped with mosaics and patterns depicting aquatic plants, symbols of a gateway to the spirit world. Such symbols appeared all over Mesoamerica in the ensuing centuries, often decorating ball-courts or ceramics.

The Olmecs also developed the ritual **ball-game** that appears in every subsequent Mesoamerican culture. Usually played in a ball-court shaped like a letter I, the game featured players, in teams of two or three, who would score points by using their thighs or upper arms to hit the ball through hoops or at markers embedded in the court walls. The penalty for losing the most important games was death – though there have been suggestions that the winners were sacrificed in some cities.

In general, the basic structure of Olmec society – a theocracy ruled over by a priestly and regal elite who communicated with and propitiated the spirit world through sacrifice and ritual blood-letting – would change little throughout Mesoamerica until the advent of Cortés, but there were some important developments. An increasing preoccupation with divining and balancing the material and the spirit world was aided by the invention of the calendar and writing.

# The calendar

For the Maya, the stars were embodiments of gods, and the constellations re-enactments of cosmic events; they regarded the three stars below the belt of Orion as the place of creation itself. Their interest in the constant shifting of the heavens was aided by the invention of the **calendar**, probably by the Zapotecs of Monte Albán in about 600 BC.

By the time of the Classic Maya (250–900 AD), the 260-day calendar, depicted as a wheel, had become the highest tool of prediction and divination. Every number and day had its own significance; each of the twenty-day names had a specific god and a particular direction, passing in a continuous anticlockwise path from one day to the next until a cycle of time was completed. This calendar was used alongside a 365-day calendar, roughly matching the solar year, but lacking the leap days necessary to give it real accuracy. This was divided into eighteen groups of twenty days plus an unlucky additional five days. Each twenty-day grouping and each solar year also had a supernatural patron. When the two calendars were set in motion and running concurrently, it took exactly 52 years for the cycle to repeat.

In addition to these two calendars, the pre-Classic Maya developed what is known as the **Long Count**, recording the total number of days elapsed since a mythological date when the first great cycle began. Under this elaborate record system, all became sacred, and every event from the planting of crops to the waging of war had to occur at the correct spiritual time.

# The pantheon

The ancient Maya worshipped a staggering number of gods who represented virtually every facet of life, from specific activities (Ek Chuah oversaw trade and commerce, for instance) to places, such as the maize fields, where squat, mischievous *aluxes* were believed to stand guard. The deities' relative importance varied across the Maya world, but typically the Sun God, most often called **K'inich Ahau**, was considered the supreme deity. As the creator, he took several forms: by night, he became the Jaguar God, guarding the way to the underworld. Characterized by crossed eyes and buckteeth, he was one of the oldest gods in the Mesoamerican tradition, also worshipped by the Olmecs. Especially in the Post-Classic era after 900 AD, he was conflated with **Itzamná**, a powerful god credited with inventing writing and the tradition of scribes. He was elderly, often depicted with a hooknose and toothless mouth and holding a pen; his consort was **Ixchel**, goddess of fertility. Also vital to the pantheon, and a highly visible god on surviving Maya buildings, was the rain god **Chac**, easily identified by a long snout, which often curls upward.

The Maya's relationship with their gods was not one of simple worship, but of struggle and outwitting. Life was not so much borrowed time, but time won by trickery from the gods of death. Maya vases, buried with the dead, often depict scenes from the Popul Vuh, the creation epic of the Quiché Maya tribe, in which the **Hero Twins**, two proto-humans with godlike powers, defeated the **Lords of the Underworld** through a series of tricks and their expertise in the ball-game.

In the Yucatán, this connection to the spirit world was made all the more tangible by the **caves** and **cenotes** that riddled the peninsula: these, it was believed, were open gateways to the underworld, and, as a result, many of them were considered sacred and the site of numerous rituals. Though the ancient Maya were not as bloodthirsty as the Aztecs of central Mexico (whose cosmology rested on the gods' seemingly insatiable appetite for human hearts), their rituals do seem to have included **human sacrifice**. When the main cenote at Chichén Itzá was dredged, for instance, it was found to contain numerous skeletons, and Fray Diego de Landa recorded details of sacrifices in his day, in the mid-sixteenth century.

The Spanish conquistadors and the Franciscan priests who accompanied them toppled a pantheon that had been in place for centuries. Hundreds of thousands of books were burnt, priests executed and temples overturned. Such is the tenacity of the traditional beliefs of the Maya, though, that even five hundred years of effort have not been enough to eradicate them entirely, as anyone who has entered a rural church in the Yucatán or witnessed the rituals of the **Day of the Dead** – called Hanal Pixan by the Maya – can attest.

# Environment and wildlife

The Yucatán Peninsula and Maya Chiapas contain some of Mexico's richest wildlife areas, with the birdlife being particularly outstanding. The lush tropical forests of **Chiapas** and **southern Yucatán** contain the remaining populations of monkeys and large cats, as well as vividly coloured parrots and toucans, while the flat uplands and coastal areas of the **Yucatán Peninsula** host a fabulous collection of migrating birds, including large flocks of greater flamingos. Snorkelling along the Mesoamerican Barrier Reef and islands in the Caribbean reveals schools of brilliantly coloured fish.

Unfortunately, as in many countries suffering economic hardship, much of this natural beauty is under threat either from direct hunting or from the indirect effects of **deforestation** and **commercialization**. It is imperative that visitors be respectful of and responsible towards the natural environment and support the vital educational programmes hoping to preserve its remnants.

It should be stressed that not only is it extremely irresponsible to buy, even as souvenirs, items that involve wild animals in their production, but it is also generally **illegal** to bring them back to the UK or the US. This applies specifically to tortoiseshell, black coral, various species of butterfly, mussels and snails, stuffed baby crocodiles, cat skins and turtle shells. Trade in living animals, including tortoises, iguanas and parrots (often sold as nestlings), is also illegal, as is the uprooting of cacti.

# Geography

The Yucatán Peninsula is a single limestone platform, one of the largest on the planet. An accretion of layers of decayed reefs, it's rarely more than a few feet above sea level. There's no visible sign of it now, but 65 million years ago, an enormous meteor slammed into the north Gulf coast near the town of Chicxulub Puerto; this is the meteor that is thought to have brought about a catastrophic climate change and the extinction of the dinosaurs. The climate, fortunately, is more stable today: the region is entirely within the **Tropic of Cancer**, and rainfall varies across the landmass, though generally there are only two seasons: a hot, wet one, from late May to October, and a temperate, dry one through most of the winter and spring. Hurricanes are a risk between late September and November, and, due to the lack of elevation, they have on occasion swept well inland: Hurricane Isidore did substantial damage to Mérida in 2002.

Most of the Yucatán's geographic interest lies underground. Despite the total lack of visible rivers, a lens of freshwater is trapped just below the limestone surface, occasionally exposed through sinkholes called **cenotes**, and filling vast and beautiful **caves**, some more than 100m deep. In 2001 and 2002, explorers discovered three human skeletons that are more than 10,000 years old in caves; several prehistoric elephants and other giant Pleistocene animals have also been brought to light. Because limestone is so porous, however, the aquifer is very easily contaminated, and scientists are only now starting to advise the government on safe modes of growth and development.

C

# Vegetation

The Yucatán Peninsula's vegetation is influenced by its low relief and the ameliorating effects of its extensive coastline, which bring regular and fairly reliable rain along with year-round warm temperatures. The northern portion is primarily **dry deciduous scrub**, filled with tamarind and bay cedar. Much of the thorny scrub has been cleared to grow maize, citrus fruits and **henequen**, a variety of agave cactus used for the production of rope. A swath of **seasonal tropical forest**, where many of the low acacias and ceibas drop their leaves in the dry season, covers the centre, mostly in Yucatán State. **Bougainvillea**, **hibiscus** and **flame trees** add dramatic colour in these areas. **Tropical rainforests** extend across the base of the Yucatán Peninsula and through Tabasco, containing mahogany, cedar, rosewood, ebony and logwood, as well as over 800 species of **wild orchid**. Extensive **mangrove forests** line much of the Gulf coast and the Caribbean. Throughout, though, charcoal cutting or slash-and-burn agriculture has substantially denuded the original forest. Similarly, tourism growth along the coast has eaten away at the mangroves – a short-sighted move, as runoff from the trees' root systems nourishes the coral reefs that draw tourists in the first place.

The tropical forests provide supplies of both **chocolate** (from the cacao trees of the Chiapas) and **vanilla**. Also harvested are **chicle**, used in the preparation of chewing gum, from the latex of the **sapodilla** tree, and **wild rubber** and **sarsaparilla**. Herbs, used in the medicinal or pharmaceutical industries, include **digitalis** from wild **foxgloves** and various **barks** used in the preparation of purges and disinfectants. The **Discorea composita** plant, unique to Mexico, is harvested in Tabasco and Chiapas, and is used in the preparation of a vegetable hormone that forms an essential ingredient of the contraceptive pill.

# Insects

Insect life is abundant, with numbers and diversity reaching their peak in the tropical rainforests. Openings in the tree canopy attract a variety of **gnats**, giant **grasshoppers** (called *langostas*, or lobsters) and colourful **butterflies**. At peak times of year, butterflies fill the air almost like snow, but, for the most part, insects makes themselves known through the variety of bites and sores incurred whilst wandering through these areas: **mosquitoes** are a particular pest, with malaria still a small risk in the jungle areas. The **garrapata** is a particularly tenacious tick found everywhere livestock exists, and readily attaches itself to human hosts. And while **scorpions** live throughout the Yucatán, they are generally not lethal (and are in fact eaten dried as a purported wart cure); **tarantulas** are also encountered in the dryer areas, and they too are not poisonous.

In the forests, long columns of **leafcutter ants** crisscross the floor in their search for tasty bits of fungus on tree bark, and surrounding tree trunks provide ideal shelter for large, brown nests of **termites**. Carnivorous **army ants** also sweep through in waves, devouring grasshoppers and other pests but leaving greenery untouched.

# Fish and reptiles

Because the Yucatán has no rivers above ground and only one substantial lake, freshwater fish are few. The Yucatán cenotes and lagoons contain two endemic species, the **Mayan cichlid** and the **banded tetra**, while deep in the underwater cave systems, several varieties of **eyeless fish** flourish. Chiapas's Río Usumacinta, however, is home to more than one hundred species.

Offshore, the Yucatán waters contain over one hundred significant marine species. Among the more prevalent are **swordfish**, **snapper**, **bonefish**, **tarpon** and **mackerel**. **Shrimp** and **spiny lobster** are also important commercial species, and deep ocean beds and coastal irregularities provide rewarding fishing in the waters of the Campeche bank on the Gulf of Mexico. The Laguna de Términos, near Ciudad del Carmen, hosts the country's largest fishing fleet. A variety of sharks cruise the reefs, but the most remarkable ones are the placid **whale sharks** congregating at the end of every summer off the coast of Isla Holbox, in perhaps the largest community in the world.

As for reptiles, **iguanas** and smaller **lizards** are at home in the forests and at seemingly every archeological site, while **crocodiles** populate the mangrove swamps and other brackish lagoon areas. **Marine turtles**, including the loggerhead, green, hawksbill and leatherback, are still found off many stretches of undeveloped waters and shores on the Gulf and Caribbean coasts. Hunting of both adults and eggs is against the law, but numbers have been greatly reduced, as illegal hunting continues. Nonetheless, programmes to protect turtle nests have been established in many of the major tourist areas, which may help boost the population in the future. Several kinds of **rattlesnake** are common in the forests, and you can find the occasional **fer-de-lance** viper in the Chiapas jungle, but generally the number of poisonous snakes is few; assorted large green **tree snakes** are more common. Amphibian life is similarly abundant; varieties include salamanders, several types of **frog** and the massive **cane toads** that have invaded nearly every continent.

# Birds

Between the marshes and scrublands of the northern Yucatán Peninsula and the dense rainforests in the south and Chiapas, this region of Mexico is a delight for birdwatchers: during the winter migratory season, some two billion birds pass through. Among the diverse species (more than five hundred in the jungles alone) are resplendent **red macaws** and **parrots**, which make a colourful display as they fly amongst the dense tree canopy. The cereal-feeding habits of the parrot family have not endeared them to local farmers, and for this reason (and their continuing capture for sale as pets), their numbers have also been seriously depleted in recent times. Larger game birds, such as **curassow**, **chachalaca** and especially the **ocellated turkey** (an essential food for the Maya for millennia) can be seen on the ground. Keel-billed **toucans** can also be spotted in the southern jungles – in a modern just-so story, Maya legend has it that the tips of their bills are red because they dipped them in the blood that covered the land during the nineteenth-century Caste Wars. Another distinctive species in the Yucatán is the large turquoise-browed **motmot** (*toh'* in Maya), called the clock bird (*pájaro reloj*) because it switches its long tailfeathers rhythmically like a pendulum.

The most familiar large birds of Mexico, however, are the carrion-eating **turkey vultures**, which migrate from North America and are often seen soaring in large groups. The Yucatán is also one of the last remaining strongholds of the small **Mexican eagle**, which features in the country's national symbol.

Large numbers of coastal lagoons serve as feeding and breeding grounds for a wide variety of aquatic birds – some of them winter visitors from the north. Foremost among these are the substantial flocks of graceful **flamingos** that can be seen at selected sites along the western and northern Gulf coasts.

# Mammals

The central Yucatán forest has traditionally teemed with **agouti, opossums** and **coatimundis**, but these have been seriously depleted by overhunting. Long-legged **pacas** (*tepescuintle*) have suffered greatly, as they have a reputation for being particularly tasty; they, at least, are now being semi-domesticated. **Spider** and **howler monkeys** inhabit the depths of the forests, though their numbers too are decreasing as their territory shrinks.

The largest ground-dwelling mammal in the region is the **tapir**, a distant relative of the horse, with a prehensile snout, usually never found far from water. Two species of **peccary**, a type of wild pig, wander the forest floors in large groups seeking their preferred food (roots, palm nuts and even snakes), and there's the smaller **brocket deer**. The **jaguar**, so revered by the Maya, is severely endangered.

The drier tropical and subtropical forests of northern Yucatán produce a more varied ground cover of shrubs and grasses, which supply food for the **white-tailed deer** and abundant small rodents such as the spiny tree **rat**, which in turn provides food for a variety of predators such as the **margay** and **jaguarundi**. Other large mammals that can still be found in small numbers are large and small **anteaters** and **armadillos**. The reefs and lagoons that run along the Quintana Roo coast have small colonies of the large aquatic **manatee** or sea cow, a docile creature that feeds on sea grass.

# Books

Most big US bookstores have an enormous array of books about, from, or set in Mexico, as well as a few novels. In the rest of the English-speaking world there's far less choice, though the best known of the archeological and travel titles below should be available almost anywhere. In the lists provided, the UK publisher is followed by the US one; where only one publisher is listed it's the same in both places, or we've specified; o/p means a book is out of print, but may still be found in libraries or secondhand bookstores. Books with a ⋆ symbol are highly recommended.

For less mainstream titles and, especially, for those covering contemporary Mexico, there are a few useful **specialist sources**. In the UK the Latin America Bureau (LAB), 1 Amwell St, London EC1R 1UL (☎020/7278 2829, fax 7278 0165, ⓦwww.lab.org.uk), publishes books featuring all aspects of the region's society, current affairs and politics. Supporters receive a 25 percent discount off LAB books and a twice-yearly copy of *Lab News*. You can freely visit Canning House Library, 2 Belgrave Square, SW1X 8PJ (☎020/7235 2303), which is the UK's largest publicly accessible collection of books and periodicals on Latin America, though you have to be a member to take books out and receive the twice-yearly *Bulletin*, a review of recently published books on the region.

# Travel

⋆ **Graham Greene** *The Lawless Roads* (Bodley Head/Viking). In the late 1930s Greene was sent to Chiapas and Tabasco to investigate the effects of the persecution of the Catholic Church. The result was this classic account of his travels in a very bizarre era of modern Mexican history; *The Power and the Glory* is an absorbing fictionalized version, centred on the exploits of a "whiskey priest" on the run from the authorities.

**Michel Peissel** *The Lost World of Quintana Roo* (Dutton, o/p). In 1958, the 21-year-old Peissel bushwhacked, on foot, through the virtually empty fringe of the peninsula. Definitely worth snapping up if you find a used copy, as it's a great depiction of an area that has changed rapidly in just a few decades.

**Nigel Pride** *A Butterfly Sings to Pacaya* (Constable, UK, o/p). The author, accompanied by his wife and 4-year-old son, travels south from the US border in a Jeep, heading through Mexico, Guatemala and Belize. Though the travels took place over 25 years ago, the pleasures and privations they experience rarely appear dated.

**John Lloyd Stephens** *Incidents of Travel in Central America, Chiapas, and Yucatán* (Dover). A classic nineteenth-century traveller, Stephens, acting as American ambassador to Central America, indulged his own enthusiasm for archeology. His journals, full of superb Victorian pomposity punctuated with sudden waves of enthusiasm, make great reading. The best editions include the fantastic original illustrations by Frederick Catherwood; the Smithsonian edition combines some of these with modern photographs.

**John Kenneth Turner** *Barbarous Mexico* (University of Texas, o/p). Journalist Turner's account of his travels through nineteenth-century

Mexico, exposing the conditions of workers in the plantations of the Yucatán, did much to discredit the regime of Porfirio Díaz.

**Ronald Wright** *Time Among the Maya* (Abacus/Grove). A vivid and sympathetic account of travels from Belize through Guatemala, Chiapas and Yucatán, meeting the Maya of today and exploring their obsession with time. The book's twin points of interest are the ancient Maya and the recent violence involving the Zapatistas.

# Fiction and poetry

**Jorge Ibargüengoitia** *The Dead Girls, Two Crimes* and others (all Chatto & Windus/Avon, o/p). One of the first modern Mexican novelists translated into English, Ibargüen-goitia was killed in a plane crash in 1983. These two are both blackly comic thrillers, superbly told, the first of them based on real events.

⭐ **Octavio Paz** (ed) *Mexican Poetry* (Grove). Edited by Paz (perhaps the leading man of letters of the post-Revolutionary era) and translated by Samuel Beckett, this is as good a taste as you could hope for of modern Mexican poets. Some of Paz's own poetry is also available in translation.

**Earl Shorris** *In the Yucatan* (W.W. Norton). This novel, the story of a Mexican-American lawyer and a Maya mystic who bond in jail, has its flaws, but its background detail is excellent, providing a good dose of political commentary and cultural information about the Maya.

⭐ **B. Traven** various works. Traven wrote a whole series of compelling novels set in Mexico. Among the best-known are *Treasure of the Sierra Madre* (Prion/Hill & Wang) and *The Death Ship* (L. Hill Books), but of more direct interest if you're travelling are such works as *The Bridge in the Jungle* and the other six books in the *Jungle* series: *Government, The Carreta, March to the Monteria, Trozas, The Rebellion of the Hanged* and *General from the Jungle* (all Allison & Busby/I. R. Dee, some o/p). These latter all deal with the state of the peasantry and the growth of revolutionary feeling in the last years of the Díaz dictatorship, and if at times they're overly polemical, as a whole they're enthralling.

# History

**Inga Clendinnen** *Ambivalent Conquests: Maya and Spaniard in Yucatán 1517 to 1570* (Cambridge UP). A product of meticulous research that documents the methods and consequences of the Spanish conquest of the Yucatán. The ambivalence in the title refers to the effectiveness of the conquest in subjugating the Maya, and the book provides insights into post-Conquest rebellions.

⭐ **Bernal Díaz** (trans J.M. Cohen) *The Conquest of New Spain* (Viking). This abridged version is the best available of Díaz's classic *Historia Verdadera de la Conquista de la Nueva España*. Díaz accompanied Francisco de Cordoba and Juan de Grijalva on their initial forays into the Yucatán, then joined Cortés for his campaign of conquest. This magnificent eyewitness account still makes compulsive reading.

**Brian Hamnett** *A Concise History of Mexico* (Cambridge UP). The book kicks off with a brief examination of contemporary issues and then jumps back to the time of the Olmecs. A combined chronological and thematic approach is used to analyse the social and political history of Mexico from then up until the present day. Some fairly large chunks of history are glossed over, but key events and issues are explored in greater detail, making for a good general introduction.

 **Nelson Reed** *The Caste War of the Yucatán* (Stanford UP).

Reed's book is the authority on this tumultuous and defining era in Yucatán history, with great detail on the Talking Cross movement. A must-read for anyone intrigued by this period.

**Hugh Thomas** *Conquest: Montezuma, Cortés, and the Fall of Old Mexico* (Touchstone); *The Conquest of Mexico* (Pimlico, UK). Same book, different title, but either way a brilliant narrative history of the Conquest by the British historian previously best known for his history of the Spanish Civil War. A massive work of real scholarship and importance but also humorous and readable, with appendices on everything from Aztec beliefs, history and genealogy to Cortés's wives and lovers.

# The ancient Maya

**Michael D. Coe** *The Maya* (Thames & Hudson). The best available general introduction to the Maya: concise, clear and comprehensive. Coe has also written several more weighty, academic volumes. His *Breaking the Maya Code* (Thames & Hudson), a history of the decipherment of the Maya glyphs, owes much to the fact that Coe was present at many of the most important meetings leading to the breakthrough, demonstrating that the glyphs actually did reproduce Maya speech. Aside from anything else, it is a beautifully written, ripping yarn, though the slagging-off of Eric Thompson gets a bit wearisome.

**M.S. Edmonson** (trans) *The Book of Chilam Balam of Chumayel* (Aegean, US, o/p). The *Chilam Balam* is a recollection of Maya history and myth, compiled by the Maya over centuries; this version was written in Maya in Latin script in the eighteenth century. Although the style is not easy, it's one of the few keys into the Maya

view of the world.

**Charles Gallenkamp** *Maya: The Riddle and Rediscovery of a Lost Civilization* (Penguin). Gallenkamp's short, accessible summary of Maya civilization also provides a history of the region's excavation, with profiles of noted archeologists and their expeditions.

**Diego de Landa** *Yucatán Before and After the Conquest* (Dover). Edited by William Gates, this is a translation of the work written by de Landa, a Franciscan monk, in 1566 as *Relación de las Cosas de Yucatán*. De Landa's destruction of almost all original Maya books as "works of the devil" assured his own account became the chief source on Maya life and society in the immediate post-Conquest period. Written during his imprisonment in Spain on charges of cruelty to the Indians (remarkable itself, given the institutional brutality of the time), the book provides a fascinating wealth of detail.

**Mary Ellen Miller** *Maya Art and Architecture* (Thames & Hudson, UK). An excellent survey of the artisanship of the Maya, organized by media, from stelae to pottery. Miller's *The Art of Mesoamerica: From Olmec to Aztec* gives a broader view.

★ **Mary Ellen Miller and Karl Taube** *The Gods and Symbols of Ancient Mexico and the Maya: An Illustrated Dictionary of Mesoamerican Religion* (Thames & Hudson). A superb modern reference on ancient Mesoamerica, written by two leading scholars. Taube's *Aztec and Maya Myths* (British Museum Press) is perfect as a short, accessible introduction to Mesoamerican mythology.

**Jeremy A. Sabloff** *New Archaeology and the Ancient Maya* (W.H. Freeman). A fascinating look at how much modern understanding of the Maya has changed in the century and a half since serious study began.

**Linda Schele, David Freidel et al.** The authors, in the forefront of the "new archeology", have been personally responsible for decoding many of the glyphs, thereby revolutionizing and popularizing Maya studies. Although their writing style, which frequently includes recreations of scenes inspired by their discoveries, is controversial to some fellow professionals, it has also inspired a devoted following. *A Forest of Kings: The Untold Story of the Ancient Maya* (Quill, US) in conjunction with *The Blood of Kings*, by Linda Schele and Mary Ellen Miller, details how the ancient Maya were ruled by hereditary kings, lived in populous, aggressive city-states, and engaged in a continuous entanglement of alliances and war. *Maya Cosmos: Three Thousand Years on the Shaman's Path* (Quill, US), by Schele, Freidel and Joy Parker is perhaps more difficult to read (dense with copious notes), but continues to examine Maya ritual and religion in a unique and far-reaching way. *The Code of Kings* (Touchstone, US), written in collaboration with Peter Matthews and illustrated with Justin Kerr's famous "rollout" photography of Maya ceramics, examines in detail the significance of the monuments at selected Maya sites.

**Robert Sharer** *The Ancient Maya* (Stanford UP). The classic, comprehensive (and weighty) account of Maya civilization, now in a completely revised and much more readable fifth edition, yet as authoritative as ever. Required reading for archeologists, it provides a fascinating reference for the non-expert.

**Dennis Tedlock** (trans), *Popol Vuh* (Touchstone). Translation of the Quiché Maya bible, a fascinating creation myth from the only ancient civilization to emerge from rainforest terrain. The Maya obsession with time can be well appreciated here, where dates are recorded with painstaking precision.

# Society, politics and culture

**Rick Bayless** *Rick Bayless's Mexican Kitchen* (Scribner/Absolute). Aimed at ambitious chefs, this tome has more than 150 recipes but no photos. The country's gastronomic heritage is explored in detail with a special focus on the myriad types of chile that form the heart of Mexican cuisine. More accessible is Bayless's *Mexico One Plate at a Time*, which focuses on the classics of the cuisine (though with no Yucatecan dishes, unfortunately), with careful instructions and thorough coaching, including a testimony in favour of lard.

**Fernández de Calderon Candida** *Great Masters of Mexican Folk Art* (Harry N Abrams). A grand and gorgeously photographed coffee-table book produced by the cultural wing of Banamex, with portraits of the artisans alongside their works.

**Macduff Everton** *The Modern Maya: A Culture in Transition* (University of New Mexico). Everton's black-and-white photographs document Maya village life with affection and dignity, with an eye to socioeconomic issues.

**Nancy and Jeffrey Gerlach** *Foods of the Maya* (University of New Mexico). A solid introduction to the Yucatecan culinary tradition, very well tested for non-Mexican kitchens.

**Diana Kennedy** *The Essential Cuisines of Mexico* (Clarkson Potter). Kennedy was a pioneer in bringing the multifaceted cuisine of Mexico to the attention of Americans, when she published her first cookbook in 1972. This book is an almost overwhelming reference, but compiled with love. Pair with *From My Mexican Kitchen: Techniques and Ingredients* if you're completely new to Mexican cooking.

**Dan La Botz** *Democracy in Mexico* (South End Press, US). Examines the political landscape of modern Mexico and puts it into historical context by equating the rise of civil society and political consciousness with the major defining events of recent decades – the 1968 student massacre, the 1985 earthquake, and the 1994 Zapatista uprising amongst others.

**Elena Poniatowska** various works. A pioneer in the field of testimonial literature and one of Mexico's best-known essayists and journalists. In *Here's to You Jesusa* (Farrar, Straus & Giroux), Poniatowska turns her attentions on her cleaning lady. Jesusa's story of her marriage, involvement in the Revolution and postwar period include her views on life, love and society. Narrated in the first person, the text is compelling, lively and at times ribald: Jesusa herself is now a celebrity on the literary circuit. Other works available in English include *Massacre in Mexico* (University of Missouri), a collage of testimonies of those present at the 1968 massacre of students in Tlatelolco; *Dear Diego* (Pantheon, US, o/p); and *Tinisima* (Farrar, Straus & Giroux/Penguin, US).

★ **John Ross** *Rebellion from the Roots* (Common Courage Press). A fascinating early account of the build-up to and first months of the 1994 Zapatista rebellion, and still the definitive book on the subject. Ross's reporting style provides a really detailed and informative background, showing the uprising was no surprise to the Mexican army. He's also the author of *Mexico in Focus* (LAB/Interlink), a short but authoritative guide to modern Mexican society, politics and culture – worth reading before a visit.

**Guiomar Rovira** *Women of Maize* (LAB). Rovira, a Mexican journalist, witnessed the Zapatista uprising in Chiapas on New Year's Day 1994. This book, which interweaves narrative, history and the personal recollections of numerous women involved in the rebellion, provides an extraordinary insight into the lives of indigenous people. The women interviewed reflect on how their previously traditional lifestyles were transformed when they joined up with the Zapatista National Liberation Army and gained access to education and other opportunities they'd never even dreamt of.

**Chloë Sayer** *The Arts and Crafts of Mexico* (Thames & Hudson/Chronicle). Sayer is the author of numerous books on Mexican arts, crafts and associated subjects, all of them worth reading.

**Joel Simon** *Endangered Mexico* (Sierra Club Books). Eloquent and compelling study documenting the environmental crisis facing Mexico at the end of the twentieth century. Accurate and very moving, it's essential reading for those wanting to know how and why the crisis exists – and why no one can offer solutions.

**Mariana Yampolsky** *The Traditional Architecture of Mexico* (Thames & Hudson). The enormous range of Mexico's architectural styles, from thatched peasant huts and vast haciendas to exuberant Baroque churches and solid, yet graceful public buildings, is encompassed in this inspired book. While most of Mariana Yampolsky's superb photographs are in black and white, a chapter on the use of colour emphasizes its importance in every area of life; the text by Chloë Sayer raises it above the level of the average coffee-table book. (For guides to ecclesiastical architecture in Mexico, see Richard Perry, below.)

# Other guides

In Mexico, the best and most complete series of guides is that published by **Guías Panorama** – they have small books on all the main archeological sites, as well as more general titles.

**Carl Franz** *The People's Guide to Mexico* (Avalon Travel). Not a guidebook as such, more a series of anecdotes and words of advice for staying out of trouble and heading off the beaten track. Perennially popular, and deservedly so.

**Joyce Kelly** *An Archaeological Guide to Mexico's Yucatán Peninsula* (University of Oklahoma). Detailed and practical guide to more than ninety Maya sites and eight museums throughout the peninsula, including many little-known or difficult-to-reach ruins; an essential companion for anyone travelling purposefully through the Maya world. Kelly's "star" rating – based on a site's archeological importance, degree of restoration and accessibility – may affront purists, but it does provide a valuable opinion on how worthwhile a particular visit might be.

**Richard and Rosalind Perry** *Maya Missions* (Espadaña Press, US). One in a series of expertly written guides to the sometimes overlooked treasures of Mexico's colonial religious architecture. *More Maya Missions* covers Chiapas. Both are illustrated by the author's simple but beautiful drawings. These specialist offerings, ideal for travellers who want more information than most guidebooks can provide, are not widely available, though you can usually find them in tourist bookstores in the areas they cover.

**Jules Siegel** *Cancun User's Guide 2005*. Siegel, a freelance journalist, moved to Mexico in 1981, then worked for the tourism ministry in the nascent resort city. His self-published tome is as much an ode to this underappreciated city and the people who built it as it is a practical guide, with shopping and eating recommendations. Affectionate, opinionated and guaranteed to change your outlook on Cancún.

# Wildlife

**Rosita Arvigo** *Sastun: My Apprenticeship with a Maya Healer* (Harper-Collins). The author established an organic herb farm in Belize, then studied with the region's best-known medicine man for five years. Her story is fascinating for anyone interested in herbal treatments; more detail can be found in her *Rainforest Home Remedies*.

★ **Les Beletsky** *Tropical Mexico: The Ecotravellers' Wildlife Guide* (Academic). An excellent field guide, with colour plates of not just birds but also reptiles and mammals found throughout the Yucatán and Chiapas.

**Ernest Preston Edwards** *A Field Guide to the Birds of Mexico and Adjacent Areas: Belize, Guatemala, and El Salvador* (University of Texas). Some 850 species are shown in colour plates, with names in English, Latin and Spanish.

**Steve Gerrard** *The Cenotes of the Riviera Maya.* This self-published full-colour guide is hard to come by outside of Mexico, but it's worth tracking down if you'll be doing any cave diving, as it's tremendously thorough.

★ **Steve Howell and Sophie Webb** *The Birds of Mexico and Northern Central America* (Oxford UP, o/p). A tremendous work, the result of years of research, this is the definitive book on the region's birds. Essential for all serious birders.

**Paul Humann and Ned DeLoach** *Snorkeling Guide to Marine Life: Florida, Caribbean, Bahamas* (New World). A clear field guide to corals, fish, plants and other underwater life off the Caribbean coast, with 280 colour photos.

**Thor Janson** *Maya Nature: An Introduction to the Ecosystems, Plants and Animals of the Mayan World* (Vista). A good complement to an illustrated field guide, as the 196 colour photographs show animals in their natural habitat.

**R.T. Peterson and E.L. Chalif** *Mexican Birds* (Houghton Mifflin). The classic ornithological guide to Mexico. The text is excellent, but drawings are limited to indigenous examples only; migratory species are included in additional (North American) guides, which can be frustratingly impractical.

**Victoria Schlesinger** *Animals and Plants of the Ancient Maya: A Guide* (University of Texas). More than a field guide, this book also examines the cultural significance of more than 100 species in the ancient Maya world.

## The music of the Yucatán

The Yucatán peninsula's historical tendency to look not to central Mexico but to the Caribbean and Europe for its culture is reflected strongly in its music, particularly *trova yucateca*, which melds European and Cuban rhythms with local heritage to produce something entirely unlike the brassy, boastful mariachi music that's most associated with Mexico.

**Trova yucateca**, the dreamily sentimental ballads performed most typically by trios of string musicians, is an outgrowth of Cuban music, fashionable in Mérida in the late nineteenth century. The city's upper class, rich from the surrounding henequen plantations, loved nothing better than to dance elegant, romantic dances like *la habanera* and *la guaracha*. At the same time, to reinforce Mérida's self-made reputation as "París en miniatura", children were also groomed for French salon society, with music lessons as part of their acculturation.

Some of these well-groomed youngsters grew up to be composers, adapting Cuba's vibrant dance music to the Yucatecan setting. This meant incorporating the Spanish-inspired rhythm of the **jarana**, danced in the Maya towns during fiestas, while Mérida's best writers penned heartfelt paeans to local Maya women. The singers conveyed their gallantry and sensitivity with oiled hair, limpid eyes and starched shirts. By the 1920s, *trova yucateca* was in full flower, and the songs of this era, such as "Caminante del Mayab", "Ojos Tristes" and "Beso Asesino", are often compiled on albums and performed by each succeeding generation.

Today's *trovadores* hew closely to tradition, though you may see trios made up of instruments other than the usual guitar, *mandolín* and *tololoche* (double bass guitar), or you may see a solo lounge crooner with more modern tousled hair and an unbuttoned shirt, rather than the crisp white guayabera. But this is still music to romance women by – or to sip a drink and lapse into reverie about the ones you've lost. In Mérida, you can do this every night of the week, as *trova* trios gather on the Plaza de la Constitución to be hired for a single serenade or an evening's show.

**Recordings** are hard to come by outside of Mexico, but consult the Arhoolie label in the US (⊛www.arhoolie.com), which distributes some recordings from the Mexican label Pentagrama, including a couple of albums by the four-decades-old Mérida trio Los Condes, and a video tribute to Pastor Cervera, one of the most famous *trova* composers. Look for others while in Mexico, where there's a very strong industry of home CD production by current *trova* artists.

# Language

# Language

# Mexican Spanish

O nce you get into it, **Spanish** is actually a straightforward language – and in Mexico people are desperately eager to understand and to help the most faltering attempt. **English** is widely spoken, especially in the tourist areas, but you'll get a far better reception if you at least try to communicate with people in their own tongue. You'll be further helped by the fact that Mexicans speak relatively slowly (at least compared with Spaniards) and that there's none of the awkward lisping pronunciation.

## Rules of pronunciation

Relative to English, the rules of **pronunciation** are clear-cut and strictly observed. Unless there's an accent, words ending in d, l, r and z are stressed on the last syllable, all others on the second last. All vowels are pure and short.

**A**  is between the A sound of "back" and that of "father"

**E**  as in "get"

**I**  as in "police"

**O**  as in "hot"

**U**  as in "rule"

**C**  is spoken like S before E and I, hard otherwise: *cerca* is pronounced "serka".

**G**  is a guttural H sound (like the ch in "loch"); before E or I, G is hard: *gigante* becomes "higante".

**H**  is always silent.

**J**  the same sound as a guttural G: *jamón* is pronounced "hamon".

**LL**  sounds like an English Y: *tortilla* is pronounced "torteeya".

**N**  often pronounced M at the ends of words in the Yucatán (Yucatám).

**Ñ**  with the tilde (accent), spoken like NY: *mañana* sounds like "manyana".

**QU**  is pronounced like an English K.

**R**  is rolled, RR doubly so.

**V**  sounds more like B, *vino* becoming "beano".

**X**  has an S sound before consonants; between vowels in place names, it has an H sound, like México ("meh-hee-ko"). In Maya words, X sounds like SH – so Xel-Ha is pronounced "shel-ha".

**Z**  is the same as a soft C, so *cerveza* becomes "servesa".

## Useful words and phrases

Although we've listed a few essential words and phrases here, if you're travelling for any length of time some kind of **dictionary** or **phrasebook** is obviously a worthwhile investment: the *Rough Guide to Mexican Spanish* is the best practical guide, correct and colloquial, and will have you speaking the language faster than any other phrasebook. One of the best small Latin American Spanish dictionaries is the University of Chicago version (Pocket Books), widely available in Mexico, although the Langenscheidt pocket dictionary is often used because its yellow plastic cover holds up to wear and tear. If you're using an older dictionary, bear in mind that CH, LL and Ñ are traditionally counted as separate letters and are listed after the Cs, Ls and Ns respectively; most current dictionaries, however, follow more familiar alphabetizing procedures, though Ñ retains its own section.

## Basics

| | | | |
|---|---|---|---|
| **Yes, No** | Sí, No | **Good, Bad** | Buen(o)/a, Mal(o)/a |
| **Open, Closed** | Abierto/a, Cerrado/a | **Here, There** | Aquí/Acá, Allí/Allá |
| **Please, Thank you** | Por favor, Gracias | **Big, Small** | Gran(de), Pequeño/a |
| | | **This, That** | Éste, Eso |
| **Push, Pull** | Empujar, Tirar | **More, Less** | Más, Menos |
| **Where?, When?** | ¿Dónde?, ¿Cuándo? | **Today, Tomorrow** | Hoy, Mañana |
| **With, Without** | Con, Sin | **Cheap, Expensive** | Barato/a, Caro/a |
| **What?, How much?** | ¿Qué?, ¿Cuánto? | **Yesterday** | Ayer |
| | | **Now, Later** | Ahora, Más tarde |

## Greetings and responses

| | |
|---|---|
| **Hello, Goodbye** | ¡Hola!, Adiós |
| **Good morning** | Buenos días |
| **Good afternoon/night** | Buenas tardes/noches |
| **How do you do?** | ¿Qué tal? |
| **See you later** | Hasta luego |
| **Sorry** | Lo siento/disculpeme |
| **Excuse me** | Con permiso/perdón |
| **How are you?** | ¿Cómo está (usted)? |
| **Not at all, you're welcome** | De nada/por nada |
| **I (don't) understand** | (No) Entiendo |
| **Do you speak English?** | ¿Habla (usted) inglés? |
| **I (don't) speak Spanish** | (No) Hablo español |
| **What (did you say)?** | Mande? |
| **My name is...** | Me llamo... |
| **What's your name?** | ¿Cómo se llama usted? |
| **I am English** | Soy inglés(a) |
| **...American*** | americano(a) |
| **...Australian** | australiano(a) |
| **...Canadian** | canadiense(a) |
| **...Irish** | irlandés(a) |
| **...Scottish** | escosés(a) |
| **...Welsh** | galés(a) |
| **...New Zealander** | neozelandés(a) |

\*Mexicans are from the Americas, too, so describing yourself as American can occasionally cause offence. Better to opt for "estadounidense" (from "Los Estados Unidos", Spanish for the United States) if you are a US American.

## Hotels, transport and directions

| | |
|---|---|
| I want... | Quiero... |
| I'd like... | Quisiera... por favor |
| Do you know...? | ¿Sabe...? |
| I don't know | No sé |
| There is... (Is there...?) | (¿)Hay...(?) |
| Give me... | Dame... |
| (one like that) | (uno así) |
| Do you have...? | ¿Tiene...? |
| ...the time | ...la hora |
| ...a room | ...un cuarto |
| ...with two beds/ double bed | ...con dos camas/ cama matrimonial |
| It's for one person (two people) | Es para una persona (dos personas) |
| ...for one night (one week) | ...para una noche (una semana) |
| It's fine, how much is it? | ¿Está bien, cuánto es? |
| It's too expensive | Es demasiado caro |
| Don't you have anything cheaper? | ¿No tiene algo más barato? |
| Can one...? | ¿Se puede...? |
| ...camp (near) here? | ¿...acampar aquí (cerca)? |
| Is there a hotel nearby? | ¿Hay un hotel aquí cerca? |
| How do I get to...? | ¿Por dónde se va a...? |
| Left, right, straight on | Izquierda, derecha, derecho |
| This way, that way | Por acá, por allá |
| Where is...? | ¿Dónde está...? |
| ...the bus station | ...la camionera central |
| ...the railway station | ...la estación de ferrocarriles |
| ...the nearest bank | ...el banco más cercano |
| ...the ATM | ...el cajero automático |
| ...the post office | ...el correo (la oficina de correos) |
| ...the toilet | ...el baño/sanitario |
| Where does the bus to . . . leave from? | ¿De dónde sale el bus para . . .? |
| I'd like a (return) ticket to . . . | Quisiera un boleto (de ida y vuelta) para . . . |
| What time does it leave (arrive in...)? | ¿A qué hora sale (llega en...)? |
| What is there to eat? | ¿Qué hay para comer? |
| What's that? | ¿Qué es eso? |
| What's this called in Spanish? | ¿Cómo se llama éste en español? |

# Numbers and days

| | | | |
|---|---|---|---|
| 1 | un/uno/una | 70 | setenta |
| 2 | dos | 80 | ochenta |
| 3 | tres | 90 | noventa |
| 4 | cuatro | 100 | cien(to) |
| 5 | cinco | 101 | ciento uno |
| 6 | seis | 200 | doscientos |
| 7 | siete | 500 | quinientos |
| 8 | ocho | 700 | setecientos |
| 9 | nueve | 1000 | mil |
| 10 | diez | 2000 | dos mil |
| 11 | once | | |
| 12 | doce | **first** | primero/a |
| 13 | trece | **second** | segundo/a |
| 14 | catorce | **third** | tercero/a |
| 15 | quince | **fifth** | quinto/a |
| 16 | dieciséis | **tenth** | decimo/a |
| 17 | diecisiete | | |
| 18 | dieciocho | **Monday** | lunes |
| 19 | diecinueve | **Tuesday** | martes |
| 20 | veinte | **Wednesday** | miércoles |
| 21 | veintiuno | **Thursday** | jueves |
| 30 | treinta | **Friday** | viernes |
| 40 | cuarenta | **Saturday** | sábado |
| 50 | cincuenta | **Sunday** | domingo |
| 60 | sesenta | | |

## Yucatec Maya basics

**Yucatec** is the variant of Maya spoken throughout the Yucatán Peninsula and northern Belize. (Maya in Chiapas and Guatemala speak other variants: Tzotzil, Tzeltal, Quiché and others.) An estimated one million people speak Yucatec, whether in small villages in central Yucatán State (which has the highest number of native Yucatec speakers) or on the city streets of Mérida. Most Maya are also at least conversant in Spanish, but they will generally appreciate any effort you make to communicate in their language. If you are interested in learning more, look for Gary Bevington's *Maya for Travelers and Students* (University of Texas Press, 1995), which provides a good introduction to the structure of the language, with a basic dictionary, as well as commentary on Maya culture. In Mexico, you may be able to find *Metodo Fácil para Leer, Escribir y Hablar la Lengua Maya*, by Jésus Rivero Azcorra and published in Mérida; it has English translation as well, and supplies more complete (though often obscure: "Clean out that iguana", for instance) phrases than Bevington's book.

For pronunciation, spelling here reflects the modern academic style, and is fairly phonetic. An X is spoken as "sh", and an apostrophe is a light glottal stop, or pause. Draw out double vowels, and try to keep stress equal on all syllables.

| | |
|---|---|
| **What's up?** | Ba'ax ka wa'alik? |
| **Not much** | Mixba'al |
| **How are you?** | Biix a beel? |
| **I'm fine** | Ma'aloob |
| **Where are you going?** | Tu'ux ka bin? |
| **I am going to Mérida** | Inka' bin a Ho |
| **What's your name?** | Ba'ax a k'aaba'? |
| **My name is...** | In k'aaba'(e)... |
| **Where are you from?** | Tu'ux ka tah? |
| **Let's go** | Ko'osh |
| **See you later** | Ka'ka't(e) |
| **See you tomorrow** | Samaal |
| **Yes** | He'le' |
| **No** | Ma' |
| **I** | Ten |
| **You** | Tech |
| **Is there...** | Yan he'? |
| **There is...** | Yan... |
| **There is no...** | Mina'an.../Na'am... |
| **What's that?** | Ba'ax lela'? |
| **How much?** | Bahuux? |
| **Thank you** | Dyos bo'otik |
| **You're welcome** | Mixba'al |
| **Bon appétit!** | Hach ki' a wi'ih! |

# Glossaries

## Terms and acronyms

**Ahorita** diminutive of *ahora* (now) meaning "right now" – but seldom applied as literally as a visitor might expect.

**Auto-da-fé** a public act of repentance, usually involving punishment or execution, and a product of the Inquisition; used most frequently in the Yucatán to refer to Fray Diego de Landa's burning of Maya texts in Maní in 1562.

**Ayuntamiento** town hall/government.

**Barrio** area within a town or city; suburb.

**Camino blanco** unpaved rural road, so called because it is paved with limestone gravel.

**Cantina** bar, usually men-only.

**Ceiba** large tropical silk-cotton tree; also the sacred tree of the Maya that represents the world.

**Cenote** a natural sinkhole in the limestone surface, and an underground water source in the Yucatán.

**Chac** Maya god of rain.

**Chac-mool** recumbent statue, possibly a sacrificial figure or messenger to the gods.

**Comal** large, round, flat plate made of clay or metal used for cooking tortillas.

**Comedor** cheap restaurant, literally dining room; also called a *cocina económica*.

**Convento** either convent or monastery.

**Cruzob** Maya followers of the Talking Cross, a nativist political movement begun during the Caste Wars of the nineteenth century.

**CTM** central union organization.

**Descompuesto** out of order.

**Don/Doña** courtesy titles (sir/madam), mostly used in letters or for professional people or the boss.

**Ejido** communal farmland.

**EPR** Ejército Popular Revolucionario, the Popular Revolutionary Army. Guerrilla group, not allied to the Zapatistas; their first appearance was in Guerrero in 1996.

**EZLN** Ejército Zapatista de Liberación Nacional, the Zapatista Army of National Liberation. Guerrilla group in Chiapas.

**Feria** fair (market).

**FONART** government agency to promote crafts.

**FONATUR** government tourism agency.

**Fray** Spanish word for friar.

**Gringo** not necessarily insulting, though it does imply North American – said to come from invading US troops, either because they wore green coats or because they sang "Green grow the rushes oh!..."

**Guayabera** embroidered Cuban-style shirt, usually for men.

**Güera/o** blonde; a very frequently used description of Westerners, especially shouted after women in the street. Not intended as an insult.

**Hacienda** plantation estate or the big house on it.

**Hacendado** plantation owner.

**Henequen** a variety of agave cactus

grown mainly in Yucatán State, the fibres of which are used to make rope.

**Huipil** Maya women's embroidered white smock dress, worn over a white petticoat, usually with a small checkered scarf.

**I.V.A.** 15 percent value-added tax (VAT).

**Jarana** a popular dance that blends Maya and Spanish styles; often performed at local *ferias*.

**Kukulkán** Maya name for Quetzalcoatl, the plumed serpent god.

**Ladino** applied to people, means Spanish-influenced as opposed to Indian; determined entirely by clothing (and culture) rather than physical race.

**Licensio** A common title, literally meaning "graduate" or "licensed"; abbreviated Lic.

**Malecón** seafront promenade.

**Malinche** Cortés's Indian interpreter and mistress, a symbol of treachery.

**Mariachi** quintessentially Mexican music, with lots of brass and sentimental lyrics; derives from northern Mexico, however, and is not particularly popular in the Yucatán; contrast *trova*.

**Maya** tribe who inhabited Honduras, Guatemala and southeastern Mexico from earliest times, and still does.

**Mestizo** mixed race, of Indian and Spanish descent.

**Metate** flat stone for grinding corn; used with a *mano*, a grinding stone.

**Milpa** a small subsistence farm plot, tended with slash-and-burn agricultural practices.

**Mirador** lookout point.

**Muelle** jetty or dock.

**NAFTA** the North American Free Trade Agreement that includes Mexico, the USA and Canada; see also TLC, right.

**Palacio** mansion, but not necessarily royal.

**Palacio de Gobierno** headquarters of state/federal authorities.

**Palacio Municipal** headquarters of local government.

**Palapa** palm thatch. Used to describe any thatched/palm-roofed hut.

**PAN** Partido de Acción Nacional (National Action Party), conservative party that took power when Vicente Fox became president in 2000.

**Paseo** a broad avenue, but also the ritual evening walk around the plaza.

**PEMEX** the Mexican national oil company.

**Planta baja** ground floor – abbreviated PB in lifts.

**PRD** Partido Revolucionario Democrático (Party of the Democratic Revolution), the left-wing opposition formed and led by Cuauhtémoc Cárdenas; has the second largest number of seats in Congress.

**PRI** Partido Revolucionario Institucional (Party of the Institutional Revolution), the ruling party for eighty years, until the surprise PAN upset in the 1999 elections.

**PT** Partido del Trabajo (Workers' Party), small party but with opposition seats in Congress.

**PVEM** Partido Verde Ecologista de México (Green Party), small opposition party.

**Quetzalcoatl** the plumed serpent – most powerful, enigmatic and widespread of all ancient Mexican gods.

**Sacbé** ancient Maya road, paved with limestone; plural *sacbeob*.

**Stele** freestanding carved monument; plural stelae.

**TLC** Tratado de Libre Comercio, the Spanish name for NAFTA.

**Toltec** tribe that controlled central Mexico between Teotihuacán and the Aztecs.

**Tope** speed-bump or other barrier on rural roads for slowing traffic.

**Trova** Romantic Yucatecan song style popular in the early twentieth century, still played by *trovadores*.

**Tula** the Toltec capital.

**Tzompantli** Aztec skull rack, or "wall of skulls".

**Wetback** derogatory term for illegal Mexican (or any Hispanic) in the US; *mojado* ("wet") is the Spanish term, without the negative connotations.

# Art and architectural terms

**Alfiz** decorative rectangular moulding over a doorway.

**Arabesque** elaborate geometric pattern of Islamic origin.

**Artesonado** intricate ceiling design, usually of jointed, inlaid wood.

**Atlantean** pre-Hispanic column in the form of a warrior – examples found at Tula and Chichén Itzá.

**Atrium** enclosed forecourt of churchyard or monastery; *atrio* in Spanish.

**Azulejo** decorative glazed tile, usually blue and white.

**Churrigueresque** highly elaborate, decorative form of Baroque architecture (usually in churches), named after the seventeenth-century Spanish architect.

**Camarín** room in a church used for storing and dressing sacred statues.

**Convento** monastery residence that includes the cloister.

**Dado** ornamental border on the lower part of an interior wall.

**Escudo** shield-shaped decoration.

**Espadaña** belfry, usually on top of the front wall of a church.

**Fluting** vertical grooves in a column.

**Fresco** technique of painting on wet or dry plaster.

**Garita** ornamental pinnacle or battlement which looks like a sentry box.

**Grotesque** ornamental style depicting fantastic birds, beasts and foliage.

**Herrerian** imperial style named after sixteenth-century Spanish architect Juan de Herrera.

**Lunette** crescent-shaped space above a doorway or beneath a vault.

**Merlón** decorative pyramidal battlement.

**Mudéjar** Spanish architectural style strongly influenced by Moorish forms.

**Ogee** curved, pointed arch.

**Pila** font or water basin; also commonly found in domestic buildings.

**Pilaster** flattened column used as decorative element.

**Pinjante** glove-shaped decorative pendant, popular in eighteenth-century architecture.

**Plateresque** elaborately decorative Renaissance architectural style.

**Portales** arcades.

**Portería** entry portico to a monastery.

**Predella** base panel of an altarpiece.

**Purista** severe Renaissance architectural style, originating in sixteenth-century Spain.

**Retablo** carved, painted wooden altarpiece.

**Zapata** wooden roof beam, often decoratively carved.

# Food and drink terms

## On the table

| | | | |
|---|---|---|---|
| **Azúcar** | Sugar | **Pimienta** | Pepper |
| **Cuchara** | Spoon | **Queso** | Cheese |
| **Cuchillo** | Knife | **Sal** | Salt |
| **Cuenta** | Bill | **Salsa** | Sauce |
| **Mantequilla** | Butter | **Servilleta** | Napkin |
| **Pan** | Bread | **Tenedor** | Fork |

## Cooking terms

| | |
|---|---|
| **Asado/a** | Broiled |
| **Al horno/horneado** | Baked |
| **A la tampiqueña** | Meat in thin strips served with guacamole and enchiladas |
| **A la veracruzana** | Usually fish, cooked with tomatoes, onions and green olives |
| **En mojo de ajo** | Fried with slow-cooked garlic |
| **Barbacoa/pibil** | Wrapped in leaves and herbs and steamed/cooked in a pit |
| **Con mole** | In mole sauce, based on a rich spice paste – *mole poblano* (with bitter chocolate) is the most common |
| **A la parilla** | Grilled over charcoal |
| **A la plancha** | Grilled on a hot plate |
| **Empanizado/a** | Breaded |
| **Frito** | Fried |
| **Poco hecho/a punto /bien cocido** | Rare/medium/well-done |

## Breakfast

| | |
|---|---|
| **Chilaquiles** | Tortilla strips with shredded chicken and tomato sauce |
| **Huevos...** | Eggs... |
| **...a la mexicana** | ...scrambled with tomato, onion and chile |
| **...con jamón** | ...with ham |
| **...con tocino** | ...with bacon |
| **...motuleños** | ...fried, served on a tortilla with beans, ham, cheese, tomato sauce, peas and fried sweet plantains |
| **...rancheros** | ...fried, served on a tortilla and smothered in a hot, red chile sauce |
| **...revueltos** | ...scrambled |
| **...tibios** | ...lightly boiled |
| **Pan dulce** | Pastries |

## Soups (sopas) and starters

| | |
|---|---|
| Botana | Any snack served with drinks; given free at traditional bars |
| Caldo | Broth (with bits in) |
| Ceviche | Raw fish pieces, marinated in lime juice and mixed with tomato and coriander |
| Entremeses | Hors d'oeuvres |
| Sopa... | Soup... |
| ...de frijoles | ...creamy black-bean soup |
| ...de lima | ...chicken soup with tortilla strips and lime |
| ...de verduras | ...vegetable soup |

## Tortilla and corn dishes (antojitos)

| | |
|---|---|
| Chiles rellenos | Stuffed peppers |
| Enchiladas | Rolled-up tacos, covered in chile sauce and baked |
| Enchiladas suizas | As above, with green chile and cheese |
| Flautas | Small rolled tortillas filled with red meat or chicken and then fried |
| Molletes | Split roll covered in beans and melted cheese, often with ham and avocado too |
| Panuchos | Like salbutes, but with black beans as well |
| Quesadillas | Toasted or fried tortillas topped with cheese |
| Queso fundido | Melted cheese, served with tortillas and salsa |
| Salbutes | Crisp-fried tortillas topped with shredded turkey, lettuce, avocado and pickled onions |
| Tacos | Soft corn tortillas with filling |
| Tacos arabes/al pastor | Tacos filled with spicy pork, sometimes served with a slice of pineapple |
| Tacos dorados | Deep-fried meat tacos |
| Tamales | Corn-meal pudding, stuffed with meat and steamed or baked in banana leaves |
| Torta | Bread roll filled with meat, lettuce and avocado |
| Tostadas | Flat crisp tortillas piled with meat and salad |
| Totopos | Crisp-fried tortilla wedges, served with salsa |

## Fish and seafood (pescados y mariscos)

| | | | |
|---|---|---|---|
| Calamares | Squid | Corvina | Sea bass |
| Camarones | Prawns | Filete entero | Whole, filleted fish |
| Cangrejo | Crab | Huachinango | Red snapper |
| Caracol | Conch | Langosta | Rock lobster |
| Cazón | Baby shark | Merluza | Hake |
| Coctel | Seafood served in a tall glass with a spicy tomato sauce and avocado | Ostión | Oyster |
| | | Pezespada | Swordfish |
| | | Pulpo | Octopus |
| | | Sábalo | Tarpon |

## Meat (carne) and poultry (aves)

| | | | |
|---|---|---|---|
| Alambre | Kebab | Filete | Tenderloin/fillet |
| Albóndigas | Meatballs | Guisado | Stew |
| Arrachera | Skirt steak | Hígado | Liver |
| Barbacoa | Barbecued meat | Lengua | Tongue |
| Bistec | Steak (not always beef) | Lomo | Loin (of pork) |
| | | Milanesa | Breaded escalope |
| Cabeza | Head | Pata | Feet |
| Cabrito | Kid | Pato | Duck |
| Carne (de res) | Beef | Pavo | Turkey |
| Carne adobado | Barbecued/spicily stewed meat | Pechuga | Breast |
| | | Pierna | Leg |
| Carnitas | Pork cooked with garlic until crispy | Pollo | Chicken |
| | | Salchicha | Sausage or hot dog |
| Cerdo | Pork | Salpicón | Shredded beef and sliced radishes seasoned with vinegar |
| Chivo | Goat | | |
| Chorizo | Spicy sausage | | |
| Chuleta | Chop (usually pork) | | |
| Codorniz | Quail | Ternera | Veal |
| Conejo | Rabbit | Tripa | Tripe |
| Cordero | Lamb | Venado | Venison |
| Costilla | Rib | | |

## Vegetables (verduras)

| | | | |
|---|---|---|---|
| Aguacate | Avocado | Hongos | Mushrooms |
| Arroz | Rice | Huitlacoche | Corn fungus, "Mexican truffles" |
| Betabel | Beetroot (often as a juice) | | |
| | | Jitomate | Tomato |
| Calabacita | Zucchini (courgette) | Lechuga | Lettuce |
| | | Lentejas | Lentils |
| Calabaza | Squash | Nopales | Cactus paddle, usually roasted or pickled |
| Cebolla | Onion | | |
| Champiñones | Mushrooms | | |
| Chícharos | Peas | Papas | Potatoes |
| Col | Cabbage | Rajas | Strips of mild green *poblano* pepper |
| Elote | Corn on the cob | | |
| Espinacas | Spinach | | |
| Flor de calabaza | Squash blossoms | Zanahoria | Carrot |
| Frijoles | Beans | | |

# Fruits (frutas) and juice (jugo)

| | | | |
|---|---|---|---|
| Cherimoya | Custard apple (sweetsop) | Melón | Melon |
| China | Orange (only in Yucatán) | Naranja | Orange |
| Ciruela | Plum | Papaya | Papaya |
| Coco | Coconut | Piña | Pineapple |
| Durazno | Peach | Pitahaya | Dragonfruit, a type of cactus fruit with a mild, tangy taste |
| Frambuesa | Raspberry | | |
| Fresa | Strawberry | Plátano | Banana/plantain |
| Guanábana | Soursop, like a large custard apple | Sandía | Watermelon |
| | | Toronja | Grapefruit |
| Guayaba | Guava | Tuna | Prickly pear (cactus fruit) |
| Higo | Fig | | |
| Limón | Lime | Uva | Grape |
| Mamey | Like a large zapote, with sweet pink flesh reminiscent of sweet potato | Zapote | Sapodilla, fruit of the chicle tree |

## Drinks (bebidas)

| | |
|---|---|
| Agua (mineral/con gas) | (Sparkling) water |
| Café de la olla | Mexican-style coffee brewed in a clay pot |
| Cerveza | Beer |
| Chelada | Beer with lime juice, ice and salt |
| Michelada | Beer with spicy lime juice, ice and salt |
| Horchata | Creamy rice-milk drink, sometimes with coconut |
| Té | Tea |
| Vino | Wine |

## Sweets (dulces)

| | |
|---|---|
| Cajeta | Caramel confection often served with... |
| ...crepas | ...pancakes |
| ...churros | ...cinnamon-covered fritters |
| Champola | Ice cream or sorbet in a tall glass filled with milk |
| Ensalada de frutas | Fruit salad |
| Flan | Crème caramel |
| Helado | Ice cream |
| Nieve | Sorbet |
| Paleta | Fruit popsicle |
| Raspada | Shaved ice with fruit syrup |

## Yucatecan specialities

| | |
|---|---|
| **Achiote** | Spice paste made with orange annatto seeds and garlic |
| **Adobo** | Chile-based spice paste similar to achiote |
| **Brazo de reina** | Large tamal filled with hard-cooked eggs and green pumpkin-seed paste |
| **Habañero** | Small, extremely hot chile pepper, made into red and green salsas |
| **Mondongo kabic** | Tripe stewed in achiote and bitter orange and green onions |
| **Papadzules** | Enchiladas filled with hard-cooked egg and topped with green pumpkin-seed sauce |
| **Poc-chuc** | Pork marinated in citrus juice, then grilled |
| **Pollo en relleno negro** | Chicken in a black, slightly burnt chile sauce |
| **Puchero** | Meaty stew with sweet potato seasoned with cinnamon and allspice |
| **Queso relleno** | round of Dutch cheese hollowed out and filled with a spicy fruit-meat filling, all topped with cream sauce |
| **Sikil-p'aak** | Spicy ground-pumpkin-seed dip |
| **Tikin xik'** | Fish with achiote and spices wrapped in banana leaves and grilled |
| **Xnipek** | Raw *habañero* salsa; literally "dog's nose," for the sweat it induces |

**L**

LANGUAGE | Food and drink terms

# Rough
# Guides
advertiser

# Rough Guides travel...

**UK & Ireland**
Britain
Devon & Cornwall
Dublin
Edinburgh
England
Ireland
Lake District
London
London DIRECTIONS
London Mini Guide
Scotland
Scottish Highlands &
   Islands
Wales

**Europe**
Algarve
Amsterdam
Amsterdam
   DIRECTIONS
Andalucía
Athens DIRECTIONS
Austria
Baltic States
Barcelona
Belgium &
   Luxembourg
Berlin
Brittany & Normandy
Bruges & Ghent
Brussels
Budapest
Bulgaria
Copenhagen
Corfu
Corsica
Costa Brava
Crete
Croatia
Cyprus
Czech & Slovak
   Republics
Dodecanese & East
   Aegean
Dordogne & The Lot
Europe
Florence directions
France

Germany
Greece
Greek Islands
Hungary
Ibiza & Formentera
Iceland
Ionian Islands
Italy
Languedoc &
   Roussillon
Lisbon
Lisbon DIRECTIONS
The Loire
Madeira directions
Madrid
Mallorca
Malta & Gozo
   directions
Menorca
Moscow
Netherlands
Norway
Paris
Paris DIRECTIONS
Paris Mini Guide
Poland
Portugal
Prague
Provence & the Côte
   d'Azur
Pyrenees
Romania
Rome
Sardinia
Scandinavia
Sicily
Slovenia
Spain
St Petersburg
Sweden
Switzerland
Tenerife & La Gomera
   DIRECTIONS
Turkey
Tuscany & Umbria
Venice & The Veneto
Venice DIRECTIONS
Vienna

**Asia**
Bali & Lombok
Bangkok
Beijing
Cambodia
China
Goa
Hong Kong & Macau
India
Indonesia
Japan
Laos
Malaysia, Singapore &
   Brunei
Nepal
The Philippines
Singapore
South India
Southeast Asia
Sri Lanka
Thailand
Thailand's Beaches &
   Islands
Tokyo
Vietnam

**Australasia**
Australia
Melbourne
New Zealand
Sydney
North America
Alaska
Big Island of Hawaii
Boston
California
Canada
Chicago
Florida
Grand Canyon
Hawaii
Honolulu
Las Vegas directions
Los Angeles
Maui directions
Miami & the Florida
   Keys
Montréal
New England

New Orleans
New York City
New York City
   DIRECTIONS
New York City Mini
   Guide
Pacific Northwest
Rocky Mountains
San Francisco
San Francisco
   DIRECTIONS
Seattle
Southwest USA
Toronto
USA
Vancouver
Washington DC
Yosemite
Yucatán

**Caribbean
& Latin America**
Antigua DIRECTIONS
Argentina
Bahamas
Barbados DIRECTIONS
Belize
Bolivia
Brazil
Caribbean
Central America
Chile
Costa Rica
Cuba
Dominican Republic
   directions
Ecuador
Guatemala
Jamaica
Maya World
Mexico
Peru
St Lucia
South America
Trinidad & Tobago

**Africa & Middle East**
Cape Town
Egypt
The Gambia

Rough Guides are available from good bookstores worldwide. New titles are
published every month. Check www.roughguides.com for the latest news.

# ...music & reference

Jordan
Kenya
Marrakesh
  DIRECTIONS
Morocco
South Africa, Lesotho
  & Swaziland
Syria
Tanzania
Tunisia
West Africa
Zanzibar

**Travel Theme guides**
First-Time Around the
  World
First-Time Asia
First-Time Europe
First-Time Latin
  America
Skiing & Snowboarding
  in North America
Travel Health
Travel Online
Travel Survival
Walks in London & SE
  England
Women Travel

**Restaurant guides**
French Hotels &
  Restaurants
London Restaurants

**Maps**
Algarve
Amsterdam
Andalucia & Costa
  del Sol
Argentina
Athens
Australia
Baja California
Barcelona
Berlin
Boston
Brittany
Brussels
Chile
Chicago

California
Corsica
Costa Rica & Panama
Crete
Croatia
Cuba
Cyprus
Czech Republic
Dominican Republic
Dubai & UAE
Dublin
Egypt
Florence & Siena
Florida
Frankfurt
Greece
Guatemala & Belize
Iceland
Ireland
Kenya
Lisbon
London
Los Angeles
Madrid
Mallorca
Marrakesh
Mexico
Miami & Key West
Morocco
New York City
New Zealand
Northern Spain
Paris
Peru
Portugal
Prague
Rome
San Francisco
Sicily
South Africa
South India
Sri Lanka
Tenerife
Thailand
Toronto
Trinidad & Tobago
Tunisia
Tuscany
Venice

Washington DC
Yucatán Peninsula

**Dictionary
Phrasebooks**
Czech
Dutch
Egyptian Arabic
European Languages
  (Czech, French,
  German, Greek,
  Italian, Portuguese,
  Spanish)
French
German
Greek
Hindi & Urdu
Hungarian
Indonesian
Italian
Japanese
Mandarin Chinese
Mexican Spanish
Polish
Portuguese
Russian
Spanish
Swahili
Thai
Turkish
Vietnamese

**Music Guides**
The Beatles
Bob Dylan
Cult Pop
Classical Music
Elvis
Heavy Metal
Hip-Hop
Irish Music
Jazz
Music USA
Opera
Reggae
Rock
Sinatra
World Music (2 vols)

**Film Guides**
Comedy Movies
Ganster Movies
Horror Movies
Sci-Fi Movies

**Reference Guides**
Books for Teenagers
Children's Books, 0–5
Children's Books, 5–11
Conspiracy Theories
Cult Fiction
Cult Football
Cult Movies
Cult TV
The Da Vinci Code
Ethical Shopping
iPods, iTunes & Music
  Online
The Internet
James Bond
Kids' Movies
Lord of the Rings
Macs & OSX
Muhammad Ali
PCs and Windows
Pregnancy & Birth
Shakespeare
Superheroes
Unexplained
  Phenomena
The Universe
Weather
Website Directory

**Football 11s Guides**
Arsenal 11s
Celtic 11s
Chelsea 11s
Liverpool 11s
Manchester United 11s
Newcastle 11s
Rangers 11s
Tottenham 11s

Also! More than 120 Rough Guide music CDs are available from all good book
and record stores. Listen in at www.worldmusic.net

# Rough Guides To
# A World Of Music

'stick to the reliable Rough Guide series' *The Guardian (UK)*

Fed by a source that runs thick and fast, the best Mexican musicians consistently express the passion that has always fired the country's music. Live music is everywhere – at parties, concerts, festivals, births, deaths, marriages, on saints' days and in the media. The range of styles in Mexico is enormous and this album features a selection including *son, ranchera, new son jarocho*, Mexican rock, mariachi and big band. What these have in common is a great irreverence, a sense of humour and a passion for life and love that is not frightened of extremes. *The Rough Guide To The Music Of Mexico* offers a highly sought after introduction to the city sounds while tracing these back to the traditional music that gave birth to them.

THE ROUGH GUIDE TO THE MUSIC OF MEXICO

Mexico

**MUSIC** **ROUGH GUIDE**

son jarocho, ranchera, mariachi, Mexican rock

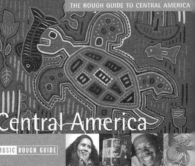

THE ROUGH GUIDE TO CENTRAL AMERICA

Central America

**MUSIC** **ROUGH GUIDE**

Latin America's best-kept secret

While Latin music has taken the world by storm in recent years, the lesser-known music of Central America remains the region's best-kept secret. The number of styles within Panama, Costa Rica, Nicaragua, El Salvador, Guatemala, Honduras and Belize is vast, and includes *marimbas*, accordion *brukdown, trova, punta* rock, reggae, salsa, cumbia, and countless local styles. The nations of Central America can hold a mantle to any country as home to some of the most diverse, dynamic and infectious music on the planet, and this Rough Guide explores the reasons why.

Hear sound samples at WWW.WORLDMUSIC.NET

Rough Guides
Radio

Now you can visit **www.worldmusic.net/radio** to tune into the exciting Rough Guide Radio Show, with a new show each month presenting new releases, interviews, features and competitions.

Available from book and record shops worldwide or order direct from
World Music Network, 6 Abbeville Mews, 88 Clapham Park Road, London SW4 7BX, UK
T 020 7498 5252  F 020 7498 5353  E post@worldmusic.net

# small print and
# Index

## A Rough Guide to Rough Guides

In the summer of 1981, Mark Ellingham, a recent graduate from Bristol University, was travelling round Greece and couldn't find a guidebook that really met his needs. On the one hand there were the student guides, insistent on saving every last cent, and on the other the heavyweight cultural tomes whose authors seemed to have spent more time in a research library than lounging away the afternoon at a taverna or on the beach.

In a bid to avoid getting a job, Mark and a small group of writers set about creating their own guidebook. It was a guide to Greece that aimed to combine a journalistic approach to description with a thoroughly practical approach to travellers' needs – a guide that would incorporate culture, history and contemporary insights with a critical edge, together with up-to-date, value-for-money listings. Back in London, Mark and the team finished their Rough Guide, as they called it, and talked Routledge into publishing the book.

That first *Rough Guide to Greece*, published in 1982, was a student scheme that became a publishing phenomenon. The immediate success of the book – with numerous reprints and a Thomas Cook prize shortlisting – spawned a series that rapidly covered dozens of destinations. Rough Guides had a ready market among low-budget backpackers, but soon also acquired a much broader and older readership that relished Rough Guides' wit and inquisitiveness as much as their enthusiastic, critical approach. Everyone wants value for money, but not at any price.

Rough Guides soon began supplementing the "rougher" information about hostels and low-budget listings with the kind of detail on restaurants and quality hotels that independent-minded visitors on any budget might expect, whether on business in New York or trekking in Thailand.

These days the guides – distributed worldwide by the Penguin Group – offer recommendations from shoestring to luxury and cover more than 200 destinations around the globe, including almost every country in the Americas and Europe, more than half of Africa and most of Asia and Australasia. Our ever-growing team of authors and photographers is spread all over the world, particularly in Europe, the USA and Australia.

In 1994, we published the *Rough Guide to World Music* and *Rough Guide to Classical Music*; and a year later the *Rough Guide to the Internet*. All three books have become benchmark titles in their fields – which encouraged us to expand into other areas of publishing, mainly around popular culture. Rough Guides now publish:

- Travel guides to more than 200 worldwide destinations
- Dictionary phrasebooks to 22 major languages
- History guides ranging from Ireland to Islam
- Maps printed on rip-proof and waterproof Polyart™ paper
- Music guides running the gamut from Opera to Elvis
- Restaurant guides to London, New York and San Francisco
- Reference books on topics as diverse as the Weather and Shakespeare
- Sports guides from Formula 1 to Man Utd
- Pop culture books from *Lord of the Rings* to Cult TV
- World Music CDs in association with World Music Network

Visit **www.roughguides.com** to see our latest publications.

SMALL PRINT

## Rough Guide credits

**Text editor**: Amy Hegarty
**Layout**: Katie Stephens
**Cartography**: Maxine Repath, Ashutosh Bharti
**Picture editor**: Jj Luck
**Proofreader**: Wendy Smith
**Cover design**: Diana Jarvis
**Photographers**: Demetrio Carrasco, Alex Robinson
**Production**: Katherine Owers

**Editorial**: **London** Kate Berens, Claire Saunders, Geoff Howard, Ruth Blackmore, Gavin Thomas, Polly Thomas, Richard Lim, Clifton Wilkinson, Alison Murchie, Sally Schafer, Karoline Densley, Andy Turner, Ella O'Donnell, Keith Drew, Edward Aves, Nikki Birrell, Helen Marsden, Joe Staines, Duncan Clark, Peter Buckley, Matthew Milton, Daniel Crewe; **New York** Andrew Rosenberg, Richard Koss, Steven Horak, AnneLise Sorensen, Amy Hegarty, Hunter Slaton
**Design & Pictures**: **London** Simon Bracken, Dan May, Diana Jarvis, Mark Thomas, Jj Luck, Harriet Mills, Chloë Roberts; **Delhi** Madhulita Mohapatra, Umesh Aggarwal, Ajay Verma,

Jessica Subramanian, Amit Verma, Ankur Guha
**Production**: Julia Bovis, Sophie Hewat, Katherine Owers
**Cartography**: **London** Maxine Repath, Ed Wright, Katie Lloyd-Jones; **Delhi** Manish Chandra, Rajesh Chhibber, Jai Prakash Mishra, Ashutosh Bharti, Rajesh Mishra, Animesh Pathak, Jasbir Sandhu, Karobi Gogoi
**Online**: **New York** Jennifer Gold, Suzanne Welles, Kristin Mingrone; **Delhi** Manik Chauhan, Narender Kumar, Shekhar Jha, Rakesh Kumar
**Marketing & Publicity**: **London** Richard Trillo, Niki Hanmer, David Wearn, Demelza Dallow, Louise Maher; **New York** Geoff Colquitt, Megan Kennedy; **Delhi** Reem Khokhar
**Custom publishing and foreign rights**: Philippa Hopkins
**Manager India**: Punita Singh
**Series editor**: Mark Ellingham
**Reference Director**: Andrew Lockett
**PA to Managing and Publishing Directors**: Megan McIntyre
**Publishing Director**: Martin Dunford
**Managing Director**: Kevin Fitzgerald

## Publishing information

This first edition published November 2005 by
**Rough Guides Ltd**,
80 Strand, London WC2R 0RL
345 Hudson St, 4th Floor,
New York, NY 10014, USA
**Distributed by the Penguin Group**
Penguin Books Ltd,
80 Strand, London WC2R 0RL
Penguin Putnam, Inc.
375 Hudson St, NY 10014, USA
Penguin Group (Australia)
250 Camberwell Rd, Camberwell
Victoria 3124, Australia
Penguin Books Canada Ltd,
10 Alcorn Ave, Toronto, Ontario,
Canada M4V 1E4
Penguin Group (New Zealand)
Cnr Rosedale and Airborne Roads
Albany, Auckland, New Zealand
Typeset in Bembo and Helvetica to an original design by Henry Iles.

1   3   5   7   9   8   6   4   2

Printed and bound in China

384pp includes index
A catalogue record for this book is available from the British Library

ISBN-13: 978-1-84353-489-1
ISBN-10: 1-84353-489-4

The publishers and authors have done their best to ensure the accuracy and currency of all the information in **The Rough Guide to The Yucatán**, however, they can accept no responsibility for any loss, injury, or inconvenience sustained by any traveller as a result of information or advice contained in the guide.

SMALL PRINT

## Help us update

We've gone to a lot of effort to ensure that the first edition of **The Rough Guide to The Yucatán** is accurate and up to date. However, things change – places get "discovered", opening hours are notoriously fickle, restaurants and rooms raise prices or lower standards. If you feel we've got it wrong or left something out, we'd like to know, and if you can remember the address, the price, the time, the phone number, so much the better.

We'll credit all contributions, and send a copy of the next edition (or any other Rough Guide if you prefer) for the best letters. Everyone who writes to us and isn't already a subscriber will receive a copy of our full-colour thrice-yearly newsletter. Please mark letters: "**Rough Guide Yucatán Update**" and send to: Rough Guides, 80 Strand, London WC2R 0RL, or Rough Guides, 4th Floor, 345 Hudson St, New York, NY 10014. Or send an email to **mail@roughguides.com**

Have your questions answered and tell others about your trip at **www.roughguides.atinfopop.com**

## Acknowledgements

**Zora O'Neill** would like to thank: Amy Hegarty for her painstaking editing, as well as Claudia Barrera and Lennard Struyk, Ry Koteen, Pia and Thed in Playa, Pedro and Eyal on Cozumel, Eliane Godement, Rob and Joanne Birce, Catriona Brown, Sandra Dayton, Andria Mitsakos, Alejandro Morelos, Guadalupe Ramos Chino, Eliane Tomasi, Andrés Limón, Janelle at Turquoise Reef, Curtis and Ashley Blogin, Jules Siegel, Claudia Pacheco, Lee Christie, Rick Bertram, Pablo DaCosta, Roger Lynn, Claudia Pacheco, Maria Laura Matta, Natalie Boden, Nicole Biscuiti, David and Ilana Randall, Jorge and Scott in Mahahual, Sonja Lillvik, Sophie and Arturo in Bacalar and Janese and the rest of the staff at IMS in Mérida.

**The editor** sends a big thank you to John Fisher, Katie Stephens, Maxine Repath, Ashutosh Bharti, Jj Luck, Demetrio Carrasco, Alex Robinson, Nikki Birrell, Wendy Smith, Steven Horak and Andrew Rosenberg.

A very special thank you goes to the fabulous Zora O'Neill and the also-fabulous Richard Koss.

## Photo credits

All photos © Rough Guides except the following:

**Cover**
Main front picture: El Castillo at Chichén Itzá © Corbis
Small front top picture: Old VW Beetle in a colourful street in Mexico © Alamy
Small front lower picture: Traditional Mexican weaves, Cancún © Alamy
Back top picture: Pink buildings, Isla Mujeres © Corbis

**Title page**
Diver in Room of Tears cave, Cenote Carwash © Gavin Newman/Alamy

**Introduction**
Mexican dresses © Robert Holmes/Corbis
Sunset on Chac-mool, Templo de los Guerreros, Chichén Itzá © Robert Harding Picture Library Ltd/Alamy
Axiote marinated pork © David Sanger/Alamy

**Things not to miss**
05 Scuba diving © Cancún Conventions and Visitors Bureau
06 Chichén Itzá © Jon Arnold Images/Alamy
10 Palenque ruins © John Fisher
11 Whale shark © Stephen Frink Collection/Alamy
13 Cenote Dzitnup © Macduff Everton/Corbis
15 Cobá – photography by Alex Robinson © Rough Guides
16 Flamingos at Celestún © DK Images
17 Ek-Balam © Barbara McKenzie/www.mayaruins.com

**Black and whites**
p.80 Isla Contoy © Isla Contoy/Corbis
p.89 Cancún coastline © Corbis
p.138 Sea turtle © George H.H. Huey/Corbis
p.153 The beach at Tulum © Jerry Dennis
p.165 Sian Ka'an Biosphere Reserve © Carl Purcell/Corbis
p.196 Ek-Balam © Alex Robinson/www.alexrobinsonphotography.co.uk
p.203 Cenote near Valladolid © Jerry Dennis
p.211 Grupo de las Mil Columnas, Chichén Itzá © Mark Thomas
p.256 Hacienda Tabi © John Fisher
p.290 Agua Azul © John Fisher
p.314 Toniná © John Fisher

# Index

Map entries are in colour.

INDEX

379

**I**

INDEX

INDEX

# Map symbols

maps are listed in the full index using coloured text

| | | | | |
|---|---|---|---|---|
| –––· | International boundary | | ♟ | Castle |
| –·–·· | Province boundary | | ⛫ | Hacienda |
| – – – | Chapter divisions boundary | | ⋏ | Camping |
| ━━━ | Motorway | | ⊙ | Monument |
| ═══ | Major road | | ✈ | Airport |
| ═══ | Minor road | | ) ( | Bridge |
| ——— | Unpaved road | | ⛽ | Petrol station |
| ▬▬▬ | Pedestrian road | | (i) | Information office |
| - - - - | Path | | ⊠ | Post office |
| ⊞⊞⊞⊞ | Steps | | © | Telephone |
| ━┿━ | Railway | | ❢ | Museum |
| — — | Ferry route | | @ | Internet access |
| ——— | River | | ★ | Transport stop |
| ▪▪▪▪ | Wall | | ⛳ | Golf course |
| ❢ | Point of interest | | ∩ | Park entrance |
| ⊻ | Viewpoint | | ■ | Building |
| ☗ | Lighthouse | | ✚ | Church |
| ⌂ | Cave | | † | Cemetery |
| ∿ | Cenote | | ▦ | Park/reserve |
| 🌿 | Waterfall | | Ⓟ | Beach |
| ﻼﻼﻼﻼ | Reef | | ꙳ | Swamp |
| ∴ | Ruins | | ⁙ | Jungle |
| ⚏ | Maya site | | | |